In the National Interest

A Chronicle of the National Film Board of Canada from 1949 to 1989

One of the cornerstones of Canadian culture, the National Film Board has throughout its history mirrored the social issues that preoccupy Canadians. Gary Evans traces the development of the postwar NFB, picking up the story where he left it at the end of his earlier work, *John Grierson and the National Film Board: The Politics of Wartime Propaganda.*

Evans points out that although Ottawa has not meddled in the operation of the NFB, outside stimuli have regularly forced the Film Board to reassess its mandate, a process which often has brought about as much confusion as light. For example, the unbridled optimism and expansion of the fifties and sixties led to English Production's desire for 'democratization' of programming, an end to the power of executive producers, and an expansion of the Film Board's core of permanent employees, all of which nearly caused the organization to founder. On the French side, despite the filmmakers' preference for the feature film rather than the *cinéma vérité* documentary, many in Ottawa regarded their 'political' films as both unfair attacks on the federal system and anachronisms coming from a federal institution. Throughout, the English-French tug of war so integral to the Canadian identity is a recurring theme.

Sources include interviews with former ministers, government film commissioners, policy-makers, and filmmakers, as well as archival documents and films. From them Evans has produced the first study to document the key trends in postwar Canadian filmmaking and to examine the role of film in the evolution of federal cultural policy.

Gary Evans is a member of the Department of History, Dawson College, and author of *John Grierson and the National Film Board: The Politics of Wartime Propaganda.*

In the National Interest

A Chronicle of the
National Film Board of Canada
from 1949 to 1989

Gary Evans

University of Toronto Press
Toronto Buffalo London

© University of Toronto Press 1991
Toronto Buffalo London
Printed in Canada
Reprinted 2001

ISBN 0-8020-2784-9 (cloth)
ISBN 0-8020-6833-2 (paper)

Canadian Cataloguing in Publication Data

Evans, Gary, 1944–
    In the national interest : a chronicle of the
    National Film Board of Canada from 1949 to 1989

    Includes index.
    ISBN 0-8020-2784-9 (bound) ISBN 0-8020-6833-2 (pbk.)

    1. National Film Board of Canada – History.
    2. Motion picture industry – Canada – History.
    3. Motion pictures – Canada.   I. Title.

PN1993.5.C2E83 1991   791.43'06'071   C91-094560-8

This book has been published with the help of a grant from the Social Science Federation of Canada, using funds provided by the Social Sciences and Humanities Research Council of Canada, and with assistance from the Canada Council and the Ontario Arts Council under their block grant programs.

For Karin

Contents

Appendices

Preface

Over five decades, the National Film Board of Canada produced 7,827 documentaries, animation shorts, feature films, and filmstrips for the education and entertainment of millions of Canadians and peoples around the world. During those years, this government-funded organization did pioneering work in the medium and created unique images in an atmosphere relatively unfettered by the political masters who paid the bills. In so doing, the Film Board earned Canada an international reputation for cinematic originality and excellence, a fact, ironically, that is unknown to most Canadians.

In other countries, artists who are also in the public service feel constrained by the agenda of the dominant political and economic regime; they envy the genuine freedom of the Film Board. More remarkable still is the fact that over the years a tradition of self-censorship, stemming from internally generated parameters, has allowed the advancement of a generally progressive philosophy. This could never have happened if the Film Board had been the puppet of various political regimes. In their wisdom, the governments of Canada have generally let the institution carve out its own raison d'être, hoping thereby to show the virtues of a free society.

The purpose of this book is to investigate the evolution of the Film Board over the last forty years and to chronicle how and to what purpose its filmmakers have used their creative freedom. Several other reasons impelled the author to undertake this study. The Film Board has been a provisioner of sorts, a living example of modern Canada's commitment to find unity in its social diversity, particularly by providing French Canadians with the means to develop an authentic Quebec cinema on their own terms and to secure their place in the English-language cultural sea of North America. The institution has also provided English Canada, particularly its schoolchildren, with the tools to survive distinct from the monolithic culture of the United States. Finally, the organization has provided a platform for minority or non-mainstream groups to express their legitimate needs nationally, encouraging them to find their rightful place in a complex and alienating society. As a national provisioner then, the Film Board has stood outside the capitalist paradigm that drives the rest of North America, thereby effectively denying the concept of a mass-consumer audience. In typical Canadian fashion, beginning with the principle of self-denial, filmmakers have suffused their productions with the ideal of public duty, that is, the still, small voice of moral integrity, justice, and honesty.

When Tom Daly, one of the major creative forces in Canadian documentary film, once asked the brilliant animator Norman McLaren how he began a project, McLaren said: 'First, set the limits, and then keep to them, because if you don't, once you start, one thing leads to a hundred other possibilities.' In considering McLaren's advice, the author determined to present the subject through a chronicle rather than an interpretive history, even though the selection of facts and films inherently constitutes a certain viewpoint. The term chronicle applies particularly to the past two decades, where not enough time has yet elapsed to allow an interpretation of events from a fixed historical perspective. In short, no one knows how the story of the Film Board (or of Canada, for that matter) will end. It also seemed fitting to pursue this tack because there was no comprehensive record of the organization; it was thought to be more useful for present and future readers and researchers to have the record of the times and atmosphere that existed. By setting the limits in this manner, the hope is that others may undertake their own investigations with a tabula rasa.

None the less, writing a chronicle of the National Film Board of Canada is analogous to making a documentary film. Of the hundreds (in this case, thousands) of different 'shots' of actuality that are part of the agency's evolution, a huge amount had to be left on the cutting-room floor. A film director will often select shots in order to create maximum emotional impact or to simplify the complex. Likewise, what follows are facts arranged in as stimulating a manner as possible to provide a tableau of the whole entity. From that composite chronology it is hoped the reader will realize that life in the Film Board was a combination of inspiration and creativity, politics and passions, overlapped by contradictions and the very raggedness of human endeavour.

There were many ways to approach the subject. In a first volume, *John Grierson and the National Film Board of Canada: The Politics of Wartime Propaganda* (University of Toronto Press 1984), the emphasis was on the institution's founder and the constellation that he made revolve around himself.

Grierson's triumphs and failures made for a tight story of the role of the Film Board in the truly great crusade of the century, the Second World War. His legacy was an affirmation of that part of the Canadian psyche which responds to ideals of public duty and public responsibility. The present volume takes up where the first left off and brings the reader to the organization's fiftieth anniversary (1989). It is coincidental and significant that the following chronicle finds Grierson appearing at critical moments to offer his opinions and insights; he remained a perpetual thread in the Film Board's tapestry until his death in 1972. Many English-language filmmakers still believe that his impact was profound. In contrast to their English colleagues, the majority of the French-language filmmakers, having arrived after the war, never quite knew what to make of him or his legacy.

The reader will find a major emphasis on the role of the government film commissioners and their relationships to the ministers and ministries they served. Surely, some may argue, the history of the organization is the work it produced, no more and no less, and not the policies and politics of film production. There were, after all, hundreds of persons who made the thousands of productions that won more than 3,000 awards over half a century. But to pursue that course would have meant describing myriad items without purpose or context. (The Film Board itself will soon publish *Comprehensive Guide*, a complete inventory of the organization's productions since 1939.) This chronicle will examine the close relationship between art and the politics of the period, a connection that will reveal diverse attitudes to work, to the organization itself, and to the government which funded it.

It will be seen how the films of each decade are the outcome of the policies, priorities, politics, arts, and passions of a chain of individuals, stretching from the minister responsible in Parliament to the film commissioner and his or her board of governors and ending with the informal leadership that helps inspire the very process of creative freedom. The film commissioner has been the barometer of all this activity, the person who tries to delineate the parameters that encompass the whole and who plays the most complex balancing act of anyone in the institution. He or she is the individual who leads, tries to lead, follows, or is ignored by the creative staff.

Over fifty years, the Film Board spent close to one billion dollars of the taxpayers' money, a much larger amount if current values are assigned. The present-day annual budget of $82 million may, as in preceding years, lead critics to ask whether the organization is worth the expense. The various facts and angles of observation that follow should enable the reader to answer that question. (That was one reason for including cost figures after the production titles in the text.)

Armed with the minutes of the board meetings of each commissioner's term, as well as relevant documentation found in the National Archives and the Film Board Archives, the author met with each commissioner to record the oral history, to ask the hard questions, and to probe the perspectives of different times. Their candidness was remarkable and, for the most part, the passage of years had enabled them to see events more objectively than before. Fortunately, too, almost all the ministers who were once responsible for the Film Board consented to be interviewed. From their vantage point, the Film Board was only one of several institutions making up the federal government's involvement in culture and was just a small part of a larger picture. The author concludes that the Film Board was a highly significant component.

It was remarkable to see how many transformations the Film Board experienced over four decades. The author's greatest advantage as an outsider was that of having a relatively unbiased opinion of the issues, politics, and films that fuelled all the activity. The exception perhaps was his recollection of how profoundly influenced he had been by the 1950 classic *How to Build an Igloo*, the first film he ever viewed as a schoolchild on the Niagara Frontier. That film established a permanent impression of the space, social diversity, and uniqueness that distinguish Canada, and helped stimulate what became an unabating desire to learn more.

In search of a wider perspective, there were hundreds of films to screen, countless production files to consult, and never enough time to interview all the players. The films described in this book are only samples that reflect a multiplicity of interests, the precedents of each decade, and the vitality of the creative process. Perhaps if Northrop Frye had seen the total output of the National Film Board of Canada, he might not have asked his famous philosophical question 'Where is Here?' because more than anything else, the Film Board has established authoritatively just where 'Here' is, particularly for generations of schoolchildren. As a minimal contribution, the Film Board record will show just who Canadians were, and like history itself, its film documents will convey to future generations the priorities and passions of the era from which they emanated.

It was fascinating to observe that what seemed important at one time was less consequential later on and that the converse also applied. The following examples illustrate. When Film Commissioner Ross McLean was 'fired' in 1949, the staff believed that Ottawa was about to close down the organization. In reality, his term was over and the government had decided to find a new man to overhaul the bureaucracy. Similarly in 1951, few understood the importance of the Massey-Lévesque Royal Commission, whose report was to relaunch the Film Board and provide it with a mission. The shift of headquarters from Ottawa to Montreal in 1956 was initiated by Commissioner Arthur Irwin, in part to escape the watchful eyes of Ottawa's politicians and in part to find an ambience more supportive of the creative process. Little did he know how effectively he had guaranteed the institution virtual immortality as long as Canada stayed a united country. Later, unbeknownst to many, commissioner Albert Trueman worked behind the scenes and failed to establish a separately funded French Production wing. His astute successor, Guy Roberge, waited until the political moment was right to pursue that policy. From 1963, Canada was on the road to becoming officially a bilingual and bicultural – and later, a multicultural – society. Those Ottawa-inspired isms were as important to the Film Board's survival as was its annual funding.

The sixties was also a decade of extremes, swinging from optimism to pessimism. Centennial Year marked Canada's hundredth birthday, and the party was celebrated at Expo '67 in Montreal, the heart and soul of French Canada. That event coincided with youthful protest, *québécois* nationalism, and world trends toward 'decolonization,' all of which coalesced to mark the birth pangs of a political movement that today challenges the very existence of Canada. At the time, the country nearly faltered in mid-step as English Canada asked its perennial question about what it was that French Canada wanted. A new generation of Quebec filmmakers found the question irrelevant as they toyed with the excitement of asserting French-Canadian nationalism, regardless of what English Canada wanted. All these phenomena are reflected variously in Film Board productions of the era.

In the wake of the Centennial celebrations, Ottawa planned across-the-board economic cut-backs. English Production had anticipated making more sponsored films for government departments and had overhired. But the fly in the ointment was the private Canadian film industry, which had developed an effective lobby for this lucrative work. Losing his gamble to make an end run for expansion, Commissioner Hugo McPherson found himself the victim of austerity, unable to work the levers to avoid a crisis. Ottawa wanted to strengthen private-sector production, and the Film Board found itself in limbo, an anachronism that needed redefinition in a new environment.

Internally, most of the battles that raged at the Film Board during the sixties were about styles of cinema. A series of emerging film genres changed the medium. One group in French Production, influenced profoundly by the auteur theories of the *Nouvelle vague /* New Wave in France, believed that features were the supreme visual art form. A number of English directors agreed. Another cluster of English and French fell in love with *cinéma vérité*, or direct cinema, as a result of the new and lightweight 16-mm film and sound equipment that made location-shooting easier. In part, their experiments led Ottawa to encourage establishment of a new expression of the documentary idea in a programme called 'Challenge for Change / Société nouvelle.' The focus was on the victims of poverty and those whom society had neglected.

From this experience, representing the unrepresented became an idea that is now welded to the Film Board's creative conscience. The present decade sees a continuation of this philosophy, especially in the work of both English and French Womens' Studios. The logical extension of this approach is that the agency is not afraid to attempt indepth analyses of important social questions; it makes film subjects where the commercial sector fears to tread. In both animation and experimental films, then, social relevance is a persistently identifiable trait.

In the seventies, commissioners Sydney Newman and André Lamy found themselves isolated from the staff as they struggled against French-Canadian 'political' films. Lamy set the pattern of the present era – an uncharismatic, but supremely efficient, assistant commissioner succeeding to the top job. Disinterested in pursuing a cult of personality, the second-in-command becomes adept at running the bureaucratic machine, proving his or her indispensability and right to succeed as the chief executive officer of the corporate complex.

In the last two decades, management has taken the hard knocks as government-imposed cutbacks threw successive regimes into a reactive mode. Lamy's successor, James de B. Domville, tried articulating a new mandate, but the staff, fearing a shutdown after the devastating Applebaum-Hébert Report of 1982, seemed reluctant to follow him. Still, no one could explain why it was that during his term the organization won more prestigious awards than ever before. François Macerola followed him and streamlined the corporate machine radically by cutting back dozens of full-time positions over five years, a necessary and painful slimming process that won him few friends from within.

Today, with production offices in six regions across the nation, the Film Board reflects a corporate image consonant with the era of privatization. It is a much leaner place than it was before, and filmmakers are resigned to the fact that private or other institutional funding is necessary for many productions to materialize. Worse, there is virtually no new hiring of permanent creative staff, and aging full-timers worry who will replace them once they leave. Others are sorry to see that the Film Board's traditional mission has changed and that government-sponsored films are now done by the private sector. Perhaps losing its unbecoming middle-age spread has had a beneficial effect, because the scarcity of production funds has taught filmmakers to take nothing for granted. As they anticipate the institution's future, these artists will need imagination and will to answer affirmatively the Film Board's archetypal question, 'Is what I do in the national interest?' For it is that phrase, 'in the national interest,' enshrined in the National Film Act of 1950, that justifies having a National Film Board.

Sawyerville and Montreal
Quebec, Canada
1990

Acknowledgments

So many people were generous with their time and information, it would be impossible to list them all. From former ministers, to film commissioners, to executive producers, to filmmakers or to the members of the Film Board infrastructure, each person's perspective made the task of bringing coherence to the whole a little less daunting.

The author gratefully acknowledges the interviews and contributions of the following former ministers: the Hon. Walter Harris, Hon. J.W. Pickersgill, Hon. Ellen Fairclough, Hon. Gérard Pelletier, Hon. Hugh Faulkner, Hon. John Roberts, and Hon. Francis Fox.

Former Film Commissioners W. Arthur Irwin, Albert W. Trueman, Guy Roberge, Hugo McPherson, Sydney Newman, André Lamy, James de B. Domville, and François Macerola and former Acting Commissioner Grant McLean were most generous with their time and analyses of their respective regimes. So too was the present commissioner, Joan Pennefather. They helped to establish the context of this chronicle.

The point of view of the board of governors was conveyed aptly in interviews with ex-members R. Gordon Robertson, David Silcox, Phyllis Grosskurth, and W.R. Jack, and former board members and presidents of the Canadian Broadcasting Corporation A.W. Johnson, Pierre Juneau, and Patrick Watson. Their insights helped to solve the riddle of the CBC–Film Board imbroglio from the late sixties to the eighties.

The role of director of production was better understood after interviewing a number of individuals who held that challenging post: they were Grant McLean, Pierre Juneau, Jacques Godbout, Frank Spiller, Robert Verrall, Ian McLaren, Peter Katadotis, Barbara Emo, and Robert Forget.

An executive producer had to have a skin of steel to operate in the difficult realms of administrator, artistic critic, adviser to filmmakers, and person responsible for the expenditure of taxpayers' money. Discussions with each of these people proved to be an excellent way to test hypotheses that the archival documentary evidence seemed to suggest. They were Tom Daly, Wolf Koenig, Colin Low, Roman Kroitor, Nicholas Balla, Guy Glover, Kathleen Shannon, Adam Symansky, Arthur Hammond, John Spotton, John Taylor, Barrie Howells, and David Verrall on the English side, and Jacques Bobet, Roger Blais, Guy L. Coté, and Josée Beaudet on the French side.

Tom Daly, who in many ways was beneficent godfather to this project, read the entire manuscript and, in his usual Socratic style, helped the author identify many patterns that lay buried in the data. This led to the discovery of various loci around which the constellation of fact could turn. The experience was probably similar to that of many filmmakers whose work Daly helped bring to fruition. The same could be said about Robert Verrall and Colin Low, whose diligence and close reading of the manuscript provided two other experienced minds to comment upon and encourage this research. These men lived the life this book describes and shared a perspective that provides a key dimension: the humanism that lies at the very foundation of the Film Board's existence. Their support and friendship were and are invaluable.

The author spoke with many filmmakers over the years of this project. Listed alphabetically, they are Donald Brittain, Marrin Canell, Gilles Carle, Marcel Carrière, Guy L. Coté, Paul Cowan, Fernand Dansereau, Ronald Dick, Jacques Drouin, Martin Duckworth, Donna Dudinsky, Robert Duncan, Guy Glover, Saverio Grana, Sturla Gunnarsson, Dorothy Todd Hénaut, Pierre Hébert, Tony Ianzelo, Albert Kish, Bonnie Sherr Klein, John Kramer, Terence Macartney-Filgate, Grant Munro, Terri Nash, Barry Perles, Pierre Perreault, Anne Claire Poirier, Peter Raymont, Boyce Richardson, Michael Rubbo, Dennis Sawyer, John N. Smith, John Spotton, Robin Spry, Julie Stanfel, Richard Todd, Giles Walker, William Weintraub, and Donald Winkler.

Of necessity, a project like this must depend upon documentary sources, and the author extends his heartfelt thanks to Film Board Archivist Bernard Lutz, whose tireless efforts to help track documents, production files, newsclippings, and a myriad of other details helped make this research as extensive as it is. To Donald Bidd, head of Library Services, the indefatigable Rose-Aimée Todd, and the staff of the Film Board library, and Hélène Tanguay of the Festivals office go special thanks for providing access to and then helping to uncover files and numerous unpublished materials. At the Film Board Film Archives, Director Marielle Cartier and her staff, including Suzanne Bouchard, Suzanne Dévy, and Lucie Charbonneau, were generous in making available films,

videos, equipment, and photos over the years of this project. Without their cooperation and services above and beyond the call of duty, this work could not have been completed. Lyle Cruickshank was especially helpful in rounding out the long-term distribution picture. With the help of Douglas Sample on the computer, he both furnished statistics and spent considerable time discussing the complexities of Film Board distribution. Gilles Roy of the personnel department helped unravel the complexity of labour relations of the past two decades by sharing both documents and insights. In Toronto, John Taylor and John Boundy provided an overview of operations, both regional and central, from the seventies to the present, while in New York City, Mary Jane Tyrrell explained how the Film Board operates in the United States. In Vancouver, Jane Gutteridge demystified current television policy, while former administrators William Cosman, Eric Cosgrove, Kirwan Cox, and Reta Kilpatrick demonstrated their continuing allegiance to the Film Board ideal.

During the years of research, the staff of the Film Board was consistently open and eager to share information. In no small part was this due to the encouragement and forthright support of Jean Claude Mahé, executive assistant to the film commissioner, secretary to the board of trustees, and director of information, who with two commissioners' approval, opened up virtually all files with no restrictions, thereby giving resounding support to the democratic ideal that the public has a right to know everything that goes on within a public institution. These individuals encouraged the sense of knowing that the twin principles of public duty and national interest are very much alive and well at the Film Board.

Thanks are also extended to film professors Peter Morris and Peter Harcourt of York University and Carleton University respectively for encouraging the author to undertake this project.

Acknowledgments

The Social Sciences and Humanities Research Council's time-release stipend funded full-time research. In Quebec, the provincial Fonds pour la formation de Chercheurs et l'aide à la Recherche provided additional release time from teaching duties to complete this work. Finally, to colleagues, members of the history department, and the administration of Dawson College, the author extends thanks for the generosity of spirit that characterized their support of this project. Special thanks go to Bruno Geslain, Martine Couture, Chantal Couture, Katie Nicholls, Bill Smith. Agathe Berthold, David Jones, Eric Bernier, and Patrick Woodsworth in this regard. To the staff of the Bibliothèque de la Cinématèque Québécois, 'Merci pour tous.'

Appreciation is extended to those individuals who welcomed the author into their homes and became unwavering supporters of this project. They include W. Arthur Irwin and his wife, P.K. Page, who read the first chapters and gave sound advice; Marjorie McKay, who was with the Film Board from its earliest days until 1964 and whose unpublished history of the Film Board was a worthy document to read at the beginning; Ron Dick, whose intellectual curiosity put meat on the bone of many of the most informative documentaries; ex-Commissioner Sydney Newman, who literally spent days untying the Gordian knot of Ottawa–Film Board politics; and Grant McLean, whose many leadership posts put him in an excellent position to comment on key elements of the fifties and sixties. Thanks too are extended to Gerald Graham, whose decades of affiliation with the Film Board, first in technical then in administrative capacities, gave him a particularly apt overview. Eddy Zwaneveld clarified much of the complexity of the technical operations set-up. Other individuals who were generous were Robert Fortier, formerly of the Department of Secretary of State; James Beveridge, of the original Film Board phalanx; Len Chatwin, whose career in distribution exemplified how the humanist element was so much a part of the agency's infrastructure; and Alexandra McHugh, who is doing her graduate work on Challenge for Change / Société nouvelle.' Also to Ruth Daly and Marion Verrall: thank you for checking grammar and spelling. The editorial staff at the University of Toronto Press has been most helpful too. Virgil Duff, managing editor, has guided this work through the complex levels of editorial production with a deft hand and constantly encouraging word. Copy-editor John St James not only offered sound suggestions; his fresh perspective and keen eye for detail were invaluable to the collaborative fine-tuning process.

In Ottawa/Hull, Dacre Cole, of the library of the Department of External Affairs, made available all documents and material relevant to the Film Board, including declassified files relating to the Psychological Warfare Committee, while Ron Fall and the staff of the National Archives of Canada helped locate ministerial files, Privy Council documents, and assorted material relating to the Film Board. To the library of the Canadian Radio and Telecommunications Commission, thanks too for providing access to the Grierson transcripts. At the Moving Images and Sound Archives, thanks to Jana Vosikovska and her staff for helping to locate still photos; the members of the Film Board Photothèque also provided a large number of the still photos contained herein.

While the author has tried diligently to be as accurate as possible, all errors of commission or omission that may be present in the text are his responsibility.

Finally, I thank Karin Doerr, project assistant, sympathetic critic, and dearest friend. No words can adequately convey how important were the patience and personal generosity she unfailingly displayed. Through fair and foul weather, she helped carry this project to its fruition.

In the National Interest

A Chronicle of the
National Film Board of Canada
from 1949 to 1989

1

Almost Derailed:
Trying to Fit the National Film Board into the Postwar World

The setting

It all began in May 1939 with a mad, frenetic, feisty, vibrant, idealistic Scotsman named John Grierson. He lived life as a modern-day Prophet of Cinema, a visionary who founded the documentary-film movement, a teacher whose primary interest in film was its potential as an agent of social change. He had a political agenda connected to no party: to use the apparatus and money of the liberal state to create universal humanitarian loyalties in the hearts of its citizenry. His was also a crusade to convince filmmakers to use the magnetism of the medium to rescue the ordinary citizen, who was perpetually adrift and seemingly inconsequential in this century of extremes. He had a personality that attracted talented men and women and he launched organizations, first in Britain, then in Canada, to make films that could create democratic loyalties, to stir the collective consciousness of society, and to teach values that would keep civilization and coherence supreme.

Grierson saw his dream of a National Film Board of Canada become a reality in May 1939. It was not to be an ambitious endeavour – just two secretaries, a manager, a producer/director, and himself housed in an abandoned lumber mill in Ottawa. The new organization was supposed to become a coordinating board and revitalize the existing

publicly owned film enterprise, the Canadian Government Motion Picture Bureau, which had been making films for various federal departments since 1923. Fifty years later, a sprawling complex in suburban Montreal, with production offices in six other regions of Canada, employing 796 full-time and dozens of other contractual employees, stands as a monument to that modest beginning.

Conceived in peacetime and born as the slumbering insular nation slipped into total war a few months later, the National Film Board was supposed to help galvanize the will of the naturally disunited country to endure the conflict. Grierson and his associates used truth as their standard and 'propaganda as education' in an effort to define 'public duty.' Total war demanded total effort, and to aid in this objective Grierson convinced the government in 1941 to transfer the Motion Picture Bureau from the Department of Trade and Commerce to the Film Board, which was under the minister of National War Services. The fledgling agency absorbed the Bureau's personnel and proceeded to increase the production and distribution of government films.

In a pre-television age, the Film Board became a multi-purpose organization, coordinating departmental information film production, distributing films both in Canada and abroad, making theatrical shorts for Canadian and American consumption, and employing internationally recognized masters of the medium to train raw Canadian talent. By 1945, the staff had mushroomed to nearly eight hundred. Some one hundred items a year reached urban and rural populations and tied them into world events. Most of all, the Film Board was making Canadians feel *connected* in a country whose devouring geography constantly conspires to make them feel disconnected.

In a television interview in 1970, Grierson recalled his handiwork: 'The Film Board was a deliberate creation to do a deliberate work, it was there to bring Canada alive to itself and to the rest of the world. It was there to declare the excellences of Canada to Canadians and to the rest of the world. It was there to invoke the strengths of Canadians, the imagination of Canadians in respect of creating their present and their future.'

From the beginning, he considered the war as a temporary diversion; the real work would be to express in peacetime the multiplicity of views that constituted the country's reality. Grierson's constant cheer-leading was about preparing for peace ('Peace must be made more exciting than war' became a favourite expression). Along the way, he found believers who shared his enthusiasm for enshrining public service as a virtue. This outlook was the glue that helped keep them, the Film Board and perhaps the country, together. In 1945 he left Canada to try launching a postwar crusade internationally.

The Canadian filmmakers whom Grierson had left behind had no difficulty in accepting his legacy: to make films as a matter of public duty as much as for the thrill of artistic expression. The calculating Scotsman had insulated the organization well – the government funded it, but had a 'hands off' policy with respect to film content and operations. With standards that were those of small-'l' liberalism, the commissioner made policy, keeping an eye on what

This aerial shot shows the newly opened Film Board headquarters in Montreal in 1956.

4

was possible to achieve without raising too many hackles. In short, he pushed a progressive agenda, but never forgot who was paying the bills. Grierson's talent as a visionary was balanced by his even greater talent as an operator who got things done. His efforts allowed the Film Board to evolve into an almost ideal example of a modern democracy – where creative freedom thrived within self-imposed limits. There would be no government censors in peacetime – trying to stay just ahead of public opinion, the institution was to set its own standards and police itself. Grierson's modus operandi had been to keep 'one inch to the Left of the Party in power.' This became the signature of many Film Board productions. Many Americans and Europeans wondered how such a philosophy could endure. But a sparsely populated nation, occupying the world's second-largest

Norman McLaren, at work on an animation film in the early fifties, died in 1987. His belief that the artist owed allegiance to the principle of public service inspired filmmakers and animators; the headquarters building now bears his name.

land mass, enjoys special conditions of freedom. The Film Board is one manifestation of that freedom.

As for the possibility of a Canadian feature-film industry, Grierson was not sanguine. First, a national film policy was unlikely, since film exhibition was a provincial responsibility and, in Canada, to obtain unanimity was (and is) improbable. Secondly, it was not feasible to alter Hollywood's worldwide preponderance, given Canadian demographics and a scarcity of experienced talent. The Liberal government had spent the war years building up the branch-plant economy; to swim against this tide was to tilt at windmills. Grierson believed the only possibility was to have Canadians make occasional films in Hollywood and hope that Film Board shorts have continued access to the American market. The operator in him thought half a loaf was better than none at all.[1]

For six years, the National Film Board of Canada had led the country through the war with its progressive film propaganda of education, inspiration, and promise of a better tomorrow. Non-theatrical film circuits in every province brought young and old Canadians together monthly in their small communities, where in separate shows they might spend an hour and a half seeing an animated sing-along film by Norman McLaren, an instructional film on nutrition, or a recently retired theatrical short or two that explained Canada's strategic place in the world conflict. They might participate in a local discussion afterwards. In urban centres, too, audiences had become accustomed to Film Board shorts in commercial cinemas, at community gatherings, at factory lunch breaks, and in church basements. True, the organization had avoided such divisive issues as conscription and the sorry tale of national indifference to Europe's Jewish refugees, but propaganda in wartime must reflect positive shared beliefs in order to achieve national unity, and such beliefs did not then exist. With the peace, audiences

believed there would still be Film Board shorts to see just before the main Hollywood feature.

Retrenchment and resentment

The audiences were wrong, because the National Film Board was careening toward possible oblivion. Grierson left for the United States, taking with him a few of the most experienced creative personnel. There was still a strong team in place, although many of them felt alone, vulnerable, and quite aware of how they had imitated other countries' film styles. They wondered if the Liberal government would continue funding their work, even though it was unlikely that the several commercial companies that made up the Canadian film industry would be able to carry on public-service filmmaking without subsidies. Politicians resumed their peacetime habits, and a number of them considered frivolous Ottawa's maintenance of a government-owned film agency. There were those who posed a question that became one of the most repeated in the next four decades, 'Should taxpayers support such an organization?' As part of the transition, the government ordered the acting film commissioner, Ross McLean, to cut his 787 staff by almost one-third. Gloom at the Film Board darkened to despair as the painful slimming process to 589 staff proceeded over almost three years. Meanwhile, the Conservative Opposition took pot-shots at the government by alleging that the Film Board was crawling with communists.

Canadian theatrical audiences had been accustomed to seeing monthly issues of the two Film Board series *Canada Carries On* and *The World in Action*. The latter appeared irregularly after 1946, and eventually disappeared. The former carried on. Budget cuts also meant there was a decrease in the number of itinerant projectionists who had run the non-theatrical rural circuits. Ironically, the number of monthly Film Board showings in community halls, church basements, and schools was actually increasing. Citizens themselves formed some 250 voluntary film councils across Canada and, besides assuming the projectionists' duties, began operating 230 film libraries. For tens of thousands in rural and urban areas, an evening of non-theatrical film still provided the catalyst for groups of ten or tens to meet, enjoy a documentary film, and discuss contemporary issues that an *Eye Witness* newsreel might suggest. Mostly, though, National Film Board films brought them together to socialize.

By its own estimate, the Film Board concluded that, in 1948, audiences at community showings totalled nine million persons annually. Abroad, it was estimated that more than 20,000 prints of Canadian films were circulating in fifty countries in diverse languages. The statistics were probably inflated, but it seemed that, as a whole, the National Film Board was serving a useful national and international function. Of its total production that year, the organization had produced 59 of 166 items for government departments, covering topics like health, nutrition, military recruitment, accidents on the job, and agriculture. The Photo Services Division provided services to government departments that were mounting exhibits, making posters, or issuing publications, while the Filmstrips Division produced 25 items, mainly for schools, selling a thousand nationally and nearly twice that number abroad. Films describing national geography, life, and institutions were also placed on Canada-bound ships carrying displaced persons and other immigrants. A few private firms wished the Film Board would disappear so they might have the market to themselves. They were jealous that it was virtually the only game in town.

The Liberal government grudgingly acknowledged the organization's impressive activities but was more concerned with the objectives of economic retrenchment and with ducking the political arrows of the Conservative Opposition.[2] The mood of the vic- tors had soured as the cold war took the glory out of victory. There was now a postwar world of two camps, with broken promises and a still-devastated European economy. This situation could hardly augur well for those at the Film Board who had created a propaganda of hope that a brave new world would be built upon the principles of internationalism. The Opposition, hungry for an issue to draw the spotlight to themselves after a decade and a half in the wilderness, found it when they continued to insinuate the unproven allegation that Grierson and his erstwhile secretary were linked to the Gouzenko spy scandal. In Ottawa, it was well known that the Film Board's creative staff tended to lean left, which in fact resembled a less-sinister small-'l' liberal vision of the world. No matter. The Progressive Conservatives took full advantage of the gift and created sizeable political capital by repeating the rumours that the Film Board was a place that harboured communist spies.

The Opposition revelled in 1948 as the government tried to control the damage. If one followed the English-language press campaign against the Film Board from February 1948, it would seem that the public had lost confidence in it. Member of Parliament G.K. Fraser's attacks in the Commons were reported in the *Ottawa Evening Citizen*, Toronto *Globe and Mail*, *Toronto Star*, *Toronto Telegram*, and *Morning Journal* on 26 February. The debate coverage continued on 24 March in the *Morning Journal* and on 5 May in the *Winnipeg Free Press*. Charges of harbouring 'fellow travellers' appeared in the *Montreal Gazette* on 29 September, and after *Le Devoir* joined in an attack on the agency's policy and work on 3 December, the *Ottawa Citizen* echoed the charges on 13 December.

The *Financial Post* climbed aboard the sour-grapes train in 1948 and published stories of Film Board excesses. One issue showed a photo of a child brushing his teeth and the caption, '$40,000? N.F.B.'[3] Commissioner Ross McLean believed that the magazine was being fed information by Hollywood interests and several independent Canadian film companies that specialized in short films. Hollywood was furious with him for having had the audacity to suggest to the government in June 1947 that the Americans invest some 30 to 40 per cent of their annual net profits of about $17 million in Canadian film production.[4] The men from Tinseltown were trying to launch the infamous Canadian Cooperation Project, a scheme whereby they would film a few features in Canada, insert favourable references to Canada in their scripts to promote tourism, and promise to encourage more distribution of Film Board shorts in the United States.[5] Hollywood's dour reaction to the Film Board (McLean's) meddling came hard on the heels of a lost antitrust battle at home: they were forced to divest themselves of their cinema chains in 1948. This ruling did not apply to Canada, where Paramount Pictures continued to control the Famous Players chain of eight hundred theatres.

Whether or not it was because the Hollywood lobby was able to reach into the heart of Ottawa, because of the press campaign or because the Canadian commercial film industry was effective in its complaints, McLean came under fire from his one-time friend and top civil-service mandarin J.W. Pickersgill, special assistant to the prime minister. Both men had been students at Oxford and had travelled around Europe together. Pickersgill remembered that McLean had had a hard time organizing a trip, let alone administering anything, so he maintained little confidence in McLean's capacity to run a five-hundred-person organization that had been run since Grierson's time as an ad-hocracy rather than as a bureaucracy.[6] Pickersgill wondered where the long-term strategies for the organization lay and he was unimpressed by a management style of reacting to stimuli and crises. Flying by the seat of one's pants had been acceptable during the emergency of war, but peacetime allowed the government to tie up loose ends. The commissioner should not have mistaken Pick-

ersgill's antipathy to him for anything other than what it was – the proverbial writing on the wall.

There was also the sticky business of the Film Board's China film *The People Between*, which Grant McLean, Ross's cousin, had shot in 1947 for the United Nations Relief and Rehabilitation Agency in civil war–torn China. Grant revelled in cultivating a Hemingway-like persona and became the first Western cameraman to record the background of the war, the famine, and the Chinese efforts with the United Nations to cope with the disastrous Yellow River floods. Ross showed the almost-finished work to Lester Pearson, the under-secretary of state for External Affairs. Pearson agreed it would be useful, but thought that the commentary should be checked with the department to ensure impartiality. The alterations were done and Ross reported that both sides were treated fairly and impartially as far as it was humanly possible. An officer of the department concurred, although Pearson at last ordered the film held up. The fact was that he and the department felt that in some sequences too much was being made of the virtues of the Communist system in China.[7]

Politicians are good at sniffing out political vulnerability, and in the cold-war atmosphere of 1948, certain government members felt that the documentary would make friends neither at home nor abroad. Dr. J.J. McCann, the minister responsible for the Film Board, ordered it withheld from distribution. He was fed up with the Film Board, having been angered recently over expenditure of $25,000 on a documentary about a hospital out west, when he thought the money might have been spent better to inoculate children.[8] Pearson must have been wondering about Ross McLean's judgment too, as he took his cue from Prime Minister King, who had requested that the Department of External Affairs have one of its members sit on the Film Board's board of governors to keep an eye on films headed for international audiences.[9] When King retired late in 1948, the External Affairs–Film Board relationship had been cemented at the board of governors level.

Things went from bad to worse for the easygoing, gentle, if hapless, film commissioner. According to a later newspaper story, his refusal to purge the Film Board in 1948 led to his undoing, when a routine check by the RCMP turned up the embarrassing evidence that a once-active Communist employee had photographed some top-secret equipment for the Canadian army. When this information reached the ears of both British and U.S. military men, the protests became louder. Subsequently, the Department of National Defence decided that the Film Board could no longer make its films.[10]

McLean felt he was left with two options. One was to forget Department of National Defence (DND) films and let the small companies like Crawley Films and Associated Screen News make them. (Both had been lobbying for more government film contracts than the few which the Film Board doled out to them occasionally.) Or he could follow DND recommendations to declare the Film Board a vulnerable agency under the terms of an earlier cabinet directive. The board of governors decided in May 1949 that the Production Division and senior administrative officers be declared vulnerable.[11] McLean requested that the RCMP conduct a security screening for those employees. Based on an assessment that came from a questionnaire to each employee (and perhaps the security officer within the Film Board), the RCMP recommended that McLean dismiss thirty-six employees. He countered by asking the RCMP to provide clear evidence of the employees' disloyalty. When they could not, he stood behind his employees.[12] The Ottawa rumour mills thrived on innuendo. An unnamed informant for the *Telegram* story explained that there was a clique in the Film Board that 'operated behind McLean's back, ran the show for him and saw to it that one way or another, one of their long-haired boys was

chosen to work on the special assignments. There seemed to be no way of stopping them.' The allegations were preposterous, but the government's priority was to avoid embarrassment.

The commissioner was in a double bind. First, the inefficient bureaucracy he had inherited had evolved during Grierson's reign and, second, in order to straighten it out, Draconian measures were necessary. He was too much the gentleman to impose the latter, and though the staff liked him, no one took his call for central discipline seriously. Therefore, if it was universally acknowledged that the machine was in need of overhaul, the fact that he would not or could not do it made it seem to outsiders that McLean was either too weak or too careless.

The Film Board security issue took the national spotlight again in November 1949, when Prime Minister Louis St Laurent and cabinet colleagues Robert H. Winters and Brooke Claxton came under fire in the Commons. At one point, a frustrated Claxton uttered some nasty off-the-record remarks about the Film Board, which found their way back to the commissioner. From 19 to 30 November, the *Ottawa Citizen*, *Montreal Gazette*, and *Ottawa Journal* reported the commotion in the House over security screenings. On 26 November an unflattering article in the *Financial Post* embarrassed the prime minister again. The people around him were already scurrying to do something about the rambunctious Film Board.

The organization had been under fire in the press for so long that many staff members feared that it hovered on the brink of extinction. They, as well as some competent outside observers, believed firmly that the small commercial film industry was the chief organizer of the campaign. A dismantled Film Board would leave those companies with government film contracts and a clear field.[13]

To make matters worse, in its arrogance, naïvety, or search for a new raison d'être, the Film Board had brought a curse upon itself by informing each province what film subjects it intended to use for tourist films. The private producers felt this was an unwarranted intrusion on their livelihoods and in 1949 they formed the Association of Motion Picture Producers and Laboratories (AMPPL) to lobby Ottawa. They became permanently suspicious of the Film Board even after private firms won the right to make tourist films.[14]

The Massey Commission

Few in the cities seemed to appreciate the Film Board's rural success story. J.J. McCann, who did not see the value of film, gladly handed over ministerial responsibilities for the Film Board to Robert H. Winters of the Department of Reconstruction and Supply in January 1949. All the while, the eccentric creative staff continued drawing public attention to itself. One staff member thought the bohemian lifestyle, including females in purple slacks, amused few in drab, strait-laced, civil-service Ottawa. If some politicians thought that film culture and culture in general did not need the public purse, one savant who understood the dynamic of culture and politics was Brooke Claxton, who had been the minister responsible for the Film Board in 1945–6.

Claxton had a long history of favouring an Ottawa-centred activist role for the support of culture and it was he who first recommended a royal commission on the arts. He had won over Lester Pearson to the idea and in November 1948 the two persuaded Prime Minister St Laurent to support the establishment of a Royal Commission on National Development in the Arts, Letters and Sciences. The Massey Commission, as it soon became known, under the chairmanship of Vincent Massey and Quebec's esteemed Dominican Father Georges-Henri Lévesque, the so-called father of the Quebec Renaissance,[15] was a non-partisan body. Its key statement that 'arts and letters lie at the roots of our life as a nation' had profound national and political significance for decades. The

Massey Commission pointed the federal government toward assuming a key role in underwriting culture. This, in turn, led to the active promotion of a bilingual and bicultural Canada. The Massey Commission stood on its head the adage that culture legitimizes the state – in this case, the state was to legitimize culture.

The vicious press campaigns of 1948 and 1949 had made good copy, but had failed to reflect the public's persistent confidence in the Film Board. When the Massey Commission began taking evidence in 1949, some 120 organizational briefs concerned themselves with the institution wholly or in part. Most of them both approved of its work and asked to see it extended. Many expressed pride in the organization and considered it a valuable and distinctive Canadian achievement, especially for its services to rural communities and its packaging of eight shows per year. They commended the Film Board's creative response to the postwar staff reductions, especially its continuing distribution of films through provincial film libraries, university extension departments, municipal libraries, and various local organizations.

Their interventions were well and good, but Canada was on the verge of the television age, and this would forever alter the Film Board's traditional distribution activity. Amidst his difficulties with the press and Parliament, McLean submitted a brief to the Massey Commission in July 1949 in which he tried unsuccessfully to bid for the promised land of television. It was the last of his failed gambits.

By this time, Winters probably associated McLean with the persistently negative press image of the institution that had become synonymous with the word 'embarrassment.' He wanted a commissioner who gave an air of efficiency and who could clean up the sloppy administration. Winters also sensed that the commissioner was out of touch with his creative staff, since it was well known that the filmmakers disliked the idea of production deadlines and generally considered television production to be inferior to their own highly polished film products.

Winters demurred and dissociated himself from McLean's brief, because the government had already decided to make the CBC responsible for television. McLean knew this and had worded his bid cautiously, having sought television production 'in relation to any other agencies which may be charged with responsibility for the development of television programs in Canada.'[16] Winters's rebuff was an ill omen and indicated that the minister was treating him like a lame duck. His term was to expire at the end of 1949 and no one was asking him his plans.

Undaunted, the commissioner appeared before the Massey Commission in August and reiterated the key points of his brief. He also admitted the need for an overhaul of the Film Board's administrative, business, and employment practices. He wanted to correct the most glaring deficiencies: Film Board contracts were non-binding, employees were deprived of superannuation benefits enjoyed by other civil servants, and expenditures were not incurred in traditional business fashion. Worse, the organization had no working capital and had to return all unspent monies to the government at the end of the fiscal year. He believed that corporate status, such as that enjoyed by the CBC, would go a long way to correcting this situation. On the plus side, McLean noted that he was helping several Canadian feature-film companies, and there was now a technical research division at his institution that served as a non-competitive element of the local film industry. But it was television that showed much more promise, as evidenced by the telecasting of Film Board films by a product-hungry United States network.[17] The commission listened politely and went on to other business. Corporate status remained an elusive goal for the next forty years.

A new role for the Film Board?

The Massey Commission aside, few knew that the government had in mind a special role for its beleaguered film agency. The pub-licly invisible Psychological Warfare Committee had been broadcasting propaganda programmes abroad from 1943 until 1947 under the aegis of the Department of External Affairs. In April 1947 the cold war took a frosty turn over the publication of the Potsdam Declaration, which the Soviet Union claimed was missing a key paragraph. It looked like propaganda was going to have an even greater role to play, and at the department Lester Pearson proposed formation of a policy committee to give general guidelines on the conduct of psychological warfare.

By October the committee proposed that the functions of the Psychological Warfare Committee were to undermine and disrupt by overt/covert means enemy morale and to 'sustain and foster the morale and spirit of resistance of our friends in enemy-occupied countries.' Late in the report there was reference to the National Film Board, which the committee was to advise and direct on the making of propaganda films for allied and neutral countries. They discussed but then rejected the idea of placing the Film Board on the committee.[18] While the Film Board role was not to be vital, this exclusion may have been a slight to McLean or yet another vote of non-confidence in him. Neither External Affairs nor the Film Board Archives has turned up evidence of McLean's knowledge of the Psychological Warfare Committee, which remained top secret.

In this period of deepening cold-war tension, Canada was following the lead of both the United States and Britain who were planning to use psychological warfare too. By 1950 the United States, anxious to combat Communism from varying angles, was spending $10 million a year on psychological-warfare films alone. The Canadians were supposed to begin to coordinate activities with their new NATO partners.[19]

Ross McLean remained ignorant of these deliberations, while hitching his hopes to the rising star of television. But in 1949 everything he touched seem to unravel. Minister Winters favoured bringing in the firm of Woods, Gordon and Company to advise on

Ross McLean, government film commissioner
from 1945 until 1950

the Board's internal reorganization and accounting procedures and the Massey Commission agreed. The fact that these irritants continued to exist seemed to reflect McLean's own poor management. In October Winters moved to create a committee of Board members to plan the administrative overhaul. By this time, he was likely already looking for a new film commissioner.

The *Financial Post* continued its attack on the Film Board in November, with an article mentioning the fact that secret films were being made outside the Film Board and that security screenings were proceeding.[20] It seemed that McLean could do nothing to keep his institution out of the public eye. He had kept silent about the screenings, lest they become an election issue and embarrass the government. Tired of the bad press, the Liberals wanted to set the Film Board on the new path they had chosen for it. In November the board of governors listened to McLean's lame explanation that Brooke Claxton had aggravated things by saying that the whole Film Board had been declared 'vulnerable' rather than just the two hundred employees in production. The members asked McLean to leave the meeting for half an hour. It was then that they probably decided to not re-engage him. When they met again in December, they confirmed that McLean would

not be reappointed at the expiration of his term in January. McLean learned the bad news officially when he phoned the minister's secretary. He then picked up a paper, to read that W. Arthur Irwin would succeed him as of 1 February 1950.[21]

Even if leadership ability had not been McLean's greatest asset, the staff reacted angrily to the cavalier manner in which he had been treated. Ralph Foster, the assistant commissioner, resigned in protest. There was talk of the whole staff quitting, but McLean dissuaded them from scuttling the ship they had worked so hard to build. They took up a collection and bought him an automobile, and presented Foster with a sound system. All eyes turned expectantly to the 'hatchet man' they expected to close the doors.

The 'Hatchet Man' saves the Film Board

W. Arthur Irwin was about as welcome as the plague. There was general consternation that he, the editor of *Maclean's* magazine, would have the effrontery to accept the direction of an organization and a medium about which he knew very little. His magazine was owned by Maclean-Hunter Publications, which also published the *Financial Post*, whose persistently inimical articles had caused so much grief. The staff asked, but never learned, who was responsible for the Irwin curse.

During the bleak autumn of 1949, Irwin had let it be known in Ottawa that after twenty-four years he was not wedded to *Maclean's* for life and might be interested in serving Canada in the Department of External Affairs. Some weeks later, he met with Norman A. Robertson, clerk of the Privy Council and secretary of the Cabinet, who offered him the National Film Board post instead. 'Good God, Norman,' Irwin replied, 'That, at the moment, is the toughest job in Ottawa.' Robertson acknowledged, 'That's it exactly. Would you see Bob Winters?' Irwin went to see the minister, who explained that

Arthur Irwin (film commissioner, 1950–3) put to rest the rumour that he was made commissioner in order to close down the agency.

the government had been having trouble with this political hot potato. They wanted someone from the outside to resuscitate and rehabilitate it. Robertson and Winters briefed him about the agency's problems. He then went to see Pearson, whom he knew on a first-name basis, and who offered him a two-year contract to pull the Film Board together. The External Affairs plum would follow. He then met Prime Minister St Laurent, who obliquely proffered the 'moral commitment' to transfer him to External Affairs later on. The die was cast and soon Ottawa was buzzing with the news of the 'bargain.' Irwin received overwhelmingly favourable press and mail responses.[22]

He recalled later that all three ministers involved in the negotiations were explicit in wanting him to fix things at the Film Board, though they did not mention psychological warfare. They had a more ambitious assignment, the 'restoration of public confidence in the Film Board ... We think you are the man who can do it ... and we want you to do it.'

Irwin sensed that part of his job was to restore the *government's* confidence in the Board, a confidence that had almost totally evaporated.[23]

The mandarins and politicos had made a shrewd choice. In part, the Film Board's new lease on life was connected to its intended use in the psychological-warfare programme. Irwin's presence, they thought, would put an end to the whole question of security risks, and after he took the job, they brought him into the larger picture. They sensitized him to other issues, like the claims by the private film companies that the Film Board was driving them out of business and the Opposition attacks in the House of Commons for profligate expenditures and bureaucratic bungling. Even government departments were bashing the agency for its arrogance and excessive billing charges for their sponsored films. Yet this litany of complaints remained unresolved for the next thirty-five years.

That Irwin came from *Maclean's*, the sister publication of the *Financial Post*, could only please (and silence the criticism of) the Maclean-Hunter group, even though Floyd Chalmers, his superior, was furious and accused him of desertion. With 'one of their own' in place to get to the bottom of the Film Board mess, the attacks on the Film Board ceased abruptly. The overnight change was also due to the fact that the unfortunate Kenneth Wilson, who had led the *Financial Post* crusade, died in a plane crash.

The government felt secure in the choice of Irwin for a good cultural reason too: he was a man who understood and expressed fully the enigma of being Canadian. As its farewell gesture, *Maclean's* published a speech titled 'The Canadian' which he had made to an American audience in June 1949. His theme, a cogent expression of Canadian national identity, was that the Canadian was one who seeks peace, liberty, and security *in his own way*; it was the quintessential statement of how being in the middle is the source of national identity. Irwin spoke of two beings in every Canadian, a geography man and a history man. The former was determined by a harsh and empty northern frontier; the latter was a natural reaction to u.s. continental expansionism and was a need to confirm the very political allegiance that the revolutionary war had severed. Canada became keeper of the bridge between the old and new worlds, thereby siring the Commonwealth idea of freedom without separateness. The Canadian nation was also born of compromise between two races, languages, and cultures. Duality had taught Canadians how to balance, to be the person in the middle, whether it was with respect to emotions, people, politics, or world powers. The Canadians' strength was to bring opposites together in a world made anarchic by the unlimited sovereignty of the modern nation-state.[24]

'The Canadian' may have been airy stuff, but prior to publication, it was read with some interest by Robert Winters as he was trying to sort out Film Board affairs; it may have turned his head.[25] The Department of External Affairs also found Irwin expressing precisely the kind of profile they were trying to cultivate internationally. Irwin had been active for over a decade in Canadian international affairs; the speech not only showed what kind of diplomat would attach himself to the department, but demonstrated too how the person in charge of the National Film Board understood and enjoyed the trust of the government.

Meanwhile, on the practical level, there was the thorny security question at the Film Board. Irwin agreed to take action, but would not initiate a wholesale purging, would not accept the premise of once a communist always a communist or of conclusive guilt by association. He insisted on the right to cross-examine the security police. There might be genuine security risks, he thought, or some people who had been just plain damn fools. Then again, there might just be some incompetents at the root of the whole matter. He vowed not to mix the first category with the second two.

Irwin's primary duty was to calm the shattered and shocked Film Board staff during the interregnum from December 1949 to February 1950. He flew to Ottawa to meet the senior staff and told them that the government had made a blanket commitment to maintain the organization. His job, he said, was to reorganize it and restore public confidence.

The RCMP gave him the 'laundry list' of thirty-six employees, which was divided into security risks, probable security risks, and possible security risks. Irwin refused to accept uncorroborated or unconfirmed allegations, and he and the police sparred over the dossiers. He insisted on one thing: that people with radical or unconventional views had a perfect right to them in a free country. He concluded there were three clear cases of people who could be real security risks. Irwin took the thirty-six dossiers to Norman Robertson and, without revealing the three names, asked him what he thought. A few days later, Robertson called back; he too had picked the same three names. Irwin conferred with Winters, who was anxious to see the security problem resolved. The commissioner made no charges when releasing the three employees, a writer/producer, an animator, and a distribution person. He told the three that since the Film Board had been declared a vulnerable agency, he could not consider them suitable candidates for employment there. None of the three protested. Soon after, the minister announced in Commons that the release of the three was not an issue of specific charges, but of their estimated trustworthiness.[26]

By June 1950 the worst was over. The Toronto *Globe and Mail* reported that the atmosphere had so changed that even the Film Board's loudest parliamentary critic, Gordon Fraser, expressed satisfaction with the new set-up.[27] After the fact, Irwin stated that it was one of the most disagreeable jobs he had ever tackled. He remained unsure as to whether these people should not have had a chance to defend themselves after being charged publicly.[28] To his credit, the liberal in him refused to fall victim to the Red-baiting hysteria then beginning to convulse the continent. The so-called purge of the Film Board was over, although more employees resigned afterwards, probably because of bitterness and discomfort with the whole offensive process of loyalty investigation.

Irwin never had a chance to respond to the various criticisms about his activities during this critical period. He learned years later that in fact there had been a Communist 'study group' at the Film Board during the mid-forties. A curious employee told him of attending one meeting. When asked about what had gone on, the employee replied, 'They knitted.'[29] No more need be said about the 'subversion' that lay at the root of the anti-Communist frenzy threatening to engulf the institution.

Restoring the government's confidence in the Film Board

The 'businessman from Toronto' scored his first breakthrough with the staff while visiting the ten different Film Board locations in Ottawa. He came upon a remote corner of a decrepit building and was shocked to discover female film inspectors working in overcoats and mittens. They told him that Public Works had refused to put in heaters for the previous three years because the building was to be condemned. Irwin told the department they had six days to put in heaters or he would call in the press to show how the Government of Canada treated its employees. The heaters were installed four days later.

By March 1950, the consultants Woods, Gordon and Company completed an internal survey of the organization. Having discussed the survey with Walter Gordon prior to its release, Irwin knew that its major recommendations called for a new structure, improved procedures in staffing, financing, and accounting, and the centralization and modernization of facilities in Ottawa.

Part of the reorganizing process was to centralize production and to have a director of production supervise the four film units which then existed: A (agricultural, French-language, foreign-language, and interpretive films), B (sponsored, scientific, cultural, and animated films), C (theatrical, newsreels, tourist, and travel films), and D (international affairs and special projects). The two leading candidates were James Beveridge and Donald Mulholland. Beveridge was part of the old Grierson phalanx, a gentle, tentative, attractive person whose only deficiency seemed to be a proneness to generalization. He had learned his editing skills from Stanley Hawes, and was best remembered for the 1941 film *Northwest Frontier*, an ethnographic documentary about the aboriginal peoples of the North. Grierson had tried and failed to make him his successor in 1945.

Mulholland, by contrast, was an import from the advertising world of Toronto, a dapper, hard-bitten, aloof, mildly cynical organizational type who smoked cigarettes in a holder. He was best known for writing and directing the 1947 ground-breaking film that blended drama and documentary, *RCMP File 1365 – The Connors Case*. The scenario, a homage to the RCMP at a time when they had the Film Board under a microscope, was based on an actual murder case. Professional and non-professional actors re-enacted the police investigation with restrained naturalism. In the end, of course, the Mounties get their man. Also notable was the first ever peacetime appearance of gunplay (one shot) in a Film Board film. Subsequently, most of the pistols seen and heard in Film Board productions were starting guns in athletic-competition films. The taboo against screen violence became a Film Board hallmark until it was broken in the brutal rape re-enactment in Anne Claire Poirier's *Mourir à tue-tête* in 1979. Absence of gunplay in dramas has been an enduring Film Board trait.[30]

Irwin settled on the unilingual Mulholland, whose devotion to hard work and clear-headedness eventually inspired loyalty from his compatriots, who were once his peers. His critical flaw, however, was to treat the film needs of French Canada shabbily. Some of the French-speaking staff came to consider him a francophobe; others thought that because French Canadians were invisible to him, he neglected them.

There were, however, mitigating circumstances. One must put this matter into the context of the time, where in Quebec the autocrat Maurice Duplessis used Communist scare tactics to exclude Film Board films from schools and continued bad-mouthing the federal agency until his death in 1959. Given this atmosphere, Mulholland was not alone in keeping French Canadians invisible to each other. A typical Duplessisism had 'le chef,' a reformed problem drinker, saying that he feared that education was like liquor, and that some could not hold it.

Another fact was the pervasive sense of social repression, as recalled by Jacques Bobet, a godfather of modern Quebec cinema, who at this time was translating English productions into French. In a Trois Rivières church basement in 1950, he was showing a 10-minute wartime documentary that celebrated the contribution of Canadian factory women working in overalls. The outraged local priest said that if the Film Board intended in the future to show other women in pants working outside the home, Quebec civilization could do without the Film Board. Period. Close quotes.[31] More content to follow demand than to create it, Mulholland was not the only person to ignore the film needs of French Canada.

Beveridge accepted a posting to London, England, graciously, although some reluctant production staff were still convinced that Irwin was out to wreck the institution. At the same time, the commissioner was quite aware that the French Canadians did not feel at home in Ottawa, despite the existence of the 'French Unit' that had allowed Jean Palardy, Pierre Petel, and Roger Blais to make their first films. Irwin began looking

for a French Canadian who could move upward in the organization. He spotted in young Pierre Juneau the very talent he thought the Board needed, and sent him to London to broaden his English, handle French distribution on the continent, and wait until the right moment for retrieval. To further strengthen the French-Canadian presence on the board of governors, Irwin persuaded Gratien Gelinas, then the top figure in the French-Canadian theatrical world, to join.

Irwin wrote to Winters in May 1950 and summarized the recommendations of the Woods Gordon report. The 1939 National Film Act needed overhauling, since the original Grierson creation was to have been a coordinating board, with production and distribution remaining with the Canadian Government Motion Picture Bureau. When the Film Board had absorbed the Bureau in 1941, the powers of the director of the Bureau to employ temporary staff were used to employ Film Board personnel. Working capital was provided for by annual appropriation and by advances recoverable at the end of each fiscal year. The organization had no power to enter into contracts, and those it had signed had no legal basis. There was even doubt whether it had the authority to produce films to be paid for by other departments.

It was obvious that the act was hopelessly outdated and Winters told Irwin to rewrite it, based on the Woods Gordon report. The original Film Act had placed a minister and a Privy Council member on the board of governors.[32] In order to keep 'politics' and political pressure at bay, Irwin placed the board under the responsibility of a single minister, who was to be responsible to Parliament for its control and direction. The new board consisted of five representatives from the main geographical areas of Canada and three from the government to represent the civil and defence services; the film commissioner was both the chairman of the board and chief executive officer. Now the organization had legal contractual powers, a working capital fund, and the power to make and distribute films. A grey area was whether or not its staff came under the Civil Service Act.[33] This proved to be the largest and most damaging loophole in the restructuring process, spinning out severe financial ramifications twenty-seven years later. The government also refused to grant crown-corporation status.

The most important language in the new act was not legal, but was Irwin's articulation of the Film Board's mandate. Clause 9a became the agency's catechism, if not catch-all justification. The phraseology became the most often repeated in the coming decades: 'The Board is established to initiate and promote the production and distribution of films in the national interest and in particular (a) to produce and distribute and to promote the production and distribution of films designed to interpret Canada to Canadians and to other nations.' When Grierson had drafted the original Film Act in 1939, the intention was the same, 'to make and distribute films designed to help Canadians in all parts of Canada to understand the ways of living and the problems of Canadians in other parts.' Irwin's words were more prosaic and expansive. He entrenched the notion of producing films for international audiences and built into the law the most open-ended phrase of all, 'in the national interest.' During fair seasons and foul, this clause became the Film Board's lifeline; for years the words began the *Annual Report*. How one interpreted 'national interest' could cause great controversy, yet in the late 1960s this phrase fell by the wayside as a new generation of filmmakers staked out another, more personal agenda. The eclipse of 'in the national interest' as a reference point coincided with a downward spiral that nearly sank the organization.

The move to Montreal

In the heady May days of 1950, the immi-

nence of a new Film Act coincided with a sense of rebirth. The law was passed in June and came into effect on 14 October. The troubling uncertainty of Irwin's first months was gone and the staff became accustomed to chatting with him, even if he seemed more the listener than talker. Irwin was concerned with myriad details, but the issue that excited people most was that of a new building.

The need for a centralized establishment had gone back to the Grierson days, when production facilities were housed in an old lumber mill on John Street, and nine other Ottawa locations accommodated the rest of the sprawling body. During the war, an architect had drawn up plans for a monumental edifice, but these lay forgotten in a filing cabinet as the McLean years became a grim struggle for survival. The Woods Gordon report had called for a new building and no one denied its necessity. The only question was: where would it go? Most people assumed the building would have an Ottawa location. Irwin slowly came to the conclusion that it could be anywhere in Canada *but* Ottawa.

His reasons were like so much of what he did, practical and to the point. Civil-service Ottawa was filled with stereotypical conservative and conventional people. The Film Board was an operation whose success depended on the effectiveness of its creative core. He feared that if it became a bureaucracy, it might stagnate and die. The unconventional behaviour of the staff had caused Ottawa tongues to wag. Irwin put it simply: 'The obvious thing was to get it somewhere where it wouldn't be so bloody conspicuous.' He believed that the staff had become so reactive that they could take neither criticism nor the government itself.

He wanted to be near a pool of talent with whom the staff would have contact and compete, while the administration wanted such a pool from which to hire staff on a per-contract basis. Their concern was to avoid building an enormous fixed overhead in the form of full-time salaries. There were only two logical places from which to choose, Toronto and Montreal. The CBC was building its core in Toronto. If the Film Board were to operate effectively within the framework of the bilingual and bicultural postulates emanating from the Massey Commission, there was only one place to go, and that was Montreal. The problem was how to persuade the government, the board of governors, and almost everybody else to accept this choice.[34]

Irwin put his case to the board and to Minister Winters at about the same time in a confidential report.[35] He argued that the creative staff found itself in a minority position of assuming a defensive attitude against all outside groups, including the government, of which it was a part. The minority group tended to turn inward, to regard itself as being superior to and misunderstood by all other groups with which it came into contact, to the point of being disinclined to receive fresh ideas from outside. (When the English-speaking wing of the Film Board recognized its status as a minority group in the Film Board in the late 1960s, some of these same observations applied to it.)

Contact with French Canada was necessary to operate effectively in French. As for the English, the commissioner argued that the English community in Montreal offered the advantages of a metropolitan area. The determining factor was that there would be immediate contact with both English- and French-speaking talent. All this had a political advantage – it would ensure the balance between the French- and English-speaking communities.

The report mentioned that Montreal was the site of one of the two initial television stations being set up by the CBC; thus, the Film Board would have access to the television main line. (Irwin had not forgotten McLean's earlier bid for the new medium, which indeed did become the major outlet for French production at the Board.)

Irwin concluded with a cost analysis of the move, noting that of the 459 on staff, some 138 were Ottawa-born, generally occupying

clerical positions, most of whom would probably not move. It was unstated, but obvious, that in Montreal these positions would be filled eventually by French-speaking people, thereby changing the very internal character of the agency.

It was not difficult for Irwin to sell Minister Winters and the board of governors. Nor was it a chore to convince the key civil-service mandarins in Ottawa, Robert Bryce, Norman Robertson, and J.W. Pickersgill. The last, whom George Woodcock has called 'that nimble Figaro of politics,' became the responsible minister some years later. Pickersgill saw no harm in putting into French Canada an institution that Quebec considered suspect. He did not want to provoke Premier Duplessis, but to create a presence, asserting the fact that Montreal was part of Canada.[36]

Winters took Irwin's submission to Cabinet, where it was accepted with few questions in September 1950, in part because there was a current notion that some functions of the government should be decentralized. When the public works department failed to find experienced studio designers, the Board of Governors engaged John and Drew Eberson of New York in June 1953. Gerald Graham, the head of Film Board Technical Operations, supervised the details of construction.

Nearly all of two dozen potential sites were eliminated immediately because they were near dense population centres, and plans called for storage in specially designed vaults of some eighteen million metres of archival film, much of which was highly explosive (and deteriorating) nitrate film. The choice was a parcel in suburban St Laurent that bordered on cow pastures and was owned by a businessman, not, as the gossip still persists, by political cronies of the government. In what was perhaps one of the greatest might-have-beens and ironies of Film Board history, headquarters could have been located in downtown Montreal. The burgeoning project costs led the Department of Public Works to order cancellation of the film vaults' construction at the last moment. The archival footage (mostly duplicate film) fell to the care of Public Works, which found makeshift storage in an old corrugated metal building in rural Kirkland, Quebec. Three years and $5.25 million later, the whole operation moved into new quarters in suburban St Laurent with hardly a ripple in the production schedule. Ever since, there has been virtual unanimity among the Film Board staff that this location, facing a busy expressway, is the worst possible place for a cultural institution to have its headquarters. As for the troublesome archival film, as predicted, spontaneous combustion caused it to go up in flames in July 1967, in a fire that consumed it all.[37]

Plans for the new facilities did not cause as much difficulty as the staff did. When they learned that Montreal was to be their new home, they opposed it overwhelmingly. Director of Production Mulholland argued against it resolutely until Irwin made it clear that this was his and the government's policy. Mulholland yielded reluctantly and then used his organizing talents to help with the move. His loyalty, however, was to Irwin only, for once the commissioner left, he again took up the employees' cry and tried to stop the move.

The Ottawa community rose up in a single voice of protest. The Film Board pariah suddenly became the city's precious jewel: the chamber of commerce passed resolutions, city council offered the agency twenty-seven acres free, and the *Ottawa Citizen* gave prominent space and support to Mayor Charlotte Whitton, who claimed that what was happening was equivalent to the expulsion of the Acadians, worse, of the Japanese Canadians from coastal British Columbia during the war. The government did not respond. No one seemed to be concerned about the economic blow that was to fall on Ottawa.

Prime Minister St Laurent was undoubtedly behind the government's silence. When Winters presented the Irwin submission, he included a secret letter to the prime minister. Television broadcast facilities would soon be built in Montreal, he said, and that city was a centre of bilingual activity in the motion-picture industry, hence the move was a good idea. However, the Government of Quebec was hindering construction of a television transmitter on Mount Royal, and Film Board films were still 'banned' in that province by Ciné Photographie, the censor board, which was another Duplessis tool.[38] While Winters had received assurance from Duplessis that the ban would be lifted in due course, the television obstruction seemed to be a closed subject with the premier. Winters reminded the prime minister that he, St Laurent, had suggested a confidential talk with Duplessis about these matters; this might be the time for it, he thought.[39]

The tête-à-tête with Duplessis was timely. The premier's Red-baiting anti–Film Board rhetoric had abated somewhat when it became known that Irwin's regime stood for a 'clean-up,' although Duplessis persisted in mocking the 'Communist' federal institution. One can only surmise that the prime minister must have used his own considerable persuasive powers to mollify the tough 'Chef' from Quebec and to solidify the foundation upon which the Film Board was to be built. Some time later, the television antenna appeared on Mount Royal, and St Laurent brooked no more arguments to stop the Film Board move. Diplomacy notwithstanding, the implacable Duplessis government prohibited the use of Film Board films in Quebec schools in 1954.

In October 1950 Irwin wrote the Massey Commission and informed them of the new National Film Act and of the decision to move the Film Board to Montreal. He believed that Quebec's Ciné Photographie no longer blocked distribution of Film Board films, although relations were not yet at the level that existed in other provinces. (In fact the Quebec censors continued to block distribution of Film Board productions for another decade.) He indicated that just over half the staff would be eligible for superannuation even though the Civil Service Act did not apply to them. Fearful of the burden of a permanent staff core, Irwin wanted to see a kind of bonus system attached to salaries in order to encourage quality and a regular turnover of creative talent. He wondered how he might get this proposal around Treasury regulations and was disappointed to learn that he could not.

Film Board operations were to cost $2.5 million for the fiscal year 1951–2, including $250,000 for production of new films to be used in the battle of ideas between the Communist and non-Communist worlds. Irwin stated that the board of governors had felt that the entertainment content of the agency's films should be increased in order to reach a wider audience. This idea was tied into the whole question of distribution, which still needed clarification, since the Film Board sometimes found itself offering the same films both for free and at a price. The question of films for CBC television was still open.[40]

Psychological warfare: The rise and fall of 'Freedom Speaks'

While the reorganization of the Film Board continued apace, with a nudge from the Department of External Affairs, Irwin turned to thinking about the possible use of films in the cold war front, for the top-secret Psychological Warfare Committee.[41] He drafted a summary of preliminary proposals for A.D.P. Heeney at External Affairs, who also sat on the newly constituted board of governors. The idea was to undertake some experimental films designed to have psychological impact in two distinct target areas, NATO countries and their friendly neighbours, and in Asian countries cooperating in the Colombo Plan.[42]

Irwin opened his brief with a line from Grierson's favourite Film Board propaganda film, *The War for Men's Minds*: 'The basic conflict in the world today is the battle for men's minds.' The rest was vintage cold war: 'We are faced with a powerful and ruthless campaign to engulf the world with a philosophy and a social system which is alien and repugnant to us. We are living in constant fear that this battle of words and ideas will turn into armed aggression and we are arming ourselves and seeking our allies to meet the threat of this aggression ... By comparison we are doing relatively little to win the battle of ideas, which, in the ultimate analysis, will determine the issue.'

In the context of the times, Irwin's brief was illuminating for its insistence that a Canadian voice could influence the war of ideas. The object was to speak to the world through film, to counter Communist propaganda with a positive re-emphasis of the advantages of democracy. He thought the major theme should be that in a democracy the state exists for the individual, not vice versa. Democracy's promise to all men remained unfulfilled, but it was still vital and growing. The promise of bread might be alluring, but democracy alone could offer bread and freedom.

The commissioner proposed a five-year programme to concentrate first on western Europe, then on India and Pakistan, and finally on Canada. The Film Board approach was to be implication, not exhortation, that is, no blatant propaganda. The point was to show an imperfect democracy growing toward an ideal. Depending on each potential audience's sophistication, there were to be differing approaches: friendly to Asia, emphasizing technical assistance; a more sophisticated approach to the cynical and pessimistic Europeans; and a didactic slant for Canadians, who needed to understand the interrelation of world problems and events in terms of their effect on Canada. He appended a list of twenty-seven film ideas. There was also to be a series of fourteen shorts (for theatrical release) describing the people of Canada, to illustrate the democratic thesis that Canada does work to the advantage of the individual.[43] Many of these film ideas did in fact become Film Board productions. Apparently very few of the staff members realized for what purposes they were investing their creative energies. To them, these were not propaganda items, but rather normal films about daily life. That, of course, is what made them unique.

External Affairs found the Irwin proposal interesting and imaginative,[44] although they thought that in order to achieve proper effectiveness the film programme should not contain more than one direct propaganda film.[45] The department thought that the programme should be called 'The Freedom Program' and waxed about adding television and Europe's 29,000 theatres to reach an annual audience of just under two billion.[46] If Irwin was generating measured enthusiasm for what was soon retitled the 'Freedom Speaks Program,' R.B. Bryce, secretary of the Treasury Board, doused cold water on matters late in January 1951. He found the plans ill-defined and doubted that sophisticated Europeans would respond to a film programme on democracy. Frankly, he wondered if all this was good enough to justify the quarter of a million dollars' expenditure. Fearing trouble from the Treasury Board (which was the perennial penurious public conscience in Cabinet), Winters discussed the proposal with Prime Minister St Laurent, who threw his weight behind the scheme.[47]

Thus was born the Ad Hoc Committee on Government Information Services, chaired by Norman Robertson, whose avowed purpose was to counter Communist propaganda outside Canada. At its first meeting, Irwin asked what sort of programmes should be undertaken with his $250,000 budget. He personally opposed a rigid propaganda approach, lest it stultify the essential feature of Western life. Robertson agreed.[48]

The committee liked his idea of producing some twelve newsreels or news magazines per year to achieve the Europe/NATO objective. If Freedom Speaks was to be a propaganda arm of Ottawa, it was typically Canadian for it to operate on the liberal basis of laisser-faire. The government had a single objective: to leave it to the Film Board to use its creative freedom to show in what way Canadians were really good at something.[49] This approach to 'propaganda' distinguished Canada from the other two major cold-war adversaries, who were carrying on their respective crusades.

The compilation film that finally emerged in 1953 was *Germany, Key to Europe*. Doing the best he could with not very stimulating stock-shot and newsreel footage, writer/director Ronald Dick synthesized the meaning of the complex events that had plunged the West into the cold war. Russia had moved quickly to fill the spiritual vacuum left behind by Hitler, the narration explained, and the Russians parroted the slogans of international Communism's campaign against the West. Russia's strategy was to pose as the champion of German unification, while accusing the Western powers of blocking it. It wanted the evacuation of all troops, after which it would count on the easily controlled Popular Front to seize power. In opposing this scenario, the West had stood firm before the Berlin blockade and hoped to turn Germany to democracy. The film concluded optimistically that the political apathy that had hung over the German people since the end of the war had begun to lift.

The film ignored the difficult question of how West Germany intended to deal with the legacy of Nazism, which the West was continuing to treat with a pall of silence. Dick had created a didactic essay; *Germany, Key to Europe* was packed with so much selective information that, at best, an average viewer could absorb only a fraction of it in twenty minutes. Though it was translated subsequently into most European languages, the film stands as an example of why the Film Board was not a particularly effective cold warrior. Irwin saw the piece from another vantage point. He confided it to no one at the time, but the making of this film signalled the achievement of his personal agenda: the government's confidence in the Film Board seemed to have been restored with no strings attached. The rest of the $250,000 was used to make fairly non-political films.

French Canada: A fair treatment or not?

From the 1940s, French Canada had complained legitimately that the Film Board did not truly serve its needs because most French-language films were translations of English originals. No one denied that authentic films from French-speaking Canada were necessary, but with a limited production budget and a closed French-Canadian market, it always came back to how to get the most from the money being spent. In 1950 Mulholland decided to stretch his production dollars and to expose English audiences to French-Canadian culture, thereby catering to both linguistic groups. He asked Bernard Devlin and Jean Palardy to direct *L'Homme aux oiseaux*, by Quebec author Roger Lemelin, which had commentary in English and dialogue in French. Shot by Grant McLean, it was an amusing folk tale of a man who lost his job because he was a bird fancier.

Film historian Pierre Véronneau has claimed that the film stands as the extreme example of the agency's assimilationist attitude to French productions. An ancillary (if more charitable) explanation might be that with distribution in Quebec hemmed in at almost every turn by the Duplessis monolith, it would be excessive for the Film Board to commit its limited production funds to an expensive film that had little chance of being seen. Until there was a secure outlet for films in French (like the soon-to-materialize Radio-Canada television network), none of the Film Board's administrators wanted to stand accused in Parliament of acting like a spendthrift. Véronneau's conclusion that the administrators did not see why they had to have francophones produce an original French production is simplistic and misleading. A more accommodating hypothesis is that *L'homme aux oiseaux* might satisfy a curiosity in English Canada to see something of the all-but-unknown society of French Canada.[50] This is not to deny that there was a long way to go until there was genuine French-Canadian production. The move to Montreal was the first step toward that goal.

The Massey report of 1951 heartily agreed. In probably its most significant observation about the Film Board, the report stated that the institution did not truly serve both language groups, that most French-language films were translations of English films, and that there was a need to give attention to producing films 'specifically for French speaking Canadians.' The need to increase French production was coupled with a call for new premises to be provided for the agency. By this time, the wheels were already in motion for the shift to Montreal.[51]

Three blockbusters secure the future

Irwin had briefed the Massey Commission in October 1950 on the planned expenditure of $250,000 for psychological-warfare films. The commission feared that this might be the beginning of the use of more of the Film Board's budget for films to be screened outside Canada and of a consequent reduction in the number of films produced for use at home. Irwin tried to assuage their concern by noting that part of the approach to psychological warfare was to produce dual-purpose films, for use at home and abroad,[52] which was something most other countries avoided.

Irwin was probably thinking of this a year later, when his nose for a good theme sniffed an opportunity to put the Film Board positively into the national and international spotlight. He and the creative staff had been looking for a means to develop an overview film on Canada, after having toyed with, then rejected, the theme of the still-unbuilt Trans-Canada Highway. Suddenly they recognized that the planned royal tour of Canada in 1951 by Princess Elizabeth and Prince Philip promised to be more than an elaborate newsreel. The visit afforded a chance to use a new 35-mm Eastman colour-film stock, not yet on the market, that differed from the traditional (sun-only) colour film by guaranteeing richness whether it was overcast, rainy, or snowy.

This was a fortuitous choice, since director David Bairstow found the fall weather typically rotten for twenty-four of the thirty-seven shooting days. The result was five reels of stunningly beautiful images. The film was to have been two reels (twenty minutes), but no one could decide what to cut. Irwin called in Harvey Harnick, the Film Board's theatrical distributor associated with Columbia Pictures, and J.J. Fitzgibbons, president of Famous Players, the largest theatre chain in Canada. After seeing the five reels of unfinished silent footage, Fitzgibbons exclaimed that it was a feature that could not be cut. He would run it with one proviso: that it be ready for Christmas week, a month away. Irwin held his breath and promised delivery, knowing full well that under normal conditions editing and music would take almost two months.

The staff worked day and night to complete the editing, and *Royal Journey* opened on time in seventeen first-run theatres in the principal cities across Canada. In the next two years over two million Canadians saw it in 1,249 cinemas, an all-time attendance record. It also played in the United States, in Britain, and in some forty countries around the world. At a cost of $88,000, this film returned a profit to the Film Board of over $150,000. With good reason Irwin believed that, more than any other single factor, *Royal Journey* restored public confidence in the Film Board. It was one reason why Grierson later praised Irwin unequivocally: 'You saved the Film Board.'[53]

There was another film conceived in 1951 that was destined to reach even greater heights than *Royal Journey*. In fact it would become the most popular Film Board film in history.[54] *Neighbours*, an 8-minute experiment in pixilation-animation technique, is inextricably linked with the genius of Norman McLaren and the world's familiarity with Canadian animation film. Irwin was the catalyst and McLaren became the creator of the unforgettable moral parable of two neighbours who destroy each other in a squabble over who is proprietor of the flower that grows on their property line.

McLaren, who joined the National Film Board in 1941, is a subject worthy of extended treatment.[55] No other person did more to bring credit to the institution than did this demure, unassuming pacifist Scotsman, who saw himself as a 'civil servant' as much as an artist who used the medium of film. He had worked for Grierson at the GPO Film Unit in England and left when war broke out in 1939. Later, he had managed to get word to his old boss in wartime Ottawa that he wanted to leave New York to work in Canada so long as he did not have to make war propaganda. It was a fortuitous moment and Grierson replied with characteristic fervour: 'Come, and you will see that you can make cinema as you understand it.' McLaren was the single talent to whom Grierson gave free rein and, in return, Canada inherited a unique legacy and predominant place in the world of animation art. From his first wartime 'message' film *Mail Early*, to the sing-along shorts *Chants populaires*, to wordless images and symbols that spoke a universal language through movement and sound, McLaren and the Film Board became synonymous with excellence. In homage to his greatness, in 1989, the NFB headquarters' main building was named after him.

McLaren founded the Animation unit in 1942, and within a decade had recruited such original animators as Colin Low, Wolf Koenig, Robert Verrall, Evelyn Lambart, George Dunning, René Jodoin, Grant Munro, James Mackay, and Jean-Paul Ladouceur. These innovative artists became the leadership core that propelled the institution for the next forty years.

In 1949, McLaren and Evelyn Lambart

had experimented with painting images on film to accompany the brilliant jazz score of Oscar Peterson in *Begone Dull Care*, which became one of the most enduring Film Board productions. The same year, McLaren joined UNESCO in China, where, as part of a project on fundamental education, he taught a group of Chinese artists simple animation and filmstrip techniques, to be used to teach rural populations the principles of health and sanitation. He witnessed the Communist takeover, and was impressed by the excitement and enthusiasm of the young people around him. He developed an empathy for them and when he returned to Canada in 1950 felt like 'a very socially aware animal,' distressed as he was by the Korean War. He intended to do a 'serious' piece, but could not resist Raymond Spottiswoode's invitation to make two stereoscopic (3-D) items for the Festival of Britain, *Now Is the Time* and *Around Is Around*. Upon returning to the Film Board, he and Grant Munro began testing a new method for animating live humans, single-framing human motion. Instead of having the camera record twenty-four frames per second, they could slow down the number to as little as one frame a second. The results, called pixilation, showed odd, stylized, capricious, and impossible behaviour, something that would be hilarious in a square-dance film. But McLaren thought square dancing was too trivial a subject.

At this critical point, Commissioner Irwin spoke to him, curious to know how he was busying himself. Mindful of this 'Freedom Speaks' commitment, Irwin suggested that McLaren turn his thoughts to a topic of some international significance. The animator mulled it over, and while rescreening the test rushes a few days later, noticed a 30-second sequence of two men exchanging what seemed to be supernaturally violent fisticuffs. At that moment the idea for *Neighbours* leapt into his mind almost full-fledged: there would be two good neighbours, a flower on the boundary of their property, mutual possessiveness by both, a dispute, a fight, and

a senseless struggle to the death of both men, their families, and the flower. There was never a script and he shot the film chronologically over the summer. Details like the neighbours' respective newspaper headlines 'Peace Certain If No War' and 'War Certain If No Peace' or the appearance of progressively uglier warpaint on each neighbour's face were improvised along the way with the help of Jean-Paul Ladouceur and Grant Munro respectively, who played the leading roles.

As McLaren explained it years later, the Korean War had its impact on the concept too. With Canada on one side and the Chinese on the other, 'I felt very strongly the effect of war on two good people who were fighting each other, and this intensity of feeling about war made me make *Neighbours*. I don't consider *Neighbours* a political film, it's primarily a moral film, it's a parable; there's a moral to it which applies to any human beings anywhere.' It did cross his mind that during the cold-war atmosphere of the time, 'it might be construed as a subversive film because it talked about peace and peace was a dirty word in that era.' When the film won an Academy Award in 1953, McLaren was on another UNESCO project, this time in India. A brief telegram heralded, 'Congratulations. Neighbours wins Oscar.' McLaren replied that he was pleased with the news, but wondered quizzically why this called for a costly telegram about someone called Oscar. Later he said it was ironic that official Hollywood, which was in the midst of enthusiastically hunting down what it considered subversives, presented the award to Canada's consul-general. Never one to direct the spotlight on himself, McLaren credited Irwin for his timely suggestion. 'It was the catalyst that linked up my deep subconscious desire to make a statement about human nature and my ability to express it through the new technique we had been toying with,' he later wrote.[56]

The irony, of course, was that *Neighbours* was to have been grain for the gristmill of psychological warfare. McLaren never knew the source of his funding and was simply using the creative freedom of the Film Board to make an earnest statement. While *Neighbours* demonstrated the futility of war and its association with human bestiality, it also said something figurative about the Canadian dilemma: Canada was itself on the border, caught powerless between the potentially annihilating nuclear powers. It is an image with which Canadians have lived for decades, one with which they are more comfortable than a world of jingoism or cynicism. Furthermore, the Film Board's association with 'peace' is part of its philosophical core reaching back to Grierson's admonition that the future of the agency would be secure if filmmakers made peace as

exciting as war. McLaren's parable, coincidentally not far from Irwin's own conception of 'The Canadian,' became the international film image that the world has associated with Canada.

It was obvious that the best films for the international audience were those without a propagandist message, and there followed some twenty films that pursued an indirect approach.[57] Because the 'Freedom Speaks' title suggested didactic propaganda, it soon became the 'International Programme.' 'Freedom Speaks' disappeared quietly at the end of 1953, with the explanation that the films produced for it had had a dual target of audiences both at home and abroad. With its demise, the special $250,000 grant ended.[58]

A third film became associated with the

Norman McLaren's wordless and pixilated animation *Neighbours* (1952) became Canada's most popular film. This Oscar-winning moral parable has brought the Film Board decades of international recognition and praise.

two above-mentioned blockbusters, an 11-minute cel-animation piece that still evokes chuckles from first-time viewers. *The Romance of Transportation in Canada* was a satirical caprice about how Canadians dealt with the historic/geographic challenge of transportation, the concept of a national image, and Canadians' own alleged love of suffering. It was a collaborative effort, involving the talents of Colin Low, Robert Verrall, Wolf Koenig, and occasionally Roman Kroitor in brainstorming sessions. For the first time, here was a frontier myth that was not American, not 'political,' and not serious. To be able to laugh at oneself may be the first step toward maturity, but when Minister Winters saw it, he was not amused. 'Who authorized that?' he barked. 'I did,' answered the cool Irwin, 'and I predict it will win international awards.' Winters ceased his carping and was gratified when it won ten awards, including an Oscar nomination, the Palme d'Or for animation at Cannes and honours at Edinburgh.

Relations with the CBC: Television

The one area that seemed to remain impervious to the Irwin magic was the Canadian Broadcasting Corporation. The Film Board's wish to have a regular television outlet had fallen on deaf ears ever since Ross McLean had broached the subject formally in 1949. Irwin talked to Davidson Dunton, his old friend and CBC chairman, and after consulting the ministers responsible, reported the terms of the Irwin-Dunton agreement to the Massey Commission in October 1950. Its key provisions were three promises: more collaboration, the mutual avoidance of monopoly, and the involvement of commercial film companies in a three-way arrangement to make films for television.

While it was still too early to tell who would do what, the Film Board was to continue to record and dramatize contemporary Canadian life on an actuality basis, but was barred from making pure entertainment films. Any films that the CBC wanted from the Film Board were to be charged according to cost, since one body was not supposed to make a profit at the expense of another. The Film Board would assemble a newsreel programme for television of around twelve minutes a week, based on half-Canadian, half-international stories. Irwin was upbeat and optimistic when he concluded that if there had been mutual suspicion in the past between the two institutions, the groundwork for the development of mutual confidence had been laid.[59]

Formalized two years later, the Irwin-Dunton agreement called for both organizations to cooperate in providing film for television and, above all, to avoid duplication. The CBC wanted more newsreel material from the Film Board and the two agreed to avoid duplicate shooting in that area too. Since the CBC could not afford to sponsor production of films for Canadian television use exclusively, there was an opening for the multiple-use Film Board films to be used by the CBC if the latter would pay a portion of the cost.

Unfortunately for the Film Board, this was not a genuine CBC offer. The corporation demurred when it was suggested that the Film Board's planned new facilities in Montreal be enlarged to encompass the additional CBC work. The network was intent upon building its own plant and facilities, so there was to be no close courtship, let alone marriage, of the two, despite their agreement to have an official liaison at the top.[60] Given the nature of modern bureaucracies, this was not surprising. Both institutions grew, and the Film Board ended up being about one-tenth the size of the CBC. The following decades were notable for the acrimonious relationship between the two.

The Irwin-Dunton agreement did, however, give rise to the *Window on Canada* series, hosted by Clyde Gilmour, a 26-week series of half-hour Film Board films edited for television, beginning in October 1953, and the *On the Spot* series, twenty-six quarter-hour *reportages* for weekly television release, both with French counterparts.[61] In 1956, these were replaced by the half-hour *Perspective* series and its French counterpart, *Passe-partout* (with half its issues straight translations from the English and the other half original French productions).

Thus, the Film Board had entered the world of television from 1953, but if the CBC seemed a reluctant partner, a good number of the Film Board creative staff felt likewise. Many of them considered television a kind of bastard medium, whose interest was not film art, but material to fill the immediacy of the void. None the less, television's strength is its requirement for economy of statement, something that Film Board filmmakers have long tended to shun.

Members of Parliament and the Film Board, 1952: They liked what they saw

Two chapters of the Massey Commission report of 1951 had referred to the Film Board positively. The report could not anticipate how the arrival of television was going to change forever that special chemistry that had helped the Film Board to become one of the essential social threads weaving through rural Canadian life. If some chambers of commerce and boards of trade had considered the agency unnecessary, the commission had ignored their few sour notes and encouraged the Film Board to commission private film production when it was in the public interest. Most pertinent was the stress on the importance of the organization carrying on experimental work in documentary films, 'especially in films designed for information and instruction.' In probably the most significant observation respecting the Film Board, the report had claimed that only a national organization protects the nation from excessive commercialization and Americanization.[62] Then and today, these were two of the most cogent arguments for having a National Film Board.

In March 1952 a confident Minister Winters announced that a Special Committee of the House was to investigate the Film Board. He was not expecting trouble and was certain the politicians would be happy with Irwin's reorganization. When the committee met two months later, the commissioner provided them with a brief historical sketch of the Grierson years and an upbeat report on contemporary successes.

He explained how the films came to be produced from the thousand or so ideas that were submitted annually. First there was close scrutiny by the production committee (made up of the director of production, his senior executive producers, distribution representatives, and the commissioner), which asked five critical questions: (1) Can it be translated on to film? (2) If so, what will the resulting film say? (3) To what audience will the film be addressed? (4) How much will it cost? and (5) Will the film fit into overall policy and the annual programme? From here, a programme pattern emerged, which the board of governors finally reviewed and decided upon. Once the programme was initiated, there were progress reports quarterly during the year. Films made for government departments, the so-called sponsored films, were decided by the sponsors. In this fashion, the 1950-1 year saw some 130 film projects, 25 of which were one-reel (10-minute) shorts for government departments and 57 of which were longer than one reel. Some 34 were for theatrical use as opposed to 96 for non-theatrical use. The creative staff of 223 produced these at a cost of $1.3 million. The annual budget of $3 million included $2.3 million voted by Parliament, $500,000 in sponsored film sales, and $250,000 from 'other' sources. To keep the financial hawks at bay, the commissioner had made sure there was a surplus, and he sent the receiver-general $37,625.

Irwin concluded his peroration by reiterating his conviction that the Film Board must nourish the paradox of unity with diversity, by interpreting the parts to the whole and the whole to the parts and by holding up images of the Canadian past and present and the path to the future.[63] Here in a nutshell was the reason d'être for the fifties. To make sure that his listeners' eyes did not glaze over with the litany of statistics, Irwin planned a surprise ending. When the committee came to headquarters for a three-hour tour, a cameraman filmed their arrival and initial tour. As they continued being briefed, the film was rushed to the laboratory, processed, and finished, just in time to show the delighted visitors upon departure. Almost a decade before instant replay, it seemed nothing less than miraculous. The gambit paid handsome dividends. A month later, the members stressed the need to consolidate the operations of the agency under one roof. Their single caveat was that Irwin could not explain why the Quebec government did not use Film Board films. He dodged the question and claimed that he wanted to present the visage of Quebec to the rest of the country and vice versa.[64] The nagging issue of Quebec was an ever-present reminder of the diversity that Irwin hoped to turn into the amalgam of unity. The hand of friendship was more easily proffered than taken. Perhaps going to Montreal would cure the problem.

But Arthur Irwin would not see the Promised Land. He had kept his part of the bargain with the government a year longer than he had promised, and in reorganizing the Film Board had also saved it. He had long been interested in the evolution of the Commonwealth, having argued that Canada had in fact invented it – so he welcomed the chance to observe its continuing development from 'down under' when he became Canada's high commissioner to Australia.

In May 1953 he announced his resignation to a shocked staff. Marjorie McKay, one of his close lieutenants, likened his leaving to losing Grierson eight years earlier. Irwin had been known as a relatively silent person and his regime had been characterized more by deeds than words. He had won over the hearts of most of the creative staff, particularly P.K. Page, whom the widower married. She left film and then became a distinguished poet and painter. Irwin admitted years later that he had longed to be more directly involved in production, but had been consumed by administrative organization. He was not to be the last film commissioner to experience this fate. But it was his vision and belief that the Montreal move would mean less friction from Ottawa politicians and, in step with the Massey Commission recommendations, a genuine and beneficial cultural cross-fertilization. Much would depend on who would succeed him. At that moment, there were very few candidates.

2

Down the Road from Ottawa to Montreal

A last attempt to stop the Montreal move

Robert Winters hoped to ensure continuity by finding a film commissioner who had been privy to policy development and who had the prestige to fill Irwin's shoes. He spotted his man in Albert W. 'Bud' Trueman, who sat on the board of governors of both the Film Board and the CBC and was president of the University of New Brunswick.

Trueman was astonished when Winters phoned him in the spring of 1953, offering the Film Board's top post. Film was not exactly his line of work, the academic protested, but, like Irwin, he agreed to do the job for a few years if there was something else to follow. He arrived in Ottawa to find that as a result of a cabinet shuffle, Walter Harris was the new minister responsible.[1]

Shortly afterward, Donald Mulholland, director of production and spokesperson for a good part of the staff, considered void his support of Irwin's planned move to Montreal and began lobbying against it. At Trueman's suggestion, he wrote a series of briefs in July and August, explaining why. The arguments are worth describing in light of what events brought three decades later. Mulholland ignored the thinking and wisdom that had pointed to the necessity of accommodating French cultural expression. His appeal was based on perpetuating the existing situation, rather than designing the Film Board of the future: 'If we were a private company seeking commercial business ... we should unquestionably set up our operations in Toronto,' he stated. Ottawa was better suited culturally than Montreal, he believed, since the capital was filled with experts in national and international problems; if skilled personnel were needed, they could be recruited from elsewhere. Besides, a move to Montreal would mean probable unionization and higher labour costs, the greatest single factor in the Film Board's budget. There was also the fact that one-quarter to one-third of the annual programme was derived from sponsored films, all from departments in Ottawa. In Montreal, it would be difficult to keep these contacts viable, even if the commissioner stayed in Ottawa, because there would be a break between himself and the rest of the organization. Mulholland predicted that this loss of closeness to the government was the most serious factor related to the whole question.[2] His fear was prescient.

Trueman took no position on the move. He believed that the film commissioner should listen to the advice of his experts, so he passed the information to Harris. But he was opening up a can of worms that the prime minister thought he had already closed after conducting personal diplomacy with Premier Duplessis. The peeved St Laurent called Winters and asked if Trueman was trying to sabotage the move. The embarrassed commissioner told Winters he was simply acquainting him with the facts of the situation.[3]

The turn of events did not reflect the fact that it was Trueman who, in October 1950, had moved the original motion to relocate the Film Board to Montreal 'with the maximum possible despatch.' The Cabinet had approved this motion and Parliament questioned neither the purchase of the Montreal site nor the $900,000 initial expenditure in 1953. Ironically, Harris had been the only cabinet member who had said in 1950 that it was unwise to move to Montreal, and he still favoured Ottawa. St Laurent inspected the proposed site with Harris and Winters and then confirmed the government's decision. Having gone through his political baptism of fire, a chastened Trueman assured Harris that he would do his best to make the move the most efficient one possible.[4]

Reports that the new building was to cost $5 million raised eyebrows early in 1953, and in December the Conservative Opposition expressed anger at how the project had crept through Parliament without much scrutiny. By March 1954 they complained that Parliament had never defined the real scope of the Film Board's activities; the Conservatives then moved to block construction. One of the last die-hard opponents warned that Montreal was a poor site because the Russians had made it the number-one target for a hydrogen-bomb attack. His paranoia was not infectious; the motion was defeated and, soon after, construction began.[5] Ottawa had lost its rambunctious child, and before long the excitement of moving gripped the staff. In two years they found themselves at the suburban Montreal site, alongside the future Trans-Canada Highway.

Harris to Trueman: 'Keep me out of trouble'

Minister Harris was much different from Winters, his predecessor, who, as an engineer-builder now in the Ministry of Public Works, liked planning and efficiency. Harris's plate was full with administration of Indian Affairs, Immigration, the National Gallery, and Public Archives. With little time to devote to the Film Board, his sole advice to the film commissioner was, 'I know nothing much about films or about the Film Board. You run the show and keep me out of trouble with the House of Commons.'[6]

Trueman believed his job was 'keeping the ship running' and he left the management to others, preferring instead to play the occasional role of adjudicator and adviser. This allowed Donald Mulholland to become an assistant commissioner in all but name. He turned over to Gerald Graham, the director of technical operations, the two-year Herculean task of coordinating building and moving. Graham's competence resulted in a move that interrupted neither the work nor output of hundreds of staff in the spring and summer of 1956.

Crawley Films, which was producing 23 per cent of the non-theatrical films made by private industry in 1952, was pressuring Harris to let private producers carry out all federal-government film production. In 1951, the Film Board had added Unit E for sponsored work and Unit F for French-language films. Trueman told Harris that he needed the sponsored work to cover the $3.6 million it cost to run the organization in 1951-2, including $1.4 million for distribution costs. (This latter 40 per cent ratio remained fairly constant for the next two decades.)

The minister realized that the private sector's struggle for these sponsored films hid the larger question of why an indigenous commercial film industry had failed to develop. In a detailed secret report to Harris, the Film Board outlined Canada's sad colonized situation, which had to do with the unwillingness of Hollywood and London, England, to share the annual hundred-million-dollar market they had in Canada. With just five English-language features produced in Canada since the Second World War, only the Film Board's documentary *Royal Jour-*

ney had been a success. A few low-budget French-language features had earned back their production costs and a couple had turned a profit.[7]

The most viable economic activity in theatrical films was the short, and most of these, made by private companies, were sport or travel films that competed with Film Board shorts. Travel films were often produced commercially and even before the infamous Canadian Cooperation Project of 1948, the Film Board had maintained travel-film libraries in the United States, where such films drew an annual audience of 3.5 million. If Canadian commercial producers rarely sought international distribution, it was the Film Board that made available select Canadian commercial films to many embassies and consulates.

The Film Board made a point of not competing with Canadian 'locals' representing u.s. and British newsreels. In fact, the Film Board sent for free its non-controversial and non-political 35-mm black-and-white silent and loosely edited material to New York, London, and Paris, where it was used as a pool by the newsreel companies, who were free to add their own commentary. It was an odd and typically colonial way for Canadians to see images of themselves, but the trade-off was that any items which ended up in the international newsreels might be seen by tens of millions. It was a humiliating situation, but better than nothing.[8]

Commercial interests posed a not-so-rhetorical question that lingered for decades: 'Should the Film Board retain its distribution and advisory roles and get out of production altogether?' Such a move would undeniably strengthen the private sector. The Film Board reply was that a core group of some fifty to seventy artists was necessary to perform the collaborative task of supplying the various films required by the government, since no single company in Canada could hope to meet that need. The Film Board's 260 creative staff produced theatrical, non-theatrical, newsreel, television, and sponsored films, without cutting corners, as the commercial companies were wont to do. This was the Board's strongest argument against either a single commercial monopoly or the fragmentation of government film production.

The organization promised to work closer with the commercial industry at all levels, and to allow outside bidding on more work. The Canadian tradition of combining public money and private enterprise became the shotgun marriage whose offspring was the hybrid called Canadian film. As for sponsored work, the Film Board's only reservation was that tendering out should never result in the agency finding itself with unused facilities or idle staff. This argument developed even more potency as a huge plant was being constructed in Montreal. The commercial industry continued its plaintive cry for the next thirty years until the Film Board relented and quit making sponsored films altogether.[9] When that occurred, rumours about an idle staff resurrected the original question of whether or not there was a need for a Film Board.

Films for what audiences?

If television, the new arrival, was beginning to transform urban Canada with a tenfold increase in telecasts from 1952 to 1954, non-theatrical distribution continued to be a Film Board mainstay. In rural Canada, audiences in church basements and community halls continued to enjoy programmes on monthly circuits as they had in the forties. How many people they constituted was a guessing game, and the unspoken secret, to which many insiders were privy and about which no one was willing to go public, was that distribution statistics were probably doctored. From 1949 until 1954 there appeared to be healthy annual rises of 10 per cent or more in both non-theatrical and theatrical statistics. The *Annual Reports* preferred to generalize total revenue, and one had to scour them carefully to find the specific figures of film sales and commercial rentals. No verification was possible for the estimated annual figure of

700,000 visitors who saw tourist films in hotels, parks, and other locations.[10] That such films were screened on a regular basis was probably more important than establishing actual numbers of filled seats.

Perhaps statistics are not as important as some might believe, since the most significant audience was the school-age group, (with the exception of Quebec) for whom teachers sought both entertainment and instructional material. Whether there were thirty-five or one hundred per screening, the fact was that in the early fifties the Film Board claimed it processed some 25,000 requests annually for its films, which it translated into an estimated audience of four to five million Canadian schoolchildren. Figures aside, there are today several generations of Canadian adults who, as children, can remember seeing such wonderful films of this period as *Ti-Jean Goes Lumbering*, *One Little Indian*, *Neighbours* (the top three non-theatrical Canadian films of all time), *The Loon's Necklace* (Crawley Films), *The Romance of Transportation in Canada*, *Teeth Are to Keep*, *The Story of Peter and the Potter*, *Age of the Beaver*, *Angotee: Story of an Eskimo Boy*, *The Pony*, *The Longhouse People*, and *How to Build an Igloo*.

Douglas Wilkinson directed and wrote *Angotee: Story of an Eskimo Boy* ($12,831) in 1953, using colour footage he had purchased from another cinematographer. This remarkable 30-minute anthropological film follows the birth, growth, and maturation of an Inuit child. Wilkinson's earlier films *How to Build an Igloo* ($7,546) in 1950 and *Land of the Long Day* ($13,848) in 1952 reinforced stereotypical beliefs about Canada. The first film demonstrates the remarkable physics involved in igloo-building, and the second follows a contemporary Inuit seal hunt. Both shorts emphasize the almost mystical relationship between the Inuit and their environment. Internationally they also did much to perpetuate in children's minds the myth that Canada was a land of Eskimos. Allan Wargon's *The Longhouse People* ($10,476) convinced millions of other children that Canada was peopled with aboriginals like the Iroquois, while Grant Munro's *One Little Indian*, a puppet film about an Indian boy who learned traffic safety rules in his first visit to the city, achieved the same unintended objective.

Whatever one might think about the impact of these films, there was a truism that was difficult to deny: the Film Board was doing a job that private industry either could not or would not do. These films were highly polished, hence expensive, and as proposed film treatments did not appear at first sight to be commercially viable. In short, if the Film Board had not made them, in all likelihood they would not have been realized.

On another level, *The Mental Mechanisms* series of 1947–50, directed by Robert Anderson for the Department of National Health and Welfare, had broken ground with respect to changing the public's attitude toward mental health. The films had also shown the possibilities of using professional actors to weave drama skillfully into the documentary text. They inspired writer-director Stanley Jackson to undertake *Shyness* in 1953, a dramatized film in which children as non-professional actors talk about their fears. One child learns through experience not to distrust others, who themselves admit that they are afraid of some things too. The film demonstrates how children learn to receive approval and encouragement. In this, as in his other films for and about children, Jackson underscored the universal humanitarian values that are the building blocks to adulthood.[11]

Quite separate from *Mental Mechanisms* was the nine-film series called *Mental Symptoms*, produced and directed by Anderson and Jackson in 1951. These films, restricted to professional audiences involved in psychiatric work, showed mental patients in situations that demonstrated their actual illnesses. The idea for the series had come from the John Huston postwar film *Let There Be Light*, a study of soldiers who suffered from various psychological disorders brought on by combat.

The Child Development series from 1951 to 1956 (*Ages and Stages*) was made by Crawley Films and distributed by the Film Board. It featured some of the most popular and best-selling Canadian instructional films and covered the typical psychological evolution of the child, from *Terrible Twos and Trusting Threes* to *Frustrating Fours and Fascinating Fives*, followed by *From Sociable Six to Noisy Nine* and then *From Ten to Twelve*. The life of a film was generally six to eight years; these colour films stayed active until the 1980s. It was not that they were the last word in child development – quite the contrary. The next generation of filmmakers, more concerned with self-expression than didactic filmmaking, resisted updating these classics until recently, despite frequent public demands.

In 1954–5, some thirty-one Film Board productions earned prizes worldwide. Among these was the 1953 children's film *Ti-Jean Goes Lumbering*, produced and directed by Jean Palardy, the first in a series of similar Ti-Jean films. This film not only proved to have staying power, but by 1990 also held first place in Canada in the top two hundred non-theatrical films. Using voice-over narration, a kindly grandfather relates to his grandchildren the fable of a French-Canadian boy who possessed superhuman powers. Grant Crabtree's clever trick photography had the little colossus outperforming all the other lumberjacks, carrying hundreds of logs, eating enough for ten men, and finally disappearing on a huge white horse. If the child/male role model (not unlike another mythological French-Canadian hero of the past, Paul Bunyan) satisfied the fantasies of countless children, the fact that filmmakers never thought to find female heroines in French-Canadian lore to translate into film regrettably confirmed the invisibility of French-Canadian women.

The dramatic short *The Grievance* ($28,601), also in 1954, was a didactic film that followed *The Shop Steward* ($28,382) in the two-part series *Labour in Canada*, written and directed by Morten Parker. This (half-hour) re-enactment of a union grievance procedure was aimed at showing unionized workers how to obtain a fair hearing if they felt victimized by employers. The film and series marked a continuation of the Film Board progressive tradition, dating back to Grierson, of portraying organized labour sympathetically and of helping to entrench workers' rights.

Science films also proved to be a popular group of documentaries. J.V. Durden's *Embryonic Development: The Chick* ($9,889) in 1953, was a fascinating observation of the development of the chick embryo through all its stages. Using time-lapse photography as well as animation technique, Durden's film opened a world of possibility to students interested in science and continues to be distributed today. Durden, who with Hugh O'Connor constituted the creative core of Unit B's Science Unit, continued his work with camera and microscope until the early sixties. In 1955, the science film *World in a Marsh*, directed by Dalton Muir, showed another example of the potential of science films. With the help of a close-up lens and underwater photography, the film described birth and death in the marsh world as a struggle for survival that 'reflected in miniature the whole world of nature, both savage and beautiful in its intricate harmony.' It remains in the top twenty Canadian non-theatrical films, but was unfortunately a singular film of its type. One of the greatest misfortunes to befall the Film Board was its failure to pursue the science-film genre with any real vigour after these classics had been made.

Norman McLaren won accolades for the institution once again, when his animation *Blinkity Blank* won the Palme d'Or at Cannes in 1955, the first of a dozen awards to follow. This 5-minute experiment in the use of intermittent animation and fitful bursts of pictures on blank film made the viewer aware of how vision and after-image affect perception. Sound was as integral to the success of the film as was light. The images set the rhythm, while a combination of Maurice Blackburn's jazz improvisation and McLaren's synthetic sound scratched on film combined to create the effect of a self-enclosed harmonious universe.

French Production: The poor relation?

In 1954 Radio-Canada, French-language CBC, gave the Film Board a 15-minute television slot, which became known as *Sur le Vif.* By the fall of 1955, it was replaced by *Passepartout*, a series of twenty-six half-hour shows combining the techniques of *Sur le Vif* and *Regards sur le Canada*, the French version of the English programme *Window on Canada*. The series ran for two years on Sunday evenings in prime time and was hosted the first year by Gérard Pelletier, who, with guests, led discussions following the film. Half the films were originals and half were recycled older films, a fact that has led some to charge that French production was a poor relation to English production. Using hindsight, one might wish that the institution had been ahead of its time, but it was not at fault for being part of its time. The most serious problem in French production was that Ottawa was not a city conducive to attracting and keeping skilled French-language personnel.[12]

Ross McLean's reorganization of production in 1948 had led to the creation of Unit A, a cultural unit responsible for dance, the arts, theatrical and non-theatrical originals, and English- and French-language versions. The latter activity, primarily the bailiwick of Jacques Bobet, led some to call it the 'French Unit,' although that was an oversimplification. Unit B was an English-speaking group that included 'diverse' and animation items. Unit C was devoted to theatrical shorts like *Eye Witness / Coup d'oeil* and newsreels, and Unit D dealt largely with sponsored films, plus Department of National Defence films. French films were noted for their eclecticism, and the theatrical series *Vigie* comprised six

films a year on the culture, industry, and agriculture of French Canada. At this point the French were receiving around 15 per cent of the production budget, excluding animation and versions.

But Unit A's product was inevitably 'folklorique,' and when French-Canadian theatre and film giant Gratien Gelinas joined the board of governors for three years in 1950, he started to lobby for better quality. Unit E, under Bernard Devlin, undertook the production of both English and French films for television. Unit F, under Roger Blais, was devoted to French production exclusively and undertook *Silhouettes canadiennes*, a French version of *Faces of Canada*.[13] A constant complaint was that the French section was suffering from lack of competent personnel. Because Arthur Irwin had designed the system to operate with more contract personnel than permanent staff, there was a high turnover of French Canadians. Besides, their unhappiness was palpable as they found themselves forced to speak, write, and think in English.[14] A standing Film Board joke was that nowhere else was there bilingualism in a federal institution in Canada – the French staff had to learn English in order to function there. Many of them punned that the letters ONF, Office National du Film, really meant Organisation non-français.

Re-enter Pierre Juneau, French adviser

Paul Theriault had been the French liaison officer at the Film Board from 1944 until 1951, during which time he had been responsible for recruiting much of the francophone staff.[15] Nearly two years later, Trueman summoned from England the Irwin appointee Pierre Juneau, who was soon called 'French Adviser,' a title nobody liked and a position with no job description. Trueman was quite aware of and sympathetic to the ferment then beginning in Quebec and considered that his elevation of Juneau fit into his policy of giving French Canadians a head start.[16]

As French adviser, Juneau had no authority to approve anything, neither to hire nor to fire, nor even to interview candidates. Thus, he had to negotiate everything as he carved out his niche. Soon he was interviewing prospective filmmakers and, before long, none was hired without his authority. He was also secretary to the board, which found him preparing agendas, attending meetings, and recording the minutes. He became an informal executive assistant to Trueman, reading his mail daily and beginning to exercise a kind of moral authority. Donald Mulholland welcomed him to production meetings, which in turn widened Juneau's perspective greatly. He observed the awkwardness of a system in which the unilingual English senior producers and administration needed to have the French proposals translated into English before considering them. It was harder still on the young French filmmakers, who had to struggle in English to defend their projects. That first year back at headquarters, Juneau made up his mind that there would have to be distinct English and French production units. His plan took nine years to realize.[17]

Meanwhile, developments on the French side must be seen in the light of continuing erratic relations with the Duplessis government and the firm hand of the new minister responsible for the Film Board, J.W. Pickersgill, who succeeded Walter Harris in July 1954.[18] He developed a style of running the ministry quite different from that of Harris, with whom he remained very close. Harris suggested that Pickersgill give Trueman the same advice he had: keep the minister out of trouble and, unless something extraordinary happened, the Film Board would get the same amount of money every year. Pickersgill tried to make it his policy not to interfere in the internal administration, but to confine himself to keeping the budget under tight control. His advice to Trueman was, 'This is the cloth you have and it's your responsibility, not mine, to decide how to cut it.' The cloth, however, included at least one wrinkle, the question of a distinct French Production group.

By November 1954 there was a move to create two posts as assistant commissioners, English and French. Mulholland was already acting in that capacity as director of operations, planning, and relations. He had expertise and the confidence of his colleagues and knew the administration. Trueman depended on his penetrating analyses of various problems. Pierre Juneau, at thirty-four, was the obvious choice for the French side, but External Affairs' board member Jules Léger thought that someone older, perhaps a prestigious outsider with a little more political experience, should hold the position.[19] Part of the problem had to do with Premier Duplessis, another with the Cabinet in Ottawa.

That same fall, Quebec censorship authorities had started to harass the Film Board again. In September, an inspector of the censorship board, Service Provincial de Cinématographie, had seized fourteen films being shown by a priest in a parish hall in Quebec City and at a tourist lodge in LaVérendrye Park. He claimed Quebec's right to charge a censorship fee.[20] It appeared that someone in Quebec City had taken a top-level policy decision regarding the federal agency, or that in typical mindless bureaucratic fashion, this was the routine formality of a censorship office vetting films. The Film Board suspected that it was being singled out and feared it would be saddled with fees of some $20,500 per year.

Trueman thought the Film Board should go along with the Quebec authorities to avoid the spectacle of having the voluntary film councils, municipal libraries, owners of projectors, or persons running them penalized. Pickersgill sought a legal opinion from the deputy attorney general, who told him that there was no legal basis on which provincial censorship boards could compel the Film Board to submit to censorship and pay fees or penalize those who showed such films.[21] In other provinces, the Film Board paid no fees for 16-mm censorship, although it had been paying censorship boards across Canada for its 35-mm theatrical films until 1951, after which time only Nova Scotia, Alberta, and Quebec continued the practice. Pickersgill took the issue up with Prime Minister St Laurent; neither wanted to snap the delicate thread that held Duplessis and Quebec to Ottawa's skein. At last they worked out a compromise strategy, which called for examination of one print of each film. Duplessis was willing to go along with the entente, providing that, if the censor condemned or modified a film, all copies of the film would have to be so modified. The minister thought he had the last word when he told Duplessis that he authorized the Film Board to go along with these arrangements, 'without entering into any discussion of the constitutional rights of either party.' The compromise read simply that the Film Board agreed to pay Quebec an annual amount of $2,500 to $3,000 for censorship fees, applied retroactively to all Film Board films.[22]

Thus did Pickersgill help keep stable Ottawa's very delicate relations with Quebec. The *Montreal Star* reported the accord in January, as part of the ongoing problem of Quebec censorship of CBC television. An unrepentant Duplessis said there was no reason to behave like a bull in a china shop, but some NFB films, meant for television, were of an objectionable nature and should never have been shown. He added that while he rarely watched television, it was a dangerous instrument, not only because it kept children from doing their homework, but also because it telecast some immoral films.[23]

The politics of censorship would have been difficult for the young Pierre Juneau to handle and this might have been one reason Pickersgill held back his promotion. Also, the question of creating two assistant commissioners was not simply a matter of bureaucratic convenience; it meant splitting programming into two linguistic branches. By March 1955 Pickersgill had refused to act. Trueman tried argument: the French programme was important but should not be seen as existing in isolation from the rest of the programme; French and English should be part of a consistent whole that served the particular needs of French Canada. But

Trueman emphasized that at all times the institution's basic purposes were national, not sectional. His rationale was an interesting one, in light of what happened when the split that occurred eight years later created two houses under one roof.

Pickersgill did not budge and a year passed. With the move to Montreal imminent, Trueman needed a senior person to deal with the anticipated increase in contacts between the Board and the French-Canadian public. Finally, André Laurendeau unleashed an attack in *Le Devoir* and condemned the Film Board's failure to construct a francophone side, thereby relegating the French Canadians to translators. He repeated another journalist's charge that Mulholland was a francophobe. Of all unlikely people, it was Duplessis himself who understood the Film Board dilemma best when he described Mulholland as 'un unilingue qui passe pour francophobe.' Trueman again tried pressuring the minister. If an outsider were chosen, probably both Juneau and Mulholland would leave, and there would be a huff in the press. Morale at the Film Board was already skittish, he warned, and a wrong move might have serious consequences.[24]

The uncharacteristically silent Pickersgill finally drew the line and refused categorically to allow creation of a separate French-language division. He delayed until February 1957 before announcing that Juneau would be executive director, in charge of financial administration and distribution, while Mulholland, the director of planning and operations, would continue heading production and technical services.[25] Both were to be paid equally, lest the French press claim that Mulholland was second in command.

It had taken two and a third years to effect this most critical structural change. Sometime later, Pickersgill admitted that he had feared that Juneau's youth would result in his being characterized as third in command or, worse, a mere token. He wanted someone who was going to matter and he was worried about an unknown who had yet to prove himself. As observer of these events, Juneau explained the hiatus decades later: 'People in authority will look for candidates of high prestige and while waiting for their ideal composite individual, will let some interesting candidates fall by the wayside'. Thus was he left to wait, undeterred if not strengthened in his belief that the Film Board had to provide an environment in which French-speaking creative people could work together without the handicap of language. He did not leave the institution until he had made that conviction a reality.[26]

Trueman on the rubber-chicken circuit: Creating an image of success

Donald Mulholland and Gerald Graham ran the operations, but Trueman excelled at public relations and speech making. He had always thought of himself as an opera star manqué, and loved using his mellifluous baritone voice to extol the institution. He criss-crossed the country in a one-man publicity campaign, almost always elucidating the same theme: the Film Board interpreted Canada to Canadians, avoided propaganda, and encouraged education. Its documentary films both provoked comparisons and showed the viewer the common denominator of human behaviour in new circumstances.[27]

Sometimes Trueman talked about specific films. His three favourites were *The Stratford Adventure*, *Farewell Oak Street*, and *Corral*. The first was an expensive ($83,000) 50-minute item released in 1953. Under director Morten Parker, the 19-man film crew followed Gudrun Parker's script, which recreated the birth of the Shakespeare Festival at Stratford, Ontario. There were cameo appearances by Alec Guinness, Tyrone Guthrie, and Irene Worth, the three internationally famous stage people who were part of its first season. Alec Guinness's advice to a rising star typified how each of the three was seen in a 'candid' moment off stage, though it was obvious they were playing to the cameras. *The Stratford Adventure* enjoyed years

of excellent national and international distribution; Trueman loved it because it was about art. When one enthusiastic, if garrulous, producer told the *Ottawa Journal* that the Film Board was planning full-length features, the annoyed commissioner contradicted him by telling the minister he did not think the Film Board could ever produce more than one a year and it was 'by no means certain that we could or should do that.'[28] English-language features remained on the back burner for another seven years.

Farewell Oak Street ($29,000) was a 20-minute dramatized piece set in Toronto. Originated by Arthur Irwin himself, it told the story of the coming of public housing to Regent Park and the end of the slums there. Gordon Burwash's script described nineteen unhappy people sharing one house and one bathroom in revolting conditions of dirt and lice. There was even a dramatized sequence of child molestation, a daring first on Canadian screens.

The strongest reaction to the film came from some of the very tenants who resented use of the term 'slum,' because they did not consider themselves poor or low people. They were angered too because they did not see it before its release in 1953. The area's member of Parliament thought the film was offensive to human dignity and wanted it withdrawn; he was probably appalled at the way his riding was being thrust into the national spotlight. The board of governors split, with some stating that the depiction of squalor was not typical of Canada or its housing problems, while others thought that seeing such conditions might help to stimulate communities to do something about their slums. Trueman wisely chose the path of least resistance and said he did not wish to withdraw the film, lest it cause more trouble and controversy than if it were left alone.[29] New prints of *Farewell Oak Street* continue to be ordered periodically by Ontario housing authorities.

No one seemed to question the dubious major premise of the film, that with new public housing there were 'no old possessions or attitudes.' Apparently class relations appeared to make no difference in this Marxless film. After the hullabaloo had settled, Trueman let it be known he was fed up with 'do good' films on housing and drugs; the latter was a reference to the planned documentary drama *Monkey on the Back*, director Julian Biggs's tragic story of a man's struggle to free himself from drug addition. Written by Gordon Burwash for the *Perspective* television series in 1956, it was in the tradition of the 1948 film by Robert Anderson, *Drug Addict* ($22,600), a predominantly voice-over dramatization that had used real drug addicts in situ. The harrowing *Monkey on the Back* used an actor to depict an addict's misery, from injecting himself, to getting arrested, to imprisonment, to the nightmare of withdrawal and cold turkey, and finally to death by overdose.

In the earlier film *Drug Addict*, the viewer also saw some gruesome examples of the misery of addiction, from actual injection by addicts to the prostitution of women to help their boyfriends afford drugs, to theft and the disintegration of a cocaine junkie in nightmarish hallucinations. This film was also brutal in its message: there was no such thing as self-cure when it came to drug addiction, and jail was no answer. Addiction cure centres and psychiatric treatment were the preferable alternatives. The film was so powerful in its frightening presentation and condemnation of drug addiction that it had been banned in the United States.[30]

How effective the two anti-drug films were is impossible to estimate. In this period, drug abuse was nothing like the pandemic it later became, but Trueman believed the Film Board's role was not to tell the country what was wrong with it. He fostered an unwritten policy and priority, the shift from social realism to the *art* of film.[31] He recalled: 'Mulholland and many others were burdened with what seemed to me an excess of social conscience, a do-the-people-good whether-they-like-it-or-not complex.' He felt that the balance between art film and educa-

tional film was not being maintained. He encouraged a new niche: more art and less social propaganda. The change occurred gradually, but perceptibly. While a few social-purpose films emerged over time, the next anti-drug film was *The Circle*, by Mort Ransen, in 1967.

Trueman found that *Corral* fit perfectly into the context he envisioned. Conceived of as a low-budget item of the *Faces of Canada* series, this was Colin Low's first non-animation film and depicted the real life of the contemporary cowboy. Home on holiday, Low followed the advice of his executive producer, Tom Daly, to go back to the place from which he had come to record an individual character portrait. He realized the mythic potential of the world he had left behind in southern Alberta and was fascinated by a man who became a cowboy instead of a mechanic or bank clerk. Such a person, he believed, was probably an incurable romantic or something of a philosopher. He hoped to capture the nuances of the craft of horsemanship in the old Spanish-American cowboy tradition, while paying homage to the Hollywood cowboy-film genre.

With Wolf Koenig's steady hand behind a new 35-mm Arriflex camera, they directed and photographed this romantic portrait of a cowboy rounding up wild horses, lassoing one of the high-spirited animals in the corral, and then going for a glorious plunging ride across the visually spectacular Rocky Mountain foothills. Eldon Rathburn's specially composed guitar music, played by Rey de la Torre, consumed $3,670 of the $4,582 budget. Music is the only sound to accentuate the Alberta sky, foothills, cowboy, and horse in their ageless pre-industrial tradition. Daly's consummate editing turned the lyricism of the silent picture into one of the purest statements of the great Canadian western myth: a humble, revolverless cowboy becomes part of a corner of the wilderness and leaves his imprint upon the world more by accommodation than by conquest.

Corral evokes nostalgia in the urban mind

In *Corral* (1954), a documentary of an idyllic Canadian West, the hero accommodates himself to the world instead of conquering it.

for the apparent peace and simplicity of that bygone era and the simple relationship between man and beast. Years later, John Grierson referred to *Corral* as a little poem about man and the perpendicular, evoked by the single rider against the sky. The 11-minute film won first prize at the Venice Film Festival in 1954 and remains one of the most widely acclaimed Canadian films.

Television: A promising outlet or suffocating monster?

Ross McLean's dream of the Film Board serving as a principal supplier of film to television had been as unrealistic as it had been grandiose. In 1950 Irwin had settled for the CBC promise of a 12-minute newsreel programme, *On the Spot*. Within three years, the Film Board's additional air time was in the form of old productions and odd-hours fillers. The other bad news about television was that it was beginning to erode the Film Board's once secure non-theatrical base. As TV proliferated, people spent more of their leisure time at home, and the organization faced years of frustration trying in vain to resurrect non-theatrical audiences. Management put on a brave face, and claimed in the *Annual Report* that films were reaching an estimated worldwide audience of 175 million.[32]

The CBC thought the Film Board was hindering its growth. As the corporation was gradually transferring its radio-public-affairs people to television, middle management assumed that for every Film Board (non-series) production accepted, a CBC person was put out of work. Many concluded that the Film Board was more than a stumbling block – it was becoming an enemy.

There were comedic missteps and tribulations over the new medium. Trueman had approved Mulholland's request to purchase five television sets for home use, so the senior filmmakers could develop a sense of what they might do. When the Treasury Board learned of the $1,500 purchase, it ordered the sets returned and sold them off as war surplus.[33]

This was not the only difficulty – most of the filmmakers resisted moving into television production.[34] Those senior producers who had demonstrated a pro-television bias, like Sydney Newman and Gordon Burwash, had been sent from the Film Board to the United States in 1948 to work for a year on all aspects of the medium. In exchange, a programme-hungry NBC television network received the right to broadcast Film Board films. Returning to Canada, both men later joined the CBC when it became clear that the Film Board was not going to move into the medium in a significant way.

The main Film Board complaint about television was that it ignored artistic quality. Filmmakers were accustomed to spending extra time to polish a production. Simply put, there was no such thing as a slipshod Film Board film. If it meant that extra weeks or even months were necessary to achieve the desired effect, nobody protested. Costs tell the story. *On the Spot* television films, for example, cost $1,200 to $2,000 each; the original crew of three, Bernard Devlin, John Foster, and Fred Davis, travelled by stationwagon across the country to find subjects as diverse as a paper mill, the RCMP crime lab, or a judo club in Hull. Their shooting ratio was two and a half to one, meaning that for every two and one-half feet shot, one foot was used. This left little room for editing. They generally picked the best takes rather than cut individual sequences.[35]

By fall 1954 the series was expanded to a half-hour and a budget of $7,000 per film.

There was a weekly deadline and the product showed it. A classic example was *The Dresden Story*, shot in 1954. The subject was racism in the town of Dresden, Ontario, whose hundred-year-old black community was reacting to the refusal of a handful of public establishments to serve them. The individual 'white man-on-the-street' opinions varied from 'no problem here' to blaming the turmoil on 'Communist-Jewish outside influences.' Two groups of representatives, one from the black and one from the white community, sat separately to answer the same questions put forward by a disarmingly cautious moderator, Gordon Burwash. The answers were as different as their skin colours; white platitudes did not mesh with the black leaders' appeal for justice. Much of the film's visual effect was lost, however, by the lack of time to edit the material in an engaging way. If the Film Board had been willing to stir the soup of complacency, it had failed to deliver the kind of programme that might have provoked many Canadian towns to examine their own attitudes toward race.

By comparison, an average 10-minute theatrical film in the Film Board's *Canada Carries On* series cost $20,000; a typical half-hour film cost between $25,000 and $30,00. Even a low-budget series like *Faces of Canada*, an Irwin concept on which the young filmmakers could cut their teeth, enjoyed a flexible deadline. Destined for theatrical release, these were short 35-mm items that showed the typical character of a Canadian region. Two of the most outstanding Film Board films of all time were products of this series, Colin Low's above-mentioned *Corral* and Roman Kroitor's *Paul Tomkowicz: Street-railway Switchman*, both released in 1954.

Half the Film Board's completed films were heading for television by the fall of 1955, yet overall prospects looked glum. There were twenty-six half-hour shows in English entitled *Window on Canada*, made up of previously completed non-theatrical or theatrical films, revised when necessary and fitted into a television framework of comment and discussion. A sampling of subjects included the Montreal Neurological Institute, the painter Frederick Varley, Newfoundland, home safety, mental illness, and immigration. *Window on Canada* was soon dropped with no tears and was replaced by a series of twenty-six half-hour shows, called *Perspective*, 'A Canadian view of Canada, its people and the world in which they live.' It resembled the *On the Spot* predecessor and was to run on Sunday afternoons at 2 p.m. This was not an auspicious hour, since only a quarter to a third of the sets in the country were on at that time. Then the CBC delayed broadcasting *Perspective* until December – football had priority.

That same year, the federal Cabinet finally approved the 1952 Irwin–Dunton agreement to foster CBC–Film Board cooperation, and both Trueman and Mulholland met with the top CBC administrators to implement it. They wanted a better deal, but the CBC claimed it had only ten hours available from the private stations, who opposed carrying serious public-service programmes. Trueman (who, ironically, had already pronounced against the 'controversial' documentary approach) and Mulholland argued that their series covered a wide variety of Canadian people and scenes and were quite distinct from the CBC's musicals, newscasts, or round-table discussions. They suggested boldly that the CBC needed and was bound to televise this kind of material. There was to be a Royal Commission on Television, the Fowler Commission, which they hoped would recommend that private stations devote more time to public-service programmes. But the royal commission did not convene until the following summer and a disheartened Mulholland feared that the Film Board might have to try to peddle its films to local stations.

That would not have been easy. The assistant CBC general manager, E.L. Bushnell, begrudged Dunton's assurance to the Film Board of an hour a week in English and

French. Bushnell wanted the Film Board to eliminate controversial subjects from its series, like the two *Perspective* films on water-supply fluoridation and difficulties in the coal industry. He feared the sponsor would be scared off if any considerable group of his prospective customers was offended. This attitude bothered Trueman, who, despite his own penchant for art and private doubts about controversial subjects, told the CBC that such rigidity meant that the Film Board would have to depart from its basic purposes. If Bushnell's proposal became policy, he wanted non-sponsored time to show the more serious programme. Dunton agreed in principle with the commissioner and said that the CBC recognized fully the need for this kind of programme. But Dunton was in no position to make binding commitments. Though he was president of the CBC, he could not overrule his middle management.

An important juncture in television history had been reached. Dunton's good intentions aside, CBC programmers were not receptive to the Film Board approach. Television demanded blandness and platitudes to mesmerize the consumer of the sponsor's product. Social realism and controversy are not very conducive to consumerism. From this time on, the promised two hours notwithstanding, the Film Board found itself almost permanently cap in hand vis à vis the CBC. 'Present indications are that we shall have difficulty in assuring ourselves of good program time,' Trueman understated.[36] He could not have known that he was speaking of the Film Board's dilemma for the next three decades. Bushnell eventually left the CBC to head Canada's private television network. His successors perpetuated the policy of non-controversy in the name of 'fairness, accuracy, and balance.'

Pickersgill as minister: A finger on the pulse

The Film Board occupied a small part of Pickersgill's sizeable portfolio, although he did not always adhere strictly to his professed policy of laisser-faire. As he put it decades later, 'I was basically sympathetic to the Film Board, but I did not want it to get itself or me into trouble that could be avoided. My interest in film making was entirely passive. I wanted no dynamic role and wanted the Board to have the greatest freedom to initiate, within limits I believed were politically defensible.'[37] Uppermost in his mind was the fact that the Film Board was not an independent corporation like the CBC, but, as a public agency, had to answer to the minister, who in turn had political responsibility to Parliament.

Yet there were several interventions. In March 1955 the Film Board invited Pickersgill, the Speaker of the House, and a few other members of Parliament to see footage of a film in progress, called *Parliament at Work*. It was not usual procedure to check with the minister on a film, but for this project the minister's advice and opinion were necessary. He had not been aware of it until then and thought several sequences were not suitable. Mulholland then cancelled the entire project. Pickersgill explained in Parliament that there were no shots of the prime minister or the leader of the Opposition and that the officers of the Film Board had suspended the project. He did not explain that his real concern was that the Opposition would say the film might be used for the government's advantage and that the Film Board might stand accused of serving bald political interests.[38] Then, too, Mulholland's neglect to organize a simultaneous French version may also have affected his decision to shelve it. The incident was soon forgotten and the footage was deposited in the Film Board's stock-shot library.

Seven months later, a more delicate issue arose when the Film Board announced its intentions to make a half-hour film on Japanese Canadians, showing how they suffered much less discrimination than a decade before, and were now better integrated into the Canadian scene. It was (and is) a subject fraught with political risk; some 20,000 Japanese Canadians had been uprooted and relocated during the Second World War without compensation. On a personal level, Pickersgill's brother had been the commissioner in charge of both removing the Japanese from British Columbia after the war and of carrying out the postwar programme of removal to Japan. The minister himself had started letting the Japanese return to Canada. The proposed film would certainly revive the controversy and cause criticism; thus he ordered the project suspended. At this point he asked Trueman how projects were initiated at the Film Board, since he wanted to learn in advance what he was expected to defend in Parliament. Trueman explained that the senior officials of the Board in committee recommended subjects which the board of governors passed. Items intended for television, like this particular film, were taken from a list made up under the supervision of the director of production.[39] Lest one think that the cancellation was significant, that year there were twenty-one cancelled or suspended projects, which was not an unusual figure.[40] None the less, ministerial involvement in cancellations was unusual.

On occasion, Trueman himself anticipated trouble and took steps to avoid it, as he did with the civil-defence film *Front Lines of Freedom*. This co-production of the United States Civil Defense Administration and Canada's Department of National Health and Welfare employed an overcharged emotional cold-war approach to civil defence. Visuals of atomic explosions accompanied by a cacophony of noise and highly dramatic music easily triggered terror and fear. Trueman and his managers doubted the wisdom of giving the film unlimited and uncontrolled circulation. Pickersgill saw the film with Paul Martin and Lester Pearson; its subsequent profile remained so low as to be all but invisible.

After the move to Montreal was complete in May 1956, in a break with tradition, Pickersgill attended a board of governors meeting to express concern over the festering CBC–Film Board relations. The Treasury Board had complained the previous fall that the Film Board was not recovering enough money from the CBC and was therefore subsidizing it. Perhaps the Fowler Commission would be the perfect vehicle to iron out the two agencies' differences and Pickersgill promised to take up the subject informally.

Prime Minister St Laurent, whose Liberal government was being squeezed and weakened by the famous Pipeline debate, was worried about any suggestion that his government was unable to settle the division of responsibility between two of its own bodies. He feared that the Opposition would reap a political windfall if the difficulties became public, so the Film Board was reduced to sending a 'strictly confidential' informal brief in September. It lay buried beneath the typical mountain of paper generated by a royal commission. The brief argued that after spending some $70,000 for experiments related to television, the Film Board had a good case for becoming a producer of public-service programmes and deserved a guaranteed two hours per week in prime time. CBC editorial control notwithstanding, it was hoped that clear lines of responsibility would be drawn.

The Film Board spokesmen seemed to have mixed emotions, however, when the Fowler Commission asked if they could produce more films for the CBC. The answer was affirmative, but lukewarm, because of a suspicion that Fowler might recommend the agency become part of the CBC. It boiled down to a question of financial trade-offs: there would be more television material if the Film Board was prepared to leave the non-theatrical and theatrical fields, but no one at the Board was prepared to abandon those traditional, albeit contracting, audiences.[41]

Then too there was the difficulty of satisfying CBC management criteria, as evidenced by the difficulties with the *Perspective* series,

now broadcast on Sundays at 5:30 p.m. in a 'family' hour. One film, *The Street*, was withdrawn because it was considered inappropriate for children to see. This tense adult drama, the product of Charles Israel's tight scriptwriting, is the story of a prostitute just out of jail, trying to go straight, but tortured by internal conflict. The temptation to resume life in the bar scene is overwhelming, and even with a job and help from the Elizabeth Fry Society, the woman hovers on the brink of sliding back into her old ways. There is no happy ending, only the possibility that she might work things out. Still preoccupied with 'art,' Trueman complained that the series was becoming too concerned with sociological problems and serious topics. The board of governors overruled him and said that the Film Board should not be forced to produce a series for a juvenile audience when that series was meant for adults. The problem was resolved when the series found a new time slot on Tuesdays at 10 p.m.[42]

By contrast, the French version of *Perspective*, *Passe-partout*, had no such difficulties with Radio-Canada. One well-crafted drama written by Fernand Dansereau was *Les Suspects*, later shot in English as *The Suspects*. It was the story of an ex-convict and his girlfriend, both of whom are picked up and interrogated by police. The scenario is untypical, in that it treats both the police and the suspects sympathetically. The psychologically brutal interrogation by a 'bad cop' is taken over by a 'good cop,' who then releases the two innocent victims. He intends to report his comrade's malfeasance, but explains that police are two steps away from death every day and that the 'bad cop', is himself a victim of the police force.[43]

Meanwhile, Pickersgill tried to make operative the Irwin-Dunton cooperation agreement of 1952. Matters came to a head in the summer of 1956, by which time the CBC had assigned only one production to the Film Board. He learned that the CBC was about to conclude a contract with an American company to make a fifty-two-week series, *The*

Last of the Mahicans, which excluded any participation by the Film Board. Worse, the CBC had just rejected a proposed Film Board series, *Jake and the Kid*, based on W.O. Mitchell's novel. Pickersgill wrote to Dr J.J. McCann, the minister responsible for the CBC, to inform him that the CBC was, strictly speaking, breaking the law, because it had been producing films for television without prior approval of the Film Board. A peeved McCann responded that the 1952 agreement was 'a clear understanding that no question be raised regarding possible control by one organization of operations of the other.' He wanted relations of the two agencies left on a businesslike basis, with each being fully answerable on its own account for its own actions. In that way there would be no danger of duplication or wasteful expenditure.

Pickersgill believed that in a showdown he could win. Strictly speaking, the statutes did not give the CBC the legal authority to make films. Dunton promised him things would improve. Pickersgill met McCann privately and said he had no more energy to continue the matter and did not wish to make this a public affair. He settled for a vague assurance from McCann and hoped they would both keep up pressure on their respective organizations.[44] But it was not to be and both organizations continued to harbour mutual ill-will.

The Film Board held its opening ceremonies in Montreal on 24 September 1956. The sober $2,000 event (no alcohol was served) for the $5.25 million building was somewhat inauspicious, since Governor-General Vincent Massey, whose commission had been partly responsible for the revitalization of the institution, did not attend on account of the controversy over the move. Robert Winters, whose Ministry of Public Works had built it, was there, as was Pickersgill, whose words of dedication crystallized the primary social aim of the federal government since the days of the Massey Commission report: 'Deux langues, deux cultures, mais une seule patrie.'[45] With its

home in Quebec, for the first time, the National Film Board of Canada was authentically L'Office National du Film. Pickersgill was still committed, however, to avoiding the creation of two houses under a single roof.

The French press campaign of 1957: L'affaire ONF

The resolution of the Pierre Juneau appointment in January 1957 did not quiet the troubled issue of French relations at the Film Board. Tensions became acute when it was realized that Juneau was not named assistant film commissioner. There followed a three-month vituperative French press campaign on behalf of creating a French section. It began with the charge that Juneau was odd man out in the triumvirate composed of himself, Mulholland, and the new director of production, Grant McLean.[46]

Three papers in particular, *Montréal Matin* (Duplessis's mouthpiece), *Le Devoir* (an independent daily), and *L'Action Catholique* (which usually disagreed with the previous two), were united in bitterness. The major premise of their polemics was that the French Canadians were victims of the English-speaking cliques running the agency. Production of French films had always been neglected and Juneau was director of a French section that had yet to come into existence. One of Juneau's first acts had been to demote French-Canadian executive producer Roger Blais. Management defended the demotion because it was believed that Blais was not a good administrator and could not provide intellectual leadership. Blais believed his demotion was on account of his having hounded Commissioner Trueman since the fall about the inequities in salaries between English and French; of the seventy-two staff earning $7,000 a year or more, only six were French Canadians.[47] Juneau himself appeared on journalist René Lévesque's television programme, 'Carrefour,' where he handled gingerly the host's blunt question about whether the French Canadians were persecuted. Fair play characterized the agency, he maintained.

But *Le Devoir*, which was leading the campaign, produced figures to show that French-Canadian salaries were lower than English. The editorialist, Pierre Vigeant, reminded readers that the previous year André Laurendeau and Gérard Pelletier had written articles demanding recognition of the French fact, but nothing had happened; he now argued for an authentic French expression. The vice-chairman of the board of governors, Léon Lortie, tried to explain in *La Presse* that· change was occurring and a whole host of French-Canadian talent was being trained. He maintained that success at the agency was measured by discipline, imagination, and team spirit; promotions were on the way.

Le Devoir was not mollified; a 'Not Well Integrated' employee wrote bitterly that the ONF had failed to create a French section after eighteen years and that the myth of French-Canadian incompetence or failure to adopt to the agency was a smokescreen. The unhappy writer concluded that the Film Board refused to recognize two cultures, each with its own means of expression. Again, the call was for the creation of an independent French section.

The charges continued unabated: there was discrimination, unfair treatment, and even brainwashing of French-Canadian employees to ensure an administration desired by English-speaking officials. Ottawa's *Le Droit* ridiculed the statement that few French Canadians wanted to work for the federal government, since those enthusiasts who acquired first-class skills often went to *Radio-Canada*.

It should be remembered that this period marked the intellectual fermentation and renaissance of postwar French Canada. With Michel Brunet's seminal essay, 'Les crises du conscience et la prise du conscience du Canada français,' in 1955, there was a strong proclivity to reflect and interpret the social and historical roots of French-Canadian so-ciety. This desire for self-expression was a natural concomitant of years of patriarchal domination of Quebec by both the Catholic church and the autocrat Duplessis. As Juneau remembered it years later, there was a kind of unanimity, a social consensus among people of that present, and younger, generation against the Duplessis years. That was as far as the 'politics' went. Thus, it would be incorrect to use the term 'separatist' or 'souveraintist' to describe events in the mid-fifties or the struggle going on at the Film Board. The thrust was that the French group wanted neither partition nor integration of the agency, only harmony and the ability to express true French-Canadian thought, or, as it was expressed in one article, 'ni cloissonement, ni integration. De l'accord.' In short, they were arguing for recognition as a distinct society.

Juneau believed the dissensions that developed subsequently were between the people who were more concerned with religious values and those who were intellectually anti-religious or areligious. By 1959 all this changed, as political consciousness took on a new meaning. Before that date, the cleavage between those interested in the whole of Canada and those who said to hell with that, had not shaped up clearly. The best way to describe the young intellectuals at the Film Board in 1957, Juneau recalled, was as largely demonstrating an aesthetic, non-political, and non-involved attitude.[48]

Bilingualism was being encouraged, if mainly to foster the understanding and use of French among the English staff in the administration and personnel areas. Not all efforts produced remarkable success in these years before French-immersion methods. One senior employee remembered the unmitigated disaster of sessions held twice weekly for two hours. When an instructor handed Director of Production Grant McLean a child's colouring book and told him to colour those parts of the body he knew in French, McLean raged, 'I don't know the French for your arsehole, but that's where I'd like to stuff these crayons!' McLean's interest in French immersion ended at that moment.[49] Unfortunately his unilingualism became a factor later in his failure to secure the position of film commissioner.

It would seem that the press campaign was having an effect on Film Commissioner Trueman. *Le Devoir* reported in March that he was resigning and was being 'kicked upstairs' because his administration had proved truly disastrous. The fact was that Pickersgill had been discussing with Trueman the possibility of making him director of the newly created Canada Council before the press campaign had begun. Trueman had originally become film commissioner with the proviso that another prestigious post would follow that tenure. Not only was it the right time to leave, but the commuting between Ottawa and Montreal had become impossible. He wrote a 'Dear Jack' letter on 6 March, telling of the press campaign and recommended a French-Canadian commissioner follow in order to work out the French-section problem without creating a French Film Board within the agency. In fact he would have said no to a French-Canadian nominee three years before, 'but now I am inclined to think that we may never secure the French assistance we need unless we at least move somewhat in that direction.' His suggestion for the post was Gérard Pelletier.[50]

The board of governors thought otherwise, and chose Guy Roberge, an official with substantial political and administrative experience, and, coincidentally, a friend of Minister Pickersgill. He could be counted upon to understand the larger cultural issues, as he had co-written the chapter in the Massey Commission report dealing with film and the Film Board. Prime Minister St Laurent had been his teacher in law school and an early employer whose firm had guided him in the practice of entertainment law. After he had served as a Liberal deputy in the Quebec legislative assembly, Roberge had come to Ottawa at St Laurent's invitation. As a law-

yer who specialized in copyright, corporation law, and industrial relations, he then served as counsel to the Massey Commission and later became a member of the government's Restrictive Trade Practices Commission.[51] He assumed his post in mid-April to the acclaim of *Le Devoir*, which called upon him to undertake the Herculean task of 'cleaning the Augean stables.' After a final parry, the press campaign against the Film Board administration vanished, as if by magic.

Trueman made a last attempt to change the structural set-up before he left and raised with Pickersgill the issue of a separate French Production wing. The minister's position had not been swayed one iota by the press campaign. He told Trueman tersely, 'I certainly think you should stall,' and the outgoing film commissioner informed Juneau and Mulholland that he would follow the minister's directions, hoping that the 'stall' would not be a long one.[52] Five days later, Trueman was at the Canada Council, where he set the course for the Council's all-important role of underwriting the national development of arts and sciences in Canada for the next generation.

The outgoing commissioner had not developed a high profile internally at the Film Board; he had travelled to Montreal once a week to consult with his four senior administrators, then took the evening train back to Ottawa.[53] He had left the management of the agency to them, while he and the board of governors set policy in consultation with the ministers, first Walter Harris and then J.W. Pickersgill. Trueman had never seen himself as a political person – it was foreign to his character. He believed in the principle that federal cultural institutions should not be partisan, and therefore subscribed to the ideal that they be liberal, imaginative, and as non-bureaucratic as possible. His point was that the government should not determine by committee what the country needed. 'I shrink from the Central Committee sitting down and deciding what is good for Canada.

Albert Trueman, centre, succeeded Irwin as film commissioner (1953–7) and in turn was followed by Guy Roberge (left, 1957–66). Both men came to the post from seats on the board of governors, whose chairman was Toronto businessman Charles Band.

To let an institution grow and shape itself is far preferable than to plan. Recognize the need but don't write the blueprint. Anyone with proven ability should be given money: let the market control the output.' He summarized his function later as 'a clearer-away of obstacles, creating and presiding over a situation in which desirable things could happen with a minimum of the frustrating delays, which can be caused by difficulties not foreseen or removed.' This attitude characterized his tenure at the Film Board where, in a milieu of lively, thinking, dreaming, provocative minds, artistic freedom became a habit. It might be added, however, that

nothing escaped the tough-minded and critical Mulholland. Trueman believed that the move to Montreal gave new life to French culture and, the French press campaign notwithstanding, thought he had encouraged the expansion of the French staff.[54] It was a slow process that obviously bothered many young filmmakers who were in a hurry to break the old mould and create a new generation's signature.

Walter Harris had devoted little energy to the Film Board because his ministerial portfolio demanded that most of his time be devoted to immigration affairs. Pickersgill also found that Immigration and Indian Affairs consumed most of his attention, but he was never too busy to keep an eye on the political implications of what was going on at the Board. If his motivation was to try to avoid embarrassment to the government, there was a real desire to direct the rising cultural ferment in Quebec toward his (and the Liberal government's) vision of a single Canada.

It is doubtful that the Conservatives made much, if any, political hay from the French press campaign of early 1957. When the federal election occurred in June, the Tories became a minority government, but had se-cured only nine seats in Quebec. The vote indicated that after almost twenty-two years of Liberal rule, Canada wanted a change. Pickersgill was replaced by E. Davie Fulton, the man often touted to be the heir apparent to the Progressive Conservative mantle. As minister of justice and acting minister of manpower and immigration, Fulton, like his predecessors, had little time for the agency. With a new film commissioner and a new minister, the Film Board slate was wiped clean; most employees have referred to what followed as the golden years.

3

The Golden Years

Guy Roberge: A new style of operating

In the wake of the *Le Devoir* press campaign, all eyes at the Film Board turned expectantly to the new commissioner to see how this lawyer, rumoured to be more a man of literature than of film, intended to operate. Roberge decided to spend three days a week in Montreal, close to production activity, while the remaining two days in Ottawa would allow him to 'mend fences' and read the various political currents.

There was a diplomatic problem in the first days – it was John Grierson. The indefatigable Scot and Film Board founder had been visiting Canada on a speaking tour and had outraged the departing commissioner by showing up late and not entirely sober for Trueman's farewell party. 'Trueman, what's the crazy idea of leaving an important organization like the Film Board to go and become the director of that money-giving bordello, the Canada Council?' he bellowed irascibly. The outraged Trueman felt like thrashing his indomitable guest.[1] Days later, a cautious Roberge assigned Grant McLean to keep Grierson busy and to shield himself from the free advice Grierson was forever willing to proffer. Yet Grierson's talents for generalizing and inspiring were useful. Roberge liked hearing the godfather of documentary film wax enthusiastic about the Film Board's magnificent, sprawling studio,

nearly 4,000 miles long, containing a variety of scenic beauty and people to record. He also learned from Grierson's own experience and recommendation that he 'keep an open door' to stay close to his employees. The new commissioner found it was good advice and, by following it, convinced the anxious staff that he intended to give everyone a piece of the Film Board cake.

The shift to Montreal was transforming the institution in numerous and felicitous ways, even though it remained a multi-purpose organization that was always in some disorder. Roberge sensed that had it been otherwise, the films would have suffered. With an even-handedness that characterized his regime, he declared that anyone could write a memorandum in either language and it was up to the recipient to be able to understand it. When a French-Canadian film-maker-poet came to his office to explain: 'Nous aussi, nous avons notre sensibilité' (We too have feelings), Roberge was sympathetic, yet he dismissed as facile propaganda the charge that Mulholland was an enemy of French Canadians and little more than an autocratic advertising executive. He liked both Mulholland's sense of national vision and his belief in the documentary film of social consciousness.[2]

Roberge attributed much of his success to good relations with the board of governors, with whom he met quarterly.[3] At their first meeting, the subject was the government's decision to freeze the budget at the 1955 figure. This fact of life made specious the charge that Mulholland and McLean were suppressing French production.[4] The truth was that despite the new multimillion-dollar building, there was not enough production money to go around. In fact, the entire budget for 1959 was $4.49 million, $100,000 less than in 1958. Roberge's problem was to reallocate funds gradually and to expand the French sector without throwing the whole machine off kilter. This adjustment process took a decade to effect.

The 1957 production operations report: A brief for the defence

A glance at the 1957 production operations report revealed to Roberge the complexity of running the financially strapped organization. Even though the CBC still complained about many Film Board documentaries, television had become a principal means of distribution, and half the sixty original films produced that year were television-bound. The French television programme had consisted entirely of versions of English films, though five original (non-television) films had been made, compared to the English side's nine. One-quarter of production had been for government departments, and because of fiscal restraints private commercial film companies received none to produce. They had had to settle for fifteen sponsored films to version into other languages for distribution abroad.

Globally, the total Film Board production budget for fiscal year 1957–8 was $2.671 million; $1.412 million was voted by Parliament, $606,000 came from the CBC (whose royalties represented half the cost of television production), and $652,000 came from the sponsored programme. The budget for 35-mm theatrical films was just under $250,000, with *Canada Carries On* (*En avant Canada*) costing $165,000 and *Eye Witness* (*Coup d'oeil*) demanding $80,000. Since 1956, Film

Board policy had been to downplay theatrical series, because based on 1955 figures the total annual theatrical audience was nine million compared to television's twenty million. Theatres were using the new wide-screen process and there was considerable pressure on the Film Board to make the same adaptation and shift to colour. Since the theatres had traditionally been accepting only twenty-four 10-minute subjects in each language per year, conversion did not make economic sense. Furthermore, since half the *En avant Canada* series had consisted of 're-makes' of non-theatrical films, to produce originals in wide-screen colour was prohibitively expensive. The other half of the series consisted of French translations of *Canada Carries On*.[5] Plans in 1957 called for four new films: a 15-minute original on the recent Royal Visit ($45,000) and three 10-minute originals on trade unions, pulp and paper, and the St Lawrence Islands, costing $20,000 each. The third was the only French original. The statistics for the *Eye Witness* and *Coup d'oeil* series were a bit better; eight 10-minute releases in each language included five English originals and four French originals, with budgets of $3,150 each.

Newsreels cost $42,000 for the year; from April to August 1957 eighteen silent stories had been shot in eastern, western, and central Canada. Subjects included Canadian armed forces in Europe, newsboys, Niagara Falls, Seaway turbines, pulp and paper, an air ambulance, a zoo nursery, a wildlife spring census, and Hungarian students. (There were no stories on Quebec.) Common wisdom still held that the silent newsreels provided the Film Board with one of the best returns on dollars invested, since they could be narrated in any language and therefore provided coverage of Canadian items internationally, both in theatres and on television.

Both English and French Production filmed half-hour low-budget documentary dramas for television. On the English side, twenty-six *Perspective* items included subjects like a Scots immigrant, the weather,

Manitoba traffic, Canadair, wheat, a log drive, scientific police, a fire brigade, a country editor, and a drama academy. With varying success, the films addressed contemporary social themes like adolescence, alcoholism, racism, native peoples, and the elderly, but filmmakers complained that there was a limited range of emotion that could be coaxed out of thirty minutes. The series terminated in 1958.

With only half as many original films as *Perspective*, Juneau called *Passe-partout* a money-starved operation in need of complete overhaul. He argued long and hard with the dubious Mulholland to replace it with the series *Panoramique*, which was to be a socio-historic introspective reflection of French-Canadian society from the 1930s. He asserted that the French should be able to take risks with their films and have the chance to 'miss' half the time like the English did.[6]

Panoramique consisted of eight shows on the thirties (Abitibi), four on white-collar workers, three on agriculture, two on the frontier, five on war, and four on postwar labour. The series had wide critical acceptance and ran until the fall of 1959. The Abitibi films, called collectively *Les Brûlés*, directed on location by Bernard Devlin, devoured a huge ($144,000) budget. Later, directors Gilles Carle and Denys Arcand claimed these had a profound influence upon their film art. Carle believed that the constant theme of subsequent French-Canadian films, solitude and the pain of life, stemmed from Les *Brûlés*.[7] Another show, *Il était une guerre*, by Louis Portugais, chronicled for the first time the reality of French-Canadian resistance to conscription during the Second World War.

There was another half-hour series that was television-bound: *Commonwealth of Nations*, a thirteen-item ($150,000) programme under the rubric *The World in Action*. It was conceived in 1953 by director Ronald Dick as part of the Irwin-inspired 'International Programme' for audiences abroad as well as at home. The Department

of External Affairs had been consulted during its production, and with a French translation of the series completed, it appeared on television simultaneously in the spring and summer of 1957.

Finally, there was a nine-item, half-hour English television series ($30,000 to $50,000 each) by Morten Parker called *The Nature of Work*, whose purpose was to consider the psychological factors that determined an employee's attitude to his job. Positions ranged from the assembly-line worker to the clerk, to the department manager, to the vice-president. Eight of these were translated into French for broadcast, excluding the vice-president programme, which perhaps says something about the socio-economic realities of Quebec at this time. Had there been originals in French, the series would not have been feasible economically.

The remainder of the budget went to the 'General' programme, allowing $200,000 to the English and $70,000 to the French, a ratio reflecting roughly the two-thirds to one-third national-population division. The subjects in English were the Trans-Canada Highway, Canadian industry, Eskimo art, changing rural life, and the story of insulin (a 20-minute dramatized film), and the programme included five 10-minute items from the *What Do You Think?* non-theatrical series begun in 1953. The latter films, directed by Gudrun Parker, were meant to provoke classroom or community discussion on fundamental democratic issues. The French were doing a 20-minute original film, *Urbanisme*, on urban life (Juneau's interest), *La Drave*, on the log-drive, and two half-hour pieces, *Les plumes aux vent* (a folkloric dance group) and *Jeunesses musicales*, directed by Raymond Garceau and Claude Jutra respectively. Translations of these French films were relatively inexpensive because the majority of them, like the rest of the Film Board's films at this time, were still not using synchronized sound.

There were also two items, 'Juvenile' and 'Science,' which consisted of a number of 20-

minute films for classroom use, including several subjects on geography and the continuing adventures of Ti-Jean, who went west in 1957 and in 1958 saved a faltering iron ore operation near Schefferville, Quebec. The animation-film budget was devoted to two films on architecture and astronomy.

Norman McLaren had just finished a new experimental pixilation work with Claude Jutra and Evelyn Lambart, the languageless fable, *A Chairy Tale*. It was the fantastic story of a man (Jutra) who found a chair with a mind of its own, unwilling to accommodate him until he proved that kindness and understanding achieve more than a will to overpower. Typically, McLaren completed it for half the $22,000 budget. When French filmmaker René Clair visited Montreal late in 1958, McLaren gave him a copy, and Clair's unsolicited praise for the institution as 'une chose absolument unique au monde,' which used cinema as an instrument of artistic creation, was wonderful for morale. Besides being nominated for an Oscar and taking first place in the experimental category at Venice, *A Chairy Tale* endured to become one of the Film Board's most popular non-theatrical films worldwide.

In 1957, there were foreign-language versions of about a dozen films in Spanish, German, Dutch, and Danish, followed by about six in Portuguese and Italian and the odd one or two in Turkish, Urdu, Bengali, Japanese, and Russian (Doukhobor).[8] These were films intended for children, indicating the wisdom of the belief that the largest and longest-lasting impact of film is on the young mind. At this time there were about 24,000 prints of Film Board films circulating abroad through embassies, consulates, and other free loan agencies.

The organization was also spending about $80,000 a year to produce sixty-eight filmstrips, both for sponsors and as part of the regular programme of subjects on geography, history, safety, folksongs, artists, learning French, biology, labour, mining, trade and commerce, and national defence. Another $150,000 was devoted to still photos, half of which were shot for government departments. The collection of stills numbered over 100,000, to which 4,300 were added per year.[9]

Reviewing this 'Production Operations Report,' Roberge now understood that his organization was not anti-French as the press campaign had insinuated, but that the greatest obstacle was the budgetary restriction. Even so, recruitment of French Canadians continued apace, and Pierre Juneau found that many of the young filmmakers he was interviewing had been seduced by film as drama, not as documentary. Theirs was almost universally an aesthetic interest, tied to the prestigious Paris periodical *Cahiers du cinéma*. The subject of 'politics' occupied a minuscule place in the French Canadians' interests, and if there was a growing unanimity or social consensus in Quebec against the Duplessis years, political consciousness among French filmmakers was still inchoate. Juneau's own penchant was for adult education and social activism of the sort being articulated in the influential review *Cité libre*. He found little response during these years to suggestions that filmmakers tackle subjects of a social nature, and recalled that it was with the greatest difficulty that he convinced Louis Portugais to make *Urbanisme*.

Remembering this period, Executive Producer Tom Daly attributed the beginnings of indigenous French-Canadian themes to the three films in the 1953-4 series *Faces of Canada: Le Bedeau* (The Beadle), a film about a Catholic churchman who chases a pig from his church; *Le Notaire* (The Notary), scripted by Raymond Garceau and directed by Pierre Arbour, about one of the three main professions of French Canada; and *Le Photographe* (The Photographer), text by Anne Hébert and directed by Pierre Arbour, about a small-town photographer who recorded such family events as births, marriages, and anniversaries.[10]

The director of production, Grant

McLean, did not tell Juneau what films to make. But given the nature of the overall Film Board programme and its orientation to television, there seemed little room for the kind of aesthetic expression the young Quebec filmmakers were advocating. To call the situation anti-French is to misread the temper of the times. Many on the French side soon argued for the use of dramatization to link what was real with what was true. And that struggle took five more years to realize, because costs, not politics, were at the heart of the problem.[11] Two more French units, 'F' and 'H,' were formed in April 1958 under Léonard Forest and Louis Portugais, while 'G,' under Jacques Bobet, remained primarily responsible for versioning. Following the telescoping of Units F and H, Fernand Dansereau became executive producer of F in March 1962, while Bobet continued to supervise G.

The board of governors and *Blue Vanguard*

At the time of the Suez Crisis of 1956, Canada had displayed its brand of helpful internationalism by aiding Britain, France, and Israel in extricating themselves from a war that the United States did not countenance. Lester Pearson earned the Nobel Peace Prize for suggesting a United Nations Emergency Force to help the two great powers withdraw with some dignity. For Israel, it meant an eleven-year lull until the next round. Then, Egypt expelled the UNEF unceremoniously and plunged into another losing war.[12]

After Pearson offered Canadian troops to the UNEF, the United Nations' Film Section asked the Film Board for a film about the operation. They shared the costs, and the film was ready by fall 1957. After seeing it, Dag Hammerskjold, the UN secretary-general, recommended some modifications, 'because of the delicate political situation in the Middle East.' Producer Tom Daly protested to Thorold Dickinson of the United Nations Film Board in New York to no avail, so he

added material on the UN debate leading to the establishment of the UNEF. The film was ready in the spring of 1958, and again, the secretary-general requested a delay in releasing it.

Blue Vanguard uses stock newsreel footage to give a day-to-day account of the Sinai campaign and the UN's mediating role. The multinational force demonstrates how international effort has brought peace, states the commentator. As British and French forces and trucks withdraw on to waiting ships, some of their remaining vehicles are painted white by UN troops. Jubilant Egyptians cheer and fire their guns in celebration. There follow scenes of the UN salvage effort, the Israeli withdrawal, more cheering in Gaza, and a closing sequence describing how opposing forces of both sides are tense on their triggers. The last words insist that the UNEF forces on the Armistice Demarcation Line had brought peace. Whatever the intention, the impression created by these images represents British and French retreat and defeat.

The film was never released. The London *News Chronicle* stated that British Foreign Office officials were behind its withdrawal and cancellation at the Berlin Film Festival because it was, by inference, critical of British policy. The United Nations Film Board suggested that the Film Board release the film at home under its own auspices. External Affairs referred the matter to the board of governors for final resolution. The members thought the film was fair and unprejudiced, but feared legal repercussions, since copyright belonged to the United Nations. They suggested that Roberge try to recover from the United Nations some of the $58,000 it cost to make. Late in 1959, the UN agreed to pay $25,000 in exchange for all copies but one, which remains in the Film Board Archives.[13] *Blue Vanguard* became an almost forgotten episode, even if the film is of historical interest for its internationalism. *Blue Vanguard*'s noble objective was all for naught, since nobody saw it. The lesson was that co-productions could be sticky affairs.

The private industry's perpetual cry for more sponsored film

Roberge had not been in the commissioner's office long before the commercial interests lodged their predictable complaint that the Film Board was retarding private industry's growth. The Association of Motion Picture Producers and Laboratories of Canada appealed to acting Minister Fulton in November, urging the government to change the Film Act, so that they might make governmental departmental films. That plum, however, was forbidden fruit because those contracts, accounting for roughly one-quarter of Film Board activity, paid many of the institution's bills.

Fulton forwarded their plea to the Film Board, where, in response, Donald Mulholland produced statistics showing why sponsored films were crucial for his agency's economic health. Without them, the Film Board stood to lose about a million dollars. The staff would then be reduced by seventy-five, saving an estimated one-third of a million dollars. Operating service costs would be reduced by $450,000, yet because of a decrease in the volume of work, overall efficiency at the new plant would decline. The core of the argument was that the quality associated with the Film Board's product (which government departments counted upon) could not be replicated by private producers who would make the cheapest possible film.[14] The private producers lost this battle, but continued to harbour their resentment until the next minister and the next thrust.

From this intervention, Roberge thought it appropriate to use his power as government film adviser to consider the future of the private industry. He recognized that commercial interests would be far more dependent in the future upon the production of features and television fare than upon shorts. In January 1958 he appointed Juneau to research a worldwide study of government practices concerning the feature-film indus-

try.[15] This was the genesis of what became his godchild a decade later, the Canadian Film Development Corporation, a ten-million-dollar loan fund to launch the Canadian feature-film industry. With such a body in existence, Roberge thought, the heat would be off the Film Board.

Production programme changes

In the spring of 1958, a committee of senior management sat for a week preparing the annual programme for the board of governors to go over with a fine-tooth comb. That was how most projects were born, although once begun, creative freedom was the rule, not the exception.

Because the theatrical programme had been losing audiences, they decided to drop the screen magazine *Eye Witness* and to double the number of *Canada Carries On* subjects, hoping to attract an international (mainly European) audience. As an afterthought, English Production set aside some funds for feature-length documentary script development.

English television material had received practically no international distribution because the all-dialogue dramatized material making up the twenty-six-part half-hour series *Perspective* was too expensive to dub into foreign languages. That series was replaced by *Frontiers*, whose purpose was to present a broad and provocative look at the frontiers of contemporary Canada, from geographical to sociological subjects. These fifteen half-hour films were shot silently so that they might be dubbed cheaply for international distribution. Another new series of seven half-hours, to be called *Candid Eye*, was to be another alternative to *Perspective* and promised to use a new filming technique to describe and interpret the people of Canada as they really were (see chapter 4). Two one-hour films to be called *Comparisons* were to round out the year; each would take a prominent feature of Canadian life and compare it to the same feature in other countries. There was to be simultaneous shooting in English and French, so that significant differences or similarities shared by both groups might also be useful nationally. The key factor in the decision to change the English television programme from drama to voice-over was the desire to reach foreign audiences through the less costly method. English drama was not ruled out altogether, and plans proceeded to produce *The Quest*, a re-enactment of the historical discovery of insulin by Banting and Best.

French television production was going in a quite different direction. The plan was to deal with French-Canadian society in a fully dramatized form, shifting from the eight half-hour subjects to four self-contained one-hour dramas. Executive producers Léonard Forest and Fernand Dansereau had pleaded with Pierre Juneau in January to end the *Panoramique* series's tiresome concentration on French Canada's sociological past and present. They wanted to be free of administrators and to create a unique French production group that could fashion its own dramatic programme and be in touch with reality. Their appeal for collective affirmation has been called the end of the traditional closed Quebec society and the beginning of a unique identity for French filmmakers at the Film Board,[16] although Juneau had been lobbying for such recognition since 1955. Just as significantly, the enlarged French group, the outcome of the spate of hiring in 1957–8, was now making its first significant collective statement.

The English and French 'General Programme' was oriented toward non-theatrical audiences at home and abroad. *The World in Action* series, no longer theatrical, was a three-year plan of films examining miscellaneous large subjects in depth. The first series on education was to be followed by one on Canadian-American relations. A film on understanding French Canada was started by English Production, in spite of the complete lack of interest on the French side to do one on understanding English Canada. They preferred instead a series of discussion films intended to emphasize the responsibilities of, and advantages in, living in a free society. For children in the classroom, there were to be several films on social geography, along with a 15-minute pilot to inaugurate a dramatic series illustrating select facts in Canadian history. A number of general films on science were under way to complement school curricula, as well as a cluster of films to parallel general-science courses in high schools and universities. Two animation films, *Universe* and *A Is for Architecture*, were also scheduled for completion. On the French side, scripts were being prepared to do another six films on the superhuman boy Ti-Jean.

This activity was aided by the increase in funds from the Department of External Affairs for foreign-language versions. From forty in 1957, to fifty-five in 1958–9, the number of versions indicated that the department was counting heavily on the Film Board to carry the Canadian image to nations abroad. Significantly, there was no doctoring of films for foreign audiences – they saw the same films Canadians saw at home. In order to relieve pressure on its employees abroad, External Affairs soon favoured a permanent Film Board officer in New Delhi to cover Southeast Asia. In 1961, another one opened in Buenos Aires to cover Latin and South America. Once those offices opened, the increasing cost to the Film Board in personnel led Distribution to request more of the annual budget. The creative staff, always short of funds, was resentful.

The Radio-Canada producer's strike of 1959: A turning point

By 1959, Quebec was in ferment against the iron-willed, but weakening Maurice Duplessis, who was in his last year of life. The preceding year, maverick law professor Pierre Trudeau had exhorted his fellow citizens publicly, 'Democracy first!' and had railed against the brutal cynicism and selfish docility of those (like Duplessis) who culti-vated the ignorance and prejudice of French Canadians. Already broad elements of so-ciety had become impatient with and imper-tinent about Duplessis's Quebec, and Tru-deau's voice reflected the desire for reform that was gripping the intelligentsia. The sen-timent soon percolated to the broad middle sector of Quebec in what would be called in 1960 'La révolution tranquille,' or the Quiet Revolution.

The producers' strike at Radio-Canada in 1959 was the most public manifestation of the changing climate, and for many Que-beckers in the media it was probably the pivotal event of the decade. Influenced by trends in France, the producers had union-ized and faced off against the corporation, whose position was that producers who di-rected others were themselves management, hence were ineligible to engage in the collec-tive-bargaining process. The argument that such unionization had been successful in Paris held no water with management, who argued that unionization in the Canadian public service was illegal.

Radio-Canada held out against the pro-ducers for ten weeks and won. Some emerg-ing French-Canadian leaders seethed at what they considered to be the indifference of Eng-lish Canada. For René Lévesque, himself a Radio-Canada contract employee, the expe-rience changed his life. He underwent a *crise de conscience* and became a nationalist. In his determination to do something about a system that was not changing fast enough, he started down the path to provincial Liberal politics, then later broke with tradition to begin a democratic struggle for Quebec inde-pendence. If, for some, the strike marked the birth of *québécois* nationalism, for others, like journalist and broadcaster Gérard Pel-letier, it signalled the beginning of a search for a counterweight to Quebec authoritar-ianism in the form of shoring up the weak-ened central state. He, Trudeau, and others (like Pierre Juneau) argued for Canadian federalism. The argument mesmerized

Quebec society for the next twenty-one years.[17]

Most of the French employees at the Film Board agonized over what they should do about the strike, since there were contracts with Radio-Canada and deadlines to meet. Some discussed joining in a sympathy strike, while others cautioned that the Film Board's legal status forbade this. Their arguments echoed many of those occurring elsewhere in Quebec. As might be expected, Roberge threaded a careful path of compromise and finally agreed to fulfil his agency's contracts up to a certain date and then cease delivery.

The board of governors met and con-firmed that the Film Board did not and could not become involved in the strike. (It mat-tered little, since it was over shortly there-after.) The union issue was particularly wor-risome, and some members argued that the proposed new Civil Service Commission procedures and rules should be extended to Film Board personnel. Roberge agreed with Marcel Cadieux of External Affairs, who thought the Film Board should be exempted from these rules. The commissioner noted that the 1939 and 1950 Film Acts had given the Film Board a free hand in regard to per-sonnel, most of whom were intended to be contract staff only. There was a legal loop-hole – the 1954 Superannuation Act brought the whole Film Board under Treasury Board control and the Civil Service Commission might think the agency came under its aegis as a result. The board and commissioner asked for total exemption, while admitting that it was possible that a staff association or union might be formed among the Board's employees. They asserted that there could be no collective bargaining with such a group, although 'collective discussions' were not precluded.[18] Neither the board of governors nor management wanted to contemplate the financial nightmare of annual budgets being consumed by a permanent and unionized staff.

Six months later, the board learned there was no legal impediment to a staff association being formed and that collective bargaining between the government and its employees was legal. A month before the decision, the staff formed a bilingual association called the Association professionel des cinéastes / Professional Association of NFB Employees and affiliated with the Quebec-based Canadian and Catholic Confederation of Labour. Not all the filmmakers were ready yet to take the plunge, as evidenced by the attendance of only twenty-five (predominantly French-speaking) persons at an organizational meeting in January 1960.[19]

The strike at Radio-Canada was the catalyst that changed political consciousness at the Film Board, as well as in Quebec and Canada, forever. Its effect on the French filmmakers had been electric. They found themselves plunging into a worldwide current embracing the popular trinity of decolonization, nationalism, and Marxism. The effects were profound, as many of them found they were carried from a very strong aesthetic bent to politics without really knowing why. Pierre Juneau, who had hired staff on the basis of talent and personality, was surprised to see the political transformation of Hubert Aquin and Michel Brault into vibrant activists.[20]

More strife with the CBC

These political developments did not diminish the ongoing tension between the Film Board and the CBC over programming. Late in 1959, Director of Operations Donald Mulholland urged a more prominent role for the Film Board in CBC public affairs. He argued that the CBC should let that sector languish, because in having to follow the new 55 per cent Canadian content rule, it had too many other interests to satisfy. Besides, when the network produced half-hour documentaries or assigned them to commercial producers, they were routine, dated stylistically, and cost more than the Film Board productions.[21] In Mulholland's view, the CBC treated public affairs like poor relations

and was subservient to sponsor pressures to produce other types of programming. The result was that Film Board films were treated like poor relations of poor relations: English productions were relegated to a Sunday afternoon time slot at 5:30 p.m., while French-language films were telecast at 10:30 p.m. on Tuesdays.

Mulholland pointed a finger of blame at lower-echelon managers. The CBC had burgeoned into a multi-departmental, decentralized operation with numerous executives and department heads, many of whom were in competition with the Film Board. He put it sarcastically, 'No program producer is going to get a raise in salary because he bought a good film from the National Film Board – his raise will come because he produced a good show himself or because he got a good time and therefore a good rating.' Perhaps top management at the CBC could force more fruitful cooperation between the two agencies. He was mollified to see a high-ranking joint policy-formulation committee created to meet twice yearly, but it bore little fruit.[22]

The other tug, however, came from within the Film Board itself, where English filmmakers continued to fear absorption by the CBC. Mulholland put on a tough face and agreed to include his organization's films in the network's series, on the firm understanding that their unique identity be retained.[23] Promises and good intentions notwithstanding, the CBC had one look at the Film Board's perplexing dramatic film on prejudice, *A Day in the Night of Jonathan Mole*, and killed the planned series on the controversial subject. Written and directed by Donald Brittain as a sponsored film for the Department of Labour, it showed the limitation of using prejudice as a means to stop prejudice. A Jew, a native Indian, and a displaced person from Europe were subjected to a revolting display of racism by a self-appointed white Christian English-Canadian judge. Each minority person was bombarded with the insults that have been platitudes repeated by age-old bigots who are fearful, hating, and stupid. The problem with the film was that it repeated big lies, and that very act could (as Joseph Goebbels had demonstrated during the Nazi period) plant the seeds of little lies, or prejudices, in the minds of those who watched. Perhaps the CBC decision was correct and liberal; using prejudice to fight prejudice is a dubious premise, no matter how well meaning it may be.

At about the same time, the network also turned down another Film Board drama based on the W.O. Mitchell book *Jake and the Kid*. In fairness to the corporation, there was good reason, since the script, *Political Dynamite*, written by the acclaimed author, was lacklustre. Jake played the fool, while the Kid was superfluous, showing none of the cuteness and innocence of the boy in the novel. Some believed English Production had not yet proved itself adept at either television drama or comedy.

Relations with the minister and the government

In the year he occupied the position of acting minister, E. Davie Fulton paid scant attention to Film Board matters. Roberge kept him informed of current developments and showed him the controversial *Blue Vanguard* and *The Ticket*, the latter film about penitentiary parole. This was not just a courtesy – he wanted to be sure the minister would not be caught flatfooted in Parliament, should questions arise. But queries about the Film Board never materialized. Fulton turned over duties to the succeeding minister, Ellen Fairclough, in May 1958, and expressed to Roberge his heartfelt appreciation and thanks.[24]

Fairclough, the first female cabinet minister in Canadian history, held her portfolio, including the Public Archives, the National Library, and the Film Board, until August 1962. She was a 'no nonsense' accountant who was reputed to have an extraordinary memory. As a way of stating that she was disinterested in the burden of operational

questions, she told Roberge that any matter could be articulated in ten lines or less. Her principal concern was to steer any relevant legislation and carry the annual estimates through Parliament. During her tenure, she never saw a Film Board film, although she did make a cameo appearance in *Women on the March*. The subject of culture was a priority neither with her nor with the Diefenbaker government during these years. Diefenbaker was following, not leading, the slow drift toward bilingualism in the federal service, and his cultural policy reflected a vague 'pan-Canadianism.' Fairclough was personable to Roberge and joked often about his 'politics' (Liberal), even though he avoided partisanship scrupulously. The softspoken, reserved gentleman only smiled at her jibes and carried out his responsibilities efficiently and circumspectly.[25]

For example, Roberge urged Fairclough to deflect a request from the commercial film industry for help in making feature films and reminded her that the minister of finance had refused a year earlier to single out the film industry for special treatment. On another occasion, when the Saskatchewan Government Film Unit requested a joint production on the South Saskatchewan Dam Project, he warned her that though it could save money, there were possible serious implications, particularly if someone wanted to make an issue of a federal institution crossing into a provincial domain. She agreed, so this and future provincial/federal co-production schemes went no further.[26] Roberge was legally correct, but it was a missed opportunity, because when the first such co-production occurred at last in 1974 with Donald Winkler's *In Praise of Hands* ($167,438), there was not a ripple of complaint.

A more serious issue arose over a two-part study of nuclear power for English television, *Atom, Servant of Man*. The film survey was to show what was being done in and outside Canada in the development of nuclear energy for peaceful purposes. Before the film was finished, Atomic Energy of Canada Limited protested the inclusion of an interview with a scientist who favoured adoption of a high-temperature-type reactor, instead of AECL's own heavy-water-type reactor. They also disliked an interview with a scientist who argued for Canadian production of enriched uranium.

AECL officials wanted the two interviews excised and threatened to withdraw their own interview. The group interested in Canadian production of enriched uranium was more ham-handed in protesting their side's possible exclusion: their menace was a public attack on the Film Board. Roberge informed Fairclough of the situation and then turned it over to the board of governors for resolution. They decided to include the interview dealing with the high-temperature-type reactor (because it related to the subject matter of the film) and to exclude the interview advocating the Canadian production of enriched uranium, because it was part of a campaign.[27] Two other points, if unstated, were coincidental: while the Film Board would not be intimidated by threatening pressure tactics, the deletion of the interview also would not ruffle the feathers of the United States, which was the principal manufacturer of enriched uranium in the Western world. Nuclear energy proved contentious once again in the 1977 film, *No Act of God*.

Black and White in South Africa: The Film Board tackles apartheid

The most controversial issue with which Roberge had to deal in his first years as commissioner was the outcry by South Africa against the film *Black and White in South Africa*, whose shock waves reverberated to the prime minister's office. It was the eleventh film in the Commonwealth series, which had appeared on television in 1957, and when all the dust had settled, it was probably one of the ancillary factors that tilted Canada to take the lead in driving South Africa from the Commonwealth in 1961.

The idea for a 20-minute film on the concept and evolution of the Commonwealth went back to 1953, when Ronald Dick suggested it to Commissioner Trueman as part of the International Program. After clearing it with External Affairs, Dick began directing the project in December 1954. The film mushroomed into a series of thirteen half-hours. South Africa furnished stock-shot footage, on the understanding that the Film Board would outline very briefly the positive element in South Africa's racial policies. That promise extended to the second film, *Portrait of the Family*, but not to the soon-to-be cause célèbre. When the whole series was completed, Norman Robertson of External Affairs had time to see the first five only, and approved of the release of all thirteen to diplomatic-post libraries.[28] It was a decision he regretted.

There was no reaction to the film or series when they appeared on CBC television in the spring and summer of 1957. A year later, the films were in South Africa, and the Canadian Government trade commissioner withdrew the film in question, on the grounds that there were a 'few unnecessary but unavoidable inaccuracies.' When it was screened in New York in September 1958, it was taken more seriously than it had been in Canada. South African officials declared it a travesty of the South African situation and complained of improper use of their country's film footage.[29]

Black and White in South Africa was a measured, not strident, attack on apartheid. Executive Producer Nick Balla considered it a 'people's view' of the subject, in which the Film Board would sit on the fence in a positive way, presenting unbiased information, which the public could then use to make decisions. The distinguished academic Edgar McInnis was the on-screen voice of authority and rectitude. Apartheid, South Africa's answer to the meeting of white civilization and Black Africa, was that country's greatest political issue, he stated, and the minority whites had elected a government that was very concerned with differences in skin pigmentation. Sequences of blacks at work and at home in the underdeveloped and primitive townships were matched by a verbal attack on the illusory 'separate but parallel' opportunities. The whole idea seems a complete fraud to many Bantu leaders, McInnis continued.

In liberal fashion, the narrator explained the anxieties of those who feared the Black majority and presented candidly the reason for South African racism that few others (then or today) have ever dared to broach publicly: 'Now these advocates of apartheid are not cruel and heartless men. Most are honest, decent, God-fearing.' The core of the matter was an 'overwhelming fear felt by whites – almost an obsession – that if racial discrimination were to be lifted, largescale intermarriage would inevitably result, and the whites would be absorbed in an inferior mixed race.' He concluded that with totalitarian Communism threatening the free world, it was urgent for the nations who believed in freedom to unite in its defence on the basis of equality, no matter what their colour or race. 'The problems of South Africa are very real and appallingly complex and there is not an easy answer. But it's more than doubtful whether a policy of discrimination provides a solution for South Africa and it is certainly impossible as a basis for the development of the Commonwealth, or even for its survival.'[30]

South Africa's ambassador in Washington fulminated and threatened a formal protest. Then in January, the *New York Times* listed the film as one of the ten best 16-mm films of 1958. A worried and embarrassed Norman Robertson wrote to Roberge that he thought the film should be withdrawn from international distribution in order to maintain friendly ties with South Africa. Long-standing department policy had been to not criticize the regime publicly, because informal statements of Canada's views were thought to be more effective.

Significantly, South African diplomats claimed later they did not recall Canada ever attempting to impress its views on their government during this period. Perhaps this is

the most trenchant remark that could be made about the effectiveness of Canada's quiet diplomacy.[31]

Canada's Department of External Affairs argued the pros and cons of withdrawal. Roberge wrote to Robertson in April, warning that the publicity storm resulting from suppressing the anti-apartheid film would harm Canada more than South Africa, but that he would go along with the department's decision. On 8 April 1959 the Film Board issued a memorandum: 'At the request of the Government of South Africa, the Department of External Affairs has asked us to immediately discontinue distribution of this film outside Canada. This means that there will be no television distribution or sales of this subject from now on.'

By fall it was decided that distribution was to be limited to Canada only; the dissatisfied South Africans continued to threaten a formal protest. When External Affairs requested the Film Board informally to withdraw it, they overstepped their authority. Citing the National Film Act's reference to films that served the national interest, the Film Board balked and said *Black and White in South Africa* was popular in Canada and was likely to have a long distribution life.

In February 1960, one month after British Prime Minister Harold Macmillan made his famous 'winds of change' speech in Capetown condemning apartheid, the grisly Sharpeville riots occurred. In Ottawa, members of Parliament called for strong diplomatic protests. At this point, Norman Robertson wrote to Canada's new minister of external affairs, Howard Green, to inform him of the background to the contentious film. The South Africans were claiming copyright infringement and meant to stop its distribution. Green decided to leave the matter alone and see what developed. But Member of Parliament Hazen Argue, at the instigation of the film's writers William Weintraub and Ronald Dick, called External Affairs. Fearful of the political windfall that could be reaped by the Opposition in Parliament, External Affairs contacted Prime Minister Diefenbaker. The prime minister, reflecting a tendency of his administration to temporize, told Green to decide on a course of action. Green told his officials not to return Argue's call.[32] On this occasion, the decision to do nothing worked in favour of the Film Board, which continued to distribute the film in Canada for the next decade. The board of governors noted that External Affairs informed South Africa at last 'that distribution of this film in Canada should not be hampered.'[33]

South Africa turned to the more serious diplomatic problem of trying, without success, to remain in the Commonwealth. They marched out when Diefenbaker threw his support behind India, Ghana, and Nigeria at the Commonwealth prime ministers' conference in March 1961. The plaintiffs interpreted Diefenbaker's position with bitter cynicism: he had been losing ground in Canada and was pandering to the anti-South African campaign carried on in the Canadian press as well as in clerical and ultra-liberal circles.[34]

Ultra-liberal or no, the Film Board had been one of the first public voices in Canada against apartheid, and *Black and White in South Africa* had helped mould public opinion, as students, professors, and other concerned citizens saw and discussed the film in hundreds of community, religious, and public-affairs groups. When it was withdrawn at last in 1972, the film had enjoyed a total of 4,952 non-theatrical bookings as well as two national television broadcasts.[35]

Most would agree that on the issue of South Africa, Diefenbaker caught up with public opinion and then led it. To what degree the contentious documentary influenced the anti-apartheid campaign one can only speculate, but the thousands of groups who saw it were part of the ground swell against South Africa in those years. One wonders too if South Africa's loud and unceasing protests over the film were not also a barometer of its impact. External Affairs, as a

functional clearing-house for film ideas that would bear on foreign policy, had learned a bitter lesson from this incident. They would have to scrutinize the Film Board productions more cautiously than ever. Early in 1960, the department withdrew its informal approval of three films on the geography, history, and people of Russia and the planned series was scrapped.[36] The next major crisis involving External Affairs was over the controversial 1964 documentary about the legendary Canadian doctor-hero of Communist China, *Bethune*.

Putting this affair into perspective, very rarely did a Film Board production stir up debate. Board secretary Ian MacNeill complained of this fact to Roberge and Mulholland when both administrators ordered deletion of a segment that ridiculed the prime minister in *Age of Dissent: Young Men with Opinions*, a piece about angry young men in Canada and England in 1959. MacNeill's position was that the Film Board was bound by its nature to be in hot water some of the time. 'The fact that we haven't been in trouble for years, however gratifying this may be when we go before Treasury Board, is an indication of the lack of significant and thought-provoking material in our film program,' he remonstrated. Mulholland defended the cut, stating that the Film Board was prepared to 'take considerable risks when the objective is worth the gamble.' Obviously, ridiculing the prime minister was not worth the gamble for a government-funded agency.[37]

Distribution: The distressing secret

No single issue in Film Board history remained more controversial than establishing accurate statistics on who was seeing the films. The simple dogma of Distribution was that if subjects were made and not seen, then public money was being squandered. Getting them to the people consumed a substantial part of the annual budget, and by the late 1950s, Distribution's expenditures were approaching those of Production. Despite this fact, no one could say with certainty just who was seeing what. Mulholland thought the whole system needed overhauling. Before he could put his ideas on to paper, however, he lost his two-year battle with cancer and died in August 1960. The loss of the tough, hard-bitten executive was profound. More for better than for worse, he seemed to have had a knack for using his authority and acerbic personality to truly lead the creative artists and to have shaped the course of Canadian documentary film in the fifties.

Inside the agency, Distribution was sometimes praised and most times damned. Statistics proved that there was a salutary effect from the non-theatrical circulation of travel films in the United States. Some 22 per cent of the tourists who came to Canada had been influenced by them. With television, there were reliable audience statistics and it was possible to monitor interest in series like *Perspective*, *Panoramique*, *World in Action*, and *Le Temps présent*. By contrast, the non-theatrical film distribution was a mystery, occupying sixty-one people in six regional offices and thirty-five district and sub-offices. It was anyone's guess as to the measurable effect of the film federations, comprising some 470 film councils, as well as the impact of voluntary citizens' groups covering cities, towns, and communities across the country.[38]

Who was seeing these films? The old method of 'spot booking' was based on a report of all showings for titles that were borrowed from a library or depot. A spot booking might mean the film was shown to a group of thirty-five or to four classes of thirty-five schoolchildren. Distribution also used the 'basic program' tabulation, which tried to count the number of audiences who viewed programmes containing varying numbers of Film Board productions. Under that system there were four to eight times *fewer* showings. In 1958–9, for example, there were 73,000 'spot' and 10,000 basic-program bookings in Ontario, compared to

12,000 'spot' and 6,000 basic-program bookings in Quebec. In descending order nationally, the audiences comprised elementary schoolchildren, then community groups, followed by high-school students. (In Quebec, twice as many [predominantly English] 'community' audiences as school audiences saw the films, the effect of years of Duplessis-ordered school boycotts of the Film Board and of the dearth of French originals.) The Film Board's own statistics in the *Annual Report, 1960–61* showed the following breakdown of what kinds of communities the Film Board reached best. Based on the 1951 census, 34 per cent of distribution was to communities of 1,000 or less; 14 per cent to communities of 1,000 to 5,000; 16 per cent to communities of 5,000 to 25,000; 13 per cent to communities of 25,000 to 100,000; 20 per cent to communities of 100,000 or more; and 3 per cent was unknown.

To achieve more accurate statistics, the organization decided to introduce a method called 'screenings,' based on mechanically processed punched cards (known as the infamous 'pink cards'). The projectionist was to indicate the number of people and what the type of audience was.[39] It was a noble intention that had an ignoble application. Some soon called it 'the great lie' because field officers often inflated statistics to demonstrate their good work. Mulholland ridiculed the inflated figures and was in the process of devising another system when he died. He had rejected the technical division's innovation, which would have marked the celluloid after each screening to allow for a specific count when the film was returned to the laboratory for periodic cleaning.[40] Not surprisingly, within a year the new statistical method showed that community distribution figures were increasing.

The figures for television bookings indicated a 30 per cent drop in 1959. The ostensible reason was that the supply of shorts was almost used up. To rectify this situation, English and French Production would have to double their output of forty half-hours per year at a cost of one million dollars. The cost-conscious government would never provide the additional funds. Besides, the CBC had a surplus of shorts it wanted to use before contracting for new programmes. At this point the Film Board had become irrelevant to the CBC, though not to Radio-Canada, which relied upon their productions more than ever.

In New York, in tribute to the Film Board's twenty-first anniversary, the Museum of Modern Art staged a five-week summer retrospective of seventeen documentaries. Richard Griffith, curator of the museum's film library, wrote warmly about the functional service the films performed for their audiences: they concentrated on the job of building a democratic community and of underlining the sense of community interest. He thought that their common characteristic was 'sober optimism,' and enthused, 'I cannot recall a single instance of technique being used, or misused, for its own sake or for the sake of momentary effect.' His praise might have seemed damning to those who favoured a more experimental approach to the medium, but since only ten of the productions shown were post-1950, someone ought to have questioned whether they presented a fair image of contemporary Canada.[41]

The versioning of 54 films into 22 foreign languages (13 European and 9 Asiatic) demonstrated the achievement of respectable international distribution by Film Board and commercial representatives as well as by diplomatic posts, although it was arguable that the agency's own worldwide lifetime audience figure of 600 million was more optimistic than realistic. Looking at the titles that were versioned in 1960, it becomes clear that these productions were aimed primarily at juvenile (school) audiences. The most popular titles chosen for versioning were *Ti-Jean Goes Lumbering*, *City of Gold*, *The Chairmaker and the Boys*, *The Rising Tide*, *The Story of the St. Lawrence Seaway*, *Wheat Country*, *World in a Marsh*, *Teeth Are to*

Keep, *Accidents Don't Happen*, and *Montreal in 1957*. (A little-known fact was that France insisted on 'versioning' the Film Board's French films itself into continental French, a practice that continued until 1962.)

According to the figures, in 1959 just less than a quarter of a million foreign screenings took place, reaching almost twenty-five million people. Almost as many productions were sold as loaned abroad, and the audience was largely school-aged. Telecasts abroad were supposed to be the main way of reaching adults; with each 'telecast' signifying a single broadcast over a single station, the United States had been the largest audience with 3,259 telecasts. But this figure did not mention that because of cut-backs in public-affairs programming, only two Film Board films, *Angotee: Story of an Eskimo Boy* and *Canadian Profile*, were televised nationally to one hundred stations on a single Saturday prime-time slot, compared to fifteen films the previous year. The United Kingdom was a distant second with 691 telecasts, while Europe had had only 70. Some 318 broadcasts had occurred in the rest of the world. Millions may have been reached, but if versioned works were largely for children, and Distribution was boasting that the BBC showed *Angotee: Story of an Eskimo Boy* and *Log Drive* twice, the film image of Canada must have looked puerile and primitive. It was also an image that was not terribly accurate, as it said nothing about contemporary urban life. *Log Drive* (*La Drave*), directed by Raymond Garceau, presented in words and music the spectacle of Quebec's fearless log-drivers, who in the annual spring ritual of danger and adventure guided countless thousands of spruce logs downstream to mills.

Canadian newsreel stories continued to receive substantial foreign distribution, including to eastern Europe. Millions may have seen the word 'Canada,' but the question of value comes to mind if one takes a sample of six stories that were distributed in commercial cinemas in eastern Europe in April and May 1960: *Seaway Opening, Er-*

nest *Lapointe Ice Breaker*, *De Gaulle in Ottawa*, *B.C. Sheep*, *Commonwealth London Conference*, and *Diefenbaker Visits Mexico*.[42] Still, the very innocuousness of the subjects confirmed an international image that the government was happy to cultivate.

Looking at distribution from another vantage point, global community statistics in Canada seemed promising. Besides the film federations composed of voluntary film councils, there were 460 film circuits, to which field representatives brought shows once a month; there were also 80 public libraries with 16-mm departments, 20 large provincial libraries, and 26 cooperative film pools, all circulating blocks of films. While resource libraries of Film Board films were being developed for each province, an ominous note was raised by one of the key Distribution officers, who admitted, 'We still do not know enough about that part of the adult Canadian audience which we are not yet reaching and are not fully informed on the part which we are reaching as to which groups are using what films in all parts of Canada.'[43]

The statistics for the most popular films of 1959–60 in community distribution present an interesting profile, despite the fact that theatrical or television releases could not be included. Contracts commonly forbade general release of theatrical subjects until some months after they had played at cinemas; as of fall 1960, one-fifth of the television material could not be released for three years. There were 678 titles in the current Film Board catalogue.[44] Scrutiny of the 'most popular title' list in Table 1 confirms again that schoolchildren were the primary audience.

TABLE 1. Most popular titles, 1959–60

ENGLISH	Total attendance to date
Released prior to 1953	
Fur Country	877,086
The Great Lakes	920,713
Grey Owl's Little Brother	864,177
Historic Highway– Upper Canada	541,887
The Loon's Necklace (Crawley Films)	1,142,227
Maple Sugar Time	662,325
Peoples of Canada	814,945
The Policeman	908,898
Teeth Are to Keep	905,154
Released during 1953–4	
Monkey Tale	721,223
Romance of Transportation	909,677
The Story of Peter and the Potter	809,844
Ti-Jean Goes Lumbering	1,109,662
The Zoo in Stanley Park	326,065
Released during 1954–5	
The Beaver Makes a Comeback	355,633
Food for Freddy	537,902
Mountains of the West	243,907
One Little Indian	994,904
Physical Regions of Canada	337,634
Released during 1955–6	
High Tide in Newfoundland	523,013
Musical Ride	1,034,344
The Pony	647,449
Who's Running Things?	115,033
Released during 1956–7	
Assignment Children	373,734
The Great Lakes– St. Lawrence Lowlands	242,019
Rythmetic	181,934
The Shepherd	362,902
World in a Marsh	485,374
Released during 1957–8	
The Atlantic Region	134,604
Being Different	16,891
City of Gold	192,920
Honey Bees and Pollination	127,063
The Sceptre and the Mace	320,639

Released during 1958–9

Animal Friends	136,616
The Changing Forest	198,364
The Legendary Judge	143,349
Safety on the Water	123,951
The Story of HMS Shannon	88,132
Trans-Canada Summer	202,696

Released during 1959–60

A Day in the Night of Jonathan Mole	
Fun for All	statistics not
Let's Look at Weeds	yet compiled
Ripple Rock	by Film Board
The Story of the St. Lawrence Seaway	
Tourist Go Home	

FRENCH	Total attendance to date

Released prior to 1953

Chantons Noël	211,063
Chants populaires no. 1	453,625
Dame truite prends la mouche	197,330
Les Moines de Saint-Benoît	221,853
Oiseaux du Canada no. 1	90,036

Released during 1953–4

Chanteurs acadiens	265,480
L'Hiver au Canada	58,794
Pierre et le potier	212,529
Sports et transports	134,700
Ti-Jean s'en va-t-aux chantiers	276,957

Released during 1954–5

Corral	164,191
Les Grandes Régions du Canada	55,304
Drôle de Micmac	247,234
Le Menu de Michel	165,039
Montagnes de l'Ouest	60,599

Released during 1955–6

Auberge Jolifou	85,771
La Feuille verte	104,541
Nous croyons au Père Noël	87,803
Pêcheurs de Terre-Neuve	130,371
Ungava	94,277

Released during 1956–7

Bassin des Grands Lacs et du Saint-Laurent	59,649
Le Berger	71,495
L'Etang	139,511
Jeunesses musicales	93,885
Regards sur l'Italie	73,155

Released during 1957–8

Bonjou' soleil	58,289
La Drave	133,777
Faune des Rocheuses	66,829
Les Grandes Plaines	61,504
Région atlantique	59,699

Released during 1958–9

Canada industriel	56,358
Félix Leclerc	46,539
La Forêt qui change	86,898
Itinéraire canadien	74,876
Le Merle	72,550
Ti-Jean au pays du fer	76,401

Released during 1959–60

Atlas du Canada	
Correlieu	Statistics not
Danses et vacances	yet compiled
Pierre Beaulieu	by Film Board
Voie maritime du Saint-Laurent	

SOURCE: M. McKay, 'The Motion Picture: A Mirror of Time' (see note 44)

This list indicates which titles were receiving the largest non-theatrical, non-television activity. Audience figures might have been somewhat skewed, as in British Columbia, where the average audience per screening was eighty-three, compared to Ontario's fifty-nine. Using figures alone as a barometer of popularity, the favourites were *The Loon's Necklace, Ti-Jean Goes Lumbering, Musical Ride, One Little Indian,* and *The Great Lakes.* In French, musical sing-alongs like *Chants populaires no. 1, Chantons Noël,* and *Chanteurs acadiens* were most popular, followed by *Drôle de Micmac* and *Pierre et le potier.* The most revealing fact from this list is that there was not much of a non-theatrical audience for adult-oriented films.

Quebec's Department of Education ban was lifted at last in February 1961.[45] More surprising perhaps was the refusal to distribute Film Board productions by boards of education and universities and their extension services in New Brunswick, Nova Scotia, Prince Edward Island, and Newfoundland. Those teachers who wanted the institution's productions had to get them on their own.

Since its founding, the Film Board had always skirted with great care the subject of education, which is one of the most jealously guarded provincial powers. Roberge wanted to be sure the federal agency would not stand accused of subsidizing provincial education departments, and this is why the Film Board had done most of its own distribution in Quebec; it also depended heavily upon film councils and depots for assistance there and in other provinces. Only in British Columbia was the Department of Education the biggest distributor of Film Board films.

It would be interesting to know if the filmmakers were cognizant of these facts about distribution statistics. There certainly was no organized internal method of informing them. The *Annual Report* was not detailed enough to make these observations, nor was it a favourite document among employees who accepted (but rarely read) it as necessary propaganda to justify perpetuation of the agency. Behind the scenes, however, the distribution people were confronting the toughest fact of all: in urban areas, Canada's key population centres, the films were not reaching the so-called groupless and rootless. In short, though rural Canada was still well covered through existing community organizations, the non-school and city populations were largely unreachable, except through television and theatres. Income from the latter was down to one-fourth of the 1953 figures, while income from the former was down almost 30 per cent from 1959. This yawning gap in distribution became the Film Board's unpublicized distressing secret.[46] Worse still was the fact that, from 1955 to 1962, Distribution had grown from 203 to 226 officers; headquarters staff had increased without reaching new audiences, and the net decrease of staff in the regions had been followed by declining field activities.[47]

The private producers lobby again

Late in 1960, the Association of Motion Picture Producers and Laboratories of Canada lodged their now-usual grievance for more sponsored films with Minister Fairclough. Roberge trotted out the old argument that his institution had to do sponsored work if it was to operate efficiently. His strongest point was that if the Film Board handed over sponsored film production entirely to the fifty-three private producers, each company would receive just enough money to make two films.[48] Fairclough accepted his explanation that some 12 per cent of the sponsored films went to private producers, although, had she looked closely at statistics, she would have learned that the Film Board had commissioned seven films from private producers in 1956–7, none the following year, and then only one per year in 1959 and 1960.[49]

The commissioner appealed to each deputy minister of government departments for more sponsored work, both to salve the bruised sensibilities of, and to help, private industry. This stemmed the industry's perennial grousing temporarily.[50] He thought that the future of private producers lay in features, not shorts, and he had been consulting with various departments since January to examine how best to provide financial help for feature and television film production.[51]

Roberge pursued his appointed role as 'adviser' to the government on film matters. After consulting with both Britain's National Film Finance Corporation and France's Centre national de la cinématographie, he recommended in 1962 co-productions as the best approach to providing impetus to a five-to-seven-million-dollar annual feature-film industry. He never mentioned the possibility of Canada imposing a quota system to nurture this new activity, because this ran contrary to Canadian historical trade patterns with the United States. There was another economic argument: of the $33 million generated by film rentals in 1959, roughly one-quarter, or $8 million, was spent on distribution in Canada. Then there was the fact that $25 million left the country annually, of which 10 per cent, or $2.5 million, was paid to the federal government as withholding tax.[52] One surmises that Roberge did not wish to wring the neck of the ten-million-dollar golden goose. His logical argument was that feature films needed to be produced first, then their intrinsic value would draw audiences to the theatres. Curiously, those favouring a quota system rarely dealt with these percentages in making their nationalist arguments. Fairclough accepted and passed on to Cabinet Roberge's recommendation for co-productions.[53] The next Liberal government picked up the ball and took credit for creating the Canadian Film Development Corporation.

The difficulties and political jockeying discussed in this chapter are indigenous to virtually all institutions and bureaucracies, but one must not lose sight of the fact that the Film Board was a very special sort of conglomeration. Unlike for most other government agencies, the results of its activity were forever being brought before the public for scrutiny and judgment. Within the organization, filmmakers engaged in jockeying of another sort, for the content and style of film. Never far from the lips of the creative personnel were questions about how effective the programming process was, what texture their films should have, and how much freedom was enough.

Some felt anchored to the Grierson tradition of making public-service films in the national interest and sought to find new ways to state universal values. Others thought that energies would be better spent in breaking out of past patterns and in anticipating future trends. Many of the Quebec filmmakers were falling under the spell of *Nouvelle vague* (New Wave) in French cinema and felt that change was at last imminent in their tradition-bound province. For both English and French filmmakers, television was the principal outlet that invited them to put familiar images before a people who were simultaneously clamouring for and fearful of change. As a whole, then, for both linguistic groups the cultural challenge of the sixties might be best expressed as a desire to wield the sword of invention and to wound, rather than slay, their respective dragons of tradition.

4

The Golden Years, Part II –
At the Heart of the Film Board:
Unit B and *L'équipe française*

Tom Daly's Unit B: 'The poets' versus 'the plumbers'

The group that perhaps had the most profound effect on English-Canadian film during the Golden Years was Tom Daly's Unit B, the second of the four units to issue from the reorganization in 1948. As executive producer since 1951, Daly bonded his creative staff together with a curious blend of Aristotelian logic, paternalism, and unwavering ethical care for each creative person. A self-described rational idealist, his intellectual roots stemmed from two major, if contrasting, influences: the esoteric philosophy of Gurdieff and the commitment to public duty as enunciated by John Grierson. The two threads combined to create a recognizably Canadian form of self-abnegation, where 'ego' was downplayed because it cut people off from each other, and consciousness was pursued for its power to create a universal quality of humanness.[1]

Daly spent an astronomical number of hours at work and was responsible for a lifetime achievement of producing over three hundred films. His Herculean capacity, combined with a method of teaching by example rather than by instruction, won him filmmakers' respect and awe. He was uncompromising personally and professionally, yet could listen and be receptive to new ideas. Responding with subtlety and feeling, he

would not tell a filmmaker something was wrong or needed fixing. He would rather ask difficult questions like 'What does the shot mean?' or suggest alterations. Invariably, he credited the filmmaker for having made the decisions and changes. He understood the paradox that one had to struggle for tolerance. Perhaps his greatest gift was that of the quintessential English Canadian: he saw good in everything.[2]

The main areas of Unit B activity were animation, art films, (including experimental and 'loners,' or single items), classroom and science films, and foreign versions. The work was divided among eighteen animators and eleven regular, six science, and six titling staff members. There was an 'inner cabinet' represented by the producer for each major area, with Daly himself supervising the 'loners.' The fact that Unit B personnel did not do much sponsored work led some jealous staff to call them 'poets,' while those who were assigned such films often thought of themselves as 'plumbers.'[3] This resentment of Unit B was a major rallying cry in the demolition of the unit system in 1964. Another explanation for the uniqueness of Unit B was that Daly attracted to himself all the people nobody else wanted, the young, bright, but difficult personalities who were anxious to break away from formal, traditional filmmaking.[4]

Always there at the editing stage, Daly

slowed things down as if he were playing a game of chess. Critics complained that in this process, where a newspaper was called for, an encyclopaedia was produced. Thoroughness and excellence were his minimum criteria, and in probing the filmmaker's footage he was apt to discuss Socrates to give context to the film images. His purpose was to stretch the artists' emotional understanding of the world and to help them focus on the individual's relationship to what he called 'organic wholeness.' It was a principle that derived from his teacher and mentor, Stuart Legg, one of the most brilliant (and forgotten) minds in the history of documentary film, who had produced the Film Board's wartime theatrical series, *Canada Carries On* and *The World in Action*. Legg taught Daly his impeccable editing skills and, with Grierson, had turned the wartime propaganda film into an internationalist, universal credo for humanitarianism. Daly believed that film should be something educational that served the public's needs. The challenge was twofold: first, to speak comprehensibly with images to which people related, and second, to understand that one's own relation to the whole preceded understanding the particular. From this philosophical approach derived the hallmark of Unit B's films – the leitmotif of suspended judgment.[5]

Daly infused Unit B with a classical approach, while trying to manage the natural conflict between the personalities. He had a remarkable talent: to bend their self-destructive impulses and use them as a source of energy for the group. As he put it with characteristic understatement, 'I myself was not the originator of film ideas; I was the aider and abettor of other people's original ideas which I knew how to help [actualize] in the editing and completion of films.'[6]

The key personnel in Unit B were (besides Norman McLaren, who was an entity on his own) Wolf Koenig, Colin Low, Roman Kroitor, and Stanley Jackson.[7] Eldon Rathburn almost always composed the music. Koenig, whose family had fled Hitler's

Germany when he was nine, was a painfully shy but gifted innovator, who had grown up on a rural Ontario farm, where originality and self-reliance were the keys to survival. John Spotton, cinematographer, unit editor, and later executive producer, described Koenig as the most brilliant mind at the Film Board, who could have more original film ideas in thirty seconds than others might have in years. Koenig joined the institution in 1946, served as cameraman on *Neighbours*, *City of Gold*, and *Corral*, and was animator on *The Romance of Transportation in Canada*. He then pioneered *The Candid Eye* series with Roman Kroitor. A reticent person publicly, Koenig conveyed through example his beliefs that the Film Board was an ethical company where human relations took precedence and responsibilities to each other underscored the higher purpose of commitment to humanist (Old Testament) ideals.

Colin Low, the Albertan son of a Mormon rancher, was shaped by frontier value of 'cooperating with your neighbours' and the communal roots of Mormonism. He had joined the Film Board as an animator in 1945, and following *Corral*, his first live-action film in 1954, probably did more to shape various documentary-film styles than any other person at the institution. He articulated the unforgettable Canadian western myth in *Corral*, continued it in *City of Gold*, and concluded its definition in *Circle of the Sun*, *The Days of Whisky Gap*, *The Hutterites*, and *Standing Alone*. Low also pioneered animation techniques in *Universe* and co-directed with Kroitor the direct-cinema *chef-d'oeuvre*, *Labyrinth*, for Expo 67. He was one of the founders of the grass-roots approach to the 'Challenge for Change' programme, and helped regionalize the institution in the 1970s. More recently, he has developed and introduced the most refined 3-D process in the world, and he continues to work on research and development of that medium for application to the giant-screen (trademark) IMAX system.

Roman Kroitor was a Saskatchewan

Ukrainian whose interest (and Master's degree) in philosophy clashed with an emotional, brash, but extremely sensitive personality. He was the object of envious ridicule by some, but was dedicated to the principle of 'public good' as he understood the term. As much an iconoclast as originator, he and Koenig became the founders and principal contributors to direct cinema in the *Candid Eye* series. Koenig described Kroitor and Daly as the polarities between which was stretched the tough strand that made Unit B functional. It was a filament extended to such a fine tautness that the rest of the unit could balance on it. Kroitor eventually left the Film Board to pioneer the giant-screen IMAX process with Graeme Ferguson and Robert Kerr, returned to the agency to produce drama in the seventies, then departed to devote his full-time talents to developing IMAX internationally and in 3-D. He continues to collaborate with the Film Board to make prestige films in that format.

Stanley Jackson, a former schoolteacher in Winnipeg and Toronto, left the profession to join the Film Board during the Second World War and became the commentary writer and voice in almost eighty Film Board documentaries. Jackson knew how difficult it was to achieve a good voice-over script, which may explain in part why so many filmmakers later abandoned the technique. Had he not shared his considerable talent, it is arguable that many of the films typifying Unit B would not have had a characteristic 'seamless look.' In *Universe*, which was an inspiration for Stanley Kubrick's film *2001: A Space Odyssey* in 1968, the visuals demonstrate humankind's insignificance in the great order, but Jackson's verbal mixture of awe and transcendence, read grandiloquently by Douglas Rain, approached the sublime: 'If we could move with the freedom of a god so that a million years pass in a second and if we went far enough past the nearest suns, beyond the star clouds and nebulae, in time they would end, and as if moving out from behind a curtain we would come to an endless sea of night. In that sea are islands, continents of stars that we have named – the galaxies ...'

Antecedents to the development of *Candid Eye*

While personality has much to do with creativity, the style that came to be recognized as Unit B's started with a book and grew from another film genre. The book was photographer Henri Cartier-Bresson's *The Decisive Moment*, which paid homage to surrealism and the principles of photojournalism in the recording of daily ephemera.[8] Cartier-Bresson used the rapid-fire 35-mm camera to document the drama of the ordinary moment, and in dealing with the photo subject's candidness, honesty, and absence of deception, eliminated the distinction between art and life. Cartier-Bresson's goal was to try to represent the absolute ambience of real life.

Kroitor and Koenig were influenced profoundly by the French master's contribution to still photography. They wondered if documentary film could not also embody the concept of 'the decisive moment,' that instant in which reality can be spontaneously and wholly rendered. Koenig considered *The Decisive Moment* his greatest influence and inspiration, and drew a line from Cartier-Bresson to John Grierson's dictum that in documentary you must serve the public and make subjects of peace as exciting as those of war.

Coincidentally, in Britain at this time there was a development in Free Cinema that showed great promise for the documentary film. *Thursday's Children*, written and directed in 1954 by Guy Brenton and Lindsay Anderson, with commentary spoken by Richard Burton, was a 22-minute film shot at the Margate School for the Deaf, in which stunning moments of truth emerged from an ordinary background. A similar experience occurred with the film *Mamma Don't Allow*, a record of a raucous Saturday night at a working-class dancehall. Both British films showed the possibilities of achieving intimacy with an omnipresent camera, an intimacy that had been documentary filmmakers' long-standing dream.

Kroitor and Koenig, along with fellow Unit B director Terence Macartney-Filgate, had long debates about these influences. They were joined by cinematographers Georges Dufaux, Gilles Gascon, Michel Brault, and John Spotton. All were conversant with the neorealism of Rossellini's *Open City* and de Sica's *Bicycle Thieves*, and were intrigued with Carol Reed's and Garson Kanin's *The True Glory*, a documentary newsreel that had shown the possibilities of merging dialogue with documentary. They agreed universally on one point: the NFB television series *Perspective* seemed wooden and unreal.

The unavailability of truly portable equipment had prevented realization of these ideas at the Film Board. After the Second World War, the heavy and aging 35-mm cameras had been converted for use in titling and animation, as Mitchell cameras, weighing 45 kilos, were bought for studio use. In 1951–2, the Film Board acquired a light, hand-held but noisy reflex camera (Arriflex) weighing 8 kilos and a 16-mm reflex weighing 3 kilos. About the same time they acquired the clattering 10-kilo Cameflex. Television production demanded a single-system, synchronized sound camera that was quiet; for this, the Auricon Filmagnetic Super 1200 was used, but it weighed an unwieldy 25 kilos. Thus, the relatively lightweight shoulder-mounted Arriflex camera was preferred in the mid-1950s for *On the Spot* television production, although its mechanical racket made close shooting difficult. The Eclair NPR appeared in 1959 and had a self-contained quartz control motor to facilitate synchronized sound. French director Jean Rouch used it to shoot *Chronique d'un été*, and soon the Film Board was using it too. In 1963, technical wizard Chester Beachell also developed for the Film Board four prototypes of a 16-mm 'silent' camera with which to experiment.

Sound was the other obstacle. Voice-over narration had characterized most productions, going back to the earliest days of the organization. When synchronized sound was used, it was usually only for a few seconds of a film because sound-recording apparatus was unwieldy, unportable, and very expensive. Filmmakers dreamed of a location sound-recording system to replace the standard 160-kilo Westrex, which dated back to the 1940s. Beachell started applying his mechanical gifts to this problem in 1954; by October 1955 he had developed an interlocked camera and sound unit (battery-powered and portable), complete with an awkward but functional chest harness for the *On the Spot* and *Passe-partout* television series. The prototype he demonstrated to the Society of Motion Picture and Television Engineers weighed a hefty 33 kilos.

In 1955–6, with weight reduced to a somewhat more portable 25 kilos (including batteries), sound was recorded on Beachell's Sprocketape behemoth, which used ¼-inch perforated magnetic recording tape, synchronized with the camera. Both camera and recorder were plugged into a line or an AC generator. By 1956, the first ten Beachell Sprocketape recorders were being used in both the *Perspective* and *Panoramique* series and for most Film Board location shooting at one-sixth the previous cost. Cameramen preferred plugging the Auricon into the German-built Mayhak recorder, though it was not a synchronized system. Synchronization became possible with the Kudelski Nagra III recorder, introduced in 1958 as the first portable, self-contained, light (16 kilo), small, and solid-state tape recorder. Sometime around the mid-sixties, the standard apparatus became the Eclair NPR, attached by cable to the Nagra.

A chance to film Igor Stravinsky en route to Europe by ship in 1963 led to another technological leap. Kroitor and Koenig were shooting in 16 mm and asked the Technical Research Division to come up with a well-balanced, 7-kilo, battery-operated, quiet camera to enable them to film the great composer. Nick Culic of the Camera Division took charge of the development team, working with Ralph Curtis and Chester Beachell. The first camera was not ready for the shoot, and while the composer stayed in his cabin for the rough voyage, Marcel Carrière, Koenig, and Kroitor spent almost all their time in the ship's engineering area, modifying the device to their needs. They reached Germany, added a few more parts, and plugged into the Kudelski Nagra. Carrière attached a wireless microphone to the composer and achieved the transcendence of which documentary filmmakers had long dreamed – the subject was freed completely from the hardware. Carrière finished perfecting the prototype while shooting the Film Board's second English feature, *Nobody Waved Goodbye*. The regular use of wireless microphones did not occur until the end of the decade.[9]

Perhaps the most important effect of the technological breakthroughs was that the new mobile techniques allowed the communications revolution to reach remote areas everywhere, especially in the Third World, providing the voiceless with a means to be heard, to become educated, and to change their local world. Some historians of communications believe that eventually these developments may be considered as important as Gutenberg's invention of the printing press.

Development of *Candid Eye*

On the heels of the breathtaking technological changes, the *Candid Eye* concept was discussed in 1957 and jelled in 1958 as a new television series. Daly encouraged his group to experiment with candid portraits by seeking a naturally interesting character or group of characters, caught up in circumstances that involved the whole person in some kind of universally significant and fascinating situation. Ideas expressed without emotional engagement, he warned, were lifeless; hence emotion had to be the principal 'hook.'

Emotion could be measured, he continued, by identifying the structure of visual images when the picture was run without sound. This was the clear and meaningful intellectual line of the medium. Above all, the emotional order and flow had to be as various, rich, and satisfying as possible. In editing later on, he discovered that it was necessary to rearrange the material frequently in order to make the candid material 'work.' Once the emotional flow could be made to function, the rest usually rearranged itself around it. The unity of these various elements produced the sense of wholeness, a vivid realization or moment of understanding. At that point, the viewer was supposed to feel an intake of energy, physical alertness, and vitality as a total experience.

Daly crystallized this philosophy when he told his personnel to search out film subjects that were about 'people who radiated wholeness from time to time.' The point was that there was to be no predetermined philosophical hook upon which to hang a film; rather, the filmmakers were to cultivate an aura of innocence using a 'candid eye.' They found their chance when Donald Mulholland, exasperated with Roman Kroitor's criticism of *Perspective*'s artistic standards, said that if Kroitor could apply Daly's principles and do one film right, he would get money for a whole series.

Kroitor and Koenig came up at last with a prototype that allowed the English and French teams to shoot simultaneous experimental sequences. The strategic thinking was that only Scrooge would dislike children telling Santa what they wanted, while equally expectant adults scurried, sang in choirs, and partied in Montreal. *The Days Before Christmas* became the first *Candid Eye* film, with directing credits going to Terence Macartney-Filgate, Stanley Jackson, and Wolf Koenig. It won over the doubtful, and the CBC agreed to run a series, beginning in the fall of 1958.

The second film, *A Foreign Language*, documented a group of foreign children learning English. Both films tried to describe and interpret Canadians as they really were, using the camera directly and perceptively to cultivate an air of innocence. They were not great films, but the directors conveyed a complex of relations to show people against their own background. They said later they were reacting to static films, where the action, as in pictorial semi-biographies, was more psychological than physical. The priority was to choose themes that contained photographable situations.[10] By the time *Candid Eye* ended, there were thirteen 24- to 28-minute films, most of which were translated into French for the television series *Temps présent.*

The English-speaking filmmakers called the new film genre 'Candid Eye' and then 'direct cinema.' The Candid Eye crews were nicknamed 'The Rover Boys,' and they relied less on tradition than on innovations with the hand-held camera and the appearance of an uncontrolled setting. Opponents bemoaned the fact that the spontaneity allowed by the new technical developments opened a Pandora's box: filmmakers lost traditional discipline as the script-writing stage no longer seemed necessary and they accepted sloppiness, or what was referred to as showing the 'seams' of a film. The filmmakers' rebuttal was that the need to light a set or plan a shot was less important than catching the moment of drama. They argued that for the same money, small crews with lightweight portable equipment, using available light as a principle, could put more time into research on the spot at small expense. That meant longer time on location and in editing, with extra footage and a richness of sound effects from which to choose. Shooting ratios leaped to 20:1, as filmmakers waited for the moment of discovery. This meant that much material was left on the cutting-room floor.[11]

L'équipe française discovers 'direct'

A cross-fertilization occurred between the English and French filmmakers because Michel Brault and Marcel Carrière served in Unit B as cameraman and soundman respectively. After Brault had shot *The Days Before Christmas* in December 1957, he and Gilles Groulx requested funds the following month to shoot a 3-minute newsmagazine clip for *Temps présent* in 'Candid Eye' technique. With Carrière as soundman, they co-directed *Les Raquetteurs* ($6,907), a film about a snowshoe congress in Sherbrooke, Quebec. Director of Production Grant McLean saw the rushes and was angered that their 3-minute piece had quintupled in length. He ordered the film broken down into stock shots, but Daly and Guy Glover intervened on Groulx's behalf and prevailed upon McLean to let the young iconoclasts finish it. Groulx called it a documentary on the social behaviour of man; Executive Producer Fernand Dansereau described it as sociological cinema. Intellectuals and critics of the time agreed, because, as an ethnographic document, it showed the common people in tribal ritual. It also had an informal 'family' atmosphere about it.[12]

Les Raquetteurs is considered the seminal film in the French group's pursuit of *cinéma direct*. It was a dramatic departure from the culture of Wilfred Pelletier and the celebration of the picturesque. The innocence, confusion, lack of decorum, country-roughness, and humour demonstrate that the key element for the French was that this was, above all, *cinéma de parole*, the arrangement of spontaneous language which cultivates an aura of innocence. Some find in *Les Raquetteurs* a reflection of the daily anarchy and fundamental humour that many Quebeckers love: the mayor addresses an uncomprehending American, an announcer blares a message scolding some mischievous children, and bystanders cheer hockey star 'Rocket' Richard while being irreverent to the Snowshoe Queen. Viewed today, the humour in *Les Raquetteurs* seems to travel a fine line between innocent self-deprecation and a trenchant mockery of Quebec commu-

Les Raquetteurs (1958) became the seminal film in French-Canadian *cinéma vérité*, reflecting spontaneity of language and the anarchic humour that many Quebeckers love.

nal attitudes and working-class people.[13] English Canadians may be forgiven if, as outsiders, they interpret this and some other *cinéma direct* films as bourgeois French Canadians ridiculing working-class French Canadians. Perhaps this aspect was not perceived at the time, since Quebec audiences, as yet unnumbed by television, were thrilled at seeing and hearing themselves.

One wonders if a new class of Quebec technocrats might have found these quaint scenes of small-town life little more than folkloric. Certainly the first films in *cinéma direct* by *l'équipe française* did much to capture music and folklore. Interpreting the film experience as good, bad, or indifferent depended on the position occupied by the viewer. One recalls, however, that a few years later, René Lévesque argued that the *québécois* should complete their leap from a colonial past to a modern nation-state, or

risk being reduced to a people who were *folklorique*.

After *Les Raquetteurs*, *l'équipe française* undertook its own direct-cinema production for the *Temps présent* series, between 1958 and 1964. They too recorded actual, unrehearsed, real-life situations without a scenario, although their subjects were well researched before shooting began. Experimentation was rife; for example, there was a 'flare period' where a light-bulb had to be seen on camera to create the 'authentic' effect. If Claude Jutra shot one film on the Film Board's shooting stage under a fluorescent light to produce the flickering normally unseen by the human eye, Michel Brault became famous for filming while sauntering with the camera held by his side.

Influenced by the *Nouvelle vague* 'auteur' theories in France, filmmaking evolved into less of a team process and more of a personal endeavour. *L'équipe française* first called it 'Candid Eye' and then, for the next decade, *cinéma direct* or *cinéma vérité*, after Jean Rouch's 1963 description of what was happening as, variously, *cinéma vérité, cinéma engagé*, and *témoignages directs*. From 1970, *cinéma direct* / direct cinema has been the most popular nomenclature. By 1964, auteur-inspired filmmakers were speaking of 'my'/'*mon*' film. So, at the moment the technology of filmmaking became most accessible, allowing the deepest penetration of the changing world, some felt the Film Board community lost the vital collaborative component of its recent successes.[14]

Representative classic films

The greatest single thing about the Film Board, said John Grierson, was its genius for portraiture, making pictures about individual people. Three of the most perfect examples of this genius are films from Unit B, which also encapsulated Daly's worldly philosophy: *Paul Tomkowicz: Street-railway Switchman* (1953), the earlier mentioned *Corral* (1954), and *Lonely Boy* (1961). A fourth, *Nahanni* (1962), directed by Donald Wilder, was made under Executive Producer Nicholas Balla of Unit C.

Paul Tomkowicz: Street-railway Switchman, Kroitor's second film as director, portrayed the night street as an arena of near fantasy, thinly disguised by the veneer of inconsequential routine. Shot in 35 mm with an Arriflex camera for $6,564, it is the 9-minute story of a Polish immigrant whose mundane job of maintaining Winnipeg streetcar switches in the dead of night becomes a gorgeous study of contrasts in black and white, washed in an audioscape of authentic street sounds. The voice-over technique underscores the wordlessness of the on-screen people and Tomkowicz's alienation in the midst of a bustling urban winter vista. The multiple images of him as an outsider emphasize the isolation of so many of the deracinated who come to Canada, a place whose climate makes extreme physical demands while leaving a spiritual soul to meander where it will. The script, derived from Tomkowicz's own words and read with an impeccable Polish accent by an actor, has moments of gentle humour. The old man softly mocks the colloquialness of Winnipeg ('Winnipeg? After Paris? ... a small village, a small street') and devours his regular morning plate of six boiled eggs after his shift. His simple dream is to retire, buy a motorcycle, and tour Canada. The commentary lifts the entire opus, from what could have been existential bleakness, to lyrical heights. It remains Kroitor's favourite film.

City of Gold ($20,771) grew out of a 1952 sponsored-film idea to promote tourism and sport in the Yukon. Low and Koenig started research, and after finding some still photos in Ottawa, decided to improve the panning method Low had employed in *Jolifou Inn*, his earlier 10-minute film of Cornelius Krieghoff paintings of nineteenth-century Quebec. The idea was to move the camera across the photos in order to give a sense of life. Then Low learned of the discovery of an exquisite record of the Yukon Gold Rush, the A.E. Hegg collection of 100 eight-by-ten glass-plate negatives in Seattle. The problem of how to animate them was solved by Kroitor, who took advantage of the presence of the British mathematical wizard Brian Salt, and developed the 'Kroitorer,' a machine that enabled one to shoot the photographs as if a hand-held camera had been there at the time. In essence, his device achieved what the computer-assisted animation camera would do when it was invented a dozen years later. (Salt's mathematical tables became the basis for the Film Board's software programme in the later 1970s.) The film hinged on contrasting the historical stills with the live-action shooting of Dawson City in the present.[15] The stunning effect was to create a paradox of living people and dead objects; a frontier city lost in time was resuscitated to life through animated photos, and the whole was encapsulated by Pierre

Berton's narration. It was a rare example of mythmaking from Canadian history.

The 21-minute story is less about gold strikes than about the cluster of restless humanity that hovered around Dawson and never found gold. Their spirit, hardiness, courage, adaptability, gusto for life, and love of the world around them became the cinematic statement. John Grierson said the film revealed the secret of the North, which was also the secret of Canada. Those luckless adventurers had found community, he believed, because the harsh climate made them dependent on one another. Because you need each other, said Grierson (if you break a leg you have a friend), you discover the secret of community, the secret of love.[16] Film critic André Bazin said at the time that *City of Gold* was a model in documentaries and was already a classic in its field. Luck was with the Film Board when the film was distributed theatrically in North America with the Brigitte Bardot film *And God Created Woman*, the acclaimed French feature that introduced the French sex symbol to North America. *City of Gold* was a curious fluke too, since it convinced many at the Film Board of the continuing possibilities of theatrical shorts when that very market was declining.

A similar quest for gold was the substance of *Nahanni* ($46,631), the 18-minute story of the Northwest Territories loner Albert Faille. This old prospector's eighth annual search for a legendary lost gold-mine, on a river known for death and mysterious disappearances, turns up fruitless once again. The viewer is struck by a double impression: one, the superbly photographed, awesome splendour and rich colour of the river and wilderness; the other, Faille's dogged, crazy determination in a hostile, humbling environment. The power of these images is such that one almost forgets the presence of camera and crew. *Nahanni* underscores the fact that success in Canada's endless space may be measured in small achievements, such as escaping with one's life, rather than by grand climaxes like realizing one's obsessive-compulsive dreams.

In 1960, Kroitor and Low completed their most ambitious project yet, *Universe* ($105,146), a classroom film on astronomy to present a picture of the universe as it might appear to a voyager in space. Kroitor's storyline explained that he hoped the film would try to make the audience feel that a journey into the universe coincides with a journey into man's soul. In short, the world was ultimately meaningful. The leitmotif became the threefold idea of *eye*: the physical eye, the intellectual 'eye of the mind,' and the eye of the soul that sees the world through the agency of love. Beginning with an astronomer in his Ontario observatory, the film shifts to animation to depict the heavenly bodies that mankind has dreamed of from time immemorial. This was the dawn of the space age, and it was fortuitous that the Soviet Union launched Sputnik just as Kroitor and Low were finishing the picture editing. In these years before horrific conceptions like the Strategic Defense Initiative, viewers could relish the excitement of contemplating the infinite in a darkened environment, then, like the film's astronomer at dawn, walk into the sunlight, accompanied by the perfect grace of a bird's morning song. *Universe* also meshes innocence and incredulousness with Oriental-like balance. Stanley Jackson's last words evoke the emotional awe of the greatness and smallness of humanity: 'In all of time on all the planets of all the galaxies in space what civilizations have risen, looked into the night, seen what we see, asked the questions that we ask?'

Universe nearly faltered in mid-production because the sky-rocketing animation costs had pushed the budget up to an exorbitant $100,000. Donald Mulholland favoured splitting it into three separate classroom films, but Kroitor, Low, and Jackson argued that the point of the film was to maintain the organic relationship of individual humans on a small planet with the whole universe. This meant condensing time and space progressively to maintain the thought, feeling, and physical relationship of one minuscule being to the total vastness. Mulholland re-

Colin Low pioneered new animation techniques in *Universe* (1960), in which the animated heavenly bodies demonstrate the puniness of humankind in the great order.

lented and the film stayed intact. Tom Daly's proudest moment occurred when a stranger called long-distance to report that he owed to the film what he considered to be his first religious experience. Even though it was primarily an animation film, Daly felt that *Universe* expressed the Candid Eye philosophy most completely, because a whole person had been touched.[17] The film became one of the most celebrated Film Board productions, won twenty-three awards worldwide, and still holds second place for NFB world sales.

Lonely Boy ($37,238), directed by Koenig and Kroitor in 1961, was a film about Ottawa-born teenage pop star Paul Anka. The filmmakers set out to show what it was that makes the songs of a crooning teenager appeal to millions. The film anticipated the adolescent 'baby boom' generation's penchant for musical heroes and the creation of musical superstars in the sixties. One angry citizen wrote to complain that the film was shocking and wicked. Commissioner Roberge assuaged the plaintiff with diplomatic language that characterized his regime and style: 'While I doubt that few people with a desire for maturity or good taste in our society would applaud this modern day phenomenon, there are many who feel there is merit in a visual study of this fact of our time.'

Lonely Boy purported to take the viewer behind the footlights to find out Anka's own attitude to his success. The hand-held camera made it possible to capture a number of spontaneously 'candid,' if innocent, moments. But there was also a degree of manipulation of subject and image. Once, the star's manager told Koenig to leave the room when some unsavoury characters in fedoras appeared. Later, at the New Jersey concert in Freedomland, the crew was told to watch a certain crooning blonde female in the crowd. Thus, when Anka did something 'unplanned,' and made her the object of 'Put Your Head on My Shoulder,' it appeared as if Koenig had anticipated events uncannily. The scene was unmediated to the extent that he did not know what was to happen, only that something was going to occur. In short, he had been ready for the spontaneous moment. But there is manipulation of another sort – of the filmmakers by Anka himself. He was neither a 'lonely boy,' nor was he trapped within the image of himself created by his manager. He was an entertainer who, in every frame of the film, was aware of his performance before the ubiquitous camera. This is the perennial problem of appearing on camera, be one a pop star or a poverty case. The pop star usually continues his or her 'show,' while the poverty case may carry on too, albeit with much less panache, but still aware of his or her 'star' quality. (This problem occurred some years later in the 'poverty film,' *The Things I Cannot Change*, which was not a Unit B production.) On reflection, years after the fact, Koenig admitted that if he had to make *Lonely Boy* again, he would have probed the issue of class to understand the socio-economic realities behind the pop phenomenon. One wonders if it would have been as rich and captivating as the film that is still considered the best of the Candid Eye approach. Koenig stressed an important element in the Unit B philosophy of candidness: the filmmaker could not exploit the people being filmed, nor could he set up a thesis to be proven. One should never steal the moment and run.[18]

Lonely Boy (1961), a Candid Eye documentary on Ottawa-born pop star Paul Anka, appeared on the eve of the Beatles phenomenon, anticipating the 'baby boom' generation's penchant for musical heroes and superstars.

The issue of exploitation is relevant if one considers that these films were characterized by what film critic Peter Harcourt called 'the innocent eye' in his highly regarded *Sight and Sound* essay on Unit B. He called it a quality of suspended judgment, of something undecided, detached and apart from the immediate pressures of existence. A more critical Bruce Elder saw these same productions as constituting passive observation, a kind of self-abandonment in the face of reality, a form of consciousness that is alienated from the world. The lack of a central focusing event created a shower of discrete particulars. Using Franz Fanon's depiction of the development of colonized art, they reflected life as seen by a colonized artist.[19]

If there is some truth to both these observations, Unit B's activity should be seen in the wider context of articulating the philosophy of making films in the national interest.

The productions confirmed one quality that characterizes how English Canada has long identified itself: denying the unifying thread of a central nexus while persistently avoiding conflict and confrontation. Some think of this as the art of accommodation, compromise, or concession; it is also the art of national self-effacement, which then saddles the individual with the responsibility to carve his or her niche in the world without the crutch of jingoism. The aphorism that art is a mirror of society creates a dilemma for Canadians: to paraphrase author Margaret Atwood, if they look in the mirror, they see either another's face or no face at all. Historically this has been the way Canada has avoided absorption by the United States, which remains disinterested in (faceless) Canadian social realities, except to complain of them when they affect business.

Roberge himself illustrated the applica-

tion of this principle of national self-effacement as national identity when he wrote to
Jules Léger, the under-secretary of state for
external affairs, requesting more money to
increase circulation of informational films
abroad. He was proud that the films were
'not regarded as propagandist and are therefore widely accepted and favourably compared to those of some other countries.' He
stated that smaller countries appreciated
being able to obtain practical authoritative
material from 'a country whose interests
tend to be humanitarian rather than strongly
economic or political.'[20] The accommodating, non-self-serving spirit of which the commissioner spoke was at the core of the Film
Board philosophy. It went back to the Grierson attitude of finding what common people
everywhere can share sincerely. Unit B was
drawn to the idea, and the *Candid Eye* films
reflected it. Being free from hypocrisy or pretence was a quality that the Film Board cultivated assiduously and naturally. The result
was a quality of cultivated innocence that
made Canada great at home and abroad.
And, typically, few Canadians ever wanted
to discuss it.

Low tried to explain some of these factors
in accounting for the success of Unit B. First,
he believed that the best film was either ten
or twenty minutes long, because terseness
made it appear convincing and precise. At-
mospherics demanded it to be short because,
in documentary, the feeling has much to do
with 'the patina of the image,' where everything has a texture of being warm and real.
There was, however, the problem of invasion
of privacy and personality, that is, the destructive elements that were possible. Low
thought that documentary had no business
playing the voyeur; it was a thin line indeed
between Cartier-Bresson and his love of his
subjects and those who wanted to look under
a rock for no other purpose but to see the
helter-skelter of creatures. Stanley Jackson,
as the conscience of Unit B, used commentary to blunt those images he thought were
aggressive invasions. Knowing that exploita-

tion was inherent in filmmaking, Low felt
that the filmmaker had to warn his subjects
of the danger of the exercise and he applied
this philosophy in *Challenge for Change* in
the late sixties. Because he had an almost
uncanny ability to feel what other people
were feeling, Low tried to put the best light on
the circumstances he found.

In short, the starting point of every film
was how to abridge, not exacerbate conflict.
In his first made-for-television piece, *The
Hutterites*, Low chose to ignore the fact that
these people were thought by some to be a
scourge on the local economy and, by forgo-
ing this angle, chose to stress how their communal values were useful and enriching to
society. Perhaps this attitude had something
to do with his Mormon teaching or perhaps it
was a mystical belief. Both Low and Unit B
reflected a tendency to reject 'scientific humanism' and materialist factors in their approach to interpreting society. From his perspective, Low felt that the films of Unit B
fitted into the mainstream of Canadian culture because Canada's was a culture of moderate expectations, not one of extravagant
expectations like that of the United States.[21]

Other gems of the golden years

The above-mentioned films could not have
been made without Tom Daly's building
Unit B into a secure laboratory in which its
members could experiment with new ideas.
A particularly innovative artist was Arthur
Lipsett, who had applied a novel approach to
film art in his 7-minute debut piece in 1961,
entitled *Very Nice, Very Nice* ($8,326), which
was nominated for an Oscar. He started by
constructing a bizarre sound track, to which
he later matched the images. In this and his
other commentaryless film collages, Lipsett
played with the idea of how people take for
granted the banality of both language and
image in everyday life. He manipulated accidental and irrational elements to create a
cascade of familiar sound and visual icons.
They flash by so quickly that the viewer

hardly has time to digest them, let alone organize them into coherence or significa- tion. The bombardment is as much a com- ment on how contemporary media-filled lives border on abstraction as it is about indi- viduals' concern with social upheaval, nu- clear war, consumerism, and alienation.

Lipsett extended this technique to *Free Fall* ($15,157) in 1964, punctuating the vis- ual/sonoral barrage with an anthropo- morphic rendition of bugs and animals. He arranged a counterpoint of the act of watch- ing as the symbol of the era. In his 1968 film *Fluxes* the image and irony were extended furthest as monkeys push buttons on ma- chines they know nothing about, while the machine of war breeds such monstrous hor- rors as mass murderer Adolf Eichmann, whose scowling countenance affronts the civilized observer. Perhaps it is all as inde- cipherable as an oriental hand dance, Lipsett concludes; a rocket blasts off with a monkey as its sole passenger. The viewer must decide if man and monkey are the selfsame objects, if morality and survival are the equal factors of life's equation, or if escape is to be found in outer space.

Donald Brittain, a member of Unit C, wrote and directed what is, after Alain Res- nais's *Night and Fog*, perhaps the best single film on Hitler's final solution of the Jewish question, *Memorandum*, an hour-long docu- mentary on the banality of evil. He followed the pilgrimage of concentration-camp in- mate Bernard Lauffer, who with his son re- turned to Germany from Canada on the oc- casion of a reunion of survivors in 1965. Brittain gropes with the incomprehensible magnitude of the Nazis' crimes without using the blood-chilling photographs most people associate with the camps. Instead, he lets words paint the grimmest picture in the viewer's imagination. Take, for example, his use of the testimony of a Jewish teacher who was forced to sort clothes of the victims. Because there was no hope, he found himself telling his own children and family, 'There's nothing to worry about,' as they entered the

Still one of the best documentaries on the subject, *Memorandum* (1965) bears witness to the barbaric efficiency of the Nazi's final solution to the Jewish Question. (Cinematographer John Spotton, left, and director Donald Brittain at Auschwitz)

gas chamber. Brittain pierces any possible remaining complacency by asking the viewer, 'Who will ever know who did the murdering by memorandum? Who did the filing and the typing from nine to five, with an hour off for lunch?' No better way has been found for placing on each person in society the burden of and responsibility for maintaining and perpetuating civilization. That concern for civilization is the founda- tion of the historical bridge between past and present which Brittain constructed in most of his documentaries.[22] His early training as a newspaperman had served him well. He de- veloped what some called the 'golden hinge.' As a hinge allows an object weighing much more than itself to open and close while swinging freely through space, so did Brit- tain's films manage to carry the viewer al- most effortlessly through time and space, with word and image tightly melded to evoke both intelligent and subconscious responses. This talent elevated him to the status of one of English Canada's foremost documentary filmmakers. He was also an uncredited 'doc- umentary doctor' who saved a number of

Film Board films that otherwise would have failed.

Also memorable were the last two films in the *Candid Eye* series, *Glenn Gould: On the Record* ($21,639) and *Glenn Gould: Off the Record* ($28,825), both directed by Kroitor and Koenig in 1959. The first finds the celebrated young pianist recording Bach in a New York studio. The 'day in the life' approach includes banter with a cabbie, drinking coffee from a thermos, reading a newspaper, and dining in a restaurant – human touches that bring an audience close to this extraordinary musician. It is part of the film's subtlety to compare and contrast genius with the ordinary. Such is the mirror that leaves the viewer both in awe of the genius, yet able to see that in every mortal body that special flame may be present. The companion film reveals a more eccentric Gould, as it finds him in New York choosing a piano, then shifts to Lake Simcoe, Ontario, where he is observed in solitude; the young artist admits his ambition to retire and become a composer. Viewing the film decades later, one knows that Gould became a recluse who performed in a studio exclusively and, just as he reached the pinnacle of his powers as one of the consummate pianists of this century, died suddenly, his ambition unrealized. The film reminds the contemporary observer of the duality of unfulfilled dreams: they both stimulate and humble civilization.

Cinéma vérité classics of *L'équipe française*

After the *Candid Eye* series ended in 1959, Unit B continued to experiment with the direct-cinema technique, culminating in the greatest and most lavish expression of that style in *Labyrinth*, at Expo 67. For *L'équipe française*, what followed *Les Raquetteurs* were classic films of the *cinéma direct* genre. The themes were not ostensibly political and the most memorable films were about recreation, sports, collective rituals, and workers: *Au bout de ma rue* (Louis-Georges Carrier,

1958), *Télésphore Légaré, garde-pêche* (Claude Fournier, 1959), *Normetal* (Gilles Groulx, 1959), *La France sur un caillou* (Gilles Groulx and Claude Fournier, 1960), *La Lutte* (Claude Jutra, Michel Brault, Claude Fournier, and Marcel Carrière, 1961), *Golden Gloves* (Gilles Groulx, 1961), *Québec-USA, ou l'Invasion pacifique* (Claude Jutra and Michel Brault, 1962), *A Saint-Henri le 5 septembre* (Hubert Aquin and a crew of twenty-eight, 1962), *Les Bûcherons de la Manouane* (Arthur Lamothe, 1962), *Jour après jour* (Clémont Perron, 1962), *Voir Miami* (Gilles Groulx, 1963), *Il y eut un soir, il y eut un matin* (Pierre Patry, 1963), *Pour la suite du monde* (Michel Brault, Marcel Carrière, and Pierre Perrault, 1964), *Un jeu si simple* (Gilles Groulx, 1964), *60 cycles* (Jean-Claude Labrecque, 1965), and *Huit témoins* (Jacques Godbout, 1965).[23]

Most of these *cinéma direct* films were made for the commercial-free television series *Temps présent*, which was telecast on Tuesdays in prime-time from 1957 until 1964. They also garnered a modest theatrical and non-theatrical distribution. The young filmmakers, as a highly educated bourgeoisie, had their films reflect both the growing awareness of class in Quebec society and their own *prise de conscience*. Seen from one angle, the documentaries mirrored a dawning democratic spirit and celebrated the forgotten urban and rural working classes. This issue of consciousness-raising and class did not, however, mean that the filmmakers were embracing radical Marxism – the second most common subject of conversation in the Film Board cafeteria was the very mundane topic of country-home renovation.[24]

Taken from another angle, the filmmakers were engaged in the perpetual generational dance of protest against those who held power. If they were expressing ethnic solidarity, the primary topic of discussion in the Film Board cafeteria was *cinéma*, not politics. This preoccupation evolved naturally into a demand for *liberté de l'expression*, or freedom of expression, and the necessity of pushing as hard as possible against the administration. This tension became part of the creative process, as necessary to the artists as a paintbrush is to a painter.

But it cost dearly. Claude Jutra wrote to Pierre Juneau late in 1959 that he 'did not want to play at the Film Board anymore'; he took his leave from 'the labyrinth' where he was always feeling angry and left Canada for some months.[25] Jutra henceforth insisted, 'Je suis un enfant perpetuel,' and in so doing set the tone not only for one group of filmmakers, but also for those who believed that youth was the symbol of the future of Quebec, the promise unrealized.[26] Youth was always enthusiastic, innocent, even naïve, and permanently on the side of what it saw as Quebec's *prise de conscience*. Political confrontation with the rest of Canada was to be the shock of the coming decade. Perhaps these tendencies, more than any 'message,' reflected the emergence of Quebec cinema.

Youth was perennially exasperating for its insubordination. In an angry outburst three years later, Fernand Dansereau told filmmakers Gilles Carle, Michel Brault, Claude Fournier, and Gilles Groulx they were fired. Jacques Bobet spoke on their behalf to director of production Grant McLean, and found the four transferred to his unit. 'On est puni; on va de vous voir,' they said gleefully as they arrived at Bobet's office, pushing each other like schoolboys.

Within twenty-four hours of their arrival, Fournier and Brault (in collaboration with Claude Jutra and Marcel Carrière) had found a subject: a professional wrestling match that was to take place two days later. Bobet had a budget drawn up immediately and the resulting film was the unforgettable *La Lutte*, a study of commercial wrestling, its phoniness, and the stereotypical men and women attracted to it. The omnipresent camera unmasked the grotesqueness of this all-show spectacle and its denizens in *cinéma direct* technique, spending half the time at ringside and the other half on close-ups of the lu-

La Lutte (1961) is a brutal portrait, in *cinéma direct* style, of commercial wrestling.

dicrous audience's emotional contortions. The innocence and naïvety of these gifted filmmakers anchored this otherwise brutal portrait. They continued to be an administrator's headache, and Bobet spent years harping upon the need for continuity and mental discipline. Because he trusted them, he felt confident they would prove themselves.[27]

Director Gilles Carle has observed astutely that in almost every case, a filmmaker's first or second *oeuvre* at the Film Board was his best.[28] As such early endeavours, the following six films not only symbolize the *équipe française*'s involvement in *cinéma direct*, but are also considered among the best of each particular director's work. Their enduring quality stems from being self-referential and reflecting the historical values and rituals that Quebec society shared.

Filming of *La Lutte* in 1961 preceded *Golden Gloves* by several months and probably influenced it, particularly the aspect of the camera watching the crowd watching the spectacle. In *Golden Gloves* ($17,620), director Gilles Groulx (assisted by Claude Jutra) emphasized the class origins of fighters and fans alike. Guy Borremans's cinematography shows the young fighting lions training feverishly as the credits roll, and a tight musical score overlaps both natural sound and silent footage. Among the fighters was an upcoming brawler and barman, Georges Thibault. He is introduced in his environment with a candidly captured spontaneous bar accident, followed by a puerile bar trick that demonstrates the 'it's-only-boys-playing' quality of men at leisure.

Boys will be boys, but they can also be killers. Like the fans in *La Lutte*, Thibault's fans surround the ring and hope for his victory in the match against a Hungarian adversary. The viewer is aware of the ringside observers watching the spectacle through the boxers' blurry feet dancing their punishing number. A too enthusiastic Thibault lands a punch after the bell and is disqualified. This leads to a childish reaction by friends and crowd. The film ends tentatively as, once

again, 'the boys' cause disarray and pandemonium after the match.

The following year, ex-lumberjack Arthur Lamothe's *Bûcherons de la Manouane* ($8,736), set the ethnographic style of filmmaking he would pursue for a lifetime. His lumberjacks were both native Indian and French-Canadian, and subsequently Lamothe turned to the native people to demonstrate that exploitation is never far from those who try to remain rooted to the land. In his film, a lumberjack trudges along an endless stack of cordwood, and the voice-over narration describes how, sixteen times per day at two dollars a cord, man and horse haul a sledgeful of cordwood, to be turned into American newspapers.

In the most sentimental scene, outside temperatures hover at Arctic lows while the men are filmed in lingering close-ups in the bunk-house during leisure time. As each is identified by name (so as to not be anonymous), the typical French-Canadian smoking ritual unfolds while they listen raptly to a comrade sweetly singing a French-Canadian ballad. It is a lyrical statement of men at peace.

Most direct-cinema films were made for the commercial-free Radio-Canada television series *Temps présent*. The ethnographic documentary *Les Bûcherons de la Manouane* (1962) incorporates Quebec filmmakers' *prise de conscience* and their dawning awareness of class in Quebec society.

Also in 1962, Claude Jutra and Michel Brault shared directing credit for *Québec-U.S.A. ou l'Invasion pacifique* ($21,705). If the ostensible theme is the three million American visitors to Quebec each year, the manipulation of the actuality footage creates a three-point subtext: it is difficult for foreigners to study and understand both French and *the* French; there is a French-Canadian tendency to be self-effacing and self-conscious about the French language in the presence of foreigners; and the relationship of French Canadians to their milieu is, at best, like being Gulliver, arms and legs pinned by the Lilliputians. The narrator states with a slight trace of cynicism, 'Ah, French culture ... You may see a display of military might anywhere, but only here will you be able to see French-speaking soldiers, disguised in English uniforms, performing a borrowed ceremony for the benefit of American cameras.'

The final sequence shows American sailors trying to pick up seductive French-Canadian girls along Quebec's famous promenade. The narrator concludes drily that, whereas two hundred years ago they sent their strongest troops and did not get very far, today they send their smartest sailors and get further. The implication in this last sequence is that not only was Quebec there for the asking, but also that Quebec acted like a prostitute waiting to be taken.

À Saint-Henri le 5 septembre ($21,564) was probably the most profound expression of *cinéma direct* and identified itself as a homage to French filmmaker Jean Rouch. Directed by Hubert Aquin, a team of twenty-eight filmmakers went into the Montreal working-class quarter and recorded 'a day in the life' in 1962. If the experience did much to consolidate the sense of collective research and team effort, Jacques Godbout and Monique Fortier had the unenviable task of turning the hours of film into forty minutes.

The film's self-reference was the intention to be a window on the city and to look at French culture in 'Amérique française.' It introduces a family which Jacques Godbout's commentary describes as one that could have stepped out of *The Tin Flute*. They were under a microscope but, like all the working-class people in the film, were treated respectfully. At 7 a.m., the family of twelve children (six at work, six at school, mother in charge of the home and father unemployed) congregate in the kitchen and go about their morning rituals, from the father helping a daughter open a medicine bottle to the girls in school uniforms having their mother braid their hair. (A similar scene occurred four years later in Tanya Ballantyne's film *The Things I Cannot Change*, which shows a more sinister view of poverty.) The narration makes its key point: the people of Saint-Henri are not angry; they hide their poverty and are revolted by dirt. In fact, judging by their 'consumer's wealth,' the workers of Saint-Henri are 'the bourgeois of the proletarian universe.'

A humorous on-camera reference to the *cinéma vérité* method occurs as a family prepares for evening prayers, and the father struggles with the radio as he tries to tune in 'Radio-Chapelet' (The Rosary). Quebec's Quiet Revolution might have captured the intellectuals and artists, but among the large working-class families it seemed that the old traditions were dying hard and slowly.

The film closes with a reference to the filmmakers seeking the light and sounds of the street and the explanation that, if the film is a homage to Jean Rouch, it is also a homage to Hitchcock; but the mystery is entirely internal, not external. Later, it was alleged that the people of Saint-Henri were angry at being filmed by outsiders; in all probability the Film Board's error was forgetting to show the film to them before it was telecast on Radio-Canada.

From 1962, the figurative battle lines were drawn between documentary and fiction. Jutra chose to leave the Film Board for the private sector to finish *A tout prendre*, a semi-autobiographical fiction piece with a documentary approach. Meanwhile, with fellow

directors Pierre Perrault and Marcel Carrière, Michel Brault shot *Pour la suite du
monde* ($82,625) over the next year. The
team then took nine months to edit and produce what is still considered the great example of *cinéma direct*, a story of some old-
timers on the St Lawrence, reviving (at the
directors' prodding) the almost forgotten
beluga whale hunt, this time to capture one
alive for an American zoo.

In a celebrated 1963 article in the influential *Cahiers du cinéma*, an enthusiastic Jean
Rouch declared *Pour la suite du monde* a
complete success, as if Dziga Vertov had
used Cartier-Bresson's camera, or if Robert
Flaherty had shot *Man of Aran* in sound.
Brault's moving camera had captured a fantastic people in an unmediated fashion, he
concluded. A more sober scientific humanist
might find peculiar in *Pour la suite du monde*

its emphasis on superstition and the tides,
the mystic influences of the dead, and the
stranglehold of religion upon the remote
population of the cultural backwater of L'Île-
aux-Coudres; an anthropologist would probably find the film a fascinating study of the
effects of generations of isolation on a rural
culture. Quebeckers accepted it instinctively
and, in celebrating it as the first (and greatest
ever) Quebec documentary feature, find in it
a means to cement language, culture, and
history on to the base of authenticity.[29]

Cinéma direct underwent some refine-
ment when it was exported to Europe. In
France, Jean Rouch became its leading expo-
nent, and in the aforementioned article, acknowledged the impact of Michel Brault,
who had gone there to spread the gospel.
Rouch claimed that it was Brault's technique
that everyone copied and that taught France

In *Pour la suite du monde* (1964), Quebec cinema's first documentary feature, Michel Brault, Marcel
Carrière, and Pierre Perrault capture the texture and sounds of a disappearing way of life.

everything about the genre. He called for the Canadian example to be followed and saluted both Dansereau and Pierre Juneau for their facilitative role. His only reservation about the technique was that the films tended to lack a subject, that is, the filmmakers tended to concentrate on the spectacle rather than thinking through what they wanted to say.[30]

The *équipe française* should have been thrilled by having achieved mention in *Cahiers du cinéma*, the ultimate recognition in the European cinema world. But Rouch was already out of touch with events that were dividing the group. As early as August 1962, fiction enthusiasts Jean-Pierre Lefebvre and Jean-Claude Pilon attacked in print those who were suffering from 'Roucheole.'[31] Dansereau disagreed and warned that the dramatic depiction of the complex French-Canadian reality could close the French Canadians into a psychological ghetto, preoccupied with collective introspection. Jacques Bobet took the middle ground and thought that fiction was a way to renew the already stale documentary form.

Gilles Groulx had found his niche in documentary work and in 1963 moved even closer to revealing contemporary French-Canadian mores in *Voir Miami* ($20,859). The film was supposed to illustrate the annual exodus of Canadians who seek sun, sports, and an American atmosphere in winter. It gives a candid glimpse of how some French Canadians are attracted to the allure of Miami and share illusions about its hedonistic life. Sensuality and sexuality are counterpoints to childlike innocence, both of which are woven into images of gross, distended, aged bodies on the verge of death. Miami is the microcosm of America, where everything is purchasable, even the moon, as a rocket poised for a Florida launch attests.

If *Voir Miami* was a mild indictment of American hedonism, the French Canadians within it are anything but appealing. Suzy, a Quebec sunbather, is disillusioned that the beauty of Miami is only to be found on postcards; Lise and Gilbert, a couple on a houseboat, pontificate about the easy and good life while sharing drinks with the film crew. They complain that Americans *like* Canadians, but do not know that Quebec exists or that they speak French. Their innocent statement reveals the subtext of the film: that the French Canadian, cut off from his people and language, is a stranger in a strange land. Groulx, dabbling in sociological cinema, leaves the viewer to wonder if politics might better explain the state of things.

Perhaps Groulx was getting too close to the difficult questions. The Film Board asked him next to turn to a documentary on hockey. The hope was that with Jean-Claude Labrecque on camera and Marcel Carrière on sound, he would make a 35-mm 'prestige' film on Canada's national sport, worthy of distribution through Canadian diplomatic posts. The intention was to show what people in 1964 see in hockey and why athletes play it. *Un jeu si simple* ($53,267) was anything but a puff piece. If players like 'Boom Boom Geoffrion' talk candidly about the precision of the game, sportsmanship, and the esteem of playing for the champions, Geoffrion also admits that the truth was that the fans wanted both violence and to see people get hurt. Groulx demonstrated the proof of this thesis by displaying the gruesome spectacle of a player fracturing his skull in a fall. Thus was hockey such a simple game.

A sequence of several minutes shows audience-reaction shots reminiscent of *La Lutte* and *Golden Gloves*. Here is the French Canada everyone can recognize, where class divisions evaporate in the democracy of the arena as all eyes are on the home team and the slippery puck. Hockey fans take their game so seriously that at times they cannot distinguish between sport and reality. To illustrate this point, Groulx used archival footage of the 1955 riot at the Montreal Forum. The ruckus happened over the suspension of the star player 'Rocket' Richard, who had hit a referee. The footage included protest signs which had read 'Injustice to

French Canada.' Pierre Juneau wanted the sequence removed, but relented when Jacques Bobet convinced him to keep the footage in the interest of historical accuracy. Watching *Un jeu si simple*, one is reminded that the historical adage 'war is sport by other means' applies as well to the reverse, that hockey as sport is war by other means.

Groulx's portrait of French Canadians as a people who prefer the role of spectator was not flattering. He was angry at French Canada for this weakness and repeated his frustration almost identically in *24 heures ou plus* in 1971. Meanwhile, a glum Department of External Affairs wondered what to do with this 'prestige' film that was remote from what they had in mind to circulate abroad. Exasperation with the Film Board was to become a familiar emotion at the department.

Preparations for Centennial Year: History into film

In 1960, the Film Board prepared to undertake a number of projects for the approaching Centennial in 1967. Their object was to make Canadians more conscious of their history and culture.[32] One of them was the *The History Makers* series, a historical reconstruction about the men who made Canadian history. The purpose of the seventeen half-hour films which cost about $40,000 each was to show the steps to Confederation in the context of the major problems of the period. The research and scripts were checked by the eminent conservative historians Donald Creighton and Guy Frégault. Only two films had francophone directors, Louis-Georges Carrier and Pierre Patry respectively for *Louis-Joseph Papineau – Le Demi-dieu* (1961) and *Louis-Hyppolite Lafontaine* (1962), which demonstrated how difficult it was to attract French-Canadian directors to participate in an affirmation of national history. A student seeing both films back-to-back might be confused by the contradictory portrayals of Papineau; but the most egregious fault in the series is its reduction of

history to the platitudes of the 'Great Man' theory and the exclusion of the roles of business, class, geography, and women. The films (which are still in circulation) have never generated much excitement, and have done little to help create a national mythology.

One explanation for the rather pedestrian approach of the series might be related to events surrounding the inclusion of the 1957 film *The Hanging Judge*, about nineteenth-century British Columbian Judge Matthew Baillie Begbie. It was withdrawn from the series and retitled (*Legendary* replaced *Hanging*) after protests from Vancouver war hero Colonel Cecil Merritt, who said that history should not be rewritten to achieve spectacular effect, nor should the Film Board be maintained at public expense 'to produce waves of Davy Crocketts for consumption by Canadians.'[33] His sentiment was correct, though one might conclude that the fear of provoking criticism reduced the series to competent, if not very memorable, dramas.[34] Between then and today, the presentation of Canadian history has fallen between the cracks and there have been few filmmakers ready to use fact and a more daring interpretive method to challenge students and help them understand the complexity, richness, and controversial nature of Canadian history, let alone answer the need for national mythmaking.

By contrast to *The History Makers*, in 1963 the first English-language feature, *Drylanders* ($211,479), appeared, an 'honest dust-bowl drama' directed by Donald Haldane, about the opening of the Canadian West in south Saskatchewan. Here was the saga of a family who endured the struggles of homesteading, isolation, and prairie winters, then drought, the Depression, and finally the death of the father-hero. Unlike a typical Hollywood barnyard film, *Drylanders* kept a close affinity to the historical record and totally avoided gratuitous violence. With the death of the hero during the decade-long drought, the story did not end; his wife continued the vital struggle to coax life from the soil. *Drylanders* is in the all-time top-fifty list and circulates today as a four-part primer for teaching English as a second language.

Drylanders spurred French production to make its case for features. As a group, French-Canadian filmmakers were peeved that the Film Board films being screened in Quebec commercial theatres were mainly translations of English productions. From 1962, there were only five original productions in French that received theatrical distribution: *Les Bûcherons de la Manouane* (Lamothe), *Paul-Emile Borduas* (Godbout), *Les Petits Arpents* (Garceau), *Patinoire* (Carle), and *Golden Gloves* (Groulx).[35]

Despite earlier misgivings, Fernand Dansereau tried his hand at historical drama in a 1965 feature co-production with Radio-Canada, *Le Festin des morts*. It was a messianic

and spiritual story of New France, based on *Jesuit Relations*, the journals of the mission life and martyrdom of some early missionaries. Dansereau attempted to re-create earlier French-Canadian mythology about ferocious Indian savages. Expenses mounted as he constructed exact models of buildings and villages. Finally, no commercial distributors in Canada or Europe were interested in the $280,000 drama, and the embarrassed Dansereau returned to the less risky documentary format.

Denys Arcand was one of the few filmmakers who tried to use a more confrontational interpretive method, and he was stung for his efforts. Arcand intended to demystify history in his short 1964 picture study of the myth of *Samuel de Champlain* ($21,162), which criticized both the man and the forced

Drylanders (1963), the first English-language Film Board feature, depicts the perilous relationship of man to nature in an unforgiving Canada.

colonization of Canada. The French Canadian Association of French-Language Educators was outraged at his impertinence and caricature of the respected Champlain. He was much more careful to hide his anti-religious and anticlerical sentiments in the next historical pieces, *La Route de l'Ouest* ($36,914) in 1964 and *Les Montréalistes* ($27,706) in 1965. Arcand has been described as one who used caricature and satire to examine Quebec's past and present both in fact and fiction. If some find his sarcastic (if not cynical) approach ungenerous and not much fun,[36] his most recent and most popular films *Le Déclin de l'empire américain* and *Jésus de Montréal* reflect a far less acerbic and more mellow personality.

On Parliament Hill: All's well that starts well

On the political front, Roberge inspired trust in most everyone he met, and Minister Fairclough made it a point to avoid interference in the Film Board on virtually all levels. When a number of members of Parliament suggested film subjects, she generally deflected them with aplomb, promising to pass their suggestions along. In 1959, she set a precedent to which most of her successors subscribed: the minister does not direct the Board's activities and cannot instruct it to make a film, because the agency is autonomous. Former Minister J.W. Pickersgill disagreed and argued that the law held the minister fully responsible for what went on at the Film Board. He may have been playing for points in the Commons, but Fairclough's attitude remained the predominant one and went a long way toward establishing what was later called the 'arm's length relationship.' As she put it briefly, 'the Minister does not interfere in the actual process of producing this and that.'[37]

Besides suggesting the occasional film subject, members of Parliament rarely concerned themselves with the Film Board. Such benign neglect was manifest when the

Film Board tried and failed to revive the old practice of Wednesday-evening screenings late in 1959 – only three members appeared. In fact, during the Diefenbaker years, in spite of government-imposed austerity, Roberge had a relatively easy time, and his annual budgets were accepted without much debate. He appeared before Treasury Board with the minister, but rarely had to reply to questions. In all, the members of Parliament generally equated the work of the Film Board with educational enrichment.

The only ripple that occurred with respect to Ottawa was over Lawrence Gosnell's anti-pollution film *Poisons, Pests and People*, which had been telecast in two-half segments in the winter of 1959–60. A shorter version, retitled *Deadly Dilemma* ($43,951), was shown at the Resources for Tomorrow conference in October 1961. Like the long version, it asked if chemical pesticides have serious long-term effects on humans and plants. Representatives of the pulp and paper industry and insecticide manufacturers who were in the audience complained that the documentary overstressed the deadly effect of chemical sprays on wildlife. (One sequence showed the destruction of salmon in New Brunswick, a side-effect of the DDT spraying of forests.) The deputy minister of the Department of Forestry wrote to the Film Board, claiming that the film was an unbalanced portrayal of the two horns of the dilemma.

Two months later, the deputy minister of the Department of Agriculture wanted to suppress the film 'because it put[s] forestry and agricultural industries in a light which is quite incompatible with the facts.' Judicious spraying, he argued, was beneficial; besides, there were some small factual errors. After the changes were made, the Agriculture representative was still unhappy, so the Film Board withdrew it altogether. The director of planning, Michael Spencer, deflected the controversy when he claimed that the film was pulled simply because there was a new documentary planned on more recent discoveries in the field. This may have been an artful dodge, but in light of subsequent information about DDT, spraying of pesticides, and environmental pollution, it was a pity that the Film Board did not allow this 'leading edge' film to alert the public to what became a major concern of society a generation later. If big-business interests had complained orally that they found the documentary unflattering to themselves, they never communicated this in writing to the Film Board – it was the two government-department representatives who agitated to withdraw it.[38] The Film Board became more involved in environmental issues a decade later, when public opinion favoured it.

There developed a financial problem in 1962 over the government's general austerity programme, which required the organization to freeze all employment and reduce expenditures by 10 per cent. The cuts added up to almost $200,000, and Roberge argued that this was unfair, since austerity meant less departmental business as well; he depended on sponsored films to pay three-quarters of salary costs. Besides, the organization was costing only about thirty cents per citizen per year. Fairclough appealed on his behalf to the Treasury Board and suggested in a flash of creative bookkeeping that the Film Board keep the salaries it saved by not filling its job vacancies. A month later, she left to become postmaster general; the new minister, R.A. Bell, went along with the plan. Roberge's success would be remembered during the next austerity crisis in 1969, which brought another commissioner down.[39]

When Bell took over the ministerial portfolio in August 1962, the director of English Production prepared for him a programme of the films most in the national interest in the past five years. It is doubtful that the busy minister ever saw them, but their titles might be a useful guide to measure the agency's performance. The absence of a single French title may have had to do with the minister's or McLean's unilingualism: *Trans-Canada Journey, Universe, Nahanni, The Quest, Corral, Kindergarten, The Settler, The Majority Vote, Introducing Canada, Charles Tupper: The Big Man, Accidents Don't Happen – Machines, Shyness, It's a Crime, Roughnecks, Circle of the Sun, Invisible Keystone, City of Gold, Vote for Michalski, Introduction to Jet Engines, Morning on the Lièvre,* and *The Sceptre and the Mace.*[40]

Bell had larger issues to worry about – the Diefenbaker government was in its death throes. As the Cabinet tore itself apart, the prime minister tried without success to hold the centre, and by April 1963 the country returned the Liberals to power in a minority government under Lester Pearson. It was just like old home week; the new minister responsible for the Film Board was Guy Roberge's old friend J.W. Pickersgill. But much had changed since 1957, and the euphoria of occupying a new home was a distant memory. As in the recent Diefenbaker government, internal divisions, invisible to the public, were pulling the agency apart, and the golden years were losing some of their lustre.

5

Art for Whose Sake?

The diminishing lustre

In 1960, the Diefenbaker government appointed the Glassco Royal Commission to find the most efficient means of organizing and operating the government bureaucracy, which had expanded with dizzying speed. One prominent question was 'To make or buy?,' as experts debated whether the government should maintain its own internal sources of supply for goods and services or look to external ones. In its general conclusion, the commission recommended the use of outside sources for support services in order to strengthen the private sector of the economy.[1]

The commission gave the Film Board a clean bill of health for its efficiency and sound budgetary control.[2] Although there was no mention of the fact that the sponsored films paid for a good part of the overhead, the commission's single allusion to them was the comment that while filmmaking activities had expanded by 50 per cent since the move to Montreal in 1956, the Film Board had tendered out only half as much sponsored work as it had in 1955.[3] The contract-hungry commercial film producers interpreted this comment as a go-ahead to pressure for review of government cultural policies and activities. Another more critical appraisal of the Film Board followed in 1966.

Within the institution, there was a near-unanimous chorus from the French-language filmmakers that they deserved their own production and funding. More worrisome was English Production's discontent with the programming process because writers, directors, editors, and executive producers were not sufficiently involved in it. By June 1962, Marjorie McKay, supervisor of production research, fumed that at the annual planning meetings there was a plethora of undeveloped and unsatisfactory ideas from which the senior administration had to make its decisions.

The philosophical division was between those who were thinking of film in terms of content and those who were thinking in terms of art. This debate cut across linguistic lines and was essentially about old and new cinema. Those who believed in the Grierson tradition believed that the functional, informational film was the essential mission of the Film Board. Others said that cinema encompassed a much larger world, reflecting the style, technique, and art of an era. It was never put in so many words, but among both English and French filmmakers there was developing an ideological split that might be summarized by the question, 'Art, but for whose sake?'

McKay, who had been with the Film Board from its first days, remembered that when Mulholland had been in charge, the planned productions had had a detailed shooting plan and were discussed thoroughly before they were started. With the adoption of direct-cinema technique, the production process began to deteriorate. When Grant McLean assumed Mulholland's responsibilities, his acceptance or rejection of an undetailed shooting plan came to have little meaning. Exasperated, McKay recommended that each unit's executive producer exercise virtual life-and-death authority over the annual programme.

Most filmmakers resented this system and their inability to make a film outside their unit. Worse, they generally considered that making a sponsored film to specific requirements was 'hack work.' Some even refused to make subjects they were assigned, arguing that they had to feel impelled creatively to produce; others argued that the filmmaker was an artist who should not be inhibited by a detailed shooting plan. McKay believed the greatest irony of all was that what had been a privilege extended to a great creative artist like Norman McLaren came to be extended to or seized by so many others. If some of the results were excellent, others were what she bitterly called 'sleazy ego-trips.'[4]

A veritable rebellion began to totter English programming and production. In 1963, filmmakers Donald Brittain and John Kemeny took a survey of their English colleagues and learned that some 87 per cent were dissatisfied with the unit system. The objective was twofold: to remove the power of executive producers and to break up Unit B, which by avoiding most sponsored films was relegating that onerous task to the rest. The agitation led to the dismantling of English Production's units in February 1964, and their replacement by an ostensibly more democratic 'pool of talent' system that spring. In short, the executive producers were 'defanged,' and directors were left with real authority in the new programme and production committees.[5] By contrast on the French side, there was still a strong allegiance to the executive producers, and a similar democratic programme committee came into existence only in September 1968.

The pool system, called 'democratization,' brought about a mind-boggling, multi-tiered bureaucratic structure made up of a programme committee, a production committee, a new category of programme supervisors, the coordinating producer, and the pool of filmmakers. The complicated tier system caught and confounded both believers and unbelievers alike.[6]

Six months later, the board of governors attempted to re-establish McKay's research functions at the programme-development level. If management had been frozen out at the production level, there was still a need to determine trends, problems, and developments in areas being considered for films. The members called for a programme group to be formed at management level to orient, lead, and inspire the programme-development groups and to assess the balance of the prospectus before the proposals were submitted as a programme.[7]

The filmmakers were not anxious to hand over their power to meddling managers who were creatures of the board of governors. By 1966, members of the board offered film suggestions that fell on deaf ears: the expansion of higher education, rural women's organizations, new members of Parliament, ethnic groups and folk arts, and a profile of timber baron H.R. MacMillan. This snub marked the end of any meaningful board input to the Film Board's programme for the foreseeable future.[8]

Cinéma direct: Obsolete before its time?

In part, the culprit may have been direct-cinema, but there were other societal forces that were causing the ferment of the early sixties. In 1962, Clémont Perron had looked at the boring repetitive life of people in a one-company paper-mill town in *Jour après jour* (*Day after Day*) ($10,783). Its framework made constant visual reference to the mechanical dissonances of factory life, reminiscent of Fritz Lang's 1926 classic *Metropolis*. The strict neutrality of the camera was supposed to present spectacle without analysis, yet one could perceive the subtlety of social criticism in the way the film caught the inane repetition of workers' life and leisure. It was up to the viewer to make sense of the monstrous incomprehensible deluge that was dwarfing modern workers, analogous to the way that the men in the film were buried in reams of paper from a runaway paper roll. This absence of analysis was becoming typical of *l'équipe française*'s expression of *cinéma direct*, although the outraged mill owners had no problem catching the director's point of view.

They complained to the minister that the film had little resemblance to what is normally found in a paper mill. Roberge reminded them that the documentary was shown to some executives of the company at an early stage, and had they taken exception to the film, the Film Board would have remedied the situation at the time. He surmised that the experimental sound effects and commentary had probably contributed to the unfavourable judgment.[9] He ordered removal of the sequences that identified the paper company.

The fact was that *cinéma direct* was causing disquiet. Executive producers on the French side were caught in the middle; they felt that *cinéma direct* was cutting actuality too close to the bone and that, as it came closer to the people, it ceased to relate much to the documentary of cultivated innocence. The several films that focused on labour exploitation or pollution had provoked company officials to demand traditional 'objective' documentaries, so the producers began to steer their filmmakers in a much safer direction.

Uncharacteristically, many francophone artists agreed without a fight, not because they were crumbling before authority, but because they believed that the new documentary technique had exhausted itself stylistically. Like Unit B, they too felt stale after two years of the same film genre. By the time that Jean-Pierre Lefebvre had asked in print, in 1962, if *l'équipe française* was not suffering from 'Roucheole,' Bobet had heard from many directors that *cinéma direct* was too constrictive and that they were beginning to repeat themselves. There was no discussion of the Grierson tradition or of alternative approaches to understanding his legacy, because he was an unknown quantity to the young French Canadians. They took their cue from the debates in *Cahiers du cinéma* and created a ground swell to use fiction to renew the documentary.[10] The subject of women became their fortuitous experimental choice.

Women as a suitable film topic had seemed an afterthought in Film Board production of the forties and fifties, especially on the French side. In 1954, there had been two traditional sociopolitical films on women with commentary by Anne Hébert: Léonard Forest's *La Femme de ménage*, about a cleaning woman at the Parliament Buildings, and Roger Blais's *Midinette*, dealing with the emancipating effect of union education. In 1960, Jacques Bobet was inspired by the success of Douglas Tunstell's *Women on the March*, two half-hours on the political emancipation of women since 1900, which had won the best-television-documentary award at Cannes in 1959. Bobet undertook *Les Femmes parmi nous*, which like the English production, concentrated on a universal approach to female emancipation and ignored reactionary Quebec's traditional attitudes to females.

In 1963 Bobet was assigned four films on women to be called *La femme et le travail*, later renamed *La femme hors du foyer*. The series did not address the question that soon came to characterize an important aspect of modern feminism: how to reconcile work, marriage, and family. Instead, the films reflected Bobet's cinematic interest in the possibility of joining *cinéma direct* with fiction. He encouraged four experimental approaches, one with actors and script, one with actors and no script, one with non-actors and a script, and one with non-actors and no script. This avant-garde approach seemed promising, especially when one of the four films, Gilles Carle's *Solange dans nos campagnes* ($23,414), using a professional actress and an improvised script, won second prize at the 1964 Festival du cinéma canadien in Montreal. The CBC refused to televise it because of its sexual inferences, but did show the other three in English versions on its *Explorations* series under the title 'Women at Work' in June 1964.[11] French Production undertook several other films on women.[12]

Innocuous beginnings: The first French features

Late in 1963, Bobet was again looking for something fresh and non-controversial. When Gilles Groulx presented him with an outline of less than one page, he assured the dubious director of production, Grant McLean, that it would be good. (French producers found McLean far more liberal and free than Pierre Juneau was after he became first director of autonomous French production in January 1964.) From that simple outline the feature *Le Chat dans le sac* ($45,982) emerged in 1964 to win the Grand Prix at the Montreal Festival du cinéma canadien.

In fact, the cat was out of the bag because the terrorist bombs of the Front de Libération du Québec (FLQ) started exploding while the feature was in progress. Set against a background of some of John Coltrane's finest jazz saxophone, the film was ostensibly a practical statement about the torment of restless urban teenagers. It was also a way for young *québécois* to recognize themselves. One Montreal newspaper claimed that *Le Chat dans le sac* had provoked a debate on the identity and aspirations of Quebec.[13]

When seen years later, Groulx's film is less a cinematic masterpiece than a reflection of the societal awakenings and unease that many artists and intellectuals were manifesting. It was derivative of contemporary French cinema and literature to see a young man (Claude Godbout) wracked by the agony of existential ennui. Perhaps it was also pretentious of the young rebel to display to

the camera book jackets of Franz Fanon and the left-wing review *Parti pris*. More difficult for the viewer to accept was the distinction between art and life, as the hero shoots a gun aimlessly into vacant woods while thinking about revolution. His escape from the city's hostile and corrupt environment to the idyllic purity of country life was hardly new to French-Canadian lore either.

Few seemed to have noticed the film's uncomplimentary portrayal of the female. She was the archetypal seductress, a self-absorbed *bourgeoise*, whom the hero claimed could not understand the French Canadian's anguish in Quebec and Canada, despite her minority status as a Jew. It was a caricature that no one protested, since the film was exclusively about the *québécois*. 'Je suis Canadien français, donc je me cherche' was the leitmotif. (This was also one of the last times the terms *Canadien français* was associated with the ferment being called *québécois* from 1964 onward.) *Le Chat dans le sac* lacked a shred of generosity to others (*les autres*). That is often the nature of adolescent self-absorption, but critics seemed willing to accept the young man's judgment that the female was a perpetual outsider, in spite of her perfect French and budding theatrical career.[14] Had observers been more critical, they might have noted that the distance between cultural affirmation and xenophobia is sometimes uncomfortably small.

At the time that Bobet had backed Groulx's project, he also asked McLean to support a four-page outline from Gilles Carle on the very Canadian subject of winter. Again, McLean gave the go-ahead, and the light-hearted feature *La Vie heureuse de Léopold Z* was born. Each carefully rehearsed scene reflects Carle's masterful comedic timing as the lovable hero, racing from scene to scene during a snowstorm on the day of Christmas Eve, pleases everyone (including himself) and thereby achieves the impossible. The background, a winter tempest in Montreal, was an original and accurate portrayal of one of Canada's meteorological facts of life, though Nature mocked Carle as it took eighteen months of sporadic filming in almost snowless winters to finish. This film too won the Grand Prix at the 1965 Festival du cinéma canadien in Montreal, proving that absurdity was as pleasing to Quebec audiences as was the ponderous cultural question.

Both *Le Chat* and *La Vie heureuse* became instant cultural icons in this heady emotional period. Because language was the critical mass and linchpin for the visuals, audiences could identify virtually all the qualities of contemporary *québécois* culture. These films gave Quebeckers a sense of pride. They stood in stark contrast to a 'special showing of outstanding films' for English audiences at Film Board headquarters in November 1963, which featured the theme 'Four Views of Quebec': *Correlieu, Morning on the Lièvre, Visit to a Foreign Country*, and *The Boy Next Door*. In these, Quebec was seen by painter Ozias Leduc, by poet Archibald Lampman, by an American tourist, and by children respectively.[15] After viewing this programme, English audiences might have been justifiably confused about what was really happening in Quebec and more apt than ever to pose the typical English question of the decade, 'What is it that Quebec wants?' It was probably coincidental, but 'Four Views of Quebec' echoed a speech Roberge had made in August, underscoring his belief that cinema should be used to initiate young people to art. (In fact, one of his favourite productions was *Morning on the Lièvre*.) His ideal was to have film serve as a museum of fine arts for the twentieth century, a kind of *cinéma musée*.[16]

Roberge was not anxious to celebrate the cinematic triumphs of Groulx and Carle. He was hard at work trying to win approval for legislation to create a financial base for the feature film in Canada. The last thing he wanted to see was the Film Board going into the business of features. His idea was to keep it producing documentary shorts, television fare, and sponsored work, while encouraging the persistently nagging private industry to go into features by means of a federally funded bank. He dismissed the above-mentioned French productions with the offhand remark to Bobet that nobody would pay to see these works. His criterion was that features should be of such quality that his sister and mother would want to see them.[17] Perhaps Montreal audiences *were* uncritical, since one Toronto newspaper complained that they responded joyfully, whether the films were good or bad.[18] Toronto's carping seemed to make little difference to loyal Montrealers who loved their familiar cityscape.

Jacques Bobet thought Juneau's attitude to the first two successful French-language features was a little less hostile than the commissioner's. Juneau had not been happy with *cinéma direct*, because despite their surface calm, those documentaries had left the Film Board vulnerable to attack from powerful economic forces. He feared that the filmmakers were on the verge of becoming iconoclasts. To avoid that, he tried to internationalize French Production, bringing in Georges Rouquier (to make *Sire le Roy n'a plus rien dit*), Gian Franco Mingozzi (whose work on Antonioni was well-known), and Enio Flaiano, Fellini's scenarist. He favoured an international atmosphere and helped organize Le Festival International du film de Montréal, which gave the filmmakers a chance to interact with cinema masters like Renoir, Lang, Truffaut, and Polanski.

Juneau was interested in features if they were done traditionally, with a script and no improvisation. As the person responsible for the expenditure, this was not an unreasonable posture. Bobet saw another facet: a scripted work was one that could be controlled at every level of production, hence Juneau, who was ideologically opposed to censorship, would never have to exercise it. Shortly after becoming director of French Production, Juneau had fifty copies of the classic film script *Les Enfants du Paradis* sent to the filmmakers to study. Many were outraged at what they called prefabricated filmmaking, but Juneau was adamant that features be scripted properly. Here is where Enio Flaiano was supposed to help, and from now on the feature films had what Bobet called disdainfully the 'Hollywood tendency'; perhaps too they lost what had been predominant in the first two, credulity and innocence.[19]

Juneau's interest in the feature was its ability to portray a country accurately. It was also one way to change the intellectual and psychological climate of both French and English Canada. In comparing both filmmaking groups, he found that the English Canadians were not menaced by temerity, anarchy, or new ideas, while the French Canadians had developed a climate of narcissism. ('Il y a ici un climat de narcissisme.') He thought that instead of a documentary on cultural relations in Canada, both the English and French should see each other's good dramatic productions. He approached the choice of subjects democratically and believed one could never go faster than the personal orientation of the filmmakers.[20]

At last, in January 1964, the indefatigable Juneau achieved the fruit of his nine-year battle, a separate production budget for French filmmakers and creation of Production française. By his ensuring this legal existence the total production budget would be split proportionately, one-third to the French and two-thirds to the English, at the beginning of the fiscal year.[21] Under Juneau's tutelage, French productions could be undertaken without having to depend on going cap in hand to McLean.[22]

The splitting off became possible after all these years with the return to power in 1963 of a minority government of Liberals under Lester Pearson and the creation of the Laurendeau-Dunton Commission, the Royal Commission on Bilingualism and Biculturalism, in July. Its terms of reference were to inquire into and report on the status of both isms and 'to recommend what steps should be taken to develop the Canadian

Confederation on the basis of an equal partnership between the two founding races.'[23] In enshrining this principle, the government could not very well continue to thwart Juneau's ambition for French Production. Roberge now supported him because the time was right politically. Responsibility for the Film Board once again fell to J.W. Pickersgill, who now held the portfolio of Secretary of State. When he spoke warmly of bilingualism in broadcasting, the Film Board felt secure that approval of the linguistic division of production was not far behind.[24]

It will be recalled that earlier delays by Pickersgill and the Liberal government had been related to a fear that by creating two separate production bases there would be two Film Boards, and Canada itself would be figuratively split. The proposition was not inconsequential. During the Diefenbaker years, the Conservatives' pan-Canadian nationalism had been characterized by 'unhyphenated Canadians.' Most agreed that the Diefenbaker government showed either a fear of or an inability to understand the French-Canadian question. The absence of any documentation about creating Production française during those years leads one to surmise that the subject was a closed one. Jacques Godbout, who joined the Film Board in 1958, explained years later he believed no government would have yielded before 1964, for fear of undermining the traditional established Anglo-Canadian authority.[25]

The changing role of the secretary of state

Perhaps Godbout's explanation was facile, because English Canada's political thrust since the days of the Massey Commission had been one of accommodation, and that attitude took as much time to percolate through the many layers of the state as through society itself. The liberals found new faces in French Canada like Maurice Lamontagne, the secretary of state from February

1964, who showed keen interest in promoting biculturalism. He had been an economic adviser to the Privy Council in the 1950s and had been instrumental, with John Deutsch and Pickersgill, in convincing the government to establish the Canada Council. Lamontagne had been one of Lester Pearson's closest advisers in Opposition, and together they had developed the concept of 'cooperative federalism.' In 1963 he and Guy Favreau had also urged Pierre Elliott Trudeau to join the Liberal party, which he did two years later.

Lamontagne recognized that culture could develop as a useful instrument of unity, if it was presented properly on both sides. In 1961 he had said that Canada had a distorted historical picture that emphasized differences and conflicts, not similarities or joint ventures. He thought that the crisis in both cultures was one of maturity; as he put the issue prosaically to R.M. Fowler, 'The irony of history is that we cannot overcome our own crises without your active support. I hope that you will solve yours soon so as to be in a better position to help us.' It was a unique way of looking at the cultural crises starting to grip the country. Lamontagne blamed Canada's cultural poverty as the root cause of separatism and the present French-English tension. His simple message was, 'Without culture we can be a country, but never a nation.'[26]

The secretary of state agreed with Quebec's Premier Lesage, who had said that this was Confederation's hour of the last chance, and something must be done. In 1965 he began to consider reorganization of the secretary of state department, so as to integrate all the heads of the cultural institutions on the policy level.[27] Soon his department burgeoned: fourteen related agencies (including the Film Board) came together under one roof, embracing almost all of the federal government's involvement in culture. Thus began the bureaucratization of Canadian culture.

Lamontagne's interest in film matters led to negotiations that ultimately gave life to Roberge's pet project, the Canadian Film Development Corporation (CFDC), under his successor. He also pursued the idea, approved in principle by Paul Martin, the secretary of state for external affairs in 1963, that the Film Board establish a film training school for people from developing countries. It was to be an inexpensive form of external aid, to provide Canada with prestige and influence as well as to benefit those aspiring Canadian filmmakers who would receive training. In 1964, he encouraged Roberge to push the scheme; it went nowhere, but remained an active policy option for the Film Board for almost two decades. Unfortunately, there was never adequate funding to bring it to life.[28]

As minister, Lamontagne was known as a thinker, and his public image was never strong.[29] (His favourite hobby was reading.) He was called Canada's first 'cultural czar' in one breath, and a 'lacklustre politician' in another. His hesitant replies in an unfamiliar language, English, had led Opposition questioners to single him out as an easy target. His successor, Judy LaMarsh, was cruellest in describing him as ineffectual. 'Of him economists said he was a good politician and politicians said he was a good economist,' she wrote. He resigned his portfolio in December 1965, amidst rumours and scandal, after he was found to have made no payment on $8,000 worth of furniture he had purchased from a company that subsequently went bankrupt.[30]

'L'affaire *Parti pris*'

The creation of French Production did not bring harmony to the Film Board, in part, because Quebec's social ferment was becoming increasingly turbulent. Some of the French-language filmmakers, who cynically called themselves 'servile servants,' rather than civil servants, found it ironic that the federal government was paying them to make films that identified the Quebec people and gave them a soul. Had they been the victims of authoritarian censorship, they could have chosen the battlefield. But they were frustrated and angry that the institution was difficult to attack because it practised the liberal idea of laisser-faire. They were free to make their films socially provocative and passionate, and it was the *québécois* audience, not the Film Board management, that passed judgment on them. Given this atmosphere, five of the most outspoken of these filmmakers, believing that Quebec had as much respect for martyrs as for heroes, planned to hurl a thunderbolt at their federal employer and achieve martyrdom.

Of course Quebec nationalism was not a new phenomenon, but it was no longer the religion-centred, rural, anti-statist object it had once been. A secular, urban-industrial society had spawned a desire for reform in education, in the public service, in labour laws, and in economic development. From 1950, a whole generation of intellectuals, including Pierre Elliott Trudeau and Gérard Pelletier, had railed against the medieval machinations of Premier Duplessis, who practised political corruption and intimidation in exercising power. As co-editors of the monthly review *Cité libre*, Trudeau and Pelletier had denounced conservative, authoritarian, dogmatic, and totalitarian nationalism, which they saw as the special preserve of vested interests who opposed social reform. They were ashamed of the backwardness Duplessis had cultivated in the name of protecting French identity, because it had deprived Quebec society of democracy. Culturally, this regime had reduced French Canadians to a 'folklorique' people, characterized by rural-religious, not urban-secular, values. The ideas expressed in *Cité libre* were liberal-left in political orientation, and the intellectuals urged a functional approach to Quebec's problems, not forgetting that national and cultural values had a secondary role to play.[31]

Their articles stood against a backdrop of daily news stories related to decolonization and the struggle of new nations. With the arrival of television in Quebec, an under-thirty French-speaking population was pierced by knowledge of global events; they too resented the authoritarian regimes that had kept the province a colonial backwater, but wanted to go further than just catching up. The new nationalism called for the state to replace the authority of the church. By 1964, at the University of Montreal, students were calling for revolutionary nationalism and were championing the rights of Quebec's working classes. They believed that state independence was the panacea that would lead to genuine decolonization and national liberation.

Trudeau and Pelletier despised the idea of Quebec becoming a separate state because they believed it would lead French Canadians to retreat into their own nationalistic shell and condemn themselves to stagnation and death by suffocation. In four key articles in *Cité libre*, from 1961 to 1966, Trudeau mocked separatists variously as alienators who were unrealistic, preposterous, self-deluding, politically reactionary, and weak petit bourgeois intellectuals who had no knowledge of basic economics and were just flapping their arms. The challenge, as he put it in his last article, was for French Canadians to hold their own as equals with the rest of Canada, not to be excluded from it.[32]

If, in the fifties, *Cité libre* and its intellectuals were far ahead of the French-Canadian filmmakers at the Film Board, by 1964 many of those same artists agreed with the radical students who believed that *Cité libre* had stood still. Some of the once-apolitical filmmakers were caught up in the emotionally appealing question of language and identity, and found little difficulty in posing the question in the terms that many Quebec students articulated, 'Un Canadien français? C'est un québécois.' Another answer was to be found in the non-ideological review *Liberté*, which became a platform for filmmakers Jacques Godbout, Hubert Aquin, André Belleau, Jacques Bobet, André Guerin, Jean LeMoyne, and Gilles Carle. Founded at the end of the fifties, *Liberté* underscored the economic and political colonization of French Canada. It tried to steer away from dogmatic nationalism and subscribed to the virtues of progressivism and freedom of expression. *Liberté* confirmed the spirit of unfettered intellectual independence that came to characterize French Production.[33]

However, outside the universities and state institutions, a fringe group like the Front de Libération du Québec adopted urban terrorism as its means of expression, and left the majority of Quebeckers, who were strangers to violence, quite puzzled. Pierre Trudeau was not among the puzzled. Following the death of an old soldier by an FLQ bomb, he published an article in *Cité libre*, in May 1964, and lashed out at 'separatist counter-revolutionaries,' whom he identified as swarming at the CBC and the Film Board, as well as in the editorial rooms of various newspapers. He jeered at their claim of being persecuted and mockingly called them terrorized terrorists who were not part of a separatist revolution, but a national-socialist (Nazi) counter-revolution.[34] Trudeau harboured these sentiments for the remainder of his political career, and one cannot help but wonder if this 1964 barb might not have had some atmospheric bearing over the following decade, when he was prime minister and his government seemed indifferent to the Film Board's financial woes.

If *Cité libre* was the intellectual engine of modern anti-Duplessist Quebec, its goal of liberalism was considered by those who dreamed of complete independence not to go far enough. The left-wing review *Parti pris* came into existence in the fall of 1963, and was meant to challenge the domination of 'nos pères ... les gens du *Cité libre*.' Its passionate articles became an overnight sensation. In April 1964 Gérard Pelletier lashed out at the journal as 'la grande illusion,' a first home-grown attempt to seriously advocate revolutionary struggle while abandoning almost all traditional values of French-Cana-

dian society. He demolished the intellectual pretensions of its contributors as nationalist dogmatism, at one point even singling out for contempt filmmaker Denys Arcand as one of those prophets who predicted that Quebec would have to become self-reliant, after independence, because it would be cut off for some years from external cultural influence.[35]

Years later, Jacques Godbout explained another aspect of this period. The young were part of a growing North American tendency to confront authority, in an epoch that was trying to deal with authority in general. Their outrage centred on the conviction that authority was medieval, because it was founded on fear, not competence. To their minds, power was equated with autocracy, and they were intent to break the vicious historical cycle. Being young, they believed it was possible to change the world. They wanted authority, but did not want to share it. The idealists thought they could break the historical pattern of the equation by refusing to assume authority once they acquired it. Godbout believed that this refusal to assume authority became the tendency of many of the French filmmakers at the Film Board, and this fact explained the future struggles of French Production.[36]

It was no small irony that in the same month as Pelletier's devastating critique was being read in *Cité libre*, *Parti pris* dedicated its issue to the Film Board and Quebec cinema. Five filmmakers from the institution wrote articles. They had the same effect as if the FLQ had detonated a bomb at NFB headquarters. As far as they were concerned, theirs was an expression of what was then being called the idea of 'collective cultural adventure.' It became known as 'L'affaire *Parti pris*.'

The five – Jacques Godbout, Gilles Groulx, Clément Perron, Gilles Carle, and Denys Arcand – each concentrated on an aspect of documentary about which he felt passion. Godbout, in 'L'année zéro,' described how the Film Board had been a factory, where the educational film was more accepted than the documentary and where the institution had only by accident stumbled into 'cinéma.' He criticized the *cinéma vérité* of Fernand Dansereau's television series *Temps présent* and its failure to probe what he called the psychoanalysis of the terrain. He wondered mockingly what the agency was to do with the new political reality and moral attitude of four million French Canadians under forty: make a film on Premier Jean Lesage in the manner of *Lonely Boy*? It was difficult to get to the heart of things, because subjects like the working class denied the official ideal of the institution. All that being said, Godbout emphasized that the Film Board was a school of filmmakers that in the next two years would determine the destiny of French-Canadian cinema.

Gilles Carle's article, 'L'ONF et l'objectivité des autres,' was no less severe. Describing the Film Board as a state organization within the capitalist system, he was aware of how easy it was to fall into gratuitousness, since the Board was a deluxe tool, a comfortable place to work. His critique of *cinéma vérité* and 'Roucheole' damned what he called the passionate appropriation of *place*, in which the picturesque was replaced by the familiar, and myth receded before reality. Documentary was already developed to excess. A filmmaker's assignment of a didactic film meant the application of objectivity (obnoxious bourgeois moralism) in which bourgeois instruction 'de-concretized' the centre, rendering it abstract, while human passions were seen as simple connectives in the graph of acquired values: 'Freedom' was the freedom of thought of the federal regime, from Halifax to Calgary. Meanwhile, Carle felt prevented from making a dramatic film about an extramarital affair, filled with sex, love, and hate. Fiction was the way to concern oneself with what was real, he concluded, because in the federal optic, love meant a vague tenderness for humanity. His dilemma was being comfortable and uncom-

fortable, the most free and the least free of filmmakers. He felt stymied and unable to give birth to a *québécois* cinema.

Clémont Perron complained in 'Un témoignage' that when he was shooting a film on the subject of drop-outs and unemployed in Sept-Îles, Quebec, in 1961, he could not shoot the sad spectacle he had witnessed because of the complicity of company, provincial, and federal officials. And Denys Arcand, in 'Des évidences,' admitted that filmmakers were too poor to work outside the Film Board and were miserably alone. French-Canadian cinema, he affirmed, bathed itself in mediocrity, and its filmmakers could only talk about the great feature they intended to make. On the question of *cinéma vérité*, he lashed out at the alleged domination of the French side by Rouch and called *Candid Eye* the subconscious life-jacket of poor types who did not want to flow in the platitudes of the soap operas of Radio-Canada. He prophesied that the destiny of Quebec cinema was glued to the destiny of French Canada.

In '28 minutes, 25 seconds,' an equally alienated Gilles Groulx made an emotional appeal for freedom of expression and denied the adequacy of a film life of formal research and technique. He felt that filmmakers were vegetating between self-censorship and compromise. He believed that the films ought to reflect the temperament and individual preoccupations of individuals and artists who needed to expand themselves. A nation awaited them.[37]

Juneau later called the articles a watershed in the history of the Film Board. Roberge agonized over them and knew he would have to answer to the minister for the audacity of their gesture. He took some time to reflect on a course of action and then called the five miscreants into his office. He read them a statement in which he said that no one was condemned to the Film Board like a prisoner – if they were allergic to the methods and policies there, they could quit. But, he added, he would be sorry to see them go elsewhere to try to realize their hopes. He was most bothered by the editorial that preceded the five articles, even though its author, Pierre Maheu, had stated that it was not necessarily the opinion of the five filmmakers.

The editorial was pure Marxist rhetoric, a manifesto that charged the Film Board with being an instrument of colonization, trying to bolster a puppet country, Canada, while negating a Quebec cinema. It asserted that the French Canadians in authority there were representatives of the colonial order, ex-Jesuits and vague liberals. The documentary film was propaganda, its camera was cold, sliding over surfaces, impersonal. Maheu argued that so-called documentary objectivity demanded a vision that must be in accord with the established order. Cleverly, films that departed from the norms, like *Voir Miami* and *Un air de famille*, were never censored, only buried gently by Distribution. At the Film Board, people were not fired, they were only worn down. The French filmmakers had turned the *Candid Eye* technique against the regime by revealing the alienation of society. Theirs was not a detached documentary, but one of passion, stretched between the acceptance and the criticism of the people it discovered. The *nouveau cinéma* rested fundamentally on a discovery of the Quebec population itself, where the filmmaker identified his people positively, thereby proving there was more than alienation, decline, and ugliness in daily life. Maheu concluded that it would be impossible for Quebec filmmakers to engage in a struggle for liberation while remaining in the framework of a colonial structure. He demanded a total repatriation of Quebec cinema.[38]

Roberge said it was impossible to believe the five filmmakers could subscribe to that editorial line in good conscience and stay at the Film Board, since their sense of honour would not permit it. He concluded that they were guilty of misconduct according to the rules which apply to public servants, and that they had discredited the Film Board, but that he would forgive them this time. If, however,

a similar incident were to occur again, he would have to take stricter action. ('Il me faudrait alors user de rigueur.') He ended the session, thanking them for their attention and wishing that other more agreeable meetings would make them forget this one.

This was vintage Roberge. If some of the filmmakers had expected martyrdom in the form of dismissal, he did not fall into their trap. He had called them on the carpet, disciplined them, and left them plenty of space to retreat. He appended his statement to the filmmakers to a letter addressed to Minister Lamontagne. In it, he explained that if he had been more severe, there might have been consequences for the country as a whole; he considered *that* course to be an inopportune one. Besides, in a creative place like the Film Board, the employees were necessarily nonconformist.[39] Roberge was right. To have dismissed them would have fuelled the fires of the nationalist cause with an *auto-da-fé*.

What he did not tell the minister was that when he had finished reading his remarks, Groulx coolly asked for a copy. The always-in-control commissioner coloured deep red and dismissed the transgressors from his office curtly. One cannot help but remember the image of the punished schoolboys, once again hooting, 'On est puni; on va de vous voir,' as they sauntered back to work. Godbout remembers feeling more amused than chastised. Some of them came to Juneau afterward and apologized, claiming they had not realized what the articles would do. In one case, the filmmaker explained it was emotion, pure personal sympathy, a gesture.

Juneau admitted years later that no one had given a serious thought to firing these artists, since they could not make films anywhere else. As he explained it, 'We're a small country, and there aren't that many people who can do the job; it's often better to try to salvage the talent. We're forced to stick together more than in bigger and richer countries, where there are more people to do what has got to be done.'[40] As for the flaming Marxist rhetoric of *Parti pris* editor Maheu, a few years later he found work as a film producer; his employer was the Office National du Film du Canada. When several of the films with which he was associated were suppressed, the ensuing publicity did the institution little good.

For those who did not support the *prise de conscience* of the French-Canadian activists, there was much puzzlement at Roberge's refusal to fire the five. If most of the sentimental expressions of this activist group were pro-*québécois* nationalism, it was quite easy to conclude that such expressions of French-Canadian nationalism were separatist. The fine line distinguishing the two positions was missed, especially on the English side, where the sense was that Canada was being torn apart. Mutual suspicion and hostility grew more intense. If even the least political of the French creative staff felt proud of the spiritual flowering of French-Canadian identity in this period, the English Canadians for their part were excluded by virtue of their language and culture. Worse, they felt they were being condemned more for their father's past sins of omission than for present-day transgressions against French Canada.

Parliamentary fallout from *Nobody Waved Goodbye*

English Production was as enamoured of the feature idea as was French Production. Its second long fiction piece was *Nobody Waved Goodbye* ($73,593), directed by Don Owen in 1964. Like Gilles Groulx's *Le Chat dans le sac*, it was about adolescent conflict, this time of youth rebelling against middle-class parental morality, conventions, and goals. But here the break was generational (Oedipal), not sociopolitical, as it was in Quebec. Owen's male and female teenagers share the ennui and stultification of suburban life and are hungry for freedom, represented by the city. The young protagonist falls into delinquency and crime, and finds himself alone at the end, pointing aimlessly down the highway. His girlfriend is left on her own to cope with an unwanted pregnancy.[41]

Both films, valuable artefacts of aspects of Canadian life in the sixties, beg for cultural comparison: *Nobody Waved Goodbye* is a scathing indictment of selfish bourgeois sterility (which gives rise to fecundity, pregnancy, and abandonment), while *Le Chat dans le sac* is a metaphor of Quebec's *prise de conscience* and potentially xenophobic fortress mentality vis-à-vis the modern urban industrial world.

Nobody Waved Goodbye was a partial pretext for what one Toronto newspaper called a parliamentary 'tongue-lashing' of the Film Board, in November 1964. Owen had made some rather ill-chosen remarks to the *Montreal Star* in August, claiming that the film had started out to be a short documentary, which he expanded into a feature. Because he was in Toronto, he said, Montreal headquarters did not know this until he had finished shooting. As he put it arrogantly, the original short documentary 'just grew ... they couldn't touch me.'[42] A month later, New Democratic Party MP Douglas M. Fisher raised two difficult questions in the Commons: Why was the Film Board making theatrical, television, and experimental film at the expense of non-theatrical films that had been used by national film councils across the country? Also, what was going on inside the agency to give rise to Owen's remarks? The secretary of state's parliamentary secretary read the Film Board's ambivalent position on features.[43]

On the second question, Roberge wrote to the minister and denied Owen's remarks categorically. This was the ebullient statement of a young director who did not operate with the complete independence his statement suggested, he claimed. Grant McLean was furious because he had signed for the extra footage to be shot and knew it was going to be a feature. So too did Tom Daly, the executive producer, and Roman Kroitor, the producer. They thought it best to let the matter lie, even if the public's sense was that Owen had pulled the wool over the Film Board's eyes.

Fisher was aware of the internal turmoil and the widespread desire to embrace 'cinema' over traditional documentary, not to mention the recent overhaul of traditional programming. He fired his heaviest salvo in Parliament that November: the serious functional documentary series, like *Ages and Stages*, *Mental Mechanisms*, and *Accidents Don't Happen*, and films on adolescence were out of date; why were comparatively few new ones being produced? Also, the extension departments of universities in western Canada 'were fed up with the NFB, and its lack of touch and lack of liaison.' The Film Board had met only twice over several years with the Canadian Education Association, which was supposed to advise on films for schools.

Fisher surmised that the problem was the split between French and English Production. The French, stimulated by their own city and new techniques, tended to be divorced from the traditional, functional documentary that had given the Film Board a name. The danger was that the organization might become oriented predominantly to the will of those who favoured art for art's sake, rather than to the needs of the audience. The former tendency was dominating the place, and it had lost sight of the great moral purpose it had experienced under Grierson.

In his October letter to Secretary of State Lamontagne, Roberge tried using analogy and optimism as he addressed the split between the French and English. It was, he confessed, 'a delicate matter,' and if the minister allowed that the Film Board was a microcosm of Canada, the whole situation now appeared to be quite sound and reasonable. There had been considerable improvement since the anxieties of 1963, he concluded, and 'if left alone, the present equilibrium will be conducive to good results and relative happiness.'[44]

This was hardly ammunition for Lamontagne to use to refute Fisher's charges. It was obvious that the traditional non-theatrical film users were upset with the new orientation of the Film Board and had complained. The school audience was still intact, although the film councils and community audiences had diminished dramatically because of television's radical effect on Canadian social relations. Lamontagne responded lamely to Fisher that the Film Board had already decided to strengthen its programme for community audiences and to undertake a study to evaluate audience needs.[45] This may have deflected the heat temporarily, but the fact was that the Film Board was no longer oriented significantly toward the non-theatrical audience.

Discretion was the likely reason the commissioner chose not to let the minister know about a new and superb community-oriented film, George Kaczender's dramatic half-hour short *Phoebe* ($33,279). Intended to warn teen audiences about unwanted pregnancy, *Phoebe* contains an innovative use of a *Rashomon*-like technique to demonstrate the various mind-sets of the pregnant teenager who agonizes over how to tell the dreaded news to her boyfriend, family, and school principal. As her imagination runs away with her, the audience too is pulled into her predicament, from which there is no escape. (The film ignores the explosive issue of abortion.) The realistic presentation of her situation makes it unnecessary to preach the virtues of sexual caution to teens. Schools and community groups in Canada and abroad found *Phoebe* an excellent vehicle to deal with the dawning sexual revolution. Brevity was one of *Phoebe*'s greatest strengths, allowing time for discussion afterward. More 16-mm prints of *Phoebe* were sold subsequently than of any other single film in Film Board history except *Universe*.

Roberge might have indicated too that commercial film companies would not likely have gone $30,000 over budget as the Film Board did in 1964, to make a 38-minute sponsored film for the Department of Veterans Affairs, *Fields of Sacrifice* ($94,890), directed by Donald Brittain. A memorial to

When Roberge spoke of improvements since the anxieties of 1963, he could have spoken of *High Steel* (1965), in which the work of Mohawk Indians from Kahnawake at dizzying skyscraper heights is contrasted with the quiet community life found on their reserve.

the 100,000 servicemen who gave their lives for Canada while serving abroad, Brittain mixed word and image to achieve just the right amount of metaphoric beauty without sinking to the maudlin. Filmed on battlefields from Hong Kong to Sicily, this poetic tribute has remained in continuous distribution.

In its twenty-fifth year, 1964, the federal film agency had become a very different place from the one John Grierson had left in 1945. Now the peripatetic Scotsman showed up once again, this time having been invited to the anniversary celebrations in August. If he seemed dwarfed physically by the microphone and old age, his grey-blue eyes, magnified by his glasses, flashed in turn playful and serious as he uttered words which had the familiar ring that many of the senior English staff remembered from nearly a quarter-century ago. 'The first principle of documentary – and it must be the first principle because I wrote it – is that you forget about yesterday. The only good film is the one you are going to make tomorrow.' One could imagine a hundred egos deflating as in a collective sigh.

Grierson had come neither to praise Caesar nor to bury him. He was still the prophet, the father, whose only progeny was the bricks, mortar, and steel around him. He reminded the audience of his perennial belief that the relationship with Ottawa was the most precious one the agency had. It was that connection, he maintained, that gave the staff a sense of satisfaction that they were artists in the service of Canada. In his estimation, to be a creative person at the Film Board was the privilege to be a great public servant.[46]

Grierson's speech likely inspired the board of governors to reconfirm a few months later that the Film Board was a part of the public service and an agency at the service of Canada.[47] For many of the new generation of

104

One of Buster Keaton's last films, *The Railrodder* (1965), takes the viewer across Canada in a wordless romp by rail, a metaphoric reminder that Canada's seemingly unlimited natural resources are not always easy for the little man to grasp.

English and French filmmakers, however, these words fell on deaf ears, since their present concern was the Canadian feature film.[48] *Nobody Waved Goodbye* and *Le Chat dans le sac* were the models to emulate, regardless of cost or the unlikelihood of significant box-office revenue. The pool system now gave the individual filmmaker such power that if he did not wish to undertake a certain project, it died. That the sponsored film had been a mainstay of English Production and had been responsible for one-fourth to one-third of total production activity left many cold. Worse, had anyone bothered to look at the statistical facts of life, the Film Board's budget was $5.5 million a year, but the real increase in production funds had been only an average of $41,000 per year since 1952.[52] As Achilles had his heel, the Film Board's

resources were finite. The single most effective argument against feature films was and remains financial. But the medium, not money, was the message of the era.

The birth of the Canadian Film Development Corporation

Since 1962 Roberge had wanted Canada, not the Film Board, to climb aboard the train of feature-film dreams because it made good business sense. Some $27 million of the $34.5 million that Canadians paid in rentals for foreign-produced films in 1961 had been remitted abroad. The commercial industry in Canada had a gross income of $10.7 million that year, yet had produced only three features. Canada's modest industry had reason to hope that features might generate an additional $5 million a year as well as employment for skilled technicians, studios, laboratories, writers, musicians, artists, actors, and filmmakers. In 1963 Roberge offered to prepare the legislation establishing a system of financial assistance and loans to encourage the development of the entertainment-film industry. The pursuit of co-productions was the least expensive way to do this, and Roberge was instrumental in promoting a Canada-France co-production agreement that year.[50]

As for creating a bank to underwrite feature films, it was too soon for Ottawa to agree to a multi-million-dollar commitment. So Roberge requested from the minister at least a decision in principle for a $3 million revolving fund, set up by government and administered by the Film Board, based roughly on the British National Film Finance Corporation structure. In his plan, an advisory committee of individuals from the Canadian film industry would allocate financial assistance to producers of good quality features.[51] A cautious government stalled and recommended more study.

In the meantime, Roberge warned against quotas, explaining (with more faith than fact) that when the time came, one could persuade hard-headed businessmen to accept good Canadian features in their distribution systems. On the more familiar legal level, he knew that the power of the federal government to introduce quotas was limited constitutionally. Besides, quotas would make the distributors hostile.[52] He did not have to state the obvious – that the United States would not stand by passively if Canada chose to confront the economic power of Hollywood and the major distributors whom the moguls manipulated.

At last, Minister Lamontagne took the occasion of twenty-fifth anniversary of the Film Board to announce the intention of the government 'to establish a loan fund for the production of feature films of high quality in Canada.' Press reaction was almost universally negative.[53] He ordered further study

and a year later, announced that a ten-million-dollar fund would be created.

Using the analogy of the achievement of the Auto Pact in 1964, which established free trade in automobile parts and assembly between the United States and Canada, Lamontagne hoped that a common market in film would replace the existing one-way arrangement dominated by the United States.[54] The new organization, the Canadian Film Development Corporation, was to be outside the aegis of the Film Board and under the watchful eye of the minister himself. Roberge was disappointed to learn he was to be an adviser only. Perhaps it was for the best, since with the exception of a few stellar productions in French, over the next two decades the CFDC squandered most of its resources on soft-core pornography and lacklustre films, the majority of which made money for the producers exclusively, The CFDC became a prime example of how the government trough is a poor place to try to teach the rapacious to honour culture. Of the few lasting benefits that came from the CFDC was its provision of practical training and jobs to those fortunate enough to find employment on the (mostly forgettable) productions. Its successor, Telefilm Canada, tightened up the lending rules in 1984, and has since tried, with varying success, to foster a recoverable-loans policy and a commercial orientation that curbs the culturally bankrupt sex-exploitation film.[55] Whatever its qualities, Roberge hoped the CFDC might deflect the commercial industry's relentless attack on the Film Board for more departmental sponsored films. Hope was no substitute for reality, however, and the commercial interests' hunger for them continued unabated.

Old friend and adversary – television

Since 1952, most of the Film Board's television transmission had been on the CBC. From 226 telecasts over three stations in the first year, by 1964 there were almost 7,000 telecasts over 69 stations, mostly in the form of 'spot bookings' or single items. The Film Board and CBC met to discuss mutual cooperation at the beginning of 1964, at which time the Film Board asked that the CBC consider using Film Board facilities as an alternative to constructing new facilities.[56] Not surprisingly, the CBC insisted on constructing its own buildings and the Film Board lost another round in the tug-of-war with its old adversary.

A rapid glance at a titles list of the most telecast English-language Film Board films of 1962 provides a measure of the impact that the institution had been having on Canada after a decade of television. The 'best sellers' are accompanied by the number of telecasts. (A telecast was one emission by one station in one city; a single national network broadcast would imply some forty telecasts.)

One Little Indian (178)
The Romance of Transportation in Canada (162)
Ti-Jean Goes Lumbering (153)
The Motorman (151)
Corral (141)
The Man in the Peace Tower (141)
How to Build an Igloo (123)
The Pony (110)
Street to the World (107)
Chantous Noël (107)
The Calèche Driver (102)
Herring Hunt (101)
Family Tree (100)
Men of Lunenberg (91)
Begone Dull Care (91)
Angotee: Story of an Eskimo Boy (89)
Maple Sugar Time (87)
Hunting with a Camera (86)
Gifted Ones (86)
Voice of the People (86)
The Salmon's Struggle for Survival (85)
Prairie Profile (84)

The corresponding titles and figures for French television best sellers were based on titles having twenty or more telecasts:

Chantons Noël (107)
Chants populaires No. 6 (48)
Cadet Rousselle (47)
Bar mitzvah (37)
Corral (36)
Il était une chaise (34)
L'Homme dans la tour (33)
Après le bagne (31)
Chants populaires No. 1 (31)
Le Cocher (31)
Chasseurs de caribou (29)
Ti-Jean s'en va-t-aux chantiers (29)
Chasseurs du Pôle Nord (28)
Comprenez mieux votre bébé (28)
Le Merle (28)
L'Age du castor (27)
Chants populaires No. 5 (27)
Montreurs de marionnettes (27)
Sur le pont d'Avignon (27)
La Drave (26)
Ombre sur la prairie (26)
St. Pierre et Miquelon (26)

The bad news that most of these shorts were used as 'fillers' in off-hours, when audiences tended to be uneven or predominantly children. There was nothing wrong with reaching the young of Canada, but many of the creative staff at the Film Board tended to act as if these audience realities did not exist. To put it another way, many were aiming their creative energies at a phantom audience. Wearing such blinkers did the organization no good in the difficult years to come.[57]

The Film Board scored in 1961–2 with the thirteen-part half-hour series *Canada at War* (*Le Canada en guerre*), a monumental history of Canadian participation in the Second World War, produced by Stanley Clish, Peter Jones, and Donald Brittain. This $318,205 compilation project began in 1958 with the indexing of almost two million metres of wartime archival film from the Canadian Army Film Unit, Associated Screen News, the RCAF, and the Film Board's earliest theatrical series, *Canada Carries On* and *The World in Action*. The epic narrative was a nostalgic reminiscence of an era, the story of Canada maturing into nationhood, a chronology of the winning of the war, a salute to its warriors, and a reminder of the horror of war. The series, the most successful in CBC history to that date, established Brittain as a masterful commentary writer and keeper of Canada's historical and cultural consciousness.

The CBC hoped to orient the Film Board to series rather than to single-item telecasts. Thus the Board's television commitment was not only broad – it had become the major pillar of its production activity.[58]

By 1964, the television production schedule was as follows:

English

'Exploding Metropolis' (6 items; 30 minutes)
'Aspects of French Canada' (10; 30 min.)
'Latin America' (1; 60 min.)
'Explorations' (5; 30 min.)
'Comparisons' (5; 30 min.)
'History' (3; 3 min.)

French

'Cité idéale' (6; 30 min.)
'Temps présent' (12; 30 min.)
'Histoire' (1; 30 min.)
'Comparisons' (4; 30 min.)
'Amérique latine' (1; 60 min.)[59]

English Production's plate was full enough with commitments to series and non-theatrical, animation, and pedagogical films. The figures did not tell of the occasional missed deadlines, which drove CBC management into a frenzy over what they thought was institutional irresponsibility. To mend fences, the Film Board offered to open its distribution network to CBC information and public-affairs programmes after they had been broadcast, but the CBC considered this plan premature, since it depended on rerunning its own programmes for up to two years after initial broadcast. As a whole then, at

this point, the English CBC was depending on the Film Board for one-fifth of its film production (13 of 65 hours), with the remainder split: 25 per cent (16 hours) produced by the CBC and the rest produced with outside assistance or completely outside the corporation. The CBC was paying 'rental' to the Film Board of around $8,000 per half-hour of film.

Television promised a respectable audience for future Film Board features even if they were financial losers. The Film Board began angling to get up to $50,000 or 49 per cent of the cost, and resented the CBC paying an average of $5,000 for English and $1,800 for French features. In 1965 shared costs were a pipedream, and when co-produced features were tried a few years later, they were disasters.[60]

A close reading of the list of television films completed in fiscal year 1964–5 (see Appendix 1) reveals that these films would probably never have been made by the private sector because they lacked commercial appeal. Had they not been made, Canada would have been the loser culturally for having no record of the varied aspects of Canadian life that were documented. That future generations would be deprived of a capsule glimpse of the era would have been sadder. If these film subjects varied, they shared a common, if unsolicited, consensus: they stand as examples in opposition to the alienating forces of pervasive consumerism that fills television and daily life. In short, each film serves in its own way as thread that ties citizens spiritually and intellectually to their society.

External Affairs tries to block *Bethune*

After Film Board producer John Kemeny had read the biography *The Scalpel and the Sword*, by Ted Allen and Sydney Gordon, he thought that the nearly unknown Canadian surgeon-hero Dr Norman Bethune would make a splendid documentary-film subject. Donald Brittain's script blended Bethune's own writings with a combination of interviews, stills, and archival footage to reconstruct the surgeon's flamboyant life. Brittain painted a mythic cinematic portrait of an authentic hero, showing Bethune as a complex and difficult individual who was an example of valid nonconformity in an age of conformity. *Bethune* took a year to finish, cost $78,874, and appeared on CBC television in January 1965. It received warm press reaction in major Canadian cities.[61]

A wary Film Board considered that the whole subject was a political tinderbox, since Bethune's political awakening grew out of his victory over tuberculosis and his support of the Loyalist cause as an anti-Fascist in civil war–torn Spain. From that experience he embraced Communism, and as Pai-Chu-An (the White One Sent), served Mao Tse Tung's forces as a surgeon in Japanese-occupied China, where he perished. Mao wrote of Bethune in his *Quotations from Chairman Mao*, ensuring him legendary status and China's enduring respect for the otherwise inscrutable Canada.

Brittain was most cautious about this aspect and wove the interviews describing Bethune in such a way as to concentrate on his personality, not his Communism: 'a meteor passing,' 'in another century he might have been a crusader or a troubadour,' 'he gave all he had or could give to the cause of the betterment of the world' were the various descriptions. Poet Frank Scott's testimony summarized it best: 'I think he was an amateur in politics, guided by his heart as much as by his head ... A surgeon was accustomed to cutting out the evil in the human body and throwing it away. About the concept of a communist, *revolution* was a sort of vast national surgery and maybe something induced him to take this more readily.' Brittain mentioned the forbidden word only once, if with equivoca-

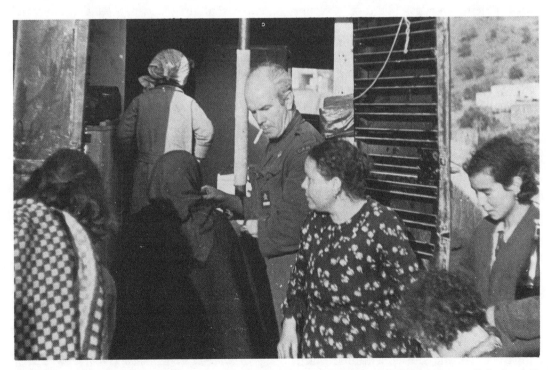

The iconoclastic Canadian surgeon Dr Norman Bethune set up his mobile blood-donor clinics in civil war–scarred Spain in 1937. Bethune's Communism displeased the Department of External Affairs, which prevented the 1964 documentary *Bethune* from being distributed abroad.

tion: 'Bethune decides to throw in with the Communist Party. However, Bethune the Marxist does not interfere with Bethune the happy wanderer.'[62]

While some thought the film did too much to support the 'great man' idea of history, a careful study of it shows that the iconoclastic surgeon's politics were secondary to his indomitable will to fight evil and like his missionary parents before him, to do good. He was caught in modern man's struggle with irreconcilable opposites, reviling the fluid atmosphere of war, yet finding it the place where his surgical freedom was greatest and where he was happiest, doing the most good. The film's universalist message of self-sacrifice for the benefit of the community far exceeds the reference to Bethune's 'politics.' The Department of External Affairs missed the point and stiffly opposed its distribution in China and other Communist countries.

It was on this issue that Roberge found himself facing an angry board of governors member, Marcel Cadieux, under-secretary of state for external affairs, with whom he had been parrying for months.[63] The urbane commissioner resented the fact that circumstances were forcing a showdown. With the support of the members, he fought bitterly to defend the Film Board's long-cherished freedom to control distribution of its films. He won his point but lost the battle.

The controversy began when Distribution suggested to the commissioner that *Bethune* would be a good film to version into Mandarin Chinese. The Film Board had been trying unsuccessfully since 1959 to get a few films into an all but closed China. When External Affairs learned of these versioning plans, Cadieux demurred, lest the film serve as a psychological weapon against Western societies. He discussed this matter with the secretary of state for external affairs, Paul Martin, who agreed and told him that only films of scientific and educational matter should be circulated in China. Roberge was out of the country at the time of these discussions.

Meanwhile, the film had been selected earlier that summer for screening in East Germany at the Leipzig International Festival in November, along with *Stravinsky* and *Eskimo Artist: Kenojuak*, two other Film Board titles. When Cadieux learned this, he was astonished because he believed Roberge had understood that the film was not to be distributed in Communist countries. To complicate matters, *Bethune* won the top award at Leipzig. Every Communist country, except the Soviet Union and Albania, wanted to show it on television, and the Film Board commercial representatives were busy signing them up. A livid Cadieux wanted an explanation.

Roberge explained that the decision to send the documentary to Leipzig had preceded Cadieux's letter and that he had already told the staff the film could not be distributed in Communist countries without consultation with the secretary of state of external affairs (*l'accord préalable du Ministre* meant literally 'the preliminary agreement of the Minister'). This being said, Roberge insisted on the Film Board's right to distribute its works abroad. He felt that it was important that people abroad see the same production as Canadians did, not a retouched one.

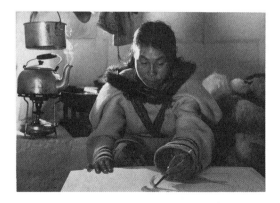

Eskimo Artist: Kenojuak (1964) shows this talented printmaker at work and at home with her family, as well as Canada's northern environment from which her creativity springs.

The commissioner carried the argument further: *Bethune* could not be used against Canada by the Communists because the film made it clear that it was less Marxism than humanitarianism that had moved Bethune to want to improve the human condition. External Affairs was not interested in fine points of interpretation. Cadieux showed Roberge a report from the Canadian ambassador in Moscow, detailing how Canadian exchange students, who had organized a showing of non-political Film Board subjects at Moscow State University, were disappointed when the Russians cancelled the show in December, one day before the exhibition.[64] He concluded that the ham-handed Communist control of information and images proved the department's point that the Communists might use *Bethune* for their own propaganda purposes.

But an important matter of principle was at issue. The dissemination of official Canadian information abroad was the ultimate responsibility of External Affairs, they argued, and had been for the past fifteen years. The Film Board position was that it had the right to decide on foreign distribution of its own films. Cadieux argued that *Bethune* could suggest that a great many Canadians shared his convictions and admired his conduct. The department opposed the regular distribution of the film in Communist countries on the grounds that it could create a false Canadian symbol and, by implication, a false appreciation of the political convictions of the majority of Canadians. Another reason for the hullabaloo was contained in the cryptic remark that the film might in certain situations trouble our relations with friendly countries. There was little doubt that External Affairs feared upsetting the United States.

If the Film Board did not like the department's position, said Cadieux, they could go to the ministerial level. Meanwhile, to allow Roberge room to manoeuvre, the department suggested that *Bethune* be the object of a country-by-country study by itself and the Film Board, with a view to evolving a special plan of distribution. Roberge would not waive publicly the general rule regarding the free distribution of films. It was a stalemate; the Film Board and External Affairs had to find a compromise. At last it was decided that *Bethune* would be released on television in Poland and Czechoslovakia. In other Communist countries, it was to be placed in Canadian embassies 'for private and evaluation screenings by the Ambassador.'

Grant McLean was enraged that after all the positive press the final decision was restriction. The Film Board staff was shocked and bewildered; many had lost respect for the management. 'Some filmmakers perceive the frightening echo of McCarthyism here without even the excuse of mass hysteria,' he fulminated. External Affairs is in the business of diplomacy and propaganda, he continued, and the Film Board is in the business of ideas; any confusion between these two functions would be downright dangerous. He felt the film would promote understanding behind the Iron Curtain and in the United States. He made his best point when he argued that the world should know that 'we have the freedom to make such a film and the United States should be reminded that our heroes are not necessarily carbon copies of theirs.'

The letter was heartfelt, although its passion might have also been a factor in the board of governors (of which Cadieux was a member) turning down McLean as permanent successor to Roberge. McLean, an outspoken personality who had fought External Affairs in the 1940s and lost over *The People Between*, could hardly be expected to play the same game as Roberge, the shrewd, suave, yet cautious diplomatic personality who could make a defeat look like victory.

The point was that Roberge had saved face, but External Affairs had obtained most of what it wanted. Upon receipt of Cadieux's first portentous letter, Roberge had told Distribution to stop promoting the film in Communist countries or Spain (the film's depiction of Bethune's participation in the civil war could open old wounds there) because External Affairs would protest. Subsequently, the Film Board cancelled its contract with Poland, although Czech television had the right of two transmissions. In the United States, distribution rights were withheld, and the Film Board decided to not promote the film actively. Only seven copies were sold in these first few years. External Affairs lifted its restrictions on the film in 1971; to date it has had one showing on Yugoslav television, in 1978; there are no contracts for commercial distribution in Communist countries.[65] Perhaps the greatest irony of all was that when diplomatic relations with China were established in the early seventies, the Chinese considered *Bethune* among the most highly valued gifts that Canada gave them.

It had been almost six years since the serious confrontation with External Affairs over *Black and White in South Africa*, which also had been withdrawn from circulation abroad. *Bethune* marked a turning point in relations with External Affairs, who insisted fanatically on non-controversy as the best way to keep Canada's international image correct. They thought the kind of international profile that suited Canada best was the department's gift, in 1964, to seven African countries of seventeen panel trucks with projectors, generators, and screens developed by the NFB for open-air screenings. (Another eighteen would be shipped to five more African countries in 1966.) The hope was that the Africans would screen innocuous Canadian films. This fundamental difference in perspective between the Film Board and External Affairs was to bring more grief.

The end of an era: Juneau and Roberge leave the Film Board

Guy Roberge, Pierre Juneau, and Grant McLean had faced a variety of obstacles nonstop since 1960, both inside and outside the agency. The struggles with External Affairs

over *Bethune* notwithstanding, from a global point of view they could claim more success than failure. Roberge had served both Liberal and Conservative governments without being partisan, had weathered austerity with finesse, and had started the mechanism to create the CFDC, a $10 million fund for private industry to forge a feature-film industry. Perhaps most significantly, he had cushioned the blow for *québécois* nationalism within the agency without creating martyrs. He did not tell anyone, but after nine years, he was ready for a change.

For Juneau, the near decade-long battle to separate production into linguistic components was a major accomplishment, though, in spite of protests, the division of production money was still roughly two-thirds English, one-third French at the end of 1965. He had seen French Production manifest a stronger proclivity toward feature than documentary, and his firm hand had tried to steer the eager neophytes toward a disciplined approach to their craft at a time when there was a profound sense of change gripping Quebec and Canadian society.

Juneau had been with the Film Board for seventeen years and was looking for new endeavours to challenge his leadership abilities in the field of communications. A tough-minded, fair, and respected Grant McLean, having inherited the mantle from Mulholland, had expanded production staff and, in response to the English side's impatience with the senior executive producers, had brought about the beginning of democratization of programming for better or for worse. He realized that the documentary no longer enjoyed its former, almost impregnable, position as a medium for the recording and interpretation of contemporary reality. It was true that the Film Board was concerning itself more and more with subject matter that was peripheral to the main issues of Canadian life 'because of Government pressure to avoid the unfamiliar, the unpleasant and the controversial.' It concerned McLean that the fundamental purposes of the agency were 'taking second place, if that, to the personal ambitions and desires of a few filmmakers.'[66] None the less, Juneau hoped that the creative talent would prove the impossible, and join discipline to freedom. Many believed that, McLean's unilingualism aside, he had the inside track to the commissioner's post, due to be filled in May 1967. He was a strong believer in the Grierson documentary tradition of making informational film in the national interest, yet had proved flexible enough to give the creative staff sufficient aesthetic freedom.

All bets were off, however, when early in 1966, Juneau, then Roberge, left in quick succession. The new secretary of state, Judy LaMarsh, had become minister in December when Pearson cast aside Lamontagne after the 'furniture scandal.' As a lifelong indefatigable and outspoken Liberal party workhorse, LaMarsh had been minister of health and welfare in the Pearson government. She had left that portfolio reluctantly because Pearson wanted someone less abrasive to bring in national medicare. (She called her successor there 'lazy' and a man 'who wouldn't do what was necessary.')[67] Anxious to keep her out of the firing line, Pearson offered her the secretary of state portfolio because someone energetic was needed to deal with broadcasting politics and the coming Centennial. LaMarsh was looking for a French-Canadian vice-chairman to sit on the Board of Broadcast Governors, a body that would soon become the Canadian Radio-television Commission (CRTC). She asked Roberge, whose easy manner and good relationship with his staff had impressed her on her visit to Film Board headquarters. Pearson had praised Roberge as the most able of public servants and said that J.W. Pickersgill was his number-one fan. But Pickersgill persuaded Roberge to wait – he told him his talents were too great to accept the post as vice-chairman. In fact, Roberge was hoping to head the CBC.

LaMarsh was still without a vice-chairman. Jean Marchand or Pierre Elliott Trudeau suggested she interview Pierre Juneau. She found him a little inflexible, but young and tough-minded, extremely capable, ambitious, and hard-working. He agreed to try and, if it worked out, to become chairman of the new CRTC. Juneau left the Film Board in March and continued his distinguished career in Canadian communications at the CRTC and, later, as president of the CBC.

On the heels of Juneau's departure, a number of filmmakers in French Production appealed to Roberge to loosen Juneau's tight organizational strings and to establish better communication within that branch. Official collective bargaining in the public service was only a year away; already many English and French filmmakers had affiliated with the newly named union, Le Syndicat général des cinéastes et techniciens. French Production saw how English Production had 'democratized' its programming and began agitating for their own separate production and programming committee to advise the director of French Production. Roberge agreed to create two positions of Assistant Government Film Commissioner (Grant McLean and Roland Ladouceur) as well as two Directors of Production, English and French (Julian Biggs and Marcel Martin).

Roberge's magnanimous accommodation could have been linked to a secret he let out at the last moment. He gave one month's notice of his intention to resign. Effective 1 April he was to become the agent general for Quebec in the United Kingdom. He had not been offered the presidency of the CBC, so he decided to accept Quebec Premier Jean Lesage's offer to go to London as Quebec's 'ambassador,' replacing Hugues Lapointe, whom Pearson wanted as lieutenant-governor of Quebec. Soon, however, Lesage's government was defeated, and Roberge accommodated himself to serving the Union Nationale regimes of Daniel Johnson and Jean-Jacques Bertrand, then the Liberal government of Robert Bourassa. He stayed in England until 1972.[68]

Upon resigning, Roberge informed the

board of governors that it would be inappropriate for him to participate in the selection of a successor.[69] Besides, the government had always gone to 'outsiders' to fill the film commissioner's position. It may have been a fortuitous time for the genial diplomatist to leave; tensions in Quebec were not easing. He had been lucky to be film commissioner when expectations were rising, and the agency was settling into a new home. With good reason had these been the 'golden years,' when a new generation of filmmakers learned their craft in an expansive atmosphere, tinged with a radical urge to challenge everything.

Roberge's great strength was that he had been a natural conciliator; yet that very quality had made it difficult for him to enunciate a mission for the Film Board. He had often called the Film Board a microcosm of Canada; perhaps his greatest contribution was making that a fact. The explosion occurring in Quebec was not so much that of mailboxes, but of folk singers and of film.[70] The Film Board was a laboratory that experienced the selfsame tensions that were pulling at the national fabric. Upon leaving, and with good reason, Roberge confided to director Ronald Dick with ominous prescience, 'The two groups in this country are going to have to separate a lot more before they come together again.'[71]

Clouds Gather
above Centennial Glamour

**Holding the fort: Grant McLean,
acting film commissioner**

Roberge's sudden departure left the organization with no heir apparent, so as a stopgap measure Minister LaMarsh appointed Grant McLean the acting film commissioner. The exiting commissioner had left the organization a full plate of activity. From November 1962, preparations had been under way in Montreal to stage the 1967 world's fair, Expo 67, an extravagant spectacular that promised to be an audiovisual bonanza. The Film Board's official contribution was to be a theme pavilion and to provide one commissioned film for the Canadian pavilion. All other film needs were left to the commercial industry to furnish. At least twenty-five pavilions would need films and equipment, not to mention the great number of related audiovisual demands that were bound to arise as sixty-two countries put their exhibits together.

The commissioner had meant Expo 67 to be a boon to Canadian companies and he facilitated this goal by persuading the organizers to let the various producers determine architectural designs. Thus the shows within, not the buildings themselves, were the centre-pieces of every exhibit, and the participants appreciated ground rules that urged them, 'Think big and use your imagination.'[1] Roberge had made things easier by offering the Film Board's advanced 35-mm colour film laboratory facilities to the private producers for all their processing; producers could then bill their sponsors for costs, adding a small mark-up for themselves. The arrangement pleased almost everyone, except those at the Film Board who thought that the Expo activity was an excuse to lock the institution into sponsored films. The great expansion of staff from 1964 conditioned many to expect that the frantic volume of private-sector activity would continue unabated after Expo was over, along with ongoing contracts for Ottawa's sponsored films.[2]

In light of this increased activity, when Grant McLean first met the board of governors in his new official capacity, he projected a five-year budgetary forecast of increasing expenditures (from $7.5 million and 997 staff in 1966–7 to $10.8 million and 1,145 staff in 1970–1) – a 42 per cent budget rise, complemented by a 15 per cent increase in staff, almost all on the English side. The figures were a perfect reflection of the era's cult of rising expectations. The greatest irony was that expansion was predicated upon doing more sponsored film work, an onus that most filmmakers hoped to shun. Current projections showed such a heavy load of sponsored films that the work could not possibly be completed unless more full-time staff were hired.[3] This became the basis for later charges that McLean was an empire-builder on behalf of English production. Further, in what seemed like approval of the agency's widening girth, the Treasury Board signalled a go-ahead for construction of a new building in Montreal to adjoin the existing plant.

McLean's other agenda item was the coming year's production activity. When the board of governors looked at the fifty-seven original titles planned, they were aghast and dismayed. Members complained that the ideas were confusing, vague, and often lacked definition. They did not state for the record which specific film ideas they disliked, but a glimpse at several titles and descriptions might help explain their anxiety:

Reality and Illusion – To explore the realms of psychology in an animation film.
Prime Time – A comedy spoofing television-watching habits.
Essai à la mille – Experimental film with the 1,000-mm lens.
Ciné crime – A story in motion using a series of very short flashes as the only clues to direct the imagination.
Situation canadienne – A study of the content of the Film Board's production programme and its relation with the various aspects of the Canadian situation.
General Strike – Conditions leading to the General Strike of 1919 and its impact on Canadian labour.
French Canada Interpretation – Analysis of current Quebec attitudes in terms of history.
A Problem of Conscience – To raise questions and stimulate discussions of honesty in the twentieth century.[4]

The filmmakers seemed unconcerned by the board members' reactions, which they considered an intrusion. Like it or not, they assumed that by accepting reorganization in 1964, the board of governors had abrogated

Grant McLean, director of English Production (1957–66) and acting film commissioner (1966–7)

its programming prerogatives, and it was too late for it to get back into the programming process. The entire institution blithely ignored external forces that were martialling against it.

Fallout from the Sheppard report

Back in July 1965, Secretary of State Lamontagne had asked independent film producer Gordon Sheppard to undertake a review of Ottawa's support of cultural policy. When finished, Sheppard's Special Report on the Cultural Policy and Activities of the Government of Canada, 1965–6, savaged the Film Board. If he believed the federal government should 'become the public entrepreneur with national, cultural dreams for sale,' the Film Board's role was peripheral. He mourned that where once there was greatness, now there was confusion, stumbling, and overcapacity. He attacked the prevailing interest in aesthetics and 'cultural films' over 'information films' and bemoaned the fact that the agency no longer considered production of films for government departments and agencies as its first task.

To better assist the development of the Canadian private film industry, Sheppard called for a drastic reduction in Film Board production; it should, he believed, 'gradually cease to staff-produce most of its films and instead have the majority of them made by private Canadian producers and freelancers on contract.' Its distribution, technical, and laboratory facilities should stay intact to serve the commercial producers. He suggested that production personnel be located in Montreal, Vancouver, Winnipeg, Toronto, and Halifax to supervise Film Board films produced by private companies there. The Film Board's exclusive domain would be experimental films. Here lay the genesis of a policy that would take two decades to be realized in its broadest form.

Sheppard's point was that the choice lay between having a strong public film industry or a strong commercial film industry; it was impossible to have both. The Film Board insisted that both were possible and angrily rebutted his unsupported statements and contradictions. It was easy to charge Sheppard with feathering his own nest as a commercial film producer.[5] But Sheppard's was not a voice in the wilderness. The Canadian commercial interests were determined to lobby until they found a responsive government prepared to nurture the private sector. From this point, the Film Board became accustomed to assuming a permanently defensive posture vis-à-vis justifying its existence. Somehow, it needed to carve out a new philosophy, though what it was to be was beyond anyone's ability to articulate.

The 'hidden agenda' in the Sheppard report was its means of dealing with the full unionization of the public sector, expected to follow in 1967. Since the Civil Service Act of 1961, the costs of job classification (promotion) and job security had escalated sharply. The price tag for collective bargaining was going to burgeon as salaries and fringe benefits were to consume a larger share of the annual budget and make a mockery of budget forecasting. The carrot that Sheppard was dangling was a means to get the Film Board out of an increasingly deepening money pit.

But this was an expansive and expensive era of optimism. If Sheppard offered a way to get rid of what the more cynical were calling 'the pensionable anarchists,' there was universal aversion within government to throttling the agency. Cut-backs would fly in the face of the 70,000-person increase in public-service employees from 1960 to 1968, which Nicole Morgan has identified as the Great Euphoria (followed by the threat of Implosion, a violent inward collapse, menacing the present era).[6] Some hoped there might be another way of blunting the full impact of unionization. In 1965, Roberge had been able to convince the Treasury Board to treat the Film Board as a 'separate employer' under the proposed Public Service Staff Relations Act.[7] The truth was that no one could predict the outcome of public-sector unionization, either monetarily or in terms of changed labour relations.

The Sheppard report had one salutary effect – it momentarily drew External Affairs close to the Film Board. Officials in Ottawa identified Sheppard as irresponsible and out to serve his own interests. Forgetting recent unpleasantries over the *Bethune* film, the department described the Film Board as a bridge-building institution, rendering essential information and educational and cultural services to the entire country. By defining and heightening Canada's image abroad, it was playing an indispensable part in the information work of Canada's diplomatic and trade posts.[8] With such powerful support, many concluded that the Sheppard report had failed to move the government. In the long run, however, External Affairs reconsidered and then abandoned its generous position. Sheppard's arguments lay at the foundation of subsequent federal policies concerning the Film Board.

Re-enter John Grierson: The father assesses the offspring

There had been infrequent reference to setting up a Film Training Centre since External

Affairs had backed the idea of training foreigners in 1963. Sheppard suggested a National Cinema School to train personnel for the private film industry. It was also a way to rationalize the Film Board's haphazard and inequitable hiring practices, where quick necessity, the old-boy network, geographical good fortune, and luck determined who was hired.[9] The whole scheme derailed, however, when the Treasury Board demurred.[10]

In 1966 the Treasury Board not only refused the institution's request for an increase, but also reduced the budget to $8.5 million from $8.9 million. The under-secretary of state, C.G.E. Steele, told Acting Commissioner McLean to prepare the higher budget, with hopes that the Treasury Board would yield.[11] It was a dangerous economic gamble that could (and did) boomerang. Meanwhile, in the absence of a Film Board mission statement, some government mandarins raised the policy issue of the role of the organization in light of Ottawa's intention to support the Canadian Film Development Corporation.

Their queries probably spurred McLean to invite John Grierson to survey the possibility of establishing the Film Training Centre. The old Scot plunged energetically into the task of examining his twenty-seven-year-old offspring and submitted his findings as a confidential report. His was probably the most perceptive analysis of the Film Board of the era, and had his admonitions received widespread circulation, much future damage might have been avoided.

Not surprisingly, he opposed a scholastic approach to the Film Training Centre because he believed that the organization was 'primarily a national information service and it is as such that it has most to teach.' He was adamant in his opposition to those creative workers who insisted upon total freedom. It was a dangerous tendency to claim to be an artist and to be financed by the state ad infinitum, since one good school of art after another had been wiped out through

such arrangements. 'Some of the very nicest films can be naive not to say ignorant and even illiterate,' was his harsh judgment. He admonished that Parliament had never thought that it was creating a body for the pursuit of strictly personal conceits; such a venture was a recurrent exercise in division and deviation. A national information service had an obligation to teach about the combination of public duty and aesthetic expression.

Grierson was not opposed to aesthetics, but they had to occur within the responsible framework of public information, which was where the government departments had their role. It was vitally important to re-establish a constructive relationship with them. Traditionally, the unique relationship with community groups and specialized audiences had been a great strength. Surprisingly, Grierson cautioned against continuing non-theatrical film, because it encouraged an over-subjective approach to filmmaking, even tempting filmmakers to opt out of their larger duties. 'At its worst, it breeds an amateur and not a professional approach,' he warned. His cautionary words were lost in the wind as the institution continued pouring resources into non-theatrical productions.

Grierson believed that animation was a field the agency could undertake with confidence to become a centre of instruction of international importance. Perhaps he spent too little space on this item; given the great prestige they have brought to the Film Board, the English and French animation departments were, and still are, taken for granted and are relatively neglected financially compared to other film areas.

He thought the Film Board was close to overextending its talents in unimportant areas like the feature film. Features should not be encouraged, he cautioned, unless they came from specific requests with guaranteed distribution, as with the CBC. The feature was a gamble on a long shot, and Grierson thought it was unfair to ask a minister to defend a long shot in Parliament.

He agreed that the private sector should get a larger slice of the national production fund. Alliances with other interests like the soon-to-be-born Canadian Film Development Corporation should be pursued too, since the Film Board needed more friends. (Later, for all intents and purposes, the CFDC froze the institution out.)

From another perspective, it seemed that Grierson envisioned the training centre as a means for the Film Board to undergo rebirth. He supported the Film Training Centre if External Affairs did and recommended that the institution should, if necessary, cut production in order to free up creative teaching talent. Management may have understood his point about relaunching the organization, but would this scheme be enough? The unspoken strategic goal was that if McLean followed Grierson's recommendations, he might rein in the programming and production committees and the pool system itself, without appearing to make a declaration of war.[12]

Grierson had understood that for any organization to remain vital and creative, a managed, periodic rebirth is essential. Ten years after the move to Montreal, he thought the Film Training Centre would be the vehicle of reinvigoration. If the scheme's hidden objective was to allow the agency to dismiss the superfluous 'second-rate' filmmakers, in the long run the first-rate Canadian graduates of the Film Training Centre would become the creative core of a rejuvenated Film Board. The only inexplicable blind side to the review was the old master's failure to address the difficult perennial 'French question' and French Production's quest for complete freedom of expression. He was not alone in this regard.

Grierson's support of the Film Training Centre notwithstanding, the plan to rededicate the Film Board was stillborn on two accounts. External Affairs learned from a number of Caribbean countries that the proposal was a low-priority item for them and, secondly, McLean failed to become commissioner. If there was a recognized need to redefine the organization's mandate, there was as yet nobody on the inside with the will to do so.

Judy LaMarsh: An enigma to herself

Another major problem was Minister Judy LaMarsh, whose standing in the government was slipping because of a tendency to speak her mind publicly. She was more honest than mischievous; but in politics, honesty can cause embarrassment, as she learned when she both mishandled the new Broadcasting Act and criticized the 'rotten management' at the CBC. Her incaution applied to the Film Board too, when, in a press interview in September 1966, she implied she was going to alter its operations radically.

LaMarsh said that the institution might be quitting production of long documentary features like *Nobody Waved Goodbye*, to which she referred hazily as 'long shorts sort of thing.' Unmindful of the Sheppard report, she suggested that the Film Board stick strictly to sponsored films, although she also expressed interest in the Film Training Centre idea that Grierson was currently studying. Did this mean no more features, co-productions with the CBC, or animation shorts? She backtracked and claimed she was in the process of trying to figure out what the agency's role should be.

In June 1966 she had tabled in the Commons the long-delayed Canadian Film Development Corporation bill. She did not know when the government would act on it, but she believed the commercial film producers who told her the ten-million-dollar fund would generate three dollars for every on invested; distributors promised her that they would distribute Canadian films if they were good. She stated that there was 'no point in producing some great artistic success which is a commercial flop ... The Film Board can make that kind of thing for its obvious merit.' When she was asked if artistic merit and lack of marketability went hand in hand, she answered, 'Not necessarily, but almost inevitably.' To compound these faux pas, she claimed she never went to the movies.[13]

The interview caused a panic at the Film Board. LaMarsh wrote to McLean and recanted, claiming that she did not want a lessened role for the organization. She promised to avoid a policy that would alter and curtail operations radically. Such policy-making was the function of the institution itself, whose recommendations she sought before making policy decisions. She then confirmed that she was still a strong supporter of Film Board work, which she considered very important in the fostering of 'Canadianness.'[14] She might have added that she had put her signature to McLean's request for a $2.27 million increase for the 1967–8 fiscal year, the first of a proposed $15 million five-year increase in total outlay. The Pearson government, nervous about skyrocketing government expenditures, then decided as a matter of policy to ask all its ministers and their deputies of cut budgets. LaMarsh left the country for a period, and it was at this point that the under-secretary of state told McLean to gamble and prepare the larger budget.[15]

Meanwhile, the minister stalled about choosing a new film commissioner. The board of governors was puzzled at her inaccessibility. Her reasons had nothing to do with the Film Board – she was being frozen out of the Cabinet's Committee on Broadcasting, which Prime Minister Pearson took a personal interest in chairing. He worked through her deputy minister and told him to tell her nothing. Soon she felt she was being undermined at every turn by the prime minister.[16] At one cabinet meeting, the querulous LaMarsh flew into a rage at J.W. Pickersgill when he corrected her on a point of law: she

was a lawyer, but he had written the law. As she stormed out, she uttered an insult and hurled a notebook at him, narrowly missing his head. Another minister grumbled chauvinistically that what she needed was a husband. An uncharitable Pearson muttered angrily, 'Be sure to put me at the bottom of the list.' In her last months as secretary of state, a colleague confirmed that Pearson considered her 'the enemy.' If LaMarsh was an enigma to her associates, she was also an enigma to herself.[17]

Her biggest public gaffes were over the CBC, which she claimed suffered from 'rotten management,' after there had occurred a national uproar over the show 'This Hour Has Seven Days.' LaMarsh became estranged from CBC President Alphonse Ouimet and began a long search for new management there.[18] While this issue was undecided, she stalled on the appointment of a Film Board commissioner.[19] She was unavailable consistently to McLean, who began to think of her as a 'flighty figure.'

LaMarsh would not be bulldozed. Grierson was asked for his advice, and he favoured McLean. Nevertheless he warned that McLean was an empire-builder with a devotion to size, and might therefore not be good at establishing the necessary outside alliances. The French press had been giving him a bad time, which might or might not continue if he were appointed commissioner. The only other possibility, Grierson concluded, was Sydney Newman, whose fault lay in having been out of the country for so long. Any outside candidate, he advised, should be 'above all someone who presents an image not only of a decent public career but of an established notable dedication to the public cause.'[20] The minister continued to dally; McLean left on a brief winter visit to study the Australian Film Board.

At the crossroads?

The impasse continued. Montreal's *La*

Presse complained of the apparent drift at the ministerial level and explained that the appointment of a Film Board commissioner was a thorn in the minister's side while she dealt with the problem of presidential succession at the CBC.[21] By spring, her under-secretary recommended that she consider resolving the Film Board issue without regard to the more perplexing CBC appointment.[22]

Meanwhile, Assistant Commissioner Roland Ladouceur went public with an unauthorized statement: the Film Board was at a crossroads, faced with a wide range of choices it was unable to take up. Unless it expanded enormously (which it did not wish to do), it must limit its interests. The choices were to pursue features, to make angry social documentaries, or to aim at educational audiences. He was upset that the organization was just marking time, waiting for someone to chair the soul-searching discussions.[23]

One of the 'crossroads' issues was the future of departmental sponsored films, which the Film Board assumed was its natural and increasing bounty. This, after all, was the reason for the spate of hiring that had occurred since 1964 in anticipation of the Centennial and Expo 67. The spending 'potlatch' had led the Pearson government to signal departments in 1966 to cut back on budgets in the coming year. If there were retrenchment, the first area to feel the pinch would be the 'frill' of sponsored films, many of which sprang to life in the last days of a fiscal year as departments stampeded to spend remaining budgets. Few at the Film Board seemed to realize that the approaching cuts might have a formidable impact.

Related to this was the organization's continuing reluctance to tender out departmental sponsored work to the commercial film industry. The private sector was busy enough enjoying the prosperity of work for the 1967 festivities, so they hardly complained about the meagre departmental contracts they had received. The trouble began after the party was over, when Film Board economics dictated that the institution could not yield to the private sector much of the multimillion-dollar annual departmental sponsored work because it was needed to pay the rent.[24] Thus, the crossroads' decision to keep most sponsored films 'in house' meant that, theoretically, the increased number of production staff would be kept busy after the extravaganzas of 1967 were over. In making this decision, McLean seemed to have forgotten Grierson's recommendation that he build alliances with commercial interests. The irony was that the majority of filmmakers felt such antipathy toward sponsored films that they considered being assigned one a form of penalty.

While the Film Board had remained headless in 1966, the CBC chose this inopportune moment to consider its existing Film Board contracts anachronistic and unsatisfactory; it decided unilaterally to terminate them. For the past decade, English Production had been furnishing the CBC with forty half-hour films per year; in 1966, this total had declined to thirteen half-hour and five one-hour films, to be supplemented by two moderately priced, colour feature co-productions. The Film Board also liked the co-production idea, since it promised to leave the institution enough money to continue making short films. CBC management believed that in the long run, however, the Film Board should become a service agency for CBC Public Affairs, which, as the legally responsible broadcaster, would exercise editorial control. Predictably, the Film Board rejected this diminution of its status.[25]

The CBC was also unhappy with the Film Board's reiteration of a policy of 'no commercials' during the broadcasting of its films.[26] Relations grew more icy when the CBC learned that the Film Board had given the commercial network a half-hour film for $800, while the CBC had been paying them $10,000 and $15,000 per half-hour of black and white and colour respectively.[27] The Film Board was about to lose its main television outlet and major audience, but few inside seemed to be concerned. Instead, English Production's filmmakers continued to wax enthusiastic about feature-length dramatic films. By early 1967, the first two co-productions were being completed, *The Ernie Game* ($321,000) and *Waiting for Caroline* ($516,000). After final costs exceeded budget, the first by $50,000 and the second by $200,000, the CBC began to wonder about the merits of co-productions.

Some months later, *Maclean's* magazine heralded the telecast of *The Ernie Game* as the 'best fiction movie Canada ever made.' Billed as a mid-winter romantic feature set in Montreal, it was the story of an alienated youth on his own, who acted as if life was little more than a lark. It was passable fare, directed by the Film Board's own flamboyant enfant terrible, Don Owen, even if it was derivative of the superior British feature *Alfie*. In a virtual replay of public remarks about *Nobody Waved Goodbye*, Owen insisted that, as a dedicated artist, he had to fight the insensitive Film Board bureaucracy to get it made. The respected Toronto critic Gerald Pratley savaged the film as 'an utter failure,' and predicted correctly that Owen's unfortunate public utterances would be seized upon by that sizeable element who had no great desire to see Canadian movies made, to trounce the two agencies as wasters of the taxpayers' money.[28] Angry Film Board managers made sure that *The Ernie Game* was the last major work Owen did for NFB.[29] Only five negative letters arrived on Minister LaMarsh's desk, making it difficult to know what the public response actually was. Her defence was that the film was the sole responsibility of management, not the government, and besides, her own personal reaction was 'very favourable.'[30]

Waiting for Caroline fared even worse. Director Ron Kelly squabbled with the producer and predicted disaster for the story about a young woman torn between two lovers, English- and French-Canadian, in Vancouver and Quebec respectively. Senator Fournier called both films indecent, immoral, and repulsive and fumed about the budget overage of more than $250,000 for both.[31] Apparently only one courageous Ottawa critic defended the films and the expenditure of tax dollars for Canadian television productions.[32]

The two co-productions led the next commissioner to promise more careful scrutiny at the supervising-producer level.[33] But for both the CBC and Film Board, the films were proof of Grierson's 1966 warning that features were a long shot that could cause the minister embarrassment. The Film Board lost both a partner and an outlet for feature co-productions as the CBC scrapped two other planned co-productions.[34]

There were altogether nine English theatrical films completed in 1966–7. One, *Helicopter Canada* ($381,640), had the unique distinction of being a sponsored film (for the Centennial Commission). It became one of the all-time top-ten favourites at home and abroad. Directed in Panavision by cameraman Eugene Boyko, with a snappy humorous narration written by Donald Brittain and Derek May, this bird's-eye view of the major land forms and cities of Canada ensures that from such a breathtaking perspective, nothing in Canada is ordinary. The narration provides several instances of a gentle self-mockery that most Canadians could embrace: Ottawa is safe from United States invasion because soldiers would get lost trying to find it; Canadians who named the over-2,000 islands in the St Lawrence the Thousand Islands did so because they were restrained and preferred understatement. West-coast weather does not escape comment either, as gorgeous footage of Vancouver is accompanied by the satiric remark, 'If and when the sun shines, it's truly the pot of gold.' *Helicopter Canada* was nominated for an Oscar and won several other awards; some might have noticed that it supported the contention that if the Film Board spent more money on fewer films, the overall benefits might be greater.

Made for the Centennial, *Helicopter Canada* (1966) is a breathtaking bird's-eye view of the major land forms and cities of Canada.

Labyrinth

Following his collaborative effort with Wolf Koenig on *Stravinsky* ($69,237) in 1965, Roman Kroitor concluded that with direct-cinema technique now being imitated at home and abroad, there was little new to discover in that genre. He, Colin Low, Wolf Koenig, and Hugh O'Connor agreed that direct cinema by definition excluded the mythic possibilities of film. A pre-existing myth seemed more attractive filmically (and less contentious nationally) than trying to develop one from Canadian history. Kroitor turned to the classic Greek legend of Theseus, who entered a labyrinth to find and kill the Minotaur, a half-man, half-bull creature that gorged itself annually on humans.

In 1963 Kroitor had developed a popular six-screen exhibit of Film Board films for the Canadian National Exhibition in Toronto, in which the screen image occupied the maximum horizontal and vertical fields of the human eye. He believed that he and his colleagues could combine these same technological ideas in presenting the famous Greek myth. Because of financial constraints, the grandiose idea went nowhere until Roberge committed the Film Board to a pavilion at Expo 67.

Then Kroitor met with Expo officials to explain his idea of this wondrous cinematic experience. The object would be to use the myth to symbolize the universality of a person's journey through the world: by confronting the legendary beast in the labyrinth he would conquer death and emerge reborn. Kroitor demonstrated how the technique might be applied with a short film called *Faces*, which used two screens side by side in interlock to show people of different cultures and nationalities in close-up. The officials responded enthusiastically and agreed to underwrite the ambitious project to be called *Labyrinth*.

In January 1964, Kroitor, Low, and O'Connor began to work on the project exclusively, with Tom Daly as the executive producer.[35] They invited the world-renowned Canadian classicist and scholar Northrop Frye to a session of 'creative tennis' to plan the scenario. Frye suggested there be seven psychological stages or steps of initiation: origins, childhood, confident youth, the desert, the battle with the dragon, death, and finally ascent or celebration through dance, all following a film structure that had a U-shaped curve. Within this U-shaped journey, there were two points of connection or recognition. The first ran from origins to death, with death as a repetition of birth; the second ran from childhood to dance and the recovery of innocence.[36] In this philosophical journey, the hero must die along with the monster he kills, a monster who is the hero's twin, symbolizing good and evil. In dying, the hero kills death and gains immortality. Through the desert, one find his way by first losing it. The twist in this film experience is to reshape the protomyth of the hero; it is not the individual hero, but society itself, that was to come into the sharpest focus. The aim of humanity is self-realization or a heightening of consciousness.

As the film possibilities began to take shape, it was obvious that the philosophic journey would have to be more felt than articulated. Architecturally, the pavilion was to contain multiple chambers with multiscreens replacing the two-dimensional format. Seven chambers were planned, through which a moving audience would realize each of the psychological stages and become aware of the paradox of *deep* past and *deep*

future as images of stone-age dance ritual contrasted with an astronaut's training ritual. But economic realities and time factors intruded; they designed instead a five-storey windowless poured-concrete building of three chambers, each relating to one aspect of 'Man the Hero.'

When the journey was realized, the visitor followed a queue of 250 at a time, entering a lobby decorated with the designs of ancient labyrinths. There, the person saw Colin Low's sculptured impression of the Minotaur and entered into a high, cathedral-like court, the Great Hall, where special lighting effects and haunting background music created an atmosphere of expectation and mystery. Elevators then distributed the visitors to one of four levels surrounding chamber I, before they were ushered into a teardrop-shaped auditorium of eight balconies on four levels on either side of the theatre. A 20-minute film presentation told of human entry into the world, childhood, and confident youth. It used the counterpoint of vertical and horizontal screens 11.3 metres in length, which forced the viewer to look alternatively from side to floor, coinciding with the 'blinkering' of human development and the tendency to see the world only in narrow and partial terms. Sound was especially important; five theatre sound systems behind the screens and 288 speakers in the balconies created a total sound environment for Eldon Rathburn's music.

The second chamber was an M-shaped maze of disorienting mirrors, prisms, and thousands of randomly flashing tiny lights, giving the confused viewer a sense of the infinity of space and evoking sensations from weightlessness to serenity. 'The Maze' was designed to symbolize the seemingly endless passages of ancient labyrinths, while the combination of music and light was to prepare the visitor for confrontation with the 'Monster' in Chamber III.

This chamber consisted of five screens four by three metres in a cruciform, almost thirteen metres wide and nine metres high, able to project in 35-mm film either a single panorama of three horizontal screens or a mixture of five interrelated compositions. The cross was meant to give reference to the tree of life, though the predominantly Christian audience would likely perceive some religious meaning.[37]

From the opening shot of hundreds of urbanites moving busily under a huge closed arcade, the viewer is made aware of the interrelatedness of humanity in the cocoon of the planet. An African, seemingly out of the Stone Age, appears on the centre screen and peers at the camera with a mixture of curiosity and incomprehension. There follows a panorama of parched desert, camels, and death, soon punctuated by a Canadian snowstorm, winter drudgery, and death. Candid shots of derelicts alternate with the desolation of the graveyard. The role of ceremony in life is stressed as various religious motifs follow, from bathing in the Ganges to African chants under the moon. An Ethiopian hunter stalks and spears a crocodile in the darkness. Death heads fill the cruciform. The film cuts to a sophisticated woman seated before a triple mirror, a section of which appears on each lateral screen. She gazes into the glass and as she wipes away her make-up, recognizes in her thrice-reflected aging countenance the flight of beauty and youth. She massages her face and holds her hands as if in prayer, with the camera close-up frozen on her sculpted fingers. From the three different angles of observation, she is an unmistakable figure of the tragic loss of youth.

From this turning point, the film plunges into death and rebirth through dance. The exquisite and breathtaking mountains of rural Crete stand as a counterpoint to extreme long shots of men at work in the fields and close-ups of playful Greek children. Then a Montreal traffic cop directs traffic as if he were choreographing a dance or directing an orchestra, followed by a ballet teacher who teaches a child a graceful pose. The scene shifts to a circus and a clown on a tightrope juggling four objects with hands

and feet. A Russian cosmonaut in training is also juggled as a rocket blasts off, while other screens are filled with natives engaged in primeval dances. Ritual is conveyed through an Eastern Orthodox baptism ceremony and a local photographer failing, then succeeding, in his portrait of a happy family. Happiness is ephemeral, as a group of tearful emigrants bids farewell to loved ones at dockside. A similar send-off occurs for the funeral of Winston Churchill, while an Eastern motif of a Buddha focuses on a man in Oriental contemplation of trees reflected in water. Faces of joy from around the world light up the cruciform as a doctor in the centre delivers a baby. A herd of horses gallops freely in the foothills of the Rocky Mountains, followed by vintage tractors on parade through an Albertan festival. Old faces are then replaced by Africans in primitive play. Saffron-robed monks proceed through columns of an Indian monastery, as the centre screen depicts the Ethiopian crocodile hunter paddling serenely downstream through verdant sun-pocked foliage. Finally, the cruciform comes alive with animated faces in communication, as a ruined column of an ancient temple occupies the central screen. The film closes with a single panorama of a sunset on the quiet waters of the sea.[38] The entire 48-minute experience has a minimal bilingual narration, written by Donald Brittain and Claude Jutra.

The crew filmed 'Stone Age' communities for their cinematic experiment in locales as remote as Ethiopia and Cambodia. Low described the shooting as deeply troubling for them, coming as they did from an advanced, wealthy, and powerful society, filming in places that seemed on the brink of disintegration. The whole experience became one of hubris; upon leaving a remote community in the corner of Crete, they learned that their guide had murdered someone in an argument over whether the Film Board had paid enough to rent the donkeys. And Hugh O'Connor, upon finishing his segment, left the Film Board to do a documentary on poverty in the Appalachians. He was shot dead on location by a seventy-year-old crank who did not want his shanties filmed.

As the project continued, footage arrived from India, Japan, Britain, the Soviet Union, the United States, and Canada; after all location work had been completed in 1965, Tom Daly turned to the Herculean year-long task of editing for multi-screens. For him, it was a near-mystical experience. The pivotal point in the film was where the sophisticated woman removed her make-up to reveal the 'real' person on whose face is etched the first hint of wrinkles. The scene was first done with an actress who could not stop acting, hence it did not work. Then a second actress tried it; she understood that, in taking off her make-up, she was supposed to reveal herself as she really was. After seven takes, the moment of truth appeared. For the viewer, it is chilling, because the artifices of theatre and cinema fall away as Mortality itself stares through the dark eyes in the mirror. Daly called the moment the most perfect-ever expression of *Candid Eye* technique.

As the deadline approached for the sponsors' screening, the film was still without a conclusion. Daly ran through every scrap of footage until he found a sequence of saffron-robed monks walking through a pillared courtyard, highlighted by natural gold light and black shadows. This had a similar texture to some unused footage of the Ethiopian crocodile hunter whose face reflected a similar light/shade aura as he made his way by boat through the trees. Daly said that conclusion was waiting to be unearthed and he attributed his discovery of the shots as proof of the mystical sense of 'wholeness' that lies at the foundation of the film experience.[39]

It is difficult to know how much of this conclusion or the philosophical journey the 1.3 million people who saw *Labyrinth* understood. The fact was that people stood in line daily that summer from one to seven hours to see it. Its single casualty was an unfortunate visitor's loss of false teeth as he/she gazed down at the giant screen. At one point,

the no longer elusive Minister LaMarsh phoned the Film Board anxiously and repeatedly to obtain VIP passes to take guests to see it. *Labyrinth* ran for 5,545 shows, some thirty per day, for six months and was one of the centrepieces of Expo 67.

A few critics noted that *Labyrinth* omitted the extreme divergences of human values, from artistic creation to the destruction of war. (Vietnam was raging on television and in the public's consciousness at this time.)[40] The overall emphasis was to make reference to human similarity rather than to the vital factors that divide people. The filmmakers chose the images to reflect varieties of human happiness connected to the centrality of a newborn infant. It was the Unit B philosophy of 'wholeness' yet again, a tradition in search of unifying, non-confrontational traits; here it affirmed the universal desire for joy and well-being. If it was a form of cultivated innocence, the experience for audiences was like any profound event, exhilarating emotionally, whether understood intellectually or not.

The impact of *Labyrinth*: Pros and cons

One beneficial development that derived from the lavish ($4.5 million) *Labyrinth* was the positive international press reaction, which gave new stature to the professional film industry in Canada. The *New York Times* praised *Labyrinth* as unique, 'as special to Expo 67 as the Eiffel Tower was to the Paris Exposition of 1889,' while *Film Quarterly* referred to it as 'the most ambitious architectural-film relationship of all ... a dazzling vision.'[41] From this fulsome publicity, many creative and technical people from the Film Board were now sought out for large projects in other countries. In Canada, their professional experience was applied to a host of cultural activities in universities, museums, and performing-arts centres.

Perhaps the most significant spin-off of *Labyrinth* was the birth of one of the most spectacular and original expressions of film

Labyrinth symbolizes humanity's journey through the world. In this chamber of the Labyrinth pavilion at Expo 67, an image of father and infant fills the sight-lines of the 250 audience members standing on eight tiered balconies. This concept gave birth to one of the most spectacular and original expressions of film presentation in this century, IMAX.

presentation this century, IMAX. Japan, which was to host the World Exposition in Osaka in 1970, had sent observers to see *Labyrinth*, and on the strength of their enthusiasm, the organizers invited Low as designer-adviser, Kroitor as producer, and Donald Brittain as director to undertake a film for the Osaka exhibition. *Labyrinth* had demonstrated that if an image filled the maximum horizontal and vertical fields of the human eyes, the impact on the audience was complete. The use of a group of images on the same screen increased the density of information, yet kept the viewers' attention from flagging. It had proved awkward technically to use multiple cameras and projectors; what was needed was a single piece of equipment and film to achieve this effect. This challenge spurred Graeme Ferguson, Roman Kroitor, and Robert Kerr to begin work on a new camera/projector system as a private-enterprise initiative. Mechanical engineer William Shaw joined them to design and build a totally new projector to handle a 70-mm film with nearly four times the normal number of sprocket holes per frame and to develop a high-intensity light source able to illuminate a screen nineteen metres across by twelve metres high. Two years of experiment and struggle led to the stunning launch of *Tiger Child* at Osaka, in 1970. From then on, the IMAX Systems Corporation began to sell the large-screen system for conventional theatre designs, then added OMNIMAX installations to domed theatres. The installations of the company continue to proliferate around the world. Colin Low became enamoured with the possibilities of 3-D in this format and directed a Canadian National–sponsored Film Board production, *Transitions*, on the theme of transportation and communication, for IMAX projection at Expo 86 in Vancouver. Of the process, Low has commented that the joining of 3-D to IMAX has restored intimacy to the big screen. His conviction is that this is the direction the film medium will take into the next century.[42] IMAX may become a principal outlet for future 'prestige' projects of the Film Board like *Labyrinth*.

There was perhaps one unfortunate effect of the success of *Labyrinth*. The vital creative energies of Kroitor, Low, and Daly were removed from English Production at precisely the time they were needed most, from mid-1964 to 1967. Years later Grant McLean wondered if *Labyrinth* was not a poor precedent because it diverted the Film Board away from its original task, to make films in the national interest.[43]

His may have been an unnecessarily harsh assessment, but there was much frustration as he tried to rally the staff in 1966 to generate enthusiasm for the 'films relevant to the burning issues and questions of our day; films about what is coming into being rather than what is going out of currency, films that will be more and more relevant to their audiences as time goes by ... We can maintain our impact only by excellence, and pointedness, and by winning the attention of the leaders in the fields we touch ... To reach the eye and the ear is not enough. Let us try always to go further and deeper, to reach the brain, the heart and the solar plexus.'[44]

Faced with the staff's general despondency in 1966, McLean was trying his best to lead. To better connect with educators he encouraged inauguration of the Screen Education Program and Summer Research Institutes of Screen Study to explore all facets of the social impact of film and television. As for the problem of sagging morale within, there was formed a Committee of Five, comprising Kroitor, John Spotton, Tom Daly, Donald Brittain, and Frank Spiller, to recommend changes to the 'pool' system. They found that enthusiasm had plummeted, there was less efficiency, and there was no sense of home or of belonging either inside the Film Board or outside, where the cultural isolation of English Quebec was profound. They suggested a number of palliatives, including a reduction in the number of productions, a better attitude to sponsored films, and a lessening of the power of directors. The committee confessed that the equilibrium that had once existed between utilitarian and interpretive films had been lost.[45] They bemoaned the tendency of filmmakers, directors, and producers to feel that after a certain point they had 'arrived' and their word was law.[46]

But English Production was not about to change. The arguments shifted back to the sponsored-film problem. 'Directors do not want to work on sponsored films,' went one theme, 'because many of the subjects are so poor.' 'Blame it on the Ottawa Liaison Officers,' cried another. But others contended that the Film Board itself was more negative about sponsored film than about the sponsor. In a backhanded reference to French Production, which was notorious for its avoidance of sponsored work, the complaint was that only some were getting the desserts while others were served up meat and potatoes.

The verbiage was dizzying, and few cared to be reminded that one-third of the annual budget, or $3.25 million, was from the sponsored work.[47] The problem was how to find a method of assigning directors to do sponsored films, in light of the coordinating producer's role as 'marriage counsellor' rather than tyrant. Perhaps director Peter Pearson put it at its blunt best when he agreed, 'To work here, that [making sponsored films] is part of the nut. The incentive is that you are given employment here. If you don't want to do that, you don't have to work here.'[48]

A glance at production statistics for the year ending 31 March 1967 demonstrates the extent of Film Board activity.[49] The list of 107 sponsored films made for various departments in 1966–7 (see Appendix 2) might demonstrate why there was such widespread hostility to them. These films may prove to be of more interest to future social scientists trying to grasp the priorities, flavour, and tempo of the era than they were to the filmmakers who referred to them as 'nuts and bolts' or 'punishment.'

Professor at the helm

By April 1967 Grant McLean learned that the minister had passed him over, and that his days as acting film commissioner were num-

bered. He never knew why, though he might have speculated on several obvious reasons. First, the commercial-film producers felt slighted and angry because he was the obstacle between themselves the multi-million-dollar sponsored-film bonanza. Since the Sheppard report, their lobby had grown stronger. Further, if either of the two strongest voices on the board of governors, R. Gordon Robertson, clerk of the Privy Council, and Marcel Cadieux, the under-secretary of state for external affairs, thought McLean was unsuitable, the candidacy would probably have gone no further. Given External Affairs concern over the *Bethune* distribution case and McLean's passionate attack on that department, he was not likely on the inside track to the commissioner's post. Also, his unilingualism was totally out of step with current government bilingualism policy, and the French side at the Film Board could be expected to make much of this flaw if he were appointed. Finally, LaMarsh was known to operate on her visceral reaction to personalities, and she had not been responsive to McLean.

She decided in favour of Hugo McPherson, a professor of English at the University of Western Ontario, whose nomination was accompanied with the words 'highly photogenic.' The appointment was greeted with consternation at the Film Board, as people wondered what political connection had led to McPherson's elevation. It did not take long to learn that there was none, which later proved to be his largest liability. Board member Phyllis Grosskurth had recommended him; her office had been near his when he taught briefly at the University of Toronto. McPherson was interested in mass media and, like so many of the day, was a recent convert to the glib gospel of Marshall McLuhan, which he had articulated eloquently to members of the board during his job interview.[50]

Toronto critic Nathan Cohen noted that McPherson had been known for his diligence, earnestness, and writing ability, but had always been strangely indifferent to

films, as witnessed when he was host of
CJBC Views the Shows. Cohen remarked
that nothing in his background suggested he
was qualified to cope with the many sensitive
problems of administration and French-English relations. He warned that there was
nothing in McPherson's past to evoke ela-
tion, and the onus was on him to prove his
appointment was not a sorry mistake.[51] It
was an inauspicious presentiment, one that
had been voiced almost exactly by ex–Film
Commissioner A.W. Trueman.

The intrepid McPherson saw the challenge
as an immense opportunity to be in charge of
one of the major cultural forces in Canadian
life. He thought he was better educated about
the arts in Canada than almost anyone else.
In one of his earliest pronouncements, he
vowed that the Film Board would remain
'right on the frontiers of communications ...
We don't want to wait for some American
magazine to tell us what is happening.' As to
'crossroads' decisions like whether to concentrate on Canadian or foreign distribution,
to specialize in documentaries or theatrical
features, he indicated that a much more open
distribution into theatres was of first importance. The only clue he gave about personal
preference was his praise of the documentary
The Things I Cannot Change and experimental abstract animations.[52]

Privately, he felt that if French Production
were not brought up to parity with English
Production, it might become a lost sister in
the organization. 'Parity' was a word that
would come to haunt him. His spoken
French was passable and he tried to befriend
and seek the opinions of Marcel Martin and
Jacques Godbout, two influential persons on
the French side. Soon he prided himself on
his good relations with them, but because
they saw him as a man of letters rather than
of film, they never placed much confidence
in him.

McPherson's was an inauspicious beginning, when on a hot July night, a fire erupted
at the Film Board's archival film depository,
a metal-sided rickety structure in Kirkland,

Quebec. The building was filled with the
highly flammable early nitrate film, as well as
the currently used 'safety film.' For years
there had been warnings that unless the nitrate film was transferred to safety stock and
stored properly in vaults, there would be a
terrible spontaneous combustion and con-
flagration that would consume everything.
Nothing had been done. When the fire occurred, 13.1 million metres or 2,150 titles,
mostly from 1940 to 1952, went up in smoke.
Luckily, the depository contained no master
films (they were kept in the Film Board's
vaults), so the loss was not as grave as it
might have been, though the films' market
value was a hefty $4.8 million.[53] Years of
sheer inertia had led to this decidedly poor
way to resolve the problem of what to do with
old films.

The senior ranks began to empty on the
heels of McPherson telling the board of governors in the same month that he intended to
reorganize the senior level as part of a plan to
reassess and redefine the institution's philosophy and aims. He thought that a high-
profile planning group should replace the
system of two assistant commissioners. Not
surprisingly, McLean tendered his resignation a month later.[54] The assistant commissioner's departure signalled the loss of
managerial know-how which the neophyte
McPherson needed badly. The director of
planning, Michael Spencer, also indicated he
would probably be leaving to head the new
Canadian Film Development Corporation.

Meanwhile, the commissioner learned of
the natural divisions within the organization: some filmmakers were operating on the
belief that the agency existed to enable them
to make 'mon film,' 'my personal film'; managers seemed most concerned about generating revenue to balance the budget, and people in Distribution were more concerned
with generating statistics than with questions
of audience and film impact. Specific problems needed specific answers.

McPherson chose the high road of generalization; in October he submitted an expan-

sive and optimistic statement of policy to the board of governors. He said that a communications explosion was occurring that would reshape society. Libraries would become media centres and before long, video cassettes would be available to users at low cost. He emphasized that the Film Board should be the government's premier adviser on new ideas in communications technology. He hoped Ottawa would both support and assist his organization in transferring some work to the private film industry.

Filmmaking would continue to be a basic activity, but it was in artistic and technical pioneering that the future lay. To remain a highly flexible bilingual organization, McPherson thought the bulk of the Film Board's employees should be hired on contract rather than become permanent members of the public service. The need was to bring in a fresh stream of young talent and to allow those who had made their contribution to go on to other things. Experimentation was important too, especially in areas where the private sector would not take risk. Finally, the distribution problem would be solved by finding specific audiences; film ideas might come from officers in the field, and the new concept of regional production might lighten the still-despondent creative atmosphere.

McPherson's other suggestions included helping government departments in their audiovisual needs, establishing the Film Training Centre, producing educational material for a planned educational television network, and establishing a better relationship and separate language contracts with the CBC. There was a need for a corporate image, a logo to promote the Board's image in Canada and to publicize its work. In arguing for this, McPherson revealed a guarded corporate secret: the Film Board was better known abroad than in Canada. At home, it was better known in rural areas and in schools than in large urban centres. As for the intractable sponsored-film problem, he promised he would tender an important amount of work

to private filmmakers if the government increased the Film Board's appropriation. He vowed he would try to convince the responsible people in Ottawa to provide this support, which was, in essence, a valuable indirect subsidy to the private sector.[55]

In their formal response three months later, the board of governors did not find McPherson's statement an impressive document because most of the material was derived from administration-generated background papers. Grierson had made many of these recommendations in 1966, and the search for a logo had preceded McPherson's arrival. There was a need for many of the changes proposed, but the members insisted that additional research and documentation be provided before the document went to the minister and Treasury Board. They said nothing about McPherson's plans to keep the majority of staff on contract rather than as permanent civil servants.

Their main caveat was that the document's recommendations were not within realistic economic terms. How, they wondered, was all this to occur within available budgets? McPherson had also forgotten that Film Board policy had to be consistent with the government's position. Should Ottawa, for example, compensate the organization for loss of income that would ensue if a larger proportion of the sponsored programme was directed to private industry? The board members wanted a solidly documented study to determine whether this route was economically practical. In short, the commissioner's ebullience and up-beat optimism did not impress them. They wanted medicine to cure the maladies, but were doubtful whether some of the proposed changes were economically or politically feasible. They told McPherson to revise his policy report.[56]

The members may have been cautious, but at the same October meeting, they had recklessly approved a request for a budgetary increase of $3 million over the existing $8.871 million budget, even though the

Treasury Board had recommended a total allocation of $10.2 million.[57] The free-wheeling aspect of this request became the Achilles' heel of McPherson's tenure.

In all probability, in his first months on the job, the commissioner had bitten off too much. His frenzied outside cultural activities took a physical toll, and in November, following a collapse with bronchial pneumonia, he could only work half-days. From this time on, the staff was aware that he suffered from serious health problems; this condition did not help him to weather the approaching storm of austerity.

The board of governors and film initiatives

The board of governors tried to assert its prerogative in programming in the wake of the co-production brouhahas over *The Ernie Game* and *Waiting for Caroline*. There were a number of films on the explosive subject of separatism, in both French and English, which needed careful handling. In French Production, director Pierre Perrault was already well along on his broad film about the metamorphosis of Quebec, a film about René Lévesque and the basic concerns being expressed by Quebeckers. Director of English Production Julian Biggs planned a film on the future of Confederation, whose purpose was to illuminate the fundamental attitudes and emotions in Canada and to help the English understand what was happening in French Canada. Canada's political topography had changed forever when former Quebec Liberal cabinet minister Lévesque organized the *Parti Québécois*, with intentions to democratically win independence for Quebec.

Interestingly, the board did not discuss the Perrault film but the one proposed by Biggs. Two board members opposed the polarization of the Confederation question. Gordon Robertson said he feared the dangers of ending up with an unbalanced film, while Marcel Cadieux of External Affairs wondered whether the Film Board should involve itself in a film on separatism from which more harm than good could come. He personally objected to 'any film which would enhance in any way, however small, the stature or importance of a person such as Lévesque or which would add to the influence which he is having on the country.' Cadieux wanted a written, detailed justification and plan for such a film or films.

McPherson blithely expressed complete confidence in the integrity of those who would work on the film and promised to pay close attention to its progress. Director of French Production Marcel Martin thought these films would bring to English Canada's attention the dissatisfaction of a large French-Canadian population; Biggs believed that the mere exposure of some of Lévesque's opinions might very well carry the seeds of their own destruction, as was the case with McCarthyism in the United States. Picking up on Robertson's continued expression of nervousness with the subject of separatism, the governors concluded that the subject of separation was too important and too controversial to undertake without close scrutiny. One member suggested that when the film reached the cutting-copy (semi-finished) stage, it should be shown to them. McPherson agreed quickly, though he said his concurrence was exceptional, and that it could not be regarded as a precedent.[58]

But it was a precedent. No board of governors had ever involved itself so intimately with a film in the institution's history. If McPherson thought his concession was responsible and fair, he was undermining the post of the film commissioner and casting serious doubt on his own executive ability. With this and the other films being made about the contemporary political crisis in Canada, McPherson was sowing the seeds of a bitter harvest that his successor would have to reap.

These extraordinary actions also demonstrated that if the Film Board were to become embroiled in controversies, some were more

Hugo McPherson (film commissioner 1967–70) found himself and the Film Board hamstrung by government austerity.

acceptable than others. There were those who argued later that the institution failed consistently to play a constructive role regarding the passionate subject of the future of Confederation because of a fear of alienating audiences. Perhaps this gap might also be explained by the role of non-confrontation that English filmmakers thought best reflected English Canada, while many of those French Canadians who had a position seemed to be leaning toward independence.

McPherson was probably out of sync with the board members from his first meeting. He had supported the idea of controversial films when it was felt that a statement should be made, and had supported the two proposed ideas, 'British Honduras' and 'The American Agony.' Cadieux of External Affairs took the safe route and warned that with budget restrictions imminent, other projects of higher priority might have to be post-

poned in order to proceed with the first film. 'British Honduras' was added to the production programme as a low priority and was never made. The governors had been even more uncomfortable with film ideas related to the Vietnam War, which was being branded on the national television audience's consciousness on the nightly news. They refused director Arthur Hammond's idea for a film about the way the war was dividing American society.[59]

On two later occasions, they considered and rejected another film proposal, 'Canada's Involvement in Arms Production,' which was to emphasize the implications of the Vietnam War for Canadians. One member derided the idea for its emotional and false treatment of a broad and highly complex policy problem, while another warned that there were degrees of freedom for a government agency which, if violated, might lead to a loss of freedom.[60] It took an innovative filmmaker like Michael Rubbo to figure out, in 1970, how to make a film about Vietnam without encountering these obstacles. *Sad Song of Yellow Skin* was his quiet, sensitive, and moving portrayal of the people of Saigon on the fringes of the war as seen by three American journalists.

A cloud on the horizon

On balance, Centennial Year had been kind to both the Film Board and the commercial film industry. The Expo extravaganza had allowed the agency to show off the leading edge in film technology with the fabulous *Labyrinth* pavilion, proof positive that 'experiment' was a justifiable institutional activity. Both Expo and related Centennial projects had provided private industry with several million dollars' worth of film work. But there was a worm of false hopes in the apple: the Film Board had depended on sponsored films for so much of its income that there were now dozens of new staff anticipating more work. With no indication that the government was going to be generous, the new commissioner had also signalled that he would give more of this work to the private sector, if Ottawa reimbursed his organization. This was a very large *if*.

At the same time, the public was unaware of the strain between the Film Board and the CBC; English feature co-productions had not worked well, although French features seemed to have fared much better at Radio-Canada, where there was a greater need for, and fewer sources of, film. The tension between the board of governors and the new commissioner was also inauspicious. The dissonance could be explained by the not-altogether-happy outcome of the 'pool' system programming procedures. As the governors tried to reassert control, a number of understanding filmmakers confirmed the public-service nature of their work while others were die-hard iconoclasts. On the French side, the politics of the era were inescapable, as several filmmakers tried to articulate what it was that Quebec wanted.

The Film Board also had to accept unionization, something that Guy Roberge had been instrumental in bringing to the whole federal public service. It all seemed controllable, even if the agency was not completely in control; most believed that a creative organization needs a certain amount of chaos if it is to function well. The one serious cloud on the horizon, which was turning darker as Centennial Year ended, was the cloud of fiscal austerity. Try as they might, the board of governors and management were having increased difficulty in juggling the figures. The cloud in 1967 became the storm in 1968 and 1969 that triggered a virtual internal rebellion.

7

Austerity

Neglected warnings

In July 1967 LaMarsh informed McPherson that there would probably be heavy cuts in all department spending in the coming fiscal year. The board of governors took the news somberly and anticipated that departmental sponsored films would be the first casualty. McPherson put on a brave face, hoped that this would not hamper things seriously, and allowed Distribution to add thirty-seven new employees.[1] In October, the Treasury Board recommended that expenses be kept at $10.2 million, but the commissioner pleaded with LaMarsh for special consideration. She signed a submission for $10.45 million, and he prided himself on his good relations with the minister.

LaMarsh may have been persuaded, but the Treasury Board was not. Two months later, officials there gave McPherson the bad news – the Film Board would have to live with only $10 million. The commissioner haggled and was able to squeeze out $200,000 more, to which there were strings attached: his institution would have to absorb the $147,000 in salary increases, thus the real augmentation was only $53,000. There was one note of optimism in March 1968, when the board members learned that Production's reserve of $40,000 might be increased and perhaps even be carried over to the new fiscal year.[2] They forgot about the Ides of March and were crestfallen when the govern-

ment announced austerity officially, along with a further budget reduction of 2 per cent. The Treasury Board had reneged on its December promise, and as anticipated, the area most likely to suffer was to be the sponsored film programme.[3]

Meanwhile, events moved swiftly on the national political front: Pierre Trudeau, who had entered federal politics in 1965, was catapulted into the national spotlight as one man who could answer the question 'What does Quebec want?' with a solution that fit into the federal concept of a united Canada. His coolness, intelligence, and belief in participatory democracy appealed to Canadians, who felt he could do *the* something that needed to be done to stem the tide of Quebec nationalism and separatism, which English Canada tended to see as one and the same phenomenon. Trudeau had tested the waters of Ottawa as minister of justice for a year. In 1968 he succeeded Lester Pearson as leader of the Liberal party and then became prime minister in the federal election that June. He chose Gérard Pelletier, his erstwhile co-founder of *Cité libre*, as secretary of state. In the aftermath of Canada's Centennial, it looked like there was a new and untried Liberal team in Ottawa. But there was a strong sense of continuity, and one of the new government's earliest decisions was to follow through on the previous Liberal regime's austerity programme.

McPherson scrambled to cut costs where

possible and considered closing the recently formed regional bureaus. As far back as mid-1957, Grant McLean had proposed one-man regional production offices to generate documentary subjects; Vancouver had been the first to open, in 1965.[4] Pelletier's executive assistant now told the commissioner not to close the offices and warned him that the minister wanted McPherson to consult with him before making public remarks that might prove embarrassing. It was not that Pelletier was trying to run the agency – he only wanted to know about public statements that he might be called upon to defend in the House.[5] The political neophyte McPherson took the easiest administrative option and closed all the regional offices but Vancouver. This move did not endear him to the new minister, who wanted to build a new film policy based on the 1965 Sheppard report recommendation for regionalization.

That summer, no one was sure about the institution's financial picture, except that the situation was bad and bound to get worse. This was confirmed in August, when in yet another thunderbolt, the Treasury Board required the Film Board to absorb built-in higher salary costs and warned management there would be less money from departments for sponsored films. It was not that the Treasury Board was making policy; rather, that the government had chosen the course of fiscal restraint, which Treasury Board was executing. 'Austerity' was being heard at all levels of government, and cost-cutting had replaced the free-spending ebullience of Centennial Year.

There seemed to be no other ulterior motive than the government's intention to reduce the deficit. McPherson's general manager, Gérard Bertrand, who had transferred to the Film Board from another department, tried reflecting this spirit when he suggested a new salary policy for the creative production staff: a base salary with additional sums possible, depending on factors of quality and quantity. This was the eastern European system, which encouraged excellence (and competition) among filmmakers. The board of governors dismissed the idea as premature, lest it jeopardize contract negotiations then in progress with the union.[6]

In 1966 the government had introduced a new procedure for passing the Film Board's annual appropriation. Before that, the commissioner sat informally with the minister and Treasury Board representatives to work out the budget, which was then brought before Parliament. The secretary of state found himself too burdened to continue the practice and was happy to see the Standing Committee on Broadcasting, Films and Assistance to the Arts replace it. Its members now queried the film commissioner at length before recommending approval of the annual budget. Grant McLean had been the first Film Board official to appear before this partisan body in the fall of 1966. The procedure had been a straightforward, uncomplicated affair that had allowed him to extol the Film Board's virtues.

McPherson went before the standing committee in November 1968. There were numerous critics who were anxious about the Leviathan that had been created in the name of culture. He was defensive as Member of Parliament Walter Dinsdale took up the cry of the commercial companies for more sponsored-film contracts. Dinsdale took a wider swipe, charging that the Film Board had a monopoly and acted as a propaganda agency for the government. The commissioner refrained from explaining that if he lost the sponsored films he would have to fire dozens of staff members. Instead, he defended his institution's responsible behaviour and insisted that he was not asked to do anything more than to make intelligent, responsible productions.[7]

Things became rougher when the committee reconvened in February 1969. Member of Parliament Barney Danson of the Finance, Trade and Economic Affairs Committee hammered at the economics of running agencies like the CBC and the Film Board, and underscored the dilemma caused by the bureaucratization of culture. Building centres for these agencies allowed them to develop bureaucracies, which hindered rather than helped the creative field, he complained. To illustrate, he charged that there was a tendency to hire people, and if they grew stale, they were pushed into a corner and kept on unending jobs. Meanwhile, fresh people were brought in and the process repeated itself, thereby developing a tremendous plant that had to be kept going.[8] A month later, the committee heard representatives from the commercial-film industry attack the Film Board monopoly and recommend that the organization be forced to compete for sponsored-film contracts.

These entrepreneurs had finally shaped their arguments into a coherent form by presenting two suggestions: first, that the Film Board become a centre of research and experimentation, an advanced school of filmmaking, which would allow it to produce only a small part of the government's work; and second, that the National Film Act be amended to give private agencies the right to produce government films.[9] The arguments took thirteen years to penetrate and returned as recommendations of the Federal Policy Review Committee (Applebaum-Hébert Committee), in 1982.

Another committee member claimed that the product delivered by the Film Board was too often over-budget and not exactly what a department had requested. It was convenient for him to forget that such cost overruns had brought about works of art with perennial appeal like *Fields of Sacrifice* and *Helicopter Canada*. Austerity or not, the Film Board soon established the Ottawa Services Branch to rectify these abuses. But departmental relations did not improve, and the commercial producers were still frozen out.

Austerity and the standing committee's hostility forced some hard decisions. The first and easiest was McPherson's own – he fired his chauffeur. Next, the administration decided to suspend its on-line computer facilities. In the name of efficiency, the agency was reduced to using inefficient manual statistical operations. Computer-animation, which was touted as a future technology, was

suspended, as was much of the initial work with a newly designed computer-operated animation stand. One heartbreaking result was that the institution failed to patent its computer-animation programming experiments, with the result that a New York company acquired the programmes for nothing and proceeded to apply for patents. Subsequent legal wrangling did not bring the Film Board much satisfaction. There were two successful experiments that came from the French Animation Studio, organized under René Jodoin in 1966. They were *Metadata* ($19,301) and *Hunger* ($38,893) done in 1971 and 1973 by Peter Foldès on the National Research Council's computer. Despite these successes, the window to the regular use of computer animation remained shut for another decade.

Television and video distribution were also put on hold for some years. The dream had been to make film and videotape documents available on demand to the urban population, largely via television. Similarly, discussions about the development of a videotape recording device that could play videos through any standard television set were suspended.[10] These promising technologies were still premature, although once developed by others, the video cassette replaced 16-mm film as the preferred distribution medium.

Meanwhile, the most difficult issue was how to deal with the projected $564,800 deficit brought on by austerity. One board member noted that because the government had increased parliamentary appropriations for most other cultural agencies while refusing a grant to the Film Board, they had lost confidence in them.[11] But Pelletier knew about the surplus group of English filmmakers and the thirty-seven new distribution officers. While he did not want to become involved in the 'specifics' of McPherson's problems, he knew they could be remedied.[12]

A frustrated McPherson asked Pelletier in June 1969 to let the Film Board overspend one-half million dollars in order to keep everyone employed, lest he have to reduce staff by up to 10 per cent. He promised to put into effect a three-pronged plan: to withdraw gradually from relying on earned income, to seek greater parliamentary appropriations, and to let the private sector produce, under the aegis of the Film Board, a large part of the sponsored programme.[13] There was silence from Ottawa.

Days later, the Treasury Board approved the collective agreement between the Film Board and the production employees' union, Syndicat général des cinéastes et techniciens (SGCT). The salary hike was similar to that negotiated by other public-service unions, but management was stunned to learn from the Treasury Board that the new salaries would have to come from existing funds. It was too late to turn back, and the government finalized the collective agreement. This was a historic moment, not only because it was the culmination of nearly a decade of unionization activities, but also because the government had left the Film Board to dangle in the wind to find the money to pay for the generous settlement. The hapless McPherson, having assumed all the while that the wage bill was separate from the bitter austerity medicine, concluded that Pelletier had done him in and had lied to him.

The CBC had promised greater prime-time exposure if the Film Board allowed commercials to be run with its films. Management now took the historic step, hoping thereby to increase revenue by up to $35,000 per hour.[14] Despite the concession that the Film Board's own personnel would edit the films to maintain their artistic integrity, the filmmakers were almost universally opposed to this policy, and felt that the Film Board leadership had failed them. McPherson was the unlucky pickle in the middle.

An appeal to higher authority

The commissioner liked and trusted the 'saintly' under-secretary of state (and former board member), Jules Léger, to whom he outlined a worst-case scenario: he would have to cut production staff, which would leave barely enough resources to carry on a few sponsored-film programmes, which in turn meant income would probably be reduced by one-third. If distribution staff were cut, this would also mean less income. In the final analysis, the Film Board would be less visible to Canadians.

It was bad enough that in 1969–70 the institution had received only $259,000 to cover the $1.249 million increase in salary costs brought about by collective bargaining. Now, for 1970–1, McPherson was told to prepare to absorb all the salary increases. In the face of already difficult relations with the unions, he saw no choice but to lay off 210, or 19.6 per cent, of the 1,070 employees. Austerity threatened to halt all current production and lead to a million-dollar loss. He might even have to close many of the Film Board's thirty-two distribution offices across Canada.

There were but four alternatives: absorb the full salary costs and lay off 210 employees; lay off 140, or 13 per cent of the staff, in the current year; lay off 35 in the last quarter of 1969–70 and 35 in the first quarter of 1970; or keep the present level of employment, expand production and distribution, and increase revenues from sources other than direct parliamentary appropriations.[15]

But Christmas did not come in July, and the Cabinet decided to stick with austerity. It made exceptions for the Department of Transport, regional expansion, health and welfare schemes, the student summer-employment programme, pensions of retired public servants, and Culture and Recreation, including increases for the Canada Council, museums, libraries, the National Arts Centre, the CRTC, citizenship activities, and the official-languages programme. The Film Board was not among the chosen few; it would have to absorb price and salary increases by reducing staff, by increasing charges for services, or by scaling down current activities. It might even have to combine all three.[16]

Why had the government forgotten its rambunctious Film Board, while boosting others? A simple answer was that a film-saturated Canadian public was nursing a collective visual hang-over following the heady expansion in film production that was part of the Centennial celebrations. But there was another perspective. The government was aware that the politics of the era were reflected at the Montreal headquarters in many subtle and not-so-subtle ways. For example, one filmmaker had been recruiting membership for the Parti Québécois until Executive Producer Jacques Bobet told him to do his politicking in the halls, not in his office. Employees had been reminded that under the provision of the Public Service Employment Act, it was forbidden to engage in any activity supporting a federal or provincial political party. Ottawa's concern was obviously the latter and less the former. For those who were waging the crusade for national unity, there was no help coming from Montreal headquarters.

There was also evidence that certain filmmakers were using the Montreal facilities for making private commercials. One administrator noted the irony of seeing the hated sponsor film become the favoured child if the filmmaker stood to gain personally.[17] Management eventually halted this practice, but decided to suppress going public with incriminating evidence of persons enriching themselves at the public's expense. There is little wonder then why the employees disdained the administration for being weak.

But the fundamental question remained: Why had the administration not cut staff earlier, after informing the board of governors of redundant personnel and the shortfall in income? Management's explanation was that they feared ongoing collective bargaining might be jeopardized if cuts were applied.[18] This was partly true. But with the first hint of austerity, the three senior administrators, General Manager Gérard Bertrand, Chief Financial Officer Ted Greenway, and Director of Planning Gerald Graham, had

designed a critical path that both French and English directors of production had accepted. Then a so-called internal revolution occurred, and McPherson allowed their document to be replaced with a more expansive one, requesting a 40 per cent budget increase. Graham claimed later that this appeared to have created in Ottawa a strong impression of management irresponsibility.[19] The evidence was overwhelming: McPherson was the architect of his own undoing, probably because he was hoping to win the love and support of his employees who had never warmed to him. By trying to be all things to all people, he found himself abandoned by the secretary of state department and left to weather the hard times alone.

The young Trudeau government, faced with serious inflation and echoing the prime minister's 'no more free lunch' attitude, had decided to reduce the size of the public service by at least 10 per cent. Pelletier had little incentive to persuade his cabinet colleagues that the Film Board was a special case, so he ignored the pleas of the film commissioner. As far as he was concerned, McPherson had painted himself into a corner. The minister privately described the situation as a 'disaster area.'[20]

A panicked McPherson met with Pelletier on 13 August, just prior to Trudeau's national television appearance to explain austerity. He told the minister that there would have to be 300 (not the 210 earlier mentioned) firings immediately or a complete halt in production. From the commissioner's perspective, the Film Board was in peril, and he had to stop the minister from destroying the organization. McPherson believed he might have some influence with President of the Treasury Board C.M. (Bud) Drury. Pelletier warned him that the Film Board and CBC would be 'durement touchés' (severely hit), but that if McPherson thought he could turn heads, he should go before the Treasury Board along with George Davidson, president of the CBC. Armed with facts and figures, McPherson went to the Treasury

Board and presented his case. Drury turned him down flat – the Film Board would have to pay its own salary bill.

Following his presentation, McPherson met both Pelletier and Léger in the hall outside the Treasury Board. Léger told him he had done well in his presentation before Drury, but reminded him that the decision to freeze the Film Board appropriation had been made at the cabinet meetings in the last days of July. Léger tried to cushion the blow: 'You wanted to take a chance on changing Drury's mind, so you had it. But in times of austerity, the arts are the first to suffer. In times of prosperity, the arts are the last to be rewarded.' At this moment, McPherson thought Pelletier had led him down the garden path by encouraging him to make his case to Drury after everything had already been decided. McPherson considered this snub the last straw. Defeated by the unfathomable rituals of Ottawa politics (which he admitted he never understood), his heart went out of the job. He felt he was being made party to devious and deceitful affairs and would not tell lies on behalf of the secretary of state; he claimed later that from this point he was waiting for a suitable moment to resign.[21]

Board member Gordon Robertson attributed part of the Film Board's isolation to the fact that Pelletier was a neophyte as minister. He was a philosophical, rather than a practical, political animal, said Robertson, an intellectual, a man of ideas who had a vision. But Pelletier was not a practical politician when it came to the political environment. Robertson thought this limited experience did not give Pelletier the wherewithal to deal with the Film Board, but he did not think Pelletier misled McPherson – it was not in his character to do so.[22]

George Davidson took the rebuff more casually. He told McPherson that the CBC had been 'stockpiling' ever since the government had indicated it was going to pursue austerity. This is a polite term for legally using all available funds to build up resources to weather a government-inspired storm or famine. A more experienced administrator, Davidson was ready to make the CBC flat-out commercial and was much better prepared for the shock than was the tiro McPherson.[23]

Bringing home bad news

The commissioner's advisers recommended that the austerity cuts be applied democratically and that each branch cut 20 per cent from its 1970–1 budget. Frank Spiller, who had taken over from Julian Biggs as director of English Production, argued that this approach was unimaginative, since it meant the lay-off of fifty-six English staff members. Ten per cent was more reasonable, he maintained.

McPherson had indeed painted himself into a corner. He called a meeting of the whole Film Board staff near the end of August to explain that this was the most serious crisis that the Film Board had ever faced. He was stuck with a $1.25 million salary bill and had told the minister that mass firings were neither acceptable nor possible. There was one last prospect to finding alternative income: the Treasury Board had a contingency fund, and a cabinet directive had said relief would be given only where an agency or department could demonstrate that 'irreparable damage' would result from austerity.

Meanwhile, he had to announce a 10 per cent cut in staff, to take place by January 1970; fifty would receive their notices on 1 November and fifty more would receive theirs on 1 January. Perhaps by then there would be new money from the Treasury Board, from new revenue-producing films, and from specially supported government programmes. The key priorities remained production and distribution, but if the agency could not pay its own way, there would be more cuts. As a gesture of goodwill, he said in conclusion that he was sorry.[24]

The employees' response: A crisis committee and work stoppage

The staff felt that, goodwill and bad news notwithstanding, McPherson's administration was effete. They formed a Crisis Committee under union president John Howe. Practically all film production came to a halt, although there was no declared strike. First they fired off identical telegrams to the prime minister, the secretary of state, the president of the Treasury Board, the minister of manpower and immigration, the minister of labour, the leaders of the Opposition, the NDP and Créditistes, and Canadian Press. In it, they accused the Treasury Board of immorality and union-busting for not providing funds to meet the first negotiated salary increases at the Film Board. Then the Crisis Committee drafted another document proposing ways to strengthen the organization in a series of unrealistic options; there was backtracking, breast-beating, and (in the present confrontational atmosphere) administration-bashing.

The sponsored-film issue could be resolved, they thought, if the government sponsors were allowed to choose whether to use the Film Board or private industry. They estimated that this would stabilize sponsored films at around half the current volume. They offered nothing to find the subsequent shortfall of income. Also, technical services might shift to a commercial operating basis, accepting outside work to generate more money. The idea of making Film Board facilities available to outsiders had last been mooted in the early fifties, when it was thought that the institution could offer the CBC its shooting stage while it was not being used. The scheme was then dismissed as impractical from a planning point of view. Nothing since had altered that judgment.

The Crisis Committee offered to reconstitute English film production, returning to a unit system to be called 'studios,' each having five to fifteen members and dealing with areas of common concern. To avoid the rigidity of the unit system, individuals with both production and distribution expertise would be integrated within these studios. This would help establish closer links with the general distribution system. It was heartening to see the staff finally concerned with the Film Board's oldest problem. But this integration took fifteen years more to effect.

The committee also suggested that distribution libraries pay for themselves. (Distribution was already considering this alternative.) Thus, fees would have to be charged to Film Board users for the first time in history. Using 1968 distribution figures of 486,000 bookings, at three dollars per booking, the Film Board would generate $1.458 million per year. McPherson thought a fee system was his single viable option; no one expected a near-universal outcry of 'foul' from across the country.

As to the sorry state of the institution, the Crisis Committee found interlocking causes and effects and a built-in resistance to change. They identified 'protectionism, power plays, distrust, deadwood, frustration and absence of creative contact' between themselves and the public. The monster, they concluded, was a mirror image and they were all in some way to blame. Their parting shot was at McPherson, whom they faulted for not consulting the staff.[25]

The Crisis Committee document sparked a heated reaction from management. Director of Planning Gerald Graham warned that the agency had to invent some unique and necessary role for itself to escape from the non-essential category it occupied in the government's eyes. He believed a rigorous pruning of programmes was the first step, in particular the filmmakers' practice of overspending budgets by 100 and 200 per cent. Without coherent objectives, activities, and achievements, the Film Board would 'at best be tolerated as wooly do-gooders, who must be treated by Treasury as charity cases ... As a continuing cinematographic playpen, designed to shield itself from the realities of the outside world the Board will become a nothing agency.' His bitterness was not without foundation, as he recalled the Film Board's rejection by the CBC, its sad record with sponsors, and the proliferation of self-indulgent little films. He advised McPherson to prepare himself for a serious and inevitable confrontation with the staff.[26] Some members of the distribution branch unleashed long-standing fury and called for the firing of all filmmakers except producers and the relinquishing of all film production to private industry.[27] It was beginning to look like the 13th of Brumaire at the unfortunate Montreal enclave.

McPherson knew he was in trouble in Ottawa. Prime Minister Trudeau, whose dream was to unite English and French Canada nationally as equals, had complained to *Maclean's* editor Peter C. Newman about the media's failure to communicate with Canadians. 'I hate like heck to see that there's nobody in the country telling the truth to the people ... The editors, commentators and just common citizens are not well informed about the country,' he said. In revealing his government's disenchantment, the prime minister was also explaining why his government had little sympathy for the Film Board or the CBC.[28]

The commissioner had asked Gordon Robertson to speak on behalf of the Film Board to Simon Reisman, an influential bureaucrat at the Treasury Board. McPherson learned that the contingency money *would* be available, but the delays in decision-making were agonizing. Pelletier and his under-secretary had chosen to take their holidays at this time and the commissioner was in the dark as to 'what policy, if any, the Government is following.' His inclination was to not react too quickly, but the staff cuts would proceed as originally planned. The greatest consolation he had in the crisis was the assurance of many people in Ottawa that the Film Board was not alone in its suffering.[29]

Late in September, the Crisis Committee threatened to tell all to the public. McPherson warned the staff that they were pursuing a suicide course by asking politicians and newspaper reporters to settle internal troubles. He took the wind out of their sails when he told them he had already sent the minister a copy of their report. He had also submitted two policy papers in the past year, in February and June, but Pelletier had not yet responded to them.[30] He did not mention that the minister had requested another point of view and had commissioned an outsider, Bram Appel, to prepare a global review of federal film activity. Appel recommended that the Film Board make the laboratory and shooting-stage cost recoverable, that is, available to private industry.[31] Some months later, Pelletier asked André Saumier, the assistant deputy minister of programming at the Department of Regional Economic Expansion, to prepare a report on federal film policy. This report was the genesis of the Global Film Policy to support the private sector.

The commissioner's attempt to defuse events was not successful, though one Film Board producer, in an attempt to reconcile all bodies, reminded him that the staff's anger at the bureaucracy stemmed from a sense of being ignored. If some filmmakers' attitudes were juvenile and divisive, the administrative and service staff and management often demonstrated an irrational hatred of them. Filmmakers were easy scapegoats and were often labelled spoiled, selfish, arrogant, irresponsible, and inefficient. This was because the quality of their productivity was easily measured. They should continue to be meddlesome, provocative, concerned and sometimes troublesome, he continued. Docile filmmakers would signal the end of a worthwhile agency.[32] The commissioner probably was wondering where his allies were; in October he reminded the staff that his responsibility was the global picture and that many did not understand the difference between what was desirable and what was possible.[33]

There had been a bizarre twist late in August. The Treasury Board approved $1 million (not the $1.25 million requested) from the contingency funds to cover the salary-revision costs.[34] This all-important decision could have led the agency out of the woods, but apparently the minister chose to keep McPherson ignorant of the details, hoping that he would begin large-scale, rather than minimal cut-backs.[35]

McPherson had helped arrange for the indefatigable John Grierson to begin teaching at Montreal's McGill University the preceding January, in spite of Grierson's professed 'contempt for the use of universities for the teaching of filmmaking, bootblacking and some of the other crap.' Teaching was more stimulating than retirement, and the Scotsman also began weekly sessions in Ottawa with the CRTC discussing communications policy. He could not talk about communications without trotting out the old Grierson gospel – he meant to preach the 'propaganda of hope and belief in a complex world ... a propaganda of the will to act and the will to order.'[36] The Film Board crisis (and a persistent reporter) convinced him to repeat publicly some of the sentiments he was expressing at McGill and in Ottawa.

Grierson climbed atop his usual soapbox and admonished that there was too much worry about winning prizes abroad. Not enough was being done to reflect the variety of the Canadian identity. This could be achieved by cultivating a new relationship with government departments and pursuing the Film Training Centre idea. Most important was remembering that the Ottawa ties were those which bound. He reiterated that the sponsored film per se was expendable. There were other films to make that would 'reflect the great stories on all the frontiers, the things that give hope, an identity, a sense of being a big guy in a big country.' The Film Board was supposed to bring Canada alive to itself and to the world, he preached. What was missing was a re-evaluation, an overall policy. The crisis was not so bad, since in contrast to its earliest Spartan leanness, the institution had developed an unbecoming middle-aged spread.[37] McPherson found little solace in Grierson's remarks and wondered if the Old Maestro was out of touch with the true nature of the commissioner's predicament.

The Toronto *Globe and Mail* soon picked up the story of the crisis and under the headline 'A Slow Dissolve for the NFB?' quoted union president Howe, who stated that the austerity cuts were greatest in the field of communications, and it was 'an indication that somebody is trying to do something ... Who knows where it will all end? Mr. Pelletier should say what he wants to do to the NFB.' The story quoted the minister as saying that the Film Board had to redefine its role and be realistic, yet Pelletier had not given any suggestions on just how that redefinition might occur. The article mentioned in passing that production had been frozen since summer.[38]

Meanwhile, Pelletier had not yet answered Opposition criticism of the Film Board's new and unprecedented policy, which he had approved, to charge rental of three to twelve dollars a day for the use of its films. The first rumblings of national protest were already being heard, and in December he explained that this policy was a way to cope with the austerity budget. The Opposition claimed that charges would affect screenings, like those on Indian reservations, where there was a great dependence on Film Board films. Another critic complained in January that these charges would cut off various regions' access to Canadian culture.[39]

Washing dirty linen in public

The union sent a letter to the prime minister on 11 December, charging the government with betraying national trust. The Film

Board not only was closing its new regional production offices, but also was a victim of austerity twice: the freeze of its annual budget and the expected decline by half in the departmental sponsored films.

Rental charges were necessary because Distribution had to become cost-recoverable for fifty salaries. This was unfortunate because the taxpayers had already paid for these films. The government's decision to force the firing of 12 to 16 per cent of the bargaining unit, so the rest could be paid their increase, was tantamount to union-busting in the public service. The minister had done nothing to rectify the double freeze and had failed to respond to the several policy papers presented to him by the Film Board over the past year.

The letter directed the severest criticism at Film Board management, who refused to make a dramatic gesture of protest over the heads of the minister and government. Jacques Godbout, who had become director of French Production in February 1969 had suggested in a typically flamboyant fashion that the entire French Production branch be cut, so as to produce a national reaction and focus on French-English relations. McPherson did not take the bait.

It was unfair, continued the union, that in applying the cuts, English Production would lose 25 per cent, while French Production would lose 11.5 per cent, of their personnel. Was it intended to start a cycle of reductions, they asked, that would end with a film commissioner at the head of a National Administration Board? Administration was cutting only 9 per cent of its staff, while Production was losing 20.7 per cent. The union had a verbal contract with management that there would be meaningful consultations with them before cuts were made. No such consultation occurred before Pelletier's statement in the Commons on 24 November; following that, the commissioner had simply shown the union the grim statistics and had confirmed that the cuts must stand.[40] This letter reflected the union's sense of outrage

and complete loss of confidence in McPherson; within days, the employees demonstrated on Parliament Hill. First in line was the most celebrated filmmaker of them all, Norman McLaren.

McPherson was being outflanked on the public-relations front. He called a general meeting of the staff on 15 December and announced that he no longer felt obliged to consult with the union because of their letter to the prime minister, which was a 'violation of normal channels of communication.' As a concession, however, before his final decision, he had asked the minister for an independent review and report on the proposed lay-offs. Pelletier asked André Saumier to investigate. The commissioner had had a meeting with the secretary of state and his deputy ministers, and they confirmed that the future of the Film Board was not in doubt. McPherson asked the staff for a moratorium on crisis meetings and special petitions as well as a resumption of production and planning. He warned that there could be no repetition of the current crisis if the agency was to survive. If the Film Board could not settle its affairs internally, then someone else would have to, a possibility fraught with danger.[41]

McPherson intended to carry out the lay-offs and tried to remain unruffled publicly. In a closed meeting of middle and upper management, he outlined the history of the crisis. All this possibly may have had to happen, he began, and might in the long run prove useful. In 1967 Grant McLean had identified the serious problem of overstaffing. The irony was that McLean had been responsible for having hired staff to handle the Centennial film binge and, some thought, to keep English Production the dominant force. The dependence on sponsored-film revenue left the organization vulnerable.[42] Austerity had found McPherson spending most of the summer in Ottawa, arguing fruitlessly for relief. When it became clear in August that the sponsor programme was falling from $2.2 million to $1.6 million, management had decided to apply the cut-backs functionally. Distribution had to opt for film rentals to ensure cost-recovery, Technical Operations was left untouched in order to avoid higher costs for services, and English Production suffered the deepest cuts since the sponsored programme was in decline. Even if the programme recovered, a large percentage of sponsored films would have to go to private industry because the pressures on Ottawa were so strong. There was no other solution but to proceed with the cuts.

In a postscript, McPherson assured the group that he was on cordial speaking terms with the minister. He confided that the present government was very consciously re-examining broad areas of Canadian life, including the Film Board. 'Trudeau wants his Ministers to govern; the Mandarins in public service are going to play a different role – there is a new measure of control at the ministerial level,' he concluded.[43] Personally, the commissioner was boiling with resentment that lingered for over a decade. Then, he castigated Ottawa politicians uncharitably for being dumb and completely unsympathetic to the arts.[44]

Meanwhile, Pelletier fielded parliamentary criticism over the rental scheme, stating that he was not in the habit of interfering with the internal management of the Film Board. He expected a second round of personnel cuts in mid-January when André Saumier's report was completed. He confirmed that there were 31 already laid off, 73 under notice, and 50 distribution personnel on notice unless user fees could pay their salaries.[45]

The key to resolving the crisis was placed in McPherson's own hands early in January, in the most unlikely fashion: the Film Board's financial staff reported they had found $500,000. From where did a half-million dollars suddenly appear? It was elementary. Low morale and labour unrest had so interfered with productivity since August that there had been a net reduction in programme expenditures. Now there was a sur-

plus. In short, by going on an undeclared strike, the union had generated enough money to finish covering the $1.25 million salary bill. It was ingenious, not to mention rare in the history of Canadian labour relations, that a strike generated enough money to save imperilled jobs. Few outsiders realized how the fiscal magic had happened. McPherson wrote to Pelletier and asked if he could apply this money to cover 1970–1 salary costs.[46]

The minister remained under fire in the Commons over the new user-fee issue and explained that the various user-agencies had been informed of the policy.[47] Letters opposed to the scheme were streaming into the Film Board from across the country. Whether they were solicited or not, the union's public pressure campaign was having an effect. Pelletier started to backtrack a month later.

The union knew their campaign had struck pay dirt when Prime Minister Trudeau rose to speak on the Film Board cuts. His words betrayed a government frustrated with its war against inflation. He supported the cuts, because exceptions for the Film Board would have to apply to almost every department. If there were no reductions in government expenditures, he would be blamed for not combating inflation. 'The Opposition should take a clear position on whether they want the Government to spend more, or less,' he parried. 'If they want us to spend more, they should state that quite clearly and we will thank them for the mandate.'[48] One wonders why, if inflation was the principal enemy, he was putting his money ($7.25 million) on the new Information Canada organization. Its mandate was to address the task of 'expanding the dimensions of democratic dialogue in this nation.'[49] Trudeau was obviously not impressed with the Film Board's version of democratic dialogue. Information Canada was a means for Ottawa to propagate national unity and national symbols on its own terms.

When the union asked the minister to intervene, Pelletier refused flatly and said that, if he did, 'then you have to have the Minister in your affairs every month or every three months ... Is that what you want? That's not what I want. I want the management to be autonomous and responsible.'[50] If he was less than satisfied with the film commissioner's performance, he was restating the long-standing historical practice, later called the 'arm's length' relationship. The government knew better than to stage a frontal political assault.

The evidence demonstrates that the government's prime concern was with cutting costs. They wanted production for 1970–1 to be scaled back to the 1964–5 level. The Saumier report repaid McPherson's inner thoughts with a severe assessment of senior management, who were accused of having 'scant knowledge of the mysterious workings of the Government in Ottawa.' Saumier warned that the 10 per cent cut-back in English Production employees might be too large for the remaining staff to be fully employed in 1970–1. What was more, French Production would need to hire additional freelance personnel to meet its production goals.

To paraphrase a great man from another era, the unrepentant McPherson had not become film commissioner in order to preside over the dismantling of the agency. He wrote to Pelletier that he had ignored the austerity danger signals because he 'considered that it [management] should state as clearly as possible its views of the national need in the domain of film and make clear the cost of expanding the Board's role.' The five-year forecast and two policy papers had expressed an expansionist view of the next decade.[51] The commissioner had chosen to ignore the fact that total salary costs were accounting for over 90 per cent of the funds that Parliament voted annually.

Six weeks later, Pelletier announced in the Commons that while production of Film Board films had been suspended for two months, all production had now resumed, and some 97 employees would be released by

summer, 34 of whom were retiring and resigning. Thus, there would be 63 lay-offs, 18 in English Production, 4 in French Production, 12 in Technical Services, 18 in Distribution, and 11 in Administration.[52] The union took the legal route and protested wrongful dismissal. When all the dust settled, seventeen English Production staff slated for lay-off were kept on. In less than a year they won their case. Caught in the middle of events and initiatives he could neither control nor deflect, McPherson had been the biggest loser. User fees had to be dropped when he was told that they were in violation of the Cabinet's anti-inflation guidelines. (Pelletier had also been the recipient of the largest-ever mail response to the cuts and fees of any secretary of state, some 450 letters from both the public and luminaries around the world.)[53] McPherson, whose staff lacked confidence in his good intentions, had been deserted by the minister; even the board of governors had proved unsupportive, and one member recommended in the midst of the crisis that he resign. The commissioner's health problems increased and he waited for the right moment to quit.

The standing committee: One of the last nails in the commissioner's coffin

McPherson's attempt to charge user fees for Film Board films had caused a Western backlash, and a number of members of the standing committee were angry when he met them in May. His was a different performance from previous appearances. Now, in 1970, he was waiting for a federal film policy, a long-term financing plan, and a way to make policy without being controlled by earned income. His presentation sounded bleak and flat and the committee criticized him for his status quo posture. He tried to retort that with its parliamentary vote frozen for the last three years, the Film Board could not make films out of air. A member went for the jugular vein and chastised him for approving a production policy that approached parity for English and French Production, rather than a financial division that reflected the two-thirds/one-third population reality. This policy would have profound financial ramifications, argued another, since every government department that operated on the parity principle would take an awful beating (through having to hire more French-language staff). Worse yet, claimed another, the move to parity would necessitate cutting back further on English production as French production increased.

McPherson was uncomfortable as he tried to argue that what he meant by 'parity' was 'flexibility'; the annoyed MP said he did not want to give any lessons in English, but the term 'parity' precluded the flexibility and balance that the commissioner intended it to mean. McPherson relented and claimed that he did not realize that 'parity' was going to be a four-letter word, so he agreed to substitute the phrase 'flexibility and balance.' It was clear that some members did not think that the Liberal government's commitment to a bilingual and bicultural country meant a fifty-fifty financial split between the two founding peoples. McPherson refrained from telling the members that as a step towards parity, the Film Board had already increased the budget in French production by $225,000, while cutting English production by $381,000, in direct contradiction to the five-year plan, which had said that French production should approach parity without taking away monies from English production – the aim was for equivalent screen-time.[54]

The commissioner argued that the concept of screen-time parity was in the best interests of the country's cultural life, and that parity meant achieving a balanced expression of the reality of Canadian culture. He produced statistics to show that the austerity crisis had left the agency with 146 English and 70 French members in production. More money was needed for language-versioning of films into English, since this better depicted French-speaking Canada to English Canada than a journalistic film essay made by English Canadians.[55] His example reflected the contemporary emphasis that English Canadians needed to better understand French Canadians. (A significantly English-Canadian fact of life was that there did not seem to be much pressure in the other direction.)

Another MP criticized the budget as a 'stand-pat and unexciting' one. McPherson complained that Parliament had denied his 1969 request for a 40 per cent hike, thus it was difficult to sound exciting if costs were up 20 per cent and the budget was frozen. The members were not impressed and another berated him, 'I would expect you, sir, to come in here and fight for what you believe in and tell us what you need in order to do the things you think need to be done.' He thought the Film Board had failed to demonstrate leadership; it should have suggested to Parliament that quotas be used to force Canadian films into commercial theatres. Here was another dangerous word, and the commissioner tried to explain that amusement taxes were provincial matters, that there were obstacles to unanimity, and that a previous commissioner had brought up the question at the cabinet level, only to have no action taken.[56]

It had been a very rough ride, and when McPherson returned before the committee two days later, his reception was worse. Members quoted the Saumier report, which stressed that being in Montreal had removed the commissioner from the thinking of the government and that he had been caught unprepared for austerity. He denied this. Another stated that there were no solid programming proposals before the committee, and the Film Board seemed to be withdrawing from television and theatrical exhibition. McPherson denied that too and emphasized that the non-theatrical audience was the most significant one.

The committee continued needling him about administration costs, which he explained had risen because technical and production services had been added. Then a member dropped a bombshell when asking about 'a certain film on the textile industry,' which representatives from that industry had seen and not liked. A befuddled McPherson turned the question over to his general manager, Gérard Bertrand, who claimed that the film was a working copy and that a prestigious member of the textile industry wanted his appearance in it excised. This had been done, and a second version would be ready in a few weeks. There had been a lunch with the said gentleman, who had a point of view, as did the filmmaker. He intended to transmit this information to the commissioner when the film was finished, at which time a decision would be taken about its final disposition. The film was *On est au coton*, directed by Denys Arcand, and when it was finished, it became one of the first of many headaches for the next film commissioner.

Another MP had saved his ammunition to probe sponsored films. The commercial film industry told the committee a year earlier that only 3 per cent of government film work went to private enterprise.[57] He put the question bluntly to McPherson: Was the Film Board going to phase out of this operation? The commissioner would have liked to tell them that in 1968 he had ordered a report on tendering procedures, involving private industry and government departments.[58] Grierson had advised him to quit sponsored films, although to keep cultivating close relationships with government departments. McPherson's advisers had recommended that some sort of phase-out programme be started to stretch over two or three years, instead of having the Film Board faced with the threat of an immediate cut-off by the masters in Ottawa.[59]

The board of governors feared that farming out sponsored films to the private sector was inviting the government to reduce the critical mass of production capacity and to turn the Film Board into an administrative and distribution agency.[60] McPherson had been shocked and enraged when a number of individuals from the private sector offered him bribes if he would favour their companies. In retaliation, he had decided to forbid the use of Film Board facilities to any but government departments. In his mind, he was being responsible to the government by refusing private deals with businessmen.[61] Now, in May 1970, McPherson skipped the complex historical explanation and offered the commercial industry the carrot it had long sought; he was ready to relinquish some sponsored work if the government reimbursed him.[62] Afterwards, he felt shaken by his torturous, maladroit performance. He crossed his fingers and hoped Pelletier would back him up. The minister remained silent.

Farewell to all that

Days after McPherson's appearance before the standing committee, Pelletier elaborated the government's broad cultural policy in response to a cabinet directive a year earlier. His was a general sketch projecting a global approach and expanded bilingualism, and he forecast an increase in cultural expenditures from $236.7 million to $540.6 million in 1974–5. He also proposed an advisory council of heads of agencies and citizens appointed by the secretary of state. In putting flesh on the bones of the culture-industry skeleton, the government was going to prop up the private sector in a way never before tried. Similarly, Pelletier intended to invite the film commissioner, the heads of other federal cultural institutions, and personalities from the cultural world to help elaborate a global film policy too. It seemed that the Film Board was about to become indistinguishable from the other trees in the forest.[63]

Austerity had led the CBC to demand that all prime-time shows have commercials. The Film Board had been without a television contract in 1969–70, which led to a shortfall in royalties of nearly $200,000. So when, in July 1969, the CBC telecast *John Cabot* with commercials, the filmmakers' union again rose up in arms. No one had told them this would happen, and McPherson, getting in his last licks, did not explain why. The union argued that Radio-Canada did not insert commercials in the Film Board's French-language films, and it was fundamental that the filmmakers control content, lest commercials distort their work. They threatened to go public yet again.

English Production chief Frank Spiller was conducting negotiations with the CBC and said that the CBC creative staff felt the same way about commercials as did their Film Board colleagues. If an exception was made for the Film Board, there would be problems. He said that the CBC would accept Film Board films without commercials, provided they were related to its public-affairs policy. But in the past few years, the Film Board was striving toward a different kind of use of films, and these different trends were not in accord with CBC philosophy.[64] The CBC's hard-hearted position would be among the first issues addressed by the next commissioner.

If it had gone poorly for the commissioner before the standing committee, life seemed worse when McPherson considered himself the victim of an insult from Pelletier's office. Unbeknownst to him, two officers from the filmmakers' union had consulted with Pelletier in June on union-management relations. McPherson fired off a letter to the minister in which he expressed his pain, though he could barely contain his anger. Collective bargaining with the union was up to Film Board management, not the minister, he said, and if the minister thought McPherson was unsatisfactory, he should dismiss him. He concluded that the credibility gap between the minister's and commissioner's offices, which had been developing since 1969, was getting wider and the other two Film Board unions might now cause dissension. He requested an early reply to his objections.[65]

Apparently there was no reply. McPherson must have been at the end of his tether, as once again it appeared that events seemed to control him. He probably thought of the conflicting advice he had received as he began his stewardship during the euphoria of the Centennial: Judy LaMarsh had told him, 'You never do anything to embarrass a minister,' and Gordon Robertson had said, 'You never do anything to embarrass a Minister unless you are about to resign.' McPherson was supposed to officiate over a cultural event in Ottawa at the Still Photography Centre. The minister waited over an hour for the commissioner, who never showed up. There was also no annual programme to submit. Shortly thereafter he resigned, a man broken by the strain of three years of almost uninterrupted crisis.

There was at least one achievement that would last beyond McPherson's tenure. Just as he left, the Film Board adopted the logo that is now synonymous with the organization. Though the idea was first mooted in 1965, it was not until early 1967 that the board of governors hired two graphics firms to come up with an appropriate corporate symbol. When their submissions had proved unsatisfactory, McPherson ordered a competition within the Film Board. Some fifty-three graphic designs were submitted, identified by number only, and after a further sifting process, the three finalists' logos were:

Georges Beaupré's 'Man Seeing' was the winner, Norman McLaren's dazzling 3-D Möbius film loop and Sidney Goldsmith's abstract seeing-eye came in second and third place. McPherson described the logo as a figure representing mankind, with echoes of the Eskimo and Indian cultures that were part of Canada's community. Its colours of green and blue are life colours, and the raised arms with clasped hands suggest celebration. The head, like the iris of an eye, symbolizes visionary man, animated man, and possibly even man *mis à nu*. From 1970, this symbol has preceded every Film Board production. In 1978 director Michael Rubbo complained that the logo was depressing; the Film Board then decided to animate it. In October 1986 Ishu Patel's colourfully animated 'Man Seeing' became the standard that adorns each film.[66]

When McPherson left that summer, there were dry eyes on all sides. Life, he later confided sadly, was a painful experience, and to understand pain was terribly important, otherwise life was superficial. One board member concluded that McPherson's lack of business experience and political know-how was the fundamental reason for his failure.[67] McPherson was also not a tough personality. As a gentle man who wanted to be liked, he claimed he never wanted to be hurtful to others. He saw his 'immense opportunity to be in charge of one of the major cultural forces in Canadian life' evaporate like an evanescent film image.[68] Primarily an academic, he had wanted to redefine the role of the Film Board in conjunction with the communications philosophy of Marshall McLuhan. The technical people encouraged him to anticipate a new distribution system that would make film and videotape documentaries widely available on demand to an urban population linked by television. But the new technology to do it was in its infancy and would take more time and expense to implement than he could afford. There were few lucky stars for the commissioner.

At the moment he resigned, McPherson should have read Professor Northrop Frye's article in *The Listener*. As an oracle himself, Frye was not jumping on the McLuhan bandwagon; he warned that the intense interest in communications and technical developments had led society to greater introversion. He cited objects like the automobile, airplane, and apartment building to demonstrate how people were more introverted than their predecessors. These objects had resulted in increased personal alienation and a decline in the sense of belonging to a community. The psychological conditions of life now reflected the easy defences of apathy and cynicism. Frye warned that they were no defences. The electronic media represented not a new order to adjust to, but a subordinate order to be contained. The gentleman-scholar concluded that it was the interdependent factors of democracy and book-culture that created the conditions of freedom.[69] Concerning film and concomitant delivery systems, the contributing architect of *Labyrinth* offered nothing but caution. This was advice proffered too late to help the unlucky McPherson, who found refuge in traditional book culture at McGill University, where he spent the rest of his illness-plagued professorial career.

In an interview a year later, McPherson could barely conceal his anger at the government for having left film and broadcasting at the bottom of its priority list. It was a contradiction he could not live with. Moreover, in moving toward a centralizing policy, the government had become too involved in the internal workings of the agency. He believed that a new film policy was needed, one that had a film commissioner, separate from the Film Board, who could prevent overlapping between the agency, the CBC, and the CFDC; one, in short, who would regulate the 'information resources' of the country.[70] Long afterwards, McPherson remained obdurate in his belief that Pelletier had let him down. There had barely been a chance to make policy or to try applying ideas about communication. His lot was to have been forced to react to one crisis after another. The staff felt he had failed in the one area in which he was supposed to have excelled: communications. And more than a few remembered Nathan Cohen's ominous presentiments upon learning of the McPherson appointment, namely, that the onus was on McPherson to prove his appointment was not a sorry mistake. Too many felt that his tenure had demonstrated precisely that. Perhaps the most important lesson for the government was that, in the future, the film commissioner might better come from the ranks of the Film Board staff. That such a course might entail another sorry mistake remained to be seen.

In Search of a Mission:
Challenge for Change/Société nouvelle

Lumbering on through hard times

Austerity had brought down the commissioner, but the bureaucracy lumbered on. In 1968, efficiency experts concluded that the Film Board suffered from a lack of policy development and planning.[1] They blamed filmmakers for ignoring the board of governors and for neglecting to assume the necessary fiscal responsibility that must accompany every project. In short, the programming system was 'a source of delusion at all levels.'[2] Relations with the departmental sponsors were poor, the experts continued, because the filmmakers resented their meddling. The way out of the impasse, they concluded, was to move out of sponsored and educational films and into 'interpretive' or cultural films.

There was puzzlement too as to why morale was lower in English than in French Production. Each group had roughly the same number of directors (eighteen and nineteen respectively), and the English had twenty producers to the French side's seven. Many of the young English filmmakers felt fettered by the authority of the producers, who had the onerous yet unofficial responsibility for the films. These young idealists believed in the freedom of the individual to find his own content.

The efficiency experts made a backhanded reference to quality when they commented that there was a gap between the Film Board's distinguished and undistinguished films. One suggestion, which remained ignored for years to come, called for the creation of a 'script bank,' to have projects ready for development when funding allowed. Even though the fault had been identified, little was done to encourage better writing; poor scripts remained the Achilles' heel of Canadian features and continue to be one of the greatest stumbling blocks to building a world-class Canadian film industry.

The consultants also criticized the filmstrip programme for having drawn the ire of the private sector, because the Film Board had undercut prices and marketed filmstrips at a loss. There was criticism too for the unplanned plunge into the 8-mm field in 1963, as well as for the organization's $100,000 investment in a Super 8-mm laboratory, which had produced some four hundred 'loop,' or single-concept films, for North American schools by 1968.[3] Easy to use, the 3-minute silent film was a continuously revolving 'loop,' contained in a cassette, that explained a science or mathematics concept. A child could load it into an inexpensive projector and proceed to become 'self-taught.' Subsequently, the Super 8 loop made a major contribution to visual education. In the United States, Ann Cooney, the originator of 'Sesame Street,' the most successful children's television show in history, designed her programme based on teaching children to read and count using the single-concept film method pioneered at the Film Board.[4] But Super 8 was a medium that was imminently obsolete as the even newer video technology arrived. In the face of austerity, the organization abandoned loop films and wrote off the costs.[5]

The efficiency experts' report also questioned the value of regional producers. Grant McLean had appointed Peter Jones to head the Vancouver office late in 1965, partly in anticipation of the Sheppard report recommendation. He told Jones to keep in touch with local writers, directors, technicians, and performers, to let them know what the Film Board was doing, and to encourage them to associate themselves with Film Board production projects to be carried out locally and elsewhere. If management was prescient enough to realize that regionalization was one way for the Film Board to help the private sector in the coming decades, the austerity drive forced this scheme on to hold, and the Winnipeg and Halifax offices closed. Jones tried to do what he could with paltry resources to help to encourage Vancouver area talent.[6] Regionalization promised an additional fillip: to lead the Film Board out of what the managers saw as the union quagmire of job security and 'democratization.' There was even stronger encouragement from the minister's office, and the scheme became the course from which there was no turning back, because it meant that new filmmakers or existing production companies could be hired on a per-contract basis. Regionalization became one of the principal aims of the government's new Global Film Policy.

In reply to the expert's recommendations, the bureaucracy was restructured with a daunting proliferation of titles, and by the spring of 1969 the new system limped into operation. Union president John Howe disdained the renovated system, calling it 'sterile and reactionary,' and said the whole edifice was reminiscent of the old unworkable

unit system of the forties and fifties.[7] If management could not win loyalty by restructuring, they assembled three task forces to moot where the Film Board's future lay. The first, headed by Anne Claire Poirier, suggested unifying production and distribution relationships in order to end internal disarray; the second, headed by Robert Forget, recommended a study of the practical application of video to create a *cinémathèque automatique*, allowing the public access to Film Board titles. (The video-cassette revolution arrived a few years later to give this idea practical application.) The third, under Tom Daly, thought the future lay in programming 'prestige' projects such as *Labyrinth*, to deliver the maximum cultural experience with the most intensity to the greatest number of Canadians. All three ideas had their merits, but, combined with a natural institutional reluctance to change and the austerity crisis that summer, nothing more came of them.

Theatrical shorts, features, or both?

After the Film Board's unprecedented financial difficulties in 1969, there was no small surprise when it was learned that two theatrical shorts, *Blake* and *Walking*, were nominated for Oscars in 1970. *Walking* ($21,676) was Ryan Larkin's animation masterpiece that described the multiple forms of that most common of human acts using a scintillating variety of animation techniques, accompanied by an engrossing contemporary musical score. *Blake* ($47,077), directed by Bill Mason, was the story of his friend and solo pilot, Blake James, whose odyssey was an endless pursuit and exploration of Canada's boundless skies and wilderness. *Blake* lets the viewer experience one element of the Canadian reality, the lone, intrepid adventurer, drawn irresistibly into the vacuum of Canada's geographic space, yet never lost, since he takes his limitations into account in fashioning a reasonably attainable personal goal. Though neither film won the coveted prize, they both confirmed that the short was what the Film Board did best.

This did not diminish English Production's interest in pursuing the feature film, despite two near-disastrous co-production experiences earlier with the CBC. Their greatest deficiency had been poor-to-indifferent scripting, which stood in contrast to the brilliant script in 1967 by New York playwright Millard Lampell. *Do Not Fold, Staple, Spindle or Mutilate* ($67,495) was a poignant 50-minute featurette directed by John Howe that starred Ed Begley. The story was about a union leader who had given his best years to the cause, only to find himself obsolete in an unfeeling world of youth and new collective-bargaining practices. The subject was a trifle close to contemporary events, since Howe was about to become the filmmakers' union president. The conflict between those with and without power was a universal and generational one.

Undaunted by the financial squeeze starting in 1968, the English Programme Committee expressed interest in developing feature ideas and scripts for future consideration.[8] Filmmaker Mort Ransen ignored script altogether as he directed *Christopher's Movie Matinee* ($81,342), an 87-minute film about a group of young people in Toronto making a film about themselves. The experience of mixing fiction with direct cinema was probably as painful for the 'actors' to shoot as it was for the audience to watch. Also in 1968, Robin Spry had tentative success with his first one-hour documentary, *Flowers on a One-way Street* ($48,545), a story that grew out of his brief observation of the hippie phenomenon which Ransen was filming in Toronto. That city's officials and press accused the Film Board crew of fomenting strife and negative publicity, when in fact the filmmakers were recording a sit-in at city hall after the first tumultuous encounter between hippies and civic authorities. In Montreal, the press furore frightened Director of Production Julian Biggs, who tried to call off the film. Commissioner

McPherson, desirous of currying favour with the filmmakers, defended the young director, and soon Biggs resigned his post. When the film was shown in the summer and fall of 1968, the press reaction was negative, even though it won a prize at the International Film Festival in Chicago. In Victoria, it was termed a blunder, and there was a call for a complete overhaul of the agency; in Toronto, the mayor called the production a misrepresentation of hippie violence.[9]

In 1969 Spry achieved a successful melding of fiction and fact in *Prologue* ($140,000), one of the Film Board's most original English films of the decade. This was the story of the sixties activists' first whiff of disillusionment before the entrenched interests of an older generation that was itself reacting to youthful revolt. A story as timeless as adolescence itself, *Prologue*'s fresh Canadian look of cultivated innocence was endearing. It was also interesting to observe how a portion of young English Canada was trying to graft the branch of United States social and political activism on to a reluctant Canadian trunk. Set in Montreal, the story has a counter-culture underground-newspaper publisher fight unsuccessfully against the city's powers-that-be, lose his girlfriend to an American draft dodger who has come to Canada to forget politics, join a commune, and then find himself in the middle of the riot-torn Democratic National Convention in Chicago during the summer of 1968. He returns to Montreal to win back his girlfriend, who has grown tired of 'dropping out' on the commune.

Spry changed the scenario when events in Chicago encouraged a blending of fiction with the actual riots to heighten the dramatic impact of the story. Thus, when the fictional hero finds himself in the middle of a Chicago police-instigated tear-gas attack, he is not unlike a wartime newsreel cameraman in the thick of the action.[10] A cameo appearance by publicity-radical Abbie Hoffman, punning about 'Lace, the new miracle weapon that makes people fornicate,' outraged Canada's conservative press. The *Calgary Herald* said the Film Board had clearly gone too far, while *Variety* criticized a friendly government that would sponsor a film that was on the side of militant activists and was a direct attack on the politics of an ally. Clyde Gilmour of the *Toronto Telegram* had no such cavils – he called it simply 'Tedium Cool.'[11]

The fiction unfolding within the actuality sequences was intended to lend authenticity to the film, emphasizing what many thought was the heroic struggle of the late sixties: fight against the authorities for idealistic principles or tune in and drop out of the adult world that is too confused and confusing to inherit. Seen in another context, the film pays unintentional homage to Canada's 'two solitudes' by ignoring totally the Montreal political context as well as the tensions being generated by both FLQ bombings and the nascent Parti Québécois. McPherson prepared a lengthy defence of the film, only to find a single member of Parliament ask one question: How much money did Hoffman receive to appear in the film? The answer was $93. An indifferent House of Commons went on to other business.[12]

Prologue was the first Canadian feature ever to be selected for the main festival at Venice, in 1969. It appeared in several other international film festivals, where it received excellent reviews, and was shown on CBS television in New York. The greatest surprise occurred when it won the best-documentary-feature award of the British Film Academy.

At the same time that *Prologue* was invited to Venice, a 99-minute Film Board feature, *Don't Let the Angels Fall* ($161,528), directed by George Kaczender and written by Timothy Findley, became the first English-Canadian feature to be invited to compete at Cannes. One critic called it a bleak and spare account of failed relationships; it was also a continuation of the theme of ennui, sandwiched between disintegrating middle-class family life and urban sterility, both of which were familiar subjects. However competent

these films were artistically, they received little or no commercial distribution inside and outside Canada.

French features

French features had a better reception at home than their English counterparts and were welcomed in Quebec theatres, although they too showed unimpressive box-office returns. In 1966, Jacques Godbout had directed *Yul 871* ($196,869), a surrealistic and romantic view of Montreal as seen for the first time by a young European engineer who was visiting for a weekend. The scenario was missing a backbone, wrote the critic from *Le Devoir*, but this was the first Canadian feature to be selected by an international film festival, in Zagreb, Yugoslavia.[13]

Le Grand Rock ($158,680), directed by Raymond Garceau in 1967, is the story of a young country boy who abandons his happy outdoor life to become a salaried employee, and then turns to a life of violence and crime. Garceau, whose earlier films had in part become the inspiration for the Film Board's new programming endeavour, 'Challenge for Change / Société nouvelle,' was concerned perennially with the social dislocation experienced by rural individuals cut off from their roots. The 72-minute drama contains all the ingredients of good fiction: love, action, beauty, and violence. Unfortunately, the film turned into a personal nightmare for Garceau after its screening in the Laurentians. The story bore a fictional resemblance to the career of a well-known local criminal. Although no proof was available, it was common knowledge in the area that this person had threatened reprisals against Garceau in the event the film was shown. After it was released, someone burned down Garceau's $12,000 country house, proving perhaps how dangerous it was to get too close to actuality.[14]

A less depressing outcome followed Claude Jutra's *Wow* ($171,886). This 1970 work attempted to combine *cinéma direct* with fiction in order to create a new form of *cinéma engagé*. Jutra subsequently called it *cinéma rêve*. He convinced a group of adolescents to make a film about themselves as a collaborative endeavour and lived with them for several months. In *Wow*, the viewer ends up looking at the world from inside out, as each member conjured up a fantasy that he or she described to the camera, then 'acted out.'[15] The descriptive sequence was shot in sepia and the 'acting out' sequence was filmed in colour. From the dynamiting of the family house, to running naked downtown, to the subtle texture of a female nude lit in blue as she floats in slow motion on a trampoline, it was clear that *l'amour*, not politics, made their world go round. Machine-age technology left them cold, but their final plea echoed young adults through the ages: 'I want to do something – but I don't know what ...' *Wow* describes youth reflecting the internal and external uncertainty and often unfocused radicalism of the late sixties. In this, as in many *québécois* films of the day, youth is a sub-text that symbolizes the unfulfilled promise of Quebec. Jutra's *Wow* was another example of how youth was becoming legitimized as one of the contemporary icons of the Quiet Revolution.

Meanwhile, from his podium at McGill University in Montreal, John Grierson was disturbed by the Film Board's expansion into features and the filmmakers' frequent enunciation of the auteur principle. Since 1966, he had been warning that aesthetics had to occur within the responsible framework of public information. Extemporizing on this theme in 1969, he declared that 'aesthetic' was a word he reserved exclusively for great things. He expressed contempt for its use with the word 'auteur,' which he said bluntly was 'an excuse for every goddam second-rate bum to inflict on us his second-rate mind, like the 8 mm camera has produced the 8 mm mind and 8 mm conceit.' Allowing filmmakers loose rein was a mistake, he admonished, 'because none of us can claim this total personal right in a medium where so much is at issue in the national interest.' He thought that such freedom reflected the worst and most trivial aspects of early-nineteenth-century romanticism.[16]

Artists were generally dangerous characters, said the ever-pontificating prophet, and he thought it was the greatest arrogance in the world to allocate to oneself the right to the greatest platform in the world for one's own personal views. 'Pulpits must be earned and occupied on terms that are publicly recognizable,' he exhorted. There was an understood condition of loyalty, and if one would come out against the public authority, one must resign. He was thinking about those who, from within the Film Board, were working toward personal agendas, political or otherwise. This was the closest he came to making any reference to French-Canadian (*québécois*) nationalist aspirations.[17] His silence on the subject was puzzling. Most young French-Canadian filmmakers reciprocated by virtually never using Grierson as a point of reference, although Claude Jutra and he seemed to have developed a warm and close personal relationship.

Canada was fundamentally a future country, he preached, and that called for epic, lyricism, and a policy that would fulfil the Film Board's mandate. The institution had been very good in its lyrical items and portraits, and he cited films like *Corral* and *Nahanni* as 'natural.' In fact, he insisted, the greatest single thing in the Film Board was its portraiture, reflecting the Canadian genius for making pictures about single men, films like *Paul Tomkowicz: Street-railway Switchman*, *Legault's Place / Le Beau Dérangement*, and *Les Bûcherons de la Manouane*.[18] He echoed the same sentiment by insisting that building something new, that pioneering, was the organization's real job.

Using another tack, Grierson suggested the Film Board might undertake poetic activity related to the fundamentals of tribal memory. He wondered why there had not been a single picture of worth about the St Lawrence River, which was central to the evolution of Canada. (He forgot Bill Mason's brilliant children's odyssey of 1966, *Paddle to the Sea* [$70,913], which had been nominated for an Oscar. Mason had an unfailing eye for Canadian landscape and wildlife and had earned premier status among the best of Canada's wilderness cinematographers.) Grierson called for a poetic piece that captured one of the greatest spectacles on earth, Nature's own 'sex show.' Every year all life depended on the river, but stopped as it froze hard, only to come alive again when it relaxed and the ice broke up in spring. The real aesthetic of Canada was its everlasting horizons of loneliness and of winter, from the North Pole to the Rockies. Those horizons represented infinite loneliness in all its manifestations.[19]

Students at McGill were spellbound by Grierson's curious blend of Scots Presbyterianism ('I derive my authority from Moses') peppered with epithets. He seemed forever on edge, caustic, and ready to hurl verbal thunderbolts to rivet in their tracks those who were brave enough to challenge his authority. Some thought these were the last gasps of an old man who had lost touch with contemporary political changes. Others saw his mind as a steel trap that could close mercilessly on the sloppy thinker and shame

Wildlife cinematographer Bill Mason sets up a complex close-up in *Paddle to the Sea* (1966). While the hand-carved Indian in a canoe drifts through the great natural space of Canada to the sea, the viewer sees how man-made pollution threatens it all.

him to silence. But Commissioner McPherson, who did not want to listen to his harangue, was forever talking about how he liked the French features. Little wonder then that Grierson's admonitions were ignored by the English filmmakers who were determined to try features too.

Roots of 'Challenge for Change / Société nouvelle'

North America was experiencing a simultaneous confluence of social and political radicalism, as 'What to do about youth?' had become the parental puzzle of the sixties. In the United States, the Kennedy administration's creation of the Peace Corps and its domestic version under President Johnson, VISTA (Volunteers in Service to America), followed by the Job Corps training of unemployed youths, had been public-relations successes. These programmes were a most effective means of channelling the energies of a postwar generation just coming of age, as the United States sidled unintentionally into an Asian conflict in a country that over half the population had never heard of, Vietnam. When President Johnson launched his 'war on poverty' in the summer of 1964, Canada had begun to mirror much of the same American social rhetoric. By 1965, Canada's War on Poverty was already an announced government programme, and in April, the government said it intended to create the Company of Young Canadians. Here was a means to put radicals to work with disadvantaged Canadians, just as VISTA volunteers were doing in the United States. It was typically Canadian that radical civil servants organized the CYC.[20]

The Film Board had also manifested radical tendencies. The 1964 restructuring of English programming and introduction of the 'pool' system had ushered in a period of experimentation in which filmmakers made use of new creative freedoms. Some believed that the auteur's role was to experiment with the medium and to be *original*. They argued that the artist's licence was to explore personal aesthetics, and to not be bound by such dead weight as traditional rigorous standards.

A number of filmmakers were making fresh and engaging films that fell into this category. In 1965, Arthur Lipsett's *Trip down Memory Lane* ($25,341) was a jumbled collage of newsreel memorabilia that yielded fresh insight into the ironies of human experience; Jean-Claude Labrecque's *60 cycles* was probably the best sports short in Film Board history, showing varied uses of the telephoto lens to observe a long-distance bicycle race in Quebec; a year later, in 1966, Derek May's seven-minute short *Angel* ($7,467) demonstrated the fascinating uses of high-contrast images in a fantasy, with poetry by Leonard Cohen. A year later, Norman McLaren's Oscar-nominated *Pas de deux* ($15,000) contained his most technically accomplished work yet, a study in multiple images of the complex choreography of ballet. These works demonstrated that artistic experimentation within the short-film genre was earning the Film Board world renown.

There were filmmakers on the other side of the spectrum who believed that their work should correlate directly to the National Film Act's fundamental clause, 'in the national interest,' which they interpreted as providing public information. They criticized the earlier Unit B films for relegating the filmmaker to the status of a perceptive and disinterested observer. These individuals saw their function as social activists as well as artists. They echoed one liberal interpretation of the era that the role of communication was to identify the forces that shaped people's daily lives. It was a short step for filmmakers to put those forces at the disposal of the people and use film to stem the apathy and cynicism that threatened to paralyse society.

Board member (and Privy Council repre-

A Film Board crew sets up a special low-angle shot to incorporate into the actuality footage of *60 cycles* (1965), which conveys the thrill of competition against a picturesque backdrop of rural Quebec.

sentative) Gordon Robertson shared this liberal goal and had written to Commissioner Roberge in 1965 that, amidst the general prosperity, there were parts of the country where poverty was real. He believed there was little understanding of the way in which poverty can blight the prospects of a child and become self-perpetuating, despite the existence of social services and of welfare programmes. He thought that a film on poverty could be of real value.

Executive Producer John Kemeny, who had been searching for film subjects that were usually ignored, responded positively to this idea. He took a proposal to the Special Planning Secretariat of the Privy Council Office, under R.A.J. Phillips, who was also a director of the CYC. The working paper on poverty proposed a one-hour film and thirteen shorter (15–20 minute) items that would involve cooperation with the CBC.[21] Thus, the film was to be a pilot project, funded by the Privy Council Office for the first time. Kemeny assigned director Tanya Ballantyne to find an archetypal poverty-stricken family to become the subject of the film. She knocked on doors at welfare and social-aid agencies in Montreal and settled on the Bailey family because a story could be built around the imminent birth of their tenth child. The Film Board paid the family $500 to film them.

The Things I Cannot Change ($34,044) was the outcome of her labours in 1966, and it was the first film in the Film Board's Poverty Program. Using direct-cinema technique, she spent three weeks with the Baileys over several months in an undirected observation of their life. From the sea of footage and a shooting ratio of at least 20 to 1, she recorded the daily life and travails of a family caught in the teeth of grinding poverty that threatened to overwhelm them. Theirs was a never-ending tale of woe: trouble with the police, not enough food, and the arrival of yet another child, to name a few.

The film revealed the physical decrepitude of paint-peeled, single-light-bulb rooms of a miserable flat, containing a bevy of children per bed, all reminiscent of turn-of-the-century photos of urban poverty. Amidst this, Mrs Bailey suffered silently, trying to keep her offspring in clean clothes and well-groomed, while the persistently unemployed and trouble-prone, but indomitable, Mr Bailey shared the household chores and tried unsuccessfully to figure out a way to escape the underclass, so that he might fit into the system.

In the tradition of Unit B's suspended judgment, Ballantyne decided there would be no narration. The film ends with the arrival of the tenth child and Bailey quoting the motto 'God grant me the serenity to accept the things I cannot change, courage to change the things I can, and wisdom to know the difference.' As Mr Bailey looks into an empty fridge, he vows that if necessary, he will steal to feed his children. When telecast on the CBC on 3 May 1967, this tour de force of the underbelly of capitalism was a shock to middle-class Canada. The estimated television audience was the largest to date for any single Film Board film. It was even said that Prime Minister Pearson saw it and was moved.[22]

Norman McLaren's *Pas de deux* (1967) is a black and white study in multiple images of the complex choreography of ballet. His innovation of exposing the same frame as many as ten times was soon copied by the world of advertising.

Although the inexperienced Ballantyne had removed some libellous comments at the advice of Film Board lawyers, the unfortunate family suffered dearly for allowing the probing camera to put on display some of their intimate feelings. The director showed the Baileys the film before it was telecast, and they did not protest. However, their subsequent notoriety led neighbours to mock the bewildered family, and the senior Bailey claimed afterwards that he did not know the origin of the motto he had quoted on-camera, which happened to be that of Alcoholics Anonymous. Ballantyne excised much footage that could have condemned the family, only to hear some call the film a fraud because it did not let the subjects pillory themselves. Ballantyne claimed that viewers brought their own biases to the film, and that

people are not so easily categorized. She thought that she was being truthful and honest, pushing the limits and going out on a limb by exposing things that people usually try to cover up, while allowing the observer to become a participant in events and not be manipulated by the voice-over narration. Others argued that the images themselves were as manipulative as words, and that the family members had become *objects*, not subjects, of the film.

When John Grierson saw *The Things I Cannot Change*, he hated it for revealing a person's private life without that person deciding that he or she be fully known. Colin Low agreed; the family was at a fundamental disadvantage because they were vulnerable and easy to exploit. Low thought it was unforgivable that a documentary film which

159

purported to be sympathetic to the subjects had exacerbated a family situation.[23] It was the last time that sensationalism played a major thread in the poverty films. From here on, the subjects became involved in the play-back and editorial process. Ballantyne had opened a Pandora's box of questions about what documentary does. She did not make another film for the Film Board for almost twenty years – and then it was a low-keyed follow-up about what happened to the Bailey family.[24]

At the Privy Council Office, R.A.J. Phillips asked Norbert Préfontaine, who was assistant secretary to the Cabinet in social policy in the Special Planning Secretariat, to take over responsibility for the work on poverty. There followed a series of conversations where he introduced people he knew in government departments who might have an interest in this issue to Film Board representatives. He invited them to offer advice to the film agency as to what areas were important, from a government point of view, for further exploration. Some were uncomfortable with the fact that direct-cinema technique did not allow sponsors to change the script. But Préfontaine was sympathetic to the idea of letting the viewer feel what it was like to be poor. It was a critical moment, and his stature and enthusiasm made it possible for two dialogues to commence. One was between departmental officials and NFB film producers, the other between citizens and government. This was a pure application of the liberal idea in an era whose byword was 'democratization.' If the citizens were in effect delegating authority to their elected representatives to inform them about important subjects, theirs was also the right to reply to people in government openly and democratically.

Robertson was impressed by the process and the possibilities and thought that the programme might lead to the Film Board assisting the various departments to tackle their particular problems.[25] In these heady and confident days of early 1967, Préfontaine was able to find enough civil servants who believed something good could come from the experiment. He invited representatives from fifteen federal departments to attend a forum held every two months in the East Block of Parliament. There, they could discuss project ideas and offer opinions that might then start to become a film or audiovisual presentation.

The plan was to have an interdepartmental committee consult with Film Board representatives and generate jointly the parameters to a given story-line or idea on subjects like Indians, poverty, and regional disparities. Eight departments and agencies responded, volunteering modest funding if the Film Board matched their contributions.[26] In this manner was the unnamed but soundly financed programme launched with great hope. The Film Board retained total control over the individual films and envisioned the project as a forerunner to initiating a regional production-distribution-advisory scheme, where films would be the catalyst to precipitate social action. The interdepartmental committee decided at last to call this experiment 'Challenge for Change.' If things went perfectly, the hope was to develop activity on a vital social issue to the point where, in a few years, the organizers might be able to step out and leave behind a body of experience and a cadre of people in university extension services to continue it. It would take about $400,000 to start up the programme, shared half by the sponsors and half by the Film Board. The interdepartmental committee consisted of key players in this field: Manpower, Health and Welfare, the Agricultural Rehabilitation and Development Agency, and the Special Planning Secretariat.

'Challenge for Change' came into existence in February 1967 as a two-year experiment. In June 1969, the interdepartmental committee broadened the concept to propose to the Cabinet an experimental multimedia project (with a French Production component), the purpose of which was to help citizens acclimatize themselves to change as a permanent feature of their lives.

Le Groupe de Recherches sociales becomes 'Société nouvelle'

Parallel to the seed-bed where Challenge for Change was germinating in 1965–6, there was another pilot being cultivated by francophone filmmaker Raymond Garceau. He produced a 23-film project in rural New Brunswick and the Gaspé Peninsula, under the Department of Forestry and the Eastern Quebec Planning Board (BAEQ). Garceau, who had originally been an agronomist, had celebrated rural life in classic documentaries like *La Drave* (on the log drive) and *Alexis Ladouceur, Métis*, and was enthusiastic about the series. The federal government's Agricultural Rehabilitation and Development Agency (ARDA) intended the films to bring to rural depressed areas a system of television education to retrain the unemployed and undereducated. Using *cinéma direct* technique, Garceau went into these forgotten, depressed corners of Quebec and gave common people the chance to express their frustrations and hopes on camera. Just as the series began to show promise as a tool of social animation, the government cancelled it peremptorily, leaving the Film Board with the bill of $95,000.

But the effectiveness of Garceau's technique lingered on, and this inspired filmmakers Fernand Dansereau, Michel Régnier, and Maurice Bulbulian to continue pursuing it. They intended to replace the random spectacle that had characterized the early *cinéma direct* experiments and to allow the people themselves, not the experts, to express the social issues that concerned them. They discovered that once people saw themselves on screen, the effect was to generate a degree of self-validation and democratization that had not existed before. Starting in 1966, the group made five films that be-

came prototypes in their varied uses of *cinéma direct*. They were *Saint-Jérôme*, *L'École des autres*, *La P'tite Bourgogne*, *82,000*, and the realistic fiction piece *Tout le temps, tout le temps, tout le temps...?* In 1967, they named their group Le Groupe de Recherches sociales.[27]

Fernand Dansereau promised the people in Saint-Jérôme that they would have the right to censor material in which they appeared before the film was telecast, in December 1966. He filmed over a nine-month period, concentrating on unemployment caused by the technological revolution. From twenty hours of film, he reduced *Saint-Jérôme* ($64,791) to two hours and subsequently split it into several dozen short pieces that became tools for social workers. Groups in the community came to question many psychological and cultural values and to reflect upon their identity as *québécois* in a world of dizzying change. This latter point about identity seemed most important to Dansereau. But such probing and criticism were not without danger for the Film Board. When Minister Jean Marchand saw derogatory footage of himself in one film, he berated Commissioner McPherson before an assembly of deputy ministers, 'If that's the kind of thing that the Film Board should do, they should cease to exist.'[28] The hapless McPherson was under fire and humiliated yet again as he tried to stand his ground before his peers. It was no small irony that the Saint-Jérôme region blossomed economically soon after General Motors Corporation constructed a major assembly plant there, with substantial financial concessions by the federal and provincial governments.

La P'tite Bourgogne ($35,552), by Maurice Bulbulian, documented a citizen's committee participating in renovation of their Montreal neighbourhood in 1967–8. (It was the Bailey's neighbourhood and had been slated for renovation before *The Things I Cannot Change* was made.) The citizens refused to be puppets of the urban-renewal professionals and insisted on having a say in the future shape of their environment. Bulbulian called the experience a collective as well as personal adventure.

In 1968, Michel Régnier made *L'École des autres* ($75,096), a trenchant documentary showing how poor social surroundings were often correlated to pupils' sorry performance in, and their dropping out of, school. CYC coordinator Peter Katadotis had helped organize a Montreal social-action programme to give the children of poor families special attention, and the film demonstrated how it was succeeding. Régnier, a one-man activist, found his *métier* as a practitioner of what he called 'functional cinema.' He spent the next twenty years in Canada and abroad making films about the underprivileged, urban renewal, and rural health care. Katadotis left the CYC to join the Film Board and eventually became the director of English Production. A similar example of Le Groupe de Recherches sociales's efforts was *82,000 (Maisonneuve-Hochelaga)*, a series of five shorts made by a Montreal citizens' committee under Film Board supervision.

Some years earlier, Léonard Forest had asked a community group in New Brunswick to write and act out a feature-length fiction piece about politics and manipulation; *La noce n'est pas finie* probably inspired Dansereau to try a similar experiment in 1969, with *Tout le temps, tout le temps, tout le temps...?* ($63,037), one of the most interesting of the five films of the Groupe de Recherches sociales. Members of a community group wrote, performed, and helped edit a piece about a contemporary scattered urban family of thirteen that has a reunion in the rural paternal home. Dansereau admitted he was influenced by the contemporary United States blacks' slogan of 'Freedom Now' as the group fashioned its archetypes, who were victims of the powers-that-be. Their fate was to eat dirt, time and time and time again (hence the title), as they mechanically played out the dramas of life, from unemployment, alcoholism, and unwanted pregnancy to in-

nocent hope, founded upon young love. Life was good, love was important, freedom was necessary, and society was rotten. It was weighty stuff that a cautious Radio-Canada aired in March 1970, in an eleven o'clock Sunday night time slot.[29]

As Challenge for Change began to flesh out its activities from February 1967, it seemed only natural to include the parallel work of Le Groupe de Recherches sociales. By June 1969 the interdepartmental committee broadened the whole concept to propose to include a French Production component. At this point, in spite of some members' reluctance to integrate, Challenge for Change became 'Société nouvelle' too, under executive producers John Kemeny and Léonard Forest. It was unfortunate that the English and French filmmakers involved in Challenge for Change and Société nouvelle tended to operate on parallel rather than coordinate lines, although there were several significant creative alliances formed.

Fernand Dansereau explained later that those francophone filmmakers who showed interest in Société nouvelle were concerned less with poverty than with building a bridge between the individual and his needs and the new technologies that had proliferated incoherently.[30] A number of people thought the French title was presumptuous because it implied that a new society had already arrived. The titles mattered little to the government, so long as they were bilingual.

Préfontaine obtained official cabinet approval in July 1969 for a five-year programme. Until then, the committee had operated through an (unauthorized) document and had bypassed specific Treasury Board approval. From this point, the committee operated essentially on the principle of parity, with equal representation (and funding) from the Film Board and the departments, all under the aegis of the secretary of state.[31] Austerity notwithstanding, the Film Board had managed to carve out a new programme mandate for itself in the coming decade.

The chairman's genius, most agreed, was

his ability to find consensus; this probably saved the experiment from death by internecine war. If the original programme was to be radical in orientation and Socratic in its method of eliciting new ideas, Préfontaine knew when to cajole and when to take a person aside in the hall. Years later, he explained that it was a matter of plain common sense and political sensitivity; he was able to assess the thin line between what is 'fair game' in the matter of public statements and education and what was not acceptable, that is, what would be either 'subversive or contrary to policy.' The Film Board people spoke for their own and their clients' interests, while the departmental representatives were speaking for departmental interests; Préfontaine was able to get most of the participants on both sides of the table to move to the ground of 'the national interest.' The process was tough, but rewarding.

Challenge for Change: First films

The first Challenge for Change films were planned in a fluid atmosphere. Peter Pearson directed a 50-minute fiction piece about poverty, *The Best Damn Fiddler from Calabogie to Kaladar* ($82,635), which later lost its Challenge for Change rubric because it did not quite fit into the framework the sponsors had envisioned. It is the story of a reckless family man from rural Ontario who prefers to not know where his next dollar is coming from, rather than to submit to the shame of depending on society's safety net of welfare. His wife gives birth to a tenth child in an atmosphere of poverty and desperation, reminiscent of the Bailey family in *The Things I Cannot Change*, and laughs at a well-meaning doctor who offers her an intrauterine device to avoid her annual bondage. The eldest daughter escapes the certain cycle of pregnancy and poverty to find work in the city as a telephone operator. The father continues his ignorant but carefree lifestyle, unheeding of all warnings of impending disaster. After its CBC telecast in March 1969,

reactions were mixed. In Ottawa, one critic called it a quiet brilliant hour of television; in Boissevin, Manitoba, they called it trash.[32] The Ottawa opinion was sounder. *Calabogie Fiddler* was named film of the year at the Canadian Film Awards in 1969, is still in distribution, and remains an example of how short English-Canadian fiction can be as good as features.

The first films to come out of Challenge for Change in 1967 were not impressive cinematically, as evidenced by the 17-minute *Encounter at Kwacha House–Halifax*, a CYC-inspired discussion between black and white youths at a community interracial club. The talking heads were visually unexciting, but one could see how potentially explosive the situation was, with discrimination at work, at school, at home, and in the community. Rex Tasker, who directed this regional production, became the founding executive producer of the Film Board's Halifax regional studio.

A similar 15-minute experiment in 1967 was *Pow Wow at Duck Lake*, by producers Barrie Howells and John Kemeny. It showed a discussion of Indian-Métis problems before a gathering of Saskatchewan Indians and whites, raising the discomfiting question about how a white man's education restricts the Indians' pursuit of native ways. Frontier College was influenced by this approach to understanding the native perspective, and in 1968 some of its teachers handed over videotape and Super 8-mm equipment to natives of the Fort Hope Ojibway reserve in northern Ontario. The experience accelerated the involvement of Indians in the social and educational work of Frontier College and generally raised both hope and expectation.[33]

The greatest success of this first year was a series of films undertaken by Colin Low in Newfoundland, in association with the Memorial University Extension Department. Called the Fogo Island Communication Experiment, this series of twenty-six short films was made in 1967 and 1968 for $83,259. They were meant to give rival factions, the poor and the established authorities, a chance to communicate. Low called the project a communication loop, where film and videotape would help teach those who were victims of misfortune first to become sensitized to articulating the problem, then to cooperate to effect a change in their condition. Unlike most films that depend on an adversarial relationship to be effective, these were meant to show that it was in the provincial government's interest to help solve the economic problem of the citizens of Fogo Island, a proud people who wanted their island fishery to provide them with a livelihood.

Low chose Fogo as his subject after examining several federal-provincial resettlement projects in another part of Newfoundland, where pork-barrelling was a way of life. He believed that to have made a film indicting the authorities would have stirred emotions, then left the population worse off than before. Such a film probably would have also meant a stillbirth for Challenge for Change. He chose Fogo Island because it had an informal improvement committee, rather than local government, and because the people were determined to resist resettlement. He arrived to discover the government freezing out services in hope that the people would partly resettle themselves.[34]

Low's method became the model for most of the future Challenge for Change films. He began discussing the substantive issues with the locals, who refused to talk on camera, since they were nervous about what friends might say or what might happen to them if the film were shown elsewhere. Low promised that he would show it to the participants before anyone else would see it. They trusted him and he kept this word. His only cut was a three-minute sequence in which the tone of the questioner sounded inquisitorial.

He shot the films in a rational, unemotional way; high emotion and conflict look interesting on national television, but he believed those two elements hindered the communication process. He thought that if he

reduced the island situation to a 'theatrical' experience, it would become so oversimplified as to exacerbate, not lessen, tensions. He saw himself as a kind of mediator, trying to find a common denominator of interest. The films were supposed to be a series of modules with relevance to Fogo Island and Newfoundland, but not much to the rest of the country. He chose film over video because the latter was technically difficult to edit at the time.

Low edited twenty hours of material to six hours of blocks on various themes, subjects, or personalities. Not all the footage was problem-oriented – a certain amount expressed life values, cultural values, or simply island attractions and entertainments. Three months later, he returned to the island and for over a month screened the documentaries in different villages, using a professional social worker to lead general discussions. Then he took the films to St John's, where he filmed a group of academic professionals at a seminar discussing the material, a sequence which he then played back to the community. Later, the ministry of fisheries made a film that was shown on Fogo. The media dialogue was continued in other parts of the province by a Film Board–trained crew from Memorial University.

The net effect of the films was that the people of Fogo Island organized to form a fishing co-op. Unemployment fell drastically, the price of fish rose, fishermen began to earn good money, and, most of all, the people felt that the changes which occurred were very much based on a catalytic community process. Some argued that the public attention surrounding the project gave the islanders their real leverage. In his usual self-deprecating way, Low would only admit that the motel where much of the meeting and filming had taken place was an important centre of communication. He was more concerned with the dilemma of film: it fixes a person's state or emotion for all time, when in fact the person might feel differently a week later and might want to be represented in another light. He concluded that the simple principles of Fogo had extensive implications for the ethical use of the visual media in general.[35]

There was a radical-activist approach to the Challenge for Change method too. In 1967 Peter Pearson and Donald Brittain filmed the American radical organizer Saul Alinksy. *Saul Alinsky Went to War* is a one-hour record of how he battled in the United States against the conditions that keep the poor in poverty. It also shows how he helped blacks in urban ghettos find an effective non-violent means to fight for their rights.

Two other Alinsky films were set in Canada in 1967, *Encounter with Saul Alinsky, Part I and II* ($10,621), also directed by Peter Pearson. Part I (29 minutes) found Alinsky in heated debate with some members of the CYC about the means and costs of securing social change. He thought good organizers should be paid well, had to be as carefully selected as an athlete for the major leagues, and should know the difference between the world as it is and as it should be. Action, sincerity, and commitment did not count; the irony was, he said, that 'the right things are done almost always for the wrong reason.' While organizers had to be free of dogma and rhetoric, change that occurs always stems from threat, which itself is a combination of power and politics. (He noted how 'the Alinsky myth' frightened the powers-that-be.) Start with the world as it is, he concluded, and change will be possible. Part II (32 minutes) shows him in intellectual combat with Indians who wished to change the Indian Act by peaceful persuasion – in opposition to his own belief that direct power was the best method to obtain this end.

Alinsky had been organizing for years. He was somewhat dubious about those Canadian social workers and animators who thought they were going to create some kind of wonderworld for those people who did not have any of the awful temptations that they as middle-class types had. He said, 'Ask the people who have nothing what they want and

they will tell you: a piece of the bourgeois pie.' If nothing else, Alinsky could always bring the pixilated idealists down to earth.

In 1968, Kemeny asked Bonnie Sherr Klein to pursue the Alinsky idea. She then directed five short films, called the *Alinsky Approach Series: Organizing for Power* ($86,835), shot in the United States. Klein, an American who was a landed immigrant to Canada, was interested in showing Canadians how Alinsky's organizing techniques might be grafted on to the Canadian trunk.[36] The Alinsky films were used in Canada to train community workers and citizen's groups.

By contrast, Colin Low did not approve of the Alinsky approach, which he thought was fundamentally cynical. He believed that the American manifested an intellectual arrogance by making determinations in the interests of other people and groups without having to live their lives. Low insisted that the best films of the Film Board reflected an interesting, thoughtful humility.[37] It was obvious that the Challenge for Change idea was not a single philosophy, but a heterogeneous approach to proliferating communications tools among the population.

George Stoney's imprint upon Challenge for Change

By 1968, John Kemeny found himself spending much of his time arguing with the Challenge for Change filmmakers about the objectives of the programme. One difficulty was that time and budget constraints led filmmakers to draw hasty conclusions because they were thrust in and pulled out of a situation before they could know the deep realities. This was one of the oldest weaknesses of documentary filmmaking. Besides, Kemeny's interest had shifted to feature films, and he soon left the Film Board to produce one. If Colin Low had demonstrated that he was at the creative heart of the enterprise and was effective with the interdepartmental committee, he did not care for administration. He produced only a few more films after the Fogo Island experience. In need of a suitable executive producer to handle the diplomacy and administration of the project, Director of Production Frank Spiller went to New York City in June to recruit the experienced documentary filmmaker George Stoney.

Stoney, who had been a professor of Bonnie Sherr Klein's at Stanford University, agreed to come, provided that his term be two years only. He had always thought well of the Film Board and in 1948 had travelled the rural circuits to learn how the unique non-theatrical distribution system of the agency functioned. When he returned in the fall of 1968, he discovered a conflict-ridden organization; he believed the tugs at Challenge for Change were between those who wanted to take the money and make their own films (having nothing to do with the programme philosophy), those who wanted to build up another bureaucracy, and those who wanted to acquire personal power. He encountered much initial acrimony from the French side, first because they refused to get involved in the programme, and then over his 60-40 per cent budget allocation, which he split in favour of the English.

An example of his difficulty was that the interdepartmental committee had programmed a film on the attitude of relief participants. No one wanted to do it, because the idea came from a particularly difficult representative from the Department of Agriculture. Stoney thought this situation was absurd because the committee could neither tell Challenge for Change how to make a film nor veto the finished product. He went outside the Film Board and recruited the first *Candid Eye* director, Terence Macartney-Filgate. Stoney's single warning to him was that he should not feel sorry for his subjects, since pity was the enemy. The object of the exercise was to make it easier for people on welfare to cope with middle-class types and vice versa. Macartney-Filgate talked to case workers at welfare agencies in Toronto and

also to welfare-rights groups, where he recorded angry relief recipients who were bitterly fighting the system. When the film was in its semi-finished state, Stoney suggested they test it on ten audiences around Montreal, a procedure that had never been done before. Three groups reacted by talking about the people on welfare, and the filmmaker felt he had missed the mark because they should have been talking about the issues. He cut the film to twenty minutes and tested it again. The film now worked because the viewers forgot their English-Canadian reserve and became angry about the welfare system.

Up Against the System ($4,830) opens with testimony about what it is like to be poor; welfare workers try to explain the vicious cycle of poverty and why the middle class seems unconcerned. As have-nots, the poor claim they have been failed by those who have; they feel victimized by an impersonal system that does not allow them freedom of speech; the poor are reduced to answering questions untruthfully to case workers who do not expect to hear the truth anyway. Poverty spawned crime, because the underprivileged were without dignity and had feelings of inferiority. One of the greatest tragedies to be feared was poverty in old age. 'The system' was being taken to task, and if the film suggests a guaranteed income might be one answer, its final point is that the government should listen, leaders were needed, and, in the words of a sweet-looking grandmother type, a revolution is needed.

Stoney asked welfare officials in Toronto to check for factual errors and prepared them for a devastating attack on the welfare system. The responsible person in the ministry swallowed his natural reserve and requested a film print to launch his upcoming regional welfare conference. *Up Against the System* was a hit there and at subsequent welfare conferences across Canada (including the Federal Task Force on Alienation in August 1969), later at all three political party conferences, and on morning talk-show television. Stoney believed the film was misused only once, when Prime Minister Trudeau attended a conference in Vancouver and, in response to a reporter's query as to why there were not more poor people present, responded with his characteristic shrug, 'But we had the film.'

When Stoney brought it to Washington, DC, incredulous officials wondered why the film was not promoting a specific programme. They asked if the Canadian government knew he had made this document and were more surprised to learn that the sponsors had used it. Americans could not see the value of listening to the people in the field; American methods depended on arm's-length relationships, where the critics were on the outside (and happy to not be beholden to people on the inside), while people on the inside did not want to hear anything outside. This adversarial relationship did not allow for a meeting of the minds, which is what Challenge for Change did. Years later, Stoney denied that the whole exercise was one of window-dressing. He felt that more people on the interdepartmental committee were committed to what they were doing than many at the Film Board.[38] In a more flippant mood, he said elsewhere that Canadian government officials believe that Canadians understood the idea of government-sponsored subversion. It is an intelligent way to mobilize social revolution without violence.[39]

Video: Another Challenge for Change tool

The first use of videotape at the Film Board had occurred in 1967, when producer Robert Forget and director Claude Jutra rented four half-inch videotape recorders to conduct research with children. They concluded that video was not an effective tool, probably because it was suffering from the normal setbacks of a new technology, that is, equipment was fragile and the tape was difficult to edit. In 1968, Bonnie Sherr Klein used video with the Citizen's Committee in Montreal's St-Jacques district, where she and her physician-husband had been volunteers. She wanted to explore the idea of letting people create their own video images. It was also unique to have an English film crew working with French subjects.

With the help of social activist Dorothy Hénaut, Klein demonstrated in *VTR St-Jacques* ($33,962) that video had great potential as an organizing tool among the poor. The Citizen's Committee assembled its own video programmes, which served to catalyse the district and to inspire positive citizens' action to confront the main problem, poor health care among the local population. In evaluating the method, Klein thought that people became more confident in themselves, sensed they were no longer alone, and felt their message would reach those authorities who could initiate solutions. One citizen's revealing comment was, 'When we watch the tapes, we don't just learn to know ourselves better; we also come to understand others better. After that, it's much more fun to work together.'[40]

In 1971, Robert Forget obtained a $40,000 grant from the Canada Council to open Vidéographe in downtown Montreal as part of an eight-month Société nouvelle experiment in video production and distribution. Forget had been inspired by the Global Village concept then being developed in New York City. He had two purposes: to allow *cinéma-documentaire électronique* to bring into play all social questions and to widen video distribution. To emphasize video's accessibility, he allowed the facility to remain open twenty-four hours a day, welcoming people for training and providing for the free use of video equipment and screening facilities. Most of what was done was called 'process videos,' as people recorded citizens' groups and public meetings. The expense of this operation was one of the main reasons for abandoning it to the Quebec Ministry of Communications in 1973. Vidéographe continued for years as an effective means for minority groups to express their problems. Forget reflected years later that the Vidéographe experiment was set up at a moment when a lot of money was made available to cool the heated social climate of youth struggling toward some form of a new social contract. He recalled that the interdepartmental committee had one abiding fear, which was not citizen-radicalism: it was that the video equipment might be used to make pornographic material. They were relieved that no such instances occurred, although Forget thought it significant that the first two productions of Vidéographe with sexual themes were shot by women. As a whole then, the experiment showed that the types of films produced by people aged thirteen to sixty-five covered a whole spectrum of subjects, what he referred to as *la pallette large*. He felt that Vidéographe was an unqualified success, and noted the fact that many people who subsequently found themselves in mainstream Quebec media had received their initial training there. Critics thought that the free-form organization of Vidéographe was its weakest link. The use of video as an organizing tool declined when major organizations and institutions found they did not have enough money to do their basic work; video was a dispensable frill.[41]

Later on, additional conflict surfaced within Société nouvelle between regional staff who favoured video and Montreal filmmakers who preferred the traditional celluloid medium. By 1974 the situation was such that, on the French side, neither the filmmakers, video workers, nor distribution people worked together any longer. The fact was that after video's newness wore off (and probably after the first video brief was presented to government), few had the patience to sit through videotapes of talking heads, since it was much more efficient to read a well-prepared written brief.

By contrast, on the English side, making films and videos, distribution, and community organizing were often carried on by the same individuals. Roles were flexible, if

somewhat confusing, because new priorities were being set constantly and there was a genuine effort to take into account the input of everybody at every level in a given project, from the government to the people who were subjects of the films. If some feared that the aura of being a filmmaker was being lost, Kathleen Shannon, who was working toward the genesis of the womens' film unit, thought the idea of giving oneself over to the community and forgetting one's ego was critical. She encouraged filmmakers to direct and become part of distribution, and believed this was one of the most positive elements to come from the Challenge for Change programme. Interactive film and video became one of the most dynamic elements of the women's unit, Studio D, and lent the Film Board new credibility as it struggled to redefine itself in coming years.[42]

Looking at the production record, from 1969 to 1973 there were fifteen VTR projects completed in English and nine in French.[43] The total expenditure during that period was $5.9 million on fifty-one films and videos in both languages, the creation of social-animation programmes in slum neighbourhoods, distribution, French and English periodicals, research, and the costs of maintaining a bureaucracy. By 1976, Société nouvelle boasted of seventy-one films and several dozen videos.[44]

Relations with the interdepartmental committee remained solid during Stoney's tenure, although there were difficulties with specific departments. Sometimes a combination of luck and strategy kept the programme on track. In one such case, Stoney helped arrange for Robert Nichol, an assistant cameraman, to leap-frog the job hierarchy and direct his first film. The interdepartmental committee representative from Agriculture, Grant Carman, wanted a film on his department's policy of removing marginal farmers on the Shield. Nichol could not finish the film with his $5,000 allotment, so Stoney had to ask the department for more money. Even in its unfinished state, *Wilf* was a beautifully photographed portrait of old Wilfred Flemming, trying stubbornly to stick it out, in spite of the impossible economics. The old farmer did not want to move, but the department had set a numerical figure of people to be uprooted without considering the human cost, especially to the aged. Upon viewing the incomplete film, Carman smiled as the lights came up and said in a subdued voice, 'Wilf is my father.' His department had received hard knocks in the critical portrait, but he provided the money to finish it. *Wilf* cost $22,607, but more importantly, Carman had finally come around to seeing Colin Low's argument that communication had to be a two-way process.[45]

One permanent change: Indian consciousness-raising

Stoney thought that *Challenge for Change* gave a boost to Indian consciousness-raising activities of the era. For example, there was an Indian film crew, sponsored by a CYC grant, and the Department of Northern Development and Indian Affairs that was at the Film Board to learn skills. The department had designed the programme to include tribes from east to west. Being chosen by well-meaning officials did not obviate the sense that they were pawns of a paternalistic system yet again. Being thrown together from diverse regions emphasized their dissimilarities, and there were also historical tribal rivalries that tugged constantly at the group. In the final analysis, though, the natives made a statement on their terms, not someone else's. Perhaps the most powerful film to come from their efforts was *Ballad of Crowfoot* ($10,324), a bitter, haunting 10-minute short in 1968, directed by Willie Dunn, a Micmac from Montreal. His intense, expressive music and words created as powerful an image as the animated arrangement of historical still photos that depicted the opening of the Canadian West. For the Indians, the coming of the white man had meant the death of the buffalo and their way of life; what remained was memory, a two-dimensional stereotyping of native people, and an empty promise of 'maybe there will be a better tomorrow.'

Another member of the Indian crew was Mike Mitchell, a Mohawk from Cornwall, Ontario. He phoned Stoney early in 1969 to tell of trouble on the St Regis reserve. The Indians there had long enjoyed a liberal interpretation of the Jay Treaty of 1791, and customs officials had let returning natives bring into Canada duty-free groceries they had bought in New York. A new officer decided he would charge duty universally. The Indians planned to protest in Ottawa and then return to block the international bridge. Mitchell asked for a Film Board crew to film the event. (The Indian crew was on location in the West.) Stoney forgot normal procedure and found a group in the Film Board cafeteria willing to help. The director of production gave him the go-ahead that afternoon, and by evening the film crew was on the reserve.

Next morning, they were first to capture the images of the bridge closure, and they continued to film for four hours. Three days later, the Indians came to the Film Board to see the freshly processed footage. Their community was in ferment over who had done what during the confrontation, which had led to scuffles and arrests. Kathleen Shannon helped put together the two hours of rushes chronicling the event. She accompanied distribution officer Anthony Kent to the reserve, where they screened the film repeatedly. The effect was electrifying as the Indians saw themselves confronting authorities soberly and effectively. Network television had aired only the clash – these rushes showed the long palavers between the violence. In effect, they explained the commotion. Shannon said later that the reactions of the people determined how she edited the final 36-minute version, *You Are on Indian*

Land ($8,432). The experience of watching those reactions and of helping the voiceless to gain their voices had catalysed her transformation to feminism.

Kent wanted to let the RCMP see the rushes. The Indians said it was *their* film and they had no intention of letting the police view it. Kent explained that the Challenge for Change idea was to encourage dialogue, and he persuaded them to acquiesce. The authorities were disappointed that the film did not contain more violence. Tony Ianzelo's handheld yet stable camera had observed events and, unlike the television station's shaky camera during scenes of scuffling, gave a very different sense of what had happened. The Film Board footage testified that there were many Indian leaders rather than one person, a fact that probably helped get the case thrown out of court. Stoney was aghast to learn, however, that in the heat of the moment, when someone called for a knife to slash the tires of cars trying to bulldoze their way through the blockade, it was the Film Board's soundman who obliged and unwittingly became an accomplice to a possible felony.

In a similar case, the Indians of the St Regis reserve contested the subdivision by whites of two islands in the St Lawrence for summer cottages. Stoney himself directed *God Help the Man Who Would Part with His Land* ($51,755), which portrayed officials of Indian Affairs viewing film footage of the dispute as representations were made by the Indians and the cottagers. The film certainly crystallized the issue, and Indian Affairs gave the Indians a sympathetic ear, probably because of a fear of notoriety and the publicity that preceded their arrival.[46]

The Indian Affairs member on the interdepartmental committee became livid over these films and habitually boycotted meetings or threatened to resign. Préfontaine brought him down to earth by telling him his department's $100,000 were going to be spent anyhow, so he had better show up. It was Préfontaine's presence on the committee that served as a buffer for the Film Board and helped deflect much departmental criticism.[47]

Cree Hunters of Mistassini and Our Land Is Our Life

Préfontaine was preparing to finish his mandate as chairman late in 1971. Before he left, the interdepartmental committee chose six priorities for the following year, among which was aboriginal people in Canadian society.[48] There were powerful forces in Ottawa (in the prime minister's office, some believed) who did not want this subject broached from a political point of view, so the Film Board decided simply to do a series about native people and their lives. This was the genesis of *Cree Hunters of Mistassini* and *Our Land Is Our Life*. Boyce Richardson, a former associate editor of the *Montreal Star*, had produced a series of hard-hitting articles on native peoples' rights and the ecological effects of white man's development in the North. With co-director/cameraman Tony Ianzelo, he set out for Mistassini, Quebec, to talk to Cree friends. The Cree and other Indians were leery about another film on Indian problems, but relented when Richardson promised that the films would let the Indians show their world through Indian eyes.

They filmed three hunting families in the bush over a five-month period in 1972–3. *Cree Hunters of Mistassini* ($95,603) was shown in rough-cut state in Mistassini in August 1973 and in semi-finished (cutting-copy) state in March 1974. Audience reactions were filmed at that time and edited into the final version of *Our Land Is Our Life* ($102,469). Producer Colin Low called the first film 'poetic anthropology.' It captured the rhythms of native life as Indians shared, rather than altered, the ecological environment. The day after its local exhibition, the men of the town left en masse for the bush to regain contact with a way of life they felt was

Cree Hunters of Mistassini (1974), a typical example of how the Challenge for Change programme was supposed to work, portrays native people in the context of their relationship to the land and deals with dominant issues such as aboriginal rights, ecology, and family relations.

fast slipping away. CBC broadcast the documentary nationally on 3 July, 1974; the French version appeared on 20 November. The more 'political' *Our Land Is Our Life* showed the Cree in a community meeting discussing their long-term future if they accepted compensation for the gigantic James Bay hydroelectric project. Their conviction was that nothing meant more to them than the land and they would not yield it. Low called this film a record of the historical erosion of that society; the Indians' problem was how to affirm themselves in the face of inexorable change.

Using the precedent of *You Are on Indian Land*, these documentaries obtained their own distribution budgets for urban and rural audiences. Animators and fieldworkers equipped with information kits made exten-

sive use of the documentaries in land-claims-settlement meetings. There was a sense that these films were an effective catalyst among natives. They stimulated action related to land issues, education, and development by transnational enterprises. More important, the experiment had proved the efficacy of settling aside special monies for distribution and promotion, although in this case the process was unwieldy and expensive. Such an approach had proved superior to the often haphazard shotgun distribution method that the Film Board normally employed. The practice of predetermined distribution budgets took more than another decade to become permanent.

At first glance, the evidence seemed to show that the immediate impact of this project as a whole was marginal. It was open to criticism for overexposing a small group who did not represent the native majority. Yet these documents did animate some native peoples; in one case a Cree band planned to return to their old homesite and abandon urban living. But that was not the point of the exercise; on average, it took 1,200 square miles to support a family by trapping, and it was unrealistic to think all the Indians could return to this way of life. The films precipitated two psychological alterations: they encouraged natives to consider their right to effect change on native rather than on white man's terms, and they drew white society's attention to the hitherto ignored implications of unlimited technological expansion. All this being said, the Cree Indians signed an agreement with the Quebec government and the authorities of Hydro-Québec in November 1975, forfeiting claim to almost one million square kilometres of land in return for apparent generous terms. Perhaps the films' strongest impact was that they encouraged white audiences to be more sympathetic to the plight of Indian people. For its part, the Film Board was pleased to have widened its native constituency, which became more interested than ever in using film.[49]

John Grierson sniffs the atmosphere of Challenge for Change

John Grierson was fond of talking about 'using art as a hammer' to his McGill University students; it was a radical phrase appropriate to a radical age. But the wiry Scotsman had his doubts about Challenge for Change, which he articulated from 1969 until 1971, and his remarks at one session, with Colin Low as guest and willing scapegoat, might be a good point from which to observe the overall impact of the programme. Using the Fogo Island experiment as his example, Grierson cautioned that the presentation of local concerns was not necessarily the real representation of local concerns, much less participatory democracy. On one level there was a particular weakness – filmmakers tended to rush to the support of protesting minorities without a due sense of responsibility to majority, established, or even constitutional viewpoints. He wondered why the intelligence, world experience, and expensive education of the filmmaker had not been brought to the people. Low ignored the ad hominem aspect of Grierson's remarks. He replied that he could not recommend anything to these people because the situation had become more complex as he looked more closely.[50]

As a whole, Grierson thought Challenge for Change lacked the broad perspective worthy of a great country – it was not 'news in depth.' He dismissed gruffly what he called subjects like 'the perplexities and sufferings of this rich Canadian people ... Fat boys being sorry for themselves is a bad joke,' he mocked. He thought the rest of the world would laugh at the absurdity of a rich country engaged in this kind of activity.[51] In a typical Grierson gesture, he found no difficulty in speaking from the other side of his mouth elsewhere that he approved of the Challenge for Change films, which were about public, not personal, things.[52]

Since 1966, Grierson had wondered about the wisdom of pursuing non-theatrical film because he thought it encouraged an over-subjective approach to filmmaking, even tempting filmmakers to opt out of their larger duties. It bothered him that young employees without authority had, by exploiting the fact that they had no power, been given access, almost loosely, to large means of production. In his unforgiving estimation, it reflected the worst and most trivial aspects of early-nineteenth-century romanticism.[53]

The biggest problem with the Challenge for Change films, Grierson continued, was their need for a consideration of the objective validity of the argument. Citing the case of an experiment in Drumheller, Alberta, *VTR Rosedale*, he thought it was marvellous that the few people left in an abandoned coal-mining town in southern Alberta were able to mobilize to bring back services they had lost. However, the forgotten fact of life was that, in Canada's wide and difficult land spaces, its boom towns were like island habitations in wide and difficult sea spaces, and often became ghost towns after the wealth was extracted. There were countless distress centres elsewhere that merited attention.[54]

By contrast, he cited the film *Nell and Fred* ($3,018), for revealing local life that to him was wonderful to behold. It was the story of two elderly people (a landlady and her rooming tenant) who considered the pros and cons of going into an institution. At the end of the film, they surprise everyone, including themselves, by deciding to stay where they originally began. Grierson called the film a complete Chekhovian experience that went beyond reporting the local problems and beyond objective discussion of the local destiny.[55]

Commenting on the controversial films that would occasionally percolate from the Film Board, Grierson cautioned that when objectivity was purposely abandoned, what remained was an excited juvenile attack. Such immature and negative criticism was provincial in nature, suburban in its background, belonging and appealing to small people. Confrontational and controversial films had long been a part of the agency's output, he admitted, even if they sometimes brought grief.[56] What worried him was the danger of losing governmental friends on account of them.

Film was meant to 'capture the dramatic implications of changes in our own day,' Grierson continued, 'of the epic possibilities, of the national achievements.' The problem was not one of survival, but of living grandly in this new technical world. Tom Daly challenged him on this point before a class at McGill. 'Technological advance as a film theme is boring,' Daly insisted. 'We are now concerned with personal problems.' Besides, Daly continued, 'The people of Ottawa are resistant to any attempt on our part to move on these high realms of activity. We have got to meet the bureaucratic complexities of modern Ottawa and they tend, of course, to make everything parochial.'[57]

Grierson would hear nothing of it. Ignoring Daly's position as the pre-eminent documentary film-shaper of Canada, he pursued his favourite guise of iconoclasm. He harangued his class, 'Don't you listen to this character, he is preaching a doctrine which he has no right to preach to a young generation.' To make his point, he accused Daly of the greatest sin of all – teaching chaos to a new generation when each generation had the right to hope for order. 'Anyone who tries to give anything else but the hope of a coherent future, cut his throat, hang him to the nearest lamppost,' he railed with dramatic flourish.[58] Daly, knowing Grierson's devastating style, did not mind much playing the scapegoat before the astonished class.

Turning to 'political' subjects, Grierson insisted that Canada was not a provincial backwater, quite the opposite. Its interest in NATO reminded him of Walt Whitman, 'embracing the world in promiscuous handfuls.' These were not the kinds of political subjects that needed articulation, he fulminated, but it was necessary to drink with the people in the right places, listen to the conversations, ask the right questions, and get the right answers.

He thought films should focus on the country and on every front, from mining to science to the human story, all revolving around Canada in the making. The best analogy was to see Canada as containing a small modest light that could be manipulated in the same way a lighthouse used a system of magnifying lenses. Thus would that modest light flash gloriously around the vast horizon. The goal of a communicator was to know either how to serve other people or how they wished to be served.[59]

Grierson concluded optimistically that there was no end to the opportunities. But Canada must start with its writers, 'the key to almost every world of expression.' The government was not the enemy; the enemy was the gloom, alarm, and despondency of teachers and talkers. He thought that with an accentuation of the positive, it would be surprising how many freedoms could be found, for the artist and for everyone else.[60]

In typical adversarial manner, Grierson had sketched with brutal and bold strokes the picture of a Film Board trying to redefine its purpose through the new flagship programme, Challenge for Change / Société nouvelle. Some thought this was the same old Second World War propagandist playing his well-worn record. Others sensed that beneath the prickly exterior he was warning that the true enemies of creativity were complacency and egotism. He died in February 1972, confident that with rededication and commitment his beloved institution could change for the better.

Another permanent change: The need to address women's roles

At the end of the first five years, the interdepartmental committee surveyed the achievement of fifty-one productions and was satisfied with statistical information that boasted over 4,000 screenings to a total audience of two million Canadians. Perhaps on the strength of this positive reception, the committee decided that it was time to probe women's issues and the contemporary question of the changing roles of women. In 1972 Anne Claire Poirier became producer of *En tant que femmes*, a programme of five films.

The series cost $64,324 and had a significant impact after it was telecast, judging from the fact that in response to the network's invitation to phone in and express reactions, the public jammed Radio-Canada's switchboards.[61] The films offered no solutions to the dilemmas they posed (like the perplexity over abortion in Poirier's own *Le temps de l'avant*), and by avoiding the rhetoric of radical feminists they probably reached more conservative women. The thirteen filmmakers adopted a sociological approach and met as a team, some seven groups of seventy women of mixed ages and professions, each week for six months. They constructed their films using varying cinematic formats of documentary, *cinéma direct*, and fiction. Their overall purpose was to build solidarity and a common identity among *les femmes québécoises*, who it was believed had not benefitted from *la révolution tranquille*, and to encourage these and other women to reappraise their capabilities and interests. The goal was to overcome their tragic isolation, to develop social consciousness among them, and to provide a vision of a better future. The filmmakers discovered they had a profound impact on the people they filmed, from the rural women (who had first appeared content with their lives at the early meetings, but who grew to question the price they had paid unwittingly for home and family) to single mothers whose need for proper day care emerged as an increasingly important national issue over the next fifteen years.[62]

In 1971 veteran Film Board distribution officer Len Chatwin had become executive producer of Challenge for Change. At about the same time that Poirier planned her series, the interdepartmental committee asked for a one-hour English film about underprivileged working mothers, who were becoming a majority in contemporary society – not only because of the increasing number of single-parent mothers, but also because in more families than ever before it now took two income earners to maintain a family's place on the social ladder. Chatwin asked Kathleen Shannon to become director because he knew how profoundly she had been sensitized by her experience with the Indians.

Shannon decided to shoot the film with the assistance of video, so the women could see what they looked like just after a sequence was recorded. It was both a psychological and practical tool because it helped them overcome their nervousness before the camera. In editing, she found that the real strength of the footage lay in modular presentation, that is, she fashioned a series of short films rather than a single one. She thought too that the male bureaucrats would likely be more responsive to individual subjects. Ultimately she constructed ten documentaries of six to fifteen minutes' length.[63] *Working Mothers* tried to come to grips with the paradoxical question of how females are to reconcile society's demands for their economic activity with the biological desire for motherhood. The films also indicated that a whole new area of social relationships needed in-depth exploration from a female perspective. To accomplish this goal, the training and hiring of women filmmakers was needed. Unlike Poirier's one-hour films, Shannon's series was not telecast, but this did not worry her because she doubted that television could change minds as they might be changed by seeing films in a live audience. When the first eight *Working Mothers* ($61,974) items were released as a set in April 1974, the five sponsoring government departments bought them for non-theatrical use to develop workshops around them.

It was evident that Challenge for Change / Société nouvelle had found a major and heretofore neglected constituency for the Film Board and one to fill the urban non-theatrical audience void. The sixties' feminist movement had planted the seeds of consciousness-raising that women would cultivate and nurture in the seventies. Both French- and English-speaking Canadian women were a clientele eager to open discussion on their long-neglected reality. Significantly, the Challenge for Change / Société nouvelle approach seemed tailor-made to having this occur. The experience of producing films by and for women convinced Shannon that a women's studio with its own budget should be formed, and she began working ceaselessly and ultimately successfully toward that end (see chapter 10). By contrast, Poirier was afraid that if she pursued a similar course, she and fellow female filmmakers would be forced into a box, making short films with a paltry budget like *Working Mothers*. Such a fate, she feared, would lead to the gradual extinction of women's films in French. Insisting on equality with her male counterparts, Poirier continued to make full-length films about women through funding from the annual French Production budget. There was no French-language women's studio until 1986.[64]

Assessing the impact of Challenge for Change / Société nouvelle

In June 1975 a somewhat deflated inter-departmental committee renewed the Challenge for Change / Société nouvelle programme for another three years.[65] By then, the whole enterprise had grown so routine with the proliferation of bureaucracy that the full committee was left sitting on its hands with nothing to do.[66] If the programme's main purpose was to promote greater inter-action between the government and those governed, as the decade wore on, the departments became less enthusiastic. The committee extended the mandate again in 1978, with the proviso that the experiment would end if departmental representation fell below four departments. The signs were not auspicious. For some of them, Challenge for Change had become more a habit than a programme. Others had been frustrated since the beginning by the constant encour-

agement of the voluntary sector to take action on social problems and issues that had no easy resolution. After an all-too-brief flirtatious swing to the left, the social pendulum was swinging back hard to the right, and fewer people in and out of government were willing to listen to non-mainstream voices. Renewed government austerity in the late seventies was the final nail in the coffin, and Challenge for Change / Société nouvelle was laid to rest quietly in 1980.

It was impossible to measure the programme's performance against some previously established model, especially since the interdepartmental committee reflected a common lack of agreement on the programme's *raison d'être*. It had become practical, controllable, and even predictable, which is the fate of many initiatives once their newness wears off. None the less, unlike the hapless Company of Young Canadians who were meant to be 'a thorn in the side of the Establishment,'[67] Challenge for Change / Société nouvelle was supposed to be part of the progressive conscience of the Establishment. It allowed a number of radical idealists to help many of the forgotten elements of Canadian society find their own voices to help themselves.

Taken as a whole, the programme's audience was composed of small, numerically few groups that were costly to reach. Distribution expenses grew so much as to threaten production, and most regional distribution representatives were let go in 1976. From then on, it was up to a heterogeneous network of animators and social workers to circulate the films voluntarily. As the sober seventies progressed, programme activity was reduced to a few large-scale projects. Video ceased being a reference point, as film, with its mystical, attractive, and enduring quality, returned to its dominant role. Films relating to specific social situations, or that showed organizations like labour unions and community and native-rights organizations at work, were thought to be the most useful teaching aids.[68]

By the time the programme wound down, Canada had earned some international acclaim and prestige as the Challenge for Change approach became a prototype for similar experiments in Australia. George Stoney tried transplanting it to New York, where he worked to encourage 'public access television,' the use of the local cable television for socially beneficial causes. Similarly, Bonnie Sherr Klein returned to Rochester, New York, where she was instrumental in propagating the 'media to the people' movement, sometimes known as 'guerrilla-TV,' an amalgam of Alinsky's ideas and the Fogo Island approach. The original ideology of Challenge for Change was that subjects were to be filmed only if there was a specific group that could use them. When one person paid a backhanded compliment that, at the very least, a practical result was 'a buoy in the Straits of Ungava,' there might be some doubt expressed about the programme's efficacy. Yet some of these films also helped encourage the formation of the Film Board's Environment Studio and anticipated the contemporary concern for ecological issues.

By 1979 there were eighty-three English films in distribution. A glance at their titles tells much about what they contain (see Appendix 3). If few of these ever appeared on network television or received theatrical distribution, they did provide a philosophical raison d'être for the Film Board for over a decade, which perhaps was their most enduring value. In spite of John Grierson's doubts and provocations, the programme had resuscitated his original concept of going to the people to help them communicate with the government and vice versa; this provided a means for the public to vent its frustration and anger, an act that is important to a democracy's health. It had also allowed a group of progressive filmmakers to relate their art to the vital issues of the day in the context of participatory democracy and to help people take charge of their own destinies and aspire to an equitable social structure in a complex bureaucratized society.[69] In short, the Challenge for Change philosophy buried Unit B's passive 'objectivity' and cleared the way for an institutional philosophy that supported the making of passionate, leading-edge films about issues that were important to people. On a less prosaic level, there was also evidence that the whole programme provided a welcome source of extra funding for financially starved Film Board operations and was a palatable alternative to the hated sponsor film of old. Ironically, those (financially critical) dinosaurs continued to be made, while the documentaries of Challenge for Change / Société nouvelle often conflicted with and undermined them.

After Challenge for Change ceased to exist, a number of filmmakers believed that it was only a matter of time before it would be unearthed, reborn, and reshaped in the next generation. When he was asked to comment on what the long-term implications of the programme were, Colin Low expressed the belief that the Challenge for Change method would return in less affluent, if not depression, times. Then, he predicted, there would be a rediscovery of community and a recognition that the mass media are fundamentally an opiate, manipulated by corporate interests who cultivate them as a social parasite of major proportions. Internationalization of the media was erosive of local community, and community programming was essentially what Challenge for Change was all about.[70] Peter Katadotis, who became the executive producer of the programme in its last years, shared the conviction that the kinds of films that had been made should become the centre of the Film Board's English programme. When he became director of English Production in 1979, that was precisely his agenda and, subsequently, the core of English production in the eighties reflected this thrust.[71]

'On a Chariot of Fire':
Sydney Newman's Tenure

Great expectations

The pall of despondency that had hovered over the Film Board for almost two years appeared to lift when Sydney Newman became commissioner in August 1970. The former Film Board director and producer had returned to Canada after twelve years in British television. He had learned to make documentaries during the war under Grierson, and then had moved into television drama until 1958, when a private British network hired him. In 1962 he took over BBC television drama and soon proved that his eye for the popular was unfailing, as he backed the successful science-fiction television series, 'Dr. No.' The staff had high hopes for the man they were calling 'the creative Film Commissioner' and agreed that if professionalism was his greatest asset, having been away from the Film Board since 1952 was his greatest liability. His was also the misfortune to arrive on the eve of the violent national trauma of the decade, the October Crisis.

Newman made his debut at a gala 'welcome home' party and said later that he felt as though he were arriving on a chariot of fire. The unilingual commissioner needed someone to both bridge the cultural barrier and help him in Ottawa, so he agreed to Minister Pelletier's suggestion that he make thirty-seven-year-old André Lamy his assistant film commissioner. The young technocrat had been associated with his brother's financially successful Onyx films and was familiar with the Quebec film scene. The French-speaking iconoclasts hereafter referred to Newman and Lamy as one person, as French communications were left entirely to the young Quebecker. From the outset, then, French Production became suspicious of the man they called 'le boss unilingue,' a phrase that Newman hated.

Everything about him seemed to contrast with his predecessor. He seemed ever-ebullient and always dressed in a sports coat and bow-tie or ascot. His glasses made his sharp brown eyes seem even larger and more alert than they already were, and when he spoke, he seemed to command attention to himself rather than to what he was saying. It was part of his natural verve, a dramatic opposite to McPherson's outwardly cool, Anglo-Saxon intellectual demeanour. Newman was neither a practitioner of honeyed words nor nervous before a crowd, and he made it clear from his first appearance before his staff that he was the chief. Older members might have nodded in approval of the 'take charge' commissioner, though the younger may have felt wary about having their freedoms curtailed. He intended to adopt as his inaugural theme, 'What now the Film Board? What for, and why?'

Minister Pelletier was supposed to attend Newman's first board meeting, in October

1970, but never made it. Two cells of the would-be revolutionary Quebec terrorist group Front de Libération du Québec (FLQ) embarked on the very un-Canadian practice of kidnapping and political murder that month, plunging the nation into crisis. Prime Minister Trudeau showed the mailed fist that Ottawa had and imposed the War Measures Act, citing an apprehended insurrection. Pelletier stayed in the capital for the parliamentary debate over the first-ever peacetime imposition of such sweeping powers.

In this tense atmosphere, Newman and Lamy tried to carry on as though it was business as usual. They spent weeks screening the work of all directors, intending to meet with each one to discuss his work. The commissioner observed drily that the films were very good, the odd one was beautiful, but many were old-fashioned and pedestrian. (He told the filmmakers bluntly and brutally that he thought their films 'stank with probity.') Few seemed aware of the new forms of documentary and actuality being developed in current television, and Newman insisted that closer collaboration between the writer and filmmaker would sharpen the editorial approach. He had little tolerance for the auteur principle and concluded that the Film Board needed a major reorganization because the supervisory system of downgraded producers was inadequate, and too many productions were over budget. He said nothing about the trouble-prone French films he was inheriting from McPherson that were in various stages of production.

As for the ever-perplexing CBC requirement for commercials, he berated the board of governors for being naïve, since the network had to earn revenue in prime time. He was willing to pay this price for a national audience if he could obtain a permanent Film Board prime-time slot. A new member of the board of governors, A.W. (Al) Johnson, made the opposing point that there needed to be a reduction of the amount of

commercialism on television.[1] He was forced to change his tune when he became CBC president later in the decade, and ideology took a back seat to financial need. Newman vowed to do whatever was necessary to have the prime-time outlet. Furthermore, in order to make the Film Board indispensable, he expected the filmmakers to 'inject a certain show-biz flair' into their films to excite mass audiences.

Newman told the staff late in November of his intention to reverse the policy of no commercials. The filmmakers' union wrote a letter to Pelletier complaining that not only had they been addressed in English, but also that Newman had said 'those who did not like it, could stuff it.' The union said that 'it' referred to Newman's unilingualism, not the policy on commercials. The irate commissioner was not going to be bullied by them as McPherson had been. He summoned the executive, reprimanded them, and demanded and then received a written apology, with a copy to Pelletier. He was angered at what he called an old-line form of unionism that was completely out of touch with a creative organization. He realized that to maintain staffing was as difficult as finding room at the bottom for new blood, and he asked the union to help. He was dreaming, since the latter was busy fighting to reinstate those who had been given lay-off notices by the previous administration. Success would be theirs as the courts determined that wholesale lay-offs violated labour law.

If union relations promised to be no better with Newman than with McPherson, there was worse budgetary news for 1971. English production had slowed so much that the prognosis was that only six of ten one-hour films for television would be completed. None of the low-budget features would be finished, and just over half of the thirty-nine planned experimental films would be ready. In sum, a public-relations disaster was in the making if the institution had to return to the government an estimated total surplus of one million dollars. Newman quickly ensured that all excess funds were committed to productions.[2]

Distribution

Being a veteran of the early years, Newman was a little dubious about the ever-optimistic distribution figures in the *Annual Report*, which estimated lifetime audiences of 82 million persons at home and 650 million persons abroad since the organization began in 1939. To get a more realistic idea of his agency's impact at home and abroad, he looked at theatrical rental contracts and non-theatrical bookings. The most-booked English theatricals had had between 800 and 1,000 bookings over four years and were (in descending order) *Gone Curling, Summer Pageantry, Get Wet, Flyway North, White Ship, What on Earth!, Animal Movie, The Drag,* and *Precision*. The top theatrical French-language attractions had averaged between 100 and 200 bookings over the same period: *La Truite de rivière, Sons et Couleurs, Dimensions, La Beauté même, La Cité de mémoire, Avec tambours et trompettes, Au hasard du temps, Art et Légende*. The theatrical figures confirmed that the films were about leisure or artistic activities.

The list of most frequently used non-theatrical titles in 1960–70 told a somewhat different story. The first place, *Paddle to the Sea*, had had 1,979 bookings; others were *I Know an Old Lady Who Swallowed a Fly, Universe, Nobody Waved Goodbye, The Ride, Neighbours, The Game, Phoebe, No Reason to Stay, The Great Toy Robbery, Bear and the Mouse, Animal Movie, What on Earth!, Pas de deux, Beaver Dam, You're No Good, The Drag,* and *Red Kite*, with an average of 1,400 bookings each; the audience was predominantly schoolchildren. Non-theatrical French films had reached a generically similar, if much smaller, audience; the most booked film was *Dimensions* (738 times), followed by *Mosaïque, Vogue à la mer, Ti-*

Jean s'en va dans l'ouest, Kénojouak, artiste esquimau, Jacquot visite le zoo, Animaux en marche, Pour un bout de papier, Felix Leclerc, troubadour, Ti-Jean s'en va-t-aux chantiers, and *Sylvie* (190 reservations). Most of these films were made before 1967. There had been only two new titles broadcast in English on the CBC, *Imperial Sunset* and *You Are on Indian Land*, while eight French titles received their first airing on Radio-Canada. There had been what looked like an impressive total of 9,456 television showings in both languages.[3] Closer scrutiny left less room for pride; most of the bookings were repeats, in non-prime time and at hours when the audience was smallest. In short, the Film Board had been reduced to supplying to CBC with 'fillers.'

Censorship of French Production: Too biased or too separatist?

Lamy brought Newman's attention to several French productions he called either too biased or too separatist in tone. Newman had no qualms about his role as final arbiter of which films would be released, since, as he later put it, 'I had to protect the agency from itself.' This belief sustained him in the storm of press controversy that later swirled around the films *Cap d'espoir, On est au coton, Un pays sans bons sens, ou 'Wake Up mes bons amis', L'Acadie, l'Acadie?!?, 24 heures ou plus,* and *Québec, Duplessis et après*. Their notoriety sealed his near-complete alienation from most of the French Production staff.

The elements embedded in each film were anger and impatience with the slowness of societal change. Given the atmosphere of confrontation, it was understandable that an English Canadian might interpret these emotions from French Canada as equivalent to propaganda against the established order, while without blinking the same person could refer to *The Things I Cannot Change* as a powerful, if ultimately benign, English-

179

Canadian documentary. Odder still was the constant lip-service that the agency paid to the *cinéma direct* style of Challenge for Change / Société nouvelle, which was evident in the films. English Canadians could vent their frustration and make radical noises, but when French Canadians did the same, it seemed that the state was in jeopardy. Such was the standard in these anything-but-normal times. As Newman put it much later, it was 'that damned French thing, day in and day out for the first two years' that wore him down.

The first film, Jacques Leduc's *Cap d'espoir* ($45,796), was produced by Pierre Maheu, former editor of the infamous *Parti pris* issue of April 1964. It reflected some of the inner violence that was stirring in Quebec in 1968–9, mainly through the feelings expressed by an on-screen university student. There was much swearing and vulgarity that McPherson had found offensive; for that reason, in April 1970, he had ordered it not to be released.[4] Newman confirmed that decision, but Luc Perreault of *La Presse* indicated there was much to be seen in this film about those who were heartsick at Quebec's slowness to change. If the film was not clear and concrete, it was fundamentally true and young.[5] In varying moods, Quebec was portrayed as sclerotic, young, old, ignorant, poorly informed, complex, frustrated, and crushed by the 'System.' Society was overwhelming, aberrant, and alienating. The consequences were discouragement, resignation, despair, irresponsibility, sadness, suicide, and death. The sum of these emotions led the on-screen young man to make a crude gesture and lash out at the viewer at one point, 'Mangez de la merde,' a gross epithet. This was too much for the genteel Film Board.

On est au coton ($152,266), by Denys Arcand, was more contentious still. If Newman appeared as a pariah to many in French Production because of this controversy, the ruckus also taught him how to handle similar film problems in the future. The French Pro-

gramme Committee approved the film's idea in 1969, at which time it was called *Les informateurs*, a three-part story of technocrats who are the backbone of the modern state. Guy Coté, the first producer, was replaced by the gadfly Pierre Maheu, who left it to Marc Beaudet when the film was in the editing stage. Meanwhile, Jacques Godbout, who had been the director of French Production since February 1969 and had approved this and the above-mentioned films, was replaced by Gilles Dignard in April 1970. What emerged amidst this game of musical chairs was a 173-minute film whose title, *On est au coton*, contained the pun 'We're fed up!' It was about the textile industry in Quebec and labour's fear of unemployment because of an imminent factory closure. The focus was on the daily life of a textile worker and on the historical legacy of strikes in that industry. Arcand intended the entire film to be a subjective view of the present and past situation from a working-class perspective exclusively.

An interview with a textile-industry executive became a self-damning instrument. The film had already become something of a cause célèbre during McPherson's tenure because of complaints from the executive, who early in 1970 had requested deletion of all references to himself. McPherson had ordered the film held back while the offending interview was excised. The feisty Arcand was willing to leave the screen black, while a narrator read the executive's letter demanding the excision.

At the same time, some textile-industry executives saw the film and described it as a violent class struggle. When they learned that poet/politico Gérald Godin was one of the principals making the film, they demanded a divorce from it. Some believed that it promoted class warfare, made the industry look predatory, and, in depicting the daily life and struggles of Quebec textile workers, abandoned any pretence of balance; others called it a Marxist propaganda tract.[6] Most ominous of all, there was a sequence in which two members of the Front de Libération du Québec were identified as they called for violence.

Newman asked Film Board lawyers for an opinion, which they delivered on 16 October 1970, as the October Crisis took its ugliest turn. Another cell of the FLQ compounded the kidnapping of the British trade commissioner in Montreal with the abduction and murder of Pierre Laporte, Quebec's minister of manpower and employment. Ottawa passed the War Measures Act, suspending civil liberties nationally – a first for peacetime Canada – and declared the FLQ an outlaw organization. (The act was rescinded six months later.) The Film Board's legal experts thought the film purported to incite violence, and sedition charges were possible. They thought a labour leader's historical references to past strikes could lead to slander charges; the FLQ members would have to

agree to be shown or they could sue the agency, since under the War Measures Act, if the sequence stayed, they could go to jail, and the Film Board could be held liable.[7]

Meanwhile, the October Crisis put the Film Board itself into a state of seige. Newman was warned that he could be a target and was given a limousine, complete with siren and chauffeur. From his office, he watched combat troops scout the perimeter of the grounds every four hours. Equally absurd was the sight of the agency's regular security, composed of aging war-veteran commissionaires, patrolling constantly around the buildings on electric golf carts. If it seemed like the stuff of a bad movie or parody, the fact was that an FLQ attack on the Film Board (or Radio-Canada) would have been outstanding guerrilla theatre.

In this atmosphere, Newman briefed Pelletier personally several times that fall. The

Director Denys Arcand, left, began the controversial *On est au coton* (1970) with poet-politician Gérald Godin, right, as his producer (seen with the film crew, Alain Dostie, in white, and Pierre Mignot).

minister was interested only in knowing what was happening and was absolutely opposed to any direct interference. As he had put it a month before the October Crisis, a government should not only respect the freedom of the artist and the scholar, but should also provide for the independence of public institutions, so that the specialists who direct them may base their actions on professional rather than political criteria.[8] That sounded fine on paper, but when Newman tried to reach out to his French-language artists, he was rebuffed. He invited them into his office for drinks and told them that he knew what it was like to be a member of a minority group; his guests seemed disinterested in being understood on such grounds, drank his alcohol, and left.

Unperturbed, Newman declared that the textile-industry executive's letter of complaint could not be included in the 'blacked out' segment. He hoped Arcand would broaden his piece to show that the cotton industry was only one example of what happens to many businesses during changing times. To be helpful, he suggested shortening the opening sequence to make it 'just as powerful and yet not boring.'[9] At this point, he had not made up his mind to suppress the film. By January, Arcand had left the screen black where the executive had appeared, identified him, omitted the reading of his damning letter, and cut the segment containing the two FLQ members. The documentary was now 162 minutes long, and there were plans to launch it at the popular Montreal club Le Patriote.

The president of the Canadian Textile Institute wrote to Newman in February that the film was dishonest, disruptive, and a gross misinterpretation of the Canadian textile industry, hence its distribution could serve no national or other legitimate interests. Newman answered him in March that he was not going to allow *On est au coton* to receive any public screenings until he had satisfied himself about it.[10] Soon he circulated a brief to the creative staff, entitled 'Responsibility and the Filmmaker,' in which he equated editorial freedom with the principle of fairness to the audience. This meant distinguishing between the fictional (personal) film and actuality films, in which the viewer was not aware of the degree of editorial control exercised by the filmmaker. 'This is the adult privilege of responsibility, of the price of membership in the Film Board,' Newman said and reminded them of the organization's right to determine its own policies and work practices.[11]

The commissioner ordered that there be no projection of *On est au coton* without permission from himself or Lamy. He tried to prevent it from being shown at the staff's own annual screening of Film Board productions, but relented after an uproar. Perhaps a letter from the production's latest producer swayed him. Marc Beaudet reminded him that the Film Board tradition was one of making difficult films, and that recent federal policy of being 'liberal' about cultural products in the name of preserving freedom assured the credibility of the system; questioning institutions sometimes did the same. His was a cunning reminder that *On est au coton* was doing precisely what Challenge for Change / Société nouvelle was trying to do. This argument did not, however, convince Newman to release it. At the end of April, the Film Board received a letter from a textile-industry division chief, indicating certain factual inaccuracies: new and quieter machines had been installed recently, the sick man in the documentary had long suffered from asthma, and, further, no French-Canadian textile executives had been shown.[12]

Not wanting to let the filmmakers choose the battlefield, Newman decided to suppress the work on these grounds, rather than those of political censorship. For example, a worker complaining about low wages in Canada erred about wages in the United States. During the shooting, there was only one giant spinning machine in Canada; in 1970 there were sixteen. Also, it was alleged that American CIO unions hated the film for no other reason than fraternal rivalry with the Quebec unions and did not wish to see their confrères on screen. (Privately, Newman thought the film was not very meticulously done and that it lacked subtlety.[13]) These may have been niggling reasons for refusing to release it, but the fact was that *On est au coton* was a painfully long, cinematically clumsy piece (with the exception of impressive tracking shots on the floors of the factories) featuring talking heads. In part, it resembled the structure of contemporary films like Fernando Solanas's four-hour underground Argentinian opus *La Hora de los Hornos*, a Marxist analysis of that country's labour history. Others saw the influence of French auteur Jean-Luc Godard. Perhaps the most trenchant element in the work was the thread of dark cynicism running through it: as a manager tries to explain the complex structure of a transnational corporation to a glassy-eyed, uncomprehending worker, the unsophisticated man, in acknowledgment, can only mutter 'extraordinaire.' Compliant workers were not on the verge of revolutionary action – they were placid, resigned to their fate, and happy to have a job.

In Parliament that April, Prime Minister Trudeau pleaded ignorance of the issue of censorship of the film when he was asked to comment. Elsewhere, Pelletier explained that he was not aware of anyone from his office having previewed it and surmised that it was withheld by the Film Board authorities who had taken the decision on their own.[14] Days later, Newman told the Film Board staff that he would not release the production because it did 'not fairly picture the textile industry it attempted to portray.' The textile executive's letter had opened a way to hold up the film on the basis of public responsibility, not censorship. Sherbrooke's *La Tribune* picked up the story shortly thereafter; *Cinéma Québec* magazine ran an article including interviews with Arcand, Godin, and Newman; there were similar articles in *Le Devoir*.[15] Meanwhile, two videotape versions had been smuggled out of the Film

Board; one was complete and uncut, and the second ran 162 minutes. Professor Louise Carrière (coincidentally the wife of reporter Luc Perreault of *La Presse*) showed the film at CEGEP (College) Vieux Montréal, from 31 May to 4 June. Perreault wrote a scathing article against censorship in July and accused the Film Board of witch-hunting and Duplessisism.[16] Soon, pirated versions of it appeared at colleges across Quebec and even at the Film Board's own creation, the Vidéographe, in downtown Montreal. It became an underground hit under the titles *The John A. Macdonald Story* and *Louis Riel*, proving that censorship can be the ultimate publicity coup for a film. By 1979, it was estimated that more than 20,000 people (mostly students) had seen it, though Arcand was bitter that the workers for whom it was made still had not.

That fall of 1971, a critical article in *Le Devoir* contained interviews with André Lamy and Pierre Gauvreau, the new head of French Production. A month later, the same newspaper published a letter from the Secretariat for Political Action of the Confederation of National Trade Unions (CSN), signed by thirty-one affiliated textile workers' unions in Quebec. It called for release of the film and demanded that the workers be allowed to decide if it was realistic. Its most inflammatory line was, 'This arbitrary and unilateral decision is unacceptable unless the NFB is actually supposed to be an instrument of propaganda for the exclusive use of the state and the employers.' Newman's advisers recommended he forget the letter, but he could not; his reply also appeared in *Le Devoir* and he repeated that the documentary did not adequately or fairly represent the textile industry. He was defending the Film Board's tradition of integrity and fairness and concluded that the agency did not win over seventy awards a year because its films lacked truth or smelled of propaganda. The organization's reputation was too valuable to lose over one production, he concluded.

Newman sent copies of the letter to major newspapers across Canada as well as to many members of Parliament. A few English papers treated the item as a brief news story, and the French press showed only slightly more interest.[17] On 16 November, the Canadian Manufacturers Association wrote him a letter expressing appreciation for his having withheld 'the so-called documentary.' A grateful Newman replied that their letter was a 'real shot in the arm' and acknowledged that relating the creative drives of individual filmmakers to national needs was a difficult problem to solve, but that given a little time it would be. His greatest satisfaction came two months later, when he had occasion to meet the prime minister for the first time. Trudeau looked him up and down and said, 'I admire your bravery and your answer to that scurrilous letter (in the French press), and I think you did the right thing.' Any doubts that Newman may have had vanished at that moment.[18]

The commissioner had drawn the line before those Quebec artists and intellects whom many suspected were burrowing within federal agencies to undermine the state. It might be argued too that he had consciously or otherwise replicated Trudeau's 'Just watch me' taunt of defiance to the FLQ terrorists a year earlier and was demonstrating that the organs of the state would and could act to protect themselves from internal strife-mongers. The price, however, was dear.

This being said, as he wrestled with *On est au coton*, Newman decided to take a less confrontational route with the film that had started out being called *Crisis in Confederation*. In 1968, the deliberations of the constitutional conference in Toronto had raised the idea of finding new ways to express 'the French question' to the English. Pierre Perreault, who had co-directed *Pour la suite du monde* and its companion piece *Le règne du jour*, was entrusted with the project, and he agreed to make a film on current questions in Quebec, using footage of René Lévesque to epitomize the nationalism issue. McPherson, it will be recalled, had made the extraor-

dinary gesture of inviting the board of governors to vet the documentary.

By March 1969, Tom Daly took over as producer of this English production. He meant to facilitate and expedite the completion of the film as a document of French attitudes and points of view, to be presented in an English version to English audiences. Daly and Perreault agreed at last that Lévesque was too 'political' a personality and decided to broaden the theme to make it into a concept of 'homeland.' Perreault introduced individual characters who represented different views and positions on current questions; Daly thought that this achieved sincere and responsible balance. A delicate process of exclusion began. Daly recommended that the English presences in the film diminish, because those English persons could not in themselves represent the multifaceted English attitudes in the way that the constellation of French characters could represent theirs. It became apparent that it was difficult to version the material effectively into English while keeping subtlety and nuance of meaning. Furthermore, the opus had stretched to a ponderous eye-glazing two hours. By March 1970, English Production withdrew from the project, and it was released under producer Paul Larose several months before the October Crisis.[19]

Un pays sans bon sens, ou 'Wake Up, mes bons amis' was a three-part album of several individuals struggling with the concept of belonging to a country, in which Perreault smoothly embraced the historical and current questions. Like Arcand, Perreault could barely restrain his frustration with the slow pace of change and called his people 'Catholic French-Canadian mice.' He did show a variety of attitudes fairly: the denial of nationalism, an English Canadian advocating Quebec separation if the people wanted it, Lévesque's stunning pro-independence performance before a hostile Manitoba audience, and a Quebec Indian claiming his people's territorial birthright.

Even if the documentary was not about

Lévesque, his shadow was everywhere. When he made his appearance late in the film, it was buried between two overly long sequences of a woman from Brittany speaking of homeland and some rural Quebeckers reminiscing about early hardships and great times past. Lévesque's performance was electrifying as he described the 'mutually sterilizing atmosphere' of modern progressive nationalism and mocked the ever-persistent English-Canadian question and answer, ' "What does Quebec want?" Answer: "More." ' He denied Quebec's interest in the melting-pot principle of the rest of Canada. If he called for French Canadians outside of Quebec to become immigrants there, he also admitted that he was a cynic. One of the on-screen protagonists called him a Jesus figure and credited this speech with his own spiritual awakening.

Another emotional centre of the film had a Franco-Manitoban recalling his youth, riding on a bus with his mother. He remembered being so ashamed of her speaking French that he felt as if she were spitting on him. It was a feeling that brought home the sense that many minorities have at one point or another if they are surrounded by a different cultural sea. It also showed how the perspectives of English and French Canada were fundamentally dissimilar: the *indépendantiste* dream was to keep Quebec's own cultural sea. (So was this also the Quebec nationalist dream, without the goal of independence, but that view was apparently too complex to express in the film.) Absent too was an articulation of Trudeau's Canadian dream: to convince an entire population to accept bilingualism and promote toleration of marginal cultural diversity within a North American English sea of heterogeneity.

Management worried that this film would become as contentious as *On est au coton*. In February 1971, Secretary of State Pelletier received the promotional sheets to *Un pays sans bons sens* and phoned Newman for more background. The question of suppression must have arisen, since that was on

Newman's mind when he wrote to explain that the film was already distributed widely across the country. He was naturally quite nervous about the ramifications that might follow if the film were to be withdrawn from circulation, and he seemed to plead with Pelletier against any interference. He admitted that the October Crisis had done much to charge the emotional atmosphere, but argued that any extreme action taken on the documentary might cause untold harm to an internal harmony (sic) that was growing within the agency. He wanted to avoid this result as much as Pelletier did.[20]

There was no other record of Pelletier's interest in *Un pays sans bons sens*, probably because a week earlier Newman had sent him a private and confidential report on his first six months as commissioner, in which he mentioned that a number of films coming out of French Production could cause problems because 'they relate to social conditions and attitudes which may be regarded as too leftist.' He warned that their handling of French-English relations might be regarded as inflammatory, but he intended to avoid a direct confrontation with the filmmakers, since 'banning [the films] would cause a major upheaval which could not be contained within the Film Board.' He intended to allow their distribution, each release spaced over a long period of time and without publicizing them, if the excesses of opinion were not too extreme. He promised that in the future editorial checkpoints would 'ensure a more balanced point of view within the films.'[21]

Weeks later, an uneasy board of governors expressed serious concern about *Un pays sans bons sens* and tried to take the high ground by denying a public agency's right to use public funds to attack the fabric of society. Yet their liberal sense told them that the strength of a democracy lies in its ability to entertain opposition to the Establishment and to examine all facets of life and thought. Newman agreed that it was an onerous problem, but he intended to ensure that, henceforth, film projects could not radically shift their theses after they were approved. He wanted the individual artists to act responsibly.[22] The members recommended the film receive wide distribution in the non-theatrical network, but not on television or in theatres.[23] *Un pays* continued circulating non-theatrically with little fanfare, except that it failed to realize its original conception, to help English Canada understand French Canada. English Canadians would find the long-winded interviews and heavily accented French almost impossible to understand, with or without subtitles, and they largely ignored it.[24]

When Newman appeared before a diffident Parliamentary Committee on Broadcasting, Films and Assistance to the Arts, he defended Perrault, stating that there were limits beyond which one would not wish to go in curbing his creative interpretation of reality. 'I can only repeat that my job is to make sure that voices of dissent are kept in balance with other voices ... Films on "touchy" subjects do not represent more than five or six percent of our total output, if that ... We need a total balance of variety of opinion and the kind of artists that we have are varied and infinite in their beliefs and opinions. I think they have done Canada really proud,' he concluded optimistically.[25] But he was personally 'touchy' about Michel Brault's idea for a fiction piece concerning the round-up and incarceration of dozens of *québécois* during the October Crisis, featuring characters who were composites of real personalities. When the French Programme Committee approved the project, he overruled them and again made the news. *Les Ordres* would have to be made as a private film venture.[26]

Early in 1971, Perrault was just finishing another 118-minute film with Brault, which again raised the issue of being French-speaking outside Quebec in the contemporary atmosphere of student confrontation. *L'Acadie, L'Acadie?!?* ($99,609) recorded the story of Acadian students' struggle at the Université de Moncton, New Brunswick.

The film accentuated the minority's demand for language rights in an intolerant, if officially bilingual, Canadian society, then switched to the students' week-long occupation of a university building and their desire to transform the institution into one that belonged to themselves and the professors. A stand-off with police ends peacefully as the students leave voluntarily. The aftermath was depression, and a student voice-over informs viewers that their leaders were dismissed, the sociology department was closed down, and Prime Minister Trudeau received an honorary doctorate, declaring Moncton living proof of the Canadian experiment. One of the defeated students concludes bitterly, 'Perhaps Acadia is a mere detail.' The film implied that francophones would find a safe home only in Quebec.[27]

A late sequence at the airport reminds the critical viewer that the filmmakers were open to a judgment of being irresponsible, as they flew in to cover the story and flew out once the action was over, leaving the students alone to cope with the fall-out of the confrontation that the Film Board had helped promote with other media. The filmmakers had contributed to the students' deflation, in spite of their attempts to use *cinéma direct* as *engaged* cinema.

Newman was getting wiser all the while. He said he liked *L'Acadie, L'Acadie?!?* very much and wanted it to be shown nationally on both CBC networks. Board member A.W. Johnson thought it would be a grave error to show it on English television and wanted another film on the subject, one that was intelligent, sophisticated, civilized, and subtle. Perrault stalled four months before agreeing to edit the English version to seventy-five minutes. This delayed national release for nearly a year; the CBC telecast was on Sunday, 28 April 1975 – in English that afternoon, and in French that night at 11:30 p.m. Once both versions were out, the film was not in great demand, and what little activity there was appeared to be with the English version.[28] *L'Acadie, l'Acadie?!?* proved that the institution's films were not having as significant an impact as some wished and many feared (and vice versa). Then again, Perrault's feelings reflected those of the more radical Quebec filmmakers when, in speaking of this film, he stated brazenly that the Canadian identity in general never interested him and that he was happy to build his own Quebec in film with federal money, an admittedly extraordinary situation.[29] Unfortunately there is no way to establish what reactions the dozens of French-Canadian federal politicians had toward the Film Board and its national usefulness after reading such a provocative statement. At the very least, they knew from what quarter there would be no help in the ongoing national debate.

Another Arcand film, *Québec: Duplessis et après* ($115,411), originated from an idea suggested to him by the ever-provocative Pierre Maheu. It was begun just as Arcand was finishing *On est au coton*. McPherson had tried to stop the project from being undertaken in April 1970, claiming without much conviction that it was a public-affairs-type programme that was not within the Film Board's mandate, but the director of French Production, Gilles Dignard, dissuaded him.[30] Arcand's thesis was to show the parallel between the 1970 electoral campaign in Quebec and the 1936 campaign that swept Maurice Duplessis into power on a wave of popular support. He reworked (if not abused) history to prove the tenuous cliché that history repeats itself. Duplessis's reform programme could not have been realized because this would have meant the reversal of the very political structure which sustained that reactionary regime. Similarly the Quiet Revolution had not really changed Quebec society, as evidenced by the 1970 defeat of René Lévesque by Robert Bourassa. There had been no opposition to Duplessis because his political breadth was such that he was the incarnation of all political parties at once. Stretching the lesson to contemporary Quebec, Arcand found but one conclusion: that provincial politics were rotten and that

over the years little had changed either in politics or for the people of Quebec. The film reflected the let-down and despair felt by many pro-*indépendantiste* activists.[31]

Newman approached this film gingerly at the end of 1971 by stating that he thought its 114 minutes were 45 minutes too long. It was well made, he said, and was 'absolutely invaluable for students of political science,' but needed to have the sources of the speeches identified. Arcand refused and waited for management's expected suppression. But Newman was not playing his game and decided to release it anyway. To no one's surprise, Radio-Canada rejected it in May 1972, on grounds that it was too long, its title was false, it was difficult to programme, and interest was hard to sustain. Arcand was now put in the position of defending both the film and the Film Board publicly. He believed it was normal that there should now and then be a film which stated that everything is rotten and that we live in a country that is corrupt from top to bottom. Realizing that he had been finessed by the commissioner, Arcand commented that censorship attracted extraordinary publicity, and that everyone wanted to see a censored film. The month before, he had told a Quebec City newspaper that before *On est au coton*, he had been a victim of internal censorship in 1963, 1964, and 1966, for the films *Champlain, Les Montréalistes,* and *Volley-ball.*[32] With *Québec: Duplessis et après*, he could claim that status no longer. The film is still in circulation and has had an unimpressive distribution record.

In spite of his intention to avoid trouble, Newman was forced to play the heavy once again, in November 1972, as Gilles Groulx served up a vitriolic diatribe against society in *24 heures ou plus*. The commissioner ordered the incomplete film stopped and locked away before a bootleg video could be made. The opus was originally titled *1461 jours*, the four years between elections, but was changed after the call for a twenty-four-hour general strike by the Quebec unions in the midst of their public-sector strife in November and December 1971. Gérald Godin called it a film-mosaic that showed the degree of alienation or political unawareness of some *québécois* and the passion of those who wanted to raise political consciousness. Newman said it lacked form, shape, and structure.[33]

Throughout the document, Groulx had appeared alternately with his political adviser, Jean-Marc Piotte; both served as participants or witnesses to the events. He also intercut newspaper headlines to punctuate the fifty-six different sequences, among them: a lock-out at *La Presse*, a fiery speech by radical labour organizer Michel Chartrand, lawyer Robert Lemieux denying the possibility of democratic change and praising the FLQ, a visit to a zoo, symbol of society's jungle, Premier Bourassa swimming laps in a pool, a triple murder of his bosses by an employee who went berserk, testimony by an FLQ member admitting to being trained by the PLO in terrorist tactics with two other *québécois*, and a description of the exploitative and repressive capitalist economy. There was a call for a reorganization of Quebec workers and a break with the system, and a statement of the essential need for Quebec socialism. Like the other documentaries that reflected frustration with the slowness of Quebeckers to change, Groulx at one point admitted accurately that most people seemed to prefer watching hockey. Accompanied by a shot of an empty hockey rink, reminiscent of the scene he had used in *Un jeu si simple*, this was supposed to be the most trenchant and revealing moment in the film.

The reference to breaking with the system was too much for Newman. He went public on 12 December: 'The film with its content and conclusion is not one which people who uphold our present democratic form of society would ever forgive the Film Board for making,' he began. The use of footage of Bourassa swimming and talking about his habit of making decisions while swimming was unfair, since it came from a physical-fitness film. The commissioner thought Groulx's conclusion that our society is entirely corrupt and needed total change was the last straw. He ordered the film withdrawn.[34]

La Presse was first to break the story about the film's suppression. After Newman's statement, the French press tended to take the idealist position: editorials supported the freedom of the artist to criticize his society. Newman was outraged at the 12 December article in *Le Devoir*, which contained the quote 'T'é mieux d'pas parler con'tes boss, pa'c'qu'on t'laissera pas faire' (Better not speak against the bosses, 'cause they won't let you do it). He told editor Claude Ryan that 'boss' was racist in this context. Ryan apologized, and the term 'boss' did not appear again in connection with the Film Board.[35] Groulx wrapped himself proudly in the robes of socialism and charged angrily that Newman ruled over the filmmakers like a Latin American dictator, was foreign to Quebec, never walked on the streets, and did not know about citizens' committees. A few months later he railed at his fellow filmmakers, most of whom he called *fonctionnaires* (civil servants) who themselves had been drawn into the strategy of capitalism: for the worst jobs the capitalists created the best working conditions.[36]

In March 1973, Groulx announced to the press that he refused to change the film, thus it would never be finished. The board of governors considered suing him for non-performance under his contract, but then thought better of it. By June the film was cancelled officially and was to be broken down into stock shots. In September Groulx offered to buy the rights to it, but the Film Board refused, citing a long-standing policy on this subject. The new minister, Hugh Faulkner, supported Newman's decision and, in the tradition of his predecessors who did not relish burned fingers, found it 'inadvisable to interfere at this level in the administration of the NFB.'[37]

The 1972–3 *Annual Report* put the issue simply: the production was halted 'because its conclusion advocates the overthrow of the political and economic system in Canada.' The English-Canadian press was both less emotional and less concerned about Newman's action. Several papers reported it simply as a news story.[38] The fact of Canada's two solitudes could not have been more distinctly expressed.

The October Crisis: Running after history with a camera

On the day federal troops poured into Montreal during the October Crisis, the English Programme Committee refused to support filmmaker Robin Spry's request to film history in the making. After the French Programme Committee gave the go-ahead to some of their people, Newman insisted that there be English participation, and soon Spry found himself 'running after history with a camera.' It intrigued him to record the range of effects the crisis was having on both rich and poor in English Quebec. In all, English Canada was agitated, vocal, and emotional. French Canada was quiet, defensive, and unexpressive. It was as if one's well-worn shoes of the last decade had been switched suddenly with those of the person next door.

The combined actuality footage by thirty Film Board staff comprised a vast assortment of perspectives. Before anyone could decide what to do with it, Newman ordered all the film sequestered because it was sub judice, on account of the trials going on in the wake of the events. By the following summer, Jacques Godbout, Mireille Dansereau, and Pierre Maheu decided to abandon the very difficult task of interpreting what had recently happened.[39] This left Spry alone on the field, and by the time he finished editing, there was a mammoth assembly that needed division. From that (and a $200,000 budget) emerged the films *Reaction: A Portrait of a Society in Crisis* ($65,728) and *Action: The October Crisis of 1970.*

The latter title tried to place events in historical perspective in an 87-minute compilation. Spry's sombre voice-over narration accompanied the confusing and twisting landscape of modern Quebec politics, concluding with the crisis and its denouement. The core of the film finds the politicians playing out their typical roles, from a befuddled and out-of-touch John Diefenbaker blaming events on American draft-dodgers, to a wise and reasonable Tommy Douglas fearing that the War Measures Act's suspension of civil liberties was excessive and unnecessary, to a grim-faced and determined Prime Minister Trudeau (in answer to the question 'How far are you [the federal government] prepared to go?'), snapping curtly 'Just watch me.'

A Film Board camera captures a remarkable moment of direct cinema as a distraught René Lévesque swears angrily at a reporter who asked him to summarize his reaction to the death of Minister Pierre Laporte in sixty seconds. 'I couldn't care less about goddam air time ... I'm not going to distort things. To hell with that ... Goddamit, we're not a soap opera ... Well, a guy dies, our opinion, ah shit ...' The interview begins and Lévesque transforms into the politician who could palpably feel how the crisis might be used to cripple the independence movement: 'We have to deplore what happened, but on the other hand let no one think wherever he is, outside Quebec or inside Quebec, that this is enough to make us a sort of cell – a collective cell of repression. We'll fight if we have to against anyone who wants to use this climate now more or less, you know, to tie up Quebec in impotence.' He elaborates for almost three minutes.

Of the two films, *Action* continues to receive the widest distribution among secondary and post-secondary school audiences, demonstrating a national appetite for subjects about the recent past. As with history itself, the angle of observation may be as important as the event. In using footage from Jean-Claude Labrecque's film on de Gaulle,

Spry was not aware that someone had doctored the soundtrack of President de Gaulle's famous 'Vive le Québec libre' exhortation of 1967 in Montreal. The viewer hears a tumultuous cheer, when in fact there had been stunned silence, as was later confirmed by René Lévesque himself.[40] In viewing the doctored sequence and thinking about events as they actually were rather than as they appeared, one is reminded that, in film as well as in print, it is the arrangement of facts that becomes history, not the facts themselves.

Spry's planned last line summed up the film's intention: 'For Canada, the arrests, the kidnappings, the killing and the removal of civil liberties have come as a sad and costly loss of innocence, and the question stands: Will Quebec separate?' Newman found some half-dozen items that made him nervous, probably as much from a political, as from a film, point of view. He asked Spry to change several voice-overs, to give equal time to spokesmen for the three principal federal parties, and to cut the last line at the phrase 'loss of innocence.' After deliberating with Tom Daly, Spry agreed to make alterations if they seemed to improve or did not change the meaning of the film. Newman agreed, probably relieved that the filmmaker was willing to respond to him without a public battle, something that French Production almost certainly would have gleefully staged.[41]

The commissioner maintained that the cut, 'Will Quebec separate?' was not made for political considerations. 'I thought it was an artistic judgment and one of broader philosophical implications than the immediacy of Quebec,' he said. Without that question, he believed, the film closed philosophically on a note of universality, on the profounder statement about the whole nature of the Canadian perception of itself. 'That a province had been invaded by the Federal army was what the film was really about ... Lurid events that normally happened in foreign countries had happened here. We had lost our innocence,' he explained.[42] Try as New-

man might to forget it, Spry's forbidden question became the national question of the decade.

Action is so dense in detail that it only touches upon the wide spectrum of French-Canadian nationalism and upon the roots of the language issue. The authorities at the time were most perplexed by the Quebec public's overwhelming approval of the contents of the FLQ manifesto, which the terrorists forced Radio-Canada television and radio to broadcast. That fact, more than the kidnappings and murder, was the real October Crisis. Ottawa was never sure if the public's enthusiastic response to the manifesto was typical of Quebec's political ambivalence or the genuine thrill of thumbing noses at federal authority.

Salvadore Allende Gossens: Un témoignage

Maurice Bulbulian, whose social-action documentaries had long addressed concerns faced by the inarticulate and forgotten classes of Quebec society, shot *Richesse des autres*, on mining from the miners' perspective, in 1972. In it, three Quebec miners journey to Chile to see how the new socialist regime of Salvadore Allende was coping with the exploitation of Chile's mines by transnational capitalists. Once the film was released, an officer of the Mining Association of Canada requested that the Film Board suspend its distribution. Newman refused and warned that by curbing it he would draw attention to the very things to which the plaintiff was objecting; it was best to let the production take its normal course.

That might have been the end of the issue, but in November 1973 Bulbulian sought to make a 20-minute companion piece from footage he had shot of President Allende as his regime was tottering. *Salvadore Allende Gossens: Un témoignage* shows an exhausted president after another day of facing demonstrations of pro- and anti-Allende crowds, of 50,000 each, able to find time to meet three miners from Quebec. They point out the contradictions of a Chilean regime committed to social justice that allowed transnationals to exploit the workers. Allende might have used this ready-made platform to condemn his country's enemies, but instead explains patiently that he wanted to bring equal opportunity to a country plagued with sickness and malnutrition.

The regime's subsequent collapse and Allende's assassination in September 1973 enhanced the historical value of the footage. On the recommendation of Lamy, Newman approved the release of the film in May 1974. A month later, the Conseil québécois pour la diffusion du cinéma asked to take both Bulbulian films to France to distribute in French cultural circuits. Newman first refused to let them out of Canada, then relented in July, but only for *Richesse des autres*. A distraught Bulbulian argued that Allende's death symbolized the murder of over 15,000 Chileans and the torture and imprisonment of another 50,000. He even offered to remove all credits, including the Film Board logo, so that the blocked work could be seen. Newman would not budge, and *Salvadore Allende* never left Canada.[43] There were no further written exchanges, but one can surmise that the commissioner made his decision based on a long-standing Film Board policy stretching back to the suppression of *Blue Vanguard* and *Black and White in South Africa*: not to comment on the problems of another country. Film Board products that circulated internationally were not supposed to draw Canada into controversy; they were non-confrontational, cultural/artistic documents cultivating innocence and symbolizing harmony.

The commissioner had been bickering constantly with French Production over the issue of bias and separatism. He was glad to see Gilles Dignard resign as director of production in September 1971, following his undiplomatic public statements about Film Board censorship. He hoped the political boil might be reduced to a simmer with his successor, Pierre Gauvreau, but after a year he left too. Yves Leduc replaced him and managed to walk the tightrope between filmmakers and management adroitly until the fall of 1976.

How much all the political ferment within the Film Board was reflective of actual social change was a fair question. Producer Paul Larose had argued in 1971 that the political climate in Quebec had changed less than one would believe and that the 'Quiet Revolution' had not occurred for the masses. If there had been one, it had been for a little group of intellectuals with whom the *québécois* could not identify.[44] Newman probably agreed, and years later concluded there were only about ten individuals on staff who were articulate, passionate, and politicized – he called them besotted emotionally. He remained unrepentant about the subject: 'I still think of myself as being more intelligently "Left" than the few cry-babies in the French branch.'[45] That being said, he was sorry he had encountered so much grief from French Production, but unlike his predecessor never thought of resigning a job he relished.[46] He had been trying to lead, but it was discomfiting to remind the staff that if they did not like the terms of reference for working for a federal agency, they could leave. It was only fair, he insisted, that if the Film Board showed films about separatism, they should be balanced by films showing a broad national viewpoint.[47] In turning to the other productions that emerged during Newman's tutelage, it was difficult to state with certainty how this criterion, heretofore phrased as 'in the national interest,' was being met.

The Chariot Disintegrates and Burns

English films in search of an audience

The film commissioner had unwillingly drawn the public's attention to the organization in Quebec, but such publicity did little to boost audience statistics. The Distribution Branch seemed unable to address the weaknesses in both theatrical and non-theatrical exhibition, and to improve the former, Newman contacted Grierson's old crony Harvey Harnick, of Columbia Pictures of Canada, who obliged him, and by 1971–2, the theatrical distribution figures grew to over 12,000 bookings, breaking the 1953–4 record. Board member Phyllis Grosskurth wondered if these theatrical films had much social significance for Canadians.[1]

Perhaps she was being too severe, since a glance at the list of twenty of the most popular 35-mm NFB films exhibited in Canada in 1971–2 reveals an assortment of quality information and entertainment subjects. The most booked film was *Boomsville / Métrofolle*, with 202 bookings, and *My Financial Career / Ma carrière financière* was last, with 140 bookings. The remaining titles in descending order were *The Catch / Capture, King Size / Au pays de King Size, Bighorn, The House That Jack Built / La maison de Jean-Jacques, Tax Is Not a Four-letter Word / Tire, Tirelire, Charley Squash Goes to Town, Aqua Rondo / Jeux d'eau, Fort Who? Mon oncle Antoine, Blake, Manhattan Odyssey / L'Odyssée du Manhattan, The Hoarder, November/Novembre, Blades and Brass / Lames et cuivres, Oskee Wee Wee / Finale de Football, Doodle Film, Great Toy Robbery / Hold-Up au Far-West,* and *I Know an Old Lady Who Swallowed a Fly.* It was impossible to know how many people saw these items, since theatres kept their attendance records to themselves. If a Film Board subject were shown with a Hollywood blockbuster, hundreds of thousands might see it; if the main feature was mediocre or worse, it was a guessing game. From the institution's point of view, what counted was having theatrical exposure. The least concern was the financial return from them, which was most always small, if not negligible.

Children's films continued to be the mainstay of the English-Canadian non-theatrical audience. McLaren's 1952 short, *Neighbours,* was the most-booked film, at 1,556. In descending order, the others were *Nobody Waved Goodbye, Paddle to the Sea, I Know an Old Lady Who Swallowed a Fly, The Rise and Fall of the Great Lakes, Carrousel, What on Earth!, Cosmic Zoom, The Great Toy Robbery, The Ride, The Game,* and *The Bear and the Mouse.* The number of viewers for each film could be as few as a dozen and as many as several hundred children, so Distribution chose a hypothetical figure of about one hundred per booking. Thus, *Neighbours* would have been seen non-theatrically by

15,560 persons a year in Canada. Taking the top twenty English titles, the total non-theatrical Canadian audience in 1971–2 would have been 229,400, while in French the figure would have been 69,600.[2] That was not a significant number of the country's twenty-three million population, though over a child's formative school years there was fair confidence that he or she would view Film Board productions many times. These statistics did not include films that had been sold previously, nor did they account for the increasing number of pirated versions on video that were being added to school libraries. Late in 1972, there was introduced a 50 per cent discount policy for schools that bought 16-mm films and made them available to the public. All this helped increase numbers, but when the agency boasted that its lifetime worldwide audience had reached one *billion* persons, it was a statistic that one could more easily doubt than believe.

A few years later, a less-than-happy fact of life was revealed in television figures that accounted for 20 and 14 per cent of French and English production respectively. The French drew fully 30 per cent of their audience from feature films, while the English were struggling to find 10 per cent. The French also reached 15 per cent of their clientele with theatrical shorts; the English reached only 6 per cent with theirs. Together, these numbers comprised the 'general' audience and totalled 65 per cent for the French and only 30 per cent for the English. Non-theatrical films comprised 35 per cent for the French and twice that figure for the English group.[3] Management tried to explain the discrepancy. English Canada provided a continuous audience for community-directed materials, while in French Canada production was geared to the general audience because it was 'a community which increasingly felt itself culturally threatened.' Budgetary limitations had forced the French to choose (low-cost) features over documentaries.

The fact was that distribution techniques had become antiquated, if not obsolete, even if the first self-service 16-mm library opened in Calgary in 1971. Procedures like counting audiences and enclosing statistics on the notorious 'pink cards' had been dropped in the sixties without replacement. McPherson's scheme to use computerized booking systems had been premature and too costly. Also in 1971, the organization took the first concrete steps to distribute films via the new three-quarter-inch video-cassette format, but this was still considered an experimental technology. Thus, the Audience Needs and Reactions Unit, created in October 1972, promised to identify thinking trends and patterns in the country, with a goal of bringing production into line with the practical needs of audiences.

When it carried out a Gallup-style survey of 3,000 people in Brant County, Ontario, to learn what the public thought about the Film Board, some 398 replied. Most did not know of its activity or function, and the fifty-four who did occupied the highest socio-economic ranks of wealth and education. The most popular subjects were the economy, ecology, and pollution, and the general feeling was that the film concerns of particular subgroups did not always interest the majority. In short, they wanted more films of more interest to more people. The respondents were *least* interested in religion, law enforcement / justice, community affairs, arts, old age, current events, and entertainment. This truth was devastating, since it flew in the face of the usual myths of necessity that the Film Board had created for itself over the years. Those polled agreed on one thing – they wanted to see more of the institution's films appear on television. This contradicted the Challenge for Change / Société nouvelle philosophy, as well as those filmmakers who thought that non-theatrical exhibition was where the agency should put its energies.[4] These suggestions did not become a programme priority, nor did the programming committee correlate seriously the findings of the Audience Needs and Reaction Unit with its own plans.[5]

This was because most creative staff believed that director-generated subjects were what they did best, and not all were meant for television. For instance, one such project was *Struggle for a Border: Canada's Relations with the United States* ($843,993), which was released in 1970 after a decade in the making. Directed by Ronald Dick and Pierre L'Amare, this series of nine one-hour history films, billed as the largest single work ever undertaken by the institution, had been a gargantuan task of weaving J.B. Brebner's classic work *North Atlantic Triangle* with 13,000 historical illustrations, cartoons, engravings, and broadsides to chronicle and dramatize the story of Canada's ability and will to survive. One of the most refreshing aspects was the series' avoidance of the usual clichés about Canada, such as 'the land God gave to Cain' or 'the impossible dream.' Its typically Canadian signature was its attempt to show the two countries doing both good and bad. There were, however, two flaws: each film was too long and dense for classroom use and was more effective in short segments. Also, Dick should have released them one at a time over the years.[6] While *Struggle for a Border* remains an example of competent and accurate historical non-fiction, it only partly fulfils the pedagogical needs of teachers of Canadian and United States history at the secondary and post-secondary level.

An example of an effective director-generated subject was Michael Rubbo's *Sad Song of Yellow Skin* ($72,484), an evocative personal account of the agony of America's war in Vietnam. Rubbo, a transplanted Australian, went to Vietnam intending to do a film on Canada's Foster Parents programme. He examined the daily lives of three non-mainstream American journalists who were themselves puzzled by the significance of the events around them. Like other Westerners, they were like men from Mars, groping futilely with an environment they could see, but not understand.

The leitmotif of incomprehension was re-peated at every level of the film: narrator Rubbo explains the American delineation of all Vietnamese as 'gooks,' signified by repetition of a U.S. soldier's nervous bravado, 'Hey, Saigon cowboy, you Saigon V.[iet]C.[ong]?' Later, a journalist's one-man aid programme of shelter to a bevy of shoe-shine children is repaid by some of the children stealing from him under the roof he gives them. A child no more than ten postures in his best Hollywood fashion with a cigarette drooping from his lips, fedora smartly tilted over his countenance, and tells brazen lies. The counterpoint is a saffron-robed monk who spent seven years in a coconut tree in a quest for peace. His acolytes cut off the ends of expended artillery shells to make flower-pots as he walks a daily ritual pilgrimage over a make-believe united country. In a down-town Saigon bar, uncomprehending patrons only half watch the Armed Forces Network television broadcast of President Nixon's contention that the American people will support the war effort if they are told why they are there, followed by the weather with 'Bubbling Bobbie,' who reports with sexy abandon the temperatures in Texas and the daily highs and lows of South Vietnam's major cities. Saigon, like the war, is a Babel of incomprehension, where Americans are known as people who either kill or give. Like-wise, the Vietnamese are portrayed as superstitious, tubercular, and drug-ridden and as prostitutes. The sad conclusion is that the only peace possible is the manipulation of the symbols of peace. A year after the Tet offensive, America's war is lost. *Sad Song of Yellow Skin* is reminiscent of the biblical story of Sodom and Gomorrah: all will be spared if there is one righteous person to be found. That person does not appear in Rubbo's film.

Sad Song of Yellow Skin was not an anti-war statement, but rather a personal testament of the general bewilderment that the war's social dislocation had brought to Saigon; all this without on-screen violence, other than one brief sequence showing the

Sad Song of Yellow Skin (1970). Cameraman Martin Duckworth films a Vietnamese monk, who spent seven years in a coconut tree in a futile quest for peace, as he walks a daily ritual pilgrimage over a make-believe united country.

aftermath of a battle. CBC Public Affairs turned it down because they did not like directors appearing in their own films. When the documentary won the Robert J. Flaherty award in England, in March 1971, the programmers changed their minds.

A few years later, in 1974, Rubbo made one of the most intriguing documentaries of the period, *Waiting for Fidel* ($123,155), a reflexive piece about documentary method and methodology. The film took place in Cuba with former Newfoundland Premier Joey Smallwood, his multimillionaire businessman-friend Geoff Stirling, and Rubbo as the on-screen director. Stirling had put up the money to make a documentary on Cuba, the cornerstone of which was to be an interview between Castro and Smallwood. He was in

the venture for profit, pure and simple. (In his week in Cuba, he became a million dollars richer because of the upward spiral of gold prices.) Rubbo wanted a film that was valuable and culturally profitable. The pugnacious Stirling attacks the Cuban revolutionary goal of socially useful work, doubting the principle of work for its own sake, when machines do it better. Rubbo, reflecting the generosity of spirit and cultivated innocence that characterized the way the Film Board embraced documentary film, is willing to accept Cuban reforms at their face value. In a sumptuous hall or on a beach where Stirling stands on his head, the film is reduced to three men waiting Godot-like for the interview that never happens before the camera. Smallwood, the self-proclaimed diplomatist and television personality, enjoys celebrity status with Castro off-screen, a frustrated Stirling attacks Rubbo and the spendthrift Film Board for wasting film footage, and a credulous Rubbo is left to show 'truth' as the Cubans and his companions reveal it to him. The film's single weakness is using the camera as a mirror on unfamiliar ground, where there is a fine line between education and manipulation. When the three Canadians 'play' themselves, documentary methodology discloses in each personality truths deeper than the surface events. *Waiting for Fidel* makes an alert audience aware of how documentary film can work.

An altogether different piece, one that Newman called spectacularly good, was telecast in January 1972. *A Matter of Fat*, written and directed by William Weintraub and narrated by Lorne Greene, was the remarkable story of French-Canadian Gilles Lorraine, a 160-kg (358-pound) obese person who undertook a hospital-supervised drastic weight-loss programme over seven and one-half months. His ordeal seems to magnify the dissonance of worshipping thinness in a society where one in four is overweight.

The direct-cinema record of Lorraine's lonely feat, showing the heartbreaking severity of his effort, cannot leave a viewer unmoved: his first food after thirty days finds him having forgotten how to eat and unable to finish the meal because his mouth hurts. After more starvation, his loss of 61 kg (150 pounds) is shown in time-lapse photography at two frames a day for seven months. In twenty-one seconds, the viewer sees him miraculously shed it all. A new man has emerged from the cocoon of fat; it is wondrous to behold as Lorraine returns home to his wife and daughters. His embrace of the children underscores how he did it for them, so that they would not ever again suffer the cruel jibes of their classmates for having a fat father. Lorraine's weight loss led him to regain religion, family, and wife. The film ends with his strong conviction that he will be the one in four dieters who can keep slim. *A*

Matter of Fat has a predictable effect on one's appetite; Weintraub himself lost so much weight subsequently that he became a wisp of his once-portly self.

There were other worthwhile documentaries being made at this time, but the filmmakers, who were often more critical than the public, tended to call them dull. They complained that directors seemed to be losing the art of orchestrating content in dramatic form. A few expressed this view about the film on John Grierson, who had succumbed to cancer in England in February 1972. *Grierson* ($242,725), a hagiographical portrait directed by Roger Blais, was filled with numerous talking heads who tried to evoke the dead master's spirit. Many who knew the Film Board founder were disappointed that the focus seemed to hover over the fiery Scot's quirks, which were easier to portray than the ideological core of public duty and public service he had instilled in his beloved agency. Yet for those who did not know Grierson, the film disclosed several of the complex facets of this extraordinary personality.

Looking on the positive side of documentary production, the new director of English Production, Robert Verrall, who had re-

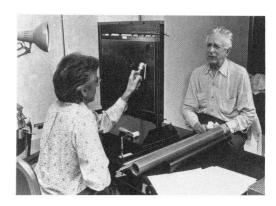

In Norman McLaren's *Pinscreen* (1973), Alexandre Alexeieff, originator of the pinscreen animation technique, observes his wife Claire Parker manipulating some of the 240,000 pins on a white rectangular board to create gradations of light and dark.

placed the one-year appointee Bernard Devlin in 1972, thought that the documentary film might be revitalized if there were a judicious mix of permanent and freelance creative staff. Such a course frightened the union, which feared that this would mean lost membership. One promising freelancer was Michael Scott of Winnipeg, who in 1973 shattered the television and movie clichés that usually stereotype policemen. With neither celebration nor condemnation, *Station 10* ($123,095) takes the viewer on an odyssey through the underbelly of midtown Montreal, as seen by the police over a two-month period. Among other events, the 'day-in-the-life' approach finds police cornering drug pushers, bumbling through a false arrest, discovering a week-old suicide, and confronting a fellow officer's brutal murder. *Station 10*, which remains a favourite in introductory sociology courses, reminds the middle-class viewer, whose usual contact with police is in the form of traffic infractions, of the policeman's all-too-human foibles in trying to enforce the law. The positive reaction to the film probably encouraged Scott and Marrin Canell to tackle in 1975 the bizarre story of a whistling officer from Vancouver, known as a tough cop with a big heart. In softer hues and tones, *Whistling Smith* shows how the officer's unorthodox style (played out fully before the camera) had earned him his sobriquet.

In 1974, a co-production with Film Australia led to *Mr. Symbol Man* ($69,432), by Bruce Moir and Bob Kingsbury. The upbeat portrait salutes Charles Bliss, whose system of fifty symbols has become the basis for teaching the linguistically handicapped how to express themselves and be understood. Bliss, a Jew who escaped Hitler's murder machine, overcame the trauma of the concentration camp by affirming life. If language can pose barriers to foster hatred, his symbols have helped demolish those barriers internationally.

A year later, Grant Munro's unique blend of humour and love of the bizarre captured

In the documentary *Whistling Smith* (1975) an unorthodox Vancouver police officer patrols a rough urban setting.

the whimsical qualities of a retired New Brunswick cemetery keeper. In *Boo-Hoo*, the straight-faced veteran takes a nostalgic traipse through the graveyard and leaves the astonished viewer unable to contemplate the finitude of life without chuckling at its absurdity. Laughter is unsuppressible when he describes a bitter wife's revenge on her once-lazy and now-deceased husband. She turned his ashes into a kitchen egg-timer, in which, every morning, she is pleased to see 'him' do his stuff.

Both the English and French Animation studios managed to excel during this period as they created exquisite works of art. In 1971, Laurent Coderre's *Zikkaron* ($14,921) won the grand prize for technique at Cannes for its novel use of cut-out animation to describe in five minutes the entire cycle of human life. Norman McLaren's *Ballet Adagio* ($25,236) of that same year was an outstanding 10-minute slow-motion study of the languor and fluidity of classical ballet, which contrasted nicely with *Street Musique* ($45,734), Ryan Larkin's visual improvisation on music as performance in 1972. The timeless parable *Balablok*, by Czech animator Bretislav Pojar (1973, $37,000), told the wordless story of human struggle in an 8-minute masterpiece. Using animated cutouts, Pojar reduced the human comedy to opposition between cubes and balls, who exhaust themselves in pointless battle until resolution is found by combining in love to produce triangles. Whether or not this is a simplistic answer to the human propensity to violence, the portrayal allows people to view objectively what Earth might look like to visitors from another planet. Once the technical means to project moving images into deep space is achieved, this film would be a good candidate to send to the galaxies to inform other intelligent life of what civiliza-

tion is likely to be found among *Homo sapiens*. *Balablok* won the Palme d'Or at Cannes in 1974.

Also in 1974, the 13-minute animated cartoon done for Information Canada, *Propaganda Message*, directed by Barrie Nelson, allowed the comic genius of Don Arioli to gush on to the screen in an irreverent glance at the complexity of Canadian society, where there are as many problems and solutions as individuals. In the scenario, the two founding peoples are likened to cats and dogs. Each animal, anxious for harmony, tries to teach the other how to bark and meow respectively – an apt description of the frustration and comedy of national accommodation. It is hard to imagine any other government in the

Propaganda Message (1974) takes an irreverent look at the complexity of Canada, whose citizens seem to prefer American television to their own national network.

world paying for a commercial on national unity, which by refusing to take its task seriously achieves the desired effect. Arioli, Kroitor, Koenig, and Verrall made up the storyboard on the train between Montreal and Ottawa as they were en route to 'sell' the project to Information Canada.

Zlatko Grgic and Arioli collaborated in a 1971 9-minute animation, *Hot Stuff*, a riotously funny sponsored film that demonstrates the human propensity to play with and be careless about fire, from its discovery to the present. Concern about fire hazards motivates the chauvinistic caveman Adam to tell Eve to tend to her apple turnovers, while the lack of concern by a contemporary television-bound lazy husband is responsible for setting his house on fire, despite his sidekick-cat's hilarious attempts to warn him.

One of the most original animation films was the computer-assisted *Hunger / La faim*, by Peter Foldès, completed in 1973, two years after his first experiment in the genre, *Metadata*. This 11-minute contemporary parable is about the inextinguishable and insatiable desire that springs from contemporary alienation. A man's once-sparing appetite is gratified perpetually, resulting in a miasma of gluttony and greed, which them-

Hunger/La Faim (1973), a parable about alienation and insatiable desire, heralded the era of computer-assisted animation.

selves lead to his being devoured by a hungry world. *Hunger* is not only a warning to the nations of the modern industrialized world, it is also a prophecy in an age that worships individual gain and pays grudging lip-service to social consciousness. *Hunger*, which won thirteen awards, including one at Cannes, heralded the future trend toward computer-assisted animation, which today is a dominant tool in animation art.

On a less sombre note the same year, E.B. White's wry New England tale *The Family That Dwelt Apart* lent itself well to the animation skills of Yvon Mallette. The 8-minute cartoon animation recounts White's tale of an island-dwelling family that attracts help it does not need from sensation-seeking media, with sad and tragic results for all concerned. The fact that one thing leads to another and to dire consequences is also the theme of *Cat's Cradle*, directed by Paul Driessen in 1974. Ten minutes of his Gothic characters' cel-animated eeriness send a chill down a viewer's spine, as one realizes the interchangeability of big and small, good and bad, and the ultimate neutrality of colour, or lack of it.

The hilarious animation *Hot Stuff* (1971) demonstrates that, if sponsored film assignments were dreaded by many NFB filmmakers, most sponsored animation pieces were handled with originality and verve.

In 1975 Veronika Soul's montage of animated photographs superimposed on actuality film footage told the story of *Tax: The Outcome of Income* ($54,300). The thesis is that one way to gauge historical time is by the numerous means governments have used to co-opt citizens' revenue. Her glimpse at Canada's modernized tax system shows just how original a sponsored film can be when the filmmaker is inspired.

From this brief survey, it is evident that animation had become one of the pillars of the institution, and in 1974 directors Rupert Glover and Michel Patenaude made *The Light Fantastick* ($59,638) to show how and why that was so. In this documentary, well-known animators described various techniques they had employed over the decades to create their world-class productions. The documentary, which included clips of some of the best animations, won three international awards.

Wildlife cinematographer Bill Mason had earned acclaim for the Film Board with his early canoe films, the children's fantasy *Paddle to the Sea* (1966), which won an Oscar nomination, and *The Rise and Fall of the Great Lakes* (1968), a geography film that has a lone canoeist living through recent geological history, only to find himself trapped in a contemporary sea of man-made pollutants. Mason left his canoe-centred subjects temporarily, and over a three-year period turned his energies to documenting the importance to nature of wolves in the wilderness. *Death of a Legend* (1971) was the first of two films on the subject. With the help of Stanley Jackson's informative commentary, Mason shattered the myth of the evil wolf, replacing that stereotype with images of the positive role the creatures play to keep the wilderness environment in balance. The film contains a cinematic first – wolf pups being born in a den and their first year of life in the wild. In the follow-up effort, *Cry of the Wild* ($74,871), Mason meant to capture the wolf on film to share with viewers the spirit of the wild. Launched in almost five hundred theatres in the United States, *Cry of the Wild* proved to be a spectacular publicity coup for the Film Board in 1973; it generated a $4.5 million gross at the box office.

Unfortunately, this film returned to the Film Board only several hundred thousand dollars, because a sloppy distribution contract allowed the American distributor literally to take the money, run, and then declare bankruptcy. Newman knew that such an accounting fiasco would not likely have occurred had his been a commercial operation, but putting on his best face, he was grateful for the widespread publicity the Film Board garnered in the United States. This and other well-known films did not, however, alter the American misnomer for the organization. They continue to this day to call it the Canadian Film Board.

The politics of federal film policy

Shortly after Gérard Pelletier became minister in 1968, he had announced the Trudeau government's intention to coordinate all cultural activities under an umbrella policy. A year later, he spelled out his objectives: democratization, decentralization, pluralism, federal-provincial and international cooperation. The three pivotal areas of culture were to be museums, publishing, and film. By January 1970 a film policy was emerging, one that was to make the commercial feature the Promised Land. The CBC had already increased its spending for features from $9.5 million to $13 million over the last six years, while the Canadian Film Development Corporation (CFDC) planned to spend more millions to aid feature-film production in 1970-1. He hoped the Film Board would establish a Festivals Office to help market Canadian film at home and abroad. Given this context, Pelletier indicated that the role of the Film Board would be changing.[7] As the glum filmmakers there saw things, the only good news was that the minister planned to require the CBC to telecast a percentage of Film Board productions.[8]

In *Cry of the Wild* (1972) Bill Mason (seen with one of his subjects in captivity) demonstrates how wolves help balance the wilderness environment.

Pelletier's commitment to democratization and regionalization was a hope to consummate the marriage of economics to culture. The commercial-film interests, whose industry now grossed $60 million to $70 million annually, were thrilled to see Ottawa now treat culture as an industry, like wheat or mining. Thus did the Federal Film Policy (later called the Global Film Policy) arrive at the Film Board from the minister's office just as Newman took over.[9] It called for creation of a Canadian Film Commission, composed of government and private-sector individuals, to assume the advisory powers that belonged to the film commissioner.[10] Those powers, intended to serve public, private, and departmental interests, had become a target of the increasingly antagonistic private sector.[11] It was of no concern to them that sponsored films paid for

one-quarter of the Film Board's annual budget; they wanted that $3–4 million plum.

The heads of the Film Board, the CBC, the CFDC, and the National Archives told the minister in December 1970 that they opposed the idea of a Canadian Film Commission. They sensed that the whole business was a misguided departmental notion from the very beginning, and their only concession was to form an ad hoc committee, the Advisory Committee on Film. Unimpressed by this resistance, the government considered it of greatest importance to see growth in the private sector.[12]

The hammer fell when Ottawa suggested that the Film Board compete with private industry for sponsored-film contracts. Newman countered and promised to tender out half of them.[13] His director of planning, Gerald Graham, had little patience with hit-

and-miss methods of filmmaking and cautioned that the Film Board's negative attitude toward sponsored-film production was well known. Relations with various departmental representatives were already miserable, and, worse, the Film Board had a reputation for rejecting sponsors' ideas and treatments almost holus-bolus; and when films were commissioned, they exceeded the quoted prices. Graham compared figures to show how the agency was 44 per cent more productive in producing its own films than the sponsored work. He suspected it was because the agency 'loaded' sponsor contracts in its time accounts. In short, the 'time' for which sponsors paid was often devoted to internal Film Board productions. This was one of the first times this long-known, but seldom-admitted fact was written.[14] Graham neglected to mention that, occasionally, some perfect gems emerged from this practice.

The germ of regionalization

The marriage of economics and culture aside, general decentralization of the federal government was a policy decision linked to the Trudeau regime's commitment to democratization. As this applied to the Film Board, Pelletier intended to establish regional production centres to allow for the discovery and development of new talent. Because the Film Board could no longer afford to hire permanent filmmakers, he hoped that regionalization would give the young the chance they needed.[15] Ironically, austerity in 1969 had forced the institution to close down the nascent Halifax and Winnipeg offices, leaving only Vancouver, where veteran producer Peter Jones's virtual one-man shoestring operation had struggled since 1965.[16] Ottawa was anxious to see regional facilities reopen in Halifax and Winnipeg, followed by a new operation in Toronto. Newman and some of his board members disapproved of the scheme, fearing it could lead to a weakening of the centre. He finally came around to

supporting the initiative, in part because it promised to bring in new creative staff without making them permanent. Regionalization was touted as one of the most positive accomplishments of the 1970s, and it became the cornerstone of the next film commissioner's regime. But Newman's original fears about a weakened centre returned to perplex the agency in the 1980s.

In 1972, the Liberal cabinet approved of Pelletier's plan to implement the Global Film Policy.[17] When he announced its first phase, he directed the CBC to broadcast increasing numbers of Canadian-produced films, the Canada Council to subsidize experimental film, the CFDC to spend usefully the $10 million increase it received, and the Film Board to regionalize and share more sponsored-film contracts with the private sector.[18]

Newman considered the Global Film Policy a sword of Damocles. He took issue with the private producers' lobby and fulminated that industry opposition to the Film Board's sponsored-film production consisted of a few Ottawa, Montreal, and Toronto companies who had easy access to government-department information and public-relations sections. He believed he had begun to improve the system in 1970 and, within two years, had softened the opposition.[19] But from now on, sponsored film was an increasingly endangered Film Board species. The private sector never ceased thinking of the Film Board staff as 'pensioners of the state,' a situation they argued was impossible in the commercial and cultural domain.[20]

One aspect of the Film Policy that was not threatening was the emphasis on the Film Board's role in education, a word that Ottawa had avoided assiduously, for fear of treading on provincial prerogative. There was no more time to be polite, however, since the paucity of Canadian audiovisual material in Canadian schools and the overwhelming predominance of foreign visual aids had created a cultural and educational crisis. In explicit terms, the Film Policy intended that

In 1971, Norman McLaren (left), Indian Prime Minister Indira Ghandi (seated, with an aide behind her), Sydney Newman, and Secretary of State Gérard Pelletier (right) observe a McLaren demonstration of animation technique at the Film Board.

the Film Board assume greater responsibility in the field of educational film. The question inside the Film Board now was, 'Who wants to make them?' Besides Donald Winkler, whose documentary *In Praise of Hands* showed the possibilities of this arrangement, there was not a long line-up of takers, and the merry-go-round whirled past the brass ring once again. Nothing could disguise the fact that too many filmmakers tended to think that making films for children was the kiss of death to a creative artist.

The Global Policy was a dismal failure in the short run, as exemplified by the ill-fated Advisory Committee on Film, which withered and died.[21] Years later, Pelletier attributed his frustration and discouragement to not having convinced the heads of his agencies of the policy's merits. In private, he and Jules Léger often asked each other rhetorically if they were not pushing the rock of

Sisyphus.[22] Yet in the long run, the objectives of the Global Policy stayed intact, and in another decade virtually all its goals had been met by Pelletier's successors.

A budget / B budget financing

The government's Draconian austerity regime of 1969–70 had led to a system of tighter fiscal rein. From the spring of 1971, the Film Board's annual budget was to be divided into two portions, called A and B budgets. The A budget was a continuation of the general or ongoing programme, films that the French and English directors chose, while the B budget covered 'ear-marked' programmes that were part of the government's policy objectives or specific departmental commissions. Thus, when the secretary of state's Film Policy called for regional production centres, the training of filmmakers and technicians, multiculturalism and language support films, the monies were part of the B budget. The subsequent budget hike from \$10.28 million in 1970–1 to \$16.42 million in 1973–4 was for earmarked projects only, and the A budget remained fixed.

The creative staff considered A/B budgeting a scourge that some likened to censorship or outside supervision of activities. They objected to management taking the money from the A budget to make up shortfalls when B budget items exceeded costs, or when income dropped, as it did with the decline of CBC rentals. In 1973, the French production group objected to its \$1.4 million A budget, which, on account of cost overruns, was about one million dollars less than the previous year. The English production group was apprehensive too, more so because filmmakers were sometimes without work. A study showed that an average of 20 per cent of their time was unallotted, and one filmmaker had found himself idle for 69 per cent or 1,073 hours of his time.[23] However, a senior filmmaker complained to English Production head Robert Verrall that the producers in English Production were like those who use credit cards as if there was no limit to available funds; overspending of budgets had become a way of life.[24] In short, one man's spree condemned another to idleness in the cafeteria coffee klatch.

In 1973 Newman tried to defuse the tension that has been generated by both the censorship issue and the B budget noose. There would be no production parity for the French Canadians, although he told them they might find things easier if they made more films dealing with Canadians other than French Canadians. Filmmakers needed to be cognizant that the length, style, and date of delivery were all important factors. Quoting Sam Steinberg from the *Corporation* series by Arthur Hammond, Newman reminded them, 'It's not the films you make, but the one you make and can't get audiences for, that gets you in trouble.'[25] An angry group of filmmakers rejected his words. 'We were amused by the paternalistic tone of your

remarks,' their letter began, and they asked Newman for a statement of the agency's philosophy or priorities.[26] An unsympathetic André Lamy put the issue more bluntly: English Production's products were too long and could not be sold, as evidenced by a drop in sales. Schools were calling for science and short films. (The Science Unit had been disbanded and forgotten in the sixties.) French Production neither had enough money to keep their staff at work nor would they shorten their feature-length documentaries.[27]

A relevant question would have been, 'Is Newman's chariot of fire about to crash and burn and does anyone care?,' but no one asked it. In part this was because Montreal was remote from those who made communication policy, but more pertinently, the cold hard fact was that Ottawa looked on the National Film Board and its problems with yawning indifference. It was only one of the eleven agencies for which the secretary of state department was responsible, and its budget of \$17.1 million was a scant 3.75 per cent of the \$455 million being spent for culture and recreation. Years later, one former board member (wishing to remain anonymous) recalled that the politicians thought about the Film Board infrequently, and then under one of three conditions; (1) a controversial film emerged and there was an explosion; (2) the budget was up for renewal; or (3) the minister went to Cabinet with something like the Film Policy, at which time great debates ensued about fundamental questions. Then the general rhetorical question was, 'What are we giving them money for?,' even though the occasional film-jewel pleased them. It was felt that the organization was an anachronism, operating not much differently from the way the Medicis had functioned. Worse, it seemed to lack any sense of direction. A minority of these dissident voices in Cabinet was a group of hard-core right-wingers who thought the agency comprised a bunch of radicals and deserved nothing.

Things changed but were still the same

after the federal election of 1972 returned a minority Liberal government. J. Hugh Faulkner, Pelletier's erstwhile parliamentary secretary, became minister. In the last days of the campaign, Faulkner promised sweeping financial assistance for the private sector, implying that the government was prepared to invest directly in Canadian culture and film through private enterprise and tax incentives.[28] He had never been enthusiastic about his predecessor's concept of a Global Film Policy and replaced it with the Capital Cost Allowance, a generous 100 per cent tax deduction to entice investors and nurture the Canadian film industry. He hoped this approach would do as much to create a critical mass of talent as the creation of the Film Board had done in its time, even if there was the possibility of abuse by those seeking tax write-offs.[29] His hope was misplaced, as dozens of producers took the money and ran, leaving much paper and few films worthy of distribution.

Along with Faulkner's policy change, sponsored-film production dropped so much that by 1973 Newman could not afford the promised fifty-fifty split with the private sector.[30] To add insult to injury, the auditor-general demanded an end to the twenty-year practice of government departments advancing money to the Film Board for films to be delivered in the following year. This new stricture was meant to force departments to be more effective in the planning of film programmes, since they had been commissioning films just prior to the end of the fiscal year in order not to have to return unspent monies to the government. Another financial blow to the institution seemed imminent.[31] Whatever the economic stress, no one could deny the real-estate needs of modern bureaucracies: Faulkner came to Montreal in the fall of 1973 to dedicate the new multimillion-dollar six-storey John Grierson Building.

It would not be an exaggeration to describe a veritable siege mentality at the Film Board, as senior management struggled to find a mission. Their document contained a cryptic statement: 'In a time of crises, NFB *can* be an essential element in Canada's "survival kit" and that "survival" – Canadian and human – is an essential central theme for the NFB.' In the absence of a coherent sense of purpose and momentum, there was a query that could be read between the lines: 'Would the agency itself survive?'[32] Privately, Newman wondered how to ensure that the organization would be serving a role that could not be performed by anyone else. Perhaps that was its mission.

From French Production: The desire for an 'authentic ONF'

Director of French Production Yves Leduc surmised that the culprit in the crisis was the whole B budget philosophy. From his group's point of view, the only alternative was to have the A budget increased, so that director-generated documentary, animation, and fiction films could continue to be made.[33] The French group suspected that management was using the B budget as a means to avoid the embarrassments of 1970–3 and to plug the philosophical gap between English and French Production. The real problem, he confessed with earnest passion, was for French Production to accept the objective of national unity because their philosophy was that 'this is a country of two nations and the [French Production] Branch is devoted first to the French Canadian nation.' He suggested glibly that there be two separate and autonomous production branches, each with its own administration, priorities, and programme guidelines. The attendant cultural consequences could fall where they would. As Quebec increasingly wished to control its own cultural affairs, so too did French Production wish to reflect the same tendency in its aspirations and films. Its filmmakers wanted to produce 'political' films, well-researched documentaries that both related to life in Quebec and made comparisons with the political philosophies of other countries.

Along with intellectuals, filmmakers were

expected to be the leading edge of opinion, Leduc affirmed. They could no longer ignore that the realities in contemporary Quebec were the preoccupations with cultural sovereignty, autonomy, and political philosophies. As for the task of interpreting French Canada to English Canada, their belief was that the differences were so great and basic that it would be useless to try. To deflect the natural English-Canadian reaction that those French filmmakers who felt this way should quit and go work for Quebec, Leduc responded nonchalantly that they *were* working for a greater national destiny, the independence of Quebec.

Hearing all this, a remarkably restrained board of governors suggested that Leduc's group objective carried with it the obligation of working within the context of the country known as Canada and within the mandate of the institution.[34] Unrepentant, seven months later, Leduc reiterated this stance as he called for the creation of 'an authentic ONF,' which meant 'complete parity and autonomy' with the English-language National Film Board. He argued that it was difficult to practise rigid objectivity when it came to films of a critical nature in social and cultural domains; his group's duty was to push freedom to the maximum. Quoting staunch federalist Marc Lalonde out of context, the filmmakers announced, 'We shall have to take the means to obtain what is our due, and to see that it is respected.'

This time, the board members forgot their normal Canadian practice of accommodation and were outraged at what appeared to them to be a virtual declaration of independence.[35] They left it to Newman to speak to the leaders, and he put it to them in his inimitable blunt fashion: would the French filmmakers rather leave *en bloc* and go to work under the aegis of the Quebec rather than the federal government? He interpreted their response as a preference to stay where they were.[36] If calling them on the carpet satisfied the board members, the truculence of the French wing could not have been unknown

and unfelt in Ottawa, despite the fact that Newman's April 1975 appearance before the Standing Committee on Broadcasting, Films and Assistance to the Arts was a tame and cordial affair. For years afterwards, he remained convinced that the separatists in French Production were 'burrowing from within' and that if they had had any integrity, they would have left the institution.

The Film Board was mirroring the same agony as Canada and, in the long run, the board members refused to play confrontational politics. They waffled instead, claiming that the policy questions Leduc had raised required serious reflection and decision. Meanwhile they could feel secure that a B budget item like the 'national unity' programme was keeping those politically committed *québécois* filmmakers from both flouting the federal presence and running away with the store.[37]

At the secretary of state department, where the minutes of board meetings were sent for perusal, an informal topic that arose rarely was what to do with the troublesome French filmmakers (if not with the institution). Minister Faulkner did not believe there was a predisposition against the film agency, which he thought at worst was still living off interest earned from its past glories. None the less, the moderate voices in the department (including Faulkner himself) were concerned about the radicals and were bothered that the organization was involving itself in politics rather than in making first-class films. That federal monies were being used to promote separatism caused anxiety, but the government had similar problems with French nationalists on so many levels and on so many fronts that the Film Board was just another voice in the chorus. When cultural-agency issues came up in Cabinet, there were ministers who raised questions about Film Board programmes, but Faulkner resisted any temptation to use censorship just because a particular production opposed a person's point of view. When some ministers went further and complained that it was not the point of view, but the film itself, that was unfair, he passed the complaint on to Newman, in whom he had great confidence to sort things out professionally. The commissioner had a feel for what the agency's mission was all about, Faulkner thought, even if he was weaker in administrative skills. The minister was disturbed that the French filmmakers would not let Newman share his expertise with them, which confirmed his own misgivings that many may have been more interested in politics than films.[38]

Helpful advice gratefully accepted: *Mon oncle Antoine*

Faulkner's bleak appraisal of French Production's relationship with the commissioner did not quite apply to Claude Jutra's feature *Mon oncle Antoine*, a co-production with

Gendron Films. The Film Board's share cost $237,214, and from its theatrical debut in November 1971 English critics variously recognized the film as original and brilliant, a universal statement about a child's loss of innocence, even as the best-ever Canadian film. French critics were less generous in their reaction and complained of a muddled script by Clément Perron, carped about a confusing point of view, and thought it handled the sociological reality superficially.[39] None the less, *Mon oncle Antoine* had a successful theatrical run beginning in December 1971, grossing $700,000 by 1974. After broadcasting it in October 1973 and August 1974 respectively, both Radio-Canada and the CBC boasted of a total audience of 2.5 million, the second-hightest rating in network history.

Many non-French speakers found the sub-

Mon oncle Antoine (1971), sometimes called the best all-time Canadian film, revolves around a young lad's coming of age. (Director Claude Jutra, left, with principal actors Benoît Marcoux and Jean Duceppe)

titled *Mon oncle Antoine* the most accessible French-language film yet because it let the viewer discover the French Canadians' perception of their own place in Canada. Later, Jutra said he had not necessarily been conscious of the symbols which others found, although he admitted that there were political implications that the viewer could derive.[40]

Set at Christmastime in a forgotten one-industry mining town in Quebec's Eastern Townships of the forties, *Mon oncle Antoine* revolves around the social hub of the general store, where a boy feels the awakening urges of adolescence. He sees the veil of childhood fall away as he confronts human frailty, sexuality, humour, depression, and death.

Jutra asked Newman to view the unfinished work late in 1970. The commissioner suggested better ways to carry out two key scenes that were the nexus of the feature, the first where the youth and his uncle Antoine lose the coffin of a dead child in the snow at night and the second when the adolescent surprises his aunt in an amorous embrace with the store clerk, played by Jutra himself. Newman suggested that Jutra delay releasing the film, do the extra shooting in February 1971, and not worry about the extra $40,000 it would cost.[41] Launched at the Moscow film festival in August 1971, the feature started its climb to fame and won the Hugo award at the Chicago film festival in November.

As the accolades poured in, the generous and encouraging Newman enthused, 'You're on a roll!' This was his way of saying he hoped Jutra would get on with another feature very soon. It was not to be. The French Programme Committee told the disconsolate director he would have to wait some years before getting another feature project, since his colleagues wanted their chance to make a feature too. Newman could do nothing to help. Jutra soon left the Film Board to make *Kamouraska* in the private sector, arguably his best film ever in its uncut version. Playing the *enfant terrible*, the direc-

tor refused the Order of Canada in November 1972, and claimed that it would mean condoning the policies of the federal government, the constitution, and so forth. It would be officially approving Canada as such, he concluded.[42] One could understand why the piqued minister had stated that many in French Production seemed more interested in politics than films.

Ottawa's policies of bilingualism and multiculturalism

Before Trudeau had become prime minister Canada was already embarked on a policy of institutional bilingualism, stemming from the recommendations of the 1963 Royal Commission on Bilingualism and Biculturalism, one of whose purposes was to try to induce more French-speaking citizens to join the federal bureaucracy and to feel free to work in either mother tongue. To fortify this principle, as well as to promote a sense of national identity and national unity, the government had introduced the Official Languages Act in 1969, a law that generated little national enthusiasm. Responding to this initiative and the possibility of additional production funds through the B budget, the board of governors tried to set Film Board policy for the seventies. They welcomed Ottawa's $200,000 initial contribution toward a three-year governmental plan of sixty Language-Learning Support films to teach French and English as they were spoken in Canada. A committee of language experts and teachers was to develop the criteria for content and the Film Board was to look after their creative execution.

Unfortunately, the results proved to be an unmitigated disaster. French Production cooperated reluctantly and English Production seemed to mock the whole enterprise with its first film, *Albert Lagrenouille*, a quixotic Rashomon-like excess. This comedy, dealing with a French Canadian's dream of winning the lottery, was very Canadian in managing to insult both the French and English simultaneously. Upon seeing the film, Lamy went white and said he thought it could destroy the organization. Newman was amused, but suspected that even retitled as *The Winner* it might do more harm than good. It was never released, although director Michael Scott and executive producer John N. Smith seemed to be the only voices to protest.[43] Another of the board of governors' ideas that met with indifference was to have English filmmakers explain French Canada to English Canada and to have French filmmakers show the rest of Canada to Quebec.[44]

If English Canada was generally resistant to the policy of bilingualism, there were those who criticized Ottawa's Official Languages Act for another reason: they claimed that it discriminated against those whose mother tongue was neither English nor French. Sensitive to the outcry, Trudeau himself had written in 1969 that this was a misconception. Taking the cue, the secretary of state department studied the issue and reported that, on the question of minorities, the country's attitude was that ethnics faced a choice, assimilation in either the anglophone or francophone melting-pot. But this was not what the bilingual and bicultural commission had intended in Book IV of its report. In accordance with the commission's recommendations then, in 1971, Ottawa decided to adopt a policy of pluralism, of providing modest ethnic cultural support while favouring integration.[45]

This sense of unease with bilingualism led directly to the policy of multiculturalism that the government inaugurated in October 1971. The prime minister claimed that, despite there being two official languages, there was no official culture, nor did one ethnic group take precedence over another. 'Indeed, cultural pluralism is the very essence of Canadian identity,' he maintained, and his policy statement said that a good deal of contemporary social unrest existed in all language groups because the need to belong had not been met. 'Ethnic pluralism can help us overcome or prevent the homogenization

and depersonalization of mass society,' he continued, and he believed that a policy of multiculturalism within the two official languages should help break down discrimination and cultural jealousies.[46]

There were those who saw multiculturalism as a means to replace the notion of exclusive ethnicity; others found it was fundamentally an anti-discrimination vehicle, attempting to harmonize race relationships in a country where the 'English' (those with British cultural roots) were no longer the majority. The general feeling evolved that this was a slogan, rather than a genuine commitment to multiculturalism. Public interest in it seemed to be as lacklustre as its regard for bilingualism. In the context of French Canada's contemporary struggle, be it framed as a struggle for equality or a struggle against the English, many French Canadians regarded 'ethnics' as competitors rather than natural allies.[47]

The overall sense was that multiculturalism was little more than voluntary marginal differentiation among people who were equal participants in society. The more critical called the policy one of ethnic-group containment. From a Machiavellian angle, they argued that multiculturalism seemed to be a device to legitimize the continued dominance of the ruling English-speaking élite. As such, it obscured the French-Canadian challenge to political power by channelling that drive in linguistic and cultural directions.[48]

Those who viewed multiculturalism from a positive sociological perspective concluded that in a country which was accustomed to defining itself in terms of what it was *not*, rather than what it was, multiculturalism might provide Canada with a symbol of nationhood without using the usual gambit of extreme nationalism or loyalty based on civics alone. It was also a suitable alternative to the violence that was poisoning national societies the world over. From yet another point of view, by adding a third component to the English-French national debate, multiculturalism promised to mitigate the linguistic polarity threatening to tear the country apart.

Whatever the diverse reactions to the policy were, multiculturalism soon became a familiar part of the Canadian social landscape. The Film Board, still seeking a raison d'être for the seventies, was happy to find itself with a newly assigned role as one of the policy's purveyors. At the outset the agency made available to major ethnic groups pre-existing versioned films intended for use abroad. From 1972, Ottawa provided almost $2 million over five years to version its films into languages other than French or English for domestic consumption and to make films about the contribution and problems of ethnic groups.[49] By 1974, 1,700 prints of 400 titles were available across Canada. The policy led also to production of original films like Albert Kish's *Our Street Was Paved with Gold* ($51,472), a nostalgic meander up Montreal's St Lawrence Boulevard, a microcosm of European cultures; Felix Lazarus's *People of the Book* ($69,811), portraying synagogue life and the efforts to perpetuate culture and tradition in small Jewish communities located in remote northern towns; and *Cousins germains* ($65,596), a French-language story of three Germans who chose Quebec as their home.

Whether or not multiculturalism had its desired effect on the national level, it would seem that exposure to these films and the teacher-directed discussions they were intended to provoke probably benefited Canadian students. On the practical level, multiculturalism was a shot in the arm for Film Board programming, and in the next few years there was a plethora of films on immigrants; the catalogue numbers seventy-five such titles in circulation today.

A permanent philosophical change: Women's films

Since its founding, the Film Board had made films about women periodically, from recruitment shorts during the Second World War, to brief propaganda pieces on women in the workplace, to the history of women's struggle for the vote in *Women on the March* (1958), to the television series of four French items on women in the mid-sixties.[50] Virtually all these works stated the clichés about the feminine condition of the particular era and, like most film documents, could be viewed as mirrors of the paternalistic middle-class social values they contained. Still, they did not praise the status quo and did contribute to the incompletely articulated, progressive dream of sexual equality. The meshing of equal opportunity with the biological desires of parenthood remained an unstated paradox until *En tant que femmes* and *Working Mothers* emerged in the early seventies.

Those documentaries were the first to reflect the impact of the feminist wave that was precipitating a profound attitudinal shift throughout Western society. The changing roles of women did not always find (male) power holders willing to share or diminish their authority, since an axiom about power is that those who have it are rarely willing to share it. Undeterred by such obstacles, progressives of both sexes understood and concurred with the need for ongoing consciousness-raising activity toward sexual equality. In Canada, the Report of the Royal Commission on the Status of Women, in 1970, was a landmark and catalyst to integrating a feminist perspective into social relations. When it was announced at the end of 1972 that 1975 would be International Women's Year, there was general optimism about change.

After filmmaker Kathleen Shannon found a responsive constituency for the *Working Mothers* series in 1974, she began a ceaseless lobby for a separate women's unit, while in French Production, Anne Claire Poirier lobbied for features dealing with women's subjects. It was a painfully slow process. Sometimes the bureaucratic bungling of the agency was unforgivable, as in the instance when Shannon and Poirier scrambled at the last moment in 1974 to present a submission to the government for $300,000 in special funds to mark International Women's Year. Their request was refused because it arrived a day after the deadline. The same year, Newman and Robert Verrall encouraged Shannon to apply for an ambitious $1.3 million for a separately funded women's budget. The Treasury Board turned the submission down flat. Undeterred, the commissioner gave Verrall the go-ahead to have Shannon organize Studio D, which began officially in August. The government's last and final 'no' to a separate budget arrived almost a year later, so Shannon had to accept a 'make do' budget. Poirier insisted on equal funding with other French Productions, and this meant there would be no French counterpart to Studio D until October 1986, when Studio B (*Regards de femmes*) was organized under Josée Beaudet.

The manifesto of Studio D was a practical 'in-house' agenda, calling for ways to bring women's influence to bear on programming, in particular through the presence of professionally qualified women in numbers equal to men. 'There are decades, centuries, millennia of repressed or forgotten history and meanings to be explored,' Studio D proclaimed, and underscored the fact that it was men's as well as women's history because current themes, now perceived as women's themes, were 'virtually universal.' The filmmakers planned a series of films on subjects like success, middle age, fatherhood, children, adolescents, women at work, and sexual discrimination.[51] No eyebrows were raised over the intended virtual segregation of this group into what critics soon called a women's ghetto. At this point, the women showed little interest in a possible contribution by progressive men who might share their outlook.

The women's audience became known as a constituency representing over 51 per cent of the population and of those components of the Film Board audience beyond the white male middle class. As for a credo, 'integrative feminism' was the praxis of their films, that is, the emphasis was on the 'otherness' of the voices that spoke to the audience – 'we' were the women and 'they' were the men.[52] Consciously or otherwise, they were in the process of drawing a direct line from Challenge for Change to Studio D, and then to the leading-edge films of the eighties and a renewed raison d'être for the organization.

Shannon took a different philosophical approach from Poirier, whose feature-length films were intended to have wide diffusion via television. She steered Studio D away from features because of their prohibitive cost and a conviction that most individuals who made them were using them to further a personal career. (She was not referring to Poirier.) She intended Studio D to make short films for non-theatrical audiences, convinced that a filmmaker should interact with her live audience. Together, surrounded in darkness and undisturbed, they would experience the film with undivided attention. She believed that such an audience could be touched and changed, as could the filmmaker herself, while a telecast, with its distractions of home life, talking, competing light sources, small screen, and easy channel selection, and commercials, rarely changed people.

Shannon thought the detached objectivity characteristic of most Film Board films was a form of bias. Such 'detachment,' she insisted, allowed people to talk about the world in the abstract, when common passion about shared vital issues was really needed. It was up to the filmmaker to serve her constituency first; to do so she would have to articulate those issues in a visionary and idealistic manner and avoid the radical feminist tack of denunciation. Shannon assumed that the approach she cultivated was in the spirit of the Grierson tradition: the filmmaker was not exploiting people, she was serving the national interest.[53]

From a similar perspective, she articulated a critique of mass culture (particularly television), whose goal is in fact too often the interest of the male, white, Anglo-Saxon, middle-class group. That body controls the levers of power and is itself demographically a minority group. To use the point of reference of Tom Daly's old Unit B, Studio D was in search of 'wholeness,' though it was not the wholeness of bringing the Canadian nation together. It was the wholeness of women articulating their own needs, just as Shannon believed that men tend to see the world from the point of view of articulating men's needs. Studio D made the 'gender' issue a familiar and accepted one in the next decade, in spite of a paucity of funds with which to do the task.

Drama development:
Another constituency

There were other 'constituencies' demanding attention too. Almost coincidental with the launching of the women's studio, Studio B began the Drama Development Programme to revitalize English Production. James de Beaujeu Domville, the executive director of Theatre de Nouveau Monde and co-founder of the National Theatre School, left his posts to become assistant director of English Production. Domville was reputed to be a wizard at administration, which helped Verrall win over Newman and Lamy to this 'outside' hiring. Domville agreed to design a more efficient and sensible budgetary system if he could then shift into drama. The plan suited him well, although he was shocked to learn upon arriving that there was no money for drama activity.

Neither was there a managerial structure to explain how finances worked, and hardly anyone had a grasp of the overall financial picture. Money that was budgeted from inside the agency was thought of as 'not real,' while income that derived from outside, like that from sponsored film, was treated as 'real.' Domville was disturbed that there was little management of people's skills and that funds were being spent without coherent purpose. Worse, there were no standards or evaluative means for hiring people; too many

had come on to staff as a result of someone on the inside having helped him or her get a film made. 'Many were called, but few could serve,' was how Domville put it drily; he wanted to see 'healthy elitism.' He did not point an accusing finger at the union, but at management, who caved in at every confrontation because of a fear of the union's threat to 'go public.' Yet to blame management entirely was not fair either. The creative staff, a mixture of talent and mediocrity, seemed generally to not have much sense of its public-service function, he thought, and carried a significant burden of responsibility. He concluded that the whole institution was only slowly coming out of a period of self-indulgent filmmaking, and it was a painful process.

Being a government department in all but name added to the muddle, because the Film Board used mechanistic accounting controls that suited the Treasury Board and not film-making purposes. The system of person-years (money allotted for one person to work for one year) took no account of freelance employees who might be working on rotating contracts on a year-round basis. The government ignored the double standard which deprived these individuals of the benefits that other full-time employees enjoyed, from sick leaves to pensions. So long as the person-year number stayed fixed, the government was happy. Over one hundred freelancers continued to work, but the administration pretended they did not exist. It was an unreal situation that needed a legal resolution. Such lopsidedness provided a strong argument for crown-corporation status, the bookkeeping practices of which would be appropriate for filmmaking.

Another absurdity was that filmmakers tended to treat inside costs as a fiction. Domville discovered that often a large sum of money was set aside for print publicity and charged to 'inside costs.' The amount was usually higher than an outside firm would charge, because the costs were spread over a year in order to keep the employees fully engaged. The director and producer might agree to 'save' money by having this work done outside at less cost. But this would mean that the employees in the Film Board's publicity department would be idle, while still drawing their pay. The money 'saved' would actually boost the cost of the production and, in turn, the cost of print publicity to other productions. Domville found that costs were being tracked in the new computerized system, but the information was not being used to manage the agency better, only to report to the government. He untied the Gordian knot and allocated resources more efficiently.[54]

Domville's was an administrative success story and his contribution to English Production was enormous. He decentralized executive responsibility for expenditures by upgrading studio administrators, just as French Production had done. He controlled the budget so tightly that Verrall showed a $250,000 surplus by the end of the first year. As a result, the feature *Why Rock the Boat?*, which had collapsed as a private-sector production, was suddenly on track.

Soon Domville took over Studio B to start the five-year experimental Drama Development Programme with erstwhile producer/director Roman Kroitor. Kroitor had left in the late sixties to set up IMAX Corporation because the times had not been right for low-budget features. He found himself put in charge of the drama programme when Domville's financial wizardry proved to be too precious to senior management, who elevated him to the post of general manager in the fall of 1975.

Kroitor's articulation of Studio B's rationale was an interesting counterpoint to that of Studio D: 'The straight documentary film must, for the most part, stop short when it approaches too close to the personal lives of individuals because it cannot invade personal privacy. Yet this is where society ultimately has its significance, the inner life of individual people.' While English Production had long sought to emulate the fiction work of French Production, tradition and budget had kept the documentary at the fore-front of English activity.

To help form the sinews of drama, Kroitor invited the noted Dutch filmmaker Nico Crama in 1974–5. Crama criticized English Production for turning out little more than ordinary television fare. The films were suffering from what he called 'the burden of *cinéma vérité* style,' lacking humour and happiness. Filmmakers should try fiction and make fewer productions better, he recommended. His nostrum was: think short, think dramatically, experiment, and smile.[55]

Crama had seen the last three English features and knew why no one was smiling. In 1972 Martin Defalco had gotten into a directorial mess with *Cold Journey* ($414,200), a film whose heart was in the right place, but whose images were not. It dealt with a young Indian's attempt to cope with an educational system whose blindness to native culture-shock was causing deracination and social

Cold Journey (1972) portrays a young Indian's attempts to cope with an unresponsive educational system. (Johnny Yesno, left, with Chief Dan George)

disintegration among native groups across the country. Its tragic ending of the youth's death by freezing left only despair. This was a cardinal sin in English Production, which was still supposed to be practising the Griersonian rule that, no matter what the circumstances, hope was the last word. Whether it was the director's intention or not, the white actors were two-dimensional at best, while the native actors, including Chief Dan George, were more convincing. The script was hopelessly muddled, and Newman became furious when more money was thrown into it after he personally ordered a halt to further expenditures. Tom Daly and Stanley Jackson gave it their best editing and verbal efforts, but neither money nor time could save it. None the less, when Indian filmmaker Alanis Obomsawin saw it, she thought it had merit because it was a rare experience for Indians to see themselves on screen as they were. The distribution branch helped set up play dates across small communities in the North, where it packed tiny rural one-theatre towns like The Pas, Manitoba. This response justified the expense at least partially, some argued.

Why Rock the Boat? ($450,000), a romantic comedy written by William Weintraub and directed by John Howe, fared not much better. In 1974 it opened in more Canadian cinemas than any Canadian film to date, though unfortunately it earned less than a quarter of its cost. Based on Weintraub's much funnier satiric novel of the same title, the film was a period piece, set in Montreal of the late forties. It was the story of a struggling newspaper reporter's eagerness for sexual and professional success, which was realized only inconclusively by the film's end. The

Why Rock the Boat? (1974), a romantic feature comedy set in Montreal of the late forties, like most English-Canadian features, earned less than a quarter of its cost.

comic seduction scene before a crackling fire was a good and memorable laugh, though the hero's desktop socialist-tirade finale seemed dissonant. Newman thought that a miscast female lead was partly responsible for the film's lukewarm acceptance.

The same year, Mort Ransen had the most disastrous result of all, after directing the 80-minute feature *Running Time*, which cost $1,166,260. The film idea grew out of Ransen's experience with *Christopher's Movie Matinee*, and he began production in 1972, just as Verrall became director of production. Billed as an exotic romp through the sixties in song and dance, it used a Bertold Brecht technique to make the viewer aware of the film as artifice rather than as an experience of reality. In trying to poke fun at social mores as well as itself, the film's net effect was to create a sense of ridiculousness. The friendship of an old lady and a young man failed to generate the kind of magnetism a contemporary American film like *Harold and Maude* was doing throughout North America. Its singular achievement was some brilliantly colourful special-effects animation by Ryan Larkin. Otherwise it was a complete loss. Martin Knelman called it 'Canadian film history's worst disaster,' and its exorbitant budget led member of Parliament Tom Cossitt to ask why public funds were being spent on such a production. At a time when other creative staff were idling in the cafeteria with nothing to do, there was no excuse for this amateurish profligacy. An embarrassed Ransen confided to Verrall years later that he wished Verrall had used his authority as director of production to stop the production. Verrall agreed. Domville concurred, and since he bore no responsibility for it, remarked that it was marvellously imaginative, totally hopeless, and a candidate to become a cult film by the year 2000.[56]

Given these formidably expensive failures, Kroitor was not going to allow any and all to take the plunge into fiction. Serious training was a firm priority. Of the twenty-five filmmakers who submitted videotape auditions, he invited only several to direct a short dramatic film. The next year he asked six more to join the programme. He stated his objective laconically: the subjects that were worthy of dramatic treatment had to be important to people and they had to inspire public feedback of 'this is worth doing,' rather than a feeling akin to the satisfaction one may have when looking at one's bankbook balance. His hope was to develop a team not unlike the original Unit B team of the 1950s, and to eventually make a blockbuster drama. He brought in Czech dramaturge Vladimir Valenta to help with scriptwriting. The discipline was brutal, and soon there were complaints that Kroitor was 'Vladimirizing' at every stage. The first 'graduates' were Giles Walker, John N. Smith, and Anne Wheeler. Kroitor then tried to expand the programme, but failed because he could not attract sufficient money. Elsewhere in the institution many staff, whose credo was still the documentary film, were dubious that drama production was 'in the national interest.'

The question of staff: To prune or not to prune?

Kroitor witnessed the problem of underutilized staff and realized that the dilemma at this time was to either pay salaries and watch the agency sink or fire staff and make films. Thinking of the ultimate responsibility to the taxpayers, he believed it was in the national interest for the administration to take the harder decision. When that course was not chosen, he left the Film Board again, disappointed at the diffuseness of its endeavours and at the atrophy of drama development.[57] He enjoyed subsequent success at IMAX and OMNIMAX and maintains an ongoing concern for the Film Board.

Verrall and Domville perceived the situation differently. They did not think that the organization was terribly overstaffed, even if Distribution could have shed some of its personnel. Management could not because more of its people were needed for the regionalization programme. Both men favoured minimal cuts in production staff. If some of the oldest members with up to thirty years' seniority were now the least productive, they reasoned that laying them off was inhumane. After all, no other government departments laid off their slow seniors, so why should the Film Board? They preferred to redeploy them, pending their retirement within the decade. As for the new talent, many of whom were on contract as freelancers, to fire them would mean terminating those who were renewing the institution. They thought that management might keep dossiers on those production people who were young and incompetent, so they could be released with cause. The next director of English Production tried this tack too, with little success.

Discussions among management reduced the staffing options to two: either all filmmakers should be freelancers, as happened in most nations, or a core should be kept to ensure continuity. Domville concurred with Colin Low that the core concept was the reason the Film Board had been able to maintain its creative continuity over the years. There was general agreement that, ideally, one-third should be a permanent core, one-third should be contracted by programme, and one-third should be genuine freelancers. If the old phrases 'interpreting Canada to Canadians' and 'in the national interest' had ceased being touted as the raison d'être of the Film Board, most employees were willing to support the assertion that they made films which the market-place did not normally support.

Relations with the minister

Meanwhile in Ottawa, Faulkner believed that he should consult his agency heads no more than three times a year, and never with respect to operations, lest he compromise the arm's-length principle.[58] When he and New-man met, they discussed broad policy issues, although the commissioner was acutely sensitive to what the minister was thinking and saying to his subordinates about the Film Board. For example, he had learned that Faulkner disliked two of the language-support films for teaching English as a second language, *The Heatwave Lasted Four Days* and *A Star Is Lost*, nor was he pleased with Ian McLaren's series *Atlanticanada*, made for the CBC.[59] Word had it that he thought the Film Board was failing at what it was supposed to do best, to make enough innovative and world-class films for the $23.5 million it was spending in 1974–5.

On one of two occasions when both men met in 1974, Newman and Faulkner discussed the overlapping of responsibilities by the eleven government bodies involved in film.[60] To evolve a clear delineation of each agency's role was easier said than done. For one, the CFDC had surveyed its achievements since its formation and concluded that a $3 million return on a total investment of $240 million meant that theatres did not want Canadian feature films. The minister had its charter altered so that, like the Film Board, it could make half-hour television documentaries. He knew this was the Film Board's traditional interpretive role, but purposely challenged its comfortable monopoly and the notion that it was a little *atelier* that was funded forever, where filmmakers produced whatever mattered to them, regardless of audience. In short, he felt that the Film Board had become a cocoon, an isolated research and development laboratory.[61]

Newman sensed that Ottawa's feature-film policy and commitment to the 250 companies that now composed the private film sector were emasculating his institution.[62] Excluding the B budget, its annual increases had been about one-half those of other agencies of comparable size, and its parliamentary appropriation was just matching inflation. Newman admitted privately that Canadian features, which he considered 'frivolous,' were not good and could not attract audiences. Because there was no critical mass of talent to form a nucleus, he thought that the money spent on them could be better spent in other film areas, such as offsetting the deluge of foreign material into schools.[63] The commissioner was a bit like a fly in the ointment when he warned about the delusions of grandeur associated with creating a Canadian feature-film industry. He knew firsthand how Britain, a culturally strong nation, had failed in its attempt to do the same. He noted ominously the proliferation of Ontario visual-arts graduates between 1968 and 1973: of three hundred who were trained, only thirty had found work in their field. His opinions made no impact upon Ottawa, where his organization continued to be viewed like old wallpaper.

As to the sticky question of union relations, Faulkner advised Newman that, if necessary, he should have it out with the union, whose actions he thought were 80 per cent politics.[64] He wanted a cap on permanent staff, and the commissioner replied that five hundred would be sufficient, with half permanent, half freelance.[65] This astounding number implied that there would have to be cut-backs, despite the fact that staff numbers were creeping up, from 859 in 1971 to 950 in 1975. A decade later, the five-hundred figure was trotted out again as a goal.

Freelancers would stimulate the creative environment and keep both staff and facilities fully occupied, said Newman. But when management's practice of hiring freelancers reduced union membership to below that of 1969, the union retained the services of labour lawyers Stanley Hartt and Mortimer Freiheit to take their case to the Public Service Staff Relations Board. The first decision went against them; on appeal, the court told the PSSRB to rehear the grievance. Management feared that a decision in favour of the union might put the last nail in the Film Board's budgetary coffin. Both sides held their breath for the denouement, which came in 1977, when the union won.

Faulkner continued to push on behalf of turning over more sponsored films to the private sector, though he thought the Film Board, not the Department of Supply and Services, should commission them. (DSS pleaded its case again in 1977 and 1984.) By the spring of 1975 the commercial producers were giving the minister plenty of flak. A typical argument was that there were around thirty-five major government film productions per year, of which only about one-third went out to tender. Supervising tendering had been the main function of the Film Board's Ottawa office since 1970. With only 12 productions to be divided between the 250 companies on the tender list, as many as 150 of them might be vying for an individual project.[66]

Sensitive to the shifting winds, Faulkner asked the Film Board to make its technical facilities available to individual private filmmakers, though not to film companies. It took until 1980 for the Program to Assist Filmmakers and Films in the Private Sector (PAFFPS) to begin officially for this purpose. In response to the suggestion that the Film Board distribute select, privately made films through its own network,[67] Newman proposed a grand scheme for a national system of distribution by computer. 'It's the kind of idiot's dream that will appeal to the Minister and has a sense of glorious vision,' he remarked cynically, and if the minister refused to provide the extra funds, it would be on his head, not the Film Board's. Faulkner did not support the costly idea,[68] although it was revised and diluted some years later to become *Format*, a computerized database of Canadian audiovisual productions available to the public. Pie-in-the-sky schemes aside, Newman warned somberly that if something was not done to help private industry, the minister would kill the Film Board.[69]

The highly vaunted Challenge for Change / Société nouvelle was also generating doubts at the ministerial level. If Faulkner favoured it for being a meaningful instrument for social change and community development, on the practical level he wondered whether the Film Board should not play a more ancillary role. He was disturbed that the filmmakers had a tendency to go into a situation, open it up, and then depart, leaving a wound that the responsible department had not made plans to dress immediately. He wanted more careful involvement with the department before the filmmakers precipitated social-action problems. Concerned about the same issue, the board of governors had earlier stressed the importance of incorporating projects into local institutional frameworks. One member kept silent for years, but thought privately that the whole programme was teary-eyed self-indulgence because it was never clear who was in charge or what it was for. Those thoughts were not unique, and in 1975 this concern led to a restructuring of the interdepartmental committee.[70]

Faulkner's support of the private sector went further than many could remember with any previous minister. He trotted out the forbidden words and told the Film Board to develop a mechanism for a quota system, which he thought was inevitable. Publicly, he remarked that quotas might be necessary at some point, but they were not the total answer to the current problems of the film industry in Canada, since there was a question as to whether films protected under such a system would attract audiences. Furthermore, he was well aware of how difficult it would be to regulate film distribution, a provincial, not federal jurisdiction.[71] The scare tactics worked. Famous Players Canada (a subsidiary of Paramount Pictures, Hollywood) volunteered more screen time for Canadian films, an informal arrangement that was short-lived.

If these various pressures were not strong enough, in June 1975 the Treasury Board informed Newman that there would be an across-the-board cut in all departments, the object being to save $1 billion. The government, having already borrowed $5 billion, needed more money to mount an employment-creating programme for the hard-pressed economy. The Film Board was about to lose $1 million, plus 1 per cent of its salary budget ($138,000). Newman pleaded special consideration, since sponsored film orders were sure to decline by 25 per cent. The struggle to win exemption proceeded through the summer, and when the dust settled in the fall, the cut was $500,000, coupled with a 2.5 per cent salary reduction over two years.[72] Regular doses of this medicine might help the gout-like Canadian government, but they increased the Film Board's misery and vulnerability.

Newman at term's end

The doubts and worries shared by many provided the backdrop for the painful decisions the government took over the next five years. One of the first was Faulkner's determination to not renew Newman's contract, which was due to expire in July 1975. The crestfallen Newman felt betrayed by the Film Board and, in paraphrasing Joyce, concluded that Canada, like Ireland, was like a sow who eats her own farrow. His bitterness was excessive, if understandable. As a unilingual Canadian who had been thrust into the cultural ferment of a much more abrasive Canada than the one he had left in the 1950s, he felt very much alone. What made it worse was that he did not seek out the comfort of people who could have told him to wait it out. He had tried to instil discipline and believed he was cut off just as he was effecting change.

Faulkner saw it differently and thought that Newman had run out of steam. The commissioner was beleaguered, seemed to have little staff support, did not appear to be in charge, and in his private life was losing his wife to fatal illness. To put it more prosaically, after half a decade, Newman's figurative 'chariot of fire' had lost a wheel and had been consumed by its own flames. But Faulkner liked Newman's perpetual ebullience, therefore the undaunted ex-commissioner landed on his feet in Ottawa as special adviser on film to the secretary of state.

There were those inside and outside the Film Board who had complained of Newman's 'band-aid management.' The minister's corporate criteria for leadership called for a chief executive officer whose role was fundamentally strategic, and secondarily operational. Most important, he wanted a leader to develop an industrial model, to point the institution toward a goal it could reach in five years, so it could evolve, take shape, and become relevant, admired, and supported. (A five-year plan followed in 1976.) In defence of Newman, Faulkner said later that if the commissioner's tenure was compromised, that was due predominantly to the staff's failure to establish a dynamic linkage between their organization and the outside talents who were begging for support.[73] None the less, during Newman's watch the Film Board had failed to convince friend and foe that it was a national necessity. By contrast, as the era of privatization was dawning, Canadian entrepreneurs were encouraged by the government's commitment to culture as an industry.

When reflecting on his tenure a decade later, Newman felt less grim. He had signed one prime-time contract with the CBC and was hopeful about concluding a second. In 1974 the Film Board's catalogue listed fifty CBC titles in an exclusive distribution agreement that promised to help increase overall audiences. He felt proud to have encouraged the formation of the women's unit, Studio D, which added great vitality to the organization over the next decade. Likewise, he had facilitated the creation of drama development while also having increased distribution of theatrical shorts, so the organization enjoyed better public exposure than it had for years. He also thought Distribution had done well by concluding agreements in 1973 with ministries of education in British Columbia, Alberta, Saskatchewan, Manitoba, and Ontario, authorizing them to reproduce Film Board films in video, the technology that was finally beginning to come of age.

On the production side, Newman was pleased that the new regional production centres promised to infuse new blood into the institution. English Production had opened in Winnipeg and Edmonton, while French Production had founded regional offices in Moncton and Winnipeg. As for Challenge for Change / Société nouvelle, he was glad to see it an ongoing concern because what it lacked in film technique it made up for in 'being a kind of safety valve to allow people to let off steam.' Finally, English Production had founded the Environment Studio under the direction of Roman Bittman, which showed promise for redefining institutional goals. All this gave him some satisfaction.

As for the staff's own judgment that their films were dull and undramatic, Newman's feeling was somewhat ambivalent. Television was 'now' oriented, rather than 'film' oriented, and he had not been able to do much about the fact that Film Board productions were often outdated by the time they were released. The CBC was also in the business of making documentaries, and because they were responsible by law for their editorial content, it was they who called the tune. This may have explained in part why many of the television series were flat, but it hurt when Faulkner, unable to restrain his own pique, criticized Film Board productions for being ordinary.

Newman had tried grappling with the challenge of directing films at a specific audience. The Audience Needs and Reaction Unit demonstrated that more money needed to be spent on market research. It took ten years more to institutionalize this element in the production process. Newman reduced the issue to its broadest common denominator: the Film Board suffered from an internal, unresolved conflict, whether directors should make films for specific purposes or for themselves. It was a conflict that could prove fatal. 'The fact is that what the Film Board lost was its sense of contributing to the country as a whole,' he admitted. Put another way, the films lacked legs. Newman recalled somewhat wistfully how Grierson had set the whole edifice moving with a strong sense that the artist was the instrument of the community. Subsequently, the concept had become denatured, and the artists enjoyed individual self-expression without a common goal. While it was legitimate to say that individual expression was just as useful to society as something that was an expression of community, Newman felt that the balance between the poles had been lost.

Newman explained the problem from an institutional viewpoint. When he gave policy to Film Board managers in various areas to execute, there was no proper system for supervisors to exert authority over ordinary staff members. As commissioner, he could have used an iron fist, yet he would have weakened the very hierarchy he hoped would control the staff. Another logical option would have been to fire staff, but he accepted management's estimate that, of the total of 268 in production, only about 15 were the so-called dead wood. Disposal might not only have created antagonism, it might also have been illegal. Most of those who had been laid off in 1969 had appealed and had won reinstatement. He preferred to look for points of strength and to encourage them to grow. He thought of dismantling the programme committees, then dismissed the idea because of the bad public relations the press would cause. Blame did not belong to the union either, to which he attributed 'the sheer fun and rambunctious ebullience of being provocative.' There was little else he could do but let the behemoth lumber on.

Aside from the above reasons, there was a general sense that certain persons in French Production had let the organization and Canada down, especially since the common reaction there to the anti-federalists who had brought embarrassment to the agency and to the government was at best silence, or at worst approval. These were years of bold posturing, and both the English and French creative staff found it hard to distinguish between French-Canadian nationalists and separatists. If many believed that the suppression of several films had been Newman's greatest mistake, the reaction from Ottawa had been one of quiet approval. Time would show that censorship had deleterious effects and that, in the future, 'death by neglected distribution' would be the preferred means to kill a film.

Meanwhile, Quebec in mid-decade was careening toward a provincial election, and the fear in Ottawa was that the ever-unpredictable Quebec voter might elect a government committed to independence and the end of Canada. Perhaps that was one of the factors that led the secretary of state to decide, with cabinet approval, that the next film commissioner should be French-Canadian. Newman had recommended that future commissioners should be appointed from within, since a loyal member was most certain to lobby for the notion of a Film Board. To no one's surprise, the mantle passed to Assistant Commissioner André Lamy.

André Lamy, Controlled by Events

Same old song and dance

At the midpoint of the 1970s, the Film Board's financial malaise seemed to have become like a stuck record. Inflation was consuming the budget voraciously, as two-thirds of every production dollar was going to salaries. The public remained largely ignorant of the ironic spectacle of too many idle staff collecting their wages while waiting for enough money to make films. Film Commissioner André Lamy inherited Newman's ever-worsening financial woes, stemming from the government's policy of cutting budgets wherever non-essential activity was identified. Sadly, the Film Board fell into this category. That fact demonstrated the ongoing failure of the organization to make itself a more visible and vital part of Canadian consciousness. The conundrum was to find a raison d'être that fit the government's commitment to foster private-sector growth and the feature film in particular. It was a no-win situation, as the agency tried keeping its traditional ideological distance from the commercial paradigm that drove the rest of society.

The new commissioner pleaded special circumstances in the fall of 1975 and took solace in having only a half-million, not one million dollars stripped from his budget. With the remaining monies he created a special discretionary fund of $800,000 to implement high priorities and develop new objectives. This promised him a margin of manoeuvrability, even if it meant that staff remained paid but underutilized. When he looked back at the period a decade later, Lamy considered the money problem a 'false agenda'; the only question was how to use it best. Seen from the cockpit of Montreal at the time of stress, the scenario was less rose-coloured. Neither the managers nor the creative group seemed willing or able to invent the elixir that would rejuvenate and relaunch the enterprise. Passing time was not healing the malady but aggravating it.

When Director of French Production Yves Leduc complained that budget increases over the past six or seven years had not covered increased costs, Lamy sympathized but did not reach into his fund. Instead, he congratulated him for his originality in working out collaboration with the Canadian International Development Agency to produce a series of films on health in Africa, as well as another series in collaboration with the Department of Education in Mexico.[1] Some months later, director Clémont Perron fulminated that the francophone operation at the Film Board was like a mushroom or fungus grafted to the main trunk of an anglophone-conceived tree, with neither the financial nor human resources to fulfil its part of the organization's cultural mandate. Lamy denied that theirs was a marginal existence and replied blandly that there was always room for improvement and that in fact the situation for the francophones was good.[2]

Lamy wanted to make regionalization a central priority, not only because it was a government objective, but also because it would allow him to transfer some underemployed Montreal staff to the new centres. His goal was to farm out up to half the annual production budget by 1980, and he began by giving the Halifax and Winnipeg production centres $300,000 each, and $500,000 each to Vancouver and Toronto. There was, however, a hidden agenda: to begin moving English Production out of Montreal altogether, 'so that English Canadian fish could swim in their own water,' as he later put it. He thought Quebec and Montreal provided no critical mass for English-speaking Canadians and that the English filmmakers could not make good films because the spark was not there; worse, they were part of a cultural ghetto.[3] If there was some truth to this thesis, the paradox was that he was (consciously or otherwise) denying both the historical vitality of the English community of Quebec and Ottawa's dream of a bilingual Canada, of which English Montreal stood as the centre-piece.

In their pursuit of excellence, the regional operations had to first learn to crawl. The initial productions from British Columbia, the Prairies, Halifax, and Toronto were probably most memorable for their earnestness, but they were not world-class. French Production, which opened up regional offices in Winnipeg, Moncton, and Toronto, found their early films reflected a like-minded seriousness. The important question was whether the expression of regional issues could appropriately address a national forum. Being cut off from each other, the regions had little chance to develop the sense of family and shared filmmaking that headquarters had once promoted.

Distribution was still the quagmire it had been in the past, and Lamy said that lack of

money, personnel, and ministerial priorities were to blame. Although there was some success with the new self-service library in Montreal, circulation of 16-mm film remained the weak link in the Film Board chain. A prototype computerized booking service was proving successful in Halifax, but it would take years to implement the system across the country. On the plus side, Distribution began marketing its films on three-quarter-inch video cassettes for the first time, and at long last there was hope that the light they saw at the end of the tunnel was not in their rear-view mirror. After the half-inch video-cassette format won the market battle in the eighties, and home video became as pervasive as television itself, cassette rentals and sales flourished. By 1984 they had surpassed film sales. But in 1975 the organization could not move faster than public demand, so it appeared that distribution woes were intractable.

Relations with the CBC were tenuous too. In spite of the Film Board's new and lower rate of $30,000 charged to the network per hour of television, their master contract collapsed by mutual consent in January 1976. Newman had been on the verge of renewing that contract for thirteen hours of Film Board programmes, but when the CBC insisted that these hours consist of a series of co-produced history films, the Film Board balked. It may have been that the filmmakers, like many Canadians, knew little about national history and wondered where to start in a country of few historical myths. They offered the lame explanation that they resented the pressure of having to complete television films under contract. For its part, the CBC preferred buying the best films on an ad hoc basis, negotiating each one separately.[4]

Finally, in addressing the sponsored-film imbroglio, Lamy promised to allocate more than half of these-films to the ever-eager commercial-film industry. Unwillingly caught in the old game, he tried to defuse tension by promising to allow the private firms to present film ideas directly to departments and agencies. If the proposal was accepted, the project would be submitted to tender through the Film Board. The spoiler was the department of Supply and Services, which pointed to its act to assert precedence over the Film Act. The truth was that both acts were (and are) in contradiction, since each agency has the power to acquire audiovisual materials for government departments. Few in Ottawa were (and are) interested in rectifying the inconsistency, lest rewriting both acts spoil or retard the government's own agenda. Lamy chose to ignore the legal contradictions when he defended his institution's sponsored-film prerogative before the Treasury Board in March 1976. Nor did he use the strongest argument for the Film Board's retention of them, that despite being over budget as a rule, they were of such high quality that they often won international awards, prestige, and recognition for Canada, all of which were priceless.[5] Supply and Services did not relent until it wrested away this long-held Film Board right almost a decade later.

Quebec law on cinema

If the internal song and dance were the same, there was a new wrinkle as the Quebec (Liberal) government assumed an activist posture on culture. Cultural Affairs Minister Jean-Paul L'Allier published a green paper entitled *Pour l'évolution de la politique culturelle*, which criticized Ottawa's role in culture. L'Allier proclaimed Quebec's pre-eminence in the field and intended to repatriate federal funds allocated to those activities. In June 1975 Quebec passed a cinema law to reinforce provincial jurisdiction in matters of censorship and related fees collection.

In response, Minister Faulkner suggested the Film Board review the 1954 agreement between the federal and provincial governments. That agreement (see chapter 2) had been an informal one that had left the Film Board off the hook on the fees issue, but kept

the door open for further debate, since it was a casual arrangement by the prime minister and Quebec's premier. Faulkner suggested a new strategy: claim exemption from censorship and fees for all films in the Film Board's distribution system except features. A cautious board of governors affirmed that the Film Board was operating under the Crown in the right of Canada and was not subject to provincial jurisdiction in this matter, and if Quebec pressed the issue, it would have to be resolved by the two governments. Board member and newly appointed president of the CBC A.W. Johnson stated unequivocally and feistily that the CBC would not comply with Quebec's law under any circumstances. He knew that federal law took precedence.[6] Lamy preferred to negotiate and had unofficial discussions with the Quebec government's Institut québécois du cinéma. He obtained their promise that, with the exception of features, neither CBC nor Film Board films would be subject to the law. He managed to resolve the matter without a formal exchange of letters between the two governments.[7]

An interesting twist in this case occurred later in 1976, when a dispute arose between Ottawa and Quebec over jurisdiction in licensing cable television in Rimouski. The Quebec government pressured the Film Board to supply films to the cable company favoured by themselves in return for agreeing to let the Film Board stop submitting its works for certification. Lamy told board members that he refused to become involved in this dispute, and in any case would order Distribution to discontinue referring films to Quebec for certification. The members agreed, although when the case remained unresolved by the courts, the commissioner reversed himself and submitted them for certification, ostensibly to no longer deny citizens access to Film Board productions. They went on the community channel, and the censorship issue was put on the back burner until the later 1980s, when it once again surfaced in a more virulent form as Quebec restricted English-only films (see chapter 13).[8]

Lifting Newman's ban on three French films

Lamy decided it was time to release the first of the so-called banned French documentaries, *Cap d'espoir*, which had been suppressed since the McPherson era. This was ironic, since it was Lamy who had first brought this and the other controversial items to Newman's attention. At the time, he had warned Newman not to stop them lest they become best sellers, but the pugnacious commissioner had decided on his own to show the flag. Lamy now argued that times had changed and that the stigma of suppression ran counter to the Film Board's overall reputation of freedom. Sensibly, he remained convinced that no film subject was so powerful that it could change society. It was a savvy decision, one that was uniquely *québécois*, since once *Cap d'espoir* was released, few persons ever booked it.

As for the more contentious *On est au coton*, the commissioner learned that Le Conseil québécois pour la diffusion du cinéma had decided to distribute a pirated version. He knew that he had the legal right to stop its exhibition, but the attendant publicity would do the Film Board no good. Again, using *politesse* rather than *politique*, he requested that the Conseil not distribute the original copy, while he checked the revised Film Board version, which had been purged of its most radical rhetoric. He favoured addition of a brief contextual explanation at the outset and convinced his board members that most of the imbalance in the film was not in the commentary, but in the words of the workers themselves. In short, it was legitimate for the workers to make claims, real or perceived. He waited until the fall of 1976 to release the film because of provincial labour strife. (The public-service unions had been threatening a general strike earlier that year.)[9] Statistics

proved his point about the dangers of suppression, since by 1988 *On est au coton* had just less than six hundred bookings.

Gilles Groulx's *24 heures ou plus* was the last of the films to be reconsidered. The maverick filmmaker now acceded to management's three-year-old request to make changes in the narration, and Lamy promised to put two prints into distribution.[10] The commissioner must have swallowed hard as he told the board of governors a year and a half later that the Quebec film critics voted *24 heures ou plus* the best film produced in Quebec during the last five years.[11] The critics may have been playing politics too. It would seem that even with two copies in circulation, the public was relatively indifferent to it, as evidenced by a total of just over five hundred bookings by 1988. By comparison, two other 'controversial' films did much better: *Québec: Duplessis et après* and *L'Acadie, L'Acadie?!?* had numbered 2,204 and 2,000 bookings respectively by the same date.

Ministerial policy tightens the screws

Minister Faulkner asked the Film Board to establish guidelines and programmes to help develop the feature-film industry. His goal, which became his successors' policy for the eighties, was to have the CFDC support private film companies rather than individuals, all of this without new legislation. One board member warned that this contradicted the whole concept of regionalization, since the small independents were in the hinterland, while the major companies that stood to benefit existed in the three largest cities, plus Ottawa. The greatest fear was that the Film Board was becoming marginalized in the process.

Faulkner was unmoved and delivered a combination body blow to the organization. To further develop the film-industry infrastructure, he proposed to transfer responsibility for the sponsor programme to the Department of Supply and Services, give the

Film Board 30 per cent of sponsored work, with the balance going to the private sector, and assign to private industry half of any future increase in the Film Board's production budget through the CFDC. An alarmed and defensive board of governors wondered why the minister did not address the main issue that confronted the Canadian film industry, foreign domination. They said that diverting funds from the public to private sector was no answer – they wanted a new national film policy.[12]

Luckily for them, deus ex machina arrived in the form of a cabinet shuffle in September 1976. Faulkner's memorandum was left to languish for the moment by his successor, John Roberts, who was not prepared to go so far in imposing a global film policy. In Roberts's opinion, the Capital Cost Allowance scheme of 1975 had largely resolved the private sector's funding problems, and he was willing to consider Lamy's recommendations as to how the Film Board could interact with the private sector. After a friendly visit to Montreal headquarters with his staff in November, he turned down his officials' suggestion that Supply and Services manage the sponsored-film programme, and instead asked Lamy to find a solution to what the private sector was calling the Film Board's 'conflict of interest.'[13] Lamy was willing to split the $4 million sponsor programme in half, if his institution might keep up to one-third of the contracts that exceeded the $4 million total. The minister preferred to establish a competition scheme for all the contracts.

Roberts believed the Film Board was not changing with the times and was sceptical because 'the real question was, in Departmental terms, whether we were getting the value for the money [$41.9 million in 1977–8] being spent in an era when feature length films were the main concern.' Most everyone associated the Film Board with documentaries, and the current belief was that the formative educative influence on people's concept of themselves was the feature film.

Using that criterion, he wondered whether or not the Film Board and its funding were relevant to that purpose. His non-cryptic conclusion was glum: for all its attributes and past glories, the institution simply did not have an important and constructive role to play in the commercial sector.[14] Neither he nor his minions questioned the dubious premise, since children's formative influences were at home and school at an age when sitting through a feature was out of the question. The short film, not the feature, probably has the greatest impact on the young mind.

Most of the English filmmakers swore fealty to the documentary. They may have been on the side of the angels, but the money was coming from elsewhere than heaven. Reflecting his colleagues' commitment to the documentary and opposition to features, veteran Colin Low objected to Roberts's position. He agreed that the fundamental role of the agency was to set technical, aesthetic, and ethical standards, so that documentary remained illumination, not deception. In a world of vested interests, he continued, there were those who wanted to deceive the public by artfully misleading them in advertising, seducing them in entertainment, and depriving them of truth by filtering news or public-affairs reportage. The Film Board's role was to resist these deformations and to pursue accurate and vigorous reportage and documentation, all in the public interest.[15] Low's opinions were heartfelt, but also turned no heads in Ottawa.

The minister forgot his priorities momentarily when Quebec delivered one of the greatest shocks in modern Canadian history as voters chose the Parti Québécois in the provincial election of 15 November 1976. René Lévesque became premier and was at last in a position to tell Canada just what it was that Quebec wanted. It was more than 'More', it was independence. On 16 November there was a raucous day-long celebration in the Film Board cafeteria. Most English staff took their lunch outside the building that day and pondered gravely the significance of it all. Ottawa was not the only place where there was perceived a clear and present danger to the future survival of Canada.

Roberts's department began preparing a series of cultural programmes to enhance national unity. Some newspapers claimed the National Unity Programme was forced on the Film Board, but both Roberts and Lamy denied it. Before long, the agency initiated *Canada Vignettes*, a series of made-for-television shorts, produced by Robert Verrall, who had just stepped down as director of English Production. The purpose of *Vignettes* was 'propaganda' in the broadest meaning of the word, namely education. More like brief commercials than shorts, the one hundred-plus *Vignettes* could vary from the CBC's most often broadcast *Faces*, an animated face drawn by Paul Bochner that went through three dozen variegated metamorphoses, to *The Performer*, a 3-minute live-action item by Norma Bailey about singer Roger Doucette, the man who sang *O Canada* at the Montreal Forum hockey games. The latter was so good that it won the Cannes Short Jury Prize in 1980. Ronald Blumer directed *The Veteran*, a former Spitfire pilot recounting to his art class his glory days during the Second World War, accompanied by stock-shot footage of aerial combat. For the $2.32 million that the entire programme cost, the return on investment was culturally incalculable, and it helped launch the careers of many talented filmmakers. The best and most predominant *Vignettes* were the animation pieces, including the riotously funny *Instant French* ('ten ways to say "I can't speak French" in French'), the charmingly humorous *Lady Frances Simpson* (the story of the first piano shipped to western Canada), and the unbelievably wacky *Spence's Republic* (about the momentary birth and death of the Republic of Manitoba in 1867). There was also the brutally frank exposé of the inequitable fur trade in *Trading Post*, a history of native exploita-

tion, while *The Horse* portrayed in graceful motion the history of that noble creature of the prairies. Animation technique against a black background captured the allure of the winners and losers in *Klondike Gold*, while the *Log Driver's Waltz* featured musical whimsy and the wild excitement of the log drive. By the time the series ended, there were seventy-seven items packaged in half-hour reels in 16-mm format, including French versions. Unfortunately, there were no screen credits for the artists. A diffident CBC broadcast the most tame and least controversial of the series, which the Film Board billed as 'convenient, captivating Canadiana.' Predictably, French Production produced only a scant few. Single-item *Vignettes* continued to be produced through 1986.

In defending the series against charges of doing either too much or too little to promote national unity, Verrall maintained that national identity was more important than national unity and that *Vignettes*' educational function was to let Canadians know about their roots. He pointed to two important aspects: (1) private industry was not likely to have undertaken them on its own because the films were not moneymakers, and (2) the participating filmmakers felt that they were using their talents primarily in the national interest. *Vignettes* also provided a great fillip to regional production.[16] Shorts like these revolving around Canadian history themes may become prototypes for expanded production in the coming years.

Speaking on national radio, Minister Roberts found the series fit neatly into his larger perception of what artists should do. It was not a matter of saving Canada, he said, but of artists reflecting and exploring their individual contexts. He approved of the Film Board filmmakers' freedom from the need for headlines and their concentration on interpreting or acting as catalysts rather than reporters. What made the organization unique and of world renown, he concluded, was the fact that the artist had time to become immersed in his on her subject and produce a more thorough in-depth presentation than was possible in daily television journalism.[17] It would seem from such public pronouncements that the minister was the organization's best friend. That may have been so, but there was no special treatment when it came to the budget.

In the doldrums searching for the Film Board mandate

When Arthur Hammond had become director of the English Programme Committee in 1975, he tried to solicit from the creative staff of 138 their ideas for film subjects. He learned that sixty-eight wanted to do a documentary, and only five opted for dramatic films. He also discovered that there was poor communication between members of the entire group as well as a need for in-house writers. The only bright light was the small multimedia group, which seemed isolated from the rest of English Production and had the happy distinction of being a net revenue-earner with its filmstrips and other non-film material.

Taken as a whole, the Programme Committee felt both a general dissatisfaction at the state of the English programme and a sense of helplessness about improving it. Hammond remarked that those who looked back at a time when Grierson alone approved or rejected every proposal 'usually back off when asked to name the autocrat they would have confidence in today.' The committee itself was in limbo, and its members criticized it for having no freelance members, not enough women, no working-class representation, no aged, and too many middle-class and middle-aged components. In exasperation, Hammond added acerbically that the lack of children on the committee demonstrated just where the search for representative members and experts led!

The committee knew it was out of touch with important elements in society and in the life of the country. Perhaps downtown Montreal would be a better location to work,

suggested some. A few wanted to know why the Halifax, Toronto, Winnipeg, and Vancouver regional offices were still without a mandate, while consuming some 20 per cent of English Production funds. Worse, the few films emerging from the regions seemed to lack reference to the rest of the nation and world. All the Film Board's films lacked cinematic qualities, the harshest critics stated. The absence of talent and energy explained why, responded others, and there was general agreement that one-fourth of the films were 'abysmal.' Some blamed it all on the priorities that came form B budgeting, because in the past the best films grew out of personal preoccupations and the talents of individuals. Most agreed, however, that films should respond to identifiable public needs and that the primary audience was the community or educational audience, not television. The committee summed up its dilemma simply, 'We are drifting. Is it a problem of procedures, or should we be here at all?'[18] The fact that such a conclusion was committed to paper underscores the depth of the filmmakers' despair and dispirit.

English Production needed a shot of adrenalin. Taking the long view optimistically, Hammond supported the idea of letting the creative people generate the programme, but he acknowledged that there was not much one could do with tenured people whose creative energy had been exhausted. He said bravely that it would be good to go through a year without talk of 'dead wood' other than as a substance that can be very effectively used to light fires, if a spark is applied to it. He charged that the union and management were weak, and that neither had an idea how to accomplish creative renewal. Both groups waited for the ravages of time, disease, and old age to take their toll. Some thought that the ship of production was in irons.[18]

The wild card in this discussion of English Production's mandate was Roman Kroitor, whose Studio B was trying to break new ground. He thought the organization's broad role was to assist in the evolution of Canadian society, not according to what had been done in the past, but according to what should be done in the future. This meant either to continue supplying a relatively small amount of 'special interest' material that no one else could or would produce, or to pursue fiction and drama. The latter was about human emotions, and since it was wrong to dissect a real human being for public consumption, drama allowed for statements about the relation between the public and private aspects of life, in short, about the values and beliefs of its individuals. Kroitor thought that contemporary Canadian dramas were mostly imitative and sterile; he recommended that dramatic films should be made on subjects that were important (reflecting social responsibility), yet made with artistic freedom and integrity.

He believed that Ottawa's regionalization policy was a means to unify the country, and he swam against the currents around him which opposed it, urging instead collaboration with regional agencies and institutions. He dreamed of training a generation of drama specialists who might realize the potentials of 10-minute and half-hour films. His assumption was that if films for different markets were made, only then could Canadians develop enough skills to make first-class drama. That would propel the Film Board into a leadership role again, for, as he concluded, 'promoting the growth of a vital, successful fiction-film capability in Canada is as important for the future as what the Film Board achieved in the documentary in the past.' The feature film, he underscored, should be reserved only for appropriate subjects.

He might have been thinking of director Robin Spry's intriguing blend of fiction and environmental concern in *One Man* ($615,283), the fast-paced story of corporate negligence and a crusading reporter's obsession to get the story out. In the scenario, the idealist newsman's struggle against the powers who create industrial pollution threatens to destroy him, his marriage, and family. As the film unfolds, the viewer realizes that the cause is noble, but too great for any one man to win. Beneath the plot is the inevitable conclusion that the need to face environmental questions is more a matter of social priority than of entertainment. Paying audiences may not have expected a feature film with such a sobering message. Despite excellent production values, *One Man* did not do well commercially in 1977. Perhaps it needed better publicity, a more fortuitous opening date, or a later release, when its message would become the public wisdom of the eighties.

From a philosophical approach complementary to Kroitor's, Colin Low resumed English Production's stock-taking debate with a typically perceptive analysis of where the filmmakers had gone. He recalled the gentle school of documentary that had evolved after the violence of the war years: the psychological films, the ordinary-people films, the family films, the educational 'how to do it' films, as well as the poetic and philosophical films. But the arrival of television brought with it an educational and cultural imperialism that threatened to overwhelm the gentler and more natural pursuits of people. Urban and industrial society turned filmmakers into specialized, unionized, and centralized individuals, preoccupied with theatrics and the dramatic film. They were no longer generalists, rather they had become persons who were struggling between regionalization and centralization, between improvisation and organization.

Low argued that television's delivery schedule made it difficult to craft the more subtle and positive social values into films. He believed that the 'auteur' had become an élite person whose product was neither analytical nor futurist. His strongest words echoed Grierson's fundamental philosophy that the filmmakers should appreciate the privilege they held. Their debt was twofold: to reflect the joy of service and to sacrifice personal self-interest to community advan-

In *One Man* (1977) a crusading reporter (Len Cariou atop the car hood) has an obsession to make the truth known about industrial pollution.

tage. Low suggested the pursuit of the triple themes of energy, environment, and social change in order to give the organization direction.[20] Once again, his words were like shouts in the wilderness of the narcissistic seventies, precisely articulated and perfectly true, but swallowed by the vacuum of space.

Tom Daly recalled these sentiments as clear, practical, thoughtful, and meaningful. By contrast, no such thinking had emanated from the commissioners and their managers, or from the ministers and their minions in the previous two and a half decades. He lay the blame for the drift on the consistent lack of leadership and vision, both at the top of the organization and in the ministerial ranks. The managerial style, he stated, consisted of words, which do not match the real need – creativity. It was sad, he lamented, that the last serious attempt to define the Film Board's mandate had come from the Massey

Commission. Since then, the government had been seeking management to fit an evolving bureaucratic managerial style, when they should have been seeking persons who understood film and could have accommodated themselves and the institution to the work that needed to be done.[21] The Film Board hungered for a leader they could respect. Putting it prosaically, Daly said the Film Board was like a comet that needed two foci – a head and a tail. Without both, it would not draw eyes toward the sky. Continuing Daly's analogy of heaven and earth, one senses his wish for the halcyon days of 'ad-hocracy', where flying by the seat of one's pants was the norm. If the contemporary era was one that demanded technocratic thinking, compartmentalization, a five-year plan, and an adversarial system of labour relations, he seemed to be saying that the efficiencies were offset by the strangulation of spontaneity. Daly had touched upon one set of truths, although he was also mourning the inevitable aging process that affects institutions as well as humans.

The new director of English Production, Ian McLaren, was in no mood for all this stock-taking. He favoured action to stem the drift and decided it was time for heads to roll. He intended to confront the creative staff and show that the managers, not the filmmakers, were going to manage. If dossiers were necessary to cut back on staff, he would compile them. He fired two people with cause and intended to dismiss five more who had been flagrant abusers of the freedom of the institution. He thought that making an example of them would galvanize discipline. Then without authorization he went public in the *Montreal Star*, on 17 January 1976, recommending that the whole staff be put on contract. He acquired an instant reputation for toughness and recklessness.

Lamy and Deputy Commissioner Domville neither chastised his youthful impertinence nor acted on his recommendations, since delay was easier. Meanwhile, the cantankerous McLaren tried to introduce a classification system and remove the staff's choice of studio affiliation, his predecessor's practice of allowing likes and dislikes to determine with whom a filmmaker would work. He redistributed the filmmakers equally to each studio and divided the total production budget almost equally. He insisted on monthly status reports for each person to account for his or her time. The biggest winner was the women's Studio D, which received substantial money as well as a handful of male filmmakers, some more reluctant than others to join. The director of English Production received no popularity award in 1976.

The fur started to fly when McLaren said the market should dictate the films to be made. What angered some was that market forces seemed to be the reason that the Film Board was still without a master contract with the CBC, which continued selecting only the specific films it wanted. Lamy explained the difficulty: the CBC's ideal was to have thirty-nine one-hour didactic films in a series rather than the Film Board's typical production of three one-hour films on a subject. The difference was that the CBC was interested neither in fine cinematic craftsmanship nor in the films' intended catalogue life of five to seven years.[22]

Yet a film like *Henry Ford's America*, a Film Board–CBC co-production in 1977, directed by the indefatigable Donald Brittain, showed that the non-series item, when good enough, deserved prime-time exposure. Some might think that the automobile, as the single icon of modern North American life, is a rather pedestrian theme. Brittain found it an open-ended opportunity and, in using the Ford dynasty as his vehicle, moulded the images around a commentary that was able to shock, entertain, and inform the viewer, all in one hour. No better account exists of how society changed to accommodate the driver and his machine. *Henry Ford's America* won nine awards, including an Emmy, American television's most coveted honour, and remained in active distribution in the late 1980s.

Some noteworthy English production in 1976–7

Perhaps part of the spiritual malaise in Montreal was due to the fact that the English-language films were not getting sufficient national exposure, nor were there enough of them. There were, however, a number of world-class films in 1976–7.

The Griersonian dictum that portraiture was what the Film Board did best never rang truer than in Donald Brittain's most ambitious ($250,000) project yet, *Volcano: An Inquiry into the Life and Death of Malcolm Lowry*, a 1976 film based on Robert Duncan's formidable research. With co-director John Kramer, Brittain re-created the atmospherics that both drove and consumed the remarkable and tragic author of *Under the*

The documentary *Volcano: An Inquiry into the Life and Death of Malcolm Lowry* (1976) portrays the multiple and opposing forces that drove and consumed this tragic author (seen here outside his shack in British Columbia).

Volcano. Richard Burton's incomparable reading of select passages helped Brittain, as narrator, lead the viewer into nether world of Lowry's tragic Consul to become, like the Consul, 'a great explorer who has discovered some extraordinary land from which he can never return to give his knowledge to the world.' He deftly and almost invisibly wove into his portrait the role of Canada in Lowry's creativity. A shack on a British Columbian inlet served as the place where Lowry could re-create in prose the 'dreadful memories of life' lived elsewhere. Thus, unspoken but present, was Canada, the anchor Lowry needed to create the art that one critic said belonged to the centuries. Wisely, the film left the viewer to grapple with the Lowry puzzle: how to explain the disparity between the calibre of his work and the wretchedness of his life. *Volcano* inspired Martin Knelman to write one of his finest reviews, in which he claimed that reading the faces in the film conveyed more about Lowry's personality than the most exhaustive book ever could.[23]

Tony Ianzelo and Andy Thomson had printmaker David Blackwood guide the viewer through the fascinating process of creating an etching in *Blackwood*, which, like *Volcano*, earned an Oscar nomination in 1976. What could have been a competent, instructive documentary on the complex process of engraving technique, narrated by Gordon Pinsent, became instead a smooth, almost mystical blending of life into art. Blackwood grounded his creation in historical events like the 1914 Newfoundland sealing disaster and in a contemporary mummers' performance upon the occasion of winter solstice. Aside from these intriguing surfaces, what remains fixed in the viewer's mind is Blackwood's unassuming modesty.

One of the most popular and celebrated films of 1976 was the animated tale by Caroline Leaf, *The Street* ($49,223), based on the short story by Mordecai Richler. While dealing with the timeless theme of aging, infirmity, and death as seen through the innocent eyes of children, the animation also exudes the warmth and sometimes self-deprecating humour of first-generation Jewish urbanites. Leaf's animation technique of continually changing washes of water-colour and ink on a glass plate created an almost cryptic rhythm of object-blending-into-object, beyond the earthbound rules of fixed observation. *The Street* won an Oscar nomination and accumulated nineteen awards.

In 1977, there were four productions that earned prestigious Oscar nominations. One was *High Grass Circus* ($62,008), a documentary feature in direct cinema by Torben Schioler and Tony Ianzelo, which tells behind-the-scenes story of a peripatetic Canadian tent circus. It is filled with bizarreness. One moment includes the brief on-screen apprenticeship of a new 'El Flamo the flame swallower' after the principal fled, followed by the barker's exaggerated phony introduction to the credulous gawkers, 'His father and mother were fire-eaters; he learned his art in the Orient.' In another scene, a female trapeze artist's leg becomes stuck, and she dangles upside down on the high wire like a sack of potatoes. The film's charm is reminiscent of Fellini's *La Strada*, where rootlessness is also a dominant theme. *High Grass Circus* is one of the most overlooked productions of the period. It is a genuine reflection of how a camera's unsparing observation can tell a truer story than artifice could ever conjure.

Another nominee, *Bead Game*, by Ishu Patel, uses thousands of beads to create scores of animated objects that change constantly into colourful and wondrous creations, devouring each other with no seeming purpose. Perhaps a five-minute version of Darwinism, *Bead Game*'s open-endedness makes it universally fascinating and appealing.

Dutch-born animator Co Hoedeman, motivated by his children building a sand castle at the beach, conceived the Oscar winner *The Sand Castle / Le Château de sable* ($82,783), a fable with a more specific storyline. Using the medium of sand and sand-covered foam-rubber puppets, he brought to life a cavorting Sandman, who becomes the visionary and creator of other functional sand creatures. To the sound of happy music and guffaws, they construct a grandiose castle under his inspiration and, like all civilizations, watch time and wind erode, then destroy, their enterprise. It is easy for both the child and adult viewer to assign meaning to this 13-minute fable, where nothing remains but spirit and memory. *The Sand Castle* won a total of twenty-two awards worldwide, the greatest number in Film Board history.

The documentary short that plucked the

Animator Co Hoedeman's Oscar-winning fable *The Sand Castle / Le Château de sable* (1977) has won 22 awards worldwide, the most in Film Board history.

heartstrings of millions and also won Hollywood's highest honour was Beverly Shaffer's *I'll Find a Way*. This was the 25-minute story of a nine-year-old girl's indomitable will to live her life as normally as possible with the crippling congenital disease spina bifida. Narrated by Nadia herself, the child's insistence on making her way in the world as an equal, despite the burden of crutches and attendant obstacles, inspires wonder more than sympathy at the triumph of will-power. In order to help groups to explore the range of emotions and thoughts that her story provokes, the film has a kit of support material.[24] Like Sandra Wilson's *He's Not the Walking Kind*, a Vancouver regional production in 1972, which tells the story of her spastic brother's life in a wheelchair and his courage to be independent, both films let the subjects speak for them-

selves and for social integration. Canada was already beginning to show an awareness of the disabled, and the documentaries went a long way toward sensitizing the public to the need for sidewalks, ramps, and lavatories to accommodate them.

In 1978, the Oscar winner for best animated short was *Special Delivery* ($35,065), a wacky, off-the-wall piece by Eunice Macaulay and John Weldon. The zany story of Ralph and Alice was modelled on typical soap-opera fare. It begins with Ralph's failure to shovel snow from his walk and ends with an accidentally dead mailman, an unfaithful wife who abandons home and town, and Ralph resigned (like many Canadians) to accept whatever fate has in store, since Life is much bigger than all mortal forces. In short, existence is better accepted than fought. If this 7-minute paper animation is a parable about the meek, weak, and torpid, Canadians loved it for combining the cultural icons they adored, especially that of cultivated innocence. Its tongue-in-cheek existential drift aside, few would have imagined that the Public Service Alliance might find pragmatic use for it in a seminar for shop stewards on how to collect evidence.

Verrall defended other high-calibre English works during this period, thinking some were as good as the Oscar winners. One, in 1977, was Derek May's *Pictures from the 1930's* ($85,536), a sponsored film based on a 1975 cross-Canada exhibition of paintings from the Depression years, with a moving counterpoint of newsreel footage depicting the social realities of that sombre period. Like his 1974 study, *Sananaguagat: Inuit Masterworks* ($96,063), which reveals the unique blending of art and nature in Inuit anthropology, the film manages to portray one of the least understood aspects of creativity – how art relates to a specific historical time and place.

In *Mother of Many Children* ($149,354), native filmmaker Alanis Obomsawin produced an album, in 1977, about native women and their matriarchal society. The

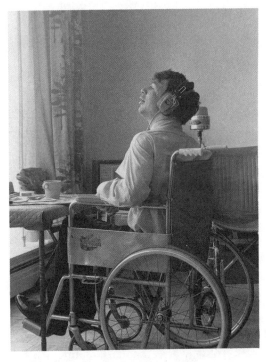

He's Not the Walking Kind (1972) reveals a growing awareness of the disabled and underscores the need to make their social integration a national priority.

The zany *Special Delivery* (1978), an Oscar winner, is a tongue-in-cheek soap opera about the meek, weak, and torpid.

film asserts that they have been under tremendous pressure to change, yet must do so within a contemporary struggle against discrimination inside and outside native society. Obomsawin does not refrain from dealing with the perennial native curse of alcohol, but puts it in a context which shows that many are not going to settle for anything less than helping themselves and each other to overcome their adversity. Because an aboriginal person has brought to bear her unique powers of cultural observation, this film is meant to help unite diverse native peoples in common purpose and hope.

Director Paul Cowan had garnered experience by filming sports for American commercial television before coming to the Film Board, where his first solo directing effort in 1976 was *Coaches* ($175,242), a glimpse of four leaders preparing their teams for pre-Olympic events. Cowan discovered that the coaches are the catalysts, teaching a mental game and the endurance to keep the athletes going. In the days before the widespread illegal use of steroids, emotion was the veritable fire of competition; in this and in the spin-off film of 1977, *I'll Go Again*, he inverted the cliché about the 'agony of defeat' to show how sport was not as much about winning as about the battle with oneself while competing. The wholesome Canadian attitude contrasts nicely with the usual American compulsion that winning is everything.

In cutting his teeth on sports films, Cowan was itching for a try at something more relevant, involving controversial social issues. He had to wait until the 1980s for a sally into the maelstrom.

When Verrall's tenure as director of English Production ended in 1977, he looked back on the prolific output for which he had been responsible and came up with a list of films he remembered best. They include a few of the films from 1973 that are mentioned above. The rest, in chronological order, are:

He's Not the Walking Kind, director Sandra Wilson, 1972

The Question of Television Violence, director Graeme Ferguson, 1972

Action, director Robin Spry, 1973

Coming Home, director Bill Reid, 1973

Grierson, director Roger Blais, 1973

The Man Who Can't Stop, director Michael Rubbo, 1973

Pinscreen, director Norman McLaren, 1973

Reaction, director Robin Spry, 1973

Ruth and Harriet: Two Women of the Peace, director Barbara Greene, 1973

Station 10, director Michael Scott, 1973

After Mr. Sam, director Arthur Hammond, 1974

Cree Hunters of Mistassini, directors Boyce Richardson and Tony Ianzelo, 1974

Mr. Symbol Man, director Bruce Moir, 1974

The New Boys, director John N. Smith, 1974

In Praise of Hands, director Donald Winkler, 1974

In Search of the Bowhead Whale, director Bill Mason, 1974

Waiting for Fidel, director Michael Rubbo, 1974

Who Are We? director Zlatko Grgic, 1974

Why Rock the Boat? director John Howe, 1974

The Working Mothers Series, director Kathleen Shannon, 1974

Bill Loosely's Heat Pump, director Kenneth McCready, 1975

Boo-Hoo, director Grant Munro, 1975

Los Canadienses, director Albert Kish, 1975

Tax: The Outcome of Income, director Veronika Soul, 1975

Temiscaming, Québec, director Martin Duckworth, 1975

The Hecklers, director Ian McLaren, 1975

TV Sale, director Ernie Schmidt, 1975

Whistling Smith, directors Michael Scott and Marrin Canell, 1975

Augusta, director Anne Wheeler, 1976

For Gentlemen Only, director Michael Scott, 1976

The Great Clean-up, director James Carney, 1976

Log House, directors Michael Rubbo and Andreas Poulsson, 1976

Moses Coady, director Kent Martin, 1976

A Sense of Humus, director Christopher Chapman, 1976

The Sword of the Lord, director Giles Walker, 1976

Amisk, director Alanis Obomsawin, 1977

Happiness Is Loving Your Teacher, director John N. Smith, 1977

Healing, director Pierre Lasry, 1977

Henry Ford's America, director Donald Brittain, 1977

No Act of God, director Ian Ball and Sidney Goldsmith, 1977

One Man, director Robin Spry, 1977

Rose's House, director Clay Borris, 1977

Some American Feminists, directors Luce Guilbeault, Nicole Brossard, Margaret Wescott, 1977

Spinnolio, director John Weldon, 1977

You're Eating for Two, director Malca Gillson, 1977

These films stand as a testament to the excellent work that English filmmakers were capable of producing.[25] But Lamy thought that a well-articulated raison d'être must precede production, and in 1977, he had Ian McLaren solicit a position paper from his

One superb example of portraiture was *Margaret Laurence, First Lady of Manawaka* (1978), which uses fact and fiction both to reveal the personality of a great Canadian writer and to create an unforgettable impression of small-town Canadian prairie life.

staff on what they thought the role of the institution should be for the next five years. From Studio C, Arthur Hammond favoured individual preferences and reminded him that some of the worst films (like the language dramas) were produced in response to very clear priorities and guidelines. He quoted the film theorist and historian Siegfried Kracauer, who said that documentary was the redemption of physical reality. Documentarians should record what is typical and significant in our society, Hammond insisted, as if for an audience a century or two later. In short, they should be ethnographers of our own society, of the central human comedy of Canada in our time. Hammond never lacked energy or optimism, and his common-sense approach to making films for the future should have fired up some enthusiasm.

Producers Robert Verrall and Guy Glover echoed similar thoughts when they remarked that many of the most distinguished and widely used films over the past three decades were single items, not from priority programmes. They observed that the successful series programmes had tended to be small ones. Thus, the present system of production and programming encouraged a miscellany of subjects, styles, and techniques, which was one of the strengths of the institution. They warned that there was a tendency to overindulge in self-flagellation, though it was true that too many films were unnecessarily expensive, in terms both of time and money. They wanted the doors kept open to permit the coming and going of filmmakers, teachers, philosophers, poets, and clowns.[26]

Derek Lamb, head of the ever-popular and highly acclaimed Animation studio, could feel positively about his animators' regular nominations for Academy Awards. If animation was the costliest form of film expression, it was also the least dated, in part because its 'language' was international. Lamb was depressed, however, at how the Film Board was scorned by the private sector and parliamentarians. He hoped for a new role, one that would be defined in terms of 'delivering the goods,' that is, making excellent and vital films. What was needed, he said, was someone at the top to inspire the place – someone like the old quarrelsome Scot, John Grierson. The public wanted information about a host of vital subjects and making such films would win back public respect and an audience. It was also important to find a way to bring on young talent.

Lamb had succeeded in the last category when he invited the animation artist Janet Perlman to make *Lady Fishbourne's Complete Guide to Better Table Manners* ($45,084) in 1976. This was an exuberant tale of four unusual table guests whose faux pas help the viewer see him/herself as others might. The film purposely does not deliver

Lady Fishbourne's Complete Guide to Better Table Manners (1976) promises an 'informal little lecture on basic table manners that we know will result in a more fulfilling life.'

on its premise of an 'informal little lecture on basic table manners that we know will result in a more fulfilling life.' It mocks such etiquette as 'what to do when something is on the plate which you don't like' by having a parrot jump up from a plate and march boldly around the table, creating general pandemonium. The film is meant to serve as a classroom provocateur to a discussion of etiquette and social mores in general. In 1979, Lamb's studio scored again with *This Is Your Museum Speaking* ($93,340), an animated sponsored film, directed by Lynn Smith, which looks at how relevant museums are to a community's sense of past and culture. An engaging meander through Western civilization as revealed by paintings and sculptures that come to life, the lesson is that museums work best by having the observer apply imagination to what is already known. Unblinded by his studio's consistent success, Lamb understood English Production's fundamental malaise, the need to find vital subjects.

Both highly motivated and directed toward community audiences, Studio D vied to become the most energetic and provocative of the English-language studios. Kathleen Shannon said that her group's cardinal rule for filmmaking was, 'Who needs it?' They first targeted their audience, which mostly consisted of groups of powerless: women, the aged, youth, and non-whites. No Studio D resources were going to serve the interest of white middle-class males, she vowed, since they were already well served by other filmmakers. The women's programme intended to cover a wide range: women's roles in history, positive female role models, undistorted feminist thinking, non-sexually stereotyped images of children and women, and examinations of broader societal issues as perceived by women.

The engine that drove her programme was neither personality nor orthodoxy, rather, a widely felt sense of 'alternative,' that is, a perspective that might be female or minority-oriented or both, and was most certainly non-mainstream. Among its first memorable efforts was *Maud Lewis: A World Without Shadows*, a film by Diane Beaudry, about the little, frail Nova Scotia artist who lived in a 3-by-3-metre house. Her paintings were strong and happy because they reflected her inner soul. Also, Beverly Shaffer's Oscar-winning *I'll Find a Way* was part of the studio's *Canadian Children* series. In 1977, Studio D produced *The Lady from Grey County*, a historical document about Agnes Macphail, the first female member of Parliament, directed by Janice H. Brown, and *Some American Feminists*, a series of interviews with six leaders of the movement, directed by Luce Guilbeault, Nicole Brossard, and Margaret Wescott.

Under fire for *No Act of God*

But 'alternative' was not the special purview of the women. In September 1977 the Film Board released a 27-minute anti-nuclear-power film, *No Act of God* ($104,000), directed by Ian Ball and Sidney Goldsmith, which takes a determined stance against the proliferation of more than 8,000 nuclear reactors worldwide. These might not be enough to satisfy growing energy needs, the narration states, and probably the documen-

tary's most radical suggestion is that humanity could live as well by using less power. After presenting the opinions of various experts who opposed the technology, the film warns that the danger of environmental catastrophe from a nuclear-power-station accident is so great that 'no act of God is permitted.' That this was no hysterical polemic was brought home when the USSR's nuclear plant at Chernobyl exploded in 1986. Meanwhile, the Canadian Nuclear Association claimed the film was inaccurate, patently biased, inflammatory, and reprehensible in approach, and maintained that it reflected the views of a small coterie of dedicated anti-nuclear zealots. In April 1978 they demanded that besides the documentary in question, all footage from three Atomic Energy of Canada sponsored films, *On the Critical Path, On Power Refuelling*, and *This Nuclear Age*, be withdrawn. They also complained to Minister Roberts, who heard similar sentiments from the Electrical and Atomic Manufacturers' Association, Ontario's Minister of Energy, and the chairman of Ontario Hydro.

Lamy responded coolly that *No Act of God* was biased in its examination of fast-breeder reactors, but that it was part of the Film Board's mandate to interpret different facets of the Canadian reality. He did not pursue the industry's suggested option of withdrawing it until a second Film Board production addressed the subject from a less impassioned perspective. When he wrote to Roberts in November 1978, he noted that the Film Board had done two other works that advanced eloquently the case for nuclear energy and the CANDU reactor. A third film, *Atomic Juggernaut*, a fascinating record of the complex delivery of a nuclear reactor's heart to India, had itself been criticized by anti-nuclear voices. Lamy concluded that he thought 'the Film Board would not be truly doing its job if we failed to present to the people of Canada different points of view on vital issues that affect our lives'.[27] Roberts was well aware of the long tradition of ministerial unwillingness to interfere with specific films. He honoured that commitment, but in the face of the nuclear industry's lobby, this might have been one of those times when he wondered whether the Film Board was a rudderless ship.

It seemed unfathomable that, by comparison, the nuclear industry remained virtually silent in 1978, when French Production released *La Fiction nucléaire.* This 86-minute political documentary was a potent left-wing attack on Quebec's plan to expand nuclear power, despite its superabundance of hydroelectric energy. Directed by Jean Chabot, the documentary not only asks pertinent questions about the reasons for the planned expansion and the principle of unlimited growth, but also probes the entire issue of Quebec as the object of covetous foreign investors. It was particularly interesting that the polemic leaves aside the independence question and addresses a critical long-range issue of Canadian national interest: Chabot believed that Quebec was the crucible of the conflict between democracy and technocracy. Despite the fact that it was

a more potent film than *No Act of God, La Fiction nucléaire* had no English version, thus did not cause a ripple nationally. Lamy probably thought it was enough to defend *No Act of God,* so he let the film go unversioned.[28]

The commissioner remained firm in his belief that his agency had to create cinematographic masterpieces that would lead politicians to believe that the Film Board *was* essential. In his opinion, the organization even needed to become arrogant about its good work and to ignore the adverse issues like lost sponsorship and monetary stringency. Lamy reduced the tangle of circumstance to a bare minimum: the public as well as the political masters in Ottawa would back and protect the Film Board if the staff produced good films like those of Donald Brittain and Norman McLaren.

Specifically, he was thinking of Brittain's two-hour CBC–Film Board co-production *The Champions* ($175,433). Using historical and stock-shot footage, as well as interviews with political personages close to both men,

La Fiction nucléaire (1978), a potent attack on Quebec's plan to expand nuclear power, depicts Quebec as the crucible of the conflict between democracy and technocracy.

it illustrated the rivalry of Pierre Trudeau and René Lévesque as a metaphor for the ongoing contemporary struggle for and against Canadian unity. The metaphor is so strong that under less competent hands, the story could have appeared burlesque or absurd. Brittain's wit works best in his succinct phrasing which, in combination with his deftness with visual nuance, leaves an impression virtually welded to an observer's consciousness.

Brittain's greatest skill was reducing the complex into simple components without creating a simplistic model. As part of the big picture, his Lévesque was less the man who would destroy Canada than the politician whose moderation and belief in democracy actually helped Canada surmount the very

challenge he had hurled. Brittain was one of the few savants of the era who could deal with politics without either betraying his own predilections or slipping into the comfortable cynicism of the age. Despite this objectivity, he was profoundly aware of contemporary politics as another form of television entertainment, and he concluded the films prophetically: 'From here, the story will be played out on the newscasts.' The ex-newsman followed his story and told it as *The Final Battle*, in 1986 ($350,659).

Lamy's other paragon of Film Board virtue was Norman McLaren, whose lifetime output of masterpieces earned Canada prestige and glory that reverberated around the world. McLaren resisted coasting on his reputation for genius and continued pushing

The political rivalry of Pierre Trudeau and René Lévesque serves as a metaphor for the ongoing struggle over Canadian unity in the three-part series *The Champions* (1978/1986).

into new fields of experimentation. In 1973 he had made the documentary *Pinscreen* ($15,269), which had demonstrated Alexandre Alexeieff's pinboard technique of film animation. From 1976–8, McLaren made *Animated Motion* ($89,977), a series of five films for students just embarking on a study of animation techniques. In them, McLaren comments upon, demonstrates, and classifies aspects of motion that the animator uses in his daily work. He then turned to the most complex and expensive production of his career, *Narcissus* ($702,607), a balletic interpretation of the Greek myth of the youth whose excessive self-love created a void of mental imprisonment. The live-action animation is a compendium of McLaren techniques gleaned from a lifetime of creativity. The project drained him, and his health, long precarious, began to wane permanently. The *Narcissus* legend symbolized the decade, although when it was finished at last in 1983, McLaren was first to admit it was structurally weak, dragged in the second half, and then dribbled off.[29] He retired in 1984 and spent his last years engrossed in listening to music with his perennial companion Guy Glover.[30] When he died in 1986, the whole of his cinematic art occupied just over three hours of screen time. McLaren's was an *oeuvre* which enriched so many lives that its full impact is still incalculable.

French Production

In 1977, Lamy also tried defending French Production as he explained the qualitative difference between the CBC and the Film Board. He referred to several recent French-language films, of Guy L. Coté on religion, *Les Deux Côtés de la médaille* ($159,655), and of George Dufaux on aging and death, *Au bout de mon âge*, as examples of the vitality of French Production.[31] The first was a two-part, 165-minute film from 1974 that suffered from lengthiness and occasional underexposed footage, but was a capable union of anthropology and sociology. The docu-

mentary shows the effects of two decades of work by three French-Canadian missionary priests in remote Bolivian villages. Peasant practices of superstition and sacrifice continue while the missionaries persist in conducting politically flammable literacy campaigns and in teaching modern animal-husbandry methods. The film allows one to stand as the peasants do, in two epochs, the modern and the primitive.

Released in 1975, Dufaux's *Au bout de mon âge* ($146,345) is a *cinéma direct* account of a reluctant and crotchety old French Canadian's last months of life, from home to hospital to hospice, comforted only by his ever-attentive wife. It was a strange choice toward which Lamy drew public attention, since the film seemed to be an unintended analogy of French Production's view of itself. Like the dying man who broke his glasses in an on-camera outburst near the end, the money-starved filmmakers too had been crying out their fear and frustration that their inevitable end was loss of freedom and creative extinction.

This being said, it was undeniable that French Production's continuing strength was the feature film. In 1976, *J.A. Martin, photographe* ($488,014) was a stellar example of a low-budget turn-of-the-century piece. Jean Beaudin directed this unhurried tale of an ambling itinerant photographer who records the lyricism of rural Quebec with a counterpoint of the combined material realities of anguish and exploitation that characterized the period. They serve as a backdrop to the main story of the photographer engaged in recording all this with a wife who, after fifteen years, has become a part of his baggage. By the end, she triggers a mutual rediscovery of their relationship and love. Monique Mercure's remarkable role won her the best-actress award at the 1977 Cannes Festival. *J.A. Martin, photographe* has been recognized as among the best films ever produced by the Film Board.

French Animation was not flagging either. In 1976, Jacques Drouin finished *Le Pay-*

J.A. Martin, photographe (1976) became one of the most renowned French-language features
of the decade.

sagiste / *Mindscape* ($38,740), one of the most effective uses of Alexeieff's pinscreen technique ever seen. (Alexeieff had donated his device to the Film Board.) Described as an invitation to come upon the place from which we started, the film has an artist entering his landscape painting, only to find symbols and signs that awaken his subconscious. The evocations are universal, and the film's wordless treatment of psychology-by-image goes substantially beyond popular culture's interest in the same subject.

Two years later, *L'Affaire Bronswik* ($106,618) emerged as one of the funniest films of the decade, a combination of live action and animation, and a send-up of documentary's talking-head technique. Directed by Robert Awad and André Leduc, its subject is the sinister power of consumerism and advertising as the controlling agents in mod-

ern life. The scenario finds typical citizens describing the overwhelming compulsion to buy that seizes them after they watch television advertising. On the serious side, the story is trying to say that the public is being victimized, since television seems to control contemporary life and habits. The film shows the viewers as victims of a sinister plot; yet there are serious thinkers who, while avoiding that notion, contend that rampant consumerism will lead our civilization to bury itself in worthless and unneeded junk. *L'Affaire Bronswik* is most potent because it unfolds as if it were a serious documentary, with tongue barely visible in cheek until late in the film. It accumulated ten international awards, and the English version became immensely popular.

Finally, there was *Jeux de la XXIe Olympiade*, the official film of the Olympic Games

L'Affaire Bronswik (1978) is both a send-up of documentary's talking-head technique and a commentary on how consumerism and advertising control modern life. Typical citizens like this poor soul describe the overwhelming compulsion to buy. (He has bought tires, but has no car.)

held in Montreal in July 1976. The cooperative project, underwritten by the Film Board and the Olympic organizing committee, had nearly triggered a full-scale revolt by members of French Production who objected to seeing the lion's share of their production funds diverted for it. By tradition, the eight previous host countries had produced the film record of the sumptuous competition, so the Film Board had little choice in the matter. Once again, many of the French filmmakers had felt that by having this project imposed from above, their individual creative freedoms were being jeopardized. A number of articles in the French press sympathized with them, but the show

had to go on. The documentary proved to be a worldwide winner, as sixty-three countries bought distribution rights in 1977. Directed by Jean-Claude Labrecque, Jean Beaudin, and Marcel Carrière. *Jeux de la XXI Olympiade* cost $1.37 million, of which the Film Board paid $470,000. The film broke with precedent and did not cover key events superficially, but chose to dwell at length on a few athletes before, during, and after their moment of Olympic trial, in order to convey what competition means. The crew of 168 shot some 100 km of film, which was edited to 117 minutes of rich and varying textures. Taken as a whole, the images of individual personalities reflect the human resoluteness that was the essence of the Olympic spirit before drug abuse turned the event into a cattle auction.

Filmmakers' inopportune court victory: Everyone into the lifeboat

The heart of Lamy's administrative problem was the lack of sufficient money for production after salaries had been paid. On the French side, there had been a 'revolving door' policy since the austerity of the late sixties: as a genuine freelancer, the Quebec filmmaker typically might work for the Film Board under contract, leave to make a film in the burgeoning Quebec private sector, and then possibly return to do another project under contract. As director of French Production from October 1976 to April 1979, the lawyer François Macerola made sure his employees could not claim permanent status.

Functioning as they did in an English cultural ghetto, the English Production personnel could not operate like their French counterparts, as there was no significant private sector for them in Montreal. It will be recalled that the original Film Board labour crisis had been sparked by the overhiring for Expo 67 and the failure to attract enough sponsored films to keep that group employed. The situation had more or less stagnated since the unhappy McPherson years. Government intentions aside, the outcome of the turbulent labour crisis of that period had found only 15, not 132, laid off because labour law protected the unionized employees well. Filmmakers continued to come and go of course, but almost 100 remained employed on a per-contract basis. Some found themselves on contracts that were renewed each year, others were hired for shorter periods or for fixed tasks; some even filled secretarial positions in order to balance the books, although they were making films. Directors of Production Devlin, and then Verrall, were unconcerned about these employees' legal status. They felt that the main point was to keep new blood coming into the

establishment and to renew the contracts of the very talented. Ian McLaren had wanted to clean house, but he had to act within the law and to show cause for each release.

If one looked at the English Production staff in 1975, then, the 'non-permanent' was fairly indistinguishable from the permanent core. The situation called for some sort of regularization, and it was at this point that the union engaged labour experts to present the case for the 'phoney freelancers' to the Public Service Staff Relations Board. The first decision went against the union. On appeal at the federal level, the court ruled there had been improper procedure and told the PSSRB to retry the case.

In September 1977, the PSSRB handed down its long-awaited decision. The judgment was both electrifying and dismaying because it ruled that 99 per cent of all freelance employees at the Film Board whose contracts had been renewed periodically over the years were in fact 'employees' by definition, unionizable, and deserving of full recognition by the Treasury Board in its person-year allotment for the Film Board. There was staff euphoria as more than 100 'contract' persons realized that they deserved permanent-employee status in the institution that had been paying them for years, but had been unable to acknowledge their infusion of creative lifeblood with the plum of job security.

To describe the picture graphically from the administration's viewpoint: think of too many survivors trying to climb into a single lifeboat. Disaster was sure to follow if the institution was forced to hire the freelancers regardless of Treasury Board controls, as this would court budgetary chaos. The administration asked the PSSRB to decide what guidelines should be applied. Meanwhile the freelancers clung to the sides of the lifeboat waiting for the decision on the terms of their employment. They had their answer in January 1979.

The union could not be faulted for its interest in doing what unions are supposed to do: save jobs and keep as many working as possible. But the administration was dismayed. Knowing that the person-year allotment was already 179 *fewer* than in 1967–8, Lamy needed to obtain additional person-years from the secretary of state and Treasury Board. If the increase was not possible, he might have to lay off 150 or cut back the high-priority regionalization programme.[32]

Lamy opposed massive lay-offs, fearful of plunging the whole organization into despair. He also felt that it was unfair to release some of the aging and less productive permanent staff who had served there for most of their professional lives. He believed that management could not create a centre of decision-making to take such drastic action in an institution that had been based on human relations for forty years. It was just too cold-blooded. He favoured a gradual solution and instituted the so-called golden handshake, a system of encouraging early retirement with a lump-sum payment. He thought it would take about a decade to effect the desired contractions. Meanwhile, this long slimming process created a pervasive sense of being in limbo and a feeling among the staff that the government did not want them.[33]

This financial nightmare grew worse when the prime minister decided to slash $4 billion from the federal budget. Robert Andras of the Treasury Board told Roberts to cut his global budget by one-third. The minister could not single out the Film Board for special treatment, and he told Lamy to pare 10 per cent off his budget, 2.5 per cent for 1979–80 and 7.5 per cent for 1980–1. The confluence of the labour decision and the across-the-board budget reduction convinced many on the inside that the organization was doomed.

Roberts spent the balance of his tenure applying fiscal restraint, rather than keeping closer contact with the boards of agencies for which he was responsible. His plan for constructing a whole variety of new cultural policies was shelved, and he resigned himself to being remembered for preventing things

from happening rather than for what he did. 'My constant concern was to allocate pain, yet to do it in a way that would preserve what was there for another day,' was how he put it. He saw himself engaged in a series of holding actions against a variety of assaults. This applied to the Film Board, to which he devoted little time, although it became known that he thought there was no reason to believe that a cultural institution should survive forever. Years later, he admitted he did occasionally think of abolishing it and using the money to support other federal activities, but it was not a practical alternative. Such a Draconian policy would have required different political times. Few could envisage the federal government withdrawing a major cultural body from Quebec while arguing for national unity. Perhaps this fact of life was the Film Board's last and permanent ace up its sleeve. To extend the old Stephen Leacock analogy, Quebec, like Confederation, was the cave into which footsteps led, but from which none emerged.[34]

Lamy resisted the pressure to lay off staff that was coming from Roberts's office. The commissioner let it be known that if the minister did not approve of his handling of the staffing problem, Roberts could replace the governors and commissioner, since the National Film Act gave the minister alone that power.[35] As it was, Roberts had enough on his plate. Life had become increasingly difficult for the Liberals after 1976, and it was the Parti québecois government that was setting the agenda for the eventual showdown by referendum. The secretary of state's main preoccupation was language policy, bilingualism in Canada to accommodate the French minority nationally, and, in Quebec, trying to shore up the sagging linguistic fortunes of the English community. When the Lévesque government passed Bill 101, outlawing the display of English signs publicly, the feeling was that the English had symbolically lost their language rights. Roberts's department furnished the funds to start the long route to testing the law in the Supreme

Court. As for separatists within the federal bureaucracy, the Film Board did not figure much in the equation because Roberts believed there were far more such persons in Radio-Canada to worry about. That was of far greater concern to him nationally than the one-tenth-the-size National Film Board.

External Affairs: The uncertain relationship

Through an informal arrangement, the Department of External Affairs had exercised responsibility for non-commercial film distribution abroad since the late 1940s. The Film Board produced and the department selected those films it thought appropriate for what was called 'prestige' screenings, either at its posts or for free screenings in host countries. External Affairs held a collection of more than 40,000 prints, for which it neither paid nor collected monies, but these outlets were worth more than money in terms of justifying the perpetuation of the film organization. Since the earliest days, post exhibitions had been considered public-relations exercises that gave Canada (and the Film Board) the kind of international image that money could not buy.

The film libraries in the posts had represented a traditional responsive, rather than an active promotional, use of film, as was best illustrated by the example of Canada's Swiss embassy film library, which was run by the legation's chauffeur. Elsewhere, the Film Board staff was accommodated in key missions in New York, London, Tokyo, and New Delhi, but by the late sixties the trend was to have the organization assume its own financial services and space requirements.

The relationship had continued until 1969, when the financial crisis caused by austerity led the Film Board to turn over the distribution of films to schools in the United States to commercial distributors like McGraw-Hill and Encyclopaedia Britannica, who could reach a large market and generate income for themselves and the hard-pressed

Film Board founder John Grierson (with newspaper), Sydney Newman (left; film commissioner 1970–5), and Newman's successor as commissioner, André Lamy (1975–9)

organization. In reacting to the changed atmosphere, External Affairs considered purchasing prints and foreign-language versions in order to begin a planned and programmed activity. Another reason for the growing physical separateness of the two was that by this time an abrasive atmosphere between them was becoming more the rule than the exception, because Film Board films tended to show Canada, 'warts and all,' while External Affairs wanted to sell Canada as a picturesque place for tourists and a sound investment for business people. Once word of a Global Film Policy from the secretary of state department began to circulate, it was clear that the Film Board's responsibility for film programmes abroad was going to decline.[36]

A product of this activity in 1969 was a Film Board–External Affairs co-production with the Department of Energy, Mines and Resources and Transport Canada of the pioneering voyage of the supertanker USS *Manhattan* through the Northwest Passage, accompanied by the Canadian icebreaker *John A. Macdonald*. Filmed from the air, from the ice, and from the vessels, *Manhattan Odyssey* captures in seven minutes the drama of testing the navigability of this waterway as a year-round commercial sea lane. The film ignored mentioning the explosive issues of accidental pollution or of u.s. refusal to recognize Canadian sovereignty over these potentially troubled waters. Given Canada's ongoing fear of souring bilateral relations, the Film Board could hardly have been expected to deviate from government policy to keep both issues far from public concern.

In another instance, External Affairs required a standard information film on Canada for all its posts. Crawley Films of Ottawa heard of the plan, submitted a planned shooting script, and bid $75,000 directly to the department in 1971. The Film Board intervened and insisted on its legal rights to undertake the film, probably because it wanted the glory as much as the work. Crawley, frozen out of a lucrative contract, believed that like other entrepreneurs it had been treated unfairly.

Here Is Canada was created by the stellar talents of two of the original Unit B team, Colin Low and Stanley Jackson. The film became the standard information film on Canada for a decade. Its $109,780 cost exceeded the External Affairs ceiling of $85,000, but the Film Board paid the difference gladly. Using descriptive colour shots of people and geography with a split-screen/voice-over technique, *Here Is Canada* came close to defining the mainstream ideal of the Canadian character: in Canada, there is room for everything and everyone. From its opening aerial shot of tundra and dogsled to its closing sequence of faces at play, sunset, ducks, horse-drawn buggy, sea, flowers, and a couple walking on a hill, the film was reminiscent of the major threads in *Labyrinth*. Tony Ianzelo's superbly photographed images of working men in isolation, cityscapes of people on the move, men and machines fused as one, creativity by art-

ists of different races and creeds, dance, sports, hockey, galloping horses before a Rocky Mountain backdrop, Quebec City Winter carnival, all knitted together by the icon of Parliament in Ottawa, leave the viewer somewhat breathless, if expecting a commercial message. Jackson's reiteration that Canada was so big, so diverse, and such a paradox emphasizes the perennial Film Board testament to cultivated innocence. External Affairs loved *Here Is Canada* and had it versioned in a multiplicity of foreign languages.

Here Is Canada improved the Film Board–External Affairs relationship temporarily. By May 1973, there was discussion of a protocol and co-financing to produce more films for 'prestige' exhibition in posts abroad. The hope was to now employ film to promote and support the department's Public Affairs Programme, and the target audiences were to be the host countries' opinion formers, decision-makers, and educators. It was expected that joint funding might produce four films that would be versioned in eight or ten languages. In 1974, three short films were produced on Canada's geography, culture, and cities.

The department had contributed $40,000 to the 10-minute animated cartoon *Who Are We?* ($118,070) in 1971. It was directed by Yugoslavian guest animator Zlatko Grgic, in Canada for only a year, and American animator Don Arioli, present for less than a decade. Both offered a tentative answer to the perplexing title: 'Who are we? Who really gives a damn? You are you and you are you – and that is what we am!' The true identity is population mixture, not homogeneity; climate and history are seen as predicaments that make for strange unifiers in a land where space scatters its people both psychologically and physically. Such qualities seemed to satisfy the Canadian insistence on an elusive, rather than particular, objective identity. *Who Are We?* became a favorite attraction of the Canadian exhibit at the Commonwealth Institute in London.

The co-financing idea looked appealing on

paper, since this promised the money-parched film agency a chance to develop proposals for the international market. But there was concern that the department was unwilling to treat the Film Board as an equal because their precise objectives and international goals often left the organization with little creative freedom to explore. To make matters worse, External Affairs had never really accepted that part of the Film Act which stipulated that the Film Board was to make films 'to interpret Canada to Canadians and to other nations.' In the department's opinion, its own omniview was far greater than the film agency's narrow 'beat' of Canada alone, thus they felt there was very little common ground.

Film Board management believed that over the past three decades a not very good client-service relationship had developed. Their differences were deeper than philosophical. First, the Film Board saw itself telling the truth, providing information about Canada at home and abroad that reflected accurately given situations, pleasing or not. But it seemed that External Affairs, in its desire to harmonize, if not homogenize, wanted propaganda free from all controversy. Second, the filmmakers demanded absolute freedom to develop their concepts, while External Affairs was insisting on the sponsor's right to editorial input.

Then too there was French Production's intransigence. They would not cooperate and had refused to respond to External Affairs' suggestions for the following subjects: Canada as seen by its artists, bread, Dr Selye on stress, the National Arts Centre, and hockey. Producer Robert Forget explained part of the dilemma: he thought the film on the National Arts Centre should be about art and not a documentary, while the department had insisted that the film be a documentary and contain an international as well as national message. 'Artistic, yes ... but artistry is not their raison d'être,' was how the department put it. In order to get the work made, English Production took it over.

In July 1974 External Affairs requested the following films be versioned: *Roughnecks* (1960), *Epilogue* (1971), some of the *History Makers* series (1960s), *Bethune* (1964), *The Voyageurs* (1964), *The Owl and the Lemming* (1971), *For You Mr. Bell* (1971), *The Builders* (1966), *The Discovery of Insulin* (1961), *If Not* (1970), and *Four Teachers* (1961).[37] With the exception of *Bethune*, which the department had kept from international distribution during the worrisome sixties, none of the films could be considered either critical or political in their orientation. These were films about Canadian 'heroes,' sung and unsung, or with special appeal to children. The turnabout on *Bethune* was a direct effect of the establishment of diplomatic relations with the People's Republic of China in 1970.

Nearly a year later, there was agreement to version the films *Plea for the Wanderer, Here Is Canada, The Long View, Oceans of Silence, A Research Brief, Sub-Igloo, The Sea,* and *Rye on the Rocks.* However, the department complained that proposed film suggestions were poor even by amateur standards and were largely unrelated to External Affairs' objectives. Worse, the 'unconscionable delays' in production and versioning of films had proved that the 'friendly informal approach' to the Film Board had met with little success. Both sides wondered whether their protocol should continue and blamed the tension on mutual misunderstanding.[38]

External Affairs evaluated the joint programme after twenty months and in September 1975 concluded that the Film Board had completed six of its own proposals and none of the eight departmental ideas, all at a cost three times as high as commercially produced films. The department repeated a litany of complaints: *Commonwealth Court* and *Deep Threat* (both on issues raised by the Law of the Sea) were poorly made; the director of information of Agriculture Canada thought *Agriculture Canada* was 'shameful'; and the *Corporation* series was a 'startling compendium of technical errors' and among the poorest films the department had ever screened.[39]

Putting it colloquially, there existed a major problem in communication between the Film Board and External Affairs. To fix things in the short run, the co-production protocol was modified to allow each party to commit its budget according to its own priorities; co-productions were to become ad hoc affairs. In 1975, the department helped to finance *Le monde s'en vient à Québec*, a travel piece about the *Francofête* at Quebec City. The same year, the department contributed to two films on the Canadian national ski teams and insisted on cutting two offending sequences from Giles Walker's *No Way They Want to Slow Down*: a team pillow fight aboard a plane and the Chilean army ski-training. Both were stricken from the international version but kept in the one that Canadians saw at home. The department refused to contribute to French Production's proposed film on three Olympic athletes from Japan, Cuba, and East Germany because it did not support any of the defined foreign-policy objectives of the countries in question.

On the cultural level, however, External Affairs was happy to order 150 copies of the 1975 film *Musicanada*, directed by Malca Gillson and Tony Ianzelo, for special distribution by all posts. It was a one-hour non-narrated conglomeration of performances by an array of musical stars from across Canada. It was a painfully slow, overly long, and repetitive piece that seems to devote as much time to children in various musical situations as to well-known professionals. By May 1976 External Affairs officers were asking for a film that portrayed performing or the visual arts. The project was undertaken three years later by Paul Cowan, who insisted on doubling its length to an hour (the Film Board paid for the second half-hour). When *Stages* was finished in 1980, the International Cultural Relations Bureau regarded it as unsatisfactory because it believed that the French-speaking performing artists were portrayed poorly.

Given the near hostile climate between the department and the Film Board, it was a wonder that anything worthwhile could be reported on films for non-commercial international distribution. In fact, the Film Board had cooperated successfully in a number of Third World projects with the department and with the Canadian International Development Agency (CIDA): family planning in India, battery-operated projectors for rural areas, cinevans for Niger, health films for Ghana, and teaching students to make and distribute agricultural training films in Tunisia. The Film Board provided ex gratia films for television in Cameroon, the Ivory Coast, Senegal, Ethiopia, and Zaïre, and similar fare for Algeria, Morocco, and Tunisia, at minimum charges.[40]

Another impressive effort was the Film Board's organization and coordination of the 250 audiovisual presentations by the Third World participants at the United Nations Habitat Conference in Vancouver in 1976. Post-production facilities and Film Board expert teams were set up in Nairobi, Kenya, and Buenos Aires, Argentina, to help inexperienced nations on the respective continents to finish their productions. The end result was a stunning array of film documentaries and audiovisual exhibits on housing around the world. The entire collection was deposited at the University of British Columbia for future researchers, who will find a wide sampling of the world of housing for the year 1976.

When Sydney Newman and a Film Board group visited China in October 1975 as guests of the China Film Corporation, they left behind some thirty-five films for preview, hopeful that the Chinese would open their theatres to foreign works other than those from North Korea, Romania, and Albania. The Canadian embassy staff had long enjoyed Film Board titles and had often shown them at receptions or to delegations about to visit Canada. In fact, the only documentary on Canada that was well known to the Chinese was the Chinese-made 8.75-mm film recording their national ping-pong team's visit to Canada in 1972. It showed the main Canadian cities and Gravenhurst, Ontario, the home of China's best-known Canadian, Dr Norman Bethune.

When the Chinese made their film interests known in January 1976, both the Film Board and External Affairs were surprised to hear specific requests for four items on nuclear power plants, two on space technology, and one on radar. 'The Chinese interest in technical films suggests an interest rather narrower than we might have hoped,' understated the communiqué from Canada's embassy. The diplomats were worried that if the documentaries were given to them, the Chinese could copy them illegally and not purchase them. Ottawa was unconcerned about pirating, since the films were available to the Chinese through other routes. The Film Board objective was exposure of the Canadian reality, including technology.[41] No one said it, but there must have been some disappointment that neither art subjects, social documentaries, animation, educational topics, nor any of the hundreds of worldwide award-winning films seemed to have any appeal to the pragmatic Chinese.[42] The long-known fact was that in Asia (and Africa), a significant commercial market for the Film Board did not exist. The worldwide language priority for post libraries was English, Spanish, and French.

There were, however, active programmes from diplomatic-post libraries. Table 2 reflects the ten most active posts in 1978-9.

By 1981 there were 1,300 titles available from post libraries in the United States. External Affairs thought the quantity to be unwieldy and wanted it pared down. That same year, the average size of film libraries internationally was down to 540 prints, and the department sought to reduce the average collection to 300, 'directly related to information objectives.'

The Film Board estimated that through the post programme a total of 27.5 million people saw its films in 1978-9. The department put the figure more realistically at one-third that number, maintaining that average audiences were fifty or less. Still, this manner of distribution to schools and organizations allowed posts to make wider contact with foreign publics than through films loaned to television stations. The posts reached 2.5 per thousand in the United States, six per thousand in Europe, seven per thousand in Latin America, one per thousand in Asia, and two per thousand in Africa and the Middle East.[44]

There was one other nearly forgotten area of distribution, the Travel Programme, which the Film Board had been carrying out for decades on behalf of the Government Office of Tourism, primarily in the United States. The travel films had been reaching an audience ten or more times larger than that of posts, and were an unsung mainstay of promoting tourism to Canada. Post activity in the United States played third fiddle to

TABLE 2 External Affairs reports from diplomatic posts: Most active film libraries, 1978-9[43]

	Inventory	Bookings	Per print	Main audience
Sri Lanka	679	15,968	23.5	post staff
Mexico	1,393	14,524	10.4	cultural groups
Rome	826	9,037	10.9	high schools
Hong Kong	684	7,714	11.3	high schools
London	1,007	6,274	6.2	high schools
Cape Town	845	6,506	7.8	high schools
Teheran	411	6,067	14.8	post staff
Detroit	961	5,112	5.3	high schools
Wellington, NZ	921	4,850	5.3	primary schools
Paris	1,276	4,709	3.7	high schools

tourism and the Film Board's own commercial activity through private distributors, but External Affairs' overall priority there was to promote the study of Canada in the schools.

By the late 1970s, the posts were complaining of a lack of new Film Board titles. This was partly due to financial restraints and to the External Affairs decision to concentrate on films that had direct information on Canada. Their objectives were to project an image of Canada's flexible federal system, a strong and resilient economy with an advanced competitive technology, a cultural life reflecting linguistic duality and diversity, and an internationally active nation.

Most of the films at posts and in the Film Board catalogue contained specialized, educational, and training material not particularly related to the Canadian situation, yet it was that very fact which created local goodwill, especially in the Third World, where an animation like *Teeth Are to Keep* had kept circulating since 1949. The department wondered if it should continue providing a free educational film service in foreign countries serving a demand for productions on women's rights, sex education, health care, sports training, industrial safety, and science education. Such wide-ranging topics as understanding glaciers, fitting artificial limbs, how to play volleyball, and puberty in boys all enhanced Canada's image, though it should be noted that a film like *The Use of Tear Gas in Riot Control*, a favourite with police forces in India, appealed to an exclusive, rather than a broad, segment of the population.

In 1977 External Affairs requested four specific items: one to replace the aging *Here Is Canada*, one on Canadian-American relations, another to explain the Canadian political system in light of the Quebec crisis, and one on Canadian-Japanese relations. The last was dropped when nothing suitable was proposed; the other three went into production. Four years later the posts received their products. Bruce Mackay and Gary Toole directed the wordless and visually poetic *Northern Composition*, which melded image and music to conjure an attractive impression of Canada at work and at play. (One sequence showing advanced satellite and microtechnology was followed by a hilarious shot of a wizened inventor demonstrating his better mousetrap, one that used a conveyor belt of raisins to lure the hapless creatures to death by drowning.) Other memorable sequences included a slow-motion comparison of the flight of wild geese to that of a jumbo airliner; a 1924 John Colin Forbes painting, *The Scarf*, which stunningly came to life; and the backstage pre-concert tension of a performer, whose subsequent look of relief and satisfaction followed a job well done. However interesting *Northern Composition* was, tradition-bound External Affairs complained that the absence of hard information about Canada left posts still relying on *Here Is Canada*.

The film for the United States had a troubled history. Derek Lamb's *What the Hell's Going On Up There?* demonstrates the difficulty of mixing satire and serious interviews. Animation sequences show a diffident Uncle Sam, with his harried domesticated eagle, trying to find out what the noisiness from Canada is all about. Comedian Marshall Efron takes on his 'Assignment Canada' with gusto, in order to learn many facets of the truth. From the Mounties, the story is that 'If Canada was not there, the Chinese could sail directly to Denmark. Think of it ... blue cheese with chopsticks.' Later, the truth appears to be that an ideal Canadian would be 'a bilingual Indian who is Jewish.' Bilingualism means that English-speaking federal civil servants were learning how to say in perfect French, 'Sorry, we have misplaced your file.' More seriously, *indépendantiste* Pierre Bourgault states the separatist threat chillingly while Canadian nationalists like Margaret Atwood, Mordecai Richler, Frank Scott, Marshall McLuhan, and Walter Stewart demonstrate their national pride unabashedly.

But the embassy and consulates in the United States had little desire to draw attention to the subject of Canadian economic nationalism, and thought it imprudent, in light of the Iran-hostage crisis, to express any anti-American tone. They asked that the film be withdrawn. Officials at External Affairs headquarters in Ottawa refused, but did persuade a reluctant Film Board to withdraw the 'offensive' sequences. In the event, posts expressed little enthusiasm for the film and the department had little to show for its $280,000 investment. *What the Hell's Going On up There* is one of the best (if neglected) contemporary impressions of Canada, whose humour is closer to Canadian hearts than the austere attempts to link childhood and innocence with the Canadian actuality.

It took two production teams to realize a half-hour film on the Canadian political system. *The Canadian Federation* ($95,454) contained a succinct overview of the politics, government, and people of Canada, with a sense of how the nation was coming to grips with changing priorities. External Affairs took the credit for reworking the script and design of the 1980 film, and was ungenerous about the Film Board's ability to take advice.

By 1981 External Affairs had engaged a commercial firm to make a half-hour general-information piece on Canada to replace *Here Is Canada*. The department's conclusion was that it had to play a close role in preparing the script and in insisting on the editorial right to make changes. In doing so, it feared that the films might fall victim to a 'propagandistic tone.'[45] Most distressing was that the National Film Board was no longer the source of production for the prestige items that projected Canada's image abroad. More than production monies had been lost: one of the legs of the Film Board's constitution had been pulled from under it. From here on, more and more people asked, 'Why have a Film Board anyway?' The eighties promised to be an inauspicious decade.

The hard questions in Lamy's last beleaguered months

As he contemplated the numbing bureaucratic malaise of 1978, the film commissioner had the unenviable task of planning the next two years, knowing that the parliamentary vote was to be decreased by at least 10 per cent. Lamy had been unable to deliver on his promise to give more sponsored films to the private sector, because like his predecessors he needed them to contribute to the Film Board's overhead. Roberts now insisted that half of them be subcontracted to private industry. Soon the Film Board was clawing tooth and nail with the private sector to win contracts. Lamy tendered out $2.3 million or 70 per cent of the sponsored work to private companies, but no one was happy. This change effectively deprived the commissioner of the primary function he and his board had held since John Grierson had founded the organization. The government film commissioner seemed to be left with a hollow title, eclipsed by the private sector and the CFDC. More than ever, events were controlling the person who wore the commissioner's hat.

To face the monetary squeeze, the board of governors discussed the possibility of closing all foreign offices and using the money to strengthen international operations at headquarters. If it boiled down to a choice of distribution or production, the governors favoured distribution. Lamy favoured production, although he concurred that the distribution branch used an outdated and antiquated system that would improve once the new technologies of computer-assisted distribution and satellite transmission were given a chance to work.[46]

The governors were divided about whether they should extend the 'user-pay' principle to national distribution. They were aware of the public furore that idea had caused when it had been tried a decade earlier, and they believed that bookings would drop by some 40 per cent. Other proposals extended to closing Research and Development or the dubious alternative of diverting the capital-equipment budget to operations. In short, there was so little manoeuvrability that the members were forced to agree at last to let management devise a coherent lay-off plan, to be applied in the worst-case scenario. Austerity looked as bleak as it had in 1969–70.

The Film Board was going to lose the several million dollars it had received for the National Unity Programme, and it expected a serious shortfall in income as other departments curtailed their information programmes in response to across-the-board budget cuts. Revenues from the CBC could be expected to drop accordingly. There would probably be a hue and cry raised from the private sector if the Film Board kept for itself the service contracts that might otherwise have gone to them; the overall film economy could be expected to reflect this negative impact.

Some hard questions were being addressed internally. On the French side, the filmmakers continued to assert their right to make their own productions and still said they did not care who saw them. They were happy that the Film Board did not fit into an identifiable slot or mould. Lamy felt they were guilty of resting on the laurels of the 1960s, when just being part of the Film Board qualified one to be part of the intellectual establishment. Quebec society had forgotten where its film industry had taken root and no longer associated its successful filmmakers with the Film Board.[47]

Resting on laurels might have also applied to English Production. Its few successes notwithstanding, the old questions were never far from being regurgitated. Was the cost of the films justified? Were budgets unrealistic? The statistics were not comforting, as they demonstrated percentages of works that went over budget and the average amounts over-budget of each: documentaries, 48 per cent ($12,000); drama, 33 per cent ($40,000); animation, 58 per cent ($29,000); features, 100 per cent ($250,000); all regional films, 66 per cent ($13,000); sponsored and co-sponsored films, 41 per cent ($26,000). Shooting ratios were roughly 20 to 1, except for animation, which was only 1.7 to 1. It took about a year and a half to produce a typical documentary, drama, animation, or regional production, and two years for a feature. Sponsored work took just over a year. The amounts were not excessive, it might be argued, though taken as a whole, they made balancing the books a magician's challenge. Besides, it was well known that no one had ever been fired for going over budget. As for the question of productivity, on average the headquarters staff was not doing anything 8.7 per cent of the time, while in the regions the figure was 6.6 per cent. But with cutbacks imminent, full productivity was impossible. These depressing statistics signified that at least management now had a basis to establish performance indicators, if indeed that was the problem.[48] Lamy also made noises about ending feature-film production altogether.

There was little else to do but hang on and hope for an economic miracle. An anxious board of governors considered another option that went back to Newman's early days as commissioner: to ask the government to rewrite the National Film Act and make the agency a crown corporation. If such a change were to occur, the old argument went, the Film Board would be entitled to carry over its surplus or deficit to the next fiscal year, to charge various departments for services now done gratis, and, most important of all, to be freed from the person-year controls exercised by the Treasury Board. It looked enticing, though there was one serious hitch – if Parliament opened the Film Act of 1950, the debate might be used to change the institution's mandate or even to sink it forever. The question of crown-corporation status remained unresolved through the eighties.[49]

Perhaps the pressure of five years as assistant commissioner and three years as commissioner had been enough for Lamy. There was not much new for him to learn in his job, other than that the budget cut for the 1979–80 year would not be $3.2 million, but $4.134 million. Roberts called together the heads of his agencies to ask what they could do to ensure the flow of money to cover inflation and to create a climate of public opinion in order to let the government know that Canadians thought these institutions were essential to Canada. It was at this point that the filmmakers' union undertook to organize a nationwide letter-writing campaign.

The board of governors ordered preparations for reduction of the workforce. About sixty-five people would have to go, most of them in production. A more stunning announcement followed when Lamy informed the board of governors, in September, that the government had approved of his intention to resign. The previous June he had seized an offer from CBC president A.W. Johnson to join the ranks of senior management and gain enough experience to eventually become the CBC's French-Canadian general manager under the English president. The minister delayed approval until September, hence the timing was such that many believed Lamy was jumping the Film Board ship because of the across-the-board cutbacks. Actually, he was jumping from one sinking ship on to another: the CBC was being asked to trim $150 million from its budget.[50] Given the depressing circumstances, Lamy's farewell to the Film Board was as upbeat as he could manage. He said he believed that the institution still constituted a major and essential cultural force in Canada and was the cornerstone of the Canadian film industry.[51] The real question was whether anyone else outside the four walls of his office believed this too.

12

The Atmosphere Changes
from Seige to Neglect

Under siege: Preparing for the
worst-case scenario

Faced with double-digit inflation, the Liberal government had dug in its heels and planned once again to apply across-the-board cuts in 'non-essential' sectors like culture, which included the beleaguered Film Board. The board of governors had almost four months to find Lamy's successor. They thought that the ideal candidate should be a high-profile outsider who could articulate a new mission and convince Canadians that the institution was indispensable. At the same time, Ottawa's demand for retrenchment made it imperative that someone who knew how to work the financial levers should assume leadership and slim down the operation as painlessly as possible. After seven years as deputy film commissioner, James de B. Domville was that someone. Rumour had it that he was a yachting friend of Prime Minister Trudeau, which, given the times, some thought could not hurt. They forgot that, in politics, everyone and no one is the politician's friend. Domville took the helm in January 1979 and braced himself for a formidable challenge – to lift the financial siege from outside and mental siege from inside. In April he made François Macerola, the director of French Production, his deputy commissioner. Producer Jean-Marc Garand then stepped in to head French Production for the

next five years, while Ian McLaren stayed on as director of English Production for one more year.

The four-month hiatus in finding a new film commissioner had aggravated the air of uncertainty. Another crisis committee wrote to Roberts to complain about the new Program to Assist Films and Filmmakers in the Private Sector (PAFFPS). The minister ignored them. He was more concerned about stories that during the previous year only half the human-resource capacity was being used in some areas and that idle filmmakers showed up at headquarters once every two weeks to collect their pay cheques. He wanted this absurdity to cease. Roberts's wishes, however, were no one else's commands because just as Domville took over, the Public Service Staff Relations Board arrived at its decision regarding the one hundred freelancers it had declared permanent employees two years before. They stated that people who were hired to direct specific projects were independent contractors and not employees; other categories of people engaged under contract were employees according to common law and were deemed to occupy positions in the public service. When asked for his opinion, Lamy, now free of Film Board responsibilities, suggested airily that Domville fire all the freelancers one day, and rehire those he wanted as independent contractors the next. That was easy for an ex-commissioner to say, but Domville considered a more humane option. He accepted the judgment, hoping the Treasury Board would guarantee the additional person-years and find the money to pay them.[1]

Since virtually all the affected freelancers were English-speaking, there was no small amount of jealousy in French Production. There, Macerola had kept a tight rein on hiring freelancers, not only because of the economics, but also because of a concern that a new permanent core in French Production might put into effect the erstwhile plans for 'an authentic Film Board.' If such a core of French-speaking directors had become entrenched, he feared they might have mirrored the independent attitudes of the Parti Québécois government and thereby have created havoc.[2]

Now with wider responsibilities, the exasperated Macerola called the January decision 'the blackest day in the history of the Film Board.' Of those freelancers who had clung to the lifeboat from the water since the second PSSRB decision in 1977, over one hundred clambered aboard in 1979. Tensions eased somewhat when the Treasury Board allowed the Film Board to engage temporary staff without them being person-year accountable. The problem then became one of how to pay them and have enough money left for film production.[3] Macerola was bitter, maintaining that for every talented person brought in, it was necessary to keep what he thought were three or four far less gifted ones. He wished Domville had had the strength to bite the bullet and let them all go.[4]

But Domville's hands were shackled. Without a single memorandum being written, he learned that the minister was now opposed on political grounds to having the Film Board cut staff. The government shuddered to think of the political damage it would suffer if headlines announced that one hundred English filmmakers would be joining the exodus of tens of thousands of Quebeckers, packing their bags for Ontario because the federal government had given up

James de B. Domville (film commissioner, 1979–84) hoped to steer the NFB toward new challenges, but he too was constrained by fiscal austerity and the private sector's growing antipathy to the Film Board's prerogatives.

on them. From the minister's bureaucrats there came a similar oral message: wholesale lay-offs were unacceptable and, in light of the successfully fought labour grievances of the seventies, probably illegal. Thus, austerity left Domville with the disagreeable task of having to close down specific functions. He could reduce neither rent nor overhead, hence his discretion to compress was greatly limited. Ten per cent austerity became equivalent to a 30 per cent cut, since once again employees were sitting around being paid, but had nothing to do. In this fashion Ottawa realized that its austerity programme was creating waste and inefficiency in almost every one of its departments. It was cold comfort to learn that this irrational outcome had not been the government's intention.[5]

Attempts to control the bureaucratic Leviathan had led to government by other means.

And so Domville found himself the reluctant captain of a ship suffering from top-heaviness and inefficiency, all because of a relatively marginal budget cut. To avoid this embarrassment again, he argued for crown-corporation status. His board members feared that opening the Film Act might sink the organization, but he was willing to take that risk. There could be no worse situation than coming to a point where there was enough money to pay salaries, but not enough to make films. This unfortunate circumstance was precisely where John Grierson had found the Canadian Government Motion Picture Bureau in the late 1930s, when he had argued for a National Film Board to be created. The irony was that, in 1979, history might be poised to repeat itself, except that no one had an idea what, if anything, would replace the Film Board. For the moment, however, the government refused to consider immortalizing the institution with corporate status.

The infernal budgetary problem yet again

A number of commercial film-industry people carped about the $5 million that had been added to the Film Board's 1978–9 budget, bringing it to $45.84 million. Theirs was an unfair swipe, since they knew that Ottawa's new bookkeeping practices now showed rent and related overheads in annual appropriations, no longer buried in the Department of Public Works budget. Production had consumed $14.68 million for the English and $7.72 million for the French studios. Distribution spent $10.35 million, and Administration took $5 million. It was easy to claim that the Film Board was a spendthrift, but a few years later, veteran producer Guy Coté used a 1981 dollar constant to show that the parliamentary appropriations in 1969 and 1979 were $33 and $40 million respectively.[6]

Finances continued to consume the daily agenda. In September the commissioner wrote to ask Roberts for an additional $3.5 million, precisely the amount in contracts that Roberts wanted him to tender out for sponsored films.[7] English Production was suffering most, but, taken as a whole, the crisis stemmed from the budget cut of 1978, the current government spending freeze, the regularization of the phoney freelancers, the loss of departmental money with the end of Challenge for Change / Société nouvelle and the loss of sponsored-film revenue. Fearing that he could not maintain the required critical mass of creative staff at headquarters, Domville argued that the Film Board faced a major lay-off in creative personnel, a reduction of all production programmes, and a threat to its very mandate. Roberts was sympathetic, but like his predecessors found himself at the mercy of the Treasury Board, which slashed the million dollars he offered to $350,000 while suggesting that Domville transfer salary costs to the operations budget. From his vantage point, Macerola thought that Roberts (and the government) did not know what to do with the organization.[8]

Spring 1979 brought about a federal election and a change that the Liberals had not planned: they were turned out of office. For the first time in nearly two decades, Canadians elected a Conservative regime, and Joe Clark became prime minister in June. He decided to shift ministerial responsibility for the Film Board from the secretary of state department, where it had lain since 1963, to the Department of Communications, under Minister David S.H. MacDonald. The new minister was a self-described 'devotee of old NFB films' and was known for having started a film society in his hometown of Charlottetown, Prince Edward Island. He may have been a sympathetic voice, yet he too joined the chorus which urged that 80 per cent of the sponsored work be made by private enterprise. He recommended that the Film Board make only those films that the private sector could not undertake.[9] MacDonald calmed some tensions and even let a ray of hope shine when he told Macerola at a first meeting that the Film Board had a function in the service of the country; it was his firm belief that Canada should have a mixture of public and private film producers. He began to organize an advisory committee under Toronto composer Louis Applebaum to study how this mixture might be best achieved. This was the beginning of Ottawa's latest investigation into the arts, later called the Federal Cultural Policy Review Committee, which published the Applebaum-Hébert report.

Before long, however, rumours about the business-oriented Conservatives began to circulate. One of the most fantastic was that they were considering an offer from Encyclopaedia Britannica to buy the National Film Board – lock, stock, and barrel – for $100 million.[10] The pall of doom over Montreal headquarters hung heavier than ever, as the bureaucratic wheels of the budget cut continued to grind. The best the personnel department could do about the surplus employee issue was to plan to reduce staff by 70, 53 of whom would go by attrition, with the balance being laid off. And the final indignity was Ottawa's demand for reimbursement of the $307,000 paid to the staff for bilingual bonus payments. Domville took it from the 1978–9 budget.

Films for what audiences? Television: Still the promised land

At a board of governors meeting, CBC President A.W. Johnson asked Domville for a paper identifying different audiences the Film Board sought to reach. That was how they did things at the CBC, where it was essential to create a demand for the subjects. His was also a subtle way of asking whether the offbeat, controversial, or leading-edge films were ever going to be seen. The CBC policy of 'balance' made it next to impossible to telecast such films nationally, since the pervading fear was that, if it took an adversarial role,

the CBC might find itself embroiled in lawsuits. Besides, the network's single channel was a popular medium that could never meet the cultural demands of minority audiences. If he was uncomfortable with the Film Board's advocacy notion, Johnson also saw himself as trying to bridge the ideological gulf between the two organizations. For its part, the Film Board refused to curtail its filmmakers' traditional freedoms.

Johnson too was not as free as many thought. The exasperated president told his underlings to resolve the two agencies' long-standing bickering over their annual contract. English CBC's programmers were planning to concentrate on drama; if they ran more documentaries in prime time, they would vacate whole fields of popular cultural expression to the Americans. However true that might be, their perception of Film Board films as not sufficiently attractive to compete with other available material for prime time viewing could be understood in two ways. Either the films were not good enough, or they did not reach the lowest common denominator, the eleven-year-old mind. That was the American, hence Canadian, ideal for attaining the best ratings. If the second explanation was truer than the first, the Film Board dilemma was hopeless.

The CBC was pleased to run *The Image Makers* (1980), a compilation of outstanding sequences from three generations of NFB filmmakers who produced over 4,000 films.

The upshot of it all was that when the Film Board asked Johnson for a fixed time slot in the coming 1981–2 seasons, he balked and said both agencies should put together packages of programmes and market them aggressively.[11] Johnson's best wishes aside, he could not override his middle management. He was not broken-hearted that the Film Board was left to earn its way on to the air waves with a good show, just like every other producer. The organization now agreed to package its productions to meet CBC standards, not knowing if it could.[12]

The CBC's current hope was a second channel, as an alternative to copycat American programming. Johnson promised that if CBC II were to materialize, there would be a great need for Film Board productions. Satisfied with this assurance, members of the board agreed that the Film Board should not submit its own application for the much ballyhooed pay-television channel, or join in any other application, since the idea was premature. Once the genie was out, however, the dream of a Film Board channel was not to be rebottled.[13]

What the advocacy films advocated

At the time that the CBC's Johnson was questioning the 'advocacy' notion, Jean-Marc Garand happened to be reporting on French Production's activities. His presentation made for an interesting counterpoint, as he mentioned that the senior French filmmakers were evolving toward the production of an increasing number of films with a definite point of view, such as *Les Enfants des normes*, *Mourir à tue tête*, and *La Fiction nucléaire*.[14]

Garand could have built his case on the outcome of the debate over the 1977 antinuclear-power film, *No Act of God*, which had reached the board of governors at the end of 1978. Then, executive producer Peter Katadotis, whose Studio E made the environmental documentaries, had defended it

to their satisfaction. The board members had taken a stance that set the tenor of their role for the next decade: they insisted that they were not an adjudicative body with respect to specific works. They thought the programmes, be they one or many films, should continue the policy already in practice, reflecting as a whole fairness, accuracy, and balance. They said it was important to continue the tradition of advocacy with a point of view on public issues.[15] In Ottawa, the reverberations were not salutary, as more than one official thought that the members were relinquishing their legal authority and, by so doing, making the Film Board accountable to no one.

Some advocacy films were laudable, others were plainly disconcerting. A year later, French Production released a series of three films on the English of Quebec under the rubric 'Ladies and Gentlemen, le Québec.'[16] Not a few wondered if one, *Le Journal de madame Wollock* ($116,119), was racist and biased. It was about an English free-advertising circular in Montreal that called itself a newspaper. Sandwiched between the ads, the conservative owner and editor, Mrs Wollock, used her platform to air conservative, right-wing, and sometimes inflammatory views prevalent in what she saw as a besieged English community, desperate to avoid being cut off from Canada. The fact that she died suddenly on the eve of the film shoot did not stop director Gilles Blais from putting a microscope to the dead woman's opinions. That Mrs Wollock's beliefs had been wrapped in the Canadian flag was one problem. That she was Jewish was another, since anti-Semitism, while quiescent in Quebec since the end of the Second World War, was not far from the rhetoric of certain right-wing nationalist elements and, in the context of the film, she (and her co-religionists) were all-too-easy targets for the unscrupulous to bait. The Toronto *Globe and Mail* claimed that the documentary was a provocation rather than an explanation of

English-Canadian attitudes and that, as a whole, the series painted an ugly picture of English Quebec.[17]

Deputy Commissioner Macerola told the board of governors that some called the film racist and biased, while others questioned the fact that it was made at all. 'Its production has been defended on the basis that it is representative of a phenomenon that exists in our society and, as such, is a valid subject for the National Film Board to study,' he explained. He thought the real problem was contextual. Furthermore, audiences had not shown great interest in it. He implied that, if left alone, the film would die an early and deserved death.

The board members wondered about suppressing it. A number of individuals around the Film Board thought it was an embarrassment, plain and simple, from its bad taste to its thinly veiled racism, not to mention its repetition of inflammatory 'anti-Quebec politics' rhetoric. The members, mindful of the McPherson/Newman precedents, argued that suppression was possible, but counterproductive, because censorship does not damage the filmmakers' reputation, but that of the Film Board. They left it to senior management to develop criteria on the merits or otherwise of the film's distribution. Domville preferred to not stop anything unless it was factually wrong. *Le Journal de madame Wollock* and its English version, *Sophie Wollock's Newspaper*, remain in distribution.

There was another point to the debate: it would be hazardous if the Film Board concluded that the spotlight could not be turned on the silly, unfair, or vicious constituents of society. 'However, in making such judgments, it was felt that creative elements that have a relevance to a substantial number of Canadians should have a higher priority than those that are of interest to only a small group.'[18] In short, the filmmakers should seek to focus on the mainstream in order to stay relevant, necessary, and visible to the people of Canada. From the other side of their mouths, the board members said they wanted increased priority for women's issues in general, which would lead then to the need to provide adequate representation in films to gender issues, visible minorities, and homosexuals. Their debate underscored how democratization is far easier to articulate as a principle than it is to put into practice. The issue became more complex in the coming decade, as choices had to be made about how to continue serving both the mainstream and non-mainstream populations.

In an era when so many social icons worshipped romantic notions of standing-pat, self-congratulation, and material affluence, the Film Board found no difficulty in turning to the emotionally wrenching crime of rape. The controversial issue had long demanded public concern, but as might be expected, the private sector feared a commercial backlash and had shunned it. The Film Board undertook the project as a co-production with the CBC. There was little or no internal agitation to suppress it, although the women's Studio D had opposed a male treatment of the subject. (They were satisfied when one of their camerapersons joined the production team.) Communities across the country may have bristled when they saw *Why Men Rape* ($279,005), an investigation of the crime from the assailant's viewpoint, directed and written by Douglas Jackson in 1979 and broadcast on the CBC in January 1980 to an audience of 1.6 million. Ten convicted rapists (in shadow) tell their stories on camera, some of random rape and violence, and others of social rape. Narrator Patrick Watson guides the viewer through the wide range of sexual behaviour and attitudes. He indicates that these women-hating men had come from environments lacking love, or were suicidal – but they themselves had made the fateful choice to rape. Other angles include the exploitation of women as sex objects, the need for better sex education, and a candid, if somewhat embarrassed, group of conventional high-school students talking about rape. 'We believe this kind of open discussion may help some men see that they can't deal with their anger against the world by taking it out on women,' Watson concludes. A panel discussion followed, and subsequently police academies used the documentary to train officers. Public television telecast it in the United States too.

Emotions also ran high after Anne Claire Poirier directed *Mourir à tue-tête* (*A Scream from Silence*) ($362,861), in 1979. She dealt with rape from the victim's viewpoint by telling a fictional story about an unfortunate nurse, based on a composite of victims' experiences. Poirier's method of dramatic re-enactment was one of the first contemporary usages of the term 'docudrama.' She reconstructed the horrific act, as well as grisly images of ritual and mass rape. The film-within-a-film technique was meant to show the agony of filmmakers trying to articulate

the issue rather than exploit it. Radio-Canada telecast it on 10 April 1980.

As a stereotype, *Mourir à tue-tête* was an overstatement because most victims of rape do not commit suicide. Critics in English Canada tended to react negatively and concluded that it was a blatant assault on the audience.[19] There was accuracy, however, in the depiction of society's (and the law's) tendency to cast some guilt upon the victims. Women make the charge of rape, but the juries decide what constitutes rape. In all, this was a discomfiting, but appropriate, subject for the Film Board to cover and for national television to telecast. But English CBC refused to touch it. These ground-breaking efforts to deal maturely with once-taboo sexual subjects soon led the Film Board to undertake a non-theatrical video series to teach children about molestation and to sensitize adults to associated crimes.

Commissioner Domville supported and

Mourir à tue-tête / A Scream from Silence (1979) deals with rape from the victim's viewpoint. The film-within-a-film technique also shows the filmmakers' agony in trying to articulate rather than exploit the issue.

justified the advocacy films as a continuation of the now-defunct Challenge for Change / Société nouvelle ideology. He requested appropriate guidelines, and they emerged at last as the 'Fairness, Accuracy and Balance' doctrine. Many disgruntled filmmakers resisted the third principle, despite management's attempt to present the case for codification of the policy.[20] Brush fires tended to erupt most often when the Film Board tried serving the broad audience of English television. For example, the chief executive officer of the War Amputees of Canada, Clifford Chadderton, objected to *Bravery in the Field* ($252,527) in an open letter to newspapers, on 8 May 1980, claiming that the hero was portrayed as an alcoholic. This half-hour fiction piece, directed by Giles Walker, was part of the CBC co-production series *Adventures in History*.[21] The story, based loosely upon common occurrences in Saint John, New Brunswick, revolved around the lack of sense and purpose in the lives of two down-and-out men, an old forgotten one-legged veteran and an adolescent ne'er-do-well who assaults and robs him of money and his medal won for 'Bravery in the Field' at Dieppe in 1942. The repentant youth returns the old man's medal and realizes he has no monopoly on hard luck and hard times. The November Remembrance Day parade restores the old soldier's pride and dignity. The film does not succumb to sentimentality, showing how the young man realizes at last that important things happened before he was born to which he owes respect.

While Walker responded ably to Chadderton's objection,[22] the best rejoinder was in the form of a nomination for an Oscar that year. The subject of veterans was especially touchy, and the Film Board ought to have taken note of the clout and emotional fire behind the war amputees' group. In a few

Bravery in the Field (1979), part of the *Adventures in History* series, portrays in an unsentimental way a down-and-out Second World War veteran and a young thug who victimizes him, only to realize he has no monopoly on hard luck.

years, Chadderton and the War Amputees mounted the most concerted, well-financed, and prolonged attack on the Film Board in its history. The subject was a film questioning the heroism of First World War Canadian ace Billy Bishop.

Kicking and screaming into the eighties

From spring until fall, the press coverage of the Film Board's fortieth anniversary conveyed the general gloom felt at headquarters.[23] Domville prepared to testify before the Parliamentary Committee on Broadcasting, Films and Assistance to the Arts, in November 1979. He considered the merits of an upbeat presentation, perhaps to mention that on the occasion of the Film Board's fortieth year he had donated to the library of the Academy of Motion Picture Arts and Sciences, the month before, copies of the forty Film Board films nominated since 1939. (See Appendix 4 for a complete list, to 1989.) But he was an administrator with his back to the wall, not a Pollyanna, and he decided to paint the sombre, bleak, and true picture. If no more monies were forthcoming, his alternatives were to close key components like the women's unit, the animation studios, or the multimedia studio, to terminate some regional production units, to limit the quantity of Film Board productions, or to reduce the percentage of sponsored films commissioned to the private sector.

The committee was not moved by his presentation. One member, probably aware of Domville's application of the PSSRB decision, claimed stingingly that the commissioner's budgetary problems were of his own making; he demanded to know the cost of each film over the last two years. Quick on his feet, Domville responded that he only provided such information in response to specific questions in Parliament. In parrying with another MP, he was not keen to show a comparison of costs of Film Board and private-sector films of a similar nature. (Nor was he interested in opening up the issue that

over half the Film Board films sold to the educational milieu were heavily discounted and undercut the commercial market.)[24] Before he could comply with the committee's queries in written form, a deus ex machina occurred in the form of Parliament being dissolved; Canada was on the way to a second federal election after just six months.[25]

If things were not going wrong enough, a fiasco in the budgeting process had left Domville with no money for the coming year. Under yet another new accounting system, the Cabinet Committee on Social Development took over the approval of projected expenditures from the Treasury Board. The Film Board expected a $2.5 million increase; however, the committee evidently confused programme figures with wage and price increases and recommended a $2 million increase. This in turn was sliced in half. The net result was no budget for 1980–1. The board members could only recommend a holding pattern until a new government was in place.[26] Managers at every level had been so inept that no single set of shoulders could be found on which to lay blame for the mess. With wry gallows humour, the French Production members resurrected Gratien Gelinas's old pun on the commissioner's name, 'James de Bidonville,' to describe their workplace. (*Bidonville* was the French-Canadian term for shanty town, home to poverty-stricken slum dwellers.)

These were emotionally charged times on another account, the imminence of the Quebec referendum, whose outcome, in April 1980, was to decide whether or not that province would embark on the road to secession and independence. To confound matters more, Canadians showed their political unpredictability by re-electing the Liberals in March 1980. It was left to Pierre Trudeau to finish the task for which he had entered politics, to wage political battle for the country's most important internal decision since Confederation in 1867.

In the new government, Francis Fox was both minister of communications and secretary of state for a brief time. This allowed him to finish David MacDonald's transfer of the Film Board and other cultural agencies from the latter to the former department. Predictably, Fox's agenda was a continuation and acceleration of the policy that MacDonald had inherited, to encourage private-sector film production. Fox also intended to define the broader question of what the federal government's role in culture was to be. Domville hoped the Film Board would have some prominence in the minister's thinking and policy. But Fox did not devote much time to the Film Board, and when he did, the questions he asked most often were, 'Is the Film Board suffering from hardening of the arteries?' and 'Is it a centre of creativity?'[27] The implied answers seemed to be 'Yes' and 'No' respectively; Fox hoped Domville could reverse them.

Institutional despondency lifted momentarily when animator Eugene Fedorenko and producer Derek Lamb accepted the Oscar in 1980 for *Every Child* ($67,778). This was a 6-minute sponsored film for the United Nations to celebrate UNICEF's Declaration of Children's Rights. Written by Lamb and Les Mimes électriques of Montreal, *Every Child* tells the story of a baby who, after appearing mysteriously, is shunted from house to house because it has no name. The animation demonstrates one of the ten principles of the Declaration, that every child is entitled to a name and a nationality. Besides the Oscar, *Every Child* won eleven other awards. There was public embarrassment, however, when the *Toronto Star* reported in April 1980 that Fedorenko was out of a job on account of the Film Board's budgetary freeze.[28]

The same year, an Oscar nomination went to *Going the Distance*, a 90-minute documentary feature, written and directed by Paul Cowan and sponsored by the Minister of State for Fitness and Amateur Sport. As the official film of the Eleventh Commonwealth Games, held in Edmonton in 1978, *Going the Distance* ($840,000) referred to the physical, emotional, and psychological stress

Every Child (1979), an Oscar-winning U.N.-sponsored animation, celebrates the universal right of every child to a name and nationality.

competitors must endure in order to compete.[29] Eight athletes from four continents were filmed training in their home countries before the event as well as performing at the Games. They were typical of the 1,980 athletes and officials who participated, and by using the microcosm of the eight, Cowan succeeded in making these games seem as interesting as the Olympics because of the viewer's ability to become intimately involved with the person as well as the sport.

Also in the running for an Oscar was *Nails*, an independent Pacific regional production completed with Film Board assistance and directed by independent filmmaker Phillip Borsos. His interest in the dialectic between man, machine, history, and myth was articulated in his near-perfect earlier 15-minute film, *Spartree*. *Nails* seems to mourn the demise of the craft of nail-making, where the artisan previously had a relationship to his work. In stark contrast, the camera moves deftly through a modern mill, with its deafening racket and machine production of countless nails. Dwarfed by mechanical behemoths, there stands the almost invisible human. With sound, music, but no commentary, *Nails* is reminiscent of the romantic and innocent-eye documentary tradition of Robert Flaherty. (It would spoil Borsos's effect to learn that nineteenth-century blacksmiths lived on average only into their forties in this most hazardous occupation.) Borsos's interest in mythic elements appeared again in *The Grey Fox*, his first, and in *Bethune: The Making of a Hero*, his most recent, commercial feature.

Yet public goodwill could be lost if a single film drew the ire of influential persons or bodies, as occurred in French Production's feature *Cordélia*, directed by Jean Beaudin. This was the true story of the 1897 trial of a woman and her lover, who were tried and executed for the murder of her husband. Superior Court justice Jules Deschênes attacked the Film Board publicly in a thirty-page document, accusing the filmmakers of

unfairly tarnishing justice. He was outraged that the scenario ignored the evidence and the three trials that had found them guilty. Deschênes's attack demonstrated the pitfalls of incomplete research and a questionable use of artistic licence; in a cavalier response, the unheeding filmmakers insisted on their right to criticize the weakness of Canadian institutions.[30]

The game of politics and the Film Board's relevance

The board of governors continued to press Domville for a definition of organizational objectives. While the principal debate was how to find an audience, they were firm in their insistence that the institution not become involved in the special distribution of political films during election campaigns.[31]

Amidst the deafening racket and machine production of a modern mill, *Nails* (1979) points to the lost relationship between an artisan and his work.

Given the fact that the Conservative government had lasted only months, and the Liberals were back in office with a not-substantial majority, their reluctance to be caught in the game of politics made sense. Films about politicians, candidates, parties, or party philosophies that were already in the catalogue would continue to be available, although they were not to be specially promoted, and during election periods new films on these subjects were not to be launched. If it seemed that this was a prudent way to avoid the pitfalls of becoming a pawn of Ottawa, the proviso that this policy applied to referenda left a few in Ottawa wondering what good was being served by the National Film Board of Canada as the crucial Quebec referendum approached.

But this was a non-issue to Fox, who had no expectation that the Film Board would become a propaganda arm of the government. If Radio-Canada was any indication, there was every reason to believe the Film Board would disappoint Ottawa.[32] English Production's principal contribution to the national debate in 1980 was the half-hour animation and live-action 'mockumentary' directed by Robert Awad and David Verrall, *The National Scream / Fièvre du castor*, a tongue-in-cheek look at Canada's passion for using the documentary to get to the truth of things. Here, the story was how the beaver became a national symbol and, in familiar documentary style, how Canada continued its search for a national identity. The punch line was the typical English Canadianism of accommodation, stated by the maven of Canadian television hosts, Elwy Yost: 'Simple humanitarianism is more meaningful than any symbol or ideology.' (Probably the most useful film in the whole contemporary political debate was Donald Brittain's 1978 documentary, *The Champions*, which was discussed earlier.)

Domville believed that the majority of French Production staff were on the 'yes' side in the debate about whether Quebec should begin negotiations toward leaving Canada

and choose sovereignty-association. Critics asked if it was in the national interest for a federal institution to support separatists. Domville thought that a civilized system should fund voices that criticized it – that was the essence of democracy. But a coterie of individuals in Ottawa was so viscerally involved in the campaign fight to save Canada that they were disappointed with the accommodating Domville. Why, they wondered, had the $2 million which Ottawa had given the Film Board to promote national unity not been spent on propaganda? They should have realized that 'no propaganda' had been a Film Board tradition since the Freedom Speaks programme of 1950 had sputtered into oblivion. The high road had been demonstrated in the *Canada Vignettes* series, which reflected the belief that national unity began with national understanding. There were several French productions that touched the referendum issue. *Le Jour du Référendum dans la vie de Richard Rohmer* was a 57-minute documentary, directed by Jacques Bensimon in 1979, that profiled the popular English-Canadian novelist, whose novel *Referendum* dramatized a worst-case right-wing scenario of English reaction to the possible effects of Quebec separation. In 1981, the bitter 108-minute *Le Confort et l'Indifférence* ($483,675) found Denys Arcand placing the entire referendum in a broad and cynical context, reminiscent of *Québec, Duplessis et après*. Among his visual juxtapositions were devices like a cleric reading Machiavelli from the heights of a luxurious office tower and a boxing match between 'Oui' (for sovereignty-association) and 'Non' (against separatism) in which the former wins in one round. There were also English-speaking matrons of wealthy Westmount contrasted with Greek immigrants who vote 'Oui' because the capitalists and monopolists say 'Non' and, finally, the pathos of simple *québécois*, whose pride rests in Bingo, custom vans, and power boats. After the *indépendantistes* lose the referendum, Lévesque urges his followers to sing 'Gens du pays.' He wins re-election, and the film closes with an empty stage, implying that the country awaits the next player on the stage of history. The final title, a quote from the exiled Soviet author Alexander Solzhenitsyn, is an ominous warning to both winners and losers: 'A lifetime is very short in the long course of history.' That such a production could come from a federal agency was remarkable and a credit to freedom of expression; that it won no friends in Ottawa at this critical historical juncture was also significant. The film attracted generally poor press reviews, yet was awarded the Quebec critics' Léo-Ernest Ouimet prize.

Opposing questions from Ottawa: A role in External Affairs? Is the Film Board worth the money?

From spring to fall in 1980, Domville waited for the promised $2 million-plus supplement,[33] while rumours swirled of yet another cut for all cultural agencies. In August, Fox announced inauspiciously that the government was undertaking a five-stage review of federal cultural policy; hearings would occur between December and the spring of 1981. The Conservatives had begun the exercise, but were defeated before they could create the committee fully. Fox asked Montreal publisher Jacques Hébert to become joint chairman with Louis Applebaum. The minister had high hopes for this first major inquiry into cultural policy since the Massey-Lévesque Royal Commission thirty years earlier. Those who anticipated that the exercise might put the organization in jeopardy were right to worry. The Applebaum-Hébert Committee lived up to their worst fears.

By the spring of 1981, Domville trotted out a Film Board 'Objectives' document, a new raison d'être with four general themes: (1) programming was to be geared toward the concept of public service; (2) there was to be improved public access to Film Board films; (3) research and development were to be pursued in conjunction with an organized training programme at the highest levels of expertise; and (4) the Film Board was to pursue an international role, especially in the Third World.[34] English Production chief Peter Katadotis thought the issue of public service was more rhetoric than reality, since no one was asking how the organization should differentiate itself from other public-service bodies; furthermore, he wondered, given the burgeoning private sector: What was the difference between public service and private enterprise? What should actually be on the screen? These philosophical questions remained unanswered in the eighties.[35]

Domville's emphasis on the Third World audience was an attempt to revitalize one of the oldest, and lately most tenuous, of ties, that with the Department of External Affairs. The department had let most Film Board productions languish in recent years because it wanted identifiable and positive propaganda, fitting into its specialized programme.[36] But the Film Board tended to believe that real prestige came from adhering to the tradition of understatement, so that the word 'Canada' appeared only in the credits as it did in Michel Régnier's highly successful *Santé Afrique* series of thirty-one films for teaching and retraining health-care personnel. The series, researched and directed with the assistance of African specialists, was an example of how the Challenge for Change / Société nouvelle idea had been propagated and nurtured abroad, and it was probably doing more to build a positive image of Canada than External Affairs realized. The Canadian public, however, remained largely ignorant of this activity.[37]

External Affairs's under-secretary of state and sitting board member, Allan Gotlieb, was brutally frank in criticizing the irrelevance of the Film Board in light of his department's current information objectives. Conveniently forgetting the major contribution the organization had made to Habitat in 1976, he said he looked in vain for films that fit into the orientation and objectives of Canadian foreign policy, emphasizing trade,

Canadian technology, and Canadian skills. There were not even any that were broadly descriptive of Canada, he complained. Gotlieb was also part of a new generation of continentalist mandarins who wanted to move Canada toward free trade with the United States. When it came to culture and broadcasting policy, he was not keen to apply a strict definition of Canadian-content quota. He thought that a free, fast-moving international involvement was necessary to achieve a certain cultural intensity.[38] Perhaps it was not coincidental that this line of thinking had been an understood tenet of each responsible minister's film policy since the end of the sixties.

Gotlieb was far more circumspect when he praised Domville before Prime Minister Trudeau at a social event. The inscrutable prime minister shot back, 'Yes, but why does he have all those separatists working for him?' Domville thought it was his friend Trudeau's way of making a joke while being half-serious.[39] Joke or not, if there was animosity in Ottawa toward the Film Board, it was because of neither an absence of films on trade and technology nor inefficiency, of which virtually all government departments could stand accused to some degree. It was coming from the same quarter as the attacks on Radio-Canada during the emotionally bitter times, from 1976 onward. For instance, in a public exchange of letters in *Le Devoir* in December and January 1980–1, between himself and some of the *indépendantiste* intellectuals and artists, Prime Minister Trudeau had criticized angrily 'these people who for years have enjoyed total freedom of expression and generous access to such federal institution as the CBC and the National Film Board to defend their thesis of sovereignty.'[40] From his perspective in Cabinet, Fox tempered the prime minister's statement by recalling that Trudeau never expressed personal displeasure with the Film Board before Cabinet; neither was there ever a cabinet discussion where the Film Board was the topic on the agenda, nor did the Cabinet charge

that the Film Board was failing to fulfil its mandate. Fox said that in Ottawa, senior-level people felt the Film Board was not producing enough to justify its expense. Politicians were particularly bothered – as many others had been before – to learn stories of filmmakers being paid, but not making films.[41] All that being said, the suspicion that French-language filmmakers were against Ottawa's national project and for Quebec's, did not elicit many charitable emotions from where it counted most.

Kudos

Abroad, it seemed again that the Film Board had more friends than it had at home. In January 1981, the intractable problems seemed to diminish temporarily when the Museum of Modern Art in New York inaugurated a six-month Film Board retrospective. The programme was a representative sample of the best animation, documentary, and feature work of the past four decades. To receive such accolades in New York is to reach the pinnacle of recognition in the art and film world. It was also million-dollar publicity for free. Minister Fox was pleased to attend the opening with his parliamentary assistant, the chairman of the Standing Committee on culture, Commissioner Domville, and the vice-chairman of his board of governors, as well as film star Donald Sutherland. They basked in the glory of the high-profile red-carpet treatment and of good coverage in both the professional press and the *New York Times*. For the moment, all was forgiven.[42] In fact, Canadian consulates made good use of the retrospective, and versions of it became the focal points of many cultural programmes.

This positive attention encouraged Domville to express once more his greatest desire – to undertake features. He said there was a certain kind of feature film, revealing something about the country, which was not likely to get off the ground without participation from the public sector. Furthermore, for the

Film Board to produce shorts exclusively was like asking a writer to produce only essays. He overturned Lamy's 'no more features' policy and intended to leap the financial barriers by embarking on two features per year, in each language, with private film producers.[43]

But it was indeed the short film that the Film Board did best, and a year later two such films received Oscar nominations: the 26-minute live-action drama *First Winter*, and the 9-minute offbeat animation *Tender Tale of Cinderella Penguin*. The latter, directed by Janet Perlman, used a medieval style of illustration to animate the ancient fairy tale as it is experienced by an exploited penguin, complete with magic flipper for the appropriate webbed foot. John N. Smith's

First Winter ($410,224) was part of the *Adventures in History* series. It was a historical drama set in 1830, telling of the hardship, disease, and death that were often part of the immigrant experience. This story of two Irish children who must survive winter alone in a log cabin in the bush after their mother dies used none of the usual romantic clichés; endurance becomes the essential Canadian quality.

At Cannes that same spring, the only Canadian film in competition was the Film Board's *Ted Baryluk's Grocery*, directed by John Paskievich and Michael Mirus of the Winnipeg regional office. They used animated black and white photos to show an aged neighbourhood Ukrainian shopkeeper's relationship with his daughter and

First Winter (1981), part of the *Adventures in History* series, eschews the usual romantic clichés about the immigrant experience; endurance is the essential quality of being Canadian.

his local environment. The distinguishing characteristic of the 10-minute item was the sense of actuality that eclipsed its sentimentality to reveal something universal in both the immigrant experience and the enduring 'village' nature of Canadian communities. The 10-minute animated version of a popular short story by Roch Carrier, *The Sweater/ Le Chandail* ($199,000), was the masterpiece of Sheldon Cohen, who won the highest animation award from the British Film Academy in 1980. This delightful nostalgic film recalls a child's glory days of street hockey in late-1940s Quebec, and helps trigger memories of thousands of Canadian childhoods, when hockey was both sport and fantasy. Then, almost every hockey-obsessed child dreamed of wearing the sweater and number

of the greatest star of the greatest team, 'Rocket' Richard of the Montréal Canadiens.

The above films were recognized and rewarded for their excellence. There were others of quality which, if they did not receive the grand prizes, demonstrated that the Film Board took seriously its policy of representing the more marginal, if forgotten, elements of society. Several representative documentaries were *Nose and Tina* and *Les Adeptes* in 1980, and *La Surditude* in 1981. *Nose and Tina*, by Norma Bailey of the Winnipeg studio, was the 27-minute true story of a native prostitute and her boyfriend, who was a train brakeman. The camera reveals select aspects of their personal lives, and a glimpse at their woes provides an inkling of how the Canadian 'system' is often stacked against the peo-

In *Ted Baryluk's Grocery* (1982) animated black and white photos are used to portray an aged Ukrainian's relationship with his daughter, with their neighbourhood store as a backdrop.

ple on the margins. *Les Adeptes* (*The Followers*) was Gilles Blais's 80-minute even-handed study of the six-month indoctrination and initiation of three Quebeckers into the Hare Krishna religious sect. *La Surditude* (*To Be Deaf*), directed by Yves Dion, was an 85-minute documentary about deaf mutes as a cultural minority group struggling to assert themselves in a society that has other priorities.

Applebaum-Hébert appearance

In May 1981 Domville hoped to make a tough verbal presentation before the Applebaum-Hébert Committee. Its members, largely from an image-conscious environment, were disappointed if not displeased that he appeared alone and with no advisers. A few of them thought it was reflective of the Film Board's arrogance. The gist of Domville's remarks was that Canada was in a national culture crisis, spending most of its money building a technologically sophisticated communications system that would improve access to American materials. If the Film Board did not receive more resources to meet the challenges posed by this crisis, it would have to withdraw from specific activities that were necessary to fulfil its public trust.[44] He wanted more money, but the committee wanted to know what his institution's role was.

He showed them the *40th Anniversary Clip*, a compilation of some of the great film moments of the past. The members' response was emotional and pleasant, since many of them had had a professional relationship with the Film Board at some point. Niceties aside, their questions were more difficult, as they wondered about the validity of the 1950 Film Act in the 1980s. Sponsored films still rankled the private sector, while the poor relations between the Film Board and the CBC were known by everyone.[45] They wondered about Domville's sally into dramatic film production and the Film Board's own rejection of the concept of a national

film school. Some regional production centres (like Moncton, NB) seemed to be exercising too much autonomy.[46] Domville thought he had communicated his agency's position well and expected the committee's written report would be fair. No one could have taken a worse reading of the wind.

Some committee members thought he should have articulated a new role for his institution. Others were unimpressed by his low-keyed, lacklustre delivery and remained unsympathetic to the plight and impasse he had inherited. They wrote their report with these facts in mind and thus probably sealed his fate as a one-term film commissioner.[47] At best, the committee could not be accused of ignoring public wants as it travelled to 18 cities and heard 500 people; about 50 of the 1,300 briefs dealt with broadcasting, film production, and distribution. There was precious little praise for the Film Board, other than the observation that it was helping to develop an indigenous commercial film industry, along with the CBC and CFDC, and was keeping the educational system Canadian.

In all, most of the comments about the Film Board were negative and can be summarized as follows: the institution was a closed shop in need of revitalizing; it should replace its own production with independent contracting; it should close or turn to training new talent; it should quit sponsored films; it should inaugurate a user-pay system; public libraries were an alternative distribution method, whereby money saved could go into production.[48] From this response, it was clear that the Film Board had failed to generate a sufficient cross-country lobby to support its goals, goals that were unarticulated or in limbo. By June 1982 the film commissioner was receiving warning signals that the committee, in taking the briefs literally, was going to recommend reducing his institution to a training school and centre for experimentation. Domville sought clarification of these points, first from committee adviser Michael Spencer and then from the committee chairman, Louis Applebaum, who allayed his concern and made him feel 'very positive.'[49] Perhaps, as one Domville aid put it later, the chemistry between the two was such that Applebaum did not like giving bad news any more than Domville liked hearing it.

French and English Production: Unity in adversity

A few months later, Deputy Commissioner Macerola met with French Production to find out why the filmmakers were dispirited. He might have recalled that Director of French Production Jean-Marc Garand had stated to *La Presse* in 1980 that the organization needed competition and that the filmmakers were too used to working in a secure climate.[50] Macerola concluded that they were suffering because of their objectives and the quality of their films, not for lack of money. If he lay the blame on the laps of the managers, he confided to no one his personal thought that, ever since the election of the Parti Québécois in 1976, French-language filmmakers ceased being critical and could not turn against friends like Gérald Godin or ex-Film Board member Pierre de Bellefeuille, both of whom were now Quebec government officials. Macerola was convinced that once French Production had ceased exercising the liberty to be critical, their films suffered in quality.[51]

The new director of English Production since January 1980, Peter Katadotis, thought that the French filmmakers were not searching for a Film Board mission like his group was.[52] He began to rationalize production planning by devoting 40 per cent of his budget to current programming procedure, 40 per cent to executive producers whose films would be based on market research and defined audience needs, and 20 per cent held by himself to be used for his own considered priorities, two or three major projects each year. Among these was a series to be called *War* and a new series based on the once-popular early childhood-specialist films,

Ages and Stages (done for the agency by Crawley Films), updated versions of which professional associations had been requesting for years.[53] Soon Studio K., emanating from Katadotis's office, became the outlet for these and other special projects.[54]

Sponsored film and distribution: The Achilles' heel

In September 1979 a crew from the People's Republic of China had been filming agricultural subjects and industrial techniques in Canada, while English and French Production were engaged in separate projects in China. A year later, Domville was pleased to find himself a guest of the Chinese government. On this junket, he was accompanied by the heads of the two groups that spoke for private industry in Canada, the Canadian Film and Television Association and the Association des Producteurs de Films du Québec. While there, he intended to try to unlock the Chinese barrier to the distribution of Canadian films and to end the back-biting over sponsored film once and for all. In a railway car somewhere in China, he offered a three-year phase-out of virtually all Film Board production of sponsored films.[55]

Pressure from both the commercial interests and the minister's office convinced the commissioner to make his generous offer. When he later told the board of governors of the deal, his single caveat was that the overall amount of such work should be substantially increased from the existing $4 million a year to around $12 million. He thought this would force the various federal departments to dismantle their audiovisual production facilities. The Film Board, as executive producer, would then be able to guarantee a level playing field for all competitors vying for the $12 million bonanza. Domville later explained his thinking. As he saw it, 'sponsored film had become a monkey on the back of English production,' whose filmmakers would go to Ottawa to drum up sponsored business in order to earn enough outside money to support the general English Production programme. Watching NFB directors beat a path to departmental sponsors' doors made the contract-hungry private entrepreneurs see red. Domville was willing to abandon all sponsored work, except that requiring a unique approach, like animation films or those like *Going the Distance*, which were sure-fire prestige earners. He admitted that, in the short run, this policy would penalize production by causing a shortfall in income, but in the long run it would help, since sponsored films had become a less significant portion of the overall production budget. Besides, the Film Board was hiring freelancers to do most of that work anyway. He defended his peacemaking policy on the China railway, believing it did not stray from the original intention of the National Film Act.[56] He asserted that he was neither yielding any of the five 'objectives' that were now part of the organization's mandate nor taking the politically unwise step of vacating the sponsored-film field altogether.[57]

Perhaps his argument was a bit too glib. A veteran like Robert Verrall thought that by quitting sponsored-film production the Film Board might have less significance than ever to Ottawa, whose politicians and bureaucrats could forget the organization more easily. This decision might prove to be the most serious, far-reaching, and perhaps damaging one of Domville's tenure. The commissioner thought he was covering his flank by insisting that his agency, not the Department of Supply and Services, remain as executive producer. His board of governors wanted to hold out for an increase in the Film Board's appropriation before relinquishing sponsored films. Domville pointed out that federal departments had already outfitted themselves with expensive in-house production facilities amounting to $7 million, in contravention of the National Film Act, and he estimated they were doing between $10 and $12 million worth of production annually. The Film Board had a right to question such illegal practices and to assert its prerogatives.

He blew the whistle, and the Treasury Board set up a committee to investigate these improprieties. The governors learned by 1982 just how much departments were bypassing the Film Act in their own production of audiovisual products. They might make items themselves or use their budget to make a contribution to a group or association, on the understanding that the money would be used to produce a film. Sometimes private producers would conclude a co-production contract with a television network and then convince a department to invest in the project. Also, television networks were competing successfully for sponsored films, this to the chagrin of the hungry private producers. Here at least was one instance where the Film Board was not responsible for the sorry state of affairs, and many commercial companies also desired to curb the abuses.[58]

That same year, Domville explained to the minister why distribution remained an Achille's heel, despite figures of about one-half million Canadian bookings per year. He claimed that the Film Board was refusing almost one in three booking requests, largely because of the unavailability of prints. With an additional $650,000 annually, he argued, the institution could add 27,000 prints to its inventory to stop the decline. There had been great success for NFB videos at the first public-library preview facilities in suburban Montreal, and there was confidence that the new video-cassette technology would provide a long-term solution to public-access problems. But the commissioner needed celluloid to ease the immediate crisis.[59]

A year later, Director of Distribution William Litwack reiterated the argument that user-fees could partly offset the costs of expansion. The board members stopped him cold, fearing a decrease in bookings. Besides, the last time this issue had been mooted, there followed a public uproar, embarrassing questions in Parliament, a chilling of relations with the minister, and the eventual resignation of the film commissioner. They told Litwack to look to video-cassette technology and electronic distribution. Achilles' heel was still exposed.[60]

Francis Fox: 'Arm's length' from the 'hands-on' minister

Francis Fox continued his predecessors' Capital Cost Allowance policy, which had resulted in the private sector's production of nearly one hundred features, the majority of which were never distributed. The pay-off (or lack of it) showed that of $277 million in paid admissions in Canada in 1979, only $2 million went to Canadian films. The abuse of the system led Fox to revise the rules so as to place more burden on the market-place; productions now had to be distributed in order to recoup costs.

The minister attended a board of governors meeting in December 1981 to explain informally where he saw the Film Board in the scheme of things. Unaccustomed to circumlocutions, he spoke directly, and when he left no members were smiling. Fox explained that in the current environment, broadcasting was everything, and the Film Board was carrying a burden that was affecting its ability to be part of this dynamic. Its distribution system was outdated and too costly, and the number of films produced for the money was low. He thought the organization could free up funds for new policy development if it dropped some non-essential activities.

He learned of a new Film Board initiative, the repackaging of existing material for cable-television broadcast, including expansion of the successful experiment with *Videotron*, where viewers could select NFB films that the cable company would then broadcast. This 'programming on demand,' and the possibilities of satellite broadcast, showed great promise. Another long-range goal that he supported was the agency's wish to obtain access to a cable channel, either exclusively or with partners, to ensure regular and consistent exposure. There were eight hundred hours of first-run material

available, but given the voracious appetite of television, even with a nightly four-hour prime-time slot, the bank of films would be exhausted in less than eight months unless they were repeated frequently. Many believed that an exclusive channel was a non-starter.[61]

But Fox liked this idea as well as that of establishing a national film school. He was also interested in films of broad popular appeal, even if it might be necessary to reorient programming away from the traditional non-theatrical audiences to achieve this goal. He complained about the recent paucity of 'excellent' films. Domville responded obliquely that the quantity question would be addressed with plans for more co-productions, if he could find more money. The minister said the money issue was not his problem to resolve because the general feeling in the cultural community was that inefficiency, not underfunding, was Domville's institutional problem. The unspoken paradox was how the commissioner was to manage human resources within existing budgets and avoid detonating the political dynamite of staff lay-offs.

As to the issue of 'arm's length,' currently a popular topic in the press, Fox said the arm's-length relationship would continue, but that he as minister had a role to articulate general cultural thrusts and broad policy direction to the boards of agencies. For example, he intended to formulate a national cultural policy after considering the Applebaum-Hébert Committee recommendations. Day-to-day administration of the cultural agencies was not his concern, however he did feel that there was a breakdown in the arms's-length relationship between boards, management, programmers, and producers. In short, he was asking where the buck stopped, since, in the Film Board case, films were too often distantly related to the agency's mandate. Some members explained that as a matter of policy, they did not involve themselves in individual films. They were content with a general film policy of excellence, balance, and objectivity. Fox repeated that it was up to the members and managers to do their jobs. His function was broad, theirs was specific. Years later, he said that the real problem was the double arm's-length relationship. He thought that the institution's malaise would cease if the board of governors truly *governed*.[62]

Domville suspected that Fox's assistant deputy ministers, David Silcox and Robert Rabinovitch, not the minister, were trying to get the department to exert more influence. Macerola sensed that those bureaucrats wanted to close down forever what they perceived as the separatist-infested Film Board.[63] Both the commissioner and his deputy were off base. Fox's deputies, who were the best and brightest of the new generation of mandarins, were working in close collaboration with the minister to tighten up the boards of governors of all cultural agencies as part of a grand design for culture. As to Ottawa's antipathy to separatists at the institution, that was a given, but the prevailing feeling was that the Film Board was an essential, if inefficient, part of the Canadian cultural scene. The inefficiency only confirmed the politicians' pre-existing disinclinations to throw more money at a place that kept drawing controversy because of the English and French 'leading-edge' films.[64] Domville's and Macerola's misperceptions of how Ottawa saw them may have confirmed the department's belief that the Film Board was failing to rejuvenate itself. In short, if the managers were hearing the wrong tune, the department believed it was because the managers were striking the wrong chords.

The aftermath of Fox's visit was not what most had expected. A sigh of relief was audible as more money did materialize for regionalization, the women's programme, and Distribution's *Format*, the Canadian audiovisual database. After inflation adjustments, the 1982 budget was $69.9 million, of which $48 million was related to the production and distribution of film and video. The employee quota was now 991 person-years, plus 175 person-years for temporary staff. Personnel consumed 54 per cent of the total operating costs. The doom-and-gloom predictions were temporarily in abeyance, but Toronto critic Gerald Pratley reminded the Film Board that the public was watching and that endemic drift characterized the whole operation.[65] The minister was pleased to hear the first shoe drop in June, when management announced a hiring freeze, intending to cut 10 per cent of the staff over two years in order to free up money for production.

Applebaum-Hébert report: The other shoe falls

The other shoe fell on 15 November, with the release of the Applebaum-Hébert Committee report (officially the Report of the Federal Cultural Policy Review Committee). Domville happened to be on holiday, racing Walter Cronkite on the waters of Chesapeake Bay, when he heard the bad news. It was the worst day of his tenure as he put into port and took the next plane to Montreal. The committee had recommended eliminating the government's role as proprietor, producer, and distributor of cultural products in favour of the private sector. In short, by advocating a free-enterprise model for Canadian cultural industries and an end to centralized production by the public sector in Canadian cultural life, the committee advocated a virtual throttling of the CBC, the National Arts Council, and the National Film Board.

The thrust of the report was that commercial filmmakers were best suited to gear production toward an export market with their copycat American-style films. The committee left untouched the age-old problem of American penetration and control of (English) Canada's cultural market; the focus was on the public-sector versus private-sector split of the Canadian market share. They wanted the commercial feature to continue to benefit from the public's largesse. This meant (1) further tax write-offs and subsidies, (2) an unstopping flow of money to the

CFDC, and (3) Canada Council support to encourage film talent. In all this, the Film Board was an afterthought left with a motherhood statement – it would become a leader, a teacher, a centre of advanced research and training.[66]

An immediate statement by the Film Board's director of public relations in the press seemed to support the committee report. This caused panic in the institution.[67] The unauthorized remark angered Domville, and the unfortunate spokesperson soon resigned to become director of public relations at a dinosaur museum. Then someone leaked to *Le Devoir* a summary of Macerola's internal document that gave his personal perception of the major problems and the future role of the agency.[68] Finally, quite unrelated to the report, the deficit-ridden government ordered another across-the-board cut for all departments. They told the Film Board to pare $1 million for each of two years, commencing the next fiscal year.

Over the next weeks, Domville tried to defend the institution's appeal to non-theatrical and structured groups.[69] He suppressed his outrage that the report did not even mention that regionalization was a significant part of current policy, or that the organization's international reputation was still considerable. He wanted some explanation for the shotgun treatment, and fingers soon pointed at commercial producers Denis Héroux and Michael Spencer. Héroux was steadfast in his assertion that with an administration consuming 20 per cent of the budget, the Film Board had lost its creativity. Spencer also defended the general thrust of the document, which stated that the Film Board's share of the federal government's resources was no longer justified, judging by the cultural benefits Canadians received from it. The organization suffered from a lack of public access, the quality of its films had declined, and it seemed irrelevant in light of television having assumed its mandate. Besides, when the committee had held cross-country hearings, hardly anyone raised

any observations about the Film Board, which in itself might have been reason enough to have an inquiry. In fact, most of the written briefs mentioning the organization had been dismal. Years later, Spencer confessed that the report's intention had not been to remove the Film Board's production function, but the text was not clear enough. He and Héroux had wanted the organization to define itself by taking into account private-sector producers and to find a new mission in the form of a film training centre.[70]

The devastated staff thought that Domville had been ineffective, both in presenting the Film Board case before the committee and in defending it publicly. Filmmakers Anne Claire Poirier, Georges Dufaux, Robert Forget, and Jacques Godbout appeared on a Radio-Canada telecast to debate with an inflexible Denis Héroux.[71] Meanwhile, in the Quebec National Assembly, there must have been a double-take at the unlikely scene of Gérald Godin, Parti Québécois government minister and *indépendantiste par excellence*, praising the Film Board. Even the aging radical columnist Pierre Bourgault proclaimed that 'national unity is better served by a great institution and by a great symbol like the NFB, than by the political speeches of our leaders.'[72]

There was help from the outside, as television journalist, commentator, and media personality Patrick Watson reacted to the report on CBC radio, stating that some of its ideas were 'nuts.' In defending the Film Board, he noted that the CBC did not do things better, because it shunned an interpretive role. He attacked the report's lack of editing and turgid prose. The document was so bad, he insisted, that journalists gave up trying to wade through it.[73] Robert Fulford of *Saturday Night* called it a well-intentioned failure that played to a series of constituencies, seemingly had no opinions of its own, and endorsed all causes. As for the Film Board, the cure was worse than the disease. He mentioned that of the forty-seven Academy Award nominations it had received since 1940, ten had been earned in the last five years. 'It remains a precious cultural asset,' he stated, 'and the suggestion that it effectively disappear is appalling.' He could not understand how the report could urge strengthening of the CFDC, whose record was for the most part dreadful.[74] Gerald Pratley, the doyen of Canadian film critics, also railed against the report for being a dismal and dreary manifesto. True, the leadership of the Film Board was weak, but it was sad in the extreme that Applebaum forgot his professional debt to the Film Board.[75] The leading independent *québécois* film directors put a union-paid advertisement in *Le Devoir*. Animosities and jealousies that they may have once had about working for a federal enterprise evaporated as they joined together in its defence. They reminded the readers that they had all started at the Film Board, that its cultural mission was unique in the world, and that its production capacities should be increased, not diminished, in order to protect the freedom of independent film-makers.[76]

A fuzzy left-wing analysis of the report in *Canadian Dimension* magazine made some astute observations. Government policy in the so-called media/communications revolution was part of a larger initiative to capture resources or markets, even when the possibilities of exploiting them successfully were limited. Cultural policies, firmly grounded within the politics of the right, were being based on the criteria of rampant individualism and consumerism. What the author addressed obliquely was the fact that culture was a commodity for sale like every other market-place item and that Canada was rushing to get into the market, lest it find itself excluded from the game. If Canada was to become part of the new market, the article continued, the CBC and Film Board, as former beneficiaries of monopoly status, needed to be restructured or to disappear. However sound this critique was, it probably reached very few eyes.[77] The mainstream

press continued hammering away at the style, rather than the meaning, of the report.

In his typical non-confrontational manner, Domville addressed the CRTC not long afterwards and began by saying that he found several positive principles in the report, even if it was contradictory and paradoxical. He agreed there was an incompatibility of cultural and industrial objectives; his remedy was a Film Board bid to become part of the annual $464 million cable-television market.[78] He tried to soothe sensitivities the following March, when he announced that he had analyzed the climate surrounding the Applebaum-Hébert report and found that it enjoyed little support in the media or among politicians, private individuals, and Film Board users. The real question was whether Fox would act on it or not. The same month, the minister revealed an outline of his new broadcasting strategy that seemed to echo the major thrust of the report. To ensure increased competitiveness in the Canadian broadcasting industry, private-sector production would become a major source of the solid core of Canadian programming; he boosted the CFDC budget from $35 million to $60 million. (That the brunt of this production was copycat synthetic American pap seemed to concern no one.)

Why was the much maligned report even given such credence? One close Domville aid suspected that its policy thrusts were formulated even before the committee sat, based on pre-existing government intentions. There was even an unfounded rumour that two key ministers had argued to scrap the Film Board, but could not because of their fear of adverse public reaction. Domville believed it was simpler than that. The senior bureaucrats thought that the high-profile, high-cost Applebaum-Hébert document could not be ignored, so they stuck its recommendations into the minister's policy. Fox told Domville privately that he did not propose to turn the Film Board into a training and experimental centre, that he would fight to retain the institution's existing level of funding, and that he would do what he could to allow the Film Board to keep the savings it would garner from the latest government-ordered, across-the-board 10 per cent ($1 million) reduction programme.[79]

But the air was filled with mixed signals; Fox's officials all but excluded the Film Board from film-policy discussions. Nor did the Treasury Board allow Domville to plough back into production the first third of a million dollars he saved by reducing the programme. Worse, Fox refused to appoint either of two candidates Domville had submitted for the vacant public-servant seat on the board of governors, which had always been filled by public servants from other ministries. Domville concluded that Assistant Deputy David Silcox and Robert Rabinovitch wanted an official from their own department.[80] (In fact, Rabinovitch advised Fox against not filling the seat.)

Domville thought he had one ace up his sleeve to blunt the extraordinary power of Fox's assistant deputy ministers: he had the minister's car-phone number, could reach him without an intermediary, and thereby could keep in frequent contact. In the long run, it made no difference, since Fox delayed and the appointment was not made. Once Domville ceased being commissioner, the battle was lost, and nine months later, Assistant Deputy Minister David Silcox became a board member. The long tradition of ostensible ministerial distance was broken for the first time since the 1950 Film Act – a representative from the department now sat on the board of governors. Fox thought he had achieved what he had set out to do: to end the double arm's length and to have Silcox, with his experience as an effective arts administrator, contribute to revitalizing the Film Board and making its members more forceful.[81] On concluding his term, however, Silcox left a board of governors with no fewer and no more teeth than it had before he arrived. The institution could not redefine and rejuvenate itself on command; the process took years and, he believed would be incomplete unless the National Film Act were rewritten and the organization began a new relationship with the private sector.[82]

It was still a no-win situation. There had been steady pressure from five successive ministers to trim the operation that they believed was becoming marginal in light of the private-sector industrial model. Events seemed to have made slimming impossible, and each commissioner worried about how best to deal with the intractable person-year problem and annual bookkeeping nightmare. Like his two predecessors, Domville had hoped to try to have the government open the Film Act to pursue crown-corporation status, which, in the best possible worlds, would guarantee the Film Board autonomy, while allowing it to serve as an instrument of broad government policy. But this was not the best of all possible worlds, and by 1989 the crown-corporation proposal was still just that.

Blueprint for the future

Domville continued to use the phrase 'public interest' to describe his institution and its work. He left it to Deputy Commissioner Macerola to use his administrative wizardry, pull a rabbit from the hat, and reduce the staff (and budget) by 10 per cent. With just over 1,000 employees, the 1983 expenditures were around $70 million, of which $31.6 million went for salaries (minus benefit plans), while total production was $31.1 million – $18.6 and $8.7 million respectively for the English and French wings and $3.8 million for sponsored film. Macerola intended to offer some one hundred staff 'golden handshakes,' cash incentives to early retirement. He thought an additional 10 per cent reduction in the infrastructure might be necessary, but that no lay-offs were yet imminent. 'No lay-offs' became his bond with the staff for the next five years.

Meanwhile, efficiency experts had been hard at work during these months analysing the structural problems. Their findings were: get better managers to manage, adopt a salary scale that closely links compensation to performance, and devise an action plan to save four to six million dollars by eliminating surplus staff, reducing temporary employees and permanent staff.[83] One item received immediate attention: one year and $1 million later, management had retired forty-nine employees, thereby effecting a long-term savings of $8 million.

Macerola rolled up his sleeves and planned to close eight distribution offices over the next eighteen months,[84] and in spite of the board of governors' misgivings, to support Distribution chief Litwack's plan to introduce user-fees for Film Board material, now being recorded on half-inch home video cassettes. The hope was that Distribution would begin to pay for itself and raise the funds to enable the organization to copy enough material on video to meet public demand. The fees came at last in 1988.

Both Domville and Macerola thought they had found the magic solution to end the distribution problem once and for all – to establish a channel dedicated to home distribution of Canadian films that were not readily available on existing television services. This 'dedicated channel' idea became a fixation upon which the organization spent considerable time and money over the next five years. A variation of the idea included the Electronic Film Library Project, with the Film Board as part of a consortium including provincial educational broadcasters. Subscribers were to receive a catalogue and have access to a multiplicity of programmes from the Film Board's library, which were to be shown in clusters and repeated.[85]

Fox was enthusiastic about the dedicated-channel idea, although the new CBC president since the summer of 1982, Pierre Juneau, resolutely opposed it. His predecessor, A.W. Johnson, had come up empty-handed in his quest for CBC II after appearing with Fox before Cabinet and an unsympathetic Prime Minister Trudeau.[86] Juneau was doggedly determined to try again; thus, he refused to discuss the Film Board plan for a specialty channel when he joined the board of governors. The hard-nosed administrator said point-blank that the Film Board was not an experienced broadcaster like the CBC. Undeterred, the board members told Domville to prepare a presentation to the CRTC for a specialty-programming licence. So instead of working together to design such a service, as Fox wished, the two agencies continued their routine of working at cross purposes. By the spring of 1985, Juneau felt compelled to resign from the board of governors over this conflict of interest.[87]

The filmmakers refused to stand behind the commissioner's plan to start a film training centre or to bring in world-renowned talent to build a better public profile. Their resistance was not from spite. About half of English Production's funding was being devoted to the regions, and the Montreal core felt its strength dwindling steadily. Forty per cent of its funding was being used for 'creator-impelled' and experimental films, and the filmmakers were miffed that this amount was to drop to 30 per cent in 1984–5. They wondered too how revitalization was to proceed, if programme planning was to evolve around the perceived needs of audiences of women and children, while the emphasis on traditional 16-mm film was to lessen. Sandwiched somewhere in this plan was Domville's favoured child, the 'culturally authentic' feature film. The multi-purposed organization was careening toward the future, adding yet more purposes. The filmmakers suspected that the money to pay for all this was to come at the expense of their own priorities. If Domville was trying to lead, they were not ready to follow.

Few could deny that the institution needed to stand on new ground. One area that was especially promising was the multi-media studio, which was producing on average about one hundred Canadian Studies items on all aspects of Canadian culture in both official languages (sound filmstrips, slide sets, and multimedia kits) for young Canadians. There was collaboration with provincial educational bodies, and projects were being planned to ensure 'curriculum fit,' particularly to provide vocabulary-enrichment materials for second-language classes and immersion programmes. While these items did not draw the spotlight in the glamour world of film, they were examples of what the Film Board was doing right, steadily, and well during these psychologically austere times. They might also point to future destinations. Plans were also afoot to create an integrated computer-animation centre in co-operation with the CBC, the National Research Council, and university research centres. The Film Board had been one of the first bodies to use computer-assisted animation techniques in the late 1960s, but had not kept up with advances in the field. It was hoped that with enough backing, this lost advantage could be regained. By the fall of 1985, French Animation, under Robert Forget, began to excel in the area.

The long tradition of reaching school-age children was continuing with little fanfare. A series of half-hour dramas based on the work of outstanding Canadian authors was planned for this market, as well as a cluster of films illustrating scientific principles, from the recently established science and technology production unit. One of the more spectacular ideas came from a British Columbia geography teacher, Geoff Goodship, who convinced the Film Board to produce a five-by-one-metre map of Canada as it might be seen by satellite, 1,000 kilometres above Texas. A thousand sets cost the agency $300,000, and each sold for $175. The impressive map adorns numerous Canadian centres and schools across the country. Prime Minister Mulroney gave President Reagan the map as a gift at the Shamrock Summit of 1984, but thought better of using the photo opportunity, lest his gift of Canada to the United States be misinterpreted by the citizens of both countries as a harbinger of what the future might bring.

But monies used for one area often meant that another suffered. The laboratory, once known as one of the finest in the world, lost its leadership position, as it was forced to absorb a disproportionate share of the budgetary cuts. Many of its excellent technicians, whose needs were as palpable as those in production, lived with the daily frustration of not having the best tools to do a job well. Others chose early retirement, leaving the laboratory in decline, struggling to regain its reputation.

Leading-edge films of the eighties

If one follows the evolution of some notable productions of the early eighties, it might be said glibly that adversity is the climate from which good films are made. This assertion is incidental to the fact that good work (and not such good work) has always characterized the Film Board. If, on one level, the bureaucratic pitfalls and institutional imperatives were daunting, on another, the filmmakers largely agreed that the dynamism of the place lay in their freedom to conceive and create the film programme.

The Last Days of Living, directed by Malca Gillson in 1980, was superficially akin to George Dufaux's *Au bout de mon âge*, some five years earlier. Here, in contrast to Dufaux's images of the despair of dying without dignity, the director observed the functioning of the Palliative Care Unit at Montreal's Royal Victoria Hospital. Techniques of listening, sharing, touching, and playing music reflect the difference between humane and uncaring treatment of the terminally ill. The subject of death is one of the most difficult in documentary, and Gillson made it accessible to both professionals and general audiences without becoming maudlin. A few cynics at

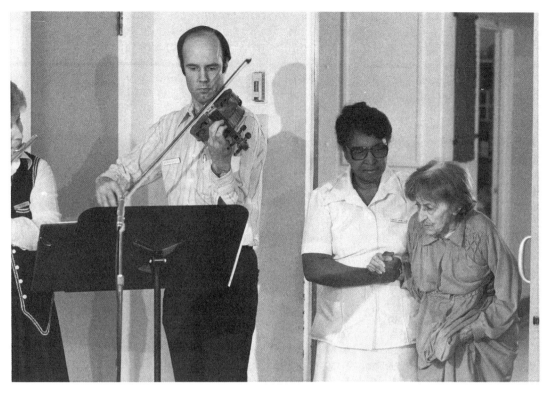

In observing the functioning of a hospital's palliative-care unit, *The Last Days of Living* (1980) treats the difficult subject of death without being maudlin.

the Film Board found *The Last Days of Living* a perfect analogy for the organization's condition.

After the Axe ($452,017) was a Toronto regional co-production with the CBC in 1981, directed by Sturla Gunnarsson. It was a variation of the docudrama, in that the lead was an actor, while the rest of the 'cast' played themselves. This Oscar-nominated story was about a manager, a composite character who, like a quarter of a million other executives a year in North America, had lost his job. His loss went deeper than employment, and the film shows how management self-help groups (here, one tied closely to fundamentalist Christianity) often succeed in helping executives find self-esteem and then work. The contrast between the 'scripted' recovery and the real ex-executives in a New York City self-help centre is perhaps too great for the viewer to accept without posing questions about dynamic and undynamic personalities. The film succeeds best in puncturing the social myth of managers not being subject to unemployment, for they too are part of the comtemporary throw-away society.

A film that hopscotched the programming process turned out to be one of the surprise hits of 1982. *Gala* was to have been a nationally televised gathering of eight of Canada's leading dance companies at the National Arts Centre in May 1981. Because of a last-minute technicians' strike, the television show was cancelled, and the Film Board decided to rush into the gap. Directors Cynthia Scott, Michael McKennirey, and John N. Smith recorded the world-class performances and took cameras backstage, before and after the event. The net effect was a stunning documentary that showed the in-

Flamenco at 5:15 (1983) – an Oscar-winner – moves seamlessly, in sight and sound, with the uninhibited flamenco rhythms shared by a teacher and her students.

tensity of creative performance as well as the many human aspects associated with, but rarely seen in, the making of art. *Gala* ($810,934) became the Film Board's pre-eminent dance film.

But the highest honours, an Oscar, went to a dance film, *Flamenco at 5:15* ($142,457), directed by Cynthia Scott in 1983. More than an impressionistic observation of a flamenco dance class at the National Ballet School of Canada, this documentary seems to ebb and flow with the very flamenco rhythms that teacher and students communicate with uninhibited joy and zest. The viewer forgets that someone is recording the event with a camera; the scene is dominated by the sensuality of music and dance, as each earnest interpreter plays out his or her moment in the spotlight as if no other moment like it will ever come again. In the tradition of the 'seamless' documentary, it is wonderful to behold the union of image, colour, sound, and movement as a single phenomenon.

A 5-minute film by brothers André and Jacques Leduc, *Zea* ($73,585), is an amazing live-action trick shot. Using a high-speed (400 feet per second) camera, a single object metamorphoses, confounding then delighting the viewer's eye. This short found a most unlikely market, the business world, where it is employed as the perfect vehicle to inaugurate think sessions in a group environment. *Zea* won a special prize at Cannes in 1982.

In the 1981–2 *Annual Report*, Domville claimed his organization's prerogative was the leading-edge film, which private film producers could not consistently afford to make. Such productions were not moneymakers, hence the Film Board had the field to itself, since the commercial sector was

Zea (1981) is an amazing live-action trick shot in which a single object metamorphoses, confounding then delighting the viewer's eye.

unlikely to scream 'foul,' even if some of the public did. Controversy was no stranger to Studio D, which by now had become well established as the only permanent women's film unit in the world and in 1981 had begun to participate in the federal Women's Program. That same year, veteran filmmaker Bonnie Sherr Klein took on the contentious issue of pornography in her documentary *Not a Love Story* ($503,519). She had begun her examination of the phenomenon as a parent who resented the way soft-core pornography on corner-store bookshelves confronted both her and her young daughter. Her investigative technique was simple: she and stripper Linda Lee Tracey embarked on a consciousness-raising quest, though Toronto critic Jay Scott called it uncharitably an 'unenlightening learn-a-long.' They descended into the demi-monde of pornographic commerce, from sleaze-parlour peep shows to fetid strip joints to Tracey's own willingness to pose provocatively before female soft-core pornographic photographer Suze Randall. (The Film Board later banned the still photo of this event.) The journey of exploration hit rock bottom as the filmmaker included a brief glimpse of a scene of imminent child pornography.

The purpose of the 'journey' was to ask questions about what pornography is, how many different forms it takes, and how it affects all aspects of social relations. More queries than answers resulted in leaving the viewer with a rather one-sided view of the subject. The on-screen interviews were weighted toward a feminist perspective which articulated that love, compassion, and responsibility were far more preferable than cool indifference toward sex as an object in itself. Unfortunately, the impression is that most of the men who appeared in the film were purveyors of pornography and were interested in it as a financial commodity alone, so there was no discussion of 'degree' in the debate. Responsible individuals who approve of erotica (non-violent artistic use of the human body) were not given a platform, nor was there reference to the United States Supreme Court decision on the parallel question of obscenity, which it said was determined by whether or not there was socially redeeming value in a work.

Nothing like *Not a Love Story* had ever come from the Film Board. Commercial distributors were quick to exploit its box-office potential. Some dubious observers thought that middle-class Canada flocked to see it less because of interest in the debate, than to view its sexually explicit material in a context that was permissible to that class. Saskatchewan's Censor Board banned it; the Ontario Censor Board refused to classify it and thereby effected the same end. The Film Board decided to appeal the Ontario decision by using the new Canadian Charter of Rights.[88] Undaunted, in the following year, an estimated 40,000 adults saw it in Ontario at three hundred private screenings, in spite of one Toronto press report that referred to it as the ultimate use of film as a panacea.[89] Meanwhile, it had opened in New York on 8–9 June 1982 for government leaders, the film community, and in a benefit for *Ms. Magazine*. Some time later, however, it was 'withdrawn from the American market following an inappropriate theatrical use of the film by the distributor.'[90] After a nine-month commercial run in Montreal, it was becom-

Not a Love Story (1981) views the world of pornography from one feminist angle. This controversial documentary by Bonnie Sherr Klein (right) contributed to the initiation by women's groups of anti-pornography activities.

ing the largest-grossing film in Film Board history. If it was effective in prompting public reflection and dialogue, Klein believed that *Not a Love Story* contributed to the surge in popular-press coverage of the pornography question and the initiation by women's groups of anti-pornography activities, including legislation to control pornography itself.[91]

In March 1982 another documentary from Studio D began its distribution life as what the board of governors called the 'hottest film since *Not a Love Story.*' Terri Nash directed *If You Love This Planet* ($70,117), which became part of the burgeoning nuclear-disarmament-related activities of the early eighties. It is a 26-minute lecture on the dangers of nuclear war, delivered by Dr Helen Caldicott of the Physicians for Social Responsibility, and was meant to be screened at the United Nations' Disarmament Conference. To boost the visually uninteresting footage, Nash inserted twenty-two different nuclear explosions and some previously unreleased ghastly newsreel clips of Hiroshima survivors. The impact on the viewer is appalling, reminiscent of Churchill's famous remark about the atomic bomb as 'the Second Coming in wrath.' The focus

cuts from shots of the transfixed Caldicott audience to the grisly footage whose impact is meant to mesmerize the viewer of the film as well. The pièce de résistance was Nash's intercutting of a Second World War propaganda item, *Jap Zero*, starring Ronald Reagan as the eager pilot who wants to get a crack at bombing the enemy. Nash, a devotee of the Grierson tradition of public-service filmmaking, never blinked as she defended *If You Love This Planet* as being very much in the other Grierson tradition of using propaganda as education. She wore her heart on her sleeve and did not intend this 'advocacy' film to give quarter to those who argue for the proliferation of nuclear weapons in the name of security.

After the CBC rejected *If You Love This Planet* for national telecast that spring, members of the board asked the CBC to explain its refusal in writing. A few months later, they were told: 'because it takes a strong position on nuclear arms and does not give a balanced and objective view of the subject.' Furthermore, the CBC told Domville that they could not counter the film's one-sidedness, since they had had difficulty in assembling a discussion panel that would include persons who favoured nuclear war.[92]

Politics intervened in the wake of absurdity. The United States Department of Justice issued an order, in 1983, under the provisions of the Foreign Agents Registration Act of 1938, requiring the American distributors of this and two other Film Board films, *Acid Rain: Requiem or Recovery* and *Acid from Heaven*, to register as agents of a foreign government. Distributors were to label these as 'political propaganda' and to report who was seeing them. The law had been all but ignored for decades, until the Americans threatened to apply it to several Film Board sex-education films in the late sixties, *Phoebe*, *The Game*, *The Merry Go Round*, and *The World of Three*, because United States conservative influences opposed the use of films in sex education. At that time, the Department of Justice had asked five

If You Love This Planet (1982), featuring a lecture by Dr Helen Caldicott on the dangers of nuclear war, stands in the Grierson tradition of using propaganda as education.

American distributors for information about the Canadian agency and had begun to determine if they were required to register under the Foreign Agents Registration Act of 1938. Before the matter got out of hand, External Affairs probably resolved the affair quietly with the Americans, and the films were distributed freely.[93] In 1974, the justice department had made a similar decision about the *Challenge for Change* film from 1972, *That Gang of Hoodlums?* by Robert Nichol, which contrasted a militant and non-militant protest demonstration in Ottawa. At that time, the Film Board withdrew it without fanfare.[94]

External Affairs was not about to intervene in the case of *If You Love This Planet*, in part because the department had opposed inclusion of the Reagan sequence, since it was against protocol to embarrass a sitting president. Meanwhile, the film won an Oscar for best documentary short of 1982, and the exuberant Nash began her acceptance speech with a thanks to the Department of Justice. Only then did the CBC telecast it on *The Journal*. The public reaction was only sixty

letters to the Film Board, most of which were positive. By comparison, *Not a Love Story* had drawn ten (generally supportive) letters a week over the year.

A few months later, a California federal district judge issued an injunction against the justice department. Many hoped this would defuse the issue, but the government pursued its case resolutely to the Supreme Court. In Canada, it was alleged that *If You Love This Planet* played a small but instrumental role in the genesis of Prime Minister Trudeau's 'peace initiative'; he invited Dr Caldicott to the Liberal party policy session on international affairs and mentioned her often thereafter. Francis Fox was unperturbed by the hullabaloo and thought this film not only reflected the national soul, but also showed that there was hope for the Film Board.[95]

Acid Rain: Requiem or Recovery and *Acid from Heaven* were two sponsored items the Film Board had commissioned to private producers on behalf of Environment Canada. The latter work was unremarkable, a filmed slide presentation of how one man lost his livelihood as a result of acid rain, while the former was a more soundly researched scientific documentary that explained the sources and dangers of the acid precipitation. The Reagan presidency came to be associated with doing little but paying lip-service to the principle of studying acid rain, despite complaints from the northeastern United States and from Canada, who were down wind of the coal-burning states that were generally believed to be generating this pollution. The reactions to these acid-rain films were evidence of just how sensitive American authorities were to both the issue and the cost of addressing it. The Reagan administration's treatment of these productions may have become a symbol of its legacy of deaf-ear and blind-eye attitudes to the accelerating environmental destruction.

Meanwhile, the three films became *causes célèbres* for civil-liberties groups and environmental organizations; Senator Edward Kennedy rallied publicly to support them.

The case went against the Film Board in a 5–3 decision, in April 1987, in which the Supreme Court upheld the justice department's argument that the 1938 law was constitutional.[96] By this time, the notoriety of the case had probably been advantageous. If a few thought that the Film Board was paying a high price for its 'leading-edge' work, others were happy to have had 'million-dollar advertising' for nothing and to have put the organization squarely in the Grierson tradition of using the documentary as a social animator.

The $3.6 million *War* series of seven one-hour documentaries made a stunning impact on both television and classroom audiences in 1983. Filmed in ten countries with the cooperation of six nations' armed forces, *War* was a sobering analysis of mankind's oldest anti-social activity, narrated with wryness, occasionally edged with cynicism, by on-camera host and analyst Gwynne Dyer. The conclusion became self-evident from the first film: that war no longer serves its purpose of settling disputes between nations. The films were directed variously by Barbara Sears (*The Road to Total War*), Paul Cowan (*Anybody's Son Will Do* and *The Deadly Game of Nations*), Michael Bryans and Tina Viljoen (*The Profession of Arms*), Tina Viljoen (*Notes on a Nuclear War*), Douglas Kiefer (*Keeping the Old Game Alive*), and the trio of Donna Dudinsky, Judith Merritt, and Barbara Sears (*Goodbye War*).

It is remarkable that at the time of filming, a new generation of Communist leadership in the Soviet Union was struggling behind closed doors to win control of the govern-

The premise of the seven-hour series *War* (1983) is that war can no longer settle disputes between nations. (Series host and analyst Gwynne Dyer, centre, on Israel's Golan Heights)

ment, having reached a similar conclusion about the usefulness of conventional and nuclear war, as well as about the Cold War. Within five years, they were in power, and world events made the idea of Cold War and nuclear Armageddon more remote than at any time since the atomic age had begun. This series, telecast in Europe as well as North America, was timely in the way it contributed to changing how Western nations and people think about the dreadful subject.

Fox's film policy and the end of Domville's term

In spite of the strength of a number of productions, it was felt internally, by the fall of 1983, that the weakest link in the Film Board was the programming process. There was an attempt to make film projects of programmes for specific audiences rather than the product of individual initiatives. Ideally, subjects would be recommended by programming committees of filmmakers, marketers, producers, and the public.

Ominously, Fox's department ignored this shift as well as other Film Board policy papers geared to finding new stratagems. All eyes turned to the minister's Strategic Overview, which dealt with the expected proliferation of systems and services in the coming decade, and its description of culture as an 'industry,'[97] The document revealed what had been propelling his department's and the government's thinking over the last decade. Communications, thrust from a national to a worldwide grid, was expected to constitute the single largest growth area in the Canadian economy. If globalization of culture threatened the Canadian culture industry, the transition to increased competition presented a tremendous opportunity to reach larger audiences. Fox hoped existing institutions like the Film Board and the CBC would adapt and aggressively market world-class products that reflected the Canadian identity and heritage.[98] He expected them to do this as they improved efficiency and accountability.

The gentle commissioner had been braving the slings and arrows of the past five years with fortitude and with as positive a disposition as he could muster. His term was up in January 1984, and feeling intrepid, he made it known to Fox that he was prepared to serve again and lead the organization into this new era. The board accepted his terms for staying, and it was finally up to the minister to approve or disapprove of his renewal. Fox remained silent and unavailable. By October, Domville decided that 'no answer' meant 'no' and he told the governors he would leave upon expiration of his mandate, three months later.[99]

Fox wanted to change horses. It had been understood that the commissioner would have to be in accord with his film policy as a condition for reappointment. Domville had an idea of its contents and indicated that he had some doubts about transferring the Film Board's international cultural activities to the newly renamed and expanded Canadian Film Development Corporation, 'Telefilm Canada.' With memories of the 'phoney freelance' court case and its outcome and the sorry Applebaum-Hébert performance and report, coupled with the sagging morale of the agency, Fox hoped another commissioner could do better.

Accepting this judgment, Domville recommended a single successor to the board of governors' search committee: Patrick Watson, a savvy, high-profile, nationally recognized personality. Watson, it will be recalled, had excoriated the Applebaum-Hébert report. He would brook no fools and most certainly would both provide continuity and defend the Film Board's best interests. Whether he would undertake cheerfully the slimming-down process was another question. The governors recommended Watson, but Fox informed them that he wanted to wait some months until his Film and Video Policy had been considered by the Cabinet. He told the search committee to suspend its activities; Deputy Commissioner Macerola became Acting Film Commissioner.

Fox had caused a vacuum because there was now no one with whom his department could deal officially. In short, Macerola was put in precisely the same position as Grant McLean in 1966. It would be up to him to convince the minister to keep him on. Domville drew Fox's attention to the low state of staff morale over the uncertainties of succession and the feared consequences of the forthcoming National Film and Video Policy. Fox tried to mollify the board members at a December meeting and reiterated that the Film Board remained a vital and central element of public cultural policy. He promised a final decision on the government's film policy in a few months; or, in a worst-case scenario, the delay would only be until the coming election period.[100] His unspoken message was clear enough – this was not the right moment for Patrick Watson to become commissioner. Watson agreed some months later to accept a vacant seat on the board of governors. In 1989 he became president of the CBC. Domville bid adieu to what he said had been the most interesting period of his professional career. As he put it wistfully some years later, 'The job of Film Commissioner was the only one I ever really wanted.'

Domville's legacy

These had been trying years for the Film Board, perhaps the most difficult of its existence. Domville had inherited an establishment that had grown less by design than by accident; some tongues wagged at his failure to have taken the hard choice of cutting staff despite the repercussions. Critics could not know that Ottawa had tied his hands. He was not a dragon-slayer and did his best while the institution lumbered on, the Oscars notwithstanding. By 1984, it was the familiar story of idle filmmakers waiting for production funds and the commercial sector waiting for the patient to die, hoping that when the last will was read, its money would go to themselves. The government had no intention of closing shop, though it wanted belt-tightening and restructuring. That Domville would not be entrusted with either responsibility was a great personal disappointment, yet he looked back with some satisfaction at the tangible things he had accomplished, especially the promotion of dramatic features. When he had first arrived, the shooting stage was hardly being used; now there were features and drama production on it all year round.[101] Another significant contribution was his insistence that the minutes of board meetings be opened to public scrutiny. The years of secrecy had contributed to the atmosphere of confrontation and misunderstanding between management and staff. Domville thought that maximum openness could promote closer cooperation in a public institution. The whole scenario of guarding the institution's innermost secrets had seemed reminiscent of the story of the far-away aborigines who closely guarded the tribal secret for generations until an outsider finally learned it by stealth – it was that there was no secret.

13

Not with a Bang or a Whimper:
Approaching a Second Half-century

The National Film and Video Policy

In his capacity as acting commissioner, Macerola met with Minister Fox a number of times, from January to May 1984, to discuss the National Film and Video Policy. The bad news was that with the production of sponsored films about to disappear to the private sector forever, Fox also determined that the Film Board should cease being their executive producer. The good news was that he said he intended to ignore the Applebaum-Hébert guillotine. The Film Board would continue as a public producer of film and video.

By the time Fox's Film and Video Policy was unveiled in May, Macerola believed he had helped to change its wording so that it became an 'auberge Espagnol,' that is, one could find in it whatever one brought to it. He feared that some unfriendly persons around the minister might read the policy in such a way as to argue that the final curtain was being brought down on the organization. By reading the policy another way, Macerola believed he had found in it a chance to fight for the Film Board's survival and to restore its credibility.[1]

Corporate language, form, and substance were the watchwords of the decade, and so Macerola assembled a Five-Year Operational Plan to complement Fox's goals. No doubt, this influenced the minister to choose him in May as the successor to Domville, since he wanted an administrator who would cut back on personnel and infrastructure without stirring up a hornet's nest of publicity. Around this time, Macerola stopped sporting his characteristic continental French-style leather jacket for more conventional attire. He was still his bearded buoyant self, with sparkling blue eyes and an ever-ready high-pitch, infectious laugh, which made it seem that however glum the situation, there was mirth to be found somewhere.

Publicly, the commissioner employed understatement to call the Fox policy a forward-looking document and a major challenge. A less sanguine staff generally considered it a coffin in which the organization would be laid to rest, Fox's assurances notwithstanding. Why, then, they wondered, was the minister proposing a bill to relieve the film commissioner of his role as first counsellor to the government? Why was Telefilm Canada (the old CFDC) assuming responsibility for promoting Canadian cultural products abroad, leaving the Film Board to market its own products? They took the half-truth of retrenchment and made it the whole truth of collapse. If fear is what the Ottawa masters had wanted to inject into the institution in order to make it shape up, they succeeded only too well – most inside thought this was the end.

Fox kept his word, however, even if the

288

François Macerola (film commissioner, 1984–8)
bit the bullet and developed a five-year plan to
cut back on full-time staff, convincing the
government that the NFB was learning to make
do with less as it reached its 50th year.

Film Board was intended to remain on the margin of the industrial model his department was promoting. His policy was meant to stake out a two-pronged territorial claim for the coming decades: (1) to address the cultural and social needs of minority and specialized audiences, that is, to undertake film and video production in those areas that the private sector ignored; and (2) to become a literary and intellectual essayist, an instrument for the high-quality, in-depth, occasionally philosophic exploration of fundamental issues, trends, and concerns of importance to Canada and the world. In continuing the unique Canadian practice of public-sector activity, the Film Board was to reflect Canada's bilingual, multicultural, and regional reality.[2]

These were fine sentiments, but how could

the institution survive without additional substantive funding? Getting down to basics, it all had a depressingly familiar ring: the policy called for more energy to be channelled into research and development, the so-called frontiers of film and video technology. It also advocated the contracting out of most filmmaking work and technical services, except those necessary for research, development, and film training. Fox also intended to transfer to the Department of Supply and Services and the Public Archives the extraneous appendages of the Still Photography Division and Film Board Archives respectively.[3]

Some doubters recognized the mailed fist of the Applebaum-Hébert report in the velvet glove of Fox's pious assurances. They worried about the fate of headquarters' core production staff if freelancers in the regions were to do most of the filmmaking. Fox's policy was silent here, except that he expected that over the next five years, some $10 million in savings would be ploughed back into the operational budget. Macerola promised that the Film Board would do what it already did best – create productions of unassailable excellence and pioneer the cutting edge of the future in film and video. An unpleasant surprise lay ahead: the government declared that the outcome of savings could not be transformed into income for production.[4]

Losing the sponsored film was a symbolic blow, since it meant removal of one of the major underpinnings upon which the whole edifice rested. Yet it also meant the end of the perennial aggravated complaints of the private sector, whose lobbyists had in turn won over the lobby-sensitive politicians. Grierson's advice to drop them had taken almost two decades to sink in. Macerola and English Production chief Peter Katadotis thought the trade-off was worth it: to give up the income in exchange for peace and the chance to reestablish the institution's credibility. Others feared, however, that without the sponsored films the government might abandon its political will to keep a Film Board.[5] They also expected the production standards for sponsored work to decline precipitously.

In a stinging denunciation, Jacques Godbout railed against the Film and Video Policy, claiming that the minister had abandoned the national character of Canadian productions in favour of the Canadian-American Auto Pact model. In short, Canadians would assemble American-style films, mostly fictional dramas (television series he called 'film disco'), made in Quebec or Ontario. As all this applied to the Film Board, Godbout found the perfect simile, when he charged that there was obviously little concern for the Film Board's 'haute couture' prestige enterprise in a ready-to-wear market. By producing television films in Canada for American consumers, he stated ironically, 'our exported films will earn money and will be seen by Canadians who watch the American networks.' Canada, he concluded, an economically underdeveloped country, will have ensured its cultural underdevelopment as well.

In a variation of this theme elsewhere, Godbout underscored the fact that the government defined Canadian content according to the nationality of the collaborators on a film and not on the basis of the authenticity of its content, as was the case in Australia. The 'policy,' he mourned, had more to do with industry than with culture. And money, which fuelled industry, had neither language, culture, nor pride. He demonstrated how the Auto Pact paradigm was firmly set: without a market sufficient to support a national cinema, Canada would negotiate with the American majors for an assembly industry, in exchange for Canadian patronage of their cinemas. Thus would an authentic cultural product be lost. And culture, he reminded the blinkered technocrats, legitimizes the state.[6]

Few persons knew that Fox was having his problems too, and that in order to get his policy through Cabinet before a planned fall election, he had had to design a scheme that would not cause confrontation with the United States. As he put it succinctly (and with a twinge of bitterness) a few years later, 'There was a United States lobbyist in the Cabinet – Canada's Department of External Affairs.' Like his predecessors, he had toyed with the idea of imposing quotas and of redressing the imbalance in the production and distribution of Canadian film and video. Predictably, External Affairs advised against conflict and warned of the danger of U.S. retaliation. The Liberal government, continuing its popularity decline and moving toward an espousal of Free Trade with its neighbour, was certainly not going to choose to initiate a Canada-United States clash prior to an election. Fox felt his hands tied in Cabinet, and the Film and Video Policy was the best he could do.[7]

Fox may have had his problems in Cabinet, but the proposed policy plummeted the Film Board into an abyss of despair. Macerola probably felt more like a hangman than the leader of a cultural organization. The only promise he could reiterate and keep was that there would be no lay-offs, but this did not mollify the distraught staff. Before the election could occur, the Ottawa scene transformed itself. Pierre Trudeau stepped down as prime minister, and with John Turner succeeding him there was a cabinet shuffle in May. Fox turned over both the Communications portfolio and the Film and Video Policy to Ed Lumley, who told Macerola to proceed with his Five Year Operational Plan. In the election that September, Canadians rejected the fledgling Turner and his Liberal government and handed the Progressive Conservatives under Brian Mulroney a mandate to govern for a full four-year term.[8] Marcel Masse became the new minister of communications in September and took the Film and Video Policy to his bosom as his own.

In October Macerola unveiled his Five-Year Operational Plan, which fit perfectly into the Fox (now Masse) Film and Video Policy. Its greatest innovation was that future production was to be undertaken after market-research methods were applied to audience needs, heralding the end of the era of exclusive director-originated programming. In short, the distribution branch was to disappear and its marketing operations were to become fully integrated into English and French Production, with distribution services now falling under Technical Services, headed by Marcel Carrière. To reach national audiences, the hope was to undertake distribution contracts with public cultural institutions like libraries and community colleges as well as with private companies. One of the first effects of this reorganization was to reduce the number of distribution offices from twenty-six to twelve. Regional production and distribution centres, now called Canadian Audio-Visual Centres, continued in Vancouver, Toronto, and Halifax. International operations were to shrink to only three offices – Paris, London, and New York.

This major reorganization signalled the resolution of the decades-old distribution imbroglio. Soon statistics would show that in 1983–4, video-cassette sales surpassed 16-mm sales for the first time. For the same period, non-theatrical distribution of videos and films reached an all-time high, with video bookings predominating. The figures for the balance of the decade would tell the story: from a modest beginning of 702 video cassettes sold in 1977–8 (compared to sales of 10,304 copies of 16-mm film), there would be 15,744 video cassettes sold in 1988–9 (compared to 1,302 copies of 16-mm film). The video format was not only more accessible, it was also cheaper than film. Purchase prices fell so much that a one-hour 16-mm film that once cost $400 now cost only $79 on video. Most staff appreciated that the five-year plan had recognized and responded to the changed distribution environment.

As for filmmaking itself, the story was different. Filmmakers were antagonistic to the plan's call for 70 per cent of annual production to be done by freelancers, with the bal-

ance being left to the core group at headquarters. They were also concerned about Macerola's anticipated expansion of a non-academic practical apprenticeship and training programme for the next generation of filmmakers. While there was a chance for the best of the new talent to make first and second masterworks at the Film Board, there was virtually no hope for their permanent employment. The serious question was who would replace the veterans as their ranks thinned over time? The commissioner had no answer, but was more concerned with the here and now – he wanted a corporate style of thinking to penetrate the organization, and his plan called for numerous title changes. The board of governors was soon the board of trustees, the heads of English and French Production became Director General of English (and French) Program, 'films' became 'products,' and similar changes in nomenclature followed throughout the agency, giving a corporate label as well as a sense of newness to everything. Not least, the new corporate mentality encouraged the staff to feel that the entire operation was now leaner and cost-recoverable. The administration expected annual sales of $1.75 million. In short, everyone was aware that everything was to have a price tag.

The Macerola plan also envisioned inauguration of the era of the accelerated 'golden handshake,' where early-retirement packages were intended to reduce numbers of both creative and technical staff. At the same time, the laboratory and shooting stage were to be opened to the private sector in a facilities-sharing scheme of co-productions. The net result of this latter change was stress: by the end of the decade, a skeleton technical staff had to cope with extensive demands on production services owing to the success of the Program to Assist Films and Filmmakers in the Private Sector and its French equivalent.

As the staff tried to digest the coming impact of the five-year plan, the document's last words implied that the long-dreaded staff cuts had to occur even if there were to be no lay-offs: 'The time has come to make choices. While some decisions will be harder than others, it is the price we must pay if we are to redefine a National Film Board that is more closely integrated into the cultural community and is on the leading edge of a new film culture.'[9]

The commissioner defended his policy on national radio a month later. The Film Board had just suffered a budgetary cut of $1.5 million, though this was not as severe as that suffered by the other cultural agencies. True, the government had removed close to $20 million of the institution's income-generating power over the next three years; however, he believed he could live with the cuts without having to reduce filmmaking. The goal of 70/30 per cent freelance/permanent staff was fair, because as 'new blood' the freelancers would end the 'beige and drab' films. Over five years, he predicted, the number of permanent directors would have to fall by nearly 50 per cent, from 54 to 30. And this did occur.[10]

Many on staff were convinced that Macerola was closing up shop, but the filmmakers would not go down without a fight. Guy Coté, who had spent a professional lifetime at the Film Board, wrote a masterful document in February 1985, charging that Macerola's plan seemed to go against the very nature of the institution. Using statistics, he attempted a historical synthesis to show that the present situation not only was the outcome of the Applebaum-Hébert report, but also stemmed from a chain of government film policies dating back to 1970.

Nationally, he insisted, the half-million Canadian bookings a year by about 50,000 clients were proof of the relevance of the Film Board to Canadian schools. Students had always been the principal Film Board audience and it was they who had the greatest need for the public-service film. But by turning over sponsored film to private industry, the government was cutting the percentage of federal expenditures on the agency to about

half of what it had been in 1968. Worse, in constant dollars as a percentage of Gross National Product, the Film Board's operating budget was 18 per cent *less* than in 1958. It was consuming a modest 4.4 per cent of federal expenditures on the arts, representing only 4 per cent of the billion-dollar film and television industry. Yet its prizes, international recognition, and innovations were far ahead of what others were achieving. Coté employed a sleight of hand here: sponsored films were not what the students generally saw; the money that sponsored films generated had, however, allowed the production of many public-service films that were school-oriented.

Coté's most revealing numerical juxtaposition was his thesis that the government's transfer of funds was going from one subsidized enterprise (the Film Board) to another subsidized, more speculative enterprise, called the private sector – an industry of freelance entrepreneurs. The private-sector production budget, created through tax incentives and other legal means, was traditionally 'skimmed' by the producers' astute use of 'administrative costs,' he charged. He pointed a finger at the Film Board's management and administration costs ($9 million) and at distribution services ($13 million), which were consuming close to half as much as the whole $50.6 million production-programme budget. His conclusion: the place was overmanaged, the proof being that since 1970 it had become more and more expensive to have the technocrats impose and increase bureaucratic control procedures. To add salt to the wound, he noted that Macerola's plan left the administrative structure untouched. In essence, then, technocracy had replaced the ad-hocracy. Critics might argue, however, that the latter's strength had never been greater than its staying power.

Headquarters had become weakened, Coté continued, since there were now nine production centres producing in two languages in six regions. Thus, regionalization had particularly diminished the national mission of English Production. Coté proposed a radical solution: that the provincial governments put up monies to support regionalization in order for headquarters to get on with the ideological mission of reflecting national concerns and international representation. In short, close the regional offices, few of whose films (except for animation) had merited national or international attention. If Coté was speaking heresy, he was reflecting the broadest spectrum of the headquarters filmmakers, who felt the centre collapsing. Their sentiment continued to be widely shared in 1989, although the defenders of regionalization claim it promotes a healthy competition between themselves and headquarters, particularly on the English side.

Macerola's planned high-profile research and development facility also irked Coté. How, he wondered, could the institution go through the training exercise and then tell those in its creative sectors that there was almost no possibility of employment or even of internal promotion? He chided that the Five Year Plan should have enunciated a more forceful mandate: to produce public-service films and to enlist the passion for filmmaking in the service of Canada's truth. Management's most egregious error was the assumption that the free-market competition and profit-oriented enterprise constituted the most favourable environment for the making of public-service films.[11]

Some months later, the union published a refutation of both the Applebaum-Hébert report and the National Film and Video Policy, using these same arguments. The author, Sandra Gathercole, warned of the 'insidious erosion' of the institution, implied by all these policies, something akin to the Chinese death of a thousand cuts. Over the years, every time the Film Board responded to criticism by accommodation, she stated, it weakened its own position. She hoped to appeal to the historical legacy of the Conservatives to communications policy, and to convince the new government to disinherit the Liberal

film policy, loosen the purse-strings, and expand public production for television. The board of trustees rejected the union's plea to scrap Macerola's Five Year Plan and renew the vitality of the permanent core; instead they supported Macerola's starvation diet. Their concern was the agency's creative drift and lack of inspiration to make films that were not being made elsewhere.[12]

The union critics forgot another truth about Canadian politics: in the past two decades, there had been little difference between Liberals and Conservatives, other than style. It might even be argued that federal politicians are relatively powerless, despite the media's focus on them for their showmanlike qualities. The critical long-range decisions are economic, and broadcasting was becoming a billion-dollar-plus transnational industry. The irony was that the Liberals had designed the Free Trade scenario (while the Conservatives opposed it), and then, when the Conservatives became the government, the shoe was on the other foot, with the Conservatives pushing free trade while the Liberals opposed it. Likewise, film policy and government investment in film culture have evolved according to a market-place-oriented, industrial model that is not predicated upon catering to Canadian audiences exclusively. Still, supporters of this model can point to a number of Canadian television series that are currently popular over the u.s. networks.

Brave plans needed action, and Macerola undertook a campaign to reinforce the institution's corporate image on Parliament Hill. He also criss-crossed the country, meeting Film Board employees, the public, politicians, and newspaper boards alike, all to generate a higher public profile. Joan Pennefather, his second-in-command (vice-commissioner, director of planning and later of corporate affairs), spent much of her time in Ottawa boosting the organization and, in the Film Board's progressive tradition, helped launch the Employment Equity Programme to guarantee women equal access to all sectors of activity at the institution. It was no easy task to plan for staff reduction while committing resources to affirmative action in the employment of women.[13]

The elusive dream: A Film Board television channel

Marcel Masse was unmoved by the union carping and told Macerola to get on with his Five Year Plan. He also approved of the institution's attempt to organize the non-profit Young Canada Television / Télé-jeunesse Canada, which planned to operate a cable channel for young viewers. The minister agreed to back a Film Board organizational loan to the fledgling corporation of a half-million, then an additional $300,000 to complete its preparations for a licence application to the CRTC. No one thought twice about the village-like aspect of Canadian cultural and political life: the letterhead declared that the chairman of the board was Francis Fox, with Yvon Deschamps and Ann Mortifee as the heads of the French and English channels respectively.

The CRTC hearings were stalled by yet another governmental examination of arts and culture in Canada, the Caplan-Sauvageau Commission. Its report, published in the spring of 1986, bolstered morale temporarily when it endorsed the Film Board as a 'feisty advocate of the public interest' and strongly encouraged the institution to continue its role as a public producer and distributor. There was also an appeal to television (both the CBC and commercial networks) to be a more effective carrier of Film Board documentary, educational, and children's films.[14] The Caplan-Sauvageau Commission found there was a serious deficiency in Canadian television: only 28 per cent of the programming available on English television was Canadian, and English-speaking teenagers spent 80 per cent of their time watching foreign programmes. Most surprising, French-speaking teens spent more than half their viewing time watching foreign pro-

grammes.[15] (This revelation led many to see the folly of Quebec's war of symbols, the complete restriction of English-language signs, when the real assimilation of French Canada was occurring daily via the melting-pot of American television.)

Such statistics provided no better argument for the type of channel the Film Board sought. The question was whether the organization was better advised to continue pursuing the possibilities of the youth channel, its own network, or perhaps a consortium. When the Department of Communications began backtracking on its promised start-up loan of $5 million, the banks reneged on their $5 million commitment, and the youth channel foundered in June 1987. The Film Board jumped immediately to TV Canada / Télécanada, a joint consortium based in British Columbia, which at least had an outside chance to win the licence. The Department of Communications supported the Film Board's expenditure of another half-million dollars to prepare the application. Pennefather presented the application in the summer of 1987 and learned that thirty-three cable companies and eleven broadcasters opposed the TV Canada application, including the Quebec cable companies, the Canadian Broadcast League, the Consumer's Association, and the CBC, which was still trying to win the licence for CBC II. The odds were too formidable, and on 30 November the CRTC rejected the TV Canada / Télécanada proposal. It was strike three and out for the Film Board's dream of its own satellite/cable-transmission outlet in the eighties.[16] Perhaps it was the wrong time to dream of relaunching a public organization in an era of privatization. The setback was not fatal; hereafter, the organization sought (and found) outlets on other cable networks at home and abroad, proving that when its films are good enough, others will pay to telecast them. The worldwide proliferation of cable-television channels may actually mean there are more opportunities than before for Film Board films to find audiences.

Ottawa: Where friends and foes meet

At the time the first application for Young Canada Television was being considered, another ominous cloud on the horizon appeared as the Conservative government's Neilsen report on culture and communications. This document stated that the Film Board's role could be carried out by slicing $20 million from its operating budget and transforming it into a training and research body. Masse thought this was going too far and, in ignoring the long knives, reaffirmed his support for the agency as a public film producer and distributor. There was no small irony in finding the minister protecting the Film Board from his own government, but having one friend in the right place made all the difference. Taking its cue from Masse, the board of trustees also rejected the Neilsen report in toto.[17] It was soon swept away in the regular torrent of paper flowing from Ottawa.

The board of trustees told Macerola to quit the cross-country political fence-mending and return to Montreal to look after internal management. The filmmakers were drifting after news that some 70 per cent of production funds had been pledged to go to freelancers exclusively.[18] Full-timers cringed at the trendy corporate phrase 'vision,' which was being used to explain the need for positioning the organization five years ahead of time. Their hunger was for leadership, a sense of belonging, and more production funding. Yet once back in Montreal, Macerola had to endure the cold-shoulder treatment at headquarters.

The Billy Bishop affair

Meanwhile at the Senate, there were disconsolate rumblings being heard at the Sub-committee on Veterans Affairs about the controversial 1982 film *The Kid Who Couldn't Miss* ($334,560), directed by Paul Cowan. In a well-orchestrated national campaign, those rumblings became an outpouring of 3,000 letters of rage on behalf of the servicemen and airmen who had risked and given their lives for Canada during wartime. The veterans were not only a formidable bunch of fighters – they also felt that the film was a slur on themselves and their fallen comrades. Their anger was white-hot because Cowan had called into question the heroic record of Billy Bishop, Canada's First World War air ace, who had been credited with seventy-two 'kills' in the carnage that had snuffed out the lives of 55,000 fliers and some ten million combatants from 1914 to 1918.

Cowan had become interested in Bishop while he was making *Stages*, a film about Canada's performing artists, famous and otherwise. The Broadway-bound *Billy Bishop Goes to War* made him think about investigating the 'underbelly of heroism,' and in its genesis, the Bishop film was to tell of the hero's glory, his gradual disillusionment, and his failure to cope with hero status.[19] While doing the research, Cowan stumbled upon tapes of pilots who had flown with Bishop's squadron, some of whom had nothing complimentary to say about the air ace; a few hinted that he may not have done everything he claimed. Cowan then learned there never was official confirmation for all of Bishop's 'kills' and particularly for the raid that earned Bishop the Victoria Cross, Britain's highest award for heroism. Further research led to people who doubted the Bishop record, but who would not go public to call the hero a liar or a cheat. The filmmaker pursued that angle by using a docudrama format, with actors playing actual persons and fact interwoven with entertainment. His method was to ask questions, rather than to make assertions. What he did assert, however, was the fact that Bishop was of more help to the cause alive than dead and that he was pulled from service to become a living incentive to encourage enlistment.[20]

By 1984 the veterans' outcry became audible as the issue was diverted from the question of heroism and its usefulness to the

The most sustained attack on any film in NFB history occurred over *The Kid Who Couldn't Miss* (1982), a docudrama about First World War air ace Billy Bishop (here posing next to his plane).

powers-that-be to whether Bishop was indeed a hero who deserved the Victoria Cross.[21] From here, the debate began its circumfluent journey that led it to the Senate Subcommittee on Veterans Affairs and the most sustained attack on any film in Film Board history. In a letter to the minister, Senator Marshall invited Macerola to answer questions before the subcommittee in the fall of 1985. The parliamentary rule was that the minister or his parliamentary secretary should answer any questions the Senate might put. If other sources were then necessary, the deputy minister could be called. Macerola had the status of deputy minister and did not have to appear until the others had testified. The board of trustees told him not to appear without the minister.

As a lawyer, Macerola was aware that Senator Marshall's invitation was precedent-

shattering. Traditionally, the government film commissioner was insulated by the minister so that he could carry out his duties without public or political interference. His public accountability extended to his readiness to appear annually before the Standing Committee on Culture and Communications in the House. But at this point, Masse had resigned his portfolio temporarily, while awaiting clearance on the charge that he had overspent the limit allowed for electioneering. While he was in 'Purgatory,' Benoît Bouchard was acting minister, and the staff of the Department of Communications thought it was better not to cause strife with the Liberal-controlled Senate; they told Macerola to accept the subcommittee's invitation.

The commissioner and Paul Cowan appeared before the Senate on 28 November

1985. Macerola tried to explain that, historically, Film Board productions had encouraged Canadians to question their destiny and place in the world. As for *The Kid Who Couldn't Miss*, the film raised pertinent questions about heroism and the people who became symbols of heroism in war. He refused to answer 'yes' to one senator's blunt question about the film, 'Aren't you ashamed of yourself?' and maintained that as commissioner he put the institution at the service of filmmaking and the Canadian public. To the chagrin of some senators, he thought it pertinent that the film asked the question, 'Do we really need heroes?' The senators were incredulous that such a question was 'in the national interest,' but they had forgotten that a long-lived Canadian trait, perhaps inspired by the fundamental role of weather in daily life, was to try to see things as they actually were, rather than how they might be. Little wonder then that afterwards Macerola drily reported to the board of trustees that he had been treated 'inelegantly.'

Cowan never denied the existence of Bishop's famous solo raid of 2 June 1917, which earned him the Victoria Cross, but used an actor to voice a compilation of legitimate questions that had the effect of puncturing the legend. The senators found Cowan's technique of blending documentary and drama to question heroism damaging to national image and pride. Senator Hartland Molson concluded that since this film suggested Bishop was a fraud, it was dishonest and not in the national interest.[22]

Macerola refused to withdraw *The Kid Who Couldn't Miss*, unless there was a factual error that could be proved. After much parrying, he was pleased when the committee accepted his recommendation that the film be labelled 'docudrama' so as not to confuse the viewers. He thought that would finish the affair, but it did not, since the Senate decided to reopen the inquiry in the summer of 1986. Veterans groups and the Bishop family meant to have the film withdrawn and destroyed and began legal proceedings, claiming that it did not satisfy the 'national interest' clause of the National Film Act. This was probably one of the rare times in the recent past when this most important clause was looked at with some earnestness by all concerned parties. The senators became more cantankerous in November 1986, when an article in the *Ottawa Citizen* seemed to treat them contemptuously. It was rumoured that, subsequently, one senator arranged a sizeable corporate donation for the War Amputees of Canada to continue fighting for the production's withdrawal.[23] Macerola, sensing the 'organized' nature of the veterans' campaign and their application to the Ontario Supreme Court for an injunction to have the work pulled, remained adamant in his refusal to suppress it.

By the summer of 1987, there was yet another new minister of communications, Flora MacDonald, member of Parliament for Kingston, where the Royal Military College was located. She told Macerola bluntly, 'Get rid of the problem, I'm fed up with it.' At headquarters in December, the commissioner met once again with H. Clifford Chadderton, the president of the War Amputees, who was on record with the statement, 'We shan't rest until Billy Bishop's memory is restored to its place in history.' Chadderton wanted the film re-edited; Macerola countered, suggesting a new film altogether as a take-it-or-leave-it proposition. The plaintiff took it. The Billy Bishop affair was on its way to being resolved once and for all, as the minutes of the Film Board read: 'there will be a historical portrait of the Canadian hero, Billy Bishop.' No filmmaker volunteered for it, however, and the documentary was going to have to be made as a private venture.

In retrospect, Macerola called the affair 'an interesting democratic experience' and believed he had had a moral obligation to explain to the public and Senate why *The Kid Who Couldn't Miss* should have been made.

He felt that he maintained the authority of the commissioner and that standing his ground was most important; he would not order the production to be re-edited or withdrawn for the Senate, because the elected Parliament was his supreme authority.[24] He did not speculate on the long- or short-range effect his appearance before the Senate might have on future Film Board trials and tribulations. For the next year, a goodly number of filmmakers were so afraid of trouble and were employing such rigourous self-censorship that at least one official in the Commissioner's Office feared the documentaries might lose their edge.

No such thing happened with one of the last Film Board-generated sponsored works, 'Excuse Me, But There's a Computer Asking For You' ($195,000), made for Revenue Canada. It demonstrated how dangerous it was for the organization to tweak the noses of those who mattered most, the members of Parliament. MPs were furious at the film's implication that an all-seeing '1984' Orwellian computer was scrutinizing all Canadian taxpayers. Tax had always been a poorly received Film Board subject – The Sloane Affair, Tax Is Not a Four-Letter Word, and Tax: The Outcome of Income had all caused some grief – and the institution had never quite learned just how close it could go to the pockets of Canadians. This short was withdrawn soon after its release by an Order in Council and was never seen by the Canadian public.

English Production: Pushing the edge of the envelope

Despite these trials, a number of filmmakers in English Production were unafraid to deal with inflammatory subjects and felt comfortable continuing the Film Board tradition of finding the middle ground and then shifting slightly to the left. Part of the agency's avowed mandate was to address the socio-cultural needs of minority and specialized audiences, and taking a progressive position on these issues was their way of continuing to push the edge of the envelope. This approach characterizes the English wing of the institution as it enters its next half-century. It is at once its greatest strength and most perilous course.

Among the last frontiers to open for public debate was human sexuality. The robes of privacy fell away in 1984, as Paul Cowan directed one of the most innovative pieces of this period, a docudrama, Democracy on Trial: The Morgentaler Affair ($506,431). Doctor Henry Morgentaler had become a national figure for his civil-disobedience crusade on behalf of a woman's right to choose safe and legal abortion. In this production, Morgentaler and his lawyer play themselves, while re-enacting their six-year legal battle against the abortion law, waged before Quebec and federal courts from 1970 to 1976. At times, the illusion of direct cinema is so complete that the distinction between documentary and drama is almost obliterated.

Cowan tied the major threads of Morgentaler's story to the doctor's experience of losing all but one of his family in the Nazi death camps. Survival, a new life in Canada, psychoanalysis, and the desire to treat all people in a humane, compassionate way characterize the doctor's life, along with a desire to help those who wish to terminate unwanted pregnancies. Inexplicably, Cowan omitted articulating another crucial point that motivated the fiercely determined and independent Morgentaler. When imprisoned in Quebec in 1975, he observed that 90 per cent of those incarcerated were originally unwanted and abused children, many of whom drifted from foster homes into a life of crime. 'If all children were desired, received with love and affection and care,' Morgentaler believed, 'they would become loving and caring individuals. If we had that for a number of generations, we would have a different kind of species, a different humankind.'[25] Understanding this outlook, there was a reasonable psychological nexus that Cowan might have

The 1980s documentary form 'docudrama' blended dramatic techniques with actuality. Here director Paul Cowan (right) prepares Dr Henry Morgentaler to re-enact his arrest at his abortion clinic in *Democracy on Trial: The Morgentaler Affair* (1984).

made: Morgentaler's lifelong fight is for the millions of civilian victims who were felled in the Second World War by those who lacked love and compassion. To Morgentaler, abortion is not about killing babies, it is about preventing potential future criminals. Perhaps verbalizing this logic would not have mattered, since, for many, the issue of abortion is impelled by visceral emotions, not intellect. After all, the anti-abortion side argues, innocence and the will to survive are the universals shared by developing life.

As early as September 1983, the Film Board had received over five hundred letters, mostly reflecting a strong negative reaction to what was termed a 'pro-abortion film.' The letters continued to come in at some forty a day, the largest number of responses to any film in Film Board history to that time. Some at headquarters believed the letters were part of an orchestrated activity by anti-abortion groups, and did not stem from a cross-section of the public. To their credit, the board of trustees agreed on the importance of the series *Democracy on Trial* and said they wanted it continued. By June 1984 they reaffirmed this stance, despite the CBC's

refusal to broadcast or be involved with the series, which it considered 'unbalanced.'[26] *Democracy on Trial* was shown on Ontario's Global Television network in January 1985, and it continues to circulate non-theatrically. The abortion debate, of which Morgentaler remains a key spokesperson and activist, continues to rage. This work was an early 'polarizer' and doubtless a signpost along the road that led the Supreme Court of Canada in 1988 to strike down the existing abortion law as unconstitutional. The Film Board intends to keep the social debate swirling, knowing that the last word on abortion will never be heard.

A much different, but sympathetic, approach to the same subject was taken in *Abortion: Stories from North and South* ($241,705) by Gail Singer of Studio D, also in 1984. She utilized a cross-cultural survey from Ireland, Japan, Thailand, Peru, Colombia, and Canada to demonstrate how abortion has been a constant historical thread, despite powerful resistance from the patriarchal structures of the church, state, and medical establishments. Throughout the documentary, witnesses attest to the fact that only a small percentage of the world's women have access to a safe, legal means of terminating unwanted pregnancy. Later, one sympathetic critic concluded that the solid research, careful sifting of evidence, and quiet calm of the film's slowly building pace served, like hardening steel, to reinforce this injustice to the worldwide majority of women.[27] The film was meant to motivate the sympathetic viewer to try to change this situation.

Cosmopolitain or not, the CBC refused to telecast *Abortion: Stories from North and South* because it too was 'unbalanced.'[28] The forces against abortion were not without ammunition either. In a nationwide press story, the president of the Canadian Conference of Catholic Bishops said it was a 'sleazy trick' for the Film Board to show the two abortion films the day before the pope's visit.[29] Macerola continued to defend Singer and other leading-edge filmmakers in a form letter to every complainant: 'The tradition of film-making at the Film Board is one which gives, within limits of factual accuracy, the film-maker the freedom to examine an issue from a personal point of view. This has resulted in an original and, we believe, invaluable body of work which touches on all aspects of Canadian life.'

Privately, however, he was becoming concerned that Studio D films were presenting only one viewpoint, when they should have been expressing other positions shared by women.[30] The Studio D 1980s philosophy is cemented in films that illustrate the principle of women's 'otherness.' They argue that patriarchal structures which are hostile and unbalanced in their own right are fair game.

When Studio D found itself strangling for want of production money, some blamed the (patriarchal) Film Board management, even though the women were not the sole victims of the budgetary squeeze. In 1987, the studio was reorganized under Rina Fraticelli, and its original group of directors were shifted to other studios, while a new core of female directors began to redefine its feminine thrust toward visible minorities.

The willingness to deal with sexuality grew out of North America's social openness and taboo-bashing that characterized the sixties and seventies. One of the last taboos, child abuse, was bridged with a number of non–Film Board productions that the agency distributed in the late seventies and early eighties: *Sexual Abuse – The Family*, *Sexual*

Feeling Yes, Feeling No (1985) teaches children, in common-sense fashion, how to prevent sexual assault.

Abuse of Children: A Time for Caring, and *Child Sexual Abuse: The Untold Secret*. The interest in the subject led Moira Simpson of the Pacific region to direct a series of four films in 1984, *Feeling Yes, Feeling No*, which included printed matter to accompany the visuals. The series was welcomed by schools, social agencies, parents, and a host of other community-oriented groups, who found them useful tools in sexual-assault-prevention programmes. With the cooperation of Health and Welfare Canada, which deposited 3,500 copies on video cassette in public libraries across the country, a brochure was included with monthly family-allowance cheques, offering a home video cassette of the series to 3.8 million Canadians at a discounted price. With over 8,000 copies sold, it became the largest-selling item in Film Board history.

The series taught children how to protect themselves from strangers as well as how to recognize sexual assault from family members and other trusted persons. The instructive, common-sense approach of these documentaries freed them from any possible charge of being exploitative in their own right. That the crime of child abuse was recognized for its pervasiveness in every social class was a leap forward in combating it; that perpetrators and their child victims were made aware of its consequences through these works put the Film Board in the vanguard of exposing one of the scourges of the age.

A natural follow-up to this disturbing topic was a 1985 production from Vancouver, *Street Kids* ($120,000), by Peg Campbell, which used an innovative docudrama technique of live action and freeze-framing to show that many victims of child abuse end up on the street selling their bodies. Perhaps the film should have revealed one of society's best-kept secrets – that most of those who turn to prostitution have been abused children (though not all child victims become prostitutes). In 1987 *To a Safer Place*, a docu-

Many victims of child abuse end up on the street, where they sell their bodies. *Street Kids* (1985) shows that these scarred juveniles often respond to child-care workers.

mentary by Beverly Shaffer, presented the testimony of one victim who spent a lifetime recovering from her childhood experience of incest. She now devotes her life to helping and encouraging those who are paralysed by the trauma. The film was seen by sixteen million people in the United States, and after being lauded in Japan, Australia, and Britain, was finally approved by the CBC for telecast in 1989.

Related to the theme of the marginal elements of society was the Pacific region series *Recovery*, four short films of less than fifteen minutes each on women who were being treated for alcoholism, heroin addiction, or both. In a struggle to overcome her unique self-destructive tendencies, each woman reveals a common desire to battle the demons of a threatening past and present. Similarly, a series of six half-hour films on services for battered women, called *The Next Step*, show how victims receive help in urban, rural, northern, and native communities. Studio D linked up with the federal Women's Film Programme as part of this activity and began working on a series of films intended as discussion starters for young audiences.

To a Safer Place (1987) presents one victim of child abuse (Shirley Turcotte, right), who now devotes her life to helping those who are paralysed by the same trauma.

The argument most often put forward on behalf of the above-mentioned pieces was that they were for constituencies that were otherwise unserved by mainstream broadcasting. The other side of the coin was the charge made in *Maclean's* magazine in 1986 that the Film Board was being held captive by pressure groups that espouse the views of a tiny minority of Canadians, to wit, the 25 per cent of the population who support the left-leaning New Democratic Party. The charge was that the Film Board was not open to all political points of view. In response to *Maclean's*, the Film Board's public-relations officer caught the author on her factual errors, but dodged the charge of leaning left on many social and political issues.[31] It would have been braver to admit that the historical record showed that the Film Board's consistent 'left' or 'radical' orientation was close to 'liberal' in its true meaning and that historically such stances often tended to become the socially accepted norm within a few years.

The future: Curriculum enhancement?

But this was no time to instruct the critics. Director General of English Program Katadotis thought that over the decades filmmakers had lost their sense of audience. He took issue with making films for small community audiences, which is what Studio D considered as its central goal. The primary fact was that schools had always been the Film Board's best audience, and he wanted to redirect English Production's energies primarily toward curriculum-enrichment films with non-violent, non-sexist, non-racist content. Although he recanted his anti-features attitude, he put most of his eggs in the non-theatrical-market basket. His most difficult leadership task was to convince filmmakers to look less for the spotlight than to the ongoing educational needs of Canadian students.[32]

One offshoot of this philosophy was the beginning of a decade-long pursuit of some of Canada's leading poets and writers by director Donald Winkler. Among these are candid portraits of F.R. Scott, Northrop Frye, Irving Layton, Earle Birney, Al Purdy, Ralph Gustavson, and P.K. Page. Their 'performances' rate as a source of enrichment to Canadian studies both at home and abroad and attest to the value of the Film Board in its assumption of the role of 'recorder and preserver' of Canadian culture.

In a completely different vein, a series of six 15- to 26-minute shorts, *Finding Our Way*, appeared in 1986-7. Children often have severe pressures placed on them in their home environments, and the films explore how they cope with such diverse subjects as the death of a sibling, budding racism, divorce, a hospitalized parent, and poverty.

Donald Winkler's candid portraits of some of Canada's leading poets and writers includes *Poet: Irving Layton Observed* (1986), in which the poet bears witness to the beauty and terror of modern life with characteristic exuberance.

Another approach to the issue of adolescence was the brainchild of veteran Wolf Koenig, who produced the series *Wednesday's Children* in 1987, six dramas costing about $225,000 each, ranging in length from twelve to seventeen minutes. The films, titled after the teenage delinquents' fictitious names, are intended as classroom pieces that should lead groups to discuss the nature and cause of delinquency. From car theft to petty crime, to drug trafficking, the youngsters are drifting variously because they are either abused, lost in suburban *anomie*, single-parent children, or born into poverty. Within this wide range of situations, the classroom audience has an opportunity to engage in exploration of their own problems of adolescent alienation and to move toward understanding and sharing.

In 1985 Koenig had been drawn to the idea of using drama to stimulate classroom discussion as he, with eight other producers, undertook production of the eight-film series *Discussions in Bioethics*. These 12- to 14-minute dramas drew attention to the contemporary ethical dilemmas of euthanasia, compulsory sterilization, health-care priorities, working on weapons development, religion versus science, and abortion. In a classroom context, they are excellent stimulants to discussion because they are open-ended rather than prescriptive. Koenig focussed the series on the need to have youngsters recognize that film is more than a palliative and escape, that it is also a means to stimulate interaction and self-discovery as viewers discuss moral issues. He continues to stand squarely in the Grierson tradition of using film as a means to ignite the fire of social responsibility, while reflecting the drama of ordinary life. He found this series had a fortuitous secondary function of allowing a group of young directors to make films, even if there was no promise of permanent employment. He and his team ignored the austerity-inspired depression that pervaded headquarters, and they plunged ahead with the hope that is associated with the young and idealistic. Grierson was their avowed model, and it pleased Koenig to hear the old Maestro's name once again in filmmakers' animated discussions. A similar series of French originals was undertaken by French Production.

One innovative experiment promised to recast the long-stagnant relationship between the Film Board and the various provincial ministries of education. By the mid-eighties the provinces recognized a national disaster in the making: students were moving away from majoring in the sciences. In the long run, the country might suffer from not having sufficient scientific training.

Guided by Koenig, director Julie Stanfel initiated the Canadian Science Video series *Perspectives in Science* and developed what was called an 'interactive' format; one-hour videos were to deal with toxic waste, biotechnology, water, agriculture, forestry, and air as environmental and sociological concerns. A 15-minute dramatic segment would be followed by 45 minutes of documentary, presenting the problem through the eyes of various parties. The 'conclusion' would be left to students and teacher to work out in a group situation. The industrial participants were given editorial control of the film segment dealing with their viewpoint. The trick was to balance carefully all options, in order to meet the requirements of the provincial ministries. Most important, the Film Board was showing initiative in this often-ignored area and was being invited to help redesign national curricula in the sciences. Studio G, the multimedia section responsible for sound-filmstrips for schoolchildren, was home to this innovation and was showing itself to be a forward-looking and energizing element in English Production.[33]

In 1985 Studio D inaugurated its planned approach to peace studies with *Speaking Our Peace*, a 55-minute documentary directed by Terri Nash and Bonnie Sherr Klein. Their attempt to link international peace initiatives by women in Canada, Britain, and the Soviet Union was a noble effort at conveying the 'otherness' of women in the nuclear-arms debate. The problem was that the Soviet participants' insistence on parroting party doctrine in the pre-Gorbachev era showed just how complex the international peace game was. This did not deter the women from launching publicity and a catalogue for educators called 'Films for a Peaceful Planet' to encourage new, socially useful and positive attitudes toward the dilemma over nuclear arms. They were part of the activist vanguard trying to find a way to end the nuclear scourge. In support of this ideal, the Film Board underwrote the half-million dollars in post-production costs for Peter

Watkins's 14-hour mega-documentary on the nuclear-arms age, *The Journey*. This was only one of the 159 private-sector projects the institution assisted in 1985–6, the sixth year of the Program to Assist Filmmakers and Films in the Private Sector (PAFFPS). These peace films seemed to lose their urgency when, by the end of the decade, the USSR's new leadership declared the Cold War over and took bold steps to reorient the industrial world away from nuclear confrontation.

But, simultaneously, the Film Board was reaching for a higher public profile on prime-time national television. By late in the decade, statistics for network telecasts reflected an upward trend, especially because of co-production agreements with the CBC. As might be expected, French Production had maintained a steady 50 per cent of output figure on Radio-Canada. On the English side, in contrast to the period 1979–85, when only 23.4 per cent of output was telecast on the CBC (213 productions were broadcast, with an additional 198 rejected), in 1985–6, Film Board productions on CBC prime time had reached 21.4 million Canadians, a figure 54 per cent higher than in 1984–5.

The gem of 1985 was *Final Offer*, a 78-minute Film Board–CBC co-production, directed by Sturla Gunnarsson. This direct-cinema documentary was a record of the historic contract negotiations in 1984 between the United Auto Workers and General Motors Corporation. Gunnarsson followed the president of the Canadian union, Bob White, as he led his membership through tortuous negotiations and finally delivered them a new contract. The stress over the months was exacerbated by the strings holding the Canadian union to the American parent union, and in the film's climax, White summons up all his charisma to lead his membership to break with the international union and achieve independent status. One has the sense, in watching *Final Offer*, that a future Canadian politician is in the making.

That same year, Donald Brittain was re-

Canadian United Auto Workers chief
Bob White, right, is the focal participant in
Final Offer (1985), a powerful direct-cinema
study of contemporary big-union contract talks.

sponsible for *Canada's Sweetheart: The Saga of Hal C. Banks*, a docudrama about the postwar Seafarers' International Union of Canada. The genesis of this Film Board–CBC co-production was Brittain's continuing interest in recent history. He had been intrigued by Canada's invitation to the well-known ham-handed American organizer, who had been brought in to wrest the SIU away from postwar Communist control. Using professional actors, he crafted his script based on court transcripts and interviews. It flowed smoothly until it came to the point of revealing who in the Canadian government put pressure on the United States to refrain from extraditing Banks for a suspected felony. Fearful of the hot water into which his colleague Paul Cowan had plunged with *The Kid Who Couldn't Miss*, Brittain demurred from telling what he knew, be-

cause playing with contemporary history is a dangerous game.

A superb three-part series in 1986, directed by Tina Viljoen, took up where the *War* series had left off. *Defence of Canada*, written and narrated by military analyst Gwynne Dyer, drew an average audience of 1.25 million viewers as it examined Canada's role in international power politics. The first of the one-hour films, *A Long Way from Home*, is a sweeping overview of two centuries of Canadian military history and of the leaders' tendency to act as if Canada was another middle-sized European country. This was followed by *Keeping the Elephants Away*, a rather cold-blooded look at military alliances and *Realpolitik*, Canadian-style. The once-famous nuclear-arms fiasco that helped catapult John Diefenbaker from the prime minister's office to oblivion is described on camera by the cunning players, affording the viewer a sense of what being a small player in a big game is all about. The final film, *The Space Between*, probably drew the most immediate attention, not only for showing that Canadian officers from time to time get to keep their 'fingers on the button' that will bring nuclear Armageddon, but also for its advocacy of neutrality and disengagement from the Western power alliance. Dyer's crusade for neutrality was taken to the national level in the press, leading Minister of External Affairs Joe Clark to respond in print to the idea negatively as he defended the NATO alliance. The first two films will have staying power for being anchored in history, something that educators particularly appreciate. The third film, and a 1987 spin-off called *Harder Than It Looks*, lost much of their punch shortly thereafter, because the contemporary scene was changing rapidly. The intention of the new Soviet Communist leadership to make obsolete the 1940s Cold War scenario was nothing short of revolutionary. It seemed a whole new world was dawning as the eighties drew to a close.

By 1988 the Film Board's prime-time television statistics remained solid, in part

Director Donald Brittain, left, discusses with Maury Chaykin the role of ham-handed American organizer Hal Banks in the docudrama *Canada's Sweetheart: The Saga of Hal C. Banks* (1985).

owing to Donald Brittain's lavish $2 million-plus Film Board–CBC docudrama co-production, *The King Chronicles*. These six hours attempted to show the highlights and political cunning of the enigmatic bachelor-politician Mackenzie King, who was Canada's longest-serving prime minister. If the drama was not always the most gripping (King's was a supremely lacklustre persona), more important, Brittain was trying to articulate a national mythology while cementing Canadian authenticity. He well understood how both those elements are central to the concept of nationhood. His untimely death in July 1989 marked the loss of a veritable national treasure. There is, as yet, no one who promises to fill the void left by this incomparable writer, director, and humanitarian.

In 1987, Katadotis had had great hopes for an educational series called *Reckoning*, five one-hour films on the political economy of Canada, hosted by political economist James Laxer. The Quebec question had momentarily receded and been replaced by the national question of free trade with the United States, hence the arrival of the series was timely. The films try to analyse the nature of the United States economy, the impact of new technologies like the microchip, the boom-and-bust historical cycle of the Cana-

dian economy, how relationships between presidents and prime ministers have affected the economy, and the alternatives to an economic marriage to the United States. Because the series clearly opposed the free-trade option, which coincided with the position of the Liberals and the New Democratic Party in the federal election of 1988, the CBC would not telecast them, lest it stand accused of being one-sided. The Conservatives were re-elected, then passed the free-trade bill in 1989.

Alternative Drama

Film Board dramas continued to draw mixed critical reviews in the eighties. From the programme called Alternative Drama came the experimental English feature *The Masculine Mystique* ($489,590) in 1984. Directors Giles Walker and John N. Smith donned the masks of comedy and tragedy as they tried to convey what four 'real men' thought of feminism and its impact on their relations with women. It was called 'the real revenge of the nerds' by one unsympathetic critic, since what was supposed to be funny evoked bathos.[34] More seriously, as a male answer to the 1980s' concerns with roles and role-playing, it shows how contemporary feminism has left many males confused and cautious in a middle-class world turned upside down. In 1985 the unflappable Walker tried the 'lost masculinity' theme again with greater success in the comedy *90 Days*, although his light touch was harder to find in the third film of the trilogy, *The Last Straw* (1987), which some thought became burlesque in parodying itself.

In 1986 another Alternative Drama feature won international recognition: John N. Smith's *Sitting in Limbo*, the story of Canadian-West Indian adolescents who stumble and fall into the all-too-familiar trap of unwanted pregnancy. The film starred non-actors, was unscripted, and had a strong documentary texture. Audiences tended to think the story-line was weak because the abortion issue never arose. But in working out the scenes, the cast members emphasized that abortion was not an option in the matriarchally oriented West Indian milieu and that, to remain 'authentic,' the female teen in the film had to continue her unwanted pregnancy.

In 1988 Smith tried the same technique again with *Train of Dreams*, an Alternative Drama story of a young ruffian's near-permanent derailment into a life of crime. The denouement unravels as the hoodlum's transformation occurs instantaneously, too quick and too permanent to be believable. Smith has a particular talent for working with non-professional actors and no script, which keeps his work fresh, engaging, and cinematically unique. The Alternative Drama features tend to cost between one-half to three-quarters of a million dollars and are alleged to be breaking even as private distributors find them a market. Despite their success, the organization may shift away from the English-language feature because the present director general of English Program, Barbara Emo, sees it as an expendable activity. Yet if low-budget features in both languages continue to earn their way, they may find a berth on the production ship. The most recent effort in the Alternative Drama feature format is Cynthia Scott's uneventful tale of seven stranded elderly women whose togetherness in a typical Canadian landscape becomes the subject of *The Company of Strangers*.

L'ONF: Twenty-five years of images of French Canada

Amidst the drift, gloom, and despondency that were synonymous with Macerola's first year, French Program marked the fall of 1984 as the twenty-fifth anniversary of French production at the Film Board, despite the fact that the French wing was formed officially under Pierre Juneau only twenty years earlier. Characteristically iconoclasts, the filmmakers chose to ignore their first

director of production and to celebrate the consolidation of *l'équipe française* around Fernand Dansereau, Bernard Devlin, Louis Portugais, and Léonard Forest, in 1958–9.

The seventy-seven films shown at the Montreal retrospective called '25 ans d'images à notre image' were a record of Quebec's profound transformation as it sought to define itself. The filmmakers paid homage to the National Film Board for having allowed the *québécois* and francophones of Canada to develop and explore their own unique images. Predictably, one could not expect them to extend the same homage to the federal government in Ottawa, whose policy had been to let it all happen. The distance between 'L'Office' and the National Film Board of Canada was further than miles, but that too was one spoke of the wheel symbolizing the Canadian national identity. The French-speaking filmmakers knew that the commercial sector would never have made these productions. Nor had the Quebec provincial government invested cultural monies for filmmaking in anywhere near the amount Ottawa had during the same period.

Jacques Godbout, the perennial conscience of French Production, claimed that twenty-five years was very little in the history of a nation, yet this was a time for sentimentality as the men and women looked back at their vanished youth and mourned that finances had determined that a new group of filmmakers had not been hired on a permanent basis. Veteran Film Board director Marcel Carrière recalled that at the beginning virtually the whole francophone creative staff had met annually in Claude Jutra's mother's living-room. Gilles Carle, who was just finishing *Cinéma, Cinéma*, a compilation film of the best of the institution's French work of the last quarter-century, maintained that diversity characterized the entire enterprise. There was no NFB style of French-language films; rather it was the filmmakers who made up the NFB. L'Office National du Film was the place where they produced their art, nothing more, nothing less.[35] He was perfectly correct on all accounts.

The list of documentaries, fiction films, and animations shown at the retrospective might be useful for a sociologist or anthropologist in the next century to gauge the evolution of French-Canadian society and art from the fifties to the eighties (see Appendix 5). *Mon oncle Antoine*, by now recognized as the best Canadian feature film of all time, was screened six times. Perhaps it is significant that Jean-Claude Labrecque's exquisite 1965 sport film *60 cycles*, about an international bicycle race run in a lush Quebec landscape, had won the most international awards (13) for live-action French production. With nineteen entries, the festival also recognized how animation had become an enduring francophone contribution to film art since the organization of a French animation unit in 1966 by René Jodoin. In the fall of 1985, Robert Forget assumed leadership at French Animation and encouraged exploration of the frontiers of the art of computer animation with a new million-dollar state-of-the-art facility at headquarters. But all was not roses and perfume. Macerola had thought that French Production had been drifting since 1976 and that filmmakers were lost in a trough, not knowing what they wanted to say.[36] He might have been thinking of the not altogether successful feature *Mario*, by Jean Beaudin, in 1984. Based on Claude Jasmin's *La sablière*, the film had gone over budget and its final costs exceeded $1 million. A story of two brothers, one mute and the other a garrulous storyteller, it follows the favourite Quebec themes of the mental prison of solitude and the anxieties of youth coming of age. Called a masterpiece of *québécois* cinema by one enthusiast, the jury at the Montreal Film Festival snubbed it, the sole Canadian entry.[37] *Mario* contains strikingly beautiful photography of the Iles de la Madeleine region of Quebec. Unfortunately, the screenplay in which the brothers are blown to bits, is so improbable that disbelief is unsuspendable. Shortly after its release, Beaudin left the Film Board.[38]

In a variation on the theme of gender roles, Yves Dion straddled the line between fiction and documentary with his *L'Homme renversé* by playing himself on camera and bringing together two actors and an actress to discuss the masculine condition. This approach enables the audience to see through gender myths and strikes a responsive chord with its exploration of men's emotional weaknesses and inability to admit vulnerability. Similarly, another more traditional fictional approach to a serious gender subject was Paule Baillargeon's *Sonia*, the story of a woman who temporarily abandons her own life to save her mother, suffering from Alzheimer's disease, from a lonely death in hospital.

An entirely different hue coloured French Production's *Passiflora*, a self-proclaimed piece of 'caustic humour' and film-hymn for dissidents, directed by Fernand Bélanger and Dagmar Teufel Gueissaz in 1985. Its premise was to find significance in the spectacle of Pope John Paul II's visit to Montreal's Olympic Stadium and the similar spectacle of pop star Michael Jackson's arrival at the same venue at a different time. Glued to this was a confused, irreverent, and irrelevant story of homosexual lust and depravity, not very flattering to homosexual actualities. Some who were sympathetic thought the film dealt with gay rights, forgetting that a minority's demand for equality does not mean the right to be offensive to the majority. The adolescent mockery of both the Catholic church and French-Canadian believers went against every tenet of fairness and decency that the federal agency had ever tried to promote.

Some thought that this unfortunate expression of bad taste was meant to wreck the Film Board; others thought that it was an example of a film that had gotten away from its producer, Jacques Vallée. There was at least one redeeming aspect, the brilliant animation of Pierre Hébert, stemming from a number of live-action sequences that he froze and then brought back to life as animated drawn figures. But it was not enough to calm the general upset that the film provoked. Within months, Daniel Pinard, director-general of French Program, left the Film Board and was replaced by documentary veteran Georges Dufaux. Macerola used his experience well as he told the board of trustees he would *not* refuse to distribute the film (nor would he subtitle it into English), lest the filmmakers become martyrs and a bad film be considered a masterpiece.[39] After practically no public demand for it, *Passiflora* earned a well-deserved death by withdrawal a year later.

Anne Trister, by Lea Pool, and *Pouvoir intime*, by Yves Simoneau were two 1986 feature co-productions that earned some critical acclaim. The first, a story of a young woman's search for meaning in the wake of her father's death, focused on her lesbian relationship and its connection to the patriarchal space in her life. *Pouvoir intime*, billed as a multilevelled *film noir* thriller, was more traditional, revolving around a bank-truck hijacking with a predictable denouement.

The darling fiction piece of the decade appeared to be *Le Déclin de l'empire américain*, a $1.8 million Film Board / Roger Frappier co-production, directed by Denys Arcand. *Le Déclin* won the Critic's Prize at Cannes in April 1986 and was nominated for an Oscar as the best foreign feature film, a first for Canada. In this slick, sardonic sex story of Quebec bourgeois-intellectual decadence, where words create the seamy atmosphere that the visuals hide innocently, Arcand's characters, in gender-role reversals, drift as aimlessly through their lives as they do through their sumptuous meal. They believe in little more than power and deceit in relationships as the modus operandi of the current age. All this is cloaked behind the blandness of a two-cheeked French-style kiss that no one believes in, yet everyone does in order to disarm the adversary while preparing to plunge in his or her verbal knife. The only punishment in the film, as one would expect from Arcand, is meted out to the character whose single crime is that of innocence. Perhaps *Le Déclin* was also his way of stating

that a generation of artists felt betrayed by the Parti Québécois government, which abandoned the independence option after the referendum defeat.[40] This stinging rebuke of contemporary *québécois* and North American morals, despite no mention of the word Quebec or Canada in the script, leaves the audience sad about the blight of alienation. On the heels of Arcand's success, in 1989, the Film Board put about $500,000 plus services into *Jésus de Montréal*, his funny, melancholy, and bitter feature about the staging of the Passion Play for contemporary Philistines. It was nominated for, but failed to win, the Palme d'Or at Cannes.

The forgotten child: Animation

As ever, the animation films garnered international stature for the organization, while the animators too often remained underfunded and unsung. Ishu Patel earned an Oscar nomination for his 1984 fable *Paradise*, the story of a blackbird's envy and inability to accept himself as he is. Once the self-deceiving bird does just that, the film explodes into a blaze of celebration by all creatures of the wild. Another Oscar nomination went to Richard Condie's 1985 animation *The Big Snit*. This Prairie region production toyed humourously with the eighties' infatuation with microcosm and macrocosm and with how a global nuclear war and a domestic quarrel may have interchangeable emotional settings. The starkness of each alternative gives the viewer a very open end to contemplate; *The Big Snit* touches upon the great imponderables of the nuclear age, though its simplistic strokes may leave audiences paralysed by a 'nothing I can do about it' attitude.

In 1986 director Les Drew animated *Every Dog's Guide to Complete Home Safety*, a public-service message of forty safety tips for homes with youngsters, delivered with hilarious effect by a didactic, lovable dog who is constantly on the edge of preventing or coping with accidents. A year later, director Bruce Mackay's 41-minute video *Eugene*

Levy Discovers Home Safety included the animations *Hot Stuff* and *The Old Lady's Camping Trip* to round out safety in the home with humour.

George and Rosemary, billed as an animated fable for those sixty-five and over, told the story in 1988 of how two golden agers find love and companionship. The upbeat story of a shy, day-dreaming man is filled with empathy and humour and is meant to help elderly people develop a positive view of themselves. Perhaps signalling that the 'youth culture' was now *passé* and that being old was the coming growth industry, this animation, produced by the sixty-five-year-old Oscar winner Eunice Macaulay and by Douglas MacDonald, directed by Alison Snowden and David Fine, was an Oscar nominee. In 1989, the Film Board had five of the eight films in competition at the respected international animation-film festival in Annecy, France. The present English Program chief, Barbara Emo, wants more flexibility for animation development and experimentation and has expanded that budget.

George and Rosemary (1987), an animated fable for those 65 and over, tells the upbeat story of how a shy, daydreaming man finds love and companionship.

Life with Flora

From Macerola's office, it appeared that the Ottawa politicians were oblivious to the Film Board's functional role, while the Department of Communications' mandarins were still hostile. When Flora MacDonald took over Marcel Masse's portfolio in the summer of 1986, she announced her support for the Film Board as 'an essential cultural resource.' She introduced a $33 million feature-film fund and allowed the Film Board to participate by co-producing with the private sector.[41] A few years later, Macerola attracted a five-year multimillion-dollar government commitment to his organization for co-productions. He thought this was a great coup, since with feature co-productions Ottawa would at least know what and for whom the institution was producing.

It remains to be seen whether this production fillip will help provide the institution with a new raison d'être; the fears are that the commercial sector will be the biggest winner and that the Film Board may drift away from its public-service function. Peter Katadotis has called this another of the perennial no-win situations thrust upon the Film Board: the Department of Communications pressures for co-productions and then asks why a Film Board is needed to do this, since other bodies can do the same task. His belief is that the organization has to sharpen its definition of *mission* and convince the masters in Ottawa of its special role, one that no one else fulfils.[42] This is the organization's task as this chronicle closes in 1989, the end of the Film Board's first fifty years.

Meanwhile, Macerola continued tightening down the nuts and bolts of his Five-Year Operational Plan. The institution had already cut back 184 full-time jobs, saving $5.5 million. The Treasury Board cuts added up to $4 million, although, unfortunately, Macerola was not allowed to plough back this savings into production. English Program's goal was to split the production budget equally between headquarters and the regions (Vancouver, Edmonton, Winnipeg, Toronto, and Halifax), rather than the existing two-thirds/one-third ratio. To reach an equal split, English Program required an additional $10 million to add on to an annual budget of $25.3 million. It was impossible to find this sum in the total Film Board budget of $73.39 million.[43] And if by some miracle the money appeared, French Program would have to be given an additional $6 million in order to maintain the nine-year average 64/36 per cent production-budget split between the English and French respectively. By 1989, with underfunding a permanent fact of life, twenty-seven directors in English drama and documentary, along with a handful of animators, were struggling to get a share of the remaining $1.5 million English Program fund. No one wanted once more to witness the scenario of filmmakers waiting in the cafeteria for deliverance. That thought sent a universal chill through the organization: thus the regions had to wait for increased monies.

Macerola was pleased with at least one set of figures: in 1986 he had gone far toward reaching his stated goal of having 70 per cent of production done by freelancers, a ratio that was split 67/57 per cent for English and French. This was all part of his objective to reduce permanent staff to 650; from 1085 in 1982, it levelled off at 753 in mid-1987 and held at 728 in 1989; there is no more 'fat' to trim.

Distribution and technology: Light at the end of the tunnel

Significant innovations have occurred during the astringent eighties, proving that in adversity the Film Board has kept its multipurpose identity alive. Probably the greatest change was the board of trustees' approval of a user-fee system for videos in 1987 and for films in 1988, which was planned to generate about $1 million income annually. Unlike the abortive effort of 1969–70, user fees were brought in gradually and with adequate

notice. This time, the public accepted them without a peep. Plans also proceeded to improve and extend the computerized booking system, complete with 1-minute video clips of available films. Another new wrinkle was a series of agreements with various public libraries to sell and deposit over three years blocks of 250 films on video cassette. By 1989, more that seventy-five such agreements were signed, thus enabling the public to have wider and better access to Film Board productions than ever before. Related to this was an increasing number of third-party agreements with independent distributors, thereby obviating the need for dozens of the Film Board's own full-time Distribution employees and allowing the closure of half the distribution offices nationally. A private firm was also engaged to distribute some hundred Film Board features in video for the U.S. market. In 1987, the CBC and Radio-Canada terminated Film Board distribution of their films, yet the contraction of 16-mm distribution will probably be offset by the introduction of the Videomatic Teller, a computerized machine containing just under two hundred titles, which allows the public to rent non-theatrical films on video cassette by using a charge card. In addition, special licensing arrangements have been made with institutions that want to reproduce Film Board films electronically. Furthermore, filmstrips are now being transferred on to video cassettes to meet educational institutions' shift to the use of video players. This too has led to a surge in sales and audiences. The new technologies have ushered in a revolution akin to the invention of the printing press, and there is little worry that distribution statistics will be doctored any longer – the national audience is actually increasing.[44] New technologies may find more individuals yet, and the future holds great possibilities.

The ever-expanding use of the computer has led to the Film Board's development of a computerized stock-shot library as well as a system of interactive video (trademark

Cleopatra) that allows students with a basic knowledge of word processing to use video, much in the way the old 'loop' process worked in the sixties, either for recording responses or, using the example of air-traffic controllers's training, for grading/certification purposes. In another application, the organization continues to refine the computerized work station and hopes to apply it soon to the filmmaking process itself. This new technology promises to shorten production time, which in turn should mean that filmmaking will be less costly.[45] The promise that had been the talk of the late 1960s has arrived at last, twenty years later.

Quebec: And yet again

But brave new worlds are sometimes blocked by tired old ones, as evidenced in 1987 when the cosmetic fell away from an old federal-provincial scar. The Quebec Liberal government threatened to put teeth into Bill 109, the Quebec Cinema Act, which the Parti Québécois regime had passed in June 1983. This law stated that any English-language film launched in Quebec must be translated into French within sixty days. The aim was to have a simultaneous release in English and French, so that Quebec distributors might benefit as much as the foreign-dominated English-language film distributors.

If the commissioner had looked at the earlier skirmishes, going back to J.W. Pickersgill's negotiations with Quebec in the fifties, he might have deduced that the Film Board could oppose the legislation and probably prevail in the courts. But Ottawa would hear nothing of it, since the Mulroney government had promised in its Meech Lake Accord to recognize Quebec as a 'distinct society'; its policy of non-confrontation took the wind out of the sails of the courtroom option. So Macerola dutifully requested additional money to cover the French versioning of English films, like the series on English-Canadian writers.[46]

When the provincial legislation was tight-

ened in December 1987, someone in Ottawa must have had second thoughts about the costs of the virtue of accommodation. Macerola went public in January 1988, claiming that the Film Board would have to pay an additional $700 to $900 thousand per year for versioning to meet provincial requirements. There were some 2,300 prints waiting for Quebec clearance, of which 450 were destined for distribution within that province's English-speaking community. The commissioner was piqued at Quebec's narrow-mindedness in not making an exception for the mostly non-theatrical Film Board films and videos. Not all these titles were of interest to the French-speaking audience and, besides, versioning of originals often followed as a matter of tradition, a year or two after the original language release. Further, he hinted sombrely, it looked like English Quebeckers could make the case that their rights were not being respected.

A verbal battle over the law ensued in the press all that winter. One theme most English and French journalists shared was that the law's unintended effect punished the Film Board. A loophole allowed Hollywood sixty days to furnish dubbed versions, by which time most films had completed their runs. Thus, they could be withdrawn before a French version had to be released.[47] At last, in May, the Quebec government caved in to public pressure when it exempted the Film Board's non-commercial films from the law's provisions. Quebec delayed implementation of the law, and in June the federal government introduced its own bill to try to curb the power of the foreign-controlled distributors while strengthening the Canadian distributors.[48] Further delays and the arrival of free trade left the issue unresolved in 1989.

Not with a bang or a whimper

By the end of 1988, Macerola felt he had achieved his primary task: to put the organization back into good stead in the eyes of the government. He had promised and delivered a belt-tightening regime without firing anyone. Since 1982–3, the Film Board had saved more than $6 million, but it was not theirs to keep. Annual production budgets have remained almost frozen. As its Jubilee year dawned, the atmosphere was one of neither wild celebration nor foreboding. In true Canadian fashion, survival had proved to be its own reward. Minister Flora MacDonald reaffirmed her support and prepared to request more production money. She never had the chance, as she went down to defeat in the federal election of November 1988.

The Conservatives were re-elected and Marcel Masse became minister of communications again. To the annoyance of many at the Film Board, he appeared at the Academy Awards ceremonies in March 1989 (before a television audience of one billion) to accept an honorary Oscar celebrating the institution's fiftieth anniversary. Having the minister speak rather than someone from the agency was a price worth paying; he not only spared the organization the cuts that extended to most every other cultural sector, but he also increased production by over $5 million in specially earmarked funds. As in every other period of the Film Board's turbulent existence, it was up to the filmmakers to use those funds creatively to satisfy the government, while carving out a unique place and mission for themselves in the nineties.

Macerola, who had decided not to seek a second term, could feel effusive too, for having hitched one of his agency's wagons to the big-budget glamour of the promising IMAX OMNIMAX technological star.[49] This latter activity grew out of the successful run of *Transitions*, which Colin Low had directed as a co-production with Canadian National, in 3-D IMAX, for Expo 86 in Vancouver.[50] Macerola interested Lavalin Industries in the giant-screen process, and the Film Board contracted to co-produce a couple of multi-million-dollar films with them. It was logical, then, if not personally fortuitous, for Macerola to leave the Film Board to join Lavalin

in December 1988, six months before the end of his term. In finding a new niche for the agency, he felt he had come close to achieving a complementary relationship between the public and private sectors.

IMAX cinemas have been proliferating around the world for a decade, and the hope is that these prestige films will bolster the reputation of the Film Board while making money. IMAX co-founder Roman Kroitor had long supported the Film Board's pursuit of the big-budget items, because artistically, socially, and politically he believed they were the things that inspired feedback from the important people, who would say, 'This is worth doing, this is what the Film Board should be all about.'[51] The $6.5 million Film Board–China 1989 IMAX co-production, *The First Emperor of China*, directed by Tony Ianzelo, is the grandest IMAX cinematic effort to date and is one of the great attractions of the new Museum of Civilization in Ottawa. Its blend of drama and documentary evoke both the excitement of a Kurosawa film and the thrill of being with an archaeologist at a once-in-a-lifetime discovery.

In September 1989 Acting Commissioner Joan Pennefather, who had presided over the fiftieth-anniversary celebrations in May, succeeded Macerola as film commissioner. She promised a regime of continuity rather than of change. Given the turbulence of the austere eighties, this might be the tonic the institution currently needs. Pennefather, a quiet-spoken, demure, yet utterly competent professional, knows her organization and hopes it will be judged by what it is rather than by what it is not. She claims to be a passionate believer in the agency's commitment to providing thought-provoking, content-filled, predominantly documentary films to the Canadian public. She is quite comfortable and fearless in manoeuvring her way around the often-arcane, bureaucratic circuits of Ottawa and is striving to find more production monies. Speaking about the institution's traditional role as *provocateur*, Pennefather acknowledges filmmakers' free-

Joan Pennefather, current film commissioner, hopes to oversee a continuation of the tradition of excellence. Her policy is to ensure that the Film Board remains accessible to visible minorities. One goal is to reach the status of professional equality between the sexes.

Pennefather holds out hope for a specialty service sent via cable television, although she is interested in doing something to fill the immediate need for more news and public affairs for the money-starved CBC, co-headed by ex–board of trustees member Patrick Watson in 1989. She knows of Watson's long-held contention that the Film Board must earn its way on to national television with good films. Where this leaves documentaries of passion, purpose, and a point of view is the great unknown. With production budgets now being distributed by province, there is also a clear and present danger to the institution in letting the natural centrifugal forces of regionalism negate the very reason for a National Film Board.

Pennefather does not express her vision in the vibrant and silvery words of a Grierson, who had railed against the 'fat-boys-feeling-sorry-for-themselves' documentary and who believed in positioning the institution 'one inch to the Left of the Party in power.' Neither does she have the old maestro's habit of using the word 'documentary' with the words 'poetry' and 'inspiration' following soon after. In the end, though, it is up to the creative staff to produce poetic films to stir the national consciousness. Their challenge is to tighten the wire of sober earnestness and visual poetry and prove that the combination supports the validity of the institution's ever open-ended raison d'être 'in the national interest.'

No doubt there will continue to be films with liberal-left progressive slants that will animate, educate, and sometimes even infuriate the public. Being provocative is in the national interest, many argue, because some of the Film Board's most controversial films have proven to be ahead of public opinion, which only later catches up to them.

'National interest' also includes the school-age audience, which perhaps remains the most important one for the organization to reach. If the battle for Canadian minds and culture via commercial television has al-

dom to be provocative, so long as they stay within the context of their original mandate, to reflect Canada to Canadians and to respond to Canadian needs. She notes that programming has evolved into a melding of bottom-to-top and top-to-bottom input, starting with a survey of audience needs as the prerequisite for every film. In accord with this philosophy, the commissioner believes present priorities revolve around public-service films for women, natives, and the handicapped. She also anticipates more collaboration with independent filmmakers.[52]

ready been lost, the last bastion of national cultural survival is the school, where there are minds who want to be provoked, not soothed. Canadian history, once the narrow preserve of a conservative university élite, and still too often the last item of concern in public-school curricula, cries out to be both scrutinized and mythologized on film. National and regional history in all its complexity may be one of the great interpretive challenges waiting to be addressed, for if national institutions like the Film Board cannot present a coherent sense of the historical past, citizens have little reason to care about a national future.

Afterword

In speaking of the glory days of the Second World War and his role as a production secretary, James Beveridge recalled that invariably, as a director was finishing a documentary opus, he or she was left holding 'six beautiful shots' that could not fit into the completed film and had to be left on the cutting-room floor. In the past thirteen chapters, there have been many such 'shots' or glimpses of the films and life of this remarkable organization that have been withheld for reasons of space and time. One wishes that the thousands of men and women who have given their vital energies to the place that Jacques Godbout has called 'une aberration magnifique' could have each been singled out as yet another 'beautiful shot' to be included as part of this chronology.

Of necessity, then, this historical portrait has been sketched with broad brush strokes. The role of the film commissioner has been central to the story because that person remains the perpetual barometer of the organization's health. He or she is also a grounded lightning-rod through whom the power of Ottawa and Canada surges, as he or she tries to play the symbolic roles of leader, visionary, public servant, protector, and executor of public duty and national interest. The creative staff have sought to recognize in their commissioner a strong and fair individual who, like Guy Roberge, is perceived as one who 'gives a slice of the cake to every-one.' The preceding story shows that circumstances and politics have largely determined how much cake there is to go around.

Some naysayers have claimed there has been a decades-long institutional drift and a consistent lack of both leadership and vision. Managerial style, they insist, comprised little more than words that did not match the real need, creativity. For the very few filmmakers who remembered, the original point of reference was Grierson, the dynamo who charted the course, left the artists alone to create, and then became a super production tyro (if not sometimes-tyrant) who forced them to defend every frame of their work. In recent memory, only Commissioner Sydney Newman had a similar ability, but he was swept aside by a political torrent that he could neither manage nor fully understand. This is not to deny that in every decade the film commissioners have had great strengths, but they usually could wear well only one of the many hats the job requires. Thus, there will always be those who bemoan the institutional drift and alleged poor administration. They should realize, however, that if the Film Board had remained an ad-hocracy, it would have been shut down long ago. In the last analysis, then, the agency is a living organism, buffeted by and reflecting the changing times. Any final judgment must be based on the quality and relevance of its films.

Why has the Film Board survived? Surely

it is because of more than inertia. Perhaps it is because the filmmakers followed a natural Canadian independence of mind and made their animations, features, and short films of sober optimism and cultivated innocence to give meaning to the original Grierson dictum that they should show how Canadians excelled at something. Over a half-century, the Film Board can boast of 4,473 English and 3,354 French productions. It has won 3,000 awards, received fifty-five Oscar nominations, and returned home with nine of the coveted trophies. At the same time, the multi-purpose organization was and is a place perpetually underfunded, constantly carping, and infuriatingly slow to respond to audience needs and to filmmakers who have a vision of the truth that they want it to fund.

One consistent pattern this book has revealed is that there has rarely been a time when the Film Board was not beleaguered. One could cite as examples Hollywood's ill will in the late forties, the CBC's frustration with and virtual abandonment of it in the late sixties, the Canadian commercial-film industry's insatiable hunger for sponsored films until the mid-eighties, and their contemporary desire for Film Board support in the form of co-productions. In every period the institution has found itself forever being reactive to besieging forces. If some entrepreneurs wish for a National Distribution Board rather than a National Film Board, Ottawa still insists that its *atelier* has a two-part facilitative role: to help the private sector succeed in the North American market and to make films that the commercial sector will not. This seemingly contradictory mandate forces a high-wire act in which the filmmakers must make themselves relevant in the commercial paradigm while pursuing their work in the national interest.

Trying to serve the national interest has not been easy either, since almost of necessity the definition of that term has remained open-ended. The original Grierson concept, which was in the Film Act of 1939, dealt with making films to help Canadians understand each other. Arthur Irwin, who put the term 'in the national interest' into the National Film Act of 1950, applied it to help resuscitate the politically battered organization and to provide it with a new home and new beginning in Montreal; after he arrived, the political powers in Ottawa hoped he would agree that it was in the national interest to steer the organization in the service of fighting the Cold War. Irwin thought artistic excellence with international appeal was the best expression of national interest and left it to an artist like Norman McLaren to take the high ground to generate the immortal *Neighbours*, rather than something akin to a ludicrous U.S. production of the same period called *Nightmare in Red*.

'In the national interest' also found meaning in two thrusts of the Massey Commission report of 1952. One was the report's demand for a national organization to protect Canada from excessive commercialization and Americanization; the other was a desire to accelerate the modern integration of Quebec into a pan-Canadian dream of bilingualism and biculturalism. Albert Trueman believed it was in the national interest to create separate English and French production wings, but he was a decade premature, so he settled for a definition that made television the major outlet of his institution's activity. Guy Roberge, who had written the part of the Massey report dealing with film, thought that the organization could escape the hostility of a nascent commercial-film industry and fulfil its mandate of being in the national interest if there were an alternative structure to support the feature-film industry. He hoped that the Film Board would then be left to do what it did best, create documentaries and art films, with separate budgets for English and French Production. In his caretaking capacity, Grant McLean tried to give meaning to 'national interest' by building momentum for the agency's service and informational-film function, while Hugo McPherson, smitten by the theories of Marshall McLuhan, thought that it was in the national interest to jump on the electronic-communications bandwagon more than a decade before society did. Because his dreams were prohibitively expensive they remained unfulfilled as government austerity froze spending.

Sydney Newman believed it was in the national interest to restrain the incautious hit-and-miss methods of filmmakers who did not wish to be held accountable; he made the office of the commissioner tougher and confrontational in an era of sharp political trial and national division. To him, 'in the national interest' meant simply protecting the organization from itself. André Lamy tried to lift the psychological malaise that seemed to be paralysing the middle-aged Film Board and helped buffer it by preferring to making films in the public rather than national interest. James de B. Domville could not use the phrase with much effect either, because it was difficult for him to swim against the hostile currents of renewed government austerity, the increasingly effective attacks of the private sector, and the referendum to decide the Quebec independence question. François Macerola also preferred to use public interest rather than national interest to justify his institution's activity, but most of his unpopular, but necessary mandate was a holding pattern to pare down its ungainly size. The present commissioner also does not use the term, perhaps because of a fear that its very utterance could bring about national division. Today 'in the national interest' is seen as a divisive phrase because the whole concept of nation appears to be on the verge of being wrestled for individually and separately by Canada and Quebec. Looking most pessimistically at the foreboding future, there may not even be a national interest for the Film Board to defend by the end of this century. The question now is whether or not the phrase deserves public resuscitation and, if it is heralded, whether national good or national pain will follow.

This book has tried to show that 'in the national interest' is still as valid as it was in 1950, because it has made the Film Board one of the few cultural life-savers Canada may point to as genuine and home-grown, a buoy that has helped prevent the nation from becoming either the largest Balkan hinterland in the world or the fifty-first member of the United States.

Put in another light, national interest has been well served by having institutional headquarters in Montreal, where almost everyone seems to feel that he or she is a member of a minority group. One is hard-pressed to find another locale in Canada where the English and French live and work creatively, mostly separately but amicably, under one roof, in both official languages. This is one authentic expression of the peculiarity of Canadian culture. Perhaps it was best that the filmmakers in the past decade never realized that Ottawa would not and could not close the institution down, lest it deny this Canadian reality. Yet if headquarters' doors have not closed, they will remain 'revolving' in the foreseeable future, in the sense that new talent will come and go, but probably will not stay because the permanent core must hereafter remain small. Likewise, with regional production centres almost exclusively geared to launch filmmakers, but not to keep them on permanently, those who remain must carry the standard on behalf of 27 million citizens, not an exclusive group or constituency.

Now that film distribution is virtually guaranteed to every Canadian home and school containing a television and video-cassette player, the Film Board is on its mettle to prove itself indispensable. How this is to be done is the most important question. The organization may confirm its usefulness by feeding an unending Canadian cultural addiction to actuality; it may also prove its worth by undertaking 'prestige' productions that give meaning to the term 'Canadian glamour.' Or it may do something for the normally drab and dry Canadian feature film which continues to beg for decent scripting.

To continue its work on the international level, the Film Board needs some top-notch diplomatists of its own to resume a connection to the work of the Department of External Affairs and to convince the mandarins there that it has something unique to offer. On the national level, the organization needs to persuade Ottawa that it deserves to make at least some of the departmental sponsored films, for it was in those productions that it showed how national distinctiveness had little to do with jingoism and much to do with quality, thoughtfulness, originality, and international appeal. One powerful argument for them is to ask just how many sponsored works done by the private sector in the past five years have won international awards. The answer is, pitifully few. Doing what needs to be done demands more public funding, the one commodity of which there has been an ongoing shortage. It is time to ask if the commercial-film sector is returning the goodwill or national honour on the investment of public funds at anywhere near the Film Board's historical record. That answer is also negative.

Many fear that if the organization continues to be stripped of its multi-purpose functions, it may be cast into oblivion. But it may also be argued that the Film Board has been in perilous straits since the late sixties, when it found itself overexpanded, underfunded, and without a national television outlet for its work. Added to this was the simultaneous unionization of the public sector, which had brought with it the Scylla of forced job security and the Charybdis of inadequate regular work for a new generation of creative talent. Navigating this passage has proved to be nearly fatal, and the institution spent almost two decades trying to deal humanely with the fact that there were too many employees for too few production dollars. It is just finishing buying back the freedom a creative organization needs in order to thrive. The critical issue today is how the artists and administrators plan to respond to the contemporary challenges hidden behind our era's masks of affluence and indifference: What can be done to stem Canada's fracturing into tribal forces? Will gender issues propagate or mitigate the age-old war between the sexes? What is to be done about the contemporary drift toward a selfish, uncivil, and unhumanitarian North America? Are the world's social and natural environments salvageable?

Some think that Challenge for Change / Société nouvelle is the ideological hook upon which the institution should form and hang its mandate. That programme's greatest strength lay in keeping close ties to the marginal elements of the population who were the forgotten flotsam of a consumer society. But as a matter of principle the CBC rejected these sorts of films because they did not meet its criterion of balance. The CBC fear of alienating wider sectors of the population means that the Film Board's pursuit of the narrowly ideological film will deprive it of a national network audience. Furthermore, the danger of designing audiovisual material solely on this principle is to put into jeopardy documentary's first principle, that the passion for truth must be linked to art and poetry. The object of the Film Board should be to help viewers gather, focus, and even change their thoughts about an issue that is in the national interest. Such activity is more subtle than the earnest presentation of fact alone. Thus, there remains one last bit of uncharted territory: the manipulation of fact and truth to articulate a national mythology. Without a fuller sense of national history and national mythology, Canadians will be left with little more than an acceptance of the world as it is, rather than having the option to dream of what it could be. And, most depressing of all, there is little reason to believe that the nation can perpetuate itself without having national history expressed in the form of legend or myth. Perhaps Ottawa is not certain for what purpose it continues to fund the organization; it is up to the creative artists to design and stake out their role in a national myth-making project, be it on the lines of *Canada*

Vignettes or a grandiose series that will show national history, warts and all. A whole generation of Canadian history and Canadian studies scholars should provide the resource material to help actualize such a project.

If mythmaking is one signpost to future activity, this book has shown that the organization has been intrepid at mirroring the pulse of historical change. After fifty years, this is perhaps the Film Board's greatest legacy, having established a fixed record of the hieroglyphics of the Canadian reality for future generations to decode. Soon, the publication of the Film Board's *Comprehensive Guide* index, containing information on every one of the 7,827 documentaries, animations, public-information shorts, and features it has made over fifty years, will help tomorrow's researchers to comprehend our present as their past.

It is fitting that the last words belong to Grierson, the prime mover. They were quoted earlier when the narrative described the institution's twenty-fifth anniversary in 1964: 'You are artists in the public service and in the service of Canada,' he told the assembled staff. 'To be a creative person at the Film Board is the privilege to be a great public servant. But you are only as good as your next film.' That single admonition by the prophet of documentary is the social contract and guarantee of excellence that should be renegotiated periodically between the creative minds at the National Film Board / Office National du Film and the Canadian public, who remain spiritual shareholders in the institution by birthright.

Appendix 1

Television films completed in fiscal year 1964–5

English (13 hours)

HALF-HOUR FILMS

'Comparisons': Five films comparing similar situations in Greece, Thailand, and Canada – *Three Country Boys, Three Fishermen, The Stage to Three, The Inner Man, City Scene*

Along Uncharted Shores: Interviews and stills on the 1936–40 British Canadian Arctic Expedition in the Foxe Basin area

David and Hazel: A Story in Communication: The importance of communication between members of a family

Jamie: The Story of a Sibling: The conflicts between the children of a family

Turn of the Century (1897–1919): The events, mood, and character of Canada between Victoria's Diamond Jubilee and the end of the First World War

Because They Are Different: An inquiry into the question of integrating native Indian children into non-Indian schools

Phoebe: The psychological state of a pregnant, unwed teenage girl and her boyfriend (see chapter 5)

The Visit: An Italian immigrant to Canada, after a number of years, returns to his homeland and realizes he belongs in Canada

Return Reservation: A portrayal of the life of a city as seen by its visitors

Blindness: To convey the feeling of blindness and to show how a blind person can live a normal life.

Every Second Car: The implications of a car on society with an emphasis on traffic safety

Joey: To convince would-be adopters that every satisfaction of parenthood can be achieved even if the child is not 'beautiful.'

John Hirsch: The theatrical personality and the Manitoba Theatre Centre, which tries to promote the acceptance of theatre

LONGER FILMS

Nobody Waved Goodbye (80 min.): See chapter 5.

The Child of the Future: How Might He Learn? (58 min.): Exploring the process of learning

Stravinsky (50 min): A portrait of the character and philosophy of this great composer

Bethune (58 min.): An interpretation through interviews, archival footage, and still photos of the life of the famed Canadian surgeon (see chapter 5)

As well, eight French originals were versioned into English for transmission: *The Lakeman, Caroline, End of Summer, Fabienne, Françoise, The Moontrap* (abridged form of *Pour la suite du monde*), *Walls of Memory*, and *Golden Gloves*.

French (5 hours)

HALF-HOUR FILMS

Le Temps perdu: A study of the middle-class teenage girl in French Canada

Vaillancourt: The sculptor, his conception of art and new style

A propos d'une plage: Anniversary film commemorating the Allied landing in Normandy in June 1944

La Fin des étés: Using flashbacks, a young girl relives fragments of her recent past.

8 Témoins (58 min.): Exploration of the world of delinquency, with reference to the delinquents themselves

Le Chat dans le sac (74 min.): See chapter 5.

Nota su una mino ranza (61 min.): In Italian, the film documents the life, problems, and hopes of Canadians of Italian origin.

One half-hour English film was versioned into French: *Les Hutterites*.

Appendix 2

Sponsored films made for various government departments and agencies, 1966–7

Agriculture

Apple Harvest: Methods of grading apples
Newfoundland Potato Disease: Review of New-foundland potato diseases and recommended preventative steps
Canadian Wheat: Principles and practices in producing this product

Atomic Energy

Rajasthan Nuclear Power Project: Record of manufacture of components for a nuclear power station for India
Radio Isotopes: What radio isotopes are and how they are used commercially

Canadian Commercial Corporation

Runway Snow Removal and *Runway Ice Control*: Two films for the U.S. Air Force dealing with runway snow and ice clearance

Canadian Government Participation, Expo 67

Canadian Pavilion, Information Wall: 8-mm demonstration loop for Communications exhibit
Canadian Pavilion (reportage): 16-mm French film on the pavilion for those unable to visit Expo

Centennial Commission

Parliament Buildings: A review of the history of the Parliament Buildings and their importance in the life of Canada
Helicopter Canada: See chapter 6.
Centennial Fever: A candid observation of the people of St Paul, Alberta, as they conceive and take part in their own Centennial projects
Participate: An athletic programme for young Canadians
Voyageur du Centenaire: Children from British Columbia and Quebec visit one another in their native provinces.
Commercials: Publicity for Centennial

Central Mortgage and Housing Corporation

Community Planning: Good planning with reference to the role of the individual municipality
Société Centrale d'Hypothèque et de Logement: Film on urban renewal in Quebec
Better Homes for the Prairies: Record of results on Prairies of implementation of the National Housing Act
National Housing Act: Record of results in Maritimes of implementation of the National Housing Act
Urbanissimo: A short trailer on urban living

323

Citizenship

The Shattered Silence: The responsibilities of citizenship in a democratic society and the need to respect law and the rights of others

En Septembre: An immigrant family in Montreal

Immigration en février: A film designed to encourage immigration from France

Au Canada: The settling of immigrants in Canada in the last few years

Les Indiens: A film designed to enhance the understanding of Indians by the Canadian public

Citizenship Centennial Project: The contribution of ethnic groups to Canada's development

The Meeting: A film to serve as a discussion opener on such questions as self-determination, the validity of majority rule, and the rights of a minority

Civil Service Commission

Enquête: Research study of the activities of the Civil Service Commission as part of a plan to recommend a long-term programme of visual-aids production

Energy, Mines and Resources

The Searching Man: How modern methods assist the present-day geologist

Geological Survey of Canada: Review of the history and objectives of the Geological Survey of Canada

Queen Elizabeth Telescope: Record of the construction of a new telescope in British Columbia

External Aid

External Aid: A film to show some key elements of an External Aid programme at work in an Asian or African country

EMO Winnipeg Flood: How EMO assisted the relief measures instituted when a disastrous flood threatened Winnipeg

Fisheries

North Pacific: Activities of the Fisheries Research Board

Atlantic Salmon in Newfoundland: Fishing in Newfoundland

Northern Fisherman: A film to impress on Indian fishermen the importance of proper methods in the handling of their product

Fish-finding Equipment: An explanation of the basic operating principles of modern electronic fish-finding equipment

Fishing Gear Technology: The use of new equipment and improved practices to help achieve better catches of inshore fish

Offshore Fisherman: A study of life at sea aboard a modern fishing trawler to aid recruitment to this occupation

Marine Safety: The basic hazards that result from non-adherence to safety precautions in small-fishing-boat operations

Forestry

Agricultural Rehabilitation and Development Association (ARDA) Study: Possible uses of film to inform people about ARDA programme

ARDA Record Film Coverage: Film illustrating various ARDA projects

ARDA – 3000 and Under: Study of a family living in a depressed rural area

Nouveau Brunswick Nord (ARDA): ARDA public-education programme in northern New Brunswick

Forest Regions of Canada: Assessment of non-renewable resources available from forest lands, highlighting their social and economic importance

Principles of Woodlot Management: Basic principles explained for benefit of small-woodlot owner

The Forester: Work of contemporary forester

Land Capability: Review of how forest land has been used historically until today

Forest Fire Clips: Television clips to alert the public to the disastrous results of forest fires

Land Computer: How modern electronic computations aid land-use assessment

Indian Affairs and Northern Development

Duck Identification Loops: Series of six 8-mm loops to assist hunters in carrying out improved duck-species identification

Ducks of Course: A review of the basic principles of duck-species identification

Louisbourg Restoration: Record of the restoration of the Louisbourg fortress

Parcs Atlantiques: National parks in the Atlantic provinces

Mountain Parks: A look at the park facilities available in British Columbia and Alberta

Northern Affairs Programme: Resources, Transport and Communications: A series of films to encourage more investment in the development and exploitation of the non-renewable resources of northern areas

La grande Hermine: Record of the reconstruction of Jacques Cartier's ship

Industry

All Systems Go: A study of Canada's technological capability in the aerospace field

Periscopter: Actuality footage and explanation of principles of a new airborne television facility

Justice

Catégorie de détenus: A training film for penitentiary officers showing various types of inmates and different psychological behaviour patterns

New Justice Series: Reception and *Inmates Training #1 and #2*: Films designed to assist in the training of personnel working in the penitentiary service

Squarejohns: A study of the difficulties of rehabilitating former criminals

Labour

Technical Education: A study of the importance of technical and vocational training for young people about to leave school

ILO Films and Slides Presentation: Audiovisual supplements in three languages designed and used for ILO Conference

Challenge of Change: A film to show the effects of technological change in our society

Impact of Change: The impact of technological change on society as a whole

Manpower and Immigration

Women in Community – Long Weekend: A study of women at work in the community in various occupations both rural and urban.

National Capital Commission

Plan de la capitale nationale: A film illustrating the National Capital plan as seen at the beginning of 1967

National Defence

A Life of Adventure: Officer recruiting film showing career opportunities available in the armed services

Nuclear Defence at Sea: Training film showing procedures and precautions on a ship under nuclear attack

Hydrofoil #1 and #2: Two films to explain the design and construction of the RCN's new hydrofoil ship

RCN Leadership Series: Short films showing typical leadership problems; for leadership training

Mapping for Defence: Comprehensive study of the army's mapping service

Bathythermograph: A technical training film for the RCN

Relative Velocities: Ideas required in the development of velocity for navigation at sea

Such Brave Men: A review of Canada's military history for schoolchildren

Infra-Red: Army technical training film

Your Parachute "SIMTELS": Videotape record of the structure and packing of a parachute (Note: This is the first-ever mention of a videotape production made for a sponsor.)

National Gallery

National Gallery: The work of the National Gallery portrayed on film

National Harbours Board

National Harbours Film: A review of the port facilities available in Canada

National Health and Welfare

Canada Youth Conference on Smoking: A record of events that took place during this conference

No Smoking for Children: A short film to discourage the use of cigarettes by children of school-going ages

Rehabilitation of the Mentally Ill: Problems associated with the rehabilitation of a patient who has undergone intensive psychiatric treatment

Northern Health Services: Recruiting and orientation films for health-care workers in the North

When Your Time Is Your Own: Community organization of recreation facilities and programmes

Get Wet: Recreation in the water

Volleyball: Two films designed to encourage the general public to take up specific sports in their leisure time

National Revenue

Tax Is Not a Four-letter Word: Public-information film extolling the need for income tax through the use of a humorous animated cartoon

Post Office

A Tale of Mail: History of the Canadian Post Office seen through animation and actuality photography

Privy Council

The Things I Cannot Change: See chapter 7.

Public Works

Oxygen Tent Therapy: A film to highlight the dangers involved in the careless handling of oxygen in hospitals

RCMP

R.C.M.P. Career Film: A film to aid recruitment to the RCMP

In Your Custody: Correct methods of escorting prisoners

Trade and Commerce

Travel Bureau: Foreign versions of films produced by provincial or private organizations for overseas use by the Travel Bureau

Harlow Housing Project: A film to show techniques used in the multi-housing development in Harlow, England

Easy Export: Animated film explaining the services available from the department to assist businessmen wishing to improve their export trade

Televisits: Films on regional subjects

Poultry Processing: A film showing the latest developments in mass poultry processing

Transport

Met Service Film: How Canada's Meteorological Service functions, giving an idea of the services it provides to Canadians in all walks of life

Canot de sauvetage: Film on life-raft technique

Civil Aviation: The status of civil aviation in Canada today, stressing particularly the services necessary to operate air-transport services effectively

Airport Construction: Record of the construction of a new airport

Launching Life Rafts: An analysis of the correct method of launching life rafts from government vessels

Air Traffic Control: A film describing the various responsibilities of air traffic controllers

UNESCO

Elément 3 l'eau: A film on the scarcity of water in the world; produced in cooperation with UNESCO

Veterans Affairs

Air Marshall W.A. Bishop, V.C.

World's Fair Corporation, Expo 67

Labyrinth: See chapter 6.

Source: Minutes of the NFB, 16–17 June 1967, Appendix

Appendix 3
Films of the
Challenge for Change programme

'... and They Lived Happily Ever After'
Andrew Britt at Shoal Bay
Ballad of Crowfoot
Billy Crane Moves Away
Building an Organization
Bus – For Us, A
Cell 16
Challenge for Change
Charley Squash Goes to Town
Child Abuse
Children of Fogo Island
Citizen Discussions
Citizen Harold
Citizen's Medicine
Community Action Theatre on Tour
Continuing Responsibility
Co-op Housing: Getting It Together
Co-op Housing: The Best Move We Ever Made
Cree Hunters of Mistassini
Cree Way
Crowded Wilderness, A
Dan Roberts on Fishing
Deciding to Organize
Do Your Thing
80 Goes to Sparta, The
Encounter at Kwacha House – Halifax
Encounter on Urban Environment
Encounter with Saul Alinsky, Parts I and II
Extensions of the Family
Fishermen's Meeting
God Help the Man Who Would Part with His
    Land

Greenlanders, The
Halifax Neighborhood Centre Project
I Don't Think It's Meant for Us
Indian Dialogue
Indian Relocation: Elliott Lake
Introduction to Fogo Island
It's Not Enough
Labrador North
Laurette
Like the Trees
Luckily I Need Little Sleep
Memo From Fogo, A
Mothers Are People
Mrs. Case
Nell and Fred
New Alchemists, The
Original Sin
Our Dear Sisters
Our Land Is Our Life
Overspill
People and Power
Pikangikum
Point: Community Legal Clinic, The
Pow Wow at Duck Lake
Prince Edward Island Development Project,
    Parts I and II, The
Promises, Promises
Question of Television Violence, The
Regina Telebus
Saul Alinsky Went to War
Some People Have to Suffer
Some Problems of Fogo

Songs of Chris Cobb, The
Specialists at Memorial Discuss the Fogo Films,
  The
Spring Like Nowhere Else, A
Temiscaming, Quebec
That Gang of Hoodlums?
These Are My People
They Appreciate You More
Things I Cannot Change, The
Through Conflict to Negotiation
Tiger on a Tight Leash
Travelling College
Up Against the System
VTR St-Jacques
'When I Go ... That's It!'

Where Do We Go from Here?
Wilf
World of One in Five
Would I Ever Like to Work
You Are on Indian Land
Young Social Worker Speaks Her Mind

This list of 83 films is taken from Garth Rustand, 'The Challenge for Change Programme: Its Use of Film and VTR,' unpublished study, Simon Fraser University, 1979. (Inexplicably, he overlooked the five films of the Alinsky Approach series, *Organizing for Power*, which have been added.)

Appendix 4
Oscar awards and nominations through 1989

Date signifies competition year for which film was nominated or awarded; date in parentheses is year of release, if different from competition year. † denotes Oscar winner.

1941 *Churchill's Island*,† Stuart Legg, director
Warclouds in the Pacific, Stuart Legg, director

1942 *High Over the Borders*, Raymond Spottiswoode, director
Inside Fighting China, Joris Ivens, director

1949 *The Rising Tide*, Jean Palardy, director

1951 *The Fight: Science Against Cancer*, Morten Parker, director

1952 *Neighbours*,† Norman McLaren, director

1953 *The Romance of Transportation in Canada*, Colin Low, director
Herring Hunt, Julian Biggs, director

1954 *The Stratford Adventure*, Morten Parker, director

1957 *A Chairy Tale*, Norman McLaren and Claude Jutra, directors
City of Gold, Wolf Koenig and Colin Low, directors

1958 *The Living Stone*, John Feeney, director

1960 *Universe*, Roman Kroitor and Colin Low, directors

1961 *Very Nice, Very Nice*, Arthur Lipsett, director

1963 *My Financial Career* (1962), Grant Munro and Gerald Potterton, directors

1964 *Christmas Cracker* (1963), Norman McLaren, Grant Munro, Jeff Hale, Gerald Potterton, directors

Eskimo Artist: Kenojuak, John Feeney, director

1966 *The Drag* (1965), Carlos Marchiori, director
Helicopter Canada, Eugene Boyko, director

1967 *What on Earth!* (1966), Les Drew and Kaj Pindal, directors
Paddle to the Sea (1966), Bill Mason, director

1968 *The House That Jack Built* (1967), Ron Tunis, director
Pas de deux (1967), Norman McLaren, director

1969 *Walking* (1968), Ryan Larkin, director
Blake, Bill Mason, director

1971 *Evolution*, Michael Mills, director

1974 *The Family That Dwelt Apart* (1973), Yvon Mallette, director
Hunger (1973), Peter Foldès, director

1975 *Whistling Smith*, Michael Scott and Marrin Canell, directors
Monsieur Pointu, Bernard Longpré and André Leduc, directors

1976 *Blackwood*, Tony Ianzelo and Andy Thomson, directors
Volcano: An Inquiry into the Life and Death of Malcolm Lowry, Donald Brittain and John Kramer, directors
The Street, Caroline Leaf, director

1977 *High Grass Circus* (1976), Torben Schioler and Tony Ianzelo, directors
Bead Game, Ishu Patel, director
The Sand Castle,† Co Hoedeman, director

330

I'll Find a Way,† Beverly Shaffer, director

1978 *Special Delivery*,† John Weldon and Eunice Macaulay, directors

1979 *Bravery in the Field*, Giles Walker, director

Going the Distance, Paul Cowan, director

Nails, Phillip Borsos, director; Mercury Films Ltd. in association with the NFB

Every Child,† Eugene Fedorenko, director

1981 *First Winter*, John N. Smith, director

The Tender Tale of Cinderella Penguin, Janet Perlman, director

1982 *If You Love This Planet*,† Terri Nash, director

After the Axe (1981), Sturla Gunnarsson, director

1983 *Flamenco at 5:15*,† Cynthia Scott, director

The Profession of Arms, Michael Bryans and Tina Viljoen, directors

1984 *Paradise*, Ishu Patel, director

The Painted Door, Bruce Pittman, director; Atlantis Films Ltd. in association with the NFB

1985 *The Big Snit*, Richard Condie, director

1986 *Le Décline de l'empire américain*, Denys Arcand, director; René Malo Films in association with the NFB

1987 *George and Rosemary*, Alison Snowden and David Fine, directors

1988 *The Cat Came Back*, Cordell Barker, director

Total: fifty-five nominations and nine Oscars, including a special Oscar for excellence in 1989, marking the occasion of the Film Board's fiftieth anniversary

Appendix 5
Chronology of the best films of French Production to 1984

La Drave, documentary, 1957, Raymond Garceau, director

Les Raquetteurs, documentary 1958, Gilles Groulx and Michel Brault, directors

Les Brûlés, fiction, 1959, Bernard Devlin, director

La Lutte, documentary, 1961, Michel Brault, Marcel Carrière, Claude Fournier, Claude Jutra, directors

Jour après jour, documentary, 1962, Clément Perron, director

Les Bûcherons de la Manouane, documentary, 1962, Arthur Lamothe, director

Patinoire, documentary, 1963, Gilles Carle, director

Caroline, fiction, 1964, Clément Perron and Georges Dufaux, directors

La Beauté même, documentary, 1964, Monique Fortier, director

A Saint-Henri, le 5 septembre, documentary, 1964, Hubert Aquin, director

Le Chat dans le sac, fiction, 1964, Gilles Groulx, director

Mémoire en fête, documentary, 1964, Léonard Forest, director

Inventaire d'une colonie (ARDA), sponsored film, 1965, Raymond Garceau, director

60 cycles, documentary, 1965, Jean-Claude Labrecque, director

La Vie heureuse de Léopold Z, fiction, 1965, Gilles Carle, director

La Fleur de l'âge: Les adolescentes, fiction, 1965, Michel Brault, director

Volley-ball, documentary, 1966, Denys Arcand, director

Ça n'est pas le temps des romans, fiction, 1968, Fernand Dansereau, director

Métrofolle, animation, 1967, Yvon Mallette, director

Le Grand Rock, fiction, 1967, Raymond Garceau, director

Un Enfant ... un pays, animation, 1967, Pierre Moretti, director

Là ou Ailleurs, documentary, 1969, Jacques Leduc and Pierre Bernier, directors

Wow, documentary/fiction, 1969, Claude Jutra, director

Le Corbeau et le Renard, animation, 1969, Francine Desbiens, Pierre Hébert, Michele Pauzé, Yves Leduc, directors

Un pays sans bon sens, documentary, 1970, Pierre Perrault, director

Mon enfance à Montréal, fiction, 1970, Jean Chabot, director

On est loin du soleil, fiction, 1970, Jacques Leduc, director

Mon oncle Antoine, fiction, 1971, Claude Jutra, director

Ixe-13, fiction, 1971, Jacques Godbout, director

Sur vivre, documentary, 1971, Yves Dion, director

Peut-être Maurice Richard, documentary, 1971, Gilles Gascon, director

César et son Canot d'écorce, documentary, 1971, Bernard Gosselin, director

Québec, Duplessis et après, documentary, 1972, Denys Arcand, director

Le Temps d'une chasse, fiction, 1972, Francis Mankiewicz, director

24 heures ou plus, documentary, 1973, Gilles Groulx, director

O.K. ... Laliberté, fiction, 1973, Marcel Carrière, director

La dernière Neige, fiction, 1973, André Théberge, director

Monsieur John Grierson, documentary, 1973, Roger Blais, director

Richesse des autres, documentary, 1973, Maurice Bulbulian and Michel Gauthier, directors

Le Mariage du hibou (Une légende eskimo), animation, 1974, Caroline Leaf and Co Hoedeman, directors

Les Filles du Roy, documentary, 1974, Anne Claire Poirier, director

Night Cap, fiction, 1974, André Forcier, director

Climats, animation, 1974, Suzanne Gervais, director

Les Tacots, fiction, 1974, André Melançon, director

Au bout de mon âge, documentary, 1975, Georges Dufaux, director

Monsieur Pointu, animation, 1975, Bernard Longpré and André Leduc, directors

Cher Théo, fiction, 1975, Jean Beaudin, director

Partis pour la gloire, fiction, 1975, Clémont Perron, director

J.A. Martin, photographe, fiction, 1976, Jean Beaudin, director

Le Paysagiste, animation, 1976, Jacques Drouin, director

Jeux de la XXIe Olympiade, documentary, 1977, Jean-Claude Labrecque with Jean Beaudin, Marcel Carrière, Georges Dufaux, directors

Les Oiseaux blancs de l'île d'Orléans, documentary, 1977, Diane Létourneau, director

Dernier envoi, animation, 1977, Francine Desbiens, director

Le Plan sentimental, documentary, 1978, Jacques Leduc, director

L'Age de la machinve, fiction, 1978, Gilles Carle, director

L'Age de chaise, animation, 1978, Jean-Thomas Bédard, director

Les Vrais Perdants, documentary, 1978, André Melançon, director

Mourir à tue-tête, fiction, 1979, Anne Claire Poirier, director

Deux épisodes dans la vie d'Hubert Aquin, documentary 1979, Jacques Godbout, director

De la tourbe et du restant, documentary, 1979, Fernand Bélanger, director

Premiers jours, animation, 1980, Clorinda Worny (died), Suzanne Gervais, Lina Gagnon, directors

Le Canot à Renald à Thomas, documentary, 1980, Bernard Gosselin, director

Zea, animation, 1981, André Leduc and Jean-Jacques Leduc, directors

'E', animation, 1981, Bretislav Pojar, director, in collaboration with Francine Desbiens

Luna, Luna, Luna, animation, 1981, Viviane Elnécavé, director

Grief 81, fiction, 1981, Jean-Guy Noël, director

L'Impossible Oubli, documentary, 1981, Harvey Spak, director

La Bête lumineuse, documentary, 1982, Pierre Perrault, director

Massabielle, fiction, 1983, Jacques Savoie, director

Un gars d'la place, fiction, 1983, Valmont Jobin, director

La Plante, fiction and animation, 1983, Thomas Vamos and Joyce Borenstein, directors

Trêve, animation, 1983, Suzanne Gervais, director

Rectangle et Rectangles, animation, 1984, René Jodoin, director

Mario, fiction, 1984, Jean Beaudin, director

Mascarade, animation, 1984, Co Hoedeman, director

Etienne et Sara, animation, 1984, Pierre Hébert, director

Opéra zéro, animation, 1984, Jacques Giraldeau, director

As shown at '25 ans d'images à notre image,' in Montreal, November–December 1984

Appendix 6
Film commissioners and directors of English and French Production, Distribution, and Technical Operations

Film Commissioners

John Grierson   October 1939–August 1945
Ross McLean   August 1945–Janury 1946 (interim); January 1946–January 1950
Arthur Irwin   February 1950–June 1953
Albert Trueman   July 1953–April 1957
Guy Roberge   May 1957–April 1966
Grant McLean   April 1966–June 1967 (interim)
Hugo McPherson   May 1967–July 1970
Sydney Newman   August 1970–August 1975
André Lamy   August 1975–January 1979
James de Beaujeu Domville   January 1979–January 1984
François Macerola   January 1984–May 1984 (interim); May 1984–December 1988
Joan Pennefather   December 1988–September 1989 (interim); September 1989–

Directors of English Production*

Stuart Legg   (Supervisor of Production) October 1939–July 1942
Raymond Spottiswoode   (Director of Production) July 1942–December 1945
James Beveridge   (Production Secretary) January 1946–May 1950
Donald Mulholland   (Director of Production) June 1950–February 1957
Grant McLean   March 1957–April 1966
Julian Biggs   April 1966–June 1968
Frank Spiller   (interim) June 1968–October 1968; October 1968–February 1971
Bernard Devlin   March 1971–September 1972

Robert Verrall   September 1972–December 1976
Ian McLaren   January 1977–December 1979
Peter Katadotis   January 1980–February 1988
Colin Neale   (interim) February 1988–September 1988
Barbara Emo   September 1988–

* Title change: Director General of English Programming, from April 1985

Directors of French Production*

Bernard Devlin   (no official title) November 1951–October 1953
Roger Blais   (no official title) 1953–1956
Pierre Juneau   January 1964–February 1965
Marcel Martin   March 1966–February 1969
Jacques Godbout   February 1969–April 1970
Gilles Dignard   April 1970–September 1971
Pierre Gauvreau   September 1971–October 1972
Yves Leduc   October 1972–September 1976
François Macerola   October 1976–March 1979
René Jodoin   (interim) April 1979–May 1979
Jean Marc Garand   May 1979–January 1984
Daniel Pinard   January 1984–December 1985
Georges Dufaux   February 1986–June 1989
Lucille Veilleux   (interim) June 1989–October 1989
Robert Forget   October 1989–

* No separate production budget until January 1964, when official title Director of French

Production was introduced; title change,
Director General of French Programming,
from April 1985

Directors of Distribution

Philéas Cote   (unofficial)
Wesley Greene   (Supervisor of Distribution)
   February 1943–May 1945
Malcom Ross   (Director of Distribution) May
   1945–August 1945
Jack Ralph   August 1945–December 1948
Len Chatwin   January 1949–July 1962
William Cosman   July 1962–May 1967
Wilf S. Jobbins   May 1967–March 1972
A.G. Vielfaure   April 1972–May 1979
William Litwack   May 1979–January 1984
Jan d'Arcy   February 1984–

Note: Through administrative reorganization in
May 1985, Distribution Branch is integrated into
English and French Program.

Directors of Technical Operations*

Raymond Spottiswoode   (Chief of Technical
   Research) To December 1945
Gerald Graham   (Chief of Technical Research)
   January 1946–January 1948; (Director of
   Technical Services) January 1948–1950;
   (Director of Technical Operations) 1950–
   February 1968
Ray W. Payne   March 1968–February 1973
Charles Prince   March 1973–February 1974
C. Douglas Ruppel   June 1974–September 1977
Creighton Douglas   October 1977–June 1980
Marcel Carrière   June 1980–

* Title change, May 1985: Director, Services
   Division, including technical and distribution
   services

Appendix 7

Museum of Modern Art 50th anniversary sampler of Film Board films (May 1989)

1939–1948

The Case of Charlie Gordon, 1939, director Stuart Legg

Mail Early, 1941, director Norman McLaren

Churchill's Island, 1941, director Stuart Legg

Dollar Dance, 1943, director Norman McLaren

High Over the Borders, 1942, directors Irving Jacoby, John Ferno

En Passant, 1943, directors Alexandre Alexeieff, Claire Parker

The Proudest Girl in the World, 1944, director Julian Roffman

The Feeling of Rejection, 1947, director Robert Anderson

1949–1958

Begone Dull Care, 1949, directors Norman McLaren, Evelyn Lambart

How to Build an Igloo, 1950, director Douglas Wilkinson

Neighbours, 1952, director Norman McLaren

Paul Tomkowicz: Street-railway Switchman, 1954, director Roman Kroitor

The Romance of Transportation in Canada, 1953, directors Colin Low, Robert Verrall, Wolf Koenig

Corral, 1954, director Colin Low

Making a Decision in the Family, 1955, director Julia Murphy

Les Raquetteurs, 1958, directors Gilles Groulx, Michel Brault

City of Gold, 1957, directors Wolf Koenig, Colin Low

1959–1968

The Back-Breaking Leaf, 1959, director Terence Macartney-Filgate

Very Nice, Very Nice, 1961, director Arthur Lipsett

Wrestling (La Lutte), 1961, directors Michel Brault, Claude Jutra, Marcel Carrière, Claude Fournier

High Steel, 1965, director Don Owen

Walking, 1968, director Ryan Larkin

Beluga Days, 1968, directors Pierre Perrault, Bernard Gosselin, Michel Brault

1969–1978

Animation from Cape Dorset, 1973, directors several Inuit artists

Hunger, 1973, director Peter Foldès

Nell and Fred, 1971, director Richard Todd

The Street, 1976, director Caroline Leaf

Pretend You're Wearing a Barrel, 1978, director Jan-Marie Martell

Travel Log, 1978, director Donald Winkler

The Sand Castle, 1977, director Co Hoedeman

1979–1988

The Sweater, 1980, director Sheldon Cohen

Ted Baryluk's Grocery, 1982, John Paskievich, Michael Mirus

Richard Cardinal: Cries from the Diary of a Metis Child, 1986, director Alanis Obomsawin

Every Dog's Guide to Home Safety, 1986, director Les Drew

Last Days of Okak, 1985, directors Anne Budgell, Nigel Markham

Wednesday's Children: Jenny, 1987, director Patricia Phillips

The Big Snit, 1985, director Richard Condie

The Cat Came Back, 1988, director Cordell Barker

Alias Will James, 1988, director Jacques Godbout

Notes

Chapter 1

1 Recent criticism of Grierson's practical approach to building the Canadian film industry rather than, as he put it, 'conjuring one out of the local sky,' has ignored these points in favour of a simplistic nationalist argument that accuses him of being a key architect of Canada's marginalization in the film world. See Peter Morris, 'Backwards to the Future: John Grierson's Film Policy for Canada.' in Gene Walz, ed., *Flashback: People and Institutions in Canadian Film History* (Montreal: Mediatext Publications 1986), 17–35.

2 For a discussion of the politics of this period, see Gary Evans, *John Grierson and the National Film Board: The Politics of Wartime Propaganda* (Toronto: University of Toronto Press 1984), 224–68.

3 The film, *Teeth Are to Keep*, written by P.K. Page and animated with cutouts by Jim Mackay, would go on to become one of the longest-running Film Board films at home and especially abroad. Page became one of the outstanding and celebrated Canadian poets of the contemporary era.

4 NFB 1067, file 1008

5 See Pierre Berton, *Hollywood's Canada* (Toronto: McClelland and Stewart 1975), 167–91; Maynard Collins, 'Cooperation, Hollywood and Howe,' *Cinema Canada* 56 (June–July 1979), 34–6; Pierre Véronneau, 'Cinéma de l'époque Duplessiste' in Carol Faucher, ed., *La production française à l'ONF* (Montreal: Cinémathèque québécoise / Musée du cinéma, 1984), 141–51; Pierre Véronneau and Piers Handling, eds, *Self-Portrait: Essays on the Canadian and Quebec Cinemas* (Ottawa: Canadian Film Institute 1980), 33–6.

6 J.W. Pickersgill interview with the author, 23 Oct. 1986

7 Tom Daly Papers, box XVI, Ross McLean to Saul Rae, Information Division, Department of External Affairs (DEA), 22 Nov. 1947; DEA to Vic Adams, NFB, 14 Sept. 1950. When the Film Board tried to distribute the film in Canada in 1950, the contract was cancelled because exhibitors thought it had a 'leftish slant.' DEA would not relax its restrictions until 1953, when it said the film could be released to film societies.

8 Marjorie McKay interview with the author, 20 May 1986. A more congenial R.H. Winters replaced him as minister responsible in January 1949.

9 Pearson's 'Dear Ross' from 'Mike' correspondence may have lulled McLean into thinking that his gaffe was not as serious as it actually was. See NFB 1067, file 1008, Pearson to McLean, 15 Mar. 1948; McLean to Pearson, 24 Mar. 1948; Pearson to McLean, 6 Apr. 1948.

10 *Telegram* (Toronto), 29 Mar. 1950. There was an unconfirmed suspicion at the Film Board that some people at Crawley Films had provided the RCMP with information that led to the 'routine check.' Michael Spencer, who had been in the Canadian Army Film Unit during the war, was the security officer and producer responsible for

all Department of National Defence films.
Years later, he denied there had been a suspect cameraman. He recalled a film crew
that was sent to the Arctic in 1948 to film
an army exercise, but all were above suspicion. Interview with the author, 27 July
1988

11 Minutes of the Meeting of the National
Film Board (hereafter, Minutes of the NFB),
23 May 1949

12 McLean told his story in 1974 when he and
four succeeding film commissioners and
several senior staff were interviewed for a
film on the history of the NFB that was
never completed. See transcripts for *N.F.B.
History*, production no. 47-031, 1974. Also,
Marjorie McKay, whose unpublished history of the Film Board yields a detailed
account of events until 1963, wrote to Tom
Daly in 1976 that from her vantage point as
supervisor of business administration, she
believed at the time that the private-indus-
try lobby created many of the problems the
Board faced in the press and in Commons.
Tom Daly Papers, box XI, no. 19, 11 Nov.
1976.

13 National Archives (NA), MG 32, B34, vol.
14, R-12-20, Confidential report on the
commercial film industry in Canada by Ian
MacNeill, secretary to the Film Board to
Albert Trueman, film commissioner, 25
Jan. 1954

14 Michael Spencer interview with the author,
27 July 1988

15 The prime minister was interested in broadcasting and the universities. The *Report of
the Royal Commission on National Development in the Arts, Letters and Sciences,
1949–1951* (Ottawa: Edmond Cloutier 1951)
has come to be regarded as the cornerstone
in the development of Canadian cultural
policy and cultural institutions. Claxton's
recommendation came in response to the
student wing of the Liberal party. When the
commission requested briefs from the public, few expected a total of 462 would come
from seven provincial governments, 87
national organizations, 262 local bodies, 32
commercial radio stations, and scores of
private individuals. Bernard Ostry, *The
Cultural Connection* (Toronto: McClelland
and Stewart 1978), 83–5; George Wood-

stock, *Strange Bedfellows: The State and the
Arts in Canada* (Vancouver: Douglas and
McIntyre 1985), 42–4; J.W. Pickersgill, *My
Years with Louis St Laurent* (Toronto:
University of Toronto Press 1975), 139.

16 NFB 1295, Film Commissioner, A-7, Brief to
the Royal Commission on National Development in the Arts, Letters and Sciences
submitted by the National Film Board of
Canada, July 1949. The brief tried to make
the case that the Film Board's film circuit
and library system were operating as a form
of *delayed* television, taking the Canadian
image to as many as one million per month,
split evenly between rural and urban audiences. It stressed that 'when television is
established in Canada, it will find ready for
use a very substantial program and a
technical capacity which could not be developed by another organization except
over a considerable period of years.'

17 NFB 1295, Film Commissioner, A-7, Ross
McLean, Witness at the Royal Commission
on National Development in the Arts,
Letters and Sciences, 24 Aug. 1949

18 DEA, file 50182, vol. 1, 11 Mar. 1948 to 28
Apr. 1950

19 Ibid., vols. 1, 2, 3. Much of the material in
this file was top secret at the time and
provides a fascinating profile of the thinking behind this aspect of the new NATO
relationship. For example, Norman A.
Robertson, clerk of the Privy Council and
secretary to the Cabinet, wrote to Escott
Reid in External Affairs, 16 Feb. 1949,
recommending a way to counter the French
position that NATO was sucking Europe into
the American war machine against the
Russians. He thought that Reid should use
Arthur Koestler's argument to paint the
Communists as a negative and destructive
element committed to wrecking this new
constructive effort. In May 1950 A.D.P.
Heeney of External Affairs gave guidelines
to the CBC for its short-wave broadcasts,
calling for true and objective news reporting, a stress on Communism as the instrument of Soviet imperialism, an appeal to
the national self-respect of subject people
without inciting them to revolt, an exposé
of Communist hypocrisy and peace propaganda, the correction of Soviet distortions

of Canadian actions, and the assertion that Canadians bring about social change without using violence or security organs that are a law unto themselves.

20 Kenneth R. Wilson and Cyril Bassett, 'Film Board monopoly facing a major test?' *Financial Post* 47, 19 Nov. 1949

21 Minutes of the NFB, 29 Nov. 1949 and 16 Dec. 1949. Irwin admitted in an interview with the author, 18 May 1986, that having Winters's secretary phone the bad news was a ham-handed thing for the minister to do. That Winters was angry there can be little doubt. Opposition Leader George Drew had asked him to quit the Film Board post on the security issue, and the *Ottawa Citizen* and *Montreal Gazette* reported this on 8 Dec.

22 Transcript of David Bairstow interview for *N.F.B. History* (uncompleted film), 11 Sept. 1974; also, Arthur Irwin interview with the author, 18 May 1986

23 Arthur Irwin letter to the author, 21 Oct. 1986

24 Arthur Irwin, 'The Canadian,' *Maclean's*, 1 Feb. 1950

25 Irwin Collection (private), Robert Winters to M. Crompton of *Maclean's* Editorial Promotion, 19 Oct. 1949

26 *Debates of the House of Commons*, vol. 2, 29 Mar. 1950, 1343–4

27 *Globe and Mail*, 23 June 1950. The headline read, 'Erstwhile critic now gives praise to Film Board,' signifying clear sailing for the Irwin regime.

28 David Bairstow interview, 11 Sept. 1974, and Irwin interview with the author, 18 May 1986

29 See Piers Handling, 'Censorship and Scares,' and Maynard Collins, 'A View from the Top: Interview with Arthur Irwin,' *Cinema Canada* 56 (June–July 1979), 25–31 and 37–41; *Has Anybody Here Seen Canada?*, co-production of the National Film Board and the Canadian Broadcasting Corporation, in association with the Great Canadian Moving Picture Company, 1978; Irwin Papers (private), handwritten notes, 'Film Board: Phone conversation with Rita Kilpatrick, August 30, 1979.'

30 A single exception occurred in the 1968 dramatic co-production *The Ernie Game*,

which had the self-destructive hero shoot his reflection in the mirror.

31 Jacques Bobet, 'Les racines cachées,' in Faucher, ed., *La production française à l'ONF*, 13–19

32 Under the National Film Act of 1939, there were eight members of the board of governors: a minister of the Crown, a member of the Privy Council, three officials of the civil or defence services, and three members not in the government's services. The governors met once a month to review and advise on production, distribution, and administration. The film commissioner, as chief executive officer, was responsible to them for the operation of the organization.

33 Arthur Irwin Papers, 'The National Film Act, 1950'

34 David Bairstow interview, 11 Sept. 1974. The fact that Irwin placed so much importance on the move to Montreal undercuts one of the primary tenets of historian Pierre Vérroneau's thesis, that the Film Board's Anglo-Saxon hierarchy had not discovered the place that francophone filmmakers should occupy. He based this facile assertion on the fact that in Marjorie Mackay's *History of the National Film Board* (unpublished NFB manuscript, 1964), only 10 pages out of 147 dealt with bicultural/bilingual aspects.

35 Arthur Irwin, *Confidential Report on the Location of the National Film Board*, Appendix 2 to Minutes of the NFB, 19 May 1950

36 J.W. Pickersgill interview with the author, 23 Oct. 1986

37 Gerald Graham interview with the author, 26 Oct. 1987, and Film Board Archives files on the Montreal move

38 On 16 Oct. 1948, Toronto's *Globe and Mail* reported that Premier Duplessis had said that Film Board films were 'impregnated if not saturated with Communist propaganda,' and that the censor board undertook censorship to guard the rights of Quebec Province 'in this domain as in others.' He declared that his government's decision to censor the Film Board 'prevented the showing of federal films with Communist tendencies.'

39 Arthur Irwin Papers, Robert Winters to

Louis St Laurent, 2 June 1950, Irwin reported to Vincent Massey on 30 Oct. 1950 that St Laurent and Duplessis had met and that the latter assured the prime minister that the Quebec government looked on the project with favour.

40 Ibid., Irwin to Massey, 30 Oct. 1950

41 DEA, file 50182, vol. 2, Escott Reid to J.A. McCordick, 4 Oct. 1950. External Affairs was also trying to arrange an exchange of ten Film Board agriculture films with Yugoslavia, but Irwin was worried about Quebec censorship, and suggested that a non-governmental organization should distribute them.

42 The Asian-bound films should be on technical assistance and on the democratic process as practised successfully in Canada. The point was to show that of the two warring ideologies, the Western democratic way of life was far more beneficial to the East than was Moscow's autocratic and materialistic system. DEA, file 50182, vol. 2, C.S.A. Ritchie for the Secretary of State for External Affairs to the High Commissioner for Canada, London, 16 Nov. 1950

43 DEA, file 50182, vol. 2, Irwin to A.D.P. Heeney, Summary of Preliminary Proposals for the Use of Film in Psychological Warfare, 16 Nov. 1950. The suggested themes appended were Human Rights, The Principle of the Opposition in a Democracy, The Secret Ballot, The Courts-Police-Citizen, The Story of a By-Election, The Canadian Compromise, Canadian Types, Canadian Children, Famous New Canadians, Canadian Outlook, International Democracy and the Canadian Position, Canada and the U.S.A., Canada and the Commonwealth, Canada and the United Nations, Canada and the North Atlantic Pact, Asian Students in Canada, Institute of Oriental Studies, Cargo from India (or Pakistan), and Technical Aids. For Canadian audiences, themes included Inside France (Germany, Italy, the Netherlands, etc.), The Culture of the East, The Hindu, and The Moslem.

The short theatrical stories included a Maritime Coal Miner, Newfoundland Pulpworker, Quebec Hydro-worker, Montreal French Businessman, Ottawa Civil Servant, Chalk River Atomic Scientist, Northern Ontario Prospector, New Canadian (Winnipeg), Rural Nurse (Saskatchewan), Alberta Oil Promoter, Okanagan Fruit Farmer, British Columbia Road Transport Driver, and The Modern Eskimo (or Indian).

44 One External Affairs officer thought he should get in touch with the information division of NATO, then under a Canadian, who might give more support if the programme were linked with defence expenditures. When the film commissioner attended the Fourth Conference on Canadian Information Abroad that same month, he found that business representatives were, on the whole, favourable to the suggested programme. DEA, file 50182, vol. 2, ibid., Irwin to Heeney, 25 Nov. 1950; J.A. McCordick (at the Canadian embassy, Washington, DC) to Irwin, 23 Nov. 1950; Paul Tremblay to Irwin Nov. 1950

45 Irwin prepared to send off his top executive producer, Tom Daly, to Washington to study the workings of the multi-million-dollar American 'truth' programme. External Affairs did not want Daly to meet the top policy makers, because they thought the department should give policy guidance, not the United States. Therefore Daly stayed home and, after discussing the American programme, External Affairs reported to Irwin that most of the State Department films were non-commissioned, or produced by outside producers. They agreed that hard-line anti-Communist material for target areas was to be limited. DEA, file 50182, vol. 2, Tom Daly to J.A. McCordick (Canadian embassy, Washington, DC), 2 Dec. 1950; McCordick to Philips, 5 Dec. 1950; McCordick to Irwin, 14 Dec. 1950

46 In January, Heeney met with Winters and Irwin to discuss films for psychological warfare. The minister said the Film Board had the facilities and know-how and would rely on External Affairs for advice on what films should be produced and how and where they should be distributed. The department would not support the programme with money, but was sympathetic to the proposal and would help wherever appropriate. They hoped to link work in this field directly with the CBC's International Service. DEA, file 50182, vol. 3,

Heeney Memo to Ritchie and McCordick, 11 Jan. 1951

47 DEA, file 50182, vol. 3, R.B. Bryce to Irwin, 24 Jan. 1951; Winters to Heeney, 26 Jan. 1951

48 DEA, file 50182, vol. 3, First meeting of the Ad Hoc Committee on Government Information Services, 1 Mar. 1951. There were hard-liners like J.A. McCordick, a Department of National Defence liaison officer, who warned a month earlier that 'cold war is war and could continue indefinitely without transition to conventional war.' He thought that in the war of ideas, Canada should formulate war aims of victory in the cold war, aims that enunciated the goal of destroying the Soviet Communist party and its foreign appendages.

Illustrating the atmosphere of that 1951 season of discontent is a top secret memo from Heeney to the minister, dated 5 Feb. 1951, which reported that a Film Board technician had developed a mechanical technique of distorting or adapting recorded speeches, so that a speech by a prominent enemy might be altered as desired or an artificial speech might be prepared. Beamed over a regular station, the enemy might think he was listening to his own radio. National Defence was interested, and after establishing the reliability of the technician, seconded him into its research facilities.

49 DEA, file 50182, vol. 3, Meeting of the Ad Hoc Committee on Government Information Services, 4 Mar. 1951

50 Pierre Véronneau, *Résistance et affirmation: La production francophone à l'ONF, 1939–1964*, Les dossiers de la cinémathèque no. 17 (Montreal: Cinémathèque québécoise / musée du cinéma (1987), 21–2

51 *Report of the Royal Commission on National Development in the Arts, Letters and Sciences, 1949–1951*, chap. 4: 50–9. Most of this chapter was written by Guy Roberge, a young Liberal member of the Quebec legislature, who had articled in Prime Minister St Laurent's law office and who became the government film commissioner in 1957. Chapter 19: 306–13 also dealt with the agency.

52 NFB 1295, Film Commissioner A-7, Royal Commission, vol. 2, Archibald Day, Secretary to the Commission to Irwin, 11 Dec. 1950; Irwin to Day, 14 Dec. 1950

53 Transcript of interview for *N.F.B. History*, 11 Sept. 1974. Arthur Irwin interview with the author, 18 May 1986. Also McKay, *History of the National Film Board*, 89. McKay quotes Grierson, 'He saved the Board. No one else could have done it.'

54 As of August 1987, *Neighbours* held first place, having been booked almost 77,000 times abroad. Its next closest competitor was *Wildlife in the Rockies*, with 69,000 bookings abroad. *Neighbours* was the third most popular non-theatrical film at home with almost 31,000 lifetime bookings, being edged out slightly by *One Little Indian* and *Ti-Jean Goes Lumbering*, which was first with 32,221 lifetime bookings. NFB Popularity List for 200 titles, 31 Aug. 1987

55 According to animator Don McWilliams, whose film *Creative Process* is the definitive documentary about McLaren's art, McLaren admired two works about himself; Maynard Collins, *Norman McLaren* (Ottawa: Canadian Film Institute 1976), and Alsio Baspiancech, *L'Opera de Norman McLaren* (Turin: Giappichelle 1980). See also the special issue on McLaren in *Séquences* 82 (Oct. 1975).

56 Irwin Papers, Norman McLaren to Arthur Irwin, 26 Feb. 1984; Transcript from *Has Anybody Here Seen Canada? A History of Canadian Movies, 1939–1953* (Montreal: National Film Board of Canada 1978); Guy Glover, *McLaren, 1980* (Montreal: National Film Board of Canada 1980). *Neighbours* cost $14,963 to make and was one of the least expensive films made in 1952.

57 Minutes of the NFB, 16 July 1951, 5 Nov. 1951, 4 Feb. 1952, 5 Aug. 1952, 3 Nov. 1952, 4 May 1953, 4 Aug. 1953. External Affairs liked a number of films: *Man in the Peace Tower, Rescue Mission, Changing Prairie, Germany, Key to Europe*, and *Canada – World Citizen*.

58 NFB, box A146, 1-M-156-3, 1952–4, Albert Trueman to Walter Harris, 15 Dec. 1953

59 NFB 1295, Film Commissioner, A-7, Royal Commission, vol. 1, Irwin to Vincent Massey, 27 Oct. 1950.

60 NA, MG 32, B34, vol. 15, R-12-21. Report on Proposals for Cooperation between the Ca-

nadian Broadcasting Corporation and the National Film Board in Respect of Provision of Film for Television Broadcasting, 23 Oct. 1952

61 The French series, *Regards sur le Canada* (half-hour) and *Sur le Vif* (quarter-hour), gave a boost to the French section, though the lack of competent personnel rather than policy slowed the evolution of that group.

62 Massey Commission report, chap. 4: 50–9

63 NFB 1298, file 666, vol. 1, 1951–2. Special Committee on the National Film Board, W.A. Robinson, chairman, 8 May 1952, 9–21

64 NFB 1298, A-368, Special Committee on the National Film Board, 3 June 1952. Irwin did not tell them how infinitely perplexing Quebec relations were. Roger Blais had directed two stereotypical films of Quebec, *Les Moines de Saint-Benoit*, a 1951 film on Benedictine monks, and *De père en fils (From Father to Son)*, a 1952 item on making maple syrup, sugar, and candy. The provincial minister responsible had to take Blais to Duplessis personally to receive approval of his use of a Quebec government airplane for an aerial shot. Duplessis kept ribbing Blais for being associated with the 'Communist' Film Board. Roger Blais interview with the author, 9 Sept. 1987

Chapter 2

1 Transcript of interview with Albert W. Trueman in *N.F.B. History* (uncompleted film), Production no. 47-031, 1974. Walter Harris became minister responsible for the Film Board in September 1953. He headed the new Department of Citizenship and Immigration, which took over many of the responsibilities heretofore exercised by the Department of Mines and Resources.

2 Irwin Papers, Donald Mulholland to A.W. Trueman, 27 July 1953, 29 July 1953, and 4 Aug. 1953

3 Winters wrote to Irwin in Australia to tell him that with the change of ministers, Trueman had had little or no guidance from July to September and that the commissioner had fallen susceptible to the pressures that Winters and Irwin would have anticipated and taken in stride. He ex-

plained that Mulholland had taken Irwin's original arguments, weighed them differently, and concluded that the move to Montreal was a bad one. He suspected collusion between the Film Board, the *Ottawa Citizen*, and the mayor of Ottawa, but was convinced that the merits of the move to Montreal would manifest themselves on reconsideration. Irwin Papers, Winters to Irwin, 19 Oct. 1953. Trueman recalled these events in his book *A Second View of Things: A Memoir* (Toronto: McClelland and Stewart 1982), 110–34.

4 National Archives (NA), J.W. Pickersgill Citizenship and Immigration Series, MG 32, B34, vol. 14, Robert Winters to Walter Harris, 21 Sept. 1953, with background memorandum dated 17 Sept. 1953; Trueman to Harris, 12 Oct. 1953; Harris to Trueman, 16 Oct. 1953. Rumours were rife that the Montreal site was even owned by St Laurent himself. Trueman wrote to Harris on 3 Oct. describing how the Montreal site was selected by the American firm Irwin had hired. They looked at twenty sites and after reducing them to five, choose the Ville St Laurent location with special consideration of the good housing accommodation available nearby. Harris told Mayor Whitton on 21 Oct. that the site would remain in Montreal. It seemed that few people anywhere approved; even the Montreal *Gazette* wrote an editorial against the proposed expenditure on 28 Oct. The following 1 Apr. 1954, a *Maclean's* article, 'You're in the Movie Business,' maintained that Irwin manoeuvred the switch to get the Film Board out from the dominating government that had rejected Crown corporate status for the agency. *Maclean's* also noted that if the Film Board was an embarrassment in Ottawa, its presence in Montreal might appease a hostile Premier Duplessis.

5 *Debates of the House of Commons*, vol. 3, 12 Mar. 1953, 2869; vol. 1, 3 Dec. 1953, 588–9; vol. 3, 2 Mar. 1954, 2584, 2601, 2681–2, 2922

6 Trueman interview in *N.F.B. History* (uncompleted film)

7 *Bush Pilot* received practically no distribution; *Whispering City*, produced in cooperation with Britain's Rank Organization,

succeeded only in its French version; *Sins of the Fathers*, on venereal disease, and *Forbidden Journey* joined the others in being financial failures. NA, Pickersgill C & I series, MG 32, B34, vol. 15, R-12-20, Confidential report on the state of the commercial film industry in Canada, Ian MacNeill to Albert Trueman, 25 Jan. 1954 (26 pp.); vol. 13, R-12-1D, E.R. Crawley to Harris, 27 Nov. 1953

8 Kay Ferris interview with the author, 28 May 1987. Ferris, who replaced Isabel Kehoe, the newsreel unit head in the fifties, remained in charge of newsreels until the major companies folded.

9 Ian MacNeill, 'Confidential report on the state of the commercial film industry in Canada,' 23–4. Also Pickersgill, C & I series, vol. 13, R-12-1D, Harris to Crawley, 1 Feb. 1954. The minister continued tradition and promised to assist private industry within the framework of the National Film Act.

10 *Annual Reports*, 1950–4

11 Jackson's previous films had been *Who Will Teach Your Child?* and *Summer Is for Kids* (1948) and *Feelings of Depression* (1951). His distinct voice became identified with some eighty Film Board documentaries and his crisply written commentaries did much to elevate and unite ordinary images into meaningful emotional experiences. He is rememberd for his peculiar lifelong desire for anonymity and a preference to remain an unsung wordsmith. His positive contribution to the art of the documentary film has been incalculable.

12 In his unpublished PhD thesis, 'La production Canadienne-Française à l'Office National du Film du Canada de 1939 à 1964,' Université de Québec, 1987 (parts of which appeared in Les dossiers de la cinémathèque, nos. 5, 14, and 17 (Montreal: Cinémathèque québécoise / Musée du cinéma 1979, 1984, and 1987), Pierre Véronneau claimed that for the 1950s, the francophones at the Film Board were in a position of assimilation by virtue of their structural immersion (p. 145). Unfortunately, he overlooked the many documents that showed how hard the administration was working to expand the French section. Time and again, management referred to a need both for better leadership within French production and for skilled personnel to fill the ranks.

13 Successful original French subjects included a rural photographer, a church beadle, and a country lawyer. According to sociologist Robert Boissonault, who interviewed some twenty-six French-Canadian filmmakers for his 1971 Master's thesis (Les cinéastes québecois: Un aperçu' [unpublished, Université de Montréal]), Blais did not show the same productive dynamism as Bernard Devlin and was eventually replaced.

14 Complaints about the French-Canadian situation appeared in print in 1955. See Louis Racine, 'La situation des Canadiens français à l'ONF,' *L'Action nationale* 44, no. 5 (Jan. 1955), 411–19.

15 In 1945, French Canadians had numbered about one-fourth of the 787 staff and 24 of the 147 production staff. Victor Jobin, Pierre Petel, Pierre Bruneau, Yves Jasmin, Raymond Garceau, and Roger Blais were in that first group; Bernard Devlin and Fernand Menard joined in 1946, to be followed by Jacques Bobet in 1947. (Guy Glover, a bilingual anglophone, had been a producer/director since 1944.)

16 Trueman recalled the story of how Father Lévesque, one of the two luminaries after whom the Massey-Lévesque Commission was named, was leaving the commissioner's office one day and, with a twinkle in his eye, drew his finger down the length of his soutane and exclaimed, '*That* has been what has kept French Canada down!' (Albert Trueman interview with the author, 22 Sept. 1986). Another important French Canadian, Jules Léger, the under-secretary of state for external affairs, joined the board of governors as Juneau was elevated. Léger became a powerful Film Board ally in government.

17 Pierre Juneau interview with the author, 6 Mar. 1987

18 Pickersgill entered Cabinet as secretary of state after being elected by Newfoundland Liberals in June 1953; in July 1954 he replaced Harris as minister for citizenship and immigration (until the St Laurent government resigned in June 1957). J.W.

Pickersgill, *My Years with Louis St Laurent* (Toronto: University of Toronto Press 1975), 209–10, 219–24

19 Pickersgill C & I series, vol. 13, R-11-10, Trueman to Pickersgill, 25 Nov. 1954

20 The history of Quebec censorship of Film Board films was complex. All theatrical films had been submitted by commercial distributors since the NFB began. In 1947, Quebec informed the Film Board it would have to submit all its 16-mm films for censorship. The antecedent that evolved was an unwritten agreement with the censor to deposit one English and one French print in the Provincial Film Library to avoid censorship. Duplessis ordered the arrangement terminated in 1950. Prime Minister St Laurent's hand had steadied relations until the fall 1954 flare-up. The films seized in the raids were on benign subjects: *Let's All Sing Together, La Pelleterie du Canada, Packaged Powder, Warp and Weft, Eye Witness No. 39, Woodwinds and Brass, Coup d'oeil No. 37, Fusée fantastique, A l'écoute de l'atome, Au pays des jours sans fin, Sing with the Commodores No. 2, Neighbours, Herring Hunt,* and *Grey Cup 1952.*

21 On 1 Feb. 1954, the deputy attorney general raised a discomfiting question that all ministers have swept under the rug each time it has arisen: Does the Film Board fall under the British North America Act regarding 'education'? If so, it has no right to interpret Canada to Canadians. There is no decided case that is conclusive on this point (Pickersgill C & I series, vol. 15, R-12-19, F.P. Varcoe to Pickersgill). No wonder then that Film Board founder John Grierson always used as his term of reference 'propaganda,' which he considered a form of education. He initiated the policy of avoiding use of the word 'education' in Film Board publications, to avoid legal ensnarements.

22 Pickersgill C & I series, vol. 15, R-12-19, Trueman to Pickersgill, 29 Sept. 1954; Pickersgill to Duplessis, 13 Oct. 1954; Duplessis to Pickersgill, 12 Nov. 1954; Pickersgill to Duplessis, 16 Nov. 1954. Minutes of the NFB, 24 Jan. 1955. Though not in direct reference to this event, St Laurent's later description of the overall relationship he enjoyed with Pickersgill summarized how pleased he was with his minister's handling of delicate matters: 'You and I did together what neither of us could do alone.' J.W. Pickersgill interview with the author, 23 Oct. 1986

23 *Montreal Star,* 21 Jan. 1955

24 Pickersgill C & I series, vol. 13, R-11-10, Trueman to Pickersgill, 28 Jan. 1955; 22 Feb. 1956; NA, MG 25, 84-85/150, box 35, file 2755, E-40, part 1, Trueman to NFB Board of Governors, 4 Nov. 1955; *Le Devoir,* 17 and 24 Feb. 1956. (Pierre Vigeant had called Mulholland a francophobe in *Le Devoir* on 16 Feb.)

25 Pickersgill C & I series, vol. 13, R-11-10, Pickersgill to Leon Lortie, board member, 25 Feb. 1956; Pickersgill to John Deutsch of the Treasury Board, 19 Apr. 1956; Trueman to NFB Board of Governors, 29 Oct. 1956; Trueman to Pickersgill, 1 Nov. 1956; Pickersgill to Trueman, 18 Dec. 1956; Pickersgill to Trueman, 14 Jan. 1957

26 Pickersgill interview with the author, 23 Oct. 1986, and Juneau interview with the author, 6 Mar. 1987

27 Over a ten-month period, he spoke to a Montreal Rotary Club, the United Nations Society in Saskatoon, the town of Harbour Grace, Newfoundland, the Department of External Affairs foreign-service officers, the Canadian Education Association, various library conferences, Queen's University, the Canadian Club, the Motion Picture Theatres Association of Toronto, and the Independent Order of the Daughters of the Empire. National Film Board Library, Albert Trueman speeches (12 on file)

28 *Ottawa Journal,* 'Film Board plans full length features,' 26 Dec. 1953; Pickersgill C & I series, vol. 13, Trueman to Harris, 28 Dec. 1953

29 The *Ottawa Journal* and Toronto *Globe and Mail* covered the story on 19 Feb. 1954, while the *Ottawa Citizen* defended the film in an editorial on 27 Feb. Meeting of the NFB, 3 May 1954; NA, Pickersgill C & I series, vol. 13, R-12-1C, Trueman to Member of Parliament Charles Henry, 24 Feb. 1954. Producer/writer Gordon Burwash wrote to a complainant on 11 February that he had amassed a body of facts and incidents after talking with residents, social workers, police, and the school principal.

He then selected the most typical and recurrent incidents and wrote the filmscript accordingly.

30 Albert Trueman interview with the author, 22 Sept. 1986. The bad press attracted by *Drug Addict* had appeared in the *Ottawa Citizen* (9 Feb.), Reuters (10 Feb.), *Globe and Mail* (10 May), and *Ottawa Citizen* (8 June 1949). It occurred at a time when the Film Board and Commissioner Ross McLean could least afford it.

31 Trueman, *A Second View of Things*, 120–1

32 *Annual Report*, 1954–5, 2

33 Albert Trueman interview for *N.F.B. History* (unfinished production)

34 Tom Daly Papers, box IX, no. 7, 'Notes for Daly talk at Edinburgh Festival, August 1979, "40 Years of the NFB"'

35 Pickersgill C & I series, vol. 13, R-12-1F, Ian MacNeill to Robbins Elliott, 8 Sept. 1953, describing the new 'On the Spot' series

36 A.W. Trueman, Report to the Board Members, 'NFB's Television Program,' 19 Sept. 1955; NA, MG 32, B34, vol. 15, R-12-26, part 1

37 Pickersgill letter to the author, 17 Feb. 1987

38 *Debates of the House of Commons*, vol. 2 (21 Mar. 1955), 2220; vol. 3 (6 Apr. 1955), 2862. J.W. Pickersgill interview with the author, 23 Oct. 1986

39 Pickersgill C & I series, vol. 14, R-12-1T, Pickersgill to Trueman, 22 Sept. 1955; Trueman to Pickersgill, 26 Sept. 1955 and 4 Oct. 1955. Interview with the author, 23 Oct. 1986. Minutes of the NFB, 25 Oct. 1955

40 Pickersgill C & I series, vol. 14, R-12-13, Trueman to Pickersgill, 30 Mar. 1955; Minutes of the NFB, 25 Apr. 1955

41 Minutes of the NFB, 17 Dec. 1956

42 Ibid., 4 Feb. 1957

43 *The Suspects*, whose script was based on real events, provoked letters of complaint and anger in Parliament. Pickersgill C & I series, vol. 15, R-12-32, Mulholland to Eric Koch. CBC Talks and Public Affairs, 28 Feb. 1957

44 Minutes of the NFB, 7 May 1956. Pickersgill, C & I series, vol. 15, R-12-26, Geoff Stirling to Pickersgill, 26 June 1956; Trueman to Pickersgill, 24 July 1956; Pickersgill to McCann, 2 Aug. 1956; McCann to Pickersgill, 4 Sept. 1956; Pickersgill to McCann, 10 and 12 Sept. 1956. National Film Board Informal Brief to the Royal Commission on Broadcasting and Television, 13 Sept. 1956. Pickersgill interview with the author, 23 Oct. 1986

45 Pickersgill C & I series, vol. 14, R-12-8, Opening ceremonies for the Film Board in Montreal, 24 Sept. 1956. Only one other member of Parliament, Guy Rouleau, showed up to celebrate, since the building was in his riding.

46 The articles were: 'Si M. Saint Laurent était sincère!' *Montréal Matin*, 18 mars 1957; 'La nomination de M. Guy Roberge à l'Office du film,' *Le Soleil*, 20 avril 1957; '"A graded system of bullying" à l'Office national du film,' *Le Devoir*, 5 avril 1957; 'Le "brainwashing" à l'ONF,' *Le Devoir*, 27 mars 1957; 'Orage sur l'ONF,' *Le Droit*, 26 mars 1957; 'Les beautés de la culture,' *Le Droit*, 2 avril 1957; 'La tête des autres,' *Le Droit*, 11 avril 1957; 'Scènes de la vie présente,' *Le Droit*, 16 avril 1957; 'Le témoignage de M. Helleur,' *Le Droit*, 18 avril 1957; 'Au pays des images,' *Le Droit*, 22 avril 1957; 'Notre cinéma national tient-il vraiment compte du fait français?' *La Presse*, 30 mars 1957; 'Avant de crier au favoritisme il faut examiner les chiffres,' *La Presse*, 2 avril 1957; 'Ce n'est pas fracassant les carreaux qu'on gagne un point,' *La Presse*, 3 avril 1957; 'Notre équipe est excellente; donnons-lui totale liberté d'agir,' *La Presse*, 4 avril 1957; 'Ce qui blesse le plus c'est l'indifférence dédaigneuse,' *La Presse*, 5 avril 1957; 'Ni cloissonnement, ni intégration; des réformes ... et tout de suite!,' *La Presse*, 6 avril 1957; 'La carrière de M. Roger Blais et la décadence de l'ONF,' *Le Devoir*, 23 avril 1957; 'Justice et culture: Guy Roberge, le nouveau président de l'ONF, *La Réforme*, 25 avril 1957; 'M. Guy Roberge à la présidence de l'ONF,' *La Presse*, 20 avril 1957; 'M. Guy Roberge aura de nombreux problèmes à régler à l'Office du film,' *Le Soleil*, 19 avril 1957; 'L'ONF, un fief interdit aux nôtres,' *L'Action catholique*, 1 mars 1957; 'A l'ONF, une section française s'impose,' *L'Action catholique*, 14 mars 1957; 'La déclaration Lortie: Un aveu I-II,' *Le Devoir*, 6–7 mars 1957; 'Le triumvirat Mulholland-Juneau-McLean à l'Office national du film,' *Le Devoir*, 26 février 1957; 'Il faut une section française à l'Office

national du film,' *Le Devoir*, 5 mars 1957; 'MM. Trueman, Lortie et Juneau se confient à la presse,' *Le Devoir*, 9 avril 1957; 'La tâche redoutable qui attend M. Guy Roberge à l'ONF,' *Le Devoir*, 23 avril 1957; 'Blocs-notes,' *Le Devoir*, 28 février, 11, 13, 18, 29 mars, 1, 3, 4, 11 avril, and 3 mai 1957. Some excerpts can be found in Pierre Véronneau, *L'Office National du Film: L'enfant martyr* (Montreal: Cinémathèque québécoise / Musée du cinéma 1979), 43–57.

47 Roger Blais interview with the author, 1 Sept. 1987. Blais thought he was demoted for having argued for equality of salaries with the English. He did not know, nor did Trueman tell him, that Film Board budgets had been frozen for years and any moves in that direction were impossible at that time. Blais stated that he neither fed information to the press nor met the columnists who wrote about him until months after the affair had quieted down.

48 Pierre Juneau interview with the author, 6 Mar. 1987

49 Desmond Dew, *Let's Try It This Way* (New York: Vantage Press 1983), 182. Dew became executive production manager under Arthur Irwin and occupied that post until the unit system was dismantled in 1964. He became a producer, then worked on sponsored films until his retirement from the agency.

50 Pickersgill C & I series, vol. 14, R-12-13, Trueman to Pickersgill, 6 Mar. 1957. Albert Trueman interview with the author, 23 Oct. 1987

51 Roberge had learned about the legal and business end of commercial cinema when he worked in St Laurent's Quebec City firm, one of whose clients was the Famous Players theatre chain.

52 NFB 1295, Film Commissioner P-32, Trueman to Juneau and Mulholland, 10 Apr. 1957

53 Grant McLean remembered Trueman's unwavering punctuality when he and a playful Mulholland came to the commissioner's office at 4:55, just as Trueman was donning his coat. 'Albert, I'm sorry to report there is a major fire raging in the film vault,' began Mulholland. 'I assume you'll look after that,' the unflappable Trueman replied as he buttoned his coat and walked out the door. Mulholland, who had tried unsuccessfully to check Trueman a number of times, sighed, 'I give up,' and he and McLean had a good laugh. Grant McLean interview with the author, 5 Aug. 1986

54 Albert Trueman interview with the author, 22 Sept. 1986; *A Second View of Things*, 133

Chapter 3

1 Pierre Juneau interview with the author, 6 Mar. 1987. Grierson had made some vituperative public comments about the state of documentary film in general, although he had said nothing of his beloved Film Board. He remarked, 'It [documentary] has such a record of boredom it hardly deserves to be resuscitated ... Take the do-goodery and long-hair out of the documentary and it will do just as much good ... Most of these long-winded, slow-moving social documentaries are nothing but navel-studying.' *Vancouver Province*, 2 Mar. 1957

2 Guy Roberge interview with the author, 20 Oct. 1986

3 High-profile French Canadians Marcel Cadieux (under-secretary of state of external affairs) and businessman Arthur Dansereau joined the board, replacing Jules Léger and Léon Lortie respectively in November 1958 and July 1959. Dansereau's term ended in February 1965, while Cadieux kept the External Affairs position until 1970, when Paul Tremblay replaced him. The most powerful board members remained the government representatives – Cadieux, Charles Stein, the under-secretary of state, and R. Gordon Robertson, deputy minister of northern affairs and national resources.

4 Minutes of the NFB, 6 May 1957

5 NFB 1315/0, A-44, Policy and Procedures 1956–68, J.W. Cosman to Mulholland and Juneau, 12 Sept. 1955; Albert Trueman wrote to Pickersgill on 2 Mar. 1956, explaining the change in Film Board policy toward theatrical production. Pickersgill C & I series, vol. 15, R-12-13

6 Pierre Juneau interview with the author, 6 Mar. 1987

7 Gilles Carle statement in the film *Cinéma,*

cinéma, ou 25 ans de production française, directed by Gilles Carle and Werner Nold; produced by Roger Frappier and National Film Board of Canada, 1984

8 The titles of the Spanish selections indicate that the intended audience was largely children: *Angotee, Story of an Eskimo Boy, Ti-Jean Goes Lumbering, Jolifou Inn, Riches of the Earth, Physical Regions of Canada, Farm Calendar, Iron from the North, 'Accidents Don't Happen,' nos. 1, 6, and 7, Herring Hunt, Montreal, The Shepherd, Peter and the Potter, World at Your Feet,* and *The Loon's Necklace.* The latter, a 1948 Crawley Films production financed by Imperial Oil and distributed by the Film Board, was a world favourite for decades.

9 Minutes of the NFB, 21–22 Oct. 1957; Appendix, '1957–58 Production Operations Report, April 1–August 31 1957'

10 Tom Daly Papers, box XI, no. 19, Daly to David Jones, 9 Nov. 1976

11 Pierre Juneau interview with the author, 6 Mar. 1987

12 The Film Board had a good realtionship with its United Nations counterpart, from whom it bought sixty-five copies of the UNFB non-theatrical film *Out,* the story of Hungarian refugees fleeing the Hungarian Revolution of 1956. Minutes of the NFB, 6 May 1957

13 Minutes of the NFB, 5–6 Sept. 1958, 21 Nov. 1958, 9–10 June 1959, 26–27 Oct. 1959. *Blue Vanguard: The Story of the First United Nations Emergency Force* (New York: United Nations Film Board 1958)

14 NFB 1298, P-32, Arthur Chetwynd to E.D. Fulton, 15 Nov. 1957; Guy Roberge to E.D. Fulton, 3 Jan. 1958. Another argument, which was not made but was as valid, was that young filmmakers could stretch their mastery of the medium with sponsored films. For example, the 1957 film *It's a Crime,* for the Department of Labour, was hilarious story by Roman Kroitor, designed by Colin Low, directed by Wolf Koenig, and animated by Gerald Potterton.

15 Minutes of the NFB, 27–28 Jan. 1958

16 Pierre Véronneau, *Résistance et affirmation: La production francophone à l'ONF, 1939–1964,* Les dossiers de la cinémathèque no. 17 (Montreal: Cinémathèque

québécoise / Musée du cinéma, 1987), 34–6

17 René Lévesque, *Memoirs,* trans. Philip Stratford (Toronto: McClelland and Stewart 1986), 140–85. For Lévesque, being a nationalist meant being fiercely for or against something or against a given situation, though never against a race. Years later, Monique Lérac recalled that when she sang 'Gens du pays' at a benefit concert during the strike, she noticed that the change in Lévesque (who was standing in the wings) was palpable. 'As It Happens' interview, CBC Radio, 2 Nov. 1987. Ron Graham, *One-Eyed Kings* (Toronto: Collins 1986), 38–45

18 Minutes of the NFB, 10–11 Mar. 1959

19 Ibid., 26–27 Oct. 1959, 26 Jan. 1969. NFB 3850, B-3, Roberge to Fairclough, 11 Dec. 1959. In *Résistance et affirmation* (p. 46) Pierre Véronneau erroneously places the beginning of the Association professionel des cinéastes in the fall of 1962. Thus, the turning point in 'group consciousness' to which he refers had probably occurred over two years earlier, reflecting the overwhelming impact of, and fallout from, the CBC producers' strike.

20 Pierre Juneau interview with the author, 6 Mar. 1987

21 Under existing financial arrangements, the Film Board recouped from the CBC half the costs of production in 'rental,' which in turn was ploughed back into production. In keeping television and other exhibition rights outside Canada, the Film Board was able to generate income to make many more films than would have been possible on its own budget. The CBC benefited in turn by having its public-affairs programming rounded out at a moderate cost.

22 Minutes of the NFB, 26–27 Oct. 1959. Appendix, 'Function and Relationship of National Film Board and Canadian Broadcasting Corporation' by Donald Mulholland, 14 Sept. 1959

23 Minutes of the NFB, 25 Apr. and 11–12 Oct. 1960. Roberge had misgivings from a different angle: making more money available for television meant reducing the 'general' programme.

24 NFB 1298, P-32, Fulton to Roberge, 19 May 1958

25 Ellen Fairclough telephone interview with the author, 25 June 1987

26 NFB 1298, P-32, Roberge to Fairclough, 10 Aug. 1958 and 13 Mar. 1961

27 Minutes of the NFB, 26 Jan. 1960

28 Department of External Affairs (DEA), Canada Films, Film Industry, Distribution, 14330-6-1, vol. 1, Nov. 1958

29 DEA, 53-337-11, M.R.M. Dale to H.B. Chandler, 7 July 1958; Hurley of South African State Information Office to Department of External Affairs, Canada, 28 Nov. 1958

30 NFB, Script: *Black and White in South Africa* by William Weintraub

31 For a complete discussion of the diplomacy of this period see J.L. Granatstein, *Canada, 1957–67: The Years of Uncertainty and Innovation* (Toronto: McClelland and Stewart 1986); John Hilliker, 'Diefenbaker and Canadian External Relations,' in J.L. Granatstein, ed., *Canadian Foreign Policy* (Toronto: Copp Clark Pittman 1986), 189–97. Brian Tennyson, *Canada's Relations with South Africa* (Washington, DC: University Press of America 1982)

32 DEA, 14330-6-1, vol. 2, External Affairs to Prime Minister Diefenbaker, 14 Apr. 1960; William Weintraub interview with the author, 23 Aug. 1985

33 Minutes of the NFB, 25 Apr. 1960

34 Tennyson, *Canada's Relations with South Africa*, 168

35 French-version bookings totalled 546; total bookings abroad numbered 336. National Film Board, Computerized distribution statistics as of 6 Sept. 1985. According to Ronald Dick, a print came into the hands of the United Nations, which showed it frequently in the 1960s to diplomats and foreign dignitaries. He alleged that early in the sixties, a Canadian diplomat was manhandled by a South African diplomat over the repeated screenings of the film there. The incident was hushed up. Ronald Dick interview with the author, 29 Aug. 1985

36 Minutes of the NFB, 23 June 1960. Roberge told Fairclough that the board of governors had considered the project favourably in January, that External Affairs had shown interest in February and March, but that the under-secretary of state for external affairs (Marcel Cadieux) had demanded the USSR's prior agreement on Canada's freedom to film, especially in the Arctic. This was doubtful, as was a broader cultural agreement with the USSR in the whole problematic atmosphere of East–West relations. While Roberge was interested in having a film give Canadians realistic facts about the USSR, and having the USSR present films about Canada or having Canadian films shown in the USSR, he decided the project should be abandoned. The fact that an American spy plane had been shot down inside the USSR in May probably contributed to Roberge's decision. One surmises that External Affairs supported him warmly. Crises aside, 1960 marked the first-ever exhibition of Film Board films in the USSR: *The Romance of Transportation in Canada, Fishermen,* and *High Arctic.*

37 NFB 1315/0, A-44, Ian MacNeill to Mulholland, Roberge, Juneau, McLean, and Glover, 27 May 1959; Mulholland to Roberge, 26 May 1959

38 Minutes of the NFB, 5–6 Sept. 1968

39 Ibid., 26–27 Oct. 1959. Taking Canada as a whole, in 1958–9, the audience was (in descending order) elementary school, community, secondary school, other, tourist, church, industrial and trade union, youth, service clubs and professional organizations, home and school, and farm. The first three categories comprised 75 per cent of the entire audience, with elementary schools representing about 50 per cent of that figure.

40 Grant McLean interview with the author, 5 Aug. 1986; Gerald Graham interview with the author, 26 Oct. 1987.

41 The films shown between 17 July and 18 Aug. 1960 were *V for Victory* (1942), *Churchill's Island* (1941), *The People Between* (1947), *The Settler* (1953), *Universe* (1960), *13 Platoon* (1942), *Chants populaires #5* (1943), *Summer is for Kids* (1948), *Paul Tomkowicz: Street–railway Switchman* (1953), *The Grievance* (1954), *The Romance of Transportation in Canada* (1953), *Neighbours* (1952), *Le Merle* (1958), *Listen to the Prairies* (1945), *The Sceptre and the Mace* (1957), *One Man's Opinion* (1953), and *City of Gold* (1957).

42 NFB 1636, A-158, Grant McLean to Guy Roberge, 23 June 1960

43 Minutes of the NFB, 23 June and 11–12 Oct. 1960

44 The 678 films were divided into eleven categories: Agriculture (45), Citizenship and Community (96), Creative Arts (108), Geography and Travel (58), Health and Welfare (86), Industry and Labour (65), Science, Resources and Wildlife (56), Sociology (62), Sports and Recreation (37), Transportation and Communication (30), World Affairs (35), and *Eye Witness* (almost 100). These statistics appeared in Marjorie McKay's document 'The Motion Picture: A Mirror of Time,' which was appended to the annual report. Minutes of the NFB, 9–10 June 1959

45 Minutes of the NFB, 10 Mar. 1961. In 1958, the Tremblay Commission, a Quebec royal commission, had shown enthusiasm for school film and wanted to offer Quebec students the same advantages that students of other countries enjoyed. It had reported favourably about the Film Board when it stated that one could not distribute too widely the films of the National Film Board. From this point there was a thaw in Quebec–Film Board relations, even though Duplessis continued to playfully mock the Film Board as a Communist organization, long after most people had forgotten about the issue. His subordinates laughed nervously at such remarks, and continued to shun the agency. Roger Blais interview with the author, 1 Sept. 1987

46 These detailed statistics were in the appendix of the Minutes of the NFB, 11–12 Oct. 1960, but board members did not discuss them.

47 NFB 1180, E.S. Coristine, Director of Administration, to Guy Roberge, 18 Jan. 1963

48 The full argument against giving out sponsored-film contracts was made in a Film Board brief attached to the appendix of Minutes of the NFB, 26 Jan. 1960. It was that the private producers had achieved remarkable expansion since 1952, in spite of the decreasing amount of work assigned by the Film Board, primarily because of television's need for commercials. The brief's argument against levying a quota system for features was interesting, in light of the occasional nationalist argument favouring it: the feature-film industry was not sufficiently established to provide features in adequate volume and quality to meet a quota. This became the basis for Roberge's argument to create the Canadian Film Development Corporation a few years later. Gerald Pratley articulated the nationalist argument in the January 1956 issue of *Vision* magazine.

49 NFB 4899, A-415, Answer to Mr. Hellyer's question in the House of Commons, March 1962

50 Minutes of the NFB, 12 Jan. 1961, Appendix 9a; 26 Jan. 1960, Appendix

51 Ibid., 26 Jan. 1960, Appendix

52 NFB 4867, A-414, vol. A, Roberge to Fairclough, 14 Feb. 1962

53 Ibid., Fairclough to Cabinet, 2 May 1962

Chapter 4

1 Tom Daly interview with the author, 8 Oct. 1987

2 These comments were made about Daly on the occasion of his retirement in May 1984 by Colin Low, Wolf Koenig, Roman Kroitor, Robert Verrall, and Guy Coté, original members of Unit B, and by Donald Brittain, Jacques Godbout, Michael Rubbo, and Paul Cowan. These artists' combined talents have created the bedrock of Canada's world-class film reputation.

3 Donald Brittain interview with the author, 19 Dec. 1988

4 John Spotton interview with the author, 1 June 1987

5 This became the central idea in the seminal essay on Unit B by Peter Harcourt, 'The Innocent Eye: An Aspect of the Work of the National Film Board of Canada,' which appeared in *Sight and Sound* 34, no. 1 (Winter 1964–5).

6 Tom Daly interview in out-takes from NFB production, *Has Anybody Here Seen Canada? A History of Canadian Movies 1939–1953* (NFB-CBC co-production, 1978), roll 8; pp. 54–9 of transcript. Wolf Koenig interview with the author, 28 July 1987. Tom Daly Papers, box XI, no. 19, Wolf Koenig to Tom Daly, 22 Oct. 1976. See also D.B. Jones, *Movies and Memoranda* (Ottawa: Canadian Film Institute 1981), 59–87.

7 See Peter Morris, *The Film Companion* (Toronto: Irwin 1984), for a brief biography and complete list of each filmmaker's films.

Morris's compendium is the most complete and satisfactory reference work on Canadian film to date.

8 Henri Cartier-Bresson, *The Decisive Moment* (New York: Simon and Shuster [in collaboration with Editions Verve of Paris] 1952)

9 Gerald Graham interview with the author, 24 Oct. 1987; see also Graham's *Canadian Film Technology, 1896–1986* (Cranbury, NJ: Associated University Presses 1989), chap. 10. John Spotton interview with the author, 1 June 1987; Spotton thinks that the first complete separation of camera and recorder occurred with *Nobody Waved Goodbye*.

10 Tom Daly Papers, box VII, no. 15, Kroitor and Koenig to Programme Planning Committee, 18 Nov. 1959. Colin Low interview with the author, 22 Oct. 1987

11 Tom Daly Papers, box VI, no. 9, Tom Daly to Peter Harcourt, 28 Aug. 1964. Daly's advice helped Harcourt to complete the above-mentioned essay on Unit B, for *Sight and Sound* (Winter 1964–5). The lessening insistence on both traditional film composition and the discipline of shooting drove to distraction some traditionalists like Denis Gillson, head of the camera department. John Spotton interview with the author, 1 June 1987

12 Louise Carrière, '25 ans plus tard: Où êtes-vous donc?' in Carol Faucher, ed., *La production française à l'ONF*, Les dossiers de la cinémathèque no. 14 (Montreal: Cinémathèque québécoise / Musée du cinéma 1984), 20–8. Also, Pierre Véronneau, *Résistance et affirmation: La production francophone à l'ONF, 1939–1964*, Les dossiers de la cinémathèque no. 17 (Montreal: Cinémathèque québécoise / Musée du cinéma 1987), 37–8 and 124–9

13 David Clandfield, *Canadian Film* (Toronto: Oxford University Press 1987), 43–5. Clandfield's historical overview of film in English and French Canada is an excellent primer.

14 John Spotton and Wolf Koenig interviews with the author, 1 June and 28 July 1987

15 Another (now forgotten) film was to come from the Dawson City footage, *Gold*, the story of modern placer gold-mining.

16 *Grierson Transcripts: Interviews Recorded with John Grierson, February 1969–July 1971*, transcribed by Sandra Gathercole, 4 vols (Ottawa: Canadian Radio and Television Commission 1972), 4: 489. An interesting variation of this theme was later developed by Gaile McGregor, *The Wacousta Syndrome: Explorations in the Canadian Langscape* (Toronto: University of Toronto Press 1985), 412–43.

17 Tom Daly, 'On Wholeness,' Tom Daly Papers, box XI, no. 19, 1 Sept. 1976

18 Wolf Koenig interview with the author, 28 July 1987. The 'universal' that *Lonely Boy* unveils was copied almost verbatim in the feature film *Privilege*, which appeared a little later. The Film Board considered suing the producers for copyright infringement, but concluded that imitation was the sincerest form of flattery.

19 Elder's article 'On the Candid Eye Movement' was reprinted with the Harcourt article in Seth Feldman and Joyce Nelson, eds, *Canadian Film Reader* (Toronto: Peter Martin Associates 1977), 67–76 and 86–93.

20 Minutes of the NFB, 21–22 Oct. 1957; Appendix 9, Roberge to Léger, 15 Oct. 1957

21 Colin Low interview with the author, 22 Oct. 1987

22 See also Ronald Blumer and Susan Schouten, 'Donald Brittain: Green Stripe and Common Sense,' reprinted in Feldman and Nelson, eds, *Canadian Film Reader*, 103–12. In this article, Brittain described the importance of editing and timing.

23 Another television series, '*Le défi*,' the brainchild of researcher Gilles Marcotte, early in 1959, intended to define the French-Canadian collectivity in sociological terms, starting with the broad theme of science, then moving on to business, the land, artists, science and industry, agriculture, and immigration. Only eight films were made before the series was dropped quietly in 1960. These topics, if well researched by university specialists, did not excite the filmmakers, who thought that intellectual subjects did not make very good cinema. Their great interest was their spontaneous use of the camera in *cinéma direct* style.

24 Marcel Carrière interview with the author, 14 Sept. 1988

25 Véronneau, *Résistance et affirmation*, 39

26 Clandfield, *Canadian Film*, 61–9

27 Jacques Bobet interview with the author, 25 Sept. 1987

28 Gilles Carle, 'La video et la mort,' in Faucher, ed., *La production française à l'ONF*, 67–9

29 In Pierre Véronneau, Michael Dorland, and Seth Feldman, eds, *Dialogue: Cinéma canadien et québécois, Canadian and Quebec Cinema*, (Montreal: Mediatexte Publications 1987), a number of articles on Perrault develop this theme: see Paul Warren, 'Les québécois et le cinéma,' and François Baby, 'Pierre Perrault et la civilisation oral traditionnelle,' 109–38.

30 Eric Rohmer and Louis Marcorelles, 'Entretien avec Jean Rouch,' *Cahiers du cinéma* 144 (June 1963), 1–22. Also, Alain Pontaut, 'Jean Rouch et *Les Cahiers du Cinéma* présentent au public français,' *La Presse*, 6 July 1963. A similar criticism about lack of thought was expressed by Yerri Kempf in 'Le cinéma canadien et ses limites,' *Cité libre* 82 (Dec. 1965), 28–31.

31 Jean-Pierre Lefebvre and Jean-Claude Pilon, 'L'équipe française souffre-t-elle de "Roucheole"?' *Objectif* 5–6 (Aug. 1962), 45–53

32 Minutes of the NFB, 23 June 1960

33 NFB 1298, P-32, Col. Cecil Merritt to Minister E. Davie Fulton, 7 Nov. 1957

34 The films in the series (in historical order) were *John Cabot – A Man of the Renaissance, The Last Voyage of Henry Hudson, Samuel de Champlain, Alexander Mackenzie – The Lord of the North, David Thompson – The Great Mapmaker, Selkirk of the Red River, Lord Durham, Lord Elgin – Voice of the People, William Lyon Mackenzie – A Friend to His Country, Robert Baldwin – A Matter of Principle, Joseph Howe – The Tribune of Nova Scotia, Louis Joseph Papineau – The Demi-God, John A. Macdonald – The Impossible Idea, Alexander Galt – The Stubborn Idealist, Georges-Etienne Cartier – The Lion of Quebec, Charles Tupper – The Big Man*, and *Louis Hyppolite-Lafontaine.*

35 The French-versioned English films were *Sky, Nahanni, The World of David Milne, Winter Rally, Lonely Boy, Morning on the Lièvre, Circle of the Sun, The Runner, My Financial Career*, and *The Ride*. The films that did not receive theatrical circulation were *Les Enfants du silence* (Brault and Jutra), *Natation* (Carle), *Voir Miami* (Groulx), and *L'Homme vite* (Borremans). The films *Jour après jour* (Perron), *Québec-USA* (Brault and Jutra), and *À Saint-Henri le 5 septembre* (Aquin) had been shown on television; the complaining filmmakers did not mention that the films could not be released theatrically for another two years because they were under contract to Radio-Canada. *L'action Québec*, 10 July 1964

36 Véronneau, *Résistance et affirmation*, 102–5; John Hofsess, 'Denys Arcand,' in *Inner Views, Ten Canadian Filmmakers* (Toronto: McGraw Hill-Ryerson 1975), 145–7; Bart Testa, 'Denys Arcand's Sarcasm,' in Véronneau, Dorland, and Feldman, eds, *Dialogue*, 203–22

37 *Debates of the House of Commons*, vol. 2, 12 Mar. 1959, 1902

38 NFB production file, *Deadly Dilemma (Poisons, Pests and People)*; Guy Roberge to Michael Spencer, 13 Nov. 1961; S.C. Barry of Department of Agriculture to Guy Roberge, 19 Dec. 1961; Spencer to Barry, 5 Mar. 1962; Peter Jones to Michael Spencer, 23 May 1962; *Globe and Mail*, 1 Feb. 1963

39 NFB 4867, A-414, vol. A. Fleming to Fairclough, 27 June 1962; Fairclough to Assistant Deputy Minister of Finance and Secretary of the Treasury Board C.G.E. Steele, 5 July 1962; Roberge memo on meeting Charette of Treasury Board, 5 July 1962; Fairclough to Steele, 5 July 1962; 4899, A-415. Response to question in Commons by Mr Matheson, 25 Oct. 1962. Minutes of the NFB, 6–7 Feb. 1963. See chapter 7 for an account of the next austerity crisis.

40 NFB 1-S, P-155, Secretary of State, 1962–73, Grant McLean to Pierre Juneau, 1 Oct. 1962

Chapter 5

1 Minutes of the NFB, 10 Mar. 1961. Nicole Morgan has noted that some observers have thought the Glassco Commission was probably responsible for more significant changes in the personnel function of the

civil service than any other event since 1867, with the possible exception of the creation of the modern Civil Service Commission in 1918. *Implosion: An Analysis of the Growth of the Federal Public Service in Canada, 1945–1985* (Montreal: Institute for Research on Public Policy 1986), 54–5

2 The *Ottawa Citizen* reported on 9 Sept. 1963 that the commission said the Film Board was supplying a maximum service to the Canadian public.

3 Canada, *Royal Commission on Government Organization*, 5 vols. (Ottawa: Queen's Printer 1962–3), vol. 2, 'Supporting Services for Government' (Report 10, January 1963), 347

4 Tom Daly Papers, box XIV, no. 7, Marjorie McKay to Michael Spencer and Grant McLean, 27 June 1962. Marjorie McKay letter to W. Arthur Irwin, 31 May 1981 (copy in possession of author)

5 Minutes of the NFB, 3 Apr. 1964. The unfortunate Marjorie McKay felt she had lost the programming battle on two accounts: first because of introduction of the pool system and second because poor health forced her to retire in 1964.

6 The production committee was to be the vital organ of the new structure, composed of the former executive producers, a representative elected from the pool, the budgetary officer, a secretary, and possible additional members. The director of production would consult with the production committee before assigning projects at the producer and programme-producer level. The producer, also called the producer-director, was to produce single films. The director of production was to seek the advice of the production committee when there was disagreement between himself and the producer with respect to script or cutting (rough-cut) copy. The production committee would also be the principal advisory authority to the director of production in recruitment and training issues. It was a strange system: the director of production had the ultimate responsibility, yet the producer or programme-producer would have the principal authority and main responsibility in script approval at the creative level. The programme supervisor

was to be an adviser to the producer; the coordinating producer would not be a boss, but an 'arranger,' responsive equally to the needs of the programme-producer and the desires and ambitions of the filmmaker. The programme-producer was also given primary responsibility for the long-term sponsor programme, which was not to be centralized.

7 Minutes of the NFB, 30 Oct. 1964
8 Minutes of the NFB, 7 Feb. 1966
9 NFB 4867, A-414, vol. B, W.D. Moffatt to Minister R.A. Bell, 3 Oct. 1962, and Roberge response attached
10 Jacques Bobet interview with the author, 25 Sept. 1987
11 One of the films, *Fabienne sans son Jules*, by Jacques Godbout, featured the rising québécoise nationalist/singer Pauline Julien and used both a non-professional actress and an improvised script. *Il y eut un soir, il y eut un matin*, by Pierre Patry, called *Françoise* in English, used professional actors and a prepared script. *Caroline*, by Georges Dufaux and Clémont Perron, employed non-professional actors and an improvised script. Joyce Goodman, 'Sociologists not consulted for NFB series on woman,' *Montreal Star*, 4 June 1964. A fifth film was given to Anne Claire Poirier, which became the drama *La Fin des étés*.
12 This same year, Monique Fortier and Anne Claire Poirier wrote *La Beauté même* and *La Fin des étés*. For the former, the subject of 'image' raised an interesting dialectic between the observation of women and the viewer's understanding of the film experience in general, while the latter set Poirier on her subsequent course of articulating the feminine perspective psychologically in a long-film format.
13 Peter Morris, *The Film Companion* (Toronto: Irwin 1984), 63–4. A much harsher judgment was levelled in an essay on the limits of Canadian cinema by *Cité libre*'s resident film critic, Yerri Kempf, who called it *puérilités 'engagées,'* or 'committed' childishness. *Cité libre* 82 (Dec. 1965), 28–31
14 See Peter Harcourt, 'The Beginning of a Beginning,' in Pierre Vérronneau and Piers Handling, eds, *Portrait: Essays on the Cana-*

dian and Quebec Cinema (Ottawa: Canadian Film Institute 1980), 64–76. David Clandfield, *Canadian Film* (Toronto: Oxford University Press 1987), 58–69. Pierre Véronneau, *Résistance et affirmation: La production francophone à l'ONF, 1939–1964*, Les dossiers de la cinémathèque, no. 17 (Montreal: Cinémathèque québécoise / Musée du cinéma 1987), 49–50

15 *Montreal Star*, 23 Nov. 1963

16 Roberge delivered his speech to the International Society for Artistic Education in Montreal; large extracts were printed in *Le Devoir*, 22 Aug. 1963

17 Jacques Bobet interview with the author, 25 Sept. 1987

18 *Toronto Telegram*, 11 Aug. 1964

19 Jacques Bobet interview, 25 Sept. 1987. Also, Michael Dorland, 'Interview: Jacques Bobet, Legends of the National Film Board: The Creation Myth and the Birth of a National Cinema,' *Cinema Canada* 106 (Apr. 1984), 7–12

20 NFB 1315/0, A-44, Policy and Procedures, 1965–8, Juneau to Roberge, 12 June 1964

21 The production statistics of 1963 had demonstrated that both English and French produced the same number of original productions, although, in addition, the English group made all the sponsored films. Minutes of the NFB, 29 June 1964, Appendix: 'Films and other visual materials completed during fiscal year ending March 31, 1964

22 Minutes of the NFB, 29 Nov. 1963. McLean's title had been Senior Assistant and Director of Production; to that was now added Director of Production (English) and General Manager of Production Operations. Juneau ahd been Senior Assistant and Executive Director; now he was Senior Assistant and Director of Production (French).

23 Canada, *Royal Commission on Bilingualism and Biculturalism*, 4 books (Ottawa: Queen's Printer 1967), book 1. The terms of reference were suggested by Michael Oliver, a political scientist (pp. 185–9). See also Ramsay Cook and Michael Behiels, eds, *The Essential Laurendeau* (Toronto: Copp Clark 1976), 30.

24 NFB 1298, P-32, Pickersgill to the Canadian Association of Broadcasters, Toronto, 1 May 1963

25 Jacques Godbout interview with the author, 5 Oct. 1987

26 Judy LaMarsh, *Judy LaMarsh: Memoirs of a Bird in a Gilded Cage* (Toronto: McClelland and Stewart 1968), 102, 311. NA, Maurice Lamontagne Papers, MG 32, B32, vol. 11, Lamontagne to R.M. Fowler, 20 July 1961. *Toronto Star*, 18 July 1964

27 This had been a recommendation of the Glassco Commission report. NA, Secretary of State, 1-S, A410, C.G.E. Steele to G.F. Davidson, Treasury Board, 18 Aug. 1965

28 Minutes of the NFB, 18 Sept. 1963: *Debates of the House of Commons*, vol. 9, 13 Nov. 1964, 10084–5; Minutes of the NFB, 27 Jan. and 1 Sept. 1965. It was estimated that the film training centre would cost between $475,000 and $600,000 for the three-year course. See chapter 6 for Grierson's discussion of the scheme.

29 Lamontagne was able to head off a potentially embarrassing clash between federal and provincial authorities over the question of film censorship, which had last arisen in 1954. Quebec's director of the Censor Bureau and president of the Office du film de la province du Québéc, André Guérin, wanted the right to charge a tariff on *each* Film Board print. He rejected the single-print arrangement agreed upon over a decade before. Guérin's position was that the Film Board should recognize in principle the right of Quebec to censor films. Roberge recalled how Pickersgill had wanted to avoid this confrontation earlier on and had settled the matter informally. This time, it was up to Lamontagne to smooth Quebec's ruffled feathers at the ministerial level, and he bought peace for the next decade. The issue was never resolved legally and would surface again to cause more grief in the 1980s. NFB 4045, Film Censorship, Guy Roberge to Secretary of State, 6 Jan. 1965. Unfortunately, no further correspondence exists, giving rise to the speculation that the problem was swept under the carpet rather than resolved.

30 *Toronto Star*, 18 July 1964; LaMarsh, *Bird in a Gilded Cage*, 49; J.L. Granatstein, *Canada, 1957–1967* (Toronto: McClelland

and Stewart 1986), 281. He made payments on the debt after the bankrupt company's creditor asked for the cash.

31 Most sources on the Quiet Revolution are in French; select translations may be found in Philip Stratford, ed., *Bilbiography of Canadian Books in Translation* (Ottawa 1977). See also Michael Behiels, *Prelude to Quebec's Quiet Revolution* (Montreal/ Kingston: McGill-Queen's 1985). Perhaps the most concise explication of the history of French-Canadian nationalism past and present is Ramsay Cook, *Canada, Quebec and the Uses of Nationalism* (Toronto: McClelland and Stewart 1986), chaps 3–7. See also J.L. Granatstein, I. Abella, D. Bercuson, and R.C. Brown, *Twentieth Century Canada* (Toronto: McGraw Hill-Ryerson 1986), 410–39.

32 L'aliénation nationaliste,' no. 35 (Mar. 1961), 3–5; 'La nouvelle trahison des clercs,' no. 46 (Apr. 1962), 3–16; 'Les séparatistes: Des contre-révolutionnaires,' no. 67 (May 1964), 2–6; and 'Le Québec est-il assiégé?' no. 86 (Apr.–May 1966), 7–10

33 Véronneau, *Résistance et affirmation*, 111–13

34 Trudeau, 'Les séparatistes: Des contre révo-lutionnaires.' His bitter words stung: 'Voyez-vous ça, les pauvres petits! Ils font nombre dans les salles de rédaction de nos journaux, ils pullulent à Radio-Canada et à l'Office du Film, ils pèsent de tout leur poids (?) sur les mass-média, mais ils trouvent néanmoins injuste la place qui leur est faite dans cette société.'

35 Gérard Pelletier, 'Parti Pris ou la grande illusion,' *Cité libre* 66 (Apr. 1964), 3–8

36 Jacques Godbout interview with the author, 5 Oct. 1987

37 *Parti pris* 7 (Apr. 1964): Godbout, pp. 6–10; Carle, 11–15; Perron, pp. 16–18; Arcand, pp. 19–21; Groulx, 22–4. The issue of the previous month had announced that Michel Brault would be contributing an article as well. It was never published.

38 Pierre Maheu, 'L'ONF, ou un cinéma québéois?,' *Parti pris* 7 (Apr. 1964), 2–5

39 NFB, 1-M, A-410, Roberge statement to the five contributors to *Partis pris*, 24 Apr. 1964; Roberge, Mémoire au Secrétaire d'Etat, 25 Apr. 1964

40 Pierre Juneau interview with the author, 6 Mar. 1987

41 *Nobody Waved Goodbye* had a very loose script; that is, the actors were following its outline, but were often ad-libbing their movements and actions. Filming with only two lights was a nightmare for cinema-tographer John Spotton, who had to antici-pate the actors' movements. Spotton considered the film a breakthrough tech-nically because it was the first time that the camera and sound recorder were separated. The female's ever-present shoulder-bag con-tained the recorder and allowed a number of interesting shots, like the opening one on a bridge on Toronto Island or the teens' departure from a subway station.

42 *Montreal Star*, 11 Aug. 1964

43 *Debates of the House of Commons*, vol. 8, 16 Sept. 1964, 8069–70. J.B. Stewart an-swered for the minister. In a typical year, he said, there were some ninety items pro-duced, including about twenty-five spon-sored films. Lengths varied from several-minute 'educational' items to 30- or 90-minute features. The board of governors stated a month later that the distinction between entertainment and the documen-tary feature film should be retained as a guide; Minutes of the NFB, 30 Oct. 1964

44 NA, 1-M, Minister's Office (M. Lamon-tagne), box A-410, 1964–6, vol. 8, Douglas Fisher to Film Board, 10 Sept. 1964; Roberge to Secretary of State, 13 Oct. 1964

45 *Debates of the House of Commons*, vol. 10, 24 Nov. 1964, 10441–4. In 1963 there had been a suggestion that the Film Board update those series that were no longer topical. Also, 'Group television study,' a kind of classroom on the air, was a coming development. There was no serious action, however, on either suggestion. NFB 1298, A-212, 'Film Board Production and Private Broadcasting Needs – A Summary,' n.d., probably early in 1964

46 Speech by John Grierson on the occasion of the National Film Board's twenty-fifth an-niversary, 5 Aug. 1964 (copy in possession of the author)

47 Minutes of the NFB, 30 Oct. 1964

48 *Canadian Film Weekly* (Toronto), 19 Aug. 1964

49 Minutes of the NFB, 30 Oct. 1964

50 External Affairs initialled this agreement with France in April 1963. Minutes of the NFB, 29 Apr. 1963. NFB 4867, A-414, vol. C, Roberge to Pickersgill, 24 Apr. 1963

51 Minutes of the NFB, 18 Sept. 1963, Appendix, Memorandum to the Secretary of State, 11 Sept. 1963

52 NA, Maurice Lamontagne Papers, MG 32, B32, vol. 11, 'Politique Culturelle,' C.G.E. Steele to Maurice Lamontagne, 29 July 1964

53 Negative editorial reaction to the proposed scheme occurred in the following newspapers: *Winnipeg Tribune*, 7 Aug.; *Globe and Mail* (Toronto), 8 Aug.; *Kitchener-Waterloo Record*, 8 Aug.; *Montreal Star*, 10 Aug.; *Pembroke Observer*, 14 Aug.; and *Ottawa Journal*, 24 Aug. 1964.

54 Excerpt from Lamontagne speech at meeting of Canadian Conference of the Arts, 13 Oct. 1965, contained in Minutes of NFB, 20 Oct. 1965, Appendix. This same comparison was used by opponents of the government's Film and Video Policy almost two decades later. They saw little use in Canada producing films for the U.S. marketplace.

55 Over the years, the executive directors of the CFDC were Michael Spencer, Michael McCabe, and André Lamy; during Lamy's term, the CFDC became Telefilm Canada, and following Lamy's departure, Peter Pearson, then Pierre des Roches, held that post.

56 Minutes of the NFB, 27 Jan. 1964, Appendix, Review of Policy Governing CBC-NFB Cooperation. In 1962, it was reported that the Film Board had only been able to deliver twenty-three out of thirty-five shows covered in its 1961–2 contract with the CBC. This fact was not included in the above-mentioned report. Tom Daly Papers, 3151, box IX, no. 3, Michael Spencer to Grant McLean and Pierre Juneau, 12 June 1962.

Spot bookings earned the Film Board about $45,000 a year in rental income, though the several television series that the agency produced for the CBC earned the greatest amount of rental income for the agency, around $440,000 per year. From a high of $622,500 in 1961–2, this amount had declined to $382,000, then risen to $448,000, and finally settled at $432,000 in 1964–5. (Private stations were paying only about $25,000 in rentals per year.)

57 NFB 4867, A-414, 'Canadian Television – 10 Year Review,' n.d. (probably 1962–3)

58 There were only six English theatrical items that year (three 20-minute and three less than 20-minute films, most in colour) and twelve French theatrical (mostly around ten minutes and in colour). Each language had its 'general' programme, which included juvenile and science films (five of ten minutes or less for the English, three for the French) and an extensive number of classroom 'loops,' 8-mm short continuous items on special cassettes. The loops could be used to teach a variety of subjects. In 1964, the English group completed themes on mathematical concepts and community responsibilities; the French produced loops on geography and physics.

That same year, the English General Programme completed twelve original films of half-hour or less duration and three animation films of less than ten minutes. The French side produced seven films for non-theatrical distribution and three history films for schools, most around thirty minutes, and a dozen 'magazine' items of less than ten minutes.

Animation was still an English-language domain, with three films finished that year and nine more to be completed the following year, when French Animation was inaugurated. Newsreels on the English and French sides numbered around twelve items for each region of Canada, or forty for the year. Most of these found their way on to television in Canada; some went abroad. The sponsored films occupied around one-fourth of the entire production programme, consisting of mostly English originals and French versions.

59 NFB 4867, A-414 Film Board–Television Distribution (CBC), 1957–64, n.d. (probably 1964)

60 NFB 4867, A-414, Michael Spencer to Guy Roberge, 23 Feb. 1965

61 *Time* magazine said, on 15 Jan. 1965, that the film both portrayed Bethune's streak of haughty egomania and explained why he was regarded as a Canadian Gandhi. Other positive reaction came from the *Telegram*

(Toronto), *Montreal Gazette*, the *Ottawa Citizen*, and *Weekend* magazine. The *Montreal Star* devoted an editorial to Bethune and stated that if the surgeon were alive in 1965, he would almost certainly not be a Communist; he was the kind of unconventional man that every age needs, yet fails to appreciate. The editorial stressed how a life of unorthodoxy and achievement might interest future generations.

62 From the script and correspondence of *Bethune*, NFB file 62-131, vol. 14

63 Earlier, Cadieux had expressed reservations about having a Czechoslovakian film crew come to make a film about Canada for showing in Czechoslovakia. He may also have been uncomfortable with the success of both countries' reciprocal national film weeks in 1964. The Film Board had shown five days of its films in Prague: 25 Sept., *Canon, Very Nice, Very Nice, (A tout prendre* was non-NFB); 26 Sept., *Opening Speech, Corral, Blinkity Blank, Circle of the Sun, Neighbours, Morning on the Lièvre*; 27 Sept., *Le Merle, Journey from Zero, The Canadians, The Romance of Transportation in Canada, Living Stone*; 28 Sept., *Rythmetic, The Ride, Trans-Canada Journey, My Financial Career, Nahanni*; 29 Sept., *Au Hazard du temps, Le monde va nous prendre pour des sauvages, Drylanders*. Minutes of the NFB, 30 Oct. 1964

64 The films to be screened were *Trans-Canada Journey, Lonely Boy, City of Many Faces, Vancouver* (non-NFB), and *Nobody Waved Goodbye*.

65 Minutes of the NFB, 7 Feb. 1966 and 21 Mar. 1966. NFB Commercial Division, Contracts for *Bethune*. See also incomplete correspondence in Bethune file, NFB, 62-121, vol. 14; Cosman to Roberge, 31 Aug. 1965; Cadieux to Roberge, 16 Sept. and 12 Nov. 1965, 21 Jan. 1966; Roberge to Cadieux, 24 Nov. and 21 Dec. 1965; Grant McLean to Roberge, 7 Feb. 1966

66 NFB 1315/0, Policy and Procedures, 1956–68, McLean document, 'Programming, 1964,' n.d. (probably spring 1964)

67 Granatstein, *Canada 1957–1967*, 195

68 LaMarsh, *Memoirs of a Bird in a Gilded Cage*, 230–1, 244–5

69 Minutes of the NFB, 21 Mar. 1966

70 Jacques Parizeau commented wryly some years later, 'For all intents and purposes, the Quiet Revolution consisted of three or four ministers, twenty civil servants and consultants – and fifty *chansonniers*.' Graham Fraser, *Parti Québécois: René Lévesque and the Parti Québécois in Power* (Toronto: Macmillan 1984), 161

71 Ronald Dick interview with the author, 2–5 Dec. 1986

Chapter 6

1 At the New York world's fair of 1964, there had been an impressive array of automation, stereo sound systems, and multiple screens, and the Film Board invited some experts to show their wares to the many producers who were to contribute to Expo 67.

2 Gerald Graham, *Canadian Film Technology, 1896–1986* (Cranbury, NJ: Associated University Presses 1989), chap. 12

3 NFB 1180, A-291, Julian Biggs to McLean, 19 May 1966

4 To be fair to the filmmakers, a number of important Film Board classics came from this mélange of titles, though not all in the coming year. They were: *Helicopter Canada, Pas de deux, Never a Backwards Step, No Reason To Stay, Paddle to the Sea, The House That Jack Built, What On Earth!*, and *Illegal Abortion*.

5 Minutes of the NFB, 9 Nov. 1966, Appendix, 'Observations by the National Film Board on "A Special Report on the Cultural Policy and Activities of the Government of Canada, 1965–66"'

6 Nicole Morgan, *Implosion: An Analysis of the Growth of the Federal Public Service in Canada, 1945–85* (Montreal: Institute for Research on Public Policy 1986), 53–61

7 NFB 3850, B-3, Film Commissioner, Roberge to George Davidson, Treasury Board, 6 May 1965

8 NFB 1180, A-279, Grant McLean Correspondence, E.R. Bellemare to Marcel Cadieux, Under Secretary of State for External Affairs, 28 Oct. 1966

9 NA, MG 6, Series 85–86/184, box 18, file

300-108/0, part 1, Gordon Sheppard to the Minister (Maurice Lamontagne), 30 Apr. 1964

10 Ibid., C.J. Lochnan to C.G.E. Steele, 20 Sept. 1965

11 Ibid., C.G.E. Steele to Secretary of State, 21 Oct. 1965; Steele to Dr George Davidson, Secretary of the Treasury Board, 19 Aug. 1966; C.J. Mackenzie to C.G.E. Steele, 19 Sept. 1966; Steele to Judy LaMarsh, 30 Sept. 1966. LaMarsh was out of the country at this time, prompting Steele to take the budgetary gamble.

12 NFB 3935, Film Training Centre, Confidential letter from John Grierson to Grant McLean, 14 Sept. 1966

13 *Globe and Mail*, 10 Sept. 1966: Bruce Lawson, 'The trials of Judy the Movie Maker.' Grant McLean ordered that this interview not be included in the Film Board's *Newsclips*, its collection of press clippings. NFB 1180, A-291, Sept. 1966

14 NFB 1180, A-291, LaMarsh to McLean, 19 Sept. 1966

15 McLean was not heartbroken about the announced cut-backs and slashed production monies for features. He confided to board member Gordon Robertson that he always felt that the National Film Act of 1950 had established the guidelines for the agency – 'national interest' and 'films to interpret Canada to Canadians and to the rest of the world.' Features could be justified if they fell within those guidelines. McLean was cautious about announcing a no-features policy because he believed that serious damage to morale would be done. NFB 1180, A-279, Grant McLean Correspondence, McLean to Robertson, 28 Sept. 1966

16 Judy LaMarsh, *Judy LaMarsh: Memoirs of a Bird in a Gilded Cage* (Toronto: McClelland and Stewart 1968), 260. There were numerous instances demonstrating how LaMarsh was the architect of her own isolation from the Cabinet. Late in 1966, she scorned Pearson's weakness openly in the Commons. When the prime minister at last agreed to proceed with Paul Hellyer's armed forces unification scheme, she snarled, 'What the hell did you do to him [Pearson]? Pour concrete down his back?' J.L. Granatstein, *Canada, 1957–1967* (Toronto: McClelland and Stewart 1986), 241.

17 J.W. Pickersgill interview with the author, 23 Oct. 1986; LaMarsh, *Bird in a Gilded Cage*, 277

18 LaMarsh, *Bird in a Gilded Cage*, 266–7

19 NA, RG 6, vol. 843, 5000-2, C.G.E. Steele to the Secretary of State, 16 May 1966

20 NA, RG 6, 85-86/184, box 6, file 177-108/0, part 1, C.G.E. Steele to John Grierson, 21 Sept. 1966; Grierson to Steele, 3 Oct. 1966

21 *La Presse*, 2 Feb. 1967. The first article was by Luc Perrault; the second was unsigned.

22 NA, RG 6, 85-86/184, box 6, file 177-108/0, part 1, C.G.E. Steele to LaMarsh, 6 Apr. 1967

23 *Globe and Mail*, 29 Apr. 1967

24 NFB 1180, A-291, Growth and the Five Year Programme, Michael Spencer to Ed Coristine, 10 Mar. 1967; Spencer to McLean, 28 Mar. 1967; Spencer to Julian Biggs and Marcel Martin, 23 May 1967; Biggs to Spencer, 25 May 1967

25 Minutes of the NFB, 15 Aug. 1966; NFB 1180, A-279, McLean Correspondence, Don Lytle, Director of Film, CBC, to Michael Spencer, Director of Planning, NFB, 3 Mar. 1967

26 Minutes of the NFB, 3 Feb. 1967; NFB, 1-S, B-53, McLean to Secretary of State LaMarsh, 11 May 1966

27 NFB 1180, A-279, McLean Correspondence, W.L. Cosman to Grant McLean, 12 Sept. 1966

28 *Toronto Telegram*, 4 Nov. 1967

29 NFB 1180, A-291, vol. 1, Gordon Burwash to Hugo McPherson, 3 and 20 Oct. 1967; Frank Spiller to McPherson, 4 Oct. 1967

30 NFB 1180, A-291, vol. 1, Judy LaMarsh letters about *The Ernie Game*, 15 Dec. 1967

31 *Montreal Star*, 21 Dec. 1967

32 *Ottawa Citizen*, 21 Dec. 1967. The journalist, Frank Penn, defended strongly the production of adult entertainment for adult hours. He predicted (correctly) that Fournier's remarks would almost certainly trigger another wave of parliamentary questions on the cost or social acceptability of this or that programme.

33 NFB, 1-S, B-53, Secretary of State, Hugo McPherson to C.G.E. Steele, 5 Dec. 1967. The commissioner insisted that cost re-coverability was not a Film Board require-ment. His most flamboyant declaration was that these features were in the public interest, in part because commercial pro-ducers would not likely have made them.

34 Minutes of the NFB, 15 Mar. 1968, Appendix 11A, English Production Programme. The CBC could not contract for payment to the NFB in 1968–9, 'for financial reasons.' The Film Board would be limited to six hour-long films, some of which were carry-ins from the previous year.

35 Five months later the core group invited Fernand Cadieux, Joan Henson, Jo Kirkpatrick, and Jean-Paul Pothier to work through the theme with them. Koenig, who was part of the original discussions, left to become head of English Animation.

36 Tom Daly Papers, VII, no. 1, Labyrinth. The group also consulted Frye's *Anatomy of Criticism*, James Frazer's *The Golden Bough*, and Robert Graves's *The White Goddess* in working out the theme.

37 The National Film Board of Canada, Tech-nical Operations Branch, Technical Bul-letin, *Labyrinthe*, no. 8, Mar. 1968. Graham, *Canadian Film Technology*, chap. 12. As director of technical operations, Graham paid tribute to the team that put the show together, including Ray Payne, Arnold Schieman, Stan Rochowicz, Rolf Epstein, Leo O'Donnell, Len Green, Chester Beachell, Ralph Curtis, Stan Cole, Ambrose Vachon, Paul Kaluski, Les Dupuis, Wally Gentleman, Jim Wilson, Dennis Gillson, and Nick Culic.

38 A 16- and 35-mm version of the cruciform film, *In the Labyrinth*, was made in 1979 and is still in distribution. It obviously loses much of its impact when five screens are compressed on to a single frame containing a grid of nine squares, but the flow of imagery certainly achieves the wholeness that Tom Daly achieved in the original.

39 Colin Low and Tom Daly interviews with the author, 8 and 21 Oct. 1987

40 Clyde Gilmour's laudatory article in the *Toronto Telegram*, 22 Apr. 1967, noted the absence of war motifs in the film as did

Judith Shatnoff in 'Expo 67: A Multiple Vision,' *Film Quarterly* 21, no. 1 (Fall 1967), 2–13. Daly was puzzled at this criticism, since he believed that disturbance, unrest, and riots came at their proper place in the psychological sequence at the end of Cham-ber I.

41 'Expo 67 and the exploding syntax of cinema,' *New York Times*, 20 Aug. 1967. There were articles also in *Photo Age*, Mar. 1967, and *Industrial Photography*, June 1967.

42 Colin Low interview with the author, 22 Oct. 1987. Low also believes that this process will allow the audience to discover the vulnerability of the characters in a way that has never before been experienced in film.

43 Grant McLean interview with the author, 5 Aug. 1986

44 Tom Daly Papers, box VI, no. 17. Pro-gramme Committee to NFB Staff, 7 Jan. 1966

45 Ibid., box VII, no. 21, The Committee of Five, Notes and Suggestions on Procedure and Organization, Spring 1966. Three or four interpretive films a year exceeded the agency's average output. They suggested multi-screen experimental films or some international products for television. As for features, there should be at least four per year, but with additional government fund-ing. Co-productions were also a possible alternative.

46 Ibid., From the Committee of Five to Pool Members, The Role and Responsibility of the Producer, 28 Oct. 1966

47 Parliament had voted the agency $3.5 mil-lion, while the Film Board itself generated $700,000 in sales and rentals. Television rentals (now called royalties) had produced only $300,000, for a total income of $4.5 million. The grand total income for the fiscal year was $7.8 million. Minutes of the NFB, 16–17 June 1967, Appendix, Produc-tion Statistics, 1 Apr. 1966–31 Mar. 1967

48 Tom Daly Papers, box XIII, no. 21, Notes on sponsored film discussion, n.d., 1966, NFB 1180, A-291, Lawrence Hyde to Julian Biggs, Grant McLean, John Howe, Frank Spiller, and Don Brittain, 1 May 1967

49 Minutes of the NFB, June 16–17, 1967. The

total number of original (non-sponsored) films was 49, 37 in English, and 12 in French; in addition, there were 12 English versions and 24 French versions of films already in existence. Two other films were bilingual. Some 82 films were versioned in foreign languages for circulation abroad in Dutch, German, Hindi, Japanese, Portuguese, Spanish, Greek, Italian, Arabic, and Norwegian. There were 37 original English and only 6 French sponsored films. Commercial film companies had completed 34 films, more than one-third of them for Expo 67 and the Centennial celebrations. There were also 227 film stories, news clips, and 8-mm 'loops' done by the agency and only one 'loop' done by a commercial company. Production of filmstrips and still photos were additional NFB activities.

50 Gordon Robertson interview with the author, 28 Jan. 1988. McPherson thought that a contributing factor to his nomination was his authorship of a study of the Canada Council, which he said was widely read in government circles and had led to further development in federal planning in the arts. NFB 1180, A-291, Film Commissioner, McPherson to Lewis Perinbam, 23 May 1968

51 *Toronto Daily Star*, 20 Apr. 1967

52 *Globe and Mail*, 18 May 1967; *Toronto Daily Star*, 18 and 19 May 1967. See chapter 8 for a discussion of *The Things I Cannot Change*.

53 NFB 1298, J.E. Ponting to Gerald Graham, 12 Oct. 1967. The final bill for the loss was issued on 18 May 1972. Insurance paid $156,407 for equipment and film and $90,430 for the building. The market value of the films was ignored.

54 Grant McLean interview with the author, 5 Aug. 1986; Minutes of Special Meeting of NFB, 28 July 1967

55 Minutes of the NFB, 20–21 Oct. 1967, Appendix, 'A Statement on Policy prepared for the Board of Governors' by Hugo McPherson, 11 Oct. 1967

56 Minutes of the NFB, 5 Jan. 1968

57 Ibid., 20–21 Oct. 1967

58 Ibid., 5 Jan. 1968

59 Ibid., 28 July 1967

60 Ibid., 15 Mar. 1968

Chapter 7

1 Minutes of the NFB, 28 July 1967. NFB 1180, A-291, McPherson to Malcolm Ross, Dean of Arts, University of Toronto, 22 Aug. 1967, acknowledging the probability of austerity in government spending.

2 Minutes of the NFB, 15 Mar. 1968. NFB 1180, A-291, Film Commissioner's Office, Leo Daigneault to Julian Biggs and Marcel Martin, 7 Feb. 1968. Daigneault reported that English Production had overspent by $20,000 while the French had *underspent* by $80,000, leaving a net surplus of $60,000.

3 Minutes of the NFB, 5 Jan. and 31 May 1968

4 NFB 1315/0, A-44, Grant McLean to Donald Mulholland and Pierre Juneau, 11 June 1957. See also Ronald Dick, 'Regionalization of a Federal Cultural Institution: The Experience of the National Film Board, 1965–79,' in Gene Walz, ed., *Flashback: People and Institutions in Canadian Film History* (Montreal: Mediatexte Publications 1986), 107–33.

5 NFB 1180, A-291, Film Commissioner's Office, 1968, J. André Ouellette to Gérard Bertrand, 4 July 1968

6 Minutes of the NFB, 28 Feb.–1 Mar. 1969. Also, NFB 1065, A-88, Film Board to Treasury Board, 29 Aug. 1969

7 NFB 1298, P-153, Minutes of the Standing Committee on Broadcasting, Films and Assistance to the Arts, 26 Nov. 1968, 386–9

8 Ibid., Minutes of the Standing Committee on Broadcasting, Films and Assistance to the Arts, 29 Feb. 1969

9 Ibid., Minutes of the Standing Committee on Broadcasting, Films and Assistance to the Arts, 27 Mar. 1969

10 Minutes of the NFB, 31 May 1968, Appendix, Programme Review Submission, 1969–70

11 Ibid., 24–25 Apr. 1969

12 Gérard Pelletier interview with the author, 3 Feb. 1988. His wife, Alec Pelletier, had worked for the Film Board and the CBC under contract for years (she had written *Le Festin des morts*), but had broken with both agencies when her husband became minister, lest the Opposition charge 'conflict of interest.'

13 NFB 1065, A-88, vol. 1, Austerity, Hugo

McPherson to the Secretary of State, 5 June 1969

14 NFB 1315/0, P-181, Policy and Procedures, vol. 2, Policy concerning the Presentation of Commercial Messages with NFB Films on Canadian Television, 27 June 1969

15 NFB 1965, A-88, Austerity, vol. 1, McPherson to Jules Léger, 7 July 1969

16 Ibid., Policy and Procedures, vol. 2, Confidential record of cabinet decisions, 25, 28, 29, and 30 July 1969, Expenditure Guidelines for 1970–71 by D.J. Leach, supervisor of cabinet documents

17 Jacques Bobet interview with the author, 27 Sept. 1987; NFB 1315/0, P-181, Policy and Procedures, vol. 2, Marc Devlin to Frank Spiller, 11 Oct. 1968

18 NFB 1065, A-88, Austerity, vol. 1, Film Board to Treasury Board, 29 Aug. 1969

19 NFB 1315/0, P-181, Policy and Procedures, vol. 2, Gerald Graham to Hugo McPherson, 19 Jan. 1970

20 Gérard Pelletier interview with the author, 3 Feb. 1988

21 Gérard Pelletier interview with the author, 3 Feb. 1988; Hugo McPherson interview with the author, 15 Sept. 1986; R. Gordon Robertson interview with the author, 28 Jan. 1988. Robertson recalled that Prime Minister Trudeau had more respect for Drury than any other minister because Drury was wise, objective, and selfless. Drury was troubled by the Centennial splurge, especially because it had occurred in Montreal, and as Robertson recalled, 'He had that hairshirt quality about him and did not want it to appear that he or his constituency were benefiting from the splurge.'

22 R. Gordon Robertson interview with the author, 28 Jan. 1988

23 Hugo McPherson interview with the author, 15 Sept. 1986

24 NFB 1065, A-88, vol. 1, Austerity, McPherson meeting with NFB staff to explain austerity, 22 Aug. 1969

25 Ibid., John Howe telegram, 25 Aug. 1969; Report of the Crisis Committee on the National Film Board of Canada, Sept. 1969. Members of the Crisis Committee were John Howe, Rex Tasker, Mort Ransen, Robert Forget, Clément Perron, and Doro-

thy Hénaut. There was some sympathetic coverage by the press. The *Montreal Star* ran a long article by Dusty Vineberg, 'Cutbacks halt work, alarm NFB' on 18 Sept. 1969, while the *Toronto Daily Star* published 'A life-or-death drama at the NFB,' by Marci McDonald, on 4 Oct. 1969.

26 NFB 1065, A-88, vol. 1, Austerity, Gerald Graham to McPherson, 12 Sept. 1969

27 NFB 1315/0, P-190, Policy and Documents, 1969, Recommendations from headquarters Distribution management to the Government Film Commissioner, 18 Sept. 1969

28 NFB 1065, A-88, vol. 1, Austerity, McPherson paper quoting the undated article to the Planning and Programme Policy Committee [3P Committee], 17 Sept. 1969

29 Ibid., McPherson to W.R. Jack, 15 Sept. 1969

30 Ibid., McPherson meeting with NFB staff, 25 Sept. 1969

31 Gérard Pelletier interview with the author, 3 Feb. 1988

32 NFB 1065, A-88, vol. 1, Austerity, Ian MacNeill to Hugo McPherson, the 3P Committee and the Crisis Committee, 30 Sept. 1969

33 Ibid., McPherson memorandum to Film Board staff, 7 Oct. 1969

34 Minutes of the NFB, 17 Oct. 1969

35 NFB 1065, A-88, vol. 1, Austerity, Treasury Board directive no. 692130, 31 Aug. 1969. The $1 million meant that the staff would decline to 866 from 1,029 and that no distribution offices would be closed. Pelletier told the Commons on 24 November that thirty-five employees, including ten in production, had been notified in October of the Film Board's intention to lay them off. Another fifty-five would have to be terminated by 15 March.

36 *Grierson Transcripts: Interviews Recorded with John Grierson, February 1969–July 1971*, transcribed by Sandra Gathercole, 4 vols (Ottawa: Canadian Radio and Television Commission 1973), 1: 14

37 Ibid., 1: 23–4. Dusty Vineberg, 'Grierson says film board over-mechanized,' *Montreal Star*, 22 Nov. 1969

38 Martin Knelman, 'A slow dissolve for the NFB?,' *Globe and Mail*, 6 Dec. 1969

39 *Debates of the House of Commons*, vol. 2,

15 Dec. 1969, 2007–8; vol. 3, 15 Jan. 1970, 2418

40 NFB 1065, A-88, vol. 1, Austerity, Copy of letter sent to the prime minister of Canada, 11 Dec. 1969. The director of French Production, Jacques Godbout, wrote subsequently to General Manager Gérard Bertrand that he refused to lay off anybody on these shoddy (administrative) grounds. He noted perceptively that of the thirteen filmmakers who might be laid off, ten were working on films whose average cost was $75,000; to save ten salaries ($100,000) the Film Board would have to throw out $750,000 worth of film.

41 NFB 1315/0, P-190, Policy Documents 1969, Hugo McPherson meeting with staff, 15 Dec. 1969. With the heads of other cultural agencies, McPherson had met the secretary of state in Montreal two days earlier. The agenda included an attempt to define Canadian culture, the roles of the agencies to help develop it and bilingualism, and discussions of a global budget for all agencies under the secretary of state. At this weekend meeting McPherson requested an outside mediator to review the situation. Minutes of the NFB, 23 Jan. 1970

42 Looking at the previous decade, in March 1960 there had been a reduction of 10, leaving a balance of 718 employees; in 1961 there was no increase; in 1962 there was a growth of 25, which in 1963 was cut back to the 718 figure; in 1964 there was a growth of 13. Then by March 1965 there was an increase of 51, followed by an increase of 69 by March 1966, an increase of 71 by March 1967, an increase of 61 by March 1968, and an increase of 12 by March 1969, for a total average increase of 53 a year over the last five years. Minutes of the NFB, 23 Jan. 1970, Appendix

43 NFB 1315/0, P-190, Policy Documents, 1969, Notes of meeting of middle and upper management about staff cuts, by Hugo McPherson, Dec. 1969. Pelletier remembers McPherson bursting into tears as he pleaded for help, 'What will I do with the filmmakers on strike?' Gérard Pelletier interview with the author, 3 Feb. 1988

44 Transcript of interview with McPherson for *History of the National Film Board* (uncom-

pleted production no. 47-031), Apr. 1980

45 *Debates of the House of Commons*, vol. 3, 15 Jan. 1970, 2418

46 NFB, 1065, A-88, vol. 1, Austerity, McPherson to Pelletier, 17 Jan. 1970

47 *Debates of the House of Commons*, vol. 3, 19 Jan. 1970, 2526

48 Ibid., vol. 3, 20 Jan. 1970, 2584

49 Ibid., vol. 4, 10 Feb. 1970, 3406. Trudeau claimed that Pelletier was aware of the Information Canada decision, but the prime minister did not answer when asked if the Film Board commissioner knew of the decision (p. 3418).

50 *Gazette* (Montreal), 30 Jan. 1970

51 NFB 1355, B-67, Film Commissioner, Saumier report, McPherson to Pelletier, 18 Jan. 1970. McPherson finally agreed to reduce the number of those laid-off by five and to inform twelve of those under notice that they would have another year. The fifty distribution personnel could stay. The cuts were announced on 30 January, when thirty-five were declared surplus: twelve filmmakers and technicians, eight film officers in Distribution, and fifteen administration and support staff. NFB 1298, A-146 (no author), Notes on the Saumier report, Jan. 1970; 1065, A-88, vol. 1, Austerity, Staff cuts, 30 Jan. 1970

52 *Debates of the House of Commons*, vol. 5, 11 Mar. 1970, 4651–2

53 Dusty Vineberg, 'NFB staff cutback under fire,' *Montreal Star*, 16 Jan. 1970

54 NFB 1315/0, A-60, Film Policy, 1969–72, McPherson's working notes for the secretary of state, 22 May 1970

55 NFB 1298, A-265, 'Parity between French and English Production; Working Notes for the Secretary of State,' 22 May 1970; also, Memo from Marie Nyez to Ted Greenway, 19 Apr. 1971. English Production was still carrying on the lion's shares of the sponsored-film work, which partly accounted for the relatively high percentage of budget distribution to the English side. In 1970, for example, there were 24 sponsored films in English and only 2 in French; of original films there were 30 in English and 34 in French (958 minutes to 1,582), a figure which demonstrates that there was already parity in the most important category.

56 NFB 1298, P-153 Commissioner-Minister file, Hugo McPherson before the Standing Committee on Broadcasting, Films and Assistance to the Arts, 12 May 1970, 1–55. In fact, McPherson had tried to recommend legislation requiring that Canadian films be exhibited in theatres and on television, but Vice-chairman of the Board of Governors W.R. Jack insisted it be dropped from the 'Statement of Policy for the Board as a Cultural Agency' in July 1969. Minutes of the NFB, 18 July 1969

57 NFB 1298, P-153, Meeting of the Standing Committee on Broadcasting, Films and Assistance to the Arts, 27 Mar. 1969. Another reason why the Film Board was being given a rough time had to do with its failure to call for public tenders for a contract to sell $200,000 worth of audiovisual equipment in Ontario. J. Patrick Nowlan, head of the committee, was peeved with the Film Board after newspaper stories in the *Toronto Telegram* and the *Toronto Daily Star* on 15 May 1970 identified three former employees, Gordon Burwash, Grant McLean, and Hans Moller, as being the beneficiaries. Nowlan claimed that the absence of public tendering 'smelled' and that other legitimate contenders should have had a chance to bid for the contract. McPherson defended the practice, claiming that they were 'the most knowledgeable group in the field.' Nowlan wanted to censure the agency.

58 Tom Daly Papers, box VII, no. 22, Woods Gordon report, 29 May 1968. The Film board told Woods Gordon early in their study that the agency proposed to shift a high percentage of the sponsored-film production to the private sector. (Austerity would make this impossible.)

59 NFB 1298, 4427/0, box A-72, Hugo McPherson to Julian Biggs, 11 Oct. 1968; 1298, 1-4-46, vol. 2, 1968, Gerald Graham to Hugo McPherson, Dec. 1968

60 NFB 1315/0, A-379, Policy and Procedures, 1967–71, 'NFB Memo: Assistance to the Private Sector–Guidelines,' 20 Mar. 1970. Minutes of the NFB, 17 Apr. 1970. Hugo McPherson interview with the author, 15 Sept. 1986

61 Ibid., P-190, Policy and Documents, 1969, Draft Statement of Policy for the National Film Board as a Cultural Agency and a 5-Year Plan of Implementation, 23 June 1969. Some members were aware that McPherson had rented the Film Board shooting stage to a private company for forty-four days and had concluded a second contract shortly thereafter. After informing the board of governors (not all of whom concurred) in August 1969, McPherson had undertaken the arrangement as a barter deal. The Film Board received $150,000 worth of laboratory services in exchange. He had justified it then as an emergency measure. Minutes of the NFB, 17 Oct. 1969. After loud protests from the president of the Association of Motion Picture Producers and Laboratories of Canada, the Film Board cancelled the agreement. Minutes of the NFB, 12 Dec. 1969

62 NFB 1298, P-153, Standing Committee on Broadcasting, Films and Assistance to the Arts, 14 May 1970, 24–59. He reminded the committee that if the 193 companies in the private sector took over the departmental film work, the average benefit to each company would be around $15,000. McPherson had stated his intentions for sponsored films a few months earlier in 'The National Film Board of Canada: Short Policy Statement Requested by the Secretary of State,' 30 Mar. 1970. NFB 1315/0, P-190

63 NFB 1315/0, A-277, Secretary of State, 'Politique culturelle du gouvernement,' 15 May 1970. Six months earlier, the Film Board language adviser claimed that, at a cost of $20,000 per year since 1963, there was serious thought of discontinuing the language-instruction programme because of austerity. A determined Cabinet decided on 30 April to accept the main recommendations of the Laurendeau-Dunton report, which was that French should become the language of work in Quebec. Prime Minister Trudeau wrote to McPherson in July 1970 that he wanted to see the public service become bilingual. Lanuage instruction would stay. NFB 1185, A-105, Bilingualism, R. Cormier to Max Yalden, 18 Dec. 1969; Prime Minister Trudeau to Hugo McPherson, 31 July 1970

64 Minutes of the NFB, 10 July 1970

65 NFB 1-S, P-155, McPherson to Pelletier, 26 June 1970

66 NFB 1315/0, P-214, General Policy and Procedures, McPherson to NFB staff, 9 July 1970

67 W.R. Jack telephone interview with the author, 7 Jan. 1987

68 Hugo McPherson interview with the author, 15 Sept. 1986

69 Northrop Frye, 'Communications,' *The Listener*, 9 July 1970

70 Dean Walker, 'Interview with Hugo McPherson: "Contradiction I couldn't live with," ' *Canadian Photography*, April 1971, 2–4

Chapter 8

1 Tom Daly Papers, box VII, no. 23A, Internal Study Group Report of the National Film Board, 30 May 1968

2 In practice this meant that programming was done by categories that had nothing to do with the product programmed. Theatres and television were considered distribution channels, filmstrip and animation were techniques, while experimental, special interest, and 'general' films represented subject areas.

3 The five series availabe were *Fragment of Life Series* (three film loops, such as 'Birth of a Caterpillar'), *Community Helpers Series* (10 loops like 'Loading a Boat'), *The Mathematics Series* (18 loops including 'Tangent'), *Série Géographie* (11 French film loops, such as 'Sedimentation'), and *Série Physique* (16 French film loops on physics) and its English equivalent, *The Physics Series*.

4 Don Arioli (cartoonist and animator) interview with the author, 21 Oct. 1988

5 Tom Daly Papers, box VII, no. 23A, Internal Study Group Report of the National Film Board, 30 May 1968, 124–5. The study also recommended budgetary and accounting reform, including the introduction of a computerized system. But there were no funds for the latter.

6 Ibid., box XIII, no. 21, Peter Jones to Frank Spiller, 'Regional Production Offices: Present and Future,' 11 July 1968. Jones argued that the agency should apportion $100,000 to regional film production per region. Austerity made this a pipedream.

7 Ibid., box VII, no. 22, Frank Spiller to staff, 10 Sept. 1968; John Howe to Frank Spiller, 18 Sept. 1968. The programme producer now had the function of the old executive producer (financial and administrative responsibility as well as the final mix of cutting copies), while the producer had the authority and responsibility for the film agreed to with the programme producer. The producer was supposed to give maximum freedom to the film director. The entire mechanism was to be overseen by the Production Control Office, which was to administer the pool of directors as well as a staff-evaluation programme.

8 Ibid., box XIII, no. 20, Julian Biggs, director of English Production to English Production staff, 23 Feb. 1968

9 *Victoria Colonist*, 10 July 1968, and *Gazette* (Montreal), 26 Nov. 1968

10 The same idea was executed by Haskell Wexler in *Medium Cool*, a Hollywood fiction film, also set at the time of the 1968 Chicago riots, which explored a well-known McLuhanism about television. Whether consciously or not, both films were articulating a premise that would come to be repeated often in subsequent years: that the camera was more than a dispassionate observer of events; it was a catalyst which then became an integral part of those events.

11 *Calgary Herald*, 24 Feb. 1970; *Variety*, 3 Sept. 1969; *Toronto Telegram*, 24 Feb. 1970. The *Toronto Daily Star* article was headlined 'The banality of Prologue is an affront to Canadians,' 23 Feb. 1970

12 *Debates of the House of Commons*, vol. 6, 13 Apr. 1970, 5766

13 Jean Basile, 'Brouilles et "YUL 871" de Jacques Godbout,' *Le Devoir*, 1 Aug. 1966

14 Minutes of the NFB, 12 Dec. 1969. In the midst of the austerity crisis, the board of governors asked the Treasury Board to provide ex-gratia relief for the unlucky filmmaker.

15 Ronald Blumer, 'Is Science Dead?' *McGill Medical Journal* (McGill University, Montreal), Spring 1970. A less enthusiastic

N.E. Story of the *Canadian Tribune*, 18 Mar. 1970, panned *Wow* for its shallowness and illusions.

16 He said that an agency like the Film Board could not afford to have more than one Norman McLaren, to whom he referred 'as our sort of court amuser' and who was, besides wheat and nickel, one of the most vital, internationally recognized products of the Canadian people. Curiously, McLaren was not politically minded and always claimed he was a public servant first. The admiring Grierson advised, 'Only trust artists who are philosopher kings.' *Grierson Transcripts: Interviews Recorded with John Grierson, February 1969–July 1971*, transcribed by Sandra Gathercole, 4 vols (Ottawa: Canadian Radio and Television Commission 1973), 4: 475; 3: 219, 249–51; 1: 56, 63, 72. See also National Film Board of Canada, *McLaren*, ed. Guy Glover (Montreal: National Film Board 1980).

17 *Grierson Transcripts*, 2: 196, 199

18 Ibid., 4: 489; 3: 370

19 Ibid., 1: 32, 129. Grierson's own words stand as a rebuttal to the tenuous thesis propounded recently by Peter Morris in 'Re-thinking Grierson: The Ideology of John Grierson,' in Pierre Véronneau, Michael Dorland, and Seth Feldman, eds, *Dialogue: Cinéma canadien et québécois, Canadian and Quebec Cinema* (Montreal: Mediatexte Publications 1987). By judging Grierson largely on a selective interpretation of some elements in Forsyth Hardy's *John Grierson: A Documentary Biography* (London: Faber and Faber 1979), while ignoring the evidence of the shrewd materialist who got things done by allowing no political label to stick, Morris concluded that the Scotsman was driven by a neoconservative ideology and élitist aesthetic. Taking this single dubious thread, Joyce Nelson wove a whole revisionist tapestry in which she asserted, rather than proved, that Grierson sold out to multinationals and monopoly capitalism (*The Colonized Eye* [Toronto: Between the Lines Press 1988]). Critic Gerald Pratley worried that Nelson's career might never recover from the self-inflicted damage caused by her book. A current tendency to confuse Grierson's political philosophy with right-wing ideology

will probably be corrected by closely studying his uncompleted book written in 1942, now published for the first time, entitled *Eyes of Democracy*, ed. Ian Lockerbie (Sterling University, Scotland: John Grierson Archive 1990).

20 For a complete account of the CYC, see Ian Hamilton, *The Children's Crusade: The Story of the Company of Young Canadians* (Toronto: Peter Martin Associates 1970).

21 Minutes of the NFB, 7 Feb. 1966

22 Peter Katadotis, at that time a fieldworker and community organizer, remembered that the film was less of a shock to those who were well acquainted with the cycle of poverty. He said that a number of his colleagues repudiated this film because it omitted what seemed to them one obvious reason for the hard luck of the principals. Katadotis interview with the author, 8 Apr. 1985. According to a board meeting in August 1968, the film was surpassed on the national ratings of CBC programmes by only the Grey Cup and Stanley Cup sports events. Minutes of the NFB, 1 Aug. 1968

23 Transcript of Colin Low interview with Alexandra McHugh, Sept. 1980. He said, 'I like making films about people I feel have something to say; [people] that are strong, that I admire, from whom you can feel a kind of energy, intelligence and guts ... I won't touch people who are angry and smoldering because that always backfires on the people.' Low's philosophy became the predominant one in the succeeding series films over the next fourteen years. See also Colin Low's 'Grierson and Challenge for Change' in McGill University John Grierson Project, *John Grierson and the NFB* (Toronto: ECW Press 1984), 95–103.

24 Transcript of Tanya Ballantyne interview with Alexandra McHugh, Sept. 1980. See also Gary Evans, 'The Future of Documentary in a TV Age,' *Cinema Canada* 119 (June 1985), 11–13. The documentary on the Baileys of the eighties was called *Courage to Change*.

25 Minutes of the NFB, 3 Feb. 1967

26 The departments were Labour, Immigration, Fisheries, and Agriculture. The agencies were Health and Welfare, Central Mortgage and Housing, Agricultural Rehabilitation and Development Agency, and

the Company of Young Canadians. In the first year, some contributed $35,000, others $5,000.

27 Jean-Yves Begin, 'Le Groupe de Recherches sociales de l'ONF,' *Séquences* 59 (Dec. 1969). Hortense Roy, a specialist in group dynamics, joined them in the experiment.

28 Hugo McPherson interview with the author, 15 Sept. 1986. McPherson was outraged because he had never heard any other instance of the Film Board being so ill-treated before government officials.

29 Begin, 'Le Groupe de Recherches sociales'; Fernand Dansereau, 'Saint-Jérôme: The Experience of a Filmmaker as Social Animator'; Patrick Watson, 'Challenge for Change'; Marie Kurchak, 'What Challenge? What Change?' (in Seth Feldman and Joyce Nelson, eds, *Canadian Film Reader* [Toronto: Peter Martin Associates 1977], 128–31; 112–19; 120–8)

30 '... aux fins de dresser un pont entre l'homme et ses besoins d'une part et les techniques qui prolifèrent dans l'incohérence d'autre part.' Quoted by Andrew Cohen, 'Challenge for Change / Société nouvelle, an Assessment,' unpublished document (Oct. 1977), 7 (in NFB 4231, 3237).

31 In fact, during the 1968 austerity crisis, the Film Board was carrying 75 per cent of the cost to the departments' 25 per cent. Each department contributed $20,000 per year until funding became more firmly grounded in 1969 at $100,000 per department.

32 *Ottawa Citizen*, 21 Mar. 1969; *The Recorder* (Boissevin, Man.), 27 Mar. 1969

33 See *Challenge for Change Newsletter* 4 (Spring–Summer 1969), ed. Dorothy Hénaut, for more detailed descriptions of these experimental projects.

34 Tom Daly Papers, box XI, no. 19, Colin Low, 'Challenge for Change and Regionalization,' 25 Oct. 1976, and 'The Fogo Island Communication Experiment,' 5 July 1972

35 Ibid., 'The Fogo Island Communication Experiment.' The impact of the films on Fogo Island was recorded in a film called *Memo from Fogo*. Low claimed that, subsequently, a large number of projects, some as far away as Tanzania and Alaska, borrowed some of the methods of the Fogo Island project. By 1972, the other change which

had occurred was that videotape (which had overcome many of its original technical limitations) was being used in most community-development media projects.

Distribution coordinator Anthony Kent explained his understanding of the uniqueness of the Challenge for Change approach: it constructed models in different kinds of circumstances for others to copy, and once that was done, never repeated them. Transcript of Anthony Kent interview with Alexandra McHugh, 8 Sept. 1980

36 *People and Power* (18 min.) had Alinsky talking about how conflict and controversy were an integral part of the Alinsky approach; *Deciding to Organize* (34 min.) showed a group of citizens from Ohio consulting Alinsky on the means of creating an effective organization; *Building an Organization* (38 min.) witnessed the difficulties encountered by a new community-action organization in Buffalo, NY; *Through Conflict to Negotiation* (46 min.) found a community-action group in Rochester, NY, confronting the Eastman Kodak company over corporate responsibility and the employment of minority groups; *A Continuing Responsibility* (42 min.) showed how Alinsky's technique creates ongoing organizations firmly rooted in the community.

37 Transcript of Colin Low interview with Alexandra McHugh, Sept. 1980

38 George Stoney interview with the author, 15 June 1987, and transcript of George Stoney interview with Alexandra McHugh, 28 Aug. 1980

39 Watson, 'Challenge for Change,' Kurchak, 'What Challenge? What Change?' and Dansereau, 'St. Jérome: The Experience of Filmmaker as Social Animator,' in Feldman and Nelson, eds, *Canadian Film Reader*, 112–31

40 Dorothy Hénaut and Bonnie Sherr Klein, 'In the Hands of Citizens: A Video Report,' *Challenge for Change Newsletter* 4 (Spring–Summer 1969), 2–5

41 Transcript of Robert Forget interview with Alexandra McHugh, 24 Mar. 1980. Robert Forget interview with the author, 29 Nov. 1988

42 Kathleen Shannon interview with the author, 16 Dec. 1988

43 English subjects were Thunder Bay, Drum-

heller, Moose Jaw, Vancouver (2), Carota Project, Saint John, MOVE/teled, Blackhead Road / Munday Pond, Forward House, vtr Training, Friendship Centres, Parallel Institute, Winnipeg, and Community Media Counsellors. The Société nouvelle projects were Region 80, Télévision communautaire: Normandin et après, Projet d'une garderie, Mines d'or, Témoignages, Milieu 70, Bobo-z-arts, Le vidéographe, and Rivière-la-paix.

44 By 1976, Société nouvelle had finished 11 films on mobility and labour, 25 on urbanization and housing, 5 on participation and communication techniques, 27 on citizenship and societal values, and 3 on environment. NFB, Challenge for Change / Société nouvelle, Reports, 1976, Appendix Q

45 George Stoney interview with the author, 15 June 1987

46 Ibid.

47 Transcript of Anthony Kent interview with Alexandra McHugh, 8 Sept. 1980

48 The other five priorities were: quality of life in urban areas, collective bargaining, welfare and jobs, human rights, and the social implications of the decline of agriculture, fisheries, and forestry.

49 NFB 4125, P-33, Distribution – Cree Hunters: Mark Zannis, *Cree Hunters of Mistassini*, Sept. 1974; Mark Zannis, '*Cree Hunters of Mistassini* and *Our Land Is Our Life*: Summary Report of Special Distribution Projects: 1974–1975,' Aug. 1975; 'Distribution Kit for *Cree Hunters of Mistassini* and *Our Land Is Our Life*,' n.d. (1974–5); n.a., 'Notes from a conversation with filmmakers Boyce Richardson and Tony Ianzelo,' n.d.; Dorothy Hénaut, 'A Production History,' extract of an article prepared for the *Journal of Communications*, n.d.

50 *Grierson Transcripts*, 4: 377–8. Low defended the method and style of Challenge for Change. 'In a community the best story is the peaceful and collaborative solution of problems. That is not theatre. The best community development is evolutionary, not revolutionary' ('Grierson and Challenge for Change,' in *John Grierson and the NFB*). A further Grierson critique occurred in the *Challenge for Change Newsletter* 8 (Spring 1972); 'Memo to Michelle about Decentralizing the Means of Production' (reprinted in Feldman and Nelson, eds, *Canadian Film Reader*, 132–43).

51 *Grierson Transcripts*, 1: 24

52 Ibid., 1: 37; 4: 512. He thought the Fogo project was a descendant of the original *cinéma vérité* tradition, going back to the great 1936 English documentary *Housing Problems*, which 'broke the goldfish bowl' and resulted in 'making films not about people but with them.'

53 Ibid., 3: 250–1. See also NFB, 3935, Film Training Centre, Confidential letter from John Grierson to Grant McLean, 14 Sept. 1966.

54 *Grierson Transcripts*, 4: 400, 380, 392–4

55 Ibid., 4: 402. What he (and other critics) ignored purposely was the complex reason for the denouement. Nell hoped Fred had returned because he missed her; but the fact was that his pension was too small to allow him to remain at the institution.

56 Ibid., 4: 492. It will be recalled that the United States had turned down the film *Drug Addict* (real addicts demonstrating drug abuse) in 1948 for being too frightening. In 1956, *Blue Vanguard* met a similar fate at the United Nations in the aftermath of the Suez campaign. In the sixties, *Poisons, Pests and People (Deadly Dilemma)*, and *Bethune* had like difficulties. In these leading-edge films, the Film Board was draped more in robes of moral purity than in the banners of *parti pris*. In reflecting a paternal sense of protection, Grierson warned that it was dangerous to move too far away from what he called 'the consensus of the House,' that is, the degree of sanction that could be expected. This put a wide chasm between himself and the activist-oriented filmmakers. He said, for example, that *Bethune* should have been made by the CBC, not the Film Board, which as a government department had responsibilities to External Affairs it should honour (4: 568).

57 Ibid., 4: 419; 435–40

58 Ibid., 4: 422–3, 440

59 Ibid., 3: 256; 4: 476; 3: 292

60 Ibid., 4: 549

61 The films in the series were *A qui appartient*

ce gage?, on children and day care; *Souris, tu m'inquiètes*, on a woman's search for identity; *J'me marie, J'me marie pas*, four women discussing their relationships with men (all in 1973); *Les Filles du Roy*, an impressionistic history of the women of Quebec; *Les filles, c'est pas pareil*, six female adolescents discussing their thoughts and feelings (both in 1974).

62 Brigitte Morissette, 'Treize femmes à la recherche des femmes,' *Le Maclean* (Montreal), Oct. 1972

63 The films were *Extensions of the Family, Luckily I Need Little Sleep, Mothers Are People, Tiger on a Tight Leash, Would I Ever Like to Work, They Appreciate You More, Like the Trees,* and *Our Dear Sisters.* Later, three other titles were added: *And They Lived Happily Ever After, It's Not Enough,* and the animated *The Spring and Fall of Nina Polanski.*

64 Anne Claire Poirier interview with the author, 23 Aug. 1988. Josée Beaudet became the head of the French women's studio, *Regards de femmes*, in October 1986.

65 The committee set priority areas in 1975: violent crime, child abuse, working poor, economy of resources, balance of economic growth, urban growth, and breaking the welfare cycle. NFB, Challenge for Change / Société nouvelle, Reports, 1969–76

66 NFB, Uncatalogued Interdepartmental Committee Correspondence, 1977–78, Charles Miller to Reta Kilpatrick, 4 Apr. 1978

67 Hamilton, *The Children's Crusade,*' 271

68 NFB, 4321, 3237, Challenge for Change / Société nouvelle; Cohen, 'Challenge for Change / Société nouvelle, 27–89

69 Grierson, 'Memo to Michelle,' in Feldman and Nelson, eds, *Canadian Film Reader*, 132–6

70 Transcript of Colin Low interview with Alexandra McHugh, Sept. 1980. Perhaps the ultimate Fogo Island postscript was discovered by an American graduate student in communications who visited the island in 1986, to learn that workers at the cooperatively-owned fish plant were angry at the low wages they were being paid; rumblings of unionization were in the air. The project had become so successful that a new group of disaffected was pitting itself against the old group of no-longer-disaffected, who had become their employers.

71 Peter Katadotis interview with the author, 11 Apr. 1989

Chapter 9

1 Minutes of the NFB, 17 Oct. 1970

2 Ibid., 11–12 Jan. 1971. Adroit use of 'creative bookkeeping' disguised these figures, and the Film Board ploughed the money back into production, returning only $17,762 to the Receiver General of Canada (*Statement of Income and Expense for the year ended March 31, 1971*).

3 Ibid., Appendix, Distribution. (A single English network telecast accounted for just under fifty bookings.)

4 NFB 1315/0, B-161, Hugo McPherson to Wilf Jobbins, 20 Apr. 1970

5 Luc Perrault, 'La bataille du socio-politique,' *La Presse*, 17 July 1971

6 Godin's credit was as assistant director and researcher. A weak left-wing analysis of these events appeared in the tract *Transformation: Theory and Practice of Social Change* 1, no. 4 (Summer 1972), under the title 'Censorship in the NFB.'

7 NFB production file, *On est au coton*, letter from Barristers Villenueve, Pigeon, Clément, and Guilbeau to Gilles Dignard, director of French Production, 16 Oct. 1970

8 Sydney Newman interview with the author, 22–25 Aug. 1986. Gérard Pelletier interview with the author, 3 Feb. 1988. Pelletier had a strong feeling for respecting the autonomy of the agency and repeated his belief that the minister must not interfere in the internal affairs of his cultural agencies, lest such action undermine the authority of those responsible and lead the minister to interfere at other levels. His consistent attitude was articulated at the address to the Canadian Conference of the Arts, on *The Development of a Cultural Policy in Canada*, Sept. 1970 (pp. 3–4), when he said that when he had to withstand the sustained fire of Opposition questions in the House, he had no illusions as to what his real powers were. Furthermore, the record showed that with the exception of a few minor incidents, no democratic government ever tried to

influence cultural organizations for political purposes or to impose its wishes on them. There has never been any government control over the cultural institutions set up by Parliament, he concluded, since in his view there was no alternative to individual creative initiative.

9 NFB file, *On est au coton*, André Lamy to Gilles Dignard, 16 Dec. 1970

10 Ibid., President of the Canadian Textile Institute to Sydney Newman, 24 Feb. 1971; Newman to president of the Canadian Textile Institute, 17 Mar. 1971

11 Tom Daly Papers, box IX, no. 12, 'Responsibility and the Filmmaker' by Sydney Newman, 12 Mar. 1971

12 NFB file, *On est au coton*, M. Chapleau to Marcel Martin, 29 Apr. 1971

13 Sydney Newman interview with the author, 22–25 Aug. 1986. Also, Tom Daly Papers, box XI, no. 19, Sydney Newman to Tom Daly, 29 Nov. 1976

14 *Debates of the House of Commons*, vol. 5, 27–28 Apr. 1971, 5259; 5314–15

15 *La Tribune* (Sherbrooke), 18 May 1971; two articles by Jean Pierre Tadros in *Le Devoir* on 17 and 19 July 1971 dealt with Newman and *On est au coton*; Tadros, the publisher of *Cinéma Québec*, ran a series of articles and interviews with Arcand, Godin, and Newman under the rubric 'La censure politique' in the June–July 1971 edition, pp. 30–5. More recently, Godin expressed the belief that *On est au coton* is very similar to Arcand's highly acclaimed 1986 fiction film *Le Déclin de l'empire Américain* (*Copie Zéro* 34–35 [December 1987 / March 1988], 45).

16 Perreault, 'La bataille du socio-politique'

17 Jean-Pierre Tadros, 'L'ONF entre censure et auto-censure,' *Le Devoir*, 25 Sept. 1971; André Heureux letter to Sydney Newman, 26 Oct., printed in *Le Devoir*, 12 Nov. 1971; Newman to Heureux, 3 Nov., published in *Le Devoir* and *La voix de l'Est* (Granby), 12 and 10 Nov. 1971. A news story appeared in *La Patrie* (Sherbrooke), on 4 and 10 Nov. In an editorial on 25 Nov. Claude Lemelin of *Le Devoir* called for release of the film.

18 NFB file, *On est au coton*, J.C. Whitelaw to Sydney Newman, 16 Nov. 1971; Newman to Whitelaw, 24 Nov. 1971; Sydney Newman interview with the author, 22–25 Aug. 1986

19 Tom Daly Papers, box VI, no. 2, Tom Daly to Sydney Newman, 5 Mar. 1971. (The production file indicates an expenditure of $34,007, but one must assume this was French Production's cost to finish it, rather than the full expense.)

20 NFB file, *Un pays sans bon sens*, Sydney Newman memorandum to the secretary of state, 5 Mar. 1971

21 NFB, 1-M, A-1, Correspondence with secretary of state, Sydney Newman to Gérard Pelletier, 26 Feb. 1971

22 Minutes of the NFB, 26–27 Mar. 1971

23 Ibid.

24 Martin Malina, 'Failing to find what Quebec wants,' *Montreal Star*, 20 Mar. 1971, was the only article in the English press about the film, according to the Film Board's press archives.

25 NFB 1298, P-153, Standing Committee on Broadcasting, Films and Assistance to the Arts, 22 Apr. 1971

26 The French Programme Committee had passed the film script in May, but Newman had overridden their decision. Robert Lévesque, 'L'ONF poursuit sa politique de censure,' *La Patrie*, week of 12 Sept. 1971. (*La Patrie* had stated on 25 July that it thought the Film Board was at a point of no return on account of censorship.) Martin Knelman, 'Sydney Newman faces NFB crisis over vetoed Quebec jail film,' *Globe and Mail*, 2 Oct. 1971

27 Peter Morris has noted that *L'Acadie, L'Acadie?!?* was widely admired in Quebec, but in Acadia itself there was criticism of the film's failure to establish a context or explain the role of New Brunswick's francophone élite. *The Film Companion* (Toronto: Irwin Publishing 1984), 3–5

28 Minutes of the NFB, 13–14 July 1972

29 Perrault, 'La bataille du socio-politique.' In this article Pierre Perrault said, L'identité canadienne en général, ça ne m'a jamais intéressé. C'est avec l'argent fédéral que j'ai bâti mon Québec à moi dans le cinéma. Je trouve ça extraordinaire.'

30 NFB file, *Québec, Duplessis et après ...*, Hugo McPherson to Gérard Bertrand, 20 Apr. 1970. On 5 May, Dignard wrote on this memo that he had changed McPherson's mind.

31 Within the film, Arcand made an interest-

ing observation about historical change: without major modifications of economic and cultural structures, the appearance and disappearance of political parties, even charismatic political personalities, are merely superficial phenomena that can only modify the historical evolution of a people, be they *québécois* or others.

32 Ghislaine Rhéault, 'Denys Arcand ... la censure,' *Le Soleil*, 20 Nov. 1971

33 Tom Daly Papers, box XI, no. 19, Sydney Newman to Tom Daly, 29 Nov. 1976

34 *Montreal Star* and *The Gazette* (Montreal), 12 Dec. 1972

35 The main articles were 'Vingt-quatre heures ou plus: Pour l'ONF et une journaliste,' *La Presse*, 4 Dec. 1972; 'Bourassa nage et l'ONF refuse un film de Gilles Groulx,' *La Presse*, 8 Dec.; 'L'ONF interdit un film de Gilles Groulx,' *Le Devoir*, 9 Dec.; 'L'ONF ne peut distribuer un film qui préconise le rejet complet du système politique,' *Le Devoir*, 12 Dec.; 'La liberté dans une cage d'or,' *La Presse*, 14 Dec.; 'L'ONF après Vingt-quatre heures ou plus,' *Le Devoir*, 13 Dec.; 'Gilles Groulx: Le pion est autonome, quand il s'agit d'un homme,' *La Presse*, 15 Dec.; 'La liberté de l'artiste,' *La Presse*, 16 Dec.; 'Vingt-quatre heures ou plus sera terminé,' *La Presse*, 16 Dec.; 'S'impliquer: Le droit du créateur,' *Le Devoir*, 16 Dec.; 'Gilles Groulx ne veut pas effacer mais charger d'avantage,' *La Presse*, 18 Dec.; 'Les cinéastes et l'affaire Groulx,' *Le Devoir*, 19 Dec.; 'L'emprisonnement temporaire des idées,' *Le Devoir*, 20 Dec.; 'Le ministre et le cinéaste,' *Le Devoir*, 27 Dec.; 'Faut-il restreindre les pouvoirs du commissaire de l'ONF?,' *Le Devoir*, 29 Dec.

36 Untitled document on censorship, 'Contre la censure politique,' probably March 1973, containing statements by Paul Larose, Pierre Perrault, Denys Arcand, Gilles Groulx, and extracts from several articles written in December 1972, in Film Board Archives file *La censure*.

37 Minutes of the NFB, 30 Mar., 28–29 June, and 21–22 Sept. 1973 (see Appendix to this source for Faulkner's remarks).

38 'NFB documentary shelved for depicting downfall of Canadian system,' *Ottawa Citizen*, 12 Dec. 1972; 'NFB cancels film urging revolution,' *Montreal Star*, 12 Dec. 1972;

'Filmmakers unhappy with ban,' *The Gazette* (Montreal), 20 Dec. 1972; 'Controversial film revised,' *Leader-Post* (Regina), 20 Dec. 1972

39 *Le Jour* (Montreal), 25 Sept. 1974

40 The voice of de Gaulle was itself recreated by an actor. Robin Spry interview with the author, 10 Feb. 1988. Lévesque was with guests behind city hall, watching on television, and heard 'the deathly silence that reigned behind us.' From the Anglos in the crowd there was a state of shock, frozen in a fury; from the French, there were 'broad, complicit smiles.' René Lévesque, *Memoirs*, trans. Philip Stratford (Toronto: McClelland and Stewart 1986), 206

41 Tom Daly interview with the author, 8 Oct. 1987

42 Sydney Newman interview with the author, 22–25 Aug. 1986

43 NFB 4163, B-137, André Lamy file, *Salvadore Allende: Un témoignage*, 14–15 Nov. 1973 to 15 July 1974

44 NFB 1298, Film Commissioner, Paul Larose memorandum, 23 Mar. 1971

45 Sydney Newman interview with the author, 22–25 Aug. 1986; Tom Daly Papers, box XI, no. 19, Newman to Daly, 29 Nov. 1976

46 Sydney Newman interview with the author, 22–5 Aug. 1986

47 Minutes of the NFB, 26–27 Mar. and 27 Aug. 1971

Chapter 10

1 Minutes of the NFB, 7 Apr. 1972

2 Ibid., 5–6 Oct. 1972, Appendix, Distribution Branch Annual Report, 8 Sept. 1972. As part of a long-standing policy, these figures were kept secret.

3 NFB 4305, B-137, 1974–75 Budget, Explanation of the 1974–75 budget of $8.8 million English and $4 million French Production, n.d.

4 'National Film Board meets Doctor Gallup,' *Audience Needs and Reactions* 4, Brant County Survey, Summer 1972. In a follow-up poll in Brant County in January 1975, a Gallup Omnibus Study reflected the views of 1,054 adults who were interviewed. There were 47 miscellaneous positive and neutral comments about the Film Board, 23 miscellaneous negative comments, 31 positive

reasons for rating the agency, 24 qualified, neutral reasons for rating the agency, and 36 negative reasons for rating it (NFB 4019/957). The main criticism was that there was too much sex in family films and they were too arty. If the latter comment had a shred of justification, the former opinion might have reflected the respondents' inability to differentiate the Film Board films from those of the CBC. If the majority of respondents made this critical error of association, then the poll was less than useful.

5 Audience Needs and Reaction Unit, 14 Aug. 1972. Another barometer was a forty-person report on the screening of the film *The Invention of the Adolescent*: 16 respondents found this 29-minute film 'plodding, slow, dated, not suitable, not appropriate, heavy-handed, drawn out, satisfactory but not relevant to their own use,' while 21 found it 'good, pretty good, interesting, excellent, and thought-provoking.' Three were non-committal. There had been only two previous studies on audience reaction, one on 30 Nov. 1945, describing how audiences fared when using the electronic 'programme analyzer' as they watched propaganda films, and a less scientific study done in 1965. There seemed to be little interest in planning films in response to the patterns that the surveys revealed.

6 Ronald Dick interview with the author, 2–5 Dec. 1986. Each film was self-contained, but part of the larger unity: *New England and New France (1490–1763), Canada and the American Revolution (1763–1783), The War of 1812 (1783–1818), Dangerous Decades (1818–1846), The New Equation: Annexation and Reciprocity (1840–1860), The Friendly Fifties and the Sinister Sixties (1850–1863), The Triumphant Union and the Canadian Confederation (1863–1867), The Border Confirmed: The Treaty of Washington (1867–1871),* and *A Second Transcontinental Nation (1872).*

7 Ben Tierney, 'Fear exists NFB will become "message maker" for govt.,' *Ottawa Journal*, 24 Jan. 1970

8 NFB 1315/0, A-60, Film Policy, 1969–72; Hugo McPherson to Gérard Pelletier, 15 June 1970; McPherson's notes on the 15 June 1970 meeting

9 Ibid., B-207, Planning and Research, 1970–1, 'Federal Film Policy,' 5 Aug. 1970

10 NFB 1-M, P-213, Secretary of State Gérard Pelletier to Sydney Newman, 4 Nov. 1971, including 1970 memorandum to Cabinet, 'Government Film Policy'

11 NFB 1315/0, A-60, Film Policy, 1969–72, Confidential letter from Marcel Martin to Sydney Newman, 6 Jan. 1971

12 Ibid., Sydney Newman to secretary of state, 27 Nov. 1970; Conference call of Film Board, CBC, and the Minister's Office, 11 Dec. 1970; Jules Léger meeting with heads of agencies, 5 Jan. 1971

13 NFB 1315/0, T-70, Film Act and Policy, 1971–74, Sydney Newman to Gérard Pelletier, 16 Dec. 1971; ibid., A-60, Film Policy, 1969–72, Marc Devlin to André Lamy, 26 Oct. 1971. Devlin warned that losing the sponsored films would have serious implications for an already sagging staff morale and that the new policy 'will be construed as one more insidious crack in the foundations' of the Film Board.

14 NFB 1315/0, A-60, Film Policy, Confidential memo from Gerald Graham to André Lamy, 22 Oct. 1971. The price differentials remained in 1976, when it was reported that an average-length Film Board sponsored film of twenty-four minutes costs $53,025 while a private-sector-produced sponsored film of seventeen minutes cost $13,065. *Debates of the House of Commons*, vol. 10, 26 Jan. 1976, 10282

15 André Fortier interview with the author, 15 Apr. 1988. Fortier was the assistant under-secretary of the secretary of state from 1969 to 1972 and the under-secretary of the secretary of state from 1975 to 1978. He and Jules Léger worked with Pelletier to devise the general Arts Policy, including the Film Policy.

16 Jones kept daily diaries from 1965 until his retirement. They provide a good view of how his activity in British Columbia became the prototype for establishing Film Board regional production offices nationally. Jones provided young filmmakers like Sandra Wilson, Al Razutis, Al Sens, and Jack Darcus with whatever practical help, guidance, and encouragement his (meagre Film Board) means allowed him to

offer. NA, Peter Jones Papers, MG 31, D210.

17 NFB 1315/0, D103, Global Film Policy, Cabinet Committee on Science, Culture and Information, Record of Committee Decision, Government Film Policy, 3 May 1972

18 André Fortier and Paul Schafer, *Development and Growth of Federal Arts Policies in the Arts, 1944–1985* (Ottawa: Department of Communications, May 1985), chap. 3 (1969–75), 27–34

19 NFB 1-M, A-1, Correspondence with secretary of state, Newman to Hugh Faulkner, 16 Apr. 1974

20 André Fortier interview with the author, 15 Apr. 1988

21 NFB 1-S, A-470, Secretary of State, 1973–4, Newman to Secretary of State J. Hugh Faulkner, 21 Jan. 1974. 1315/0, D-250, Newman to Jean Boucher, Under-Secretary of State, 29 Mar. 1974

22 NFB 1315/0, D-103, Global Film Policy, Notes for a speech by the Honorable Gérard Pelletier, 4 July 1972. Also, Pelletier interview with the author, 3 Feb. 1988

23 Tom Daly Papers, box IX, no. 23, Notes of meeting of Unit C, 8 Nov. 1973

24 NFB 2615, A-392, X Budget, 1973, Robert Verrall to André Lamy, 10 July 1973

25 Director Arthur Hammond was responsible for the seven half-hours film series in 1973–4, which was promoted extensively to the business and education communities and consumer groups. Steinberg Corporation of Montreal gave Hammond free access to all company operations, including top management board meetings. Hammond admitted that few other Canadian companies would have been so generous. The film titles explain each area of concentration: *Bilingualism, Growth, International Operations, The Market, Motivation, Real Estate, After Mr. Sam.*

26 Minutes of the NFB, 14–15 Dec. 1973, Appendix, Sydney Newman to the Filmmakers of French and English Production, 31 Oct. 1973

27 NFB 2615, A-392, X Budget, 1973, Lamy to Newman, 24 July 1973. A year and a half later, an exasperated director of programming, Arthur Hammond, commented that the continuing criticism was that the films were too long, no matter what their length,

and there was too much emphasis on talking heads rather than on the more dramatic cinematic presentation of reality. Tom Daly Papers, box IX, no. 20, Annual Programme Guidelines, 1975–6

28 NFB 1-M, A-1, Correspondence with the minister, Faulkner to Newman, 20 Aug. 1974. Faulkner informed Newman that the feature film was to be aided by a 115 per cent capital-cost allowance, while the CFDC was to increase its participation in promotion and distribution of Canadian films. He told the Film Board to undertake more programmes with private companies for showing on television and in theatres and schools.

29 Hugh Faulkner interview with the author, 4 May 1988. Faulkner's other major contribution to Canadian publishing was the long-awaited imposition of a burden on *Time* and *Reader's Digest* magazines, whose advertisers could no longer write off advertising costs. This was meant to help Canadian publications, which were starved for advertising revenue.

30 Newman told the Standing Committee on Broadcasting, Films and Assistance to the Arts, on 23 Apr. 1974, that in 1971–2 34 per cent of the sponsored films ($1 million) were contracted out, in 1972–3 42 per cent ($1.3 million) were contracted out, and in 1973–4, 50 per cent ($1.5 million) were supposed to be contracted out. NFB 1298, P-213

31 Minutes of the NFB, 14–15 Dec. 1973. Not to be forgotten either was that a number of departments in Ottawa had their own studios to make films, even if it meant using devious (and under the terms of the National Film Act, sometimes illegal) means to exclude Film Board involvement in them. This was another proof that, good intentions notwithstanding, the secretary of state had obtained minimal coordination on may film matters. NFB 1-M, A-146, Meeting with Minister Faulkner, Gerald Graham memo to Newman on upcoming meeting with Faulkner, 19 Nov. 1973

32 NFB 1315/0, T-70, Film Act and Policy, 'Redefining the National Film Board' (revised draft), 4 Dec. 1973

33 Minutes of the NFB, 30 Mar. 1973

34 Minutes of the NFB, 20 Sept. 1974. Leduc's honesty could be just as brutal toward his own filmmakers. He admitted frankly to Lamy the following April that freelancing was the only way of renewing the agency's creative personnel 'because current employment policy has made it virtually impossible to break the coterie of permanent filmmakers and bring in young, less paranoiac and more dynamic recruits.' He reminded Lamy that the last full-time filmmaker hired in French Production was in 1967. NFB 1-M, P-213, Meeting with the minister, Yves Leduc to André Lamy, 10 Apr. 1975

35 Minutes of the NFB, 5–6 Mar. 1975

36 Ibid., 13–14 June 1975

37 These were not his words, though they were the sentiments expressed by André Fortier as he explained how the secretary of state department intended the B budget to function. (Interview with the author, 15 Apr. 1988)

38 Hugh Faulkner interview with the author, 4 May 1988

39 For a partial list of press reviews, see Peter Morris, *The Film Companion*, 200–1. Morris neglected to include Vincent Canby's qualified praise for the film in the *New York Times* on 18 Apr. 1972. Canby's critical observation deserves mention because it remains valid with the passage of time; he thought that a film so calculated to evoke humour, nostalgia, sadness, and regret left little room for self-discovery.

40 Jutra interview in the *Calgary Herald*, 22 Dec. 1971

41 Sydney Newman interview with the author, 22–25 Aug. 1986

42 *Montreal Star*, 28 Nov. 1972, Geneviève Bujold turned down the prestigious award too, with a curt and impolite remark, 'I stick to my own kind.'

43 Robert Verrall interview with the author, 20 May 1988. When Verrall showed the film to the assembled filmmakers at the year-end screening, Newman was ready to relieve him of his duties.

44 Minutes of the NFB, 22–23 Oct. 1971

45 NFB 1-S, P-155, Secretary of State, Memo to Cabinet from secretary of state department, 26 Feb. 1971. Trudeau had written an article for Canadian Press entitled 'Why are they forcing French down our throats?' which was published on 15 July 1969. Many believe that English Canada's resentment of bilingualism was expressed in the federal election of 1972, when Trudeau won only enough seats for a minority government. For a thought-provoking discussion of bilingualism and multiculturalism, see Ronald Wardhaugh, *Language and Nationhood* (Vancouver: New Star Books 1983), chapters 2 and 9.

46 'Trudeau pledges Canada to multi-racial culture,' *Toronto Daily Star*, 8 Oct. 1971

47 Wardhaugh, *Language and Nationhood*, 210–11

48 For a synthesis of the debate about ethnicity and multiculturalism, see Karl Peter, 'The Myth of Multiculturalism and Other Political Fables,' in J.L. Granatstein, I.M. Abella, D.J. Bercuson, R.C. Brown, and H.B. Neatby, eds, *Twentieth-Century Canada: A Reader* (Toronto: McGraw Hill-Ryerson 1986), 289–304. A materialist analysis of the ideological imperatives behind Canada's so-called search for 'identity' is found in Tony Wilden, *The Imaginary Canadian* (Vancouver: Pulp Press 1980).

49 The Film board proposed production of six films per year for four years for and about ethnic groups for some $390,000 per year. Versions were an additional activity; by January 1973 there were foreign-language versioned films available in Canada in 24 languages: the top six (in descending order by titles) were Spanish (91), Italian (31), Portuguese (15), German (15), Greek (10), and Dutch (10). Five titles in Ukrainian were to be added that year. Minutes of the NFB, 11–12 Jan. 1973; Appendix, Report on activity of the Distribution Branch of the National Film Board in the Multicultural Program, 1972–3

50 *The Home Front* (1940), *Women Are Warriors* (1942), *Proudly She Marches* (1943), and *Wings on Her Shoulder* (1945) are the best-known films of the war, while *Is It a Women's World?*, *Needles and Pins*, *Service in the Sky*, and *Women at Work* were a 1958 series of films concentrating on employment issues. The same year, *Women on the March* gave a two-part, one-hour history of the women's movement from 1900 and the struggle for equal political rights. See

chapter 4 for a description of the four French films on women in the sixties. See also Teresa Nash, 'Images of Women in NFB Films during World War II and the Postwar Years, 1939–49,' unpublished PhD thesis, McGill University, Montreal, 1982.

51 Minutes of the NFB, 5–6 Mar. 1975. The studio system on the English side now appeared as follows: Studio A, animation; Studio B, sponsor and television films along with the drama development programme; Studio C, documentary films; Studio D, women; Studio F, television series; and Studio G, filmstrips and multimedia kits.

52 See also Chris Scherbarth, 'Studio D of the National Film Board of Canada: Seeing Ourselves through Women's Eyes,' unpublished Master of Arts thesis, Carleton University, Ottawa, 1986.

53 Kathleen Shannon interview with the author, 16 Dec. 1988. Among the books that she considered seminal in helping her articulate and broaden the Studio D philosophy was Tony Wilden's *The Imaginary Canadian*.

54 James de B. Domville interview with the author, 9 June 1988

55 At the board meeting of 13–14 June 1975, the governors decided to formalize the practice of bringing in distinguished filmmakers for short periods of time. In the past few years the Film Board had hosted a number of world-class animators like Lotte Reininger, the brilliant silhouette animator, Alexander Alexeieff, Bretislaw Pojar, Zlatko Grgic, and Peter Foldès.

56 Robert Verrall interview with the author, 18 May 1988, and James de B. Domville interview with the author, 9 June 1988. The film's self-referentiality is mildly interesting, though so overdone as to resemble *Christopher's Movie Matinee* gone berserk. Sydney Newman bears some responsibility for this misadventure, since it was he who said he found the earlier film charming and approved of the same method of shooting in *Running Time*. Martin Knelman, 'Canadian Film History's Worst Disaster,' *Saturday Night*, May 1978

57 Roman Kroitor interview with the author, 25 Nov. 1987

58 This relationship was explained in detail to a small unit in the Privy Council Office called 'Machinery of Government,' which itself was symptomatic of the phenomenon of proliferating bureaucracy. This division prepared papers for the clerk of the Privy Council on subjects like the concept of the ministry system and the allocation of functions between departments and boards. One keen observation was that while the members of this office had a good theoretical appreciation of government, they had no real feel or understanding of how things actually turn out in operation. NFB 1-M, A-146, Meeting with Minister Faulkner, Nov. 1974; Reta Kilpatrick to Sydney Newman/André Lamy, 11 Oct. 1974

59 NFB 1-M, A-146, Meeting with the minister, Apr. 1975, Notes on meeting with the minister, 10 Apr. 1975, by Reta Kilpatrick. Newman had been informed in another document that in test screenings, reaction to the Language Support series was split evenly between positive, neutral, and negative feelings. The French-language films, called *Toulmonde parle français*, were in *joual* and were almost incomprehensible to students, who were not expected to learn it. The ten films were *Branch et Branch, 'Les Oreilles' mène l'enquête, Les Tacots, Le Violon de Gaston, Le Temps d'une vente, Les 'Troubbes' de Johnny, Un fait accompli, La Dernière Neige, Par une belle nuit d'hiver,* and *Pris au collet.*

Faulkner had difficulty with two English films, one about a television-news cameraman whose weakness for wine, women, and fast cars led him to crime (*Heatwave*), and the other a musical comedy about the trials and tribulations of making an old-time musical spectacular in the Busby Berkeley tradition (*Star*). He probably did not see *A Case of Eggs*, a spoof about hens on strike, stolen eggs, and a broken heart, which was just being completed. The 1963 production *Drylanders* was probably the best-received language-support film.

60 The six principal federal agencies were the Film Board, the CBC, the CFDC, Information Canada, the Canada Council, and the Department of Communications. There was also the Department of Secretary of State, including the Arts and Culture then Citizenship branches, followed by the National Film Archives and the CRTC. NFB 1-M,

A-146, 'The Headlong Rush to Film: Overlapping Film Responsibilities among
Federal Cultural Agencies,' 17 Apr. 1974
61 Hugh Faulkner interview with the author, 4
May 1988
62 Minutes of the NFB, 5–6 Apr. and 20 Sept.
1974. At the latter meeting, board member
Jack Wasserman suggested the Film Board
should undertake a dramatic reassessment
of its role and decide whether it should
make a case to the government to recover
responsibilities that were rightfully those of
the agency, both legally under the Film Act
and according to the national film philosophy that had created the organization. He
thought it was imperative that the Film
Board determine its objectives and role and
develop a strategy to make its case.
63 Ibid., 13–14 Dec. 1974
64 Hugh Faulkner interview with the author, 4
May 1988
65 NFB 1-M, A-146, Meeting with the minister,
29 Nov. 1974, Minutes
66 Minutes of the NFB, 13–14 June 1975,
Appendix, Contracts tendered
67 The open-door policy to private companies
had been mooted in 1968 when Bram
Appel, a chartered accountant, examined
the Film Board administratively and recommended renting facilities to the private
sector so that monies could be added to the
institution's annual production. Pelletier
rejected the scheme. The distribution idea
probably grew out of the purchase in 1974
of 163 prints of eight privately produced
films for distribution abroad. NFB 1315/0,
D-250, Director of Distribution Anthony
Vielfaure to Newman, 27 Nov. 1974.
Gérard Pelletier interview with the author,
3 Feb. 1988
68 Minutes of the NFB, 13–14 June 1975,
Appendix, Hugh Faulkner to Jean Chrétien,
president of the Treasury Board, 27 May
1975
69 NFB 1-M, A-146, Minutes of meeting of
branch directors, 2 Apr. 1975.
70 NFB 1M, A-46, Meeting with the minister,
7–8 Feb. 1974. Reta Kilpatrick, Notes on
meeting with the minister in Peterborough
on 7–8 Feb. 1974. In December 1974, there
were plans to upgrade departmental representation on the interdepartmental committee to the deputy-minister or assistant-

deputy-minister level. The new group was
to be an advisory body, meeting several
times a year to establish guidelines and
review projects. Minutes of the NFB, 13–14
Dec. 1974. The board member has requested anonymity.
71 Faulkner was well aware that in six years
the CFDC had loaned $13.5 million for
features while having only $1.8 million
repaid, for a loss of 86.4 per cent on
investment. He thought it needed to build
on its strengths and work on areas like
script development and distribution. NFB
1-M, A-1, Correspondence with the minister, Notes prepared for interview with the
Vancouver Sun, 14 Nov. 1974. Hugh
Faulkner interview with the author, 4 May
1988
72 Minutes of the NFB, 12–13 Dec. 1975
73 Hugh Faulkner interview with the author, 4
May 1988

Chapter 11

1 Michel Régnier's series, *Santé Afrique*, was
a primer on health standards, and in a
departure from Film board tradition, was
never released in Canada because of its
specificity to Africa. The films generated
priceless goodwill in developing Africa,
while the co-production *Canada-Mexique*,
released in both nations, concentrated variously on Mexican exploitation of Indians,
farm workers, and dispossessed peasants,
and on the Canada-Mexico migrant agri-
cultural-labour exchange. The Canadian directors were Paul Leduc (*Ethnocidio*), Gilles
Groulx (*Première question sur le bonheur*),
and Maurice Bulbulian (*Tierra y Libertad*).
Ethnocidio was invited to appear in the
Critic's Week at the 1977 Cannes Film
Festival.
2 Minutes of the NFB, 18–19 June and 10–11
Sept. 1976
3 Michael Wash, 'Film commissioner out-
lines plan for NFB,' *Vancouver Province*, 22
Mar. 1976. Also, André Lamy interview
with the author, 10 May 1988
4 Tom Daly Papers, box X, no. 6, CBC-NFB
Relations, 12 Jan. 1976
5 Minutes of the NFB, 5–6 Sept. and 12–13
Dec. 1975 and 19–20 Mar. 1976
6 As the person who had been responsible for

developing the guidelines for bilingualism in the public service while at the Treasury Board, Johnson was trying to resist making the Ottawa-Quebec power struggle his consuming preoccupation, as it was almost everywhere else in the public service.

7 The election of the Parti Québécois government in November 1976 marked the apogee of the postwar independence movement. It built upon L'Allier's ideas and designed a cultural-development policy that managed to both supersede and duplicate federal activity. A super ministry of cultural development under Dr Camille Laurin was intended to become the intellectual engine of the Quebec independence movement. André Fortier and Paul Schafer, *Development and Growth of Federal Arts Policies in the Arts, 1944–1985* (Ottawa: Department of Communications, May 1985), 37–9

8 Minutes of the NFB, 19–20 Mar. and 10–11 Sept. 1976. The cable company (which had eight channels) had programmed films selected by subscribers from a library of 1,600 films, of which 256 were from the Film Board. In six months, there were 10,000 requests for Film Board films. From this time on, the future possibilities of cable television promised to be one possible elixir to resolve distribution woes. Minutes of the NFB, 18–19 June 1976

9 Ibid., 19–20 Mar., 18–19 June, and 10–11 Sept. 1976. Also Luc Perrault, 'A l'ONF: Fin des interdits,' *La Presse*, 12 Apr. 1976; ' "On est au coton" en première à la Bibliothèque,' *Le Devoir*, 7 Oct. 1976

10 Minutes of the NFB, 10–11 Sept. 1976. By 1988, there were thirteen prints available for distribution.

11 Ibid., 17–18 Mar. 1978

12 Ibid., 10–11 Sept. 1976. Deputy Film Commissioner James de B. Domville was arguing privately that the Capital Cost Allowance did not create actors, directors, or writers. The scheme only encouraged the borrowing of second-rate dregs from Los Angeles or of Canadian expatriates there. He thought the minister either did not understand the degree to which the Canadian film industry was subservient to the Americans or did not pay attention to reality; Domville interview with the author, 9 June 1988. Faulkner left politics later to

become a president of a transnational Canadian aluminum company.

13 Minutes of the NFB, 18–19 Mar. 1977

14 John Roberts interview with the author, 29 Mar. 1988

15 NFB 1-M, A-146, Meeting with the minister, Apr. 1975; Robert Verrall to André Lamy, 1 Apr. 1975, quoting Low's general statement.

16 Robert Verrall interview with the author, 18 May 1988. There were a total of 121 vignettes produced by 1986. The Cineplex Odeon circuit began running four *Vignettes* on an experimental basis in 1988, holding out the slim possibility of renewed theatrical exposure for some Film Board shorts.

17 *Annual Report, 1977–78*, quoting a Roberts radio interview in July 1977

18 Tom Daly Papers, box IX, no. 20, Arthur Hammond survey of filmmakers' ideas for 1975–6

19 Ibid., Arthur Hammond to the Programme Committee, 12 Jan. 1976; Programme Guidelines, 1976–7, 13 Apr. 1976

20 Tom Daly Papers, box X, no. 1, Derek Lamb to Ian McLaren, 14 Feb. 1977; Kathleen Shannon to Ian McLaren, 19 Jan. 1977; 'Studio B and the Film Board's Mandate' by Roman Kroitor, 21 Feb. 1977; Colin Low to David Novek, 17 Jan. 1977

21 Tom Daly interview with the author, 16 Feb. 1989

22 L.B. (sic), 'Où en est l'Office national du film?,' *Séquences* 88 (Apr. 1977), 21–7

23 Martin Knelman, *Weekend Magazine*, 3 Apr. 1976, See also Janet Maislin's less enthusiastic review in the *New York Times*, 20 Oct. 1977, and Ronald Blumer's effusive 'among the greatest movies I have ever seen' review in *Cinema Canada* 28 (1976), 46–8.

24 This film and *Veronica* were part of the *Children of Canada* series and shared the same budget. Together they cost $86,223.

25 Verrall thinks the following films (with their directors) deserve mention as worthy successors to the above list: *Blowhard* (Brad Caslor and Christopher Hinton, 1978); *Development without Tears* (Tina Viljoen, 1978); *Small Is Beautiful* (Douglas Kiefer, Barrie Howells, Donald Brittain, 1978); *What the Hell's Going On Up There?* (Derek Lamb, 1979); *Wood Mountain Poems*

(Harvey Spak, 1979); *The Biosphere* (William Pettigrew, 1979); *Horse Drawn Magic* (Dorothy Todd Hénaut, 1979); *Nails* (Phillip Borsos, 1979); *This Is an Emergency* (Derek Lamb and Terence Macartney-Filgate, 1979); *Twice upon a Time* (Giles Walker, 1979); *Gulfstream* (Bruce Mackay and William Hansen, 1980); *The Strongest Man in the World* (Halya Kuchmij, 1980); *The Sound Collector* (Lynn Smith, 1982).

26 Tom Daly Papers, box IX, no. 21, Arthur Hammond to Ian McLaren, 15 Feb. 1977; Robert Verrall and Guy Glover to Ian McLaren, 21 Jan. 1977

27 Minutes of the NFB, 17–18 Mar. and 16–17 June 1978. David Balcon, ed., 'Notes From Siberia' (special file), Research and Policy Development, National Film Board, Oct. 1981, section IX, *No Act of God*. Colin Low had thought the Film Board was 'very late' in making this film.

28 When Chabot made the film available to the Energy Committee of the Quebec government's Planning and Development Council, a spokesman for that group said simply that the film would initiate a constructive discussion concerning the subject of the nuclear option. Production file, *La Fiction nucléaire*, P. André Sauvageau to Guy Fournier, 28 Mar. 1979

29 McLaren was quoted in a Canadian Press story released on 4 Dec. 1983. In 1990, Don McWilliams of English Animation directed the definitive screen documentary on McLaren's work, entitled *Creative Process*.

30 McLaren went to India in 1953 on a UNESCO project dealing with fundamental education. He contracted a serious illness there and upon returning to Canada was hospitalized with severe rheumatic fever that permanently damaged his heart and health.

31 L.B., 'Où en est l'Office national du film?'

32 Gilles Roy (director of personnel, NFB) interview with the author, 23 Aug. 1988. Minutes of the NFB, 16–17 Sept. and 9–10 Dec. 1977 and 16–17 June 1978. A person-year is the total number of hours one person works for one year.

33 To make labour relations worse, the Anti-Inflation Board (AIB) told the Film Board it

should stop paying the (federal government) Bilingual Bonus to its employees because the payments exceeded the AIB guidelines. Furthermore, it told the NFB to recover $307,000 in payments from the employees who had received it. Together, management and the unions appealed the AIB decision. Minutes of the NFB, 17–18 Mar. and 16–17 June 1978

34 John Roberts interview with the author, 29 Mar. 1988. It was a shock to the Film Board staff to hear the rumour that Ottawa felt there was no special reason to perpetuate the agency. François Macerola interview with the author, 8 Sept. 1988

35 André Lamy interview with the author, 10 May 1988. Roberts did not remember making any such recommendation (interview with the author, 29 Mar. 1988), although it is probable that pressure was coming from his deputy ministers to Lamy to put his administrative house in order and fire excess staff.

36 L.A.D. Stephens, *Study of Canadian Government Information Abroad, 1942–1972: The Development of the Information, Cultural and Academic Divisions and Their Policies* (Ottawa: Department of External Affairs 1977), chap. 13, 1–39. The larger backdrop to this activity was that External Affairs gained membership in May 1970 on the new Interdepartmental Committee on External Relations (ICER), whose purpose was to advise the government on the allocation of resources for external operations. ICER's members – the key personnel in the senior civil service – tried and failed to coordinate the external operations of four departments around an integrated foreign policy. Kim Richard Nossal, *Canadian Foreign Policy* (Scarborough, Ont.: Prentice-Hall 1985), 139–40. The Film Board tried and failed to obtain a seat on ICER.

37 Department of External Affairs (DEA), 56-20-7, B-0142, A.B. Rogers, director, Information Division, External Affairs, to T.E. Farley, deputy director, Creative Services, Information Division, External Affairs, 10 Oct. 1974; Farley to Rogers, 22 Oct. 1974

38 DEA 56-20-1-4, B-0540, External Affairs liaison with NFB, 13, 14, 16 May 1975. Also,

NFB 1298, 1E, B-137, Film Commissioner's Office and External Affairs, 30 Jan. 1975, Joint meeting on viability of protocol

39 DEA 56-20-1-4, B-0540, External Affairs liaison with NFB, Note on the NFB/EA co-funded film program (Feb. 1974–Sept. 1975), 25 Sept. 1975. *Deep Threat*, a clever and entertaining 7-minute animation by Don Arioli and Zlatko Grgic, showed how the onslaught of men, machines, and pollution was threatening to kill aquatic life. Perhaps its final message, 'The sea has its own laws and man is accountable,' was too strong and provocative for External Affairs' liking. Later, *A Promise for Tomorrow*, on the Law of the Sea theme, covered the exploits of the *Nora and Gladys*, the schooner that carried a floating exhibit which articulated Canada's position on that topic.

40 NFB 1298, 1E, B-137, Film Commissioner's Office and External Affairs, André Lamy to Neil Overend of CIDA, Jan. 1976

41 DEA, 56-20-1-4, B-0540, J. Stoddart report on China trip, 22 Oct. 1975; Canadian Embassy, Peking to External Affairs, Ottawa, 26 Jan. 1976; Ottawa to Peking, 29 Jan. 1976

42 It was reported from the Canadian Commission in Hong Kong that the following Mandarin-versioned Film Board films were on deposit for prestige screenings: *The Chairmaker and the Boys, Eskimo Artist: Kenojuak, Introducing Insects, The Living Stone, Snow, The St. Lawrence Seaway, Wildlife of the Rocky Mountains, World at Your Feet,* and *World in a Marsh*. DEA 56-20-1-4, B-0540, External Affairs liaison with NFB, telex, 14 Dec. 1976. Three years later, a five-man Chinese film crew visited Canada for four months at the invitation of the Film Board. They covered agriculture, industry, forestry management, communications, geography, and Canadian lifestyles. They took back to China the following stock-shot footage: *The Living Stone* (67 feet of Inuit dancing), *Life in a Woodlot* (33 feet), *Circle of the Sun* (67 feet of Indians dancing), *Moisson* (433 feet of seeding and farming in Saskatchewan), and *Eskimo Artist: Kenojuak* (230 feet). Significantly, the most recent footage was fifteen

years old. Tom Daly Papers, box IV, no. 7, Chinese delegation memo

43 DEA 56-20-1-4, B-0540, External Affairs liaison with NFB, A. Blair, External Affairs, to Lyle Cruickshank, 28 Aug. 1979

44 Annual sales in the United States for non-theatrical use exceeded the number of prints in all post libraries, and the cumulative sale of 145,000 Film Board films there meant that the total audience was much higher. The same applied to western Europe's total audience.

45 DEA 56-20-1-4, B-0540, External Affairs liaison with NFB, S. Beattie, A Study of the Department of External Affairs Post Film Program, 10 Sept. 1981

46 André Lamy interview with the author, 10 May 1988

47 Ibid.

48 Minutes of the NFB, 8–9 Sept. 1978, Appendix, 'Quantifiable Measures for the NFB'

49 Ibid., 8–9 Sept. 1978, Appendix, Discussion of Crown Corporation status

50 Ibid., 23 Sept. 1978. André Lamy interview with the author, 10 May 1988

51 Minutes of the NFB, 15–16 Dec. 1978. The CPC plan was not realized, since by the fall of 1980, the new minister, Francis Fox, asked him to become the executive director of the CFDC, which was about to get an infusion of over $100 million.

Chapter 12

1 Minutes of the NFB, 16–17 Mar. 1979, Appendix 4, Person Year Problem. Prior to Domville's official appointment, there had been continuous lobbying to try convincing the Treasury Board to withdraw the planned 65-person-year cut and to even raise slightly the 1978–9 allotment. The Treasury Board made no promises. Minutes of the NFB, 15–16 Dec. 1978, Appendix 2b. The PSSRB decision affected 121 freelancers and mocked the Treasury Board's planned cuts.

2 François Macerola interview with the author, 8 Sept. 1988. Macerola, a lawyer by training, had joined the institution in 1972 and became the director of French Production in 1976.

3 Some 34 persons were offered continuous

positions, 35 obtained temporary positions, and 35 others received a lump-sum payment. Continuous employees in production positions were subject to a two-year probation. Temporary employees were not to be employed for longer than three years. By March 1982 there were 1,010 continuous and 72 temporary employees, compared to 986 continuous and 84 temporary the previous year (hired: 140; transferrred: 52; promoted: 38; retired or resigned: 98). Minutes of the NFB, 18–19 June 1982, Appendix 5a, 'Personnel Branch Report for 1981–82'

4 François Macerola interview with the author, 8 Sept. 1988

5 Minutes of the NFB, 16–17 Mar. 1979; James de B. Domville interview with the author, 9 June 1988

6 Other figures showed that the agency's parliamentary appropriations as a percentage of total Gross National Product were stable from 1958 to 1968, rose slightly from 1968 onwards, then dropped in 1979 to the 1958 percentage, where they remained until 1984. Guy Coté, *Figuring It Out: Twenty-Five Years of Filmmaking at the National Film Board* (Montreal: SGCT/ONF, February 1985), 5–6

7 Minutes of the NFB, 15–16 June 1979. Roberts's directive of 11 Apr. 1978 had told the Film Board 'to contract out to the private sector 50% of the first $4 million (in constant 1977 dollars) of films sponsored annually by departments or agencies of the government, plus 75% of the value of sponsored film production in excess of $4 million.'

8 Minutes of the NFB, 14–15 Sept. and 14–15 Dec. 1979. François Macerola interview with the author, 8 Sept. 1988

9 D.B. Jones, 'Kicking the Car When It's Out of Gas,' *Variety*, 9 Jan. 1980

10 Hugo McPherson, 'No Guarantees, No Culture,' *Maclean's*, 16 June 1980, 6

11 Minutes of the NFB, 12–13 Dec. 1980, Appendix 2, A Description of NFB's Relationship with the English and French Networks of the CBC. A.W. Johnson interview with the author, 14 Apr. 1988

12 Minutes of the NFB, 20–21 Mar. 1981

13 Ibid., 12–13 June 1981. David Balcon and Réal Gauthier soon began a tentative explo-

ration of cable/satellite possibilities, and reported to the governors at the end of 1981. Subsequently Balcon headed a task force to try to obtain partners in a bid for a Film Board cable channel.

Twice in the previous year, the commissioner had gone public with a call for a second national channel. James de B. Domville, *Selected Speeches of the Government Film Commissioner James de B. Domville, 1979–1983* (Montreal: NFB 1986): 'To a Committee of the CRTC on Extension of Service to the Northern and Remote Communities,' 11 April 1980, and 'To the CRTC on CBC-2/Tele-2 Licence Applications,' 15 Jan. 1981

14 Minutes of the NFB, 15–16 June 1979. *Les Enfants des normes*, directed by Georges Dufaux, was an eight-part series, shot in *cinéma direct* style, on the vocational high school, as seen from the viewpoint of teacher, parent, student, and man on the street.

15 Minutes of the NFB, 15–16 Dec. 1978

16 The other films were *Le Jour du référendum dans la vie de Richard Rohmer (Richard Rohmer and His Referendum – A View from Quebec)*, directed by Jacques Bensimon, and *Feu l'objectivité (Double Vision)*, directed by Jacques Godbout. Both films dealt with the dynamic of English/French relations and mutual perceptions of politics.

17 Richard Cleroux, 'Films paint ugly picture of English Quebec,' *Globe and Mail*, 27 Feb. 1980; William Johnson, 'NFB view of English Canada a mixed bag,' *Globe and Mail*, 28 Feb. 1980

18 Minutes of the NFB, 14–15 Mar. 1980

19 Adele Freedman, 'Rape film is a blatant assault on the audience,' *Globe and Mail*, 9 Feb. 1980; Clyde Gilmour, 'A Scream from Silence is far from an award winner,' *Toronto Star*, 11 Feb. 1980

20 A wide-ranging discussion of the history of the Fairness, Accuracy and Balance issue was circulated to employees from the Policy, Research and Development Office in 1981. David Balcon, ed., *Notes from Siberia (Special File)*, Internal Film Board document, Oct. 1981

21 The other titles in the series, co-produced with the CBC, National Museum of Man, National Museums of Canada, ATEC, OECA,

and Access Alberta were *First Winter, Gopher Broke, The Machine Age, The Red Dress, Revolution's Orphans, Strangers at the Door, Teach Me to Dance, Voice of the Fugitive,* and *The War Is Over.*

22 The *Montreal Star,* 16 May 1980. Walker denied that the veteran was a wino, 'because I created the character and directed the actor.' The *Telegraph Journal, New Brunswick,* agreed with him, in an article on 17 May.

23 A sample of articles ran as follows: Martin Malina, 'Reeling into the future,' *Montreal Star,* 28 Apr.; Sid Adilman, 'Loved abroad, but shunned at home,' *Toronto Star,* 29 Apr.; Richard Gay, 'Pour les 40 ans de l'ONF,' *Le Devoir,* 26 May; Luc Perrault, 'Le défi de l'ONF: Survive à ses 40 ans,' *La Presse,* 15 Sept.; Angèle Dagenais, 'Les nouveaux défis de l'ONF,' *Le Devoir,* 15 Sept.; Pierre Bourgault, 'Sad birthday for the NFB,' *The Gazette* (Montreal), 29 Sept.; Holly Dressel, 'The National Film Board at forty,' *Take One,* Fall 1979, 37–9.

24 Roberts had asked, in April 1978, that the Film Board revise its pricing structure and correct any instances where its sales policy was operating to the disadvantage of the private sector. Subsequently, the Film Board raised its prices 30 per cent, but they were still almost 25 per cent lower than the average price of a privately distributed film. The Film Board suggestion that the government subsidize the private sector to match the Film Board's pricing technique had gone nowhere. Minutes of the NFB, 14–15 Mar. 1980, Appendix 5, Relations with the Private Sector

25 Domville appeared before the committee on 15 Nov. 1979. Minutes of the NFB, 14–15 Dec. 1979. In 1978, Member of Parliament Tom Cossitt had asked why public funds were spent on a film like *Running Time,* which had taken four years to finish, cost over a million dollars, and was so terrible that it could not find theatrical distribution.

26 Minutes of the NFB, 14–15 Dec. 1979 and 14–15 Mar. 1980. The A budget was $44,446 million (the $2.5 million increase requested in September had not materialized) and the B budget was $3.935 million. By the time the new system was fully in place in 1981, the A budget was replaced by an Opera-

tional Plan, covering the current level of activities, and a Strategic Overview, covering new and expanded programmes that the minister would assess and possibly incorporate into a larger overview that would be forwarded by him to the appropriate cabinet policy committee.

27 Francis Fox interview with the author, 22 Sept. 1988

28 Sid Adilman, 'Oscar winner out of a job,' *Toronto Star,* 26 Apr. 1980

29 Gary Evans, 'The games athletes play,' *Montreal Star,* 28 July 1979

30 Toutefois le film *Cordélia* a trahi le dossier et causera à la justice un dommage difficilement réparable,' the esteemed judge concluded. 'Le juge Deschênes se porte à la défense de la Justice,' stated *L'Echo du nord* (St-Jerôme), 15 Oct. 1980.

31 Minutes of the NFB, 14–15 Mar. 1980

32 Fox fumed privately about being powerless to change Radio-Canada's unobjective coverage of the whole debate. Francis Fox interview with the author, 22 Sept. 1988

33 Julian Hicks, 'NFB funding may be restored,' *Edmonton Journal,* 24 Apr. 1980. Baneful economics had led to a hiring freeze, which lasted through the summer of 1980. As of 31 Mar. 1980, there were 945 continuous employees. Over the whole of 1980, some 167 employees were hired, 74 were transferred from one job to another, and 101 resigned or retired. Director of English Production Peter Katadotis, hoping to inspire the existing creative group toward the original Grierson concept of the 'public service' film, shifted half his programme toward themes that addressed the identified needs of specific audiences and targets. Minutes of the NFB, 13–14 June 1980

34 James de B. Domville, *Selected Speeches of the Government Film Commissioner,* 'To the Standing Committee on Communications and Culture, April 9, 1981.' Minutes of the NFB, 13–14 June 1980. This new committee replaced the Standing Committee on Broadcasting, Films and Assistance to the Arts.

35 Peter Katadotis interview with the author, 10 Apr. 1989

36 L.A.D. Stephens, *Study of Canadian Government Information Abroad, 1942–1972: The Development of the Information,*

Cultural and Academic Divisions and Their Policies (Ottawa: Department of External Affairs, Mar. 1977), chap. 13

37 Minutes of the NFB, 18–19 Sept. 1981, appendices 9a and 9b, 'Distribution Activities Abroad' and 'NFB Production Activities Abroad,' Aug. 1981. This tradition has continued in the new animated film *Karate Kids*, a video aimed at Third World street children that warns them how to avoid contracting the HIV virus and AIDS. Directed by Derek Lamb and Kaj Pindal, this production will be in ten languages. External Affairs also showed much interest in exporting films about dance in Canada.

38 Ibid., 12–13 Sept. 1980. Gotlieb, who is now chairman of the Canada Council, may have been unduly harsh, since an examination of television export sales that fall showed that 121 films were bought by Albania, Brunei, Bulgaria, Cyprus, Denmark, Finland, France, Greece, Iceland, India, Japan, Malta, the Netherlands, New Zealand, Portugal, Romania, Scotland, Sweden, Switzerland, the United Kingdom, and the United States. Albania bought *Games of the XXI Olympiad, Electronic Fish Finders, The Flower and the Hive, Sub-Igloo, Adventure in Newfoundland, To the Edge of the Universe, The Peep Show, Satellites of the Sun, Down to the Sea*, and *On Power Refuelling*. The United States, by comparison, bought *An Easy Pill to Swallow, Bill Loosely's Heat Pump, Christmas at Moose Factory, Climates, Colour of Life, Descent, Maud Lewis, Who Will I Sentence Now?, Would I Ever Like to Work, An Old Box, Hot Stuff, Games of the XXI Olympiad, Going the Distance, Ladies and Gentlemen, Mr. Leonard Cohen. High Grass Circus, Buster Keaton Rides Again, The Eye Hears and the Ear Sees, J.A. Martin, Photographer, Summerhill, Los Canadienses, Best Damn Fiddler from Calabogie to Kaladar, Sun, Wind and Wood, Flight, Post Partum Depression, Best Friends, Ballet Adagio*, and *Centaur*.

39 James de B. Domville interview with the author, 9 June 1988

40 Trudeau hurled the first volley at a fundraising dinner in Montreal, on 30 Nov. claiming the *independantistes*, intellectuals, and artists were against his plans for repatriating the constitution. They answered him in *Le Devoir*, on 11 Dec. and he replied on 21 Jan. 1981, denying that he wanted to silence their criticism, since they had had generous access to federal institutions. *Sudbury Star*, 23 Jan. 1981

41 Francis Fox interview with the author, 22 Sept. 1988.

42 The MOMA retrospective began with a series of five different programmes of animated films that ran from 22–30 Jan. 1981. This was followed by two months of documentaries and concluded with two months of features. A truncated version of the MOMA retrospective opened in Los Angeles and Chicago that spring, again to great praise. Minutes of the NFB, 20–21 Mar. 1981

43 Marshall Delaney, (Robert Fulford), 'Featured Role,' *Saturday Night*, Mar. 1981, 61

44 James de B. Domville, *Selected Speeches of the Government Film Commissioner*, 'To the Applebaum-Hébert Committee, May 11, 1981'

45 In 1980–1, only 18 Film Board films were shown in prime time on the CBC; 33 were broadcast on Radio-Canada. A total of 31 received national telecast on CBC; 44 appeared on Radio-Canada. Ten years earlier the figure had been 85 on the CBC and 84 on Radio-Canada.

46 The administrative staff had occupied the Moncton Film board offices, demanding $200,000 for annual production with no strings. The crisis was terminated by closing the office down, then reopening it with new staff. Under a new process, the regions (not headquarters' filmmakers) determined the pertinence of film projects, with the final decision resting with the deputy film commissioner. Minutes of the NFB, 12–13 June 1981

47 Michael Spencer interview with the author, 27 July 1988. Other informed persons have expressed similar thoughts, but wish to remain anonymous.

48 NFB 2944, Applebaum-Hébert Committee, NFB and the Applebaum/Hébert Committee (synopsis of 50 briefs applying to broadcasting, film production, and distribution), n.d.

49 Minutes of the NFB, 18–19 June 1982;

Michael Spencer interview with the author, 27 July 1988. Spencer, who had been a Film Board manager until leaving in 1968, was a staff member of the commission.

50 Jean-Marc Garand, 'Il faut introduire la compétition à l'ONF,' *La Presse*, 21 June 1980

51 François Macerola interview with the author, 8 Sept. 1988

52 Peter Katadotis interview with the author, 10 Apr. 1989

53 Minutes of the NFB, 18–19 June 1982

54 From 'Studio K' Katadotis sent filmmakers to several Third World hot spots to bring out unfiltered information from the village level about regional conflicts. Such forays into the Third World could be fraught with political danger, since that arena was the forum in which the superpowers were waging their respective political games. In hot spots like Nicaragua and the Philippines there was always the danger of becoming involved in someone else's political football match. Film Board management subsequently ordered a halt to the practice of having the director of production serve as his own executive producer. François Macerola interview with the author, 8 Sept. 1988

55 Minutes of the NFB, 12–13 Sept. 1980

56 Ibid., 20–21 Mar. 1981, Appendix, 1982–83 Strategic Overview, p. 13. The Cabinet Committee on Social Development declared on 3 Dec. 1980 that the Film Board should be the executive producer of all sponsored film (Appendix 12b, Proposed Revisions of National Film Board Policy Regarding Execution of Film, Videotape and AV Productions for Federal Government Departments and Agencies). This policy was adopted at the board of governors meeting on 12–13 June 1981.

57 James de B. Domville interview with the author, 9 June 1988

58 Ibid.

59 Minutes of the NFB, 12–13 Dec. 1980. Appendix, Memorandum, Resource Allocation to the National Film Board: Minister of Communications, 15 Nov. 1980 (This was a Film Board appeal to the minister for a $2.5 million increase.)

60 Changes in distribution came, but slowly. Litwack fine-tuned the earlier Telidon experiment to develop *Format*, a bilingual, nationwide computerized library system, capable of storing information on all Canadian-produced audiovisual material for greater public access. In 1982, the NFB catalogue was restructured to resemble *Format*'s organization. Litwack also took the first steps toward inaugurating a video-cassette rental policy, which the Film Board finalized in 1988, along with a user-pay policy for film bookings. Ibid., 17–18 Sept. 1982

61 The arguments for increasing television exposure were spelled out in a discussion paper by the Research and Policy Development Branch, 'Options for an Increased NFB Presence on English-Language Television,' 3 Dec. 1981. Domville presented a brief to the CRTC on 5 Dec. See *Speeches of the Government Film Commissioner*, 'To the CRTC on Canadian Content, December 5, 1981.' The race to obtain a cable-television channel licence summed up the major external thrust of the Film Board in the eighties until the CRTC finally and unceremoniously slammed the door closed on this option, in November 1987.

62 Minutes of the NFB, 11–12 Dec. 1981. Francis Fox interview with the author, 22 Sept. 1988

63 James de B. Domville interview with the author, 9 June 1988. François Macerola came to perceive Rabinovitch, Lynn Macdonald, and, to a lesser degree, Silcox as the flies in the ointment with respect to effective relations with the minister. He viewed their primary concern as to help the commercial industry get a firm footing. François Macerola interview, 8 Sept. 1988

64 Francis Fox interview with the author, 22 Sept. 1988; David Silcox interview with the author, 6 Apr. 1989

65 Gerald Pratley, 'Drifting along with the NFB,' *Toronto Sun*, 7 Apr. 1982. He claimed the organization had been living off its reputation for so long that there was almost nothing left to sustain it.

66 Canada, *Report of the Federal Cultural Policy Review Committee* (Ottawa: Information Services, Department of Communications 1982)

67 Actually, the headline 'National Film Board

backs criticism in study' did the most damage. The article in the *Ottawa Citizen* (16 Nov. 1982) by Aileen McCabe and Jamie Portman put the remark in context, that the Film Board intended to take the recommendations as positively as possible, since it knew it had to realign itself to its objectives and recapture its audiences.

68 Entitled 'On Creativity and Effectiveness' ('De l'efficacité créatrice'), the document summary appeared on 27 Nov. and became the blueprint for policy development and practice for the balance of the 1980s.

69 Sid Adilman, 'Doesn't anyone love the NFB?' *Toronto Sunday Star*, 21 Nov. 1982. A few months later, Serge Losique, the flamboyant president of Montreal's World Film Festival, attacked the agency for 'being frozen with an army of bureaucrats who, like gangrene, have rendered it impotent.' He suggested that grants destined for the Film Board be given to private filmmakers. *La Presse*, 13 Feb. 1982. In a low-keyed interview in *Cinema Canada* 92 (Jan. 1983), Domville refused to berate the report, but insisted that the Film Board would renew itself and make its position known to the federal government (pp. 33–4). In the same issue, Film Board producer Arthur Hammond was less diplomatic. He called the report 'ignorant, foolish, biased and insulting' (36–41).

70 Nathalie Petrowski, 'Héroux s'explique mal l'indignation de l'ONF,' *Le Devoir*, 25 Nov. 1982; transcript of Spencer interview from *Sunday Morning* (CBC Radio), 16 Jan. 1983; Michale Spencer interview with the author, 27 July 1988. Spencer also thought that if the agency were relieved of its sponsored-films role (which it no longer was performing well) it could then devote itself to producing excellent films.

71 Transcription de l'émission *Premier Page* télédiffusée au réseau de Radio-Canada le mardi 30 novembre 1982 à 21 h 30. Filmmakers Denys Arcand, Michel Brault, Gilles Carle, Claude Jutra, Jean-Claude Labrecque, and Arthur Lamothe published an open appeal to Fox in *Le Devoir* on 30 Dec. calling for an increase in production funding and a continuation of the cultural mission of the institution that they called unique in the world.

72 '... une institution fédérale dont nous sommes tous fiers, Québécois et Canadiens, l'Office national du film, un lieu de liberté et de création au sein duquel il s'est épanoui pour le plus grand bien de tous. On dit souvent ici que c'est la faute du fédéral; dans son cas, on peut dire que c'est grâce au fédéral.' *Débate de l'Assemblée nationale*, 25 nov. 1982, 6105; Pierre Bourgault, 'Sign a reprieve for the Film Board,' *The Gazette* (Montreal), 8 Jan. 1983

73 Transcript from *Sunday Morning* (CBC Radio), 21 Nov. 1982

74 Robert Fulford, 'Plenty of Nothing,' *Saturday Night*, Feb. 1983, 3–7

75 Gerald Pratley, 'Preoccupied with Culture,' *Toronto Sun*, 21 Nov. 1982

76 *Le Devoir*, 30 Dec. 1982. The filmmakers were Denys Arcand, Michel Brault, Gilles Carle, Claude Jutra, Jean-Claude Labrecque, and Arthur Lamothe.

77 Liora Salter, 'Stepping Back from Applebert: Politics and the Cultural Debate,' *Canadian Dimension* 17 (Nov. 1983), 35–8

78 James de B. Domville, *Speeches of the Government Film Commissioner*, 'To the Canadian Radio-Television and Telecommunications Commission, December 2, 1982'

79 *Maclean's* reported that the report had so demoralized Fox's department that Prime Minister Trudeau had to set up a top-level cabinet task force directed by Senator Jack Austin to evaluate it. The article hinted that Fox and Pierre Juneau wanted to undermine the report. Mark Czarnecki, 'A New Blueprint for Culture,' *Maclean's*, 29 Nov. 1982, 36–40

80 Minutes of the NFB, 11–12 Mar. 1983, Appendix, Francis Fox (Minister of Communications), 'The Situation Is Urgent, the Time Opportune.' The million-dollar cut was to be felt most in the distribution and international wings, which would close offices. Minutes of the NFB, 10–11 Dec. 1982

81 Minutes of the NFB, 11–12 Mar., 23–24 Sept., and 9–10 Dec. 1983. James de B. Domville interview with the author, 9 June 1988. In July 1981 Silcox became president of the CFDC. Francis Fox interview with the author, 22 Sept. 1988

82 David Silcox interview with the author, 6 Apr. 1989

83 Minutes of the NFB, 10–11 Dec. 1982, Appendix 8, Executive Summary of C.G.I. Study (7 Dec. 1982). The study cost $90,000, and the findings were anything but surprising: (1) surplus staff comprised some 4.5 per cent of the total workforce; (2) there had been no major administrative reorganization for fourteen years; (3) too many people reported to the deputy commissioner; (4) the distribution branch was susceptible to fostering and expanding the conflict between the English and French cultures; and (5) office automation (data processing) needed to assume more priority. The jewel in the crown of their report was a suggestion to form a new position of planning coordinator for administrative renewal, which would cost a half-million dollars to achieve.

84 Ibid., 17–18 June 1983. Ironically, when the Film Board appeared before the House of Commons Standing Committee on Communications and Culture on 28 April and 10 May, the committee criticized the agency for closing distribution offices.

85 James de B. Domville, *Speeches of the Government Film Commissioner*, 'To the Standing Committee on Communications and Culture, April 28, 1983.' After having taken a national survey of 2,000 persons, Domville concluded that there was sufficient support for a satellite/cable channel that would be an interactive national electronic film library. Sixty-eight per cent were interested in children's programmes in the daytime and information/documentary programmes in the evenings. Fifty-four per cent could pay two dollars per month for the service and 65 per cent would pay fifty cents a month for it.

86 When Trudeau assumed his most professorial tone and asked them to explain the broader context in which the new channel would operate, Fox knew the time was not right. Francis Fox interview with the author, 22 Sept. 1988

87 Fox asked Domville on 11 July 1983 to work with the CBC toward a cable-television-station proposal. Minutes of the NFB, 8 Aug. 1983. Before going their separate ways, Juneau hired former Acting Film Commissioner Grant McLean to draft a blueprint of how the two organizations might combine

resources, with the Film Board becoming the documentary-film arm of the CBC. The report never saw the light of day. Juneau's resignation from the board was announced at the meeting of 31 Mar.–1 Apr. 1985. By 1987 the Film Board's 'consortium approach' lost out to the CBC, which found itself having to share a licence with private entrepreneurs. By the spring of 1989, the new channel was still not ready to go on air. A year later, the all-news channel was broadcasting, but was not attracting significant numbers of viewers.

88 Minutes of the NFB, 18–19 June 1982. Klein commented: 'This kind of censorship nurtures the climate of sexual repression on which pronography feeds and in which violence and brutality are, by omission, fully acceptable to community standards.' Dorothy Hénaut, Bonnie Sherr Klein, and Linda Lee Tracy, '*Not a Love Story*, Personal Insights and Public Responses,' unpublished typescript (1983), chap. 6. *Not a Love Story*, Production file

89 'Banned here, anti-porn film won't go away,' *Toronto Sunday Star*, 29 Aug. 1982. Jay Scott's harsh comments about this film and Irene Angelico's *Dark Lullabies* appeared in the *Globe and Mail*, 31 Aug. 1985.

90 Minutes of the NFB, 11–12 Mar. 1983, Appendix 8a, Notes on the Statement of Income and Expense for the ten months ending January 31, 1983. Gerald Pratley had condemned the film for its New York point of reference in the *Toronto Sun*, 7 Apr. 1982, while Robert Fulford's article in the *Toronto Star*, on 5 June 1982, 'NFB film ignites anti-porn movement,' was a much more positive critique.

91 Bonnie Sherr Klein interview with the author, 8 Dec. 1988

92 Minutes of the NFB, 18–19 June and 17–18 Sept. 1982, and James de B. Domville interview with the author, 9 June 1988

93 NFB 1E, A-105, External Affairs, Wilf Jobbins to Hugo McPherson, 2 June 1969. According to the files, each of the films had a normal distribution contract with American distributors, enjoying a long distribution life both in the United States and abroad. It may have been from this time that American distributors of Film Board films registered annually as agents of a

foreign government, simply by filling out a form and informing the authorities of the titles they were distributing.

94 'NFB VS. USA,' *Cinema Canada* 94 (Mar. 1983), 3, 11. There is no other documentation about the *That Gang of Hoodlums?* troubles in its production file. It cost $12,875.

95 Minutes of the NFB, 17–18 June 1983. Richard and Sandra Gwyn, 'The Politics of Peace,' *Saturday Night*, May 1984, 23. Francis Fox interview with the author, 22 Sept. 1988

96 Stuart Taylor, 'Court backs "propaganda" label for 3 Canadian films,' *New York Times*, 29 Apr. 1987

97 See Paul Audley, *Canada's Cultural Industries: Broadcasting, Publishing, Records and Film* (Toronto: James Lorimer 1983)

98 Minutes of the NFB, 23–24 Sept. 1988, Appendix B, Francis Fox, *Strategic Overview, 1983*

99 James de B. Domville interview with the author, 9 June 1988

100 Minutes of the NFB, 9–10 Dec. 1983

101 Sid Adilman, 'Film Board's top man to move on in January,' *Toronto Star*, 2 Nov. 1983

Chapter 13

1 François Macerola interview with the author, 8 Sept. 1988. Fox ignored the legal contradiction of amending the Department of Supply and Services law while not simultaneously modifying the National Film Act.

2 Francis Fox, *The National Film and Video Policy* (Ottawa: Department of Communications, May 1984), 9–18

3 The 150,000 photos in the Still Photography Division were to find a permanent home and museum in Ottawa at the multimillion-dollar Canadian Museum of Contemporary Photography, slated to open in 1991.

4 This decision shattered many of the hopes of English Production to relaunch the institutional ship properly. Barbara Emo (director general of English Programming) interview with the author, 13 Apr. 1989

5 Fox had been deaf to Domville's argument that Supply and Services' overhead was higher than the Film Board's and that because the film business was unpredictable financially, there was the possibility of skulduggery in the commission and execution of millions of dollars in film contracts by a department that had no knowledge of the complexities of film production. James de B. Domville interview with the author, 9 June 1988. Macerola chose to ignore what his legal side was telling him: that there was a case of conflict between two pieces of legislation.

6 Jacques Godbout, 'De Gérard Pelletier à Francis Fox,' *Le Devoir*, 22 Oct. 1983. A variation of this article, called 'Francis Fox's Silent Film Policy,' appeared in *Cinema Canada* 109 (July–August 1984), 21.

7 Francis Fox interview with the author, 22 Sept. 1988

8 Fox thought that one reason he and the Liberals went down to defeat was that the ministers had gotten too close to their deputy ministers, listening to them in frequent tête-à-têtes, rather than telling them what the government wanted. Francis Fox interview with the author, 22 Sept. 1988

9 François Macerola, *Five Year Operational Plan* (Montreal: National Film Board, Oct. 1984). Macerola did not protest the Trudeau Cabinet's planned shift of the Still Photography Division to the National Museums Corporation in October. The division that had cost the Film Board $400,000 per year would have its budget trimmed to a meagre $75,000 in its new home. The decision had taken the Trudeau Cabinet less than twenty seconds, according to Senator Jack Austin. Christopher Hume, 'Film Board shuffle worries artists,' *Toronto Star*, 21 Sept. 1984

10 *Stereo Morning* (CBC FM Radio), 'NFB Cutbacks,' 14 Nov. 1984

11 Guy Coté, *Figuring It Out: Twenty-Five Years of Filmmaking at the National Film Board* (Montreal: SGCT/ONF [Syndicat général du cinéma et de la télévision / Office National du Film], Feb. 1985)

12 Sandra Gathercole, *Setting the Record Straight* (Montreal: SGCT/ONF, Aug. 1985). Minutes of the NFB, 6 Mar. 1986. Sitting as a trustee, Patrick Watson confirmed the board's attitude; he personally thought that

Macerola's was the right approach and that ultimately it would save the institution. Patrick Watson interview with the author, 19 Oct. 1988

13 Men were paid on average $4,000 to 6,000 more than women and the percentages of women at work were 22 in management, 31 in filmmaking, 15 as technicians, 34 in information and distribution, and 72 as support staff.

14 Gerald L. Caplan, *Task Force on Broadcasting Policy* (Ottawa: Ministry of Supply and Services 1986), 343–8

15 Minutes of the NFB, 28–29 Jan. 1987

16 Ibid., 27–28 Aug. 1986, Background document on Film Board and television by Kirwan Cox; 28–29 Jan., 26 June, 11 Sept., and 10 Dec. 1987; 11 Feb. 1988

17 Ibid., 18–19 Dec. 1985 and 6 Mar. 1986

18 Patrick Watson interview with the author, 19 Oct. 1988

19 Minutes of the NFB, 12–13 Dec. 1980

20 Eloise Morin, 'Billy Bishop movie shows the dark side of war,' *The Gazette* (Montreal), 8 Jan. 1983

21 Ron Lowman, 'Angry airmen want Billy Bishop film banned,' *Toronto Star*, 6 Jan. 1984; Glenn Bohn, 'Top Allied ace believes Bishop,' *Vancouver Sun*, 9 Jan. 1984

22 Senate Sub-committee on Veterans Affairs, 26 Nov. and 10 Dec. 1985

23 H. Clifford Chadderton, ed., *Hanging a Legend: The National Film Board's Shameful Attempt to Discredit Billy Bishop, VC* (Ottawa: War Amputations of Canada 1986). The special 371-page digest distributed free of charge to the public, tried to exonerate Bishop while castigating Cowan and the Film Board. There were a number of factual errors in the film, though the publication could not prove that Cowan had erred factually in posing his questions about heroism. The battle was fought in the national press in the Kingston *Whig Standard*, the St Catharine's *Standard*, Peterborough *Examiner*, Windsor *Star*, Montreal *Gazette*, Fredericton *Gleaner*, Edmonton *Sun*, Moncton *Times Transcript*, Kitchener-Waterloo *Record*, and the *Globe and Mail* on 4 Nov. 1986, the Regina *Leader Post* on 5 Nov., as well as at least six other newspapers in Canada. One of the most

vicious diatribes against the Film Board was written by McKenzie Porter of the *Toronto Sun*, who called the filmmakers 'a gaudy motley of artistic charlatans who belonged to the loony left ... pacifist-socialists ... chicken-hearted poltroons and geriatric hippies.'

24 François Macerola interview with the author, 8 Sept. 1988. The fragments of the Billy Bishop saga may be pieced together in the Minutes of the NFB, 18–19 Dec. 1985; 6 Mar., 26 Apr., 26–27 June, and 1–2 Nov. 1986; and 10 Dec. 1987. The film is still in distribution, though to purchase it, one must receive clearance from the commissioner's office.

25 Wayne Grady, 'The Abortionist,' *Saturday Night* 99 (July 1984), 30–9. Also, see *Democracy on Trial* production file for the transcripts of Cowan's fascinating discussions with Morgentaler, which reveal more than the documentary ever could.

26 Minutes of the NFB, 23–24 Sept. and 10 Dec. 1983; 23–24 Mar. and 18–19 June 1984. The other films in the series, which dealt with equally controversial subjects, were never made. They were to have been about a homosexual racetrack judge, a fisherman struggling for the right to unionization, an Indian woman who lost her Indian status for marrying a white man, and fishing lodge owners who fought a mercury-polluting company.

27 Donna Gollan, 'Abortion: A Reality, Not an Issue,' *Broadside*, Oct. 1984

28 *Daybreak* (CBC Radio), comments of Barrie Zwicker, 13 Nov. 1984

29 Canadian Press, ' "Sleazy trick" to show two abortion films day before Pope's visit.' *The Gazette* (Montreal), 16 Aug. 1984

30 NFB production file, *Abortion: Stories from North and South*, François Macerola form letter to complainants. Macerola interview with the author, 8 Sept. 1988

31 Barbara Amiel, 'A radical approach to the NFB,' *Maclean's*, 28 Apr. 1986, 9; 23 June 1986, 4. Amiel had neglected to perceive that the films also happened not to compete with commercial producers, who found the subjects unrewarding economically.

32 Peter Katadotis interview with the author, 10 Apr. 1989

33 The titles of a few sound filmstrips of Studio G put a contemporary face on favourite Canadian visual themes: *Canadian Arctic, Tell Me a Story, Everyday Things in Early Canada, Multicultural Education, Women in Canadian History*, and *The Immigration Experience*.

34 Ron Base, 'Film Board unveils real revenge of the nerds,' *Toronto Star*, 8 Sept. 1984

35 Carrière named the key creative group as Jutra, Brault, Perrault, Nold, Dufaux, Gosselin, Bobet, Fournier, Carle, Forest, Blais, Garceau, Devlin, Groulx, Portugais, Lamothe, Giraldeau, and Fortier. Richard Gay, 'L'ONF: 25 années d'images à notre image,' *Le Devoir*, 17 Nov. 1984

36 François Macerola interview with the author, 8 Sept. 1988

37 Claude Robert, ' "Mario"; Chef d'oeuvre du cinéma québécois,' *Journal de Québec*, 3 Nov. 1984

38 L'adieu de Beaudin à l'ONF,' *La Presse*, 20 Oct. 1984

39 Minutes of the NFB, 6 Mar. 1986

40 Martin Kenlman, 'Triumphant Loser,' *Saturday Night*, Nov. 1989, 103–6. Arcand's pessimism is evident as he sneers at the lost referendum and promises to never vote again unless there were a Nazi threat.

41 Minutes of the NFB, 27–28 Aug. 1986

42 Peter Katadotis interview with the author, 10 Apr. 1989. He left for Telefilm Canada in 1988 and, like so many Film Board veterans, keeps his eye on the organization's health.

43 Minutes of the NFB, 28–29 Jan. 1987. Only 13 per cent of French production was regional emanating from Winnipeg, Toronto, and Moncton. In 1987, Winnipeg's French production studio closed.

44 Lyle Cruickshank interview with the author, 31 Mar. 1989

45 The *Editroid* is one example of using video for editing purposes. Other refinements using the computer may automate part of the film-cutting process. *Cleopatra*, for multimedia editing, allows an operator to access a minimum of four hundred hours of video with fully automatic robot retrieval; this will speed the editing process by making all shots and sound in a production easily accessible. In short, transfers, authoring, storyboarding, editing, and playback simulation can now be done on one all-purpose workstation that can handle video-cassette, videodisc, compressed video, filmstrip, or slide series singly or simultaneously. Also, sound effects are more easily added to a production, since some 40,000 are now stored digitally and are retrievable via computer. There is too a transportable computerized robot-controlled system for complex and precise motion control for camera, dolly, and object movement planning, memorization, and execution trademark *The Brain*. It is being used to achieve effects that formerly were achievable at formidable cost; certain effects that were even beyond the capacity of a human operator are available on a computer keyboard.

46 Minutes of the NFB, 26 June 1987

47 Matthew Fraser, 'Narrow minded Quebec film law has NFB in turmoil,' *Globe and Mail*, 13 Jan. 1988. The law irked filmmaker Donald Winkler, whose excellent series on English-Canadian poets was pulled from distribution because it had not been translated into French. The well-known translator Philip Stratford complained that Quebec's Bill 109 amounted to blacklisting films on the work of Canadian poets writing in English.

48 Lysiane Gagnon, 'Une loi nationaleuse,' *La Presse* (Montreal), 3 Jan. 1988; Fraser, 'Narrow minded Quebec film law'; 'Hitting wrong target,' *The Gazette* (Montreal), 18 Jan. 1988; Don MacPherson, 'Big sister knows what's best for us,' *The Gazette*, 23 Feb. 1988; 'MacDonald tables stronger Film Bill,' *Globe and Mail*, 9 June 1988. These articles contributed to the souring mood of English Canada. In 1990, the Meech Lake Accord failed to receive unanimous provincial support and died.

49 Minutes of the NFB, 10 Dec. 1987

50 More a visual spectacle than a traditional narrative, *Transitions* concentrated on the importance of transportation as a major Canadian theme and was screened to over three million visitors.

51 Roman Kroitor interview with the author,

25 Nov. 1987. As he put it, a person who is dying experiences a film with a definite perspective of life and death and what is in between; such a person knows that what is 'in between' should be art. To Kroitor,

every work of art is a philosophical statement coming from a set of beliefs. 'Art' in film is what makes a film 'work.'

52 Joan Pennefather interview with the author, 4 Oct. 1989

Index

Index

Index

403